HANDBOOK OF PUBLIC FUNDING OF RESEARCH

Handbook of Public Funding of Research

Edited by

Benedetto Lepori

Institute of Communication and Public Policy, Faculty of Communication, Culture and Society, Università della Svizzera Italiana, Switzerland

Ben Jongbloed

Center for Higher Education Policy Studies (CHEPS), Faculty of Behavioural, Management and Social Sciences (BMS), University of Twente, the Netherlands

Diana Hicks

School of Public Policy, Georgia Institute of Technology, USA

EE Edward **Elgar**
PUBLISHING

Cheltenham, UK • Northampton, MA, USA

Published by
Edward Elgar Publishing Limited
The Lypiatts
15 Lansdown Road
Cheltenham
Glos GL50 2JA
UK

Edward Elgar Publishing, Inc.
William Pratt House
9 Dewey Court
Northampton
Massachusetts 01060
USA

A catalogue record for this book
is available from the British Library

Library of Congress Control Number: 2023930298

This book is available electronically in the **Elgar**online
Political Science and Public Policy subject collection
http://dx.doi.org/10.4337/9781800883086

MIX
Paper | Supporting
responsible forestry
FSC® C013604

ISBN 978 1 80088 307 9 (cased)
ISBN 978 1 80088 308 6 (eBook)

Printed and bound by CPI Group (UK) Ltd, Croydon, CR0 4YY

Contents

Contributors

Aixa Y. Alemán-Díaz works at the Copenhagen Business School, Denmark. Her research focuses on the politics and policy of science, technology and innovation with an interest in the governance of emerging fields like nanotechnology. She has ample experience advising governments and international organizations on matters related to economic development and health. She holds BA and MPP degrees from the University of Chicago, and expects her PhD in 2023.

Stefan Arora-Jonsson is Professor of Organization at Uppsala University, Sweden. He has published on the role of institutionalized norms on the competitive behaviour of organizations, the diffusion of ideas and blame, and the identity work of political parties, and he currently devotes his time to questions of the organization of competition – in particular among schools and political parties. His earlier work is published in *Administrative Science Quarterly*, *Organization Science*, *Sociological Theory* and the *Strategic Management Journal*.

Olivier Bégin-Caouette, PhD, is Assistant Professor of Comparative Higher Education at the Department of Administration and Foundations of Education, at Université de Montréal, Canada. His research focuses on the interactions between higher education systems and political–economic structures, as well as on the internationalization of higher education. He is a founding member of the Laboratory for Interdisciplinary Research on Higher Education, and an associate member of the Interuniversity Research Center on Science and Technology.

Carter Bloch, PhD, is Professor and Center Director at the Danish Centre for Studies in Research and Research Policy, Department of Political Science, Aarhus University, Denmark. His research spans a number of areas within research and innovation policy, including how funding influences research and research performance, innovation ecosystems, and public–private research collaboration. He currently leads the project 'Promoting the socio-economic impact of research – the role of funding practices (PROSECON)' and participates in the Horizon2020 GLOBALINTO project on intangible assets.

Barry Bozeman is Regents' Professor and Arizona Centennial Professor of Technology Policy and Public Management at Arizona State University, Phoenix, AZ, USA. He conducts research on science policy and organization theory. Recent books include *Public Values Leadership* (with Michael Crow, Johns Hopkins University Press, 2021) and *Strength in Numbers: The Science of Team Science* (with Jan Youtie, Princeton University Press, 2019). Bozeman is an elected fellow of the American Association for the Advancement of Science and the National Academy of Public Administration.

Nils Brunsson is Professor of Management and is affiliated with Uppsala University and with the Stockholm Centre for Organizational Research (Score), Sweden. He has published numerous articles and authored, co-authored or edited 30 books in the field of management and organization studies. The list of books includes *A World of Standards* (2000), *Mechanisms of Hope* (2006), *The Consequences of Decision-Making* (2007), *Meta-organizations* (2008), *Reform as Routine* (2009), *Decisions* (2017), *Organizing and Reorganizing Markets* (2018),

Organization outside Organizations (2019) and *Competition: What it is and Why it Happens* (2021).

Susanne Bührer has worked at Fraunhofer ISI, Germany since 1996. Before this, she studied politics, sociology and history at the University of Stuttgart and completed her PhD at the University of Mannheim. Her specialized research fields include program evaluations, impact analysis (including societal impacts), the evaluation of institutional funding measures, gender and innovation, and responsible research and innovation. As a project manager, she has a wide range of experience working on and managing third party-funded projects for national and international clients.

Giliberto Capano is Professor of Public Policy at the University of Bologna, Italy. He specializes in public administration, public policy analysis and comparative higher education. His research focuses on governance dynamics and performance in higher education and education, policy design and policy change, policy instruments' impact, the social role of political science, the policy impact of COVID-19 and leadership as an embedded function of policy making. His recent books are: *A Modern Guide to Public Policy* (coedited with M. Howlett, Edward Elgar, 2020); *Convergence and Diversity in the Governance of Higher Education* (co-edited with D. Jarvis, Cambridge University Press, 2020); and *Trajectories of Governance: How States have Shaped Critical Policy Sectors in the Neoliberal Age* (co-authored with J. Rayner, F. Toth and A. Zito, Palgrave, 2022).

Joanna Chataway is Head of Department for Science, Technology, Engineering and Public Policy at University College London, UK. She is Principal Investigator of the ESRC-funded International Public Policy Observatory. Previously, she was Deputy Director of Science Policy Research Unit (SPRU) and Professor of Science and Technology Policy at SPRU, University of Sussex. She has also worked as the Director of the Health, Innovation and Science research group at RAND Europe and Professor of Biotechnology and Development at the Open University. She has expertise in the areas of science and technology policy, international development, health research and innovation policy and evaluation approaches and methodologies.

Josie Coburn is a doctoral researcher in science and technology policy studies at SPRU, University of Sussex, UK. She is investigating how and why biomedical research changes direction or remains on target, funded by the ERC H2020 Serendipity in Research and Innovation project. She also works on the Multicriteria Mapping initiative and has an interest in opening up complex decision making including consideration of uncertainties. She has a BA in artificial intelligence and MScs in evolutionary and adaptive systems and public policies for science, technology and innovation.

Laura Cruz-Castro is CSIC Senior Researcher at the Institute of Public Goods and Policies in Madrid, Spain. Her area of research is science and innovation policy. She has studied evaluation systems, research careers and the dynamics of research organisations. She is currently interested in the funding of research and its interaction with scientific careers, as well as in organisational characteristics fostering scientific innovations.

Peter Edlund is a postdoctoral researcher at the Department of Business Studies, Uppsala University, Sweden. His current work focuses on the organising of status and competition in and among public sector organisations, such as universities, nursing homes, and upper secondary schools. Edlund's latest book is *Science Evaluation and Status Creation: Exploring the European Research Council's Authority* (Edward Elgar, 2020).

Donna K. Ginther is the Roy A. Roberts and Regents Distinguished Professor of Economics and the Director of the Institute for Policy and Social Research at the University of Kansas, USA. She is also a Research Associate at the National Bureau of Economic Research. She has studied the economic and scholarly impact of research funding on scientific careers as well as race and gender differences in research funding success.

Magnus Gulbrandsen is Professor at TIK Centre for Technology, Innovation and Culture at the University of Oslo, Norway. His research addresses broad themes within science and innovation policy such as quality, impact and interaction between researchers and users, commercialization of research and internationalization. A main interest for him is how and under which conditions research-based knowledge is taken up and used in society. This is also the topic of the Oslo Institute for Research on the Impact of Science, an eight-year project that Gulbrandsen has led since its startup in 2016. He has published in leading scientific journals and worked with industry and policymakers.

Thomas Heinze is Professor of Sociology and Director at the Interdisciplinary Center for Science and Technology Studies at the University of Wuppertal, Germany. He *studied* sociology and economics (Diploma 2000), holds a PhD in administrative science (2005) and a habilitation in sociology (2010). He was Guest Professor at the following universities: Gothenburg (2013), Arizona State (2017) and Caltech (2018). His research interests include the emergence and diffusion of scientific breakthroughs, research organizations, theories of institutional change and organizational theory.

Diana Hicks is Professor in the School of Public Policy, Georgia Institute of Technology, USA, specializing in metrics for science and technology policy. She was the first author on the Leiden Manifesto for research metrics published in *Nature*, translated into 25 languages and awarded the 2016 Ziman award of the European Association for the Study of Science and Technology for collaborative promotion of public interaction with science and technology. She co-chairs the biennial international Atlanta Conference on Science and Innovation Policy and was an editor of Research Evaluation. Professor Hicks has also taught at the Haas School of Business at the University of California, Berkeley; SPRU, University of Sussex; and worked at National Institute of Science and Technology Policy in Tokyo. In 2018 she was elected Fellow of the American Association for the Advancement of Science.

Hugo Horta is an Associate Professor at the Faculty of Education, University of Hong Kong. His main topics of interest refer to academic research processes, outputs and outcomes (including research agendas), mobility and academic inbreeding, and career trajectories of PhD holders. He serves in the editorial/advisory boards of several international higher education and science policy journals.

Arlette Jappe is Senior Researcher at the Interdisciplinary Center for Science and Technology Studies at the University of Wuppertal, Germany. She studied psychology at Free University Berlin (Diploma 2001) and holds a PhD in sociology from Bielefeld University (2007). She was researcher at the Fraunhofer Institute for System and Innovation Research, Karlsruhe (2001–2012) and has broad experience in science and innovation policy research. Her current research interests include research organizations and institutional renewal, higher education institutions, and professionalization of bibliometrics.

Ben Jongbloed is Senior Research Associate in the Center for Higher Education Policy Studies (CHEPS) of the University of Twente in the Netherlands. He has worked at CHEPS for almost 30 years and has published extensively on governance and resource allocation in higher education. Ben also teaches public policy and higher education economics in the University of Twente and Oslo University, and he regularly supervises students and PhD candidates working on their thesis. Ben has been involved in several national and international research projects for clients such as the European Commission, the Organisation for Economic Co-operation and Development (OECD) and national ministries. Ben was part of the team that developed U-Multirank – an alternative to the existing global rankings in higher education. His recent work is on performance-based funding and embedding entrepreneurship and sustainability in higher education.

So Young Kim is a Professor and the former Head of the Graduate School of Science and Technology at Korea Advanced Institute of Science and Technology in South Korea. As an academic and a public intellectual interested in high-stake issues at the interface of Science and Technology (S&T) and public policy, she has conducted large-scale S&T policy projects and served numerous committees providing S&T policy advice for the Korean government. Her work has been recognized by various awards including the National Assembly Award for the Contribution to S&T Policy.

Jussi Kivistö is a Professor in the Higher Education Group, Faculty of Management and Business at Tampere University, Finland. His research focuses on higher education policy, management and funding. Dr Kivistö has lead several development and evaluation projects related to higher education in national and international level and served as a part-time consultant in the World Bank. Dr Kivistö has published over 100 publications, mostly in the field of higher education research.

Alexander Kladakis is a PhD Fellow at the Danish Centre for Studies in Research and Research Policy, Department of Political Science, Aarhus University, Denmark. He has a background in sociology and is currently working on a dissertation that compares the career trajectories of elite researchers in Denmark and the UK. His research interests include the scientific workforce, career paths in academia, scientific elites, science funding and problem choice.

Silvia Mirlene Nakano Koga has a bachelor's degree in educational sciences and a master's degree in public administration from the University of Buenos Aires, Argentina. She is a PhD candidate in educational sciences at Université de Montréal, Canada and her doctoral thesis focuses on the analysis of research coordination in federal countries. She's a student member of the Laboratory for Interdisciplinary Research on Higher Education.

Quintin Kreth is a doctoral student in the School of Public Policy at the Georgia Institute of Technology School of Public Policy, USA. His research examines scientific careers, training and workplaces. He has particular interests in how research activities and related productivity vary across institutional settings in the USA, particularly among the less elite and lower-resourced.

Grit Laudel is a Senior Researcher in the Department of Sociology at the Technical University Berlin, Germany. She is a sociologist of science who investigates the influence of institutions on the conduct and content of research.

Benedetto Lepori obtained is PhD at the Faculty of Communication of the Università della Svizzera Italiana in Lugano, Switzerland, with a thesis on the Swiss research policy and is currently Titular Professor at the Institute of Communication and Public Policy of the same university. He is a recognized scholar in the field of research policy and higher education; among his major contributions have been the development of indicators for the analysis of public research funding and the development of the European Tertiary Education Register, the reference database of European higher education. He has published nearly 100 papers in leading international journals in the field, such as *Research Policy, Organization Studies, Accounting, Organization and Society, Studies in Higher Education* and *Science and Public Policy*.

Huan Li is a PhD candidate at the Faculty of Education, University of Hong Kong. His main research interests include the postgraduate education, academic profession, academic entrepreneurship and science and technology studies. Much of his current work aims to gain in-depth understanding of factors influencing doctoral talents' intended and actual career trajectories in Greater China.

Émanuelle Maltais has a bachelor's degree in political science from Laval University and a master's degree in Educational Sciences at TÉLUQ University, Canada. She is a PhD candidate in educational sciences at Université de Montréal and her doctoral thesis focuses on the effects of research funding mechanism on university research production. She is a student member of the Laboratory for Interdisciplinary Research on Higher Education.

Charles Mathies is an Assistant Professor in the Higher Education and Community College Leadership program at Old Dominion University, USA. He also holds ancillary appointments at the Finnish Institute for Educational Research in the University of Jyväskylä and Tampere University in Finland. Dr Mathies's research focuses on the role of global markets, politics and infrastructures in the movement of knowledge, data and people across borders.

Julia Melkers is Professor in the School of Public Policy and leads the ROCS lab (Research on Careers in Science) at the Georgia Institute of Technology, USA. Her funded research examines issues relevant to careers in science and engineering, from early to established career stages. Her interests are in the social and institutional factors that matter in career progression. As of August 2022 she will be Director of the Center for Organization Research and Design at Arizona State University.

Irene Ramos-Vielba is a Senior Researcher at the Danish Centre for Studies in Research and Research Policy, Aarhus University, Denmark. With a background in political science and sociology, she has worked in various research institutions and countries. Her research interests include science-society interconnections, research funding and the societal relevance of research. She has participated as an advisor/consultant for governmental agencies and as an expert on science and innovation policy for the European Commission.

Emanuela Reale is research director and currently director of the Research Institute on Sustainable Economic Growth IRCRES CNR, Italy. Her main areas of interest are higher education policy, governance, R&D funding, Science, Technology and Innovation indicators, research evaluation and impact assessment, with a special focus on Social Sciences and Humanities research. Emanuela has been Principal Investigator in several national and European projects and Coordinator of European Commission tenders on transnational interdisciplinary academic research and government R&D funding. She has published in and is a referee for many international journals dealing with research policy, research evaluation and higher education studies.

Juan D. Rogers is Professor of Public Policy at the School of Public Policy, Georgia Institute of Technology, USA. He received his professional engineer degree in electrical engineering from the University of Buenos Aires and PhD in science and technology studies from the Virginia Polytechnic Institute and State University. He specializes in the analysis and evaluation of science, technology and innovation policies in economic development, competitiveness and the uses of science and technology to address special social or economic needs.

Luis Sanz-Menéndez is CSIC Research Professor at the Institute of Public Goods and Policies in Madrid, Spain. He has also been involved in science and technology policy making at the Spanish Ministry of Science and Technology and Chairing the OECD Committee for Scientific and Technological Policy between 2007 and 2015. His research relates to research and innovation policies including research funding, public research organisations and universities, academic careers and program evaluation.

Thomas Scherngell is Senior Scientist and Head of the research group Innovation Dynamics and Modelling at the Center for Innovation Systems and Policy of the Austrian Institute of Technology (AIT). He is also Lecturer at the Vienna University of Economics and Business (WU) and holds a *venia docendi* (habilitation) in economic geography and regional science, received from WU in 2012. Before joining AIT in 2007, Thomas Scherngell was a full-time university assistant at the Department of Economic Geography and GIScience at WU (2002–2007). He also held a post-doc fellowship at the University of Macau, China (2012–2013).

Sarah Seus has worked at Fraunhofer ISI, Germany since 2014. Her work focuses on the evaluation of science and innovation policies where she is specifically interested in evaluating the societal impacts of research and transition processes. She has been the project manager of several evaluations of research programmes. She currently leads the Responsible Research Innovation activities in the H2020 funded project 'Shared Green Deal'. Sarah Seus studied political science in Germany (Catholic University of Eichstätt) and France (IEP Rennes/IEP Lille; MA in 2008).

Gunnar Sivertsen is Research Professor at the Nordic Institute for Studies in Innovation, Research and Education in Oslo, Norway. Sivertsen contributes to research on research and to science-based innovation in the development of research evaluation, research funding and the use of indicators. He has advised the development of the research evaluation and funding systems in several countries.

Mads P. Sørensen, PhD, is Senior Researcher at the Danish Centre for Studies in Research and Research Policy, Department of Political Science, Aarhus University, Denmark. He has a background in the history of ideas and has specialised in meta-research, research integrity and social theory. His current research interests include research integrity, key concepts/ideas in research policy, changing conditions of knowledge production, non-knowledge, risk society and social theory. He is presently coordinating a large European project on research integrity: SOPs4RI (https://sops4ri.eu/).

Duncan A. Thomas is a Senior Researcher at the Danish Centre for Studies in Research and Research Policy, Aarhus University, Denmark. He is interested in how excellence, quality and societal impacts of research interrelate with policy, funding, evaluation and organisational conditions. He has researched various fields, at small scales and national levels, explored instances of supranational, multilateral cooperation and studied massively collaborative global science, like CERN-LHC particle physics. He has also advised UK, European and US industries, regulators and policymakers.

Inga Ulnicane is Senior Research Fellow at De Montfort University, UK. Her interdisciplinary expertise is in areas of science, technology and innovation politics, policy and governance. Her publications focus on topics such as artificial intelligence, dual use, European integration in research and innovation, grand societal challenges and responsible research and innovation. She has also prepared commissioned studies for the European Parliament and European Commission, and contributed to a number of international projects including the Human Brain Project.

Rainer Walz is Deputy Director of Fraunhofer ISI, Germany and Head of the Competence Center Sustainability and Infrastructure Systems. He studied economics and political science at the University of Freiburg and at Brock University, Canada. He has a PhD and 'habilitation' in economics. His research focuses on sustainability and innovation, environmental and natural resources policy, dynamics and competitiveness in green markets, interaction between economic development, globalization and the environment, and the analysis of impacts of new technologies.

Richard Woolley is a sociologist working at INGENIO (CSIC-UPV) in Valencia, Spain.

Ohid Yaqub works on research policy and biomedical innovation. In previous work, he has examined the rate and direction of vaccine innovation. His current focus is on the desirability and feasibility targeting research, and the idea of serendipity in research. Neglected diseases caught his attention in the 1990s, after which he studied for a BSc in biochemistry, and an MSc and PhD in science policy.

1. Introduction to the *Handbook of Public Funding of Research*: understanding vertical and horizontal complexities

Benedetto Lepori, Ben Jongbloed and Diana Hicks

1.1   BACKGROUND AND OBJECTIVES

Scientific research requires resources – financial, human, infrastructural, legal, social, and cultural, whose provision is an ever more expensive and complex undertaking. This *Handbook* explores the financing of scientific research by national governments and the European Union. Since WWII, the increasing importance of knowledge for society and the economy has encouraged governments to adopt research policy and funding as a 'new' core task of the state. Research policy bridges the state and the science system (Guston, 2000) mainly through the distribution of public subsidies (Braun and Gilardi, 2006). According to the Organisation for Economic Co-operation and Development (OECD) estimates, OECD governments spent $497 billion on research and development in 2020, an amount that has doubled over the past 15 years (OECD, 2021). This expanding commitment speaks to governments' hopes that research will support economic growth, create jobs, enhance social welfare, protect the environment, and expand the frontiers of human knowledge.

The level of public resources invested in science differs between countries (Larrue et al., 2018) depending on the challenges the country faces, its government's ambitions, and political leaders' beliefs about the function of the state in research and innovation systems – on how much direction should be given by the state and how much funding should be made available for which objectives (and challenges). This *Handbook* discusses the underlying ideas and rationales for investing public funds in the research activities carried out by universities, public research organizations (PROs), and government labs. It compares the political economy of science funding (e.g. Martin and Nightingale, 2000) and the various coordination roles governments play in research funding systems (Lepori, 2011) to better understand countries' research funding regimes.

Government provides research funding to universities, the leading research performers, as recurrent funds, selective, competitive funds, or combinations of the two. Various governmental agencies working at (or in-between) different levels, semi-public organizations, and research councils are involved in deciding on research resources and the purposes and conditions attached (Larrue et al., 2018). This *Handbook* analyses the types and channels of funding, modalities to distribute funds, eligibility requirements, and other conditions connected to the research funds. The chapters also discuss how resource allocation functions at the level of the research performers – the universities, PROs, research groups, and individual researchers – and what strategies these entities employ in reaction to trends and reforms in their funding environment. Universities and PROs are encouraged to generate and (to different degrees) compete for these financial resources (Krücken, 2021). However, they are increasingly

1

required to collaborate with other public and private partners and work across disciplinary borders to develop social and technological innovations.

Most governments aim to achieve multiple goals by funding research-performing organizations. In broad terms, they look for: (1) excellent ('breakthrough') research (Dasgupta and David, 1994), (2) research used by society (e.g. Hessels and Freeman, 2010), (3) the build-up of research capacity and research skills (Boud and Lee, 2009), and (4) efficiency in the use of public resources (Hicks, 2012). In this mix, fostering excellence in science has been a critical objective of many governments (Moore et al., 2017). The funding instruments employed to encourage breakthroughs in research and the creation of clusters of excellence are therefore also discussed in this *Handbook*, along with the accompanying excellence initiatives and their effects – intended as well as unintended.

The objectives of encouraging excellence in science and, simultaneously, encouraging research that contributes to technological and social innovation are closely connected to the balance between a top-down versus a bottom-up approach in science funding. The top-down approach relates to funding earmarked by funding agencies for specific research projects. In contrast, bottom-up approaches leave considerably more degrees of freedom to researchers and research groups to set their own research agenda.

The top-down approach is finding favor as research and innovation systems worldwide undergo fundamental change owing to new societal challenges. To tackle those challenges – also known as the Sustainable Development Goals – governments are enlisting universities and PROs using targeted research programs and other financial incentives. Researchers and their organizations are challenged to reposition themselves – even transform themselves – in this new funding environment to perform their public duty. Here the idea of mission orientation has become increasingly popular (Mazzucato, 2018). Mission-oriented research and innovation policies address the grand societal challenges, such as climate change, energy transition, and the digital divide in societies. Mission-oriented funding encourages stakeholders from different backgrounds (both public and private) to collaborate on tackling big challenges ('missions').

The contributors to this book offer a critical analysis of the changing rationales for public support for research. They present insights into how the mechanisms of public research funding have changed over time and how funding arrangements interact with other elements in national research and innovation systems. The authors employ a range of theoretical perspectives, using approaches from economics (e.g. innovation economics, institutional economics, principal–agent theory), sociology (i.e. sociology of organizations, sociology of science), political theory, and public administration.

Handbooks that collect the multiple perspectives, strategies, and viewpoints related to the public funding of science do not exist. There are handbooks on science and public policy (e.g. Simon et al., 2019a), on innovation (e.g. Fagerberg et al., 2005), and on the economics of innovation (Hall and Rosenberg, 2010). And this *Handbook* overlaps with them, for example, regarding the governance of science, technology, and innovation systems (e.g. Kuhlmann and Ordóñez-Matamoros, 2017). Still, these books primarily focus on the role of public funding and R&D tax incentives for industrial innovation or on support for entrepreneurship and innovators. Therefore, we believe that this *Handbook* fills a critical gap given the state's prominent role in supporting science.

As we highlight in the following sections, the research policy and funding landscape have become increasingly complex and differentiated in terms of the underlying rationales (Elzinga,

2012), of the mix of instruments adopted to implement policies (Flanagan et al., 2011; Capano et al., 2020) and of actors and organizational arrangements involved in the management of funding (Simon et al., 2019b). We offer this *Handbook* as a first attempt to grapple with the complexity of public research systems in order also to help grounding future work on research funding systems.

1.2 IDEAS AND NARRATIVES: FROM THE ENDLESS FRONTIER TO GRAND CHALLENGES

The chapters in this *Handbook* address questions raised by structural shifts in the research funding system over the past several decades (Elzinga, 2012). After the success demonstrated by science in WWII with the invention of penicillin, radar, and the nuclear bomb, governments came to believe that supporting research was essential and would lead to health and prosperity. Spurred by Vannevar Bush's work in WWII and his subsequent report *Science: The Endless Frontier*, the US government established research grant funding in many agencies and founded the National Science Foundation as the focus for basic research across all fields of science. European governments provided universities with core, block, or institutional funding based on historical factors and a size-based formula. Under these arrangements, the research community had professional autonomy. Competitively awarded research grants were also available to fund specific, expensive projects. The post-war era is often looked back upon as a kind of golden age for science when growth in budgets could accommodate growth in the scientific community, and university expansion offered faculty jobs for most new PhDs (Stephan, 2013).

At this time, the foundational justifications for public science funding were articulated in the seminal work of Nelson (1959) and Arrow (1962). Their research pointed to market failures in the production of scientific research and stressed the need for governments to support research – in particular, the types of research for which there is little immediate demand in the market. Governments allocate public funding to researchers and to the universities and PROs that employ them in hopes of societal benefits, and scientists were granted autonomy to pursue those goals with integrity. Governments' expectations of something in return, high-quality research and useful knowledge, meant that a mutual dependency between funders and research performers developed, with mutual benefits. This relationship has often been referred to as a social contract (Guston and Keniston, 1994).

The classic classifications of research activity were also established in this era. In 1963 a group of OECD and science indicator experts met in Frascati, Italy, and produced the first edition of the Frascati Manual to set out a standard methodology for collecting statistics about research funding. The Frascati Manual classification of research activities into basic, applied, and development has featured in research funding statistics ever since (OECD, 2015).

After several decades, international economic competition heightened, government budgets tightened, and research funding arrangements evolved in directions less congenial for the research community (Geuna, 2001; Martin, 2003). Concepts such as 'academic capitalism' (Slaughter and Rhoades, 2004) and New Public Management (Ferlie et al., 2008) emerged to frame thinking on how to allocate public research funding. These policy models promoted the notion that competition and economic incentives are better ways to achieve policy goals, even in research and higher education (Capano, 2011). They generated a move from institutional funding based on block grants (with significant degrees of freedom for those receiving the funds) to funding increasingly tied to measures of performance and policy goals (Geuna, 2001; Stephan, 1996; Hicks, 2012). At the same time, a tendency could be observed to make research performing organizations rely more on funding for research projects, awarded based on competition between proposals submitted by investigators. Such project funding is limited in scope, budget and time (Lepori et al., 2007). With the increase in project funding, we see the emergence of a mixed model, where universities and public research organizations are increasingly competing for funds and therefore influenced by research priorities and conditions set by funders.

When the emphasis on project grants increased, so did the competition, resulting in lower overall success rates for grant proposals (Lepori et al., 2007). Funders' increased research evaluation and specification of goals reduced researcher autonomy (Whitley et al., 2018). Many chapters in this *Handbook* examine the resulting tensions: concentration of resources (Bloch, Kladakis, and Sørensen, Chapter 8; Jappe and Heinze, Chapter 13), increased competition (Arora-Jonsson, Brunsson, and Edlund, Chapter 11), effects on universities (Kivistö and Mathies, Chapter 12) and public research institutes (Cruz-Castro and Sanz-Menéndez, Chapter 14) and researchers (Laudel, Chapter 16), as well as the complexities of designing such public funding instruments (Sivertsen, Chapter 6).

Governments also began to focus on the results achieved by national research enterprises (Reale, Gulbrandsen, and Scherngell, Chapter 7). In the US, the discussion was of the changing social contract, expecting university research to develop a more direct relationship to innovation and the market, for example, universities patenting their research results. In Europe, the European Framework programs exemplified government interest in new technology and innovation, funding projects directed to specified goals. The classic basic, applied, and development classification began to seem too limited. Alternatives were proposed, such as Pasteur's Quadrant, which recognized that research could be motivated by both the quest for fundamental understanding and considerations of use (Stokes, 1997), or Mode 2, which emphasized research conducted in the context of application (Gibbons et al., 1994). Both frameworks transcended the basic/applied research categorization and allowed for research that addressed combinations of intellectual and practical problems (Hicks, 2016).

Through the Framework program, the EU also hoped to raise European research spending to 3% of GDP, strengthen the research efforts of weaker countries, and close the technology gap with the US and Asia. In Chapter 4, Ulnicane tracks the advent and growth of these programs attending to the extent to which their goals were achieved. In Asia, countries successfully built high-tech economies through strategic support of applied research and innovation. Kim (Chapter 22) explores the extent to which current research funding programs in Asian countries reflect these historical origins and the tensions that result. The differences between funding systems and their evolution can be understood with reference to broader differences in the type of capitalism and governance in each country (Bégin-Caouette, Nakano Koga, and Maltais, Chapter 20).

Currently, we are witnessing another addition to research funding rationales, with attention turning to grand societal challenges, UN Sustainable Development Goals, and fostering a transition to a greener energy mix (Simon et al., 2019b; Mazzucato, 2018). Research funding statistics increasingly include breakdowns by purpose of funding. Bozeman (Chapter 2) reminds us of the importance of this move towards framing research in terms of more than economic gain and addressing broader public values. However, the complexity of engaging research with these goals raises challenges for the design of funding programs. Previous, similarly motivated, research programs to develop cures for neglected diseases have not lived up to expectations. Coburn, Yaqub, and Chataway (Chapter 10) identify their many challenges. The lessons learned should be heeded by those attempting to solve other societal challenges through research. Bührer, Seus and Walz delineate exactly how much a substantial funding program can by itself transform research into a transdisciplinary effort addressing grand challenges and argue for broader efforts to reform research institutions and incentives (Chapter 9).

Research funding is also challenged to incorporate other dimensions into program design. Diversity, equity, and inclusion are receiving increased attention as well as responsible research. Several chapters examine the current state of support and programs that target different types of researchers. Cruz-Castro, Ginther, and Sanz-Menéndez (Chapter 17) provide a thorough review of our understanding of the extent to which women and underrepresented groups are disadvantaged under current funding policies. Melkers, Woolley, and Kreth (Chapter 18) itemize the American and European programs that offer support targeted to different stages of research career development.

None of these rationales has gone away; each shift simply adds another element to the mix. The complexity of funding program design is thus increasing (Reale, Gulbrandsen, and Scherngell, Chapter 7; Thomas and Ramos-Vielba, Chapter 15). Scholars and policymakers tend to take for granted the high level capacity needed to administer constellations of modern research funding instruments. Rogers (Chapter 21) makes visible this complexity in examining cases of countries that struggle to implement the programs that characterize modern research systems. As we demand that research funding address ever more dimensions of research systems, Rogers' chapter is a helpful reminder that we demand ever more capacity from government agencies.

1.3   POLICY MIXES AND THE COMPLEXITY OF FUNDING INSTRUMENTS

As highlighted in the previous section, current science policies have become layered in their conceptual content and goals. While supporting basic science remains essential, funding systems also aim to foster economic innovation and enable societies to respond to grand challenges such as climate change. Moreover, while research inherently requires risk-taking and accepting failures and duplications, the research funding policy discourse also focuses on efficiency and evaluating the return on investment in public research. These inherent tensions generate complexities in the design of policy interventions that have to serve multiple ideologies and goals. Diversity of national contexts (Bégin-Caouette, Nakano Koga, and Maltais, Chapter 20) and the tendency of policy interventions to persist and accumulate over time further increase complexity. Therefore, current research funding systems are by and large incoherent accumulations of instruments (Aagaard, 2017) that have been mostly reformed rather than replaced as thinking shifted (Reale, Gulbrandsen, and Scherngell, Chapter 7).

Therefore, beyond individual interventions, the 'policy mix' matters for achieving policy goals (Kern et al., 2019). Reale, Gulbrandsen, and Scherngell (Chapter 7) suggest that differentiation of instruments and organizational settings is an important strategy to keep apart the potentially conflicting logics and goals of science policy (Skelcher and Smith, 2015). Yet most studies of research funding focus on single funding instruments, while how different instruments complement each other and interact at the performer level remains under-investigated.

The notion of 'funding configurations' put forward by Thomas and Ramos-Vielba (Chapter 15) may represent a helpful tool in this direction. However, we still lack systematic studies of policy interactions in research funding and analytical categories to reduce the observed complexity (Capano and Pritoni, 2019; Cocos and Lepori, 2020).

As for individual instruments, a prominent characteristic of research funding instruments is the complexity of their 'delivery package' (Salamon, 2002), i.e. the concrete ways in which the instrument works. As shown extensively by Reale, Gulbrandsen and Scherngell (Chapter 7), research funding programs vary in their goals and modes of intervention to select proposals, manage projects and evaluate results. These functions are managed in a complex setting characterized by different types of research funding organizations. Care is required when comparing national systems because the delivery of seemingly similar programs can be quite different (Flanagan et al., 2011). In the *Handbook*, Sivertsen (Chapter 6) provides a rich account of the delivery of performance-based funding to universities. He demonstrates that how a university involves faculty and implements a national scheme largely accounts for the effects of the government's instrument and for its ability to affect research performers' behavior.

Along the same lines, both Kivistö and Mathies (Chapter 12) and Reale, Gulbrandsen, and Scherngell (Chapter 7) display the lasting influence of principal–agent theory in the design of policy interventions in research funding and argue that in most situations encountered in research funding its core behavioral assumptions are not warranted, therefore potentially jeopardizing the achievement of policy goals. When analyzing the processes leading to the launch of research initiatives on rare diseases (Coburn, Yaqub, and Chataway, Chapter 10), and the impact on research of programs oriented towards ecological transition (Bührer, Seus, and Walz, Chapter 9), the authors indeed show that the assumption that research performers do what is requested by policymakers is simplistic. Instead, researchers deploy a wide range of strategies to 'capture' programs and exploit them to their own benefit (see Laudel, Chapter 16).

As suggested by Capano (Chapter 5), these remarks call for analysts of research funding systems to make use of concepts developed by political science to analyze policy mixes and instrument systems (Salamon, 2002) and their behavioral effects on performers (Vedung et al., 1998). Reale, Gulbrandsen, and Scherngell (Chapter 7) observe that research funding instruments are not just practical measures to distribute resources but are social institutions that convey cultural and normative contents to the actors in the field (Lascoumes and Le Galès, 2007). These institutional effects might be more potent than (and not always aligned with) direct economic incentives and, for instance, provide legitimacy to the notion that scientists are competing against each other (Arora-Jonsson, Brunsson, and Edlund, Chapter 11; Squazzoni et al., 2013). Horta and Li (Chapter 19) show that the adverse effects of such a competitive culture might well outweigh the direct benefits of economic incentives.

1.4   STRUCTURAL DISPARITIES AND ACTORS' STRATEGIES

Public funding is not an end in itself. The financial transfers that governments make to research funding agencies, universities, PROs, and researchers are meant to advance knowledge and contribute to technological and societal innovation. However, funding allocations will also affect the distribution and concentration of financial resources across researchers and organizations. Some of these effects may be welcomed and are indeed intended by the entities responsible for funding allocations. This is the case for performance-based funding systems, which send research funds to places where performance is outstanding, or where there is the promise of excellent research. However, funding allocations may also lead to other, less desired and unintended effects. We suggest that policy and instruments' design should try to anticipate these unintended effects.

Quite a few of the chapters in this *Handbook* note disparities and inequities created by research funding policies that may favor certain types of institutions, research teams, researchers – and possibly also regions and countries. Competition for research funding may lead to a concentration of funds among fewer researchers.

Promoting excellent research is paramount in an increasing number of financing instruments (Basri and Glass, 2014). The excellence initiatives undertaken by national governments (e.g. in Germany, France, Australia, and in several Nordic countries) aim to increase research quality within the science system by providing selective support to a limited number of researchers or organizations that perform exceptionally well or show the potential to do so. These initiatives to concentrate resources coincide with a tendency toward increasing grant sizes and larger grant forms such as Centres of Excellence (see the chapter by Bloch, Kladakis, and Sørensen, Chapter 8).

The concentration of resources and the increased competition for research grants might reinforce the Matthew effect (Merton, 1968; Bol et al., 2018) – the tendency for a scientist's past success to generate yet more success. This exacerbates uneven resource distribution, favoring those with early funding success and coming at the expense of less-well-established researchers. The distribution of research funding thus inevitably creates disparities at different levels: at the level of the science system, as well as at the level of individual researchers, institutions, regions, and disciplines. Alternatives models for status-based competition aiming at redistributing resources in ways that can counteract the 'Matthew effect' (the so-called 'Mark effect', Bothner et al., 2011) have been proposed and would be worth exploring,

The tension between the goals of research excellence in science and an egalitarian distribution of resources is fundamental in science policy (Hicks and Katz, 2011). It appears in several places in this *Handbook*. For instance, the chapter by Jappe and Heinze (Chapter 13) discusses prestige hierarchies at the organizational and individual levels in university systems that tend to predict funding concentrations (e.g. Lepori et al., 2015). The inequities in access to research funding for researchers in different stages of their careers are addressed by Melkers, Woolley, and Kreth (Chapter 18). The chapter by Cruz-Castro, Ginther, and Sanz-Menéndez (Chapter 17) reviews the relationship between research funding applications and grant recipients, on the one hand, and socioeconomic characteristics such as gender and ethnic background, on the other.

To prevent uneven funding allocations across institutions and regions, the stratification in research systems would need to be taken into account when designing research funding policies, such as the ones employed by the European Commission for allocating its Framework Programme funds and its structural funds across institutions and recipients located in the various EU Member States (Quaglio et al., 2020). To curb tendencies toward uncontrolled resource concentration, funding agencies may design grants policies in ways that provide a more equitable allocation of funding, for instance by targeting researchers at different career stages, both for purposes of broader inclusion and to satisfy distinct career-building objectives. As argued by Cruz-Castro, Ginther, and Sanz-Menéndez (Chapter 17), research remains largely inconclusive as to whether disparities are mainly the result of structural differences, self-selection, or the effect of different types of discrimination or bias during the review and allocation processes. This prompts a further examination of the sources of the disparities.

At the level of the individual researcher, Laudel (Chapter 16) argues that the strategies employed by individual researchers for securing research funding are all about balancing the research portfolio with the external interests expressed in the funding instruments. The outcome will have consequences for the direction and quality of research. Therefore, she argues that the researchers' strategic responses – but also the potential strategies of research organizations (i.e. higher education institutions, PROs) – would have to be taken into account when funding instruments are designed.

Furthermore, organizations and scientists are not just passive recipients of policy interventions, but help shape the research and resource environment and, to some extent, co-design the funding policies (see the chapters by Sivertsen and Laudel in this *Handbook*). For instance, although public authorities can influence the intensity of the competition for research funds, the research community itself very much defines the criteria for and indicators of excellence. Researchers – again, overwhelmingly the more established and senior researchers – sit on funding councils and assessment committees and help decide who should be awarded grants and receive tenure or other forms of recognition (see also Braun, 1998). The degree and origin of the competition for funding and the resulting disparity in funding allocations for different types of researchers and institutions is an issue discussed, for instance, in the chapter by Arora-Jonsson, Brunsson, and Edlund (Chapter 11).

Involving the academic community in designing funding policies is vital to achieving policy goals. From the chapter by Coburn, Yaqub, and Chataway (Chapter 10), we learn that the different degrees of involvement of particular communities and representatives in determining national research agendas are central to explaining the researchers' attention to particular grand societal challenges. Their chapter examines research programs targeting neglected tropical diseases that affect developing countries but receive relatively little funding support in rich countries. Research funding priorities thus can lead to disparities because priority setting is embedded in a wider governance system where multiple actors have different degrees of power to influence research agendas and public budgets.

Normative issues, political will and power, stakeholder interests, prioritization, and the role of international donors and multinational corporate actors are addressed in a few places in this *Handbook*, such as in the chapters by Coburn, Yaqub, and Chataway (Chapter 10) and Bozeman (Chapter 2). In many ways, this is about the political economy of science funding (e.g. Tandberg, 2010). One could argue that, similar to the discussion around innovation policy (Kuhlmann et al., 2010), the priorities, rationales, and instruments of research policy are the result of interactions between the actors involved in research, policy-making, and studying and overseeing research. As argued in the chapter by Bozeman, the research enterprise does not generally seek solutions to problems of broader public concern, as opposed to problems faced by corporations or the military. Hence, the calls for research funding that addresses the grand societal challenges (see above) and pays attention to the world's structural inequities. The chapter by Rogers (Chapter 21), in particular, addresses the challenges faced by countries that do not possess a well-resourced and well-equipped research system and where there are multiple governance deficiencies in the research and innovation systems.

Internationally, disparities in scientific progress at the country level and – partly owing to that – economic performance are evident and lead to the question of how countries that lag can catch up with the rest of the world. The targeted public investments in education, research, and innovation made by some of the countries in Eastern Asia have often been studied. The chapter by Kim (Chapter 22) and also the chapter by Rogers (Chapter 21) highlight the different elements in the development strategies and trajectories of these countries, such as priority setting for research funding in terms of foci and the different types of public research, as well as the need to build up sufficient analytical and professional capacity in the (government) institutions supporting the academic research enterprise.

Countries and equally research organizations at various levels must make multiple trade-offs between the objectives of excellence, equity, relevance, efficiency, selectivity, and diversity in research funding. The chapters in our *Handbook* provide multiple examples of strategies and research policies to address these objectives while trying to remedy the disparities that might result from the distribution of research funds.

1.5   PUBLIC RESEARCH FUNDING: A PRIMER AND A GUIDE TO THE *HANDBOOK*

A helpful way to map the contents of this *Handbook* locates components of public research funding systems in organizational layers and allocation channels. More precisely, Figure 1.1 (based on Lepori, 2011) distinguishes between the following layers.

- *Four organizational layers:*
  - at the top, a policy design process where the amount of public research funding is decided and funding instruments are devised;
  - next, a layer of instruments where funding schemes by the state and dedicated Research Funding Organizations are administered;
  - followed by recipients and allocators, research organizations such as higher education institutions (HEIs) and PROs obtain research funds from governments and disburse them;
  - and, finally, research performers, research groups, and individual researchers acquire funding (from institutional and project funds) to conduct research.
- *Two main allocation modes:*
  - institutional funding allocated to research organizations (primarily HEIs and PROs) as part of their 'regular' budget;
  - project funding, awarded directly to research groups and individuals for research activities limited in scope and duration (Lepori et al., 2007).

While we have highlighted cross-cutting themes in the previous sections, it is helpful to locate the individual chapters of this *Handbook* in such a map (Figure 1.1) to visualize the book's structure.

1.5.1   The Policy Design Layer

The *policy design layer* deals with the overall public funding policies within countries and/or at the international level. While the design of policy and the associated regulatory frameworks have been seen as a struggle between actors and actor coalitions for power and resources (Sabatier, 2007), policy scholars also highlight the central importance of the ideational dimension, i.e. the cultural assumptions, the norms and policy goals, which (should) underlie the

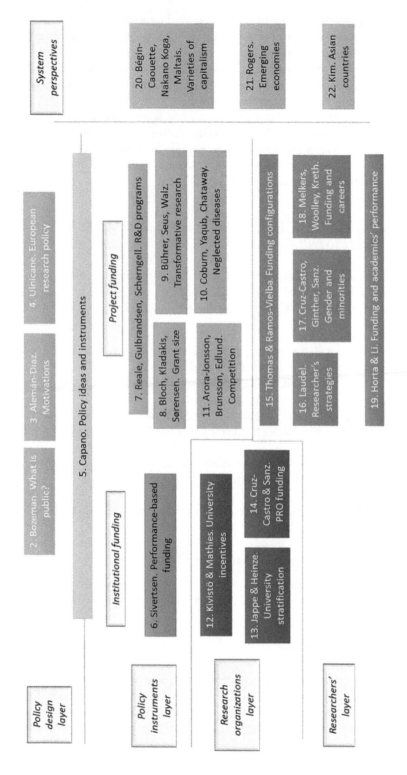

Figure 1.1   Mapping the Handbook chapters

design of policy interventions (Surel, 2000). In Chapter 5, Capano takes stock of the political sciences literature to elaborate on the roles of policy ideas in policy design and to show the impact of managerial ideas such as performance evaluation in the selection and design of policy instruments and, specifically, of performance-based funding (Hicks, 2012).

Focusing more specifically on ideas and narratives driving public research funding, the chapter by Alemán-Díaz (Chapter 3) analyzes the competing motivations for research funding as a persistent tension between the 'autonomy of creativity' and the 'politics of purpose' (see also Stephan, 2013). In turn, Ulnicane's chapter (Chapter 4) analyzes how these motivations came into play in developing EU funding policies and programs, showing that a plurality of motivations spurred the rapid growth of EU engagement with research.

The policy layer also deals with politics, i.e. the processes and negotiations that decide goals, priorities (Thurmaier and Willoughby, 2001), funding levels (Li and Zumeta, 2015) and the distribution of funding between different types of performers and agencies (Tandberg, 2010; Weerts and Ronca, 2012). While several chapters deal with priority setting and the underlying rationales, such as Coburn, Yaqub, and Chataway (Chapter 10), this *Handbook* does not include a chapter on the politics of public research funding, i.e. how actors' interests and power influence the competition for funding between science policy and other policy domains (Thurmaier and Willoughby, 2001; Li and Zumeta, 2015). Such a chapter might have explored why changes in policy rationales and funding instruments do not necessarily imply shifts in the final allocation of funding, noting how the relative power of the involved actors shapes outcomes. There is indeed empirical evidence of such political games in US higher education funding (McLendon, 2003). Nevertheless, we have a better understanding of how the science budget is embedded in national political contexts (see Larédo and Mustar, 2001; Chubin et al., 1990) and how it reflects the vested interests of actors.

1.5.2 The Policy Instrument Layer

The *policy instrument layer* deals with the mix of channels and instruments through which funding is allocated (Flanagan et al., 2011) and the allocation criteria applied, as well as the respective organizational arrangements (Lepori and Reale, 2019). A broad distinction has been drawn between recurrent institutional funding provided to research organizations (Lepori and Jongbloed, 2018) and project funding awarded to research groups and individuals for specific activities (Lepori et al., 2007). However, within these broad categories, differentiation has occurred (Larrue et al., 2018; Cocos and Lepori, 2020) as an outcome of layering processes (Aagaard, 2017).

The *Handbook* includes two chapters dealing with institutional funding and the introduction of performance elements in higher education funding. Sivertsen (Chapter 6) and an overview of project funding schemes and research funding organizations by Reale et al. (Chapter 7). Additionally, three chapters deal with emerging issues in grant funding. Bloch, Kladakis, and Sørensen (Chapter 8) discuss whether the observed trend towards large grants and centers of excellence is beneficial to research. Bührer, Seus, and Walz (Chapter 9) examine the potential and risks of program funding to support the transformation of research systems and to address societal needs. Coburn, Yaqub, and Chataway (Chapter 10) analyze the history of efforts to develop treatments for neglected diseases. These chapters highlight deep questions about the policy mix in research funding raised by the (re-)emergence of societal topics in research policy and funding (see Section 1.2).

Finally, the section on policy instruments includes a conceptual chapter on the meaning and construction of competition by Arora-Jonsson, Brunsson, and Edlund (Chapter 11). Competition has become a 'mantra' in public research funding. Competition's benefits are expected to include inducing responsiveness to funders' priorities and greater efficiency (Musselin, 2018; Krücken, 2021). Yet sociological theory suggests that competition is not given but socially constructed by the actors in the field (Arora-Jonsson et al., 2020) and, indeed, researchers and research organizations are involved in the design and implementation of research funding programs (Braun, 2003). The state does play a distinct role in organizing competition, but Chapter 11 argues that its concrete enactment also depends on how research actors engage with the state-defined rules (Edelman et al., 1999). The chapter, therefore, highlights a critical bridge between policy design, implementation and the strategies of research organizations and researchers.

1.5.3   The Research Organizations Layer

The *research organizations layer* deals with how research organizations such as higher education institutions and public research organizations obtain institutional funding from the state and distribute it to their research groups. The construction of public research organizations, notably HEIs, as organizational actors capable of their own strategies (Brunsson and Sahlin-Andersson, 2000) and of competing for resources (Deiaco et al., 2010) represents a significant change in European public research systems in recent decades, where HEIs had tended to be rather weak strategic actors (Whitley, 2008).

Core concerns are funding strategies and resourcing differences between organizations (Sanz-Menéndez and Cruz-Castro, 2003; Lepori et al., 2019) and whether research organizations follow national strategic priorities and criteria when distributing money internally (Moll and Hoque, 2011). Kivistö and Mathies (Chapter 12) review the empirical evidence on how HEIs respond to national incentivization schemes, whose design is discussed in Sivertsen's chapter (Chapter 6). They show that performance-based funding builds on strong assumptions about behavioral responses of the treated organizations based on mainstream economic thinking; if these are not warranted, there is no guarantee that incentives trickle down as expected (Aagaard, 2015). Taking a structural perspective, Jappe and Heinze (Chapter 13) show how the allocation of public funding is driven mainly by persistent reputational hierarchies within higher education systems and by competition between HEIs for talented academics. They argue that the supply side of funding (White, 2001) should be taken into account to avoid funding reforms simply ending up strengthening inherited disparities.

Finally, while most of the research on changes in public research funding has focused on HEIs, PROs remain a vital research actor in many countries in basic and applied research (Crow and Bozeman, 1998; Larédo and Mustar, 2001). Cruz-Castro and Sanz-Menéndez (Chapter 14) argue that the PROs' funding model fundamentally differs from that of HEIs in being closely aligned with their underlying mission and authority structure (Cruz-Castro and Sanz-Menéndez, 2018). Their exploratory chapter identifies an important gap in our understanding of public funding systems.

1.5.4 The Research Group and Individual Researchers Layer

At the level of the *research group and individual researchers* funding is transformed into scientific output, generating cumulative cycles of reputation, which may lead to a very unequal distribution of resources (Latour and Woolgar, 1979), the so-called Matthew effect (Merton, 1968). The contributions in this *Handbook* section focus exclusively on individual researchers. While there have been some studies of funding strategies and portfolios of research groups (Latour and Woolgar, 1979; Joly and Mangematin, 1996), we lack a systematic overview of how research groups are funded. Research groups are challenging to study because their research domains, missions, and organization vary widely and because they can be fluid, with membership shifting between projects. Many groups, especially within universities, are led by a senior professor who acquires funds for their graduate students and junior colleagues. Hence, the chapters explore individual researchers' funding strategies. Yet, with the increase in project funds, we also witness the professionalization of funding acquisition and the tendency of group leaders to act as project managers, a particularly strong tendency in natural and medical sciences.

Laudel argues that researchers and research groups should be considered strategic actors, developing different funding acquisition strategies (Laudel, 2006) and juggling different funding sources, such as projects and institutional funding (Lepori et al., 2016). Understanding how researchers might drive funding helps explain the outcome of funding policies and potentially unintended effects.

To bridge funding instruments and funding strategies, the chapter by Thomas and Ramos-Vielba (Chapter 15) introduces the concept of *funding configurations* to connect the multiplicity of project funding schemes with researchers' strategies for acquiring funding analyzed in Laudel's chapter (Chapter 16). Two additional chapters focus on specific aspects and dimensions of researchers' funding: Melkers, Woolley, and Kreth (Chapter 18) provide an extensive review of grant schemes targeting different career stages, while Cruz-Castro, Ginther, and Sanz-Menéndez (Chapter 17) analyze in a differentiated manner the empirical evidence on gender and minority gaps. The last chapter in this section, by Horta and Li (Chapter 19), assumes a broad view of the impact of funding changes on academic work, covering the consequences for research outputs and other scholarly activities such as teaching and research collaboration.

Finally, the *Handbook* includes three chapters adopting a broader national systems perspective. Bégin-Caouette, Nakano Koga, and Maltais (Chapter 20) adopt a comparative perspective, showing how similarities and differences between OECD countries in the organization of research funding can be associated with the emergence of academic capitalism (Slaughter and Rhoades, 2004) and with institutional variation associated with different countries' welfare regimes (Esping-Andersen, 1990). They provide a nuanced approach to the ongoing debate on the convergence of national research policies. In the same vein, two chapters highlight challenges and institutional structures for specific groups of countries. Rogers (Chapter 21) shows how the lack of specific competencies in the administrative structures of middle-income countries hampers the development of the research system. Kim (Chapter 22) discusses the strong commitment of Asian countries to science and technology, rooted in their successful latecomer developmental strategies executed through multi-year S&T plans.

1.6   FINAL REMARKS: UNDERSTANDING COMPLEXITY AND ITS IMPLICATIONS

It has been observed that public research funding systems have moved from relatively simple configurations with a clear division of tasks, for example, between universities and mission-oriented research centers, to more complex structures with overlapping functions (Aagaard, 2017). As documented in this *Handbook*, complexity has been appearing at the level of ideas and policy rationales (Alemán-Díaz, Chapter 3; Ulnicane, Chapter 4), in the mixes of instruments adopted (Reale, Gulbrandsen, and Scherngell, Chapter 7), in the ecology of research performers such as universities (Jappe and Heinze, Chapter 13) and public research organizations (Cruz-Castro, Ginther and Sanz-Menéndez, Chapter 14), and in the positions and strategies of researchers competing for funding (Laudel, Chapter 16; Cruz-Castro and Sanz-Menéndez, Chapter 17; Melkers, Woolley, and Kreth, Chapter 18).

Our *Handbook* provides evidence that vertical interactions across layers also generates complexity – an aspect frequently disregarded in a literature primarily organized by levels (Cocos and Lepori, 2020). Examples of such cross-level relations are the recursive interaction between policy ideas and policy instruments (Capano, Chapter 5), the enactment of competition organized by the state (Arora-Jonsson, Brunsson, and Edlund, Chapter 11), researchers recomposing different funding instruments in coherent funding portfolios (Thomas and Ramos-Vielba, Chapter 15) and universities becoming involved in the design and implementation of performance-based funding (Sivertsen, Chapter 6).

Beyond this general observation, our final remarks concern challenges and pathways in dealing with forms of complexity at the scholarly level, in policy design, and in the management of research funding instruments.

As scholars, to move beyond 'a night where all cows are black', we suggest developing theoretical lenses so that concepts such as policy narratives, policy instruments, funding markets, and competition can be delineated and disentangled analytically into their different dimensions to become amenable to empirical investigation. Some chapters in our *Handbook* suggest adopting theoretical lenses from related fields, such as the sociology of markets (Arora-Jonsson, Brunsson, and Edlund, Chapter 11) or public policy (Capano, Chapter 5). Many concepts used in the study of research funding, such as strategy, stratification, and policy mixes, have been the object of in-depth theoretical development in other fields. While acknowledging that research policy and funding differs from management or other policy domains, we contend that more can be borrowed from studies in other areas. We also recommend moving beyond the descriptive and inductive approach that characterizes many studies in our field towards theory-led empirical designs, and theoretically informed definitions of objects of study. This, too, will help in disentangling complexity.

As for the design of policies and the selection of instruments, we suggest devoting more attention to (a) the complementarities and interactions between (funding) instruments and (b) designing policies based on a realistic conceptualization of the instruments' interaction with strategic responses of performers. On the former, the traditional policy perspective of addressing a single policy goal with a dedicated instrument and then evaluating the effects in isolation is generating decreasing returns. In the real world, performers interact with multiple instruments and create dependencies between them. For instance, funding instruments targeting the transfer of knowledge from universities to companies critically depend on the working of instruments that support the production of new knowledge. In contrast, excellence instruments for advanced researchers build upon the outcomes of support to early career researchers. This is not to say that all instruments should be designed and analyzed together, but that it is essential to identify the most critical interdependencies for each (new or redesigned) policy intervention. On the latter, we feel that policy design and evaluation still largely rely on a (uniform) top-down action logic derived from principal–agent theory. Many chapters of this *Handbook* suggest that project funding markets may work upstream from the existing hierarchy of performers (White, 2001), while performers, such as research organizations, have considerable leeway in responding to policy interventions. A more realistic representation of this interaction would acknowledge that the 'agents' face a range of often conflicting incentives and, therefore, seek to pursue their own goals within a complex technical, legal, bureaucratic, and cultural landscape. Recognizing this might help in designing more effective public policy (and in understanding what works in research funding).

Finally, we feel that the traditional recipe of multiplying research funding organizations and instruments to target ever more policy goals and performers might be reaching its limits. We ground this view on three observations. First, the long phase of growth in public research funding, which started with WWII, has ended (Lepori and Jongbloed, 2018). Therefore, resources for new instruments are becoming scarce, and accordingly, there is a risk of launching instruments with such limited budgets that management costs are likely to exceed benefits. Second, in many countries, funding instruments increasingly overlap, with the result that similar projects might be submitted to different instruments – at the expense of targeting and increasing the burden on the evaluation system. In the US, Federal agencies are increasingly pushing this administrative complexity onto performers by funding large, multi-year networks and demanding performers meet ever more goals and be responsible for managing the yearly allocation of funding and accountability.

Third, perhaps, more importantly, new challenges, such as achieving Sustainable Development Goals, can be addressed only by synergistic action combining different instruments and through hybrid instruments, targeting both the development of new knowledge and its orientation to broader societal goals. Hence, we suggest that managing the funding instruments portfolio (at the system's and research funding organization level) might require very different approaches than in the past.

These final remarks emphasize the Janus-faced nature of our *Handbook*. On the one hand, it looks back to provide colleagues with a synopsis of the existing body of knowledge on public research funding, thereby filling a notable gap in our domain. On the other hand, it looks forward to new questions and challenges generated by changing contexts and suggests some pathways to begin to address them.

REFERENCES

Aagaard, Kaare. 2015. How incentives trickle down: Local use of a national bibliometric indicator system. *Science and Public Policy*, 42(5), 725–737.

Aagaard, Kaare. 2017. The evolution of a national research funding system: Transformative change through layering and displacement. *Minerva*, 55(3), 1–19.

Arora-Jonsson, Stefan, Nils Brunsson and Raimund Hasse. 2020. Where does competition come from?: The role of organization. *Organization Theory*, 1, 1–24.

Arrow, Kenneth. 1962. Economic welfare and the allocation of resources for invention. In *The Rate and Direction of Inventive Activity: Economic and Social Factors*, pp. 609–626. Princeton University Press.

Basri, Ester and Anna Glass. 2014. Promoting research excellence: New approaches to funding. In *The State of Higher Education*, p. 87. OECD.

Bol, Thijs, Mathijs de Vaan and Arnout van de Rijt. 2018. The Matthew effect in science funding. *Proceedings of the National Academy of Sciences*, 115, 4887–4890.

Bothner, Matthew S., Joel M. Podolny and Edward Bishop Smith. 2011. Organizing contests for status: The Matthew effect vs. the Mark effect. *Management Science*, 57, 439–457.

Boud, David and Alison Lee. 2009. *Changing Practices of Doctoral Education*. Routledge.

Braun, D. (1998). The role of funding agencies in the cognitive development of science. *Research Policy*, 27(8), 807–821.

Braun, Dietmar. 2003. Lasting tensions in research policy-making – a delegation problem. *Science and Public Policy*, 30, 309–321.

Braun, Dietmar and Fabrizio Gilardi. 2006. *Delegation in Contemporary Democracies*. Routledge.

Brunsson, N. and K. Sahlin-Andersson. 2000. Constructing organizations: The example of the Public Sector Reform. *Organization Studies*, 21, 721–746.

Capano, Giliberto, Andrea Pritoni and Giulia Vicentini. 2020. Do policy instruments matter? Governments' choice of policy mix and higher education performance in Western Europe. *Journal of Public Policy*, 40(3), 375–401.

Capano, Giliberto. 2011. Government continues to do its job. A comparative study of governance shifts in the Higher Education Sector. *Public Administration*, 89, 1622–1642.

Capano, Giliberto and Andrea Pritoni. 2019. Exploring the determinants of higher education performance in Western Europe: A qualitative comparative analysis. *Regulation and Governance*, 14(4), 764–786.

Chubin, Daryl E., Edward J. Hackett and Edward J. Hackett. 1990. *Peerless Science: Peer Review and US Science Policy*. SUNY Press.

Cocos, Marta and Benedetto Lepori. 2020. What we know about research policy mix. *Science and Public Policy*, 47, 235–245.

Crow, Michael and Barry Bozeman. 1998. *Limited by Design: R&D Laboratories in the US National Innovation System*. Columbia University Press.

Cruz-Castro, Laura and Luis Sanz-Menéndez. 2018. Autonomy and authority in public research organisations: Structure and funding factors. *Minerva*, 56, 135–160.

Dasgupta, Partha and Paul A. David. 1994. Toward a new economics of science. *Research policy*, 23, 487–521.

Deiaco, Enrico, Magnus Holmén and Maureen McKelvey. 2010. 12. What does it mean conceptually that universities compete? In *Learning to Compete in European Universities: From Social Institution to Knowledge Business*, ed. M. McKelvey and M. Holmén, pp. 300–327. Edward Elgar.

Edelman, Lauren B., Christopher Uggen and Howard S. Erlanger. 1999. The endogeneity of legal regulation: Grievance procedures as rational myth. *American Journal of Sociology*, 105, 406–454.

Elzinga, Aant. 2012. Features of the current science policy regime: Viewed in historical perspective. *Science and Public Policy*, 39, 416–428.

Esping-Andersen, Gosta. 1990. *The Three Worlds of Welfare Capitalism*. Princeton University Press.

Fagerberg, Jan, David C. Mowery and Richard R. Nelson. 2005. *The Oxford Handbook of Innovation*. Oxford University Press.

Ferlie, Ewan, Christine Musselin and Gianluca Andresani. 2008. The steering of higher education systems: A public management perspective. *Higher Education*, 56, 325.

Flanagan, Kieron, Elvira Uyarra and Manuel Laranja. 2011. Reconceptualising the 'policy mix' for innovation. *Research Policy*, 40, 702–713.

Geuna, Aldo. 2001. The changing rationale for European university research funding. *Journal of Economic Issues*, 35, 607–632.

Gibbons, Michael, Camille Limoges, Helga Nowotny, Simon Schwartzman, Peter Scott and Martin Trow. 1994. *The New Production of Knowledge. The Dynamics of Science and Research in Contemporary Society*. SAGE.

Guston, David H. 2000. *Between Politics and Science: Assuring the Integrity and Productivity of Research*. Cambridge University Press.

Guston, David H. and Kenneth Keniston. 1994. Introduction: The social contract for science. In *The Fragile Contract*, ed. D. H. Guston and K. Keniston, pp. 1–41. MIT Press.

Hall, Bronwyn H. and Nathan Rosenberg. 2010. *Handbook of the Economics of Innovation*. Elsevier.

Hessels, Laurens K. and J. Freeman. 2010. *Science and the Struggle for Relevance*. Uitgeverij BOXPress.

Hicks, Diana. 2012. Performance-based university research funding systems. *Research Policy*, 41, 251–261.

Hicks, Diana. 2016. Grand challenges in US science policy attempt policy innovation. *International Journal of Foresight and Innovation Policy*, 11, 22–42.

Hicks, Diana and J. Sylvan Katz. 2011. Equity and excellence in research funding. *Minerva*, 49, 137–151.

Joly, Pierre-Benoit and Vincent Mangematin. 1996. Profile of public laboratories, industrial partnerships and organisation of R&D: the dynamics of industrial relationships in a large research organisation. *Research Policy*, 25, 901–922.

Kern, Florian, Karoline S. Rogge and Michael Howlett. 2019. Policy mixes for sustainability transitions: New approaches and insights through bridging innovation and policy studies. *Research Policy*, 48, 103832.

Krücken, Georg. 2021. Multiple competitions in higher education: A conceptual approach. *Innovation*, 23(2), 163–181.

Kuhlmann, Stefan and Gonzalo Ordóñez-Matamoros. 2017. *Research Handbook on Innovation Governance for Emerging Economies: Towards Better Models*. Edward Elgar.

Kuhlmann, Stefan, Philip Shapira and Ruud Smits. 2010. Introduction. A systemic perspective: The innovation policy dance. In *The Theory and Practice of Innovation Policy. An International Research Handbook*, pp. 1–22. Edward Elgar.

Larédo, Philippe and Philippe Mustar. 2001. *Research and Innovation Policies in the New Global Economy: An International Comparative Analysis*. Edward Elgar.

Larrue, Philippe, Dominique Guellec and Frédéric Sgard. 2018. New trends in public research funding. *OECD Science, Technology and Innovation Outlook 2018 – Adapting to Technological and Societal Disruption*, pp. 185–204. OECD.

Lascoumes, Pierre and Patrick Le Galès. 2007. Introduction: Understanding public policy through its instruments? From the nature of instruments to the sociology of public policy instrumentation. *Governance*, 20, 1–21.

Latour, Bruno and Steve Woolgar. 1979. *Laboratory Life. The Construction of Scientific Facts*. Princeton University Press.

Laudel, Grit. 2006. The art of getting funded: How scientists adapt to their funding conditions. *Science and Public Policy*, 33, 489–504.

Lepori, Benedetto. 2011. Coordination modes in public funding systems. *Research Policy*, 40, 355–367.

Lepori, Benedetto and Ben Jongbloed. 2018. National resource allocation decisions in higher education: objectives and dilemmas. In *Handbook on the Politics of Higher Education*, ed. B. Cantwell, H. Coates and R. King, pp. 211–228. Edward Elgar.

Lepori, Benedetto and Emanuela Reale. 2019. The changing governance of research systems. Agencification and organizational differentiation in research funding organizations. In *Handbook on Science and Public Policy*, ed. S. Kuhlmann, D. Simon, W. Canzler and J. Stamm, pp. 448–463. Edward Elgar.

Lepori, Benedetto, Valerio Veglio, Barbara Heller-Schuh, Thomas Scherngell and Michael Barber. 2015. Participations to European Framework Programs of higher education institutions and their association with organizational characteristics. *Scientometrics*, 105, 2149–2178.

Lepori, Benedetto, Michael Wise, Diana Ingenhoff and Alexander Buhmann. 2016. The dynamics of university units as a multi-level process. Credibility cycles and resource dependencies. *Scientometrics*, 109, 2279–2301.

Lepori, Benedetto, Aldo Geuna and Antonietta Mira. 2019. Scientific output scales with resources. A comparison of US and European universities. *PloS One*, 14(10), 20223415.

Lepori, Benedetto, Peter van den Besselaar, Michael Dinges, et al. 2007. Comparing the evolution of national research policies: what patterns of change? *Science and Public Policy*, 34, 372–388.

Li, Amy Y. and William Zumeta. 2015. State support for higher education. In *The Palgrave International Handbook of Higher Education Policy and Governance*, pp. 463–482. Springer.

Martin, Ben R. 2003. The changing social contract for science and the evolution of the university. In *Science and Innovation: Rethinking the Rationales for Funding and Governance*, ed. A. Geuna, A. Salter and E. Stienmueller, pp. 7–29. Edward Elgar.

Martin, Ben R. and Paul Nightingale. 2000. *The Political Economy of Science, Technology and Innovation*. Edward Elgar.

Mazzucato, Mariana. 2018. Mission-oriented innovation policies: challenges and opportunities. *Industrial and Corporate Change*, 27, 803–815.

McLendon, Michael K. 2003. State governance reform of higher education: Patterns, trends, and theories of the public policy process. In *Higher Education: Handbook of Theory and Research*, pp. 57–143. Springer.

Merton, Robert K. 1968. The Matthew effect in science. The reward and communication systems of science are considered. *Science*, 159(3810), 56–63.

Moll, Jodie and Zahirul Hoque. 2011. Budgeting for legitimacy: The case of an Australian university. *Accounting, Organizations and Society*, 36, 86–101.

Moore, Samuel, Cameron Neylon, Martin Paul Eve, Daniel Paul O'Donnell and Damian Pattinson. 2017. 'Excellence R Us': University research and the fetishisation of excellence. *Palgrave Communications*, 3, 1–13.

Musselin, Christine. 2018. New forms of competition in higher education. *Socio-Economic Review*, 16, 657–683.

Nelson, Richard R. 1959. The simple economics of basic scientific research. *The Journal of Political Economy*, 67, 297–306.

OECD. 2015. *Frascati Manual 2015: Guidelines for Collecting and Reporting Data on Research and Experimental Development*. Paris: OECD.

OECD. 2021. *Main Science and Technology Indicators*. Paris: OECD.

Quaglio, Gianluca, Sophie Millar, Michal Pazour, et al. 2020. Exploring the performance gap in EU Framework Programmes between EU13 and EU15 Member States. In-Depth Analysis. European Union.

Sabatier, P. 2007. *Theories of the Policy Process*. Westview Press.

Salamon, Lester. 2002. *The Tools of Government: A Guide to the New Governance*. Oxford University Press.

Sanz-Menéndez, Luis and Laura Cruz-Castro. 2003. Coping with environmental pressures: public research organisations responses to funding crises. *Research Policy*, 32, 1293–1308.

Simon, Dagmar, Stefan Kuhlmann, Julia Stamm and Weert Canzler. 2019a. *Handbook on Science and Public Policy*. Edward Elgar.

Simon, Dagmar, Stefan Kuhlmann, Julia Stamm and Weert Canzler. 2019b. Introduction: Science and public policy-relations in flux. In *Handbook on Science and Public Policy*, ed. S. Kuhlmann, D. Simon, W. Canzler and J. Stamm. Edward Elgar.

Skelcher, Chris and Steven Rathgeb Smith. 2015. Theorizing hybridity: Institutional logics, complex organizations, and actor identities: The case of nonprofits. *Public Administration*, 93, 433–448.

Slaughter, Sheila and Gary Rhoades. 2004. *Academic Capitalism and the New Economy: Markets, State, and Higher Education*. John Hopkins University Press.

Squazzoni, Flaminio, Giangiacomo Bravo and Károly Takács. 2013. Does incentive provision increase the quality of peer review? An experimental study. *Research Policy*, 42, 287–294.

Stephan, Paula. 1996. The economics of science. *Journal of Economic Literature*, 34(3), 1199–1235.

Stephan, Paula. 2013. The endless frontier: Reaping what Bush sowed? In *The Changing Frontier: Rethinking Science and Innovation Policy*, ed. A. B. Jaffe and B. F. Jones, pp. 321–370. Chicago University Press.

Stokes, Donald E. 1997. *Pasteur's Quadrant. Basic Science and Technological Innovation*. The Brookings Institution.

Surel, Yves. 2000. The role of cognitive and normative frames in policy-making. *Journal of European Public Policy*, 7, 495–512.

Tandberg, David A. 2010. Politics, interest groups and state funding of public higher education. *Research in Higher Education*, 51, 416–450.

Thurmaier, Kurt M. and Katherine G. Willoughby. 2001. *Policy and Politics in State Budgeting*. ME Sharpe.

Vedung, Evert, Marie-Louise Bemelmans-Videc and Ray C. Rist. 1998. Policy instruments: Typologies and theories. In *Carrots, Sticks, and Sermons: Policy Instruments and their Evaluation*, ed. M. Bemelmans-Videc, R. C. Rist and E. Vedung, pp. 21–58. Transaction.

Weerts, David J. and Justin M. Ronca. 2012. Understanding differences in state support for higher education across states, sectors, and institutions: A longitudinal study. *The Journal of Higher Education*, 83, 155–185.

White, H. C. 2001. *Markets from Networks: Socioeconomic Models of Production*. Princeton University Press.

Whitley, Richard. 2008. *Constructing Universities as Strategic Actors: Limitations and Variations*. Manchester Business School.

Whitley, Richard, Jochen Gläser and Grit Laudel. 2018. The impact of changing funding and authority relationships on scientific innovations. *Minerva*, 56(1), 109–134.

PART I

PUBLIC POLICIES AND RESEARCH FUNDING

2. What is *public* about public research? The case of COVID-19 R&D

Barry Bozeman

INTRODUCTION

Acting on the premise that the meaning of "public" not only affects perspectives on public funding of research but also fundamentally affects policy emphases, this chapter seeks to analyze some diverse notions of "public" and their respective implications for research policies. The concepts examined here include (1) public as sector or legal status, (2) public as dimensional publicness or configurations of political and economic authority, (3) public as public choice and (4) public as public values.

Since three of these perspectives are familiar, the chapter gives special attention to the public values meaning of public. But what is a public values perspective? In an emerging literature, in both public policy and in science policy, the term public values can be defined as "those values providing normative consensus about (a) the rights, benefits, and prerogatives to which citizens should (and should not) be entitled; (b) the obligations of citizens to society, the state, and one another; and (c) the principles on which governments and policies should be based" (Bozeman, 2007, 13).

To illustrate the relation of various concepts of public funding, and especially the public values notion of public funding of research, the chapter examines the case of research funding and policies for COVID-19, chiefly but not exclusively in the US. The US is an especially interesting instance of COVID-19 funding because it touches on all the concepts of "public funding" on offer in this chapter. Related, US public funding of research is of special interest because of the many gaps between level of investment and derived outcomes. This is exemplified in the area of public health outcomes.

ALTERNATIVE MEANINGS OF "PUBLIC FUNDING" OF SCIENCE

As mentioned above, four distinct meanings of "public" are examined here, with special emphasis placed on one of these. The four meanings of public include: (1) sector based, also known as ownership; (2) dimensional publicness; (3) public goods; and (4) public values. Each is considered in turn, along with their very different implications for various dimensions of research funding and research policy. Since the public values concept of public has especially stark implications for public research funding, especially the impacts of such funding on economic growth, inequality, and citizens' well-being, this concept receives particular attention. However, it is important to note that each concept of public plays a prominent role in thinking about science, technology and innovation policy.

Sector Boundaries and Public Research

One may bring any of a variety of analytical lens to understanding public funding of research (see Ulnicane, Chapter 4, this *Handbook*), but the current chapter focuses on government policy and performance, with government of private sector servings as legal boundaries worth maintaining and using in analysis. Those focused chiefly on sector recognize, of course, processes of public–private partnerships and hybridization but view these as "off types," departures from the norm, and maintain that sector differences remain a good guide to activities and outcomes.

As mentioned, the chief concern here is with a public values approach, one that leads to quite different issues than a legal boundary-focused sector approach. Thus, it is important to emphasize the compelling evidence of the dangers of equating government or, in the sense most often used, "public" research funding with public values. From the First World War until at least the ratification of the Geneva Protocol in 1975 the US government invested in tens of millions of dollars in research on biological weapons, research that was public in the sense of government sponsorship and provision but that had little bearing on any generally recognized public values. During that period, government researchers and government-sponsored researchers developed bacteria designed to destroy wheat crops, nerve gases, bacteria, including anthrax, delivered through fluorescent particles, and a variety of pathogens including equine encephalitis, melioidosis, glanders, and Q fever, among others. According to one report, one public research project focused on inoculating tics and other parasites with germs that could then be conveyed to a hypothetical enemy once released in their general population (Etukudoh et al., 2020).

To be sure, a sector focus need not be in contradiction to a public values concept of public (or to the other concepts presented here), rather it is a matter of emphasis. Those taking a sector focus on research funding focus primarily and in most respects beneficially on issues related to what government and industry, respectively, are doing with respect to the funding and performance of research.

Dimensional Publicness and Public Research

My own work regarding "publicness" has taken two different but ultimately intersecting routes, each relevant to public research. One stream of work has focused on the limitations of sharp institutional distinctions among sectors, arguing that the rise of hybrid organizations, massive contracting out, government regulation of business, public–private partnerships and, indeed, all manner of institutional and organizational design complexities, conspires to diminish the legal and formal meaning of "public" and "private" and suggests the need for different ways to use the terms productively. The argument is posed as a general one (Bozeman, 1987; Bozeman and Bretschneider, 1994; Walker and Bozeman, 2011), but has also been demonstrated to have considerable relevance to science organizations and institutions (Crow and Bozeman, 1987). The basic idea runs through these diverse works – that publicness and privateness should be thought of as dimensional rather than fixed and that we learn more about organizations by understanding the extent to which they are either government controlled or market controlled than we do by examining only formal legal status.

Perhaps the best example of the application of dimensional publicness to science and technology policy is in the study of scientific institutions. In case studies and documentary analysis of more than 300 US research and development organizations, ones chosen from every sector (public, private, nonprofit) we find that knowing the sources of funding tells us a great deal about behavior. Thus, research organizations that are legally private vary considerably according to the percentage of their funds coming from government contracts and grants. By the same token, research organizations that are formally public behave differently if they have a high degree of private contracts or private service compared with those who exist chiefly on government funding (see Crow and Bozeman, 1998; Bozeman, 2013). Thus, in considering the impacts of government funding, it may be useful to understand not only the source of funding but also the recipient of the funding and the possibility of using policy levers to shape changes in the organizational and institutional designs of research performers.

Public Goods and Public Research

When we discuss "public funding of research," as mentioned, we are in most instances using the term as a shorthand for government funding of research, but the routine parlance does not diminish the importance of public goods conceptualization in "public funding." Indeed, public goods concepts permeate much of thinking about public funding and science policy (e.g. Sanz-Menéndez and Cruz-Castro, 2003; Cruz-Castro et al., 2020).

The term "public goods" is part and parcel of positive political economy theory in general and public choice in particular. It also one of the most common terms in applied policy analysis, popular because it is part of a theoretical formulation that provides guidance for making judgments about public funding and public investment and for allocation functional activities between public and private sector. According to one leading textbook, public goods are "in varying degrees, *nonrivalrous* in consumption, *nonexcludable* in use, or *both*" (Weimer and Vinings, 2017, 72). These authors note that nonrivalrous consumption indicates that if one person consumes a good then the quantity available to other persons is undiminished. Likewise, excludable ownership is another way of saying that an individual or group has control over the use of the good (though, note, with no implication of the justness, beneficence or legitimacy of such control).

From the standpoint of public funding of research, public goods theory highlights a long-standing thesis about the efficient allocation of resources, namely that government should fund research and technology goods deemed public, whereas business should fund research that is private, in the sense of rivalrous, excludable and appropriable. Since so-called basic research is viewed has having special public goods aspects and because results of basic research are generally disseminated in open sources (or ones with minimal charges), most basic research should be supported by government and most development and commercially relevant applied research by industry. Throughout the world, most large government funding research has tended to follow this pattern, focusing more on what is perceived as basic research, doing so either self-consciously or not.

The sector-spending criteria suggested by public goods theory are closely related to market failure theory, the idea that the role of government, should there be a role, should be confined to "interfering" in the market if and only if there is market failure. Market failure theory (Bator, 1958) prescribes use of markets, not government, unless one or more of the following "failures" occur: monopoly, imperfect information to consumers, or the inability for providers of goods and services to protect against "free riders" (those who benefit from a good or service but do not for one reason or another pay for it). For the moment let's not delve deeply into such limitations as, for example, there is almost never perfect information, just as in public goods theory there is almost never a pure public good but, rather, decisions to be made about goods along a spectrum of private (rival, exclusive to degrees) and public (nonrival, nonexclusive to degrees).

Since this chapter's concerns are not with theoretical or operational descriptions of the technical efficiencies of resource investments, there is no reason to go much further in reviewing a widely familiar set of criteria and arguments derived from variants of classical, neoliberal political economy theory. Suffice to say that most such public goods and market failure approaches are more ambiguous than they seem, less rooted in evidence than one might expect, and sometimes include internal logical flaws (Randall, 1983; Cowen, 1985; Joseph and Johnston, 1985; Zerbe and McCurdy, 1999; Furton and Martin, 2019).

Public Values and Public Research

One view of publicness is described above, dimensional publicness which seeks to understand the joint impacts of political and market authority affecting organizations and policies. A different, but not entirely unrelated, meaning of publicness is the publicness of values. Unlike the above-described "dimensional publicness" the normative publicness of public values theory relates more closely to public philosophy and, particularly, to public interest theory than to institutional and organizational relations per se. However, the two interact when we ask, in one form or another, this question, "What mix of political and economic authority best severs the achievement of specific public values?"

A public values focus, whether aimed a science, technology, research and innovation or whether brought to any other public policy and governance domain, always starts with one core assumption: that the purpose of legitimate public action should, first and foremost, be to advance public values, as defined above (Bozeman, 2007, 13). One implication of the public values definition is that public values are not the same thing as "objectives or actions of government policy" nor, for that matter is "legitimate public action," the same as "government action." With respect to research performed by the private sector, public value theory takes no normative positions and, instead, remains agnostic about the role and impacts of privately sponsored research. However, it is important to note that private sector research often makes enormous contributions to public values, whether or not the specific objective to make such contributions or whether the outcomes are a "positive externality" (to reframe that term) from work undertaken primarily for other purposes such as by government mandate or regulation, in search of profit or stock value, or curiosity.

In the case of government science, public value theory is not agnostic with respect to objectives and focus. If research is publicly financed, it is assumed not only that the research should result in public benefit but also that (1) the benefits should be, practically speaking, not just theoretically speaking, as widely distributed as possible, and (2) any negative effects from the research should not only be minimized but when unavoidable should, likewise, be fairly distributed.

There has been some research and theory focused directly on public values-focused science and "public value mapping" (e.g. Bozeman and Sarewitz, 2005, 2011; Joly et al., 2015; Molas-Gallart, 2015; Matt et al., 2017; Bozeman, 2020) but there is a much more expansive literature (or literatures) focused on closely related topics. Scholars from around the world (Ulnicane, 2016; McNie et al., 2016; Mazzucato, 2018; Uyarra et al., 2019; Birch, 2020) have begun to question the aims of innovation and have begun to focus on science policy approaches reinforcing not only economic benefit but also social, including much of the work under the "responsible innovation" rubric (Stilgoe et al., 2013; Hartley et al., 2019). Some documents espouse public values. For example, the *Healthy People 2030* document produced by NIH (2021), although it does not use the term public values, is decidedly a move in that direction.

In Table 2.1 we consider possible strengths and weakness of the four meanings of "public" as pertaining to research. Each has a distinctive contribution to understanding public policy for research policy.

CONCEPTS OF PUBLIC RESEARCH: HEALTH AND MEDICAL RESEARCH PRE-PANDEMIC

Before discussing the case of US public research spending on the COVID-19 vaccine, let us first consider the broader framework for spending on health and medical research. Doing so suggests why the US case is an especially fertile one.

The US spends prodigious amounts of public research funding on health and medical research, usually with the express intention of improving public health. In 2019, *before* the advent of the COVID-19 pandemic, the US spent more than any other nation on health care, both in absolute numbers and per capita. Of the more than $11 trillion dollars spent, a significant amount was devoted to public funded research, with the US National Institutes of Health (NIH) receiving $39.1 billion for health and medical research, substantially more than requested in the President's budget, the largest science investment in the federal budget, and the largest such investment in the world. The NIH research budget is more than six times the US National Science Foundation budget, which funds all areas of science and social science excepting health and medical research, and the NIH alone represents more than one-quarter of federal expenditures for research and development (R&D) and more than half the money spend on basic and applied research, that is, excluding the sizeable Department of Defense budget for technology development (Congressional Research Service, 2020).

While NIH research includes considerable "curiosity-driven" research within its overall research portfolio, most of its research seeks to serve to public benefit objectives, including those specified in the agency's planning documents such as *Healthy People 2030* (NIH, 2021), which includes 355 "measurable objectives" indexed by topic. However, not everyone believes that large-scale investment necessarily yields commensurate benefit, either in the US (Sarewitz, 2010) or other industrialized nations (Chatterjee, 2014; Grant and Buxton, 2018). One indirect indicator is that despite eclipsing other nations' spending on all categories of health and medical spending, including research, the US life expectancy was, in 2015, less than that of 43 other nations, all with much less spending per capita (World Data, 2019). For example, the UK spends only about $3,749 per person and the US spends $9,237. Nonetheless, US life expectance in 2019 was 80.9 years in the UK compared with 79.1 in the US.

The research-health outcomes gap in the US is notable. One major impact study (Bowen and Casadevall, 2015) has shown an increasing gap between spending for R&D and benefits in terms of medical gains to public health. The authors speculate that reasons for this gap include the focus on genetic models in general and especially ones that may not be applicable to human beings (i.e. mouse models that have convenient if perhaps not relevant genetic properties), an increasing tendency to focus on chronic rather than fatal diseases, and the fact

Table 2.1   *Four meanings of "public" in public research*

Theory lens	Core research funding question	Assumptions about public research	Policy guidance strengths and weaknesses	Illustrative literature*
Sector	What research should be publicly funded and what privately funded?	Typically includes no explicit normative assumptions, tends to view "public" and "private" as same as "government" and "business" and provides of prescriptions about allocation	Analytical simplicity; corresponds to popular usage and to most policymakers' perspectives	The vast majority of existing work pertaining to "public funding of research." Literature reviews include Salter and Martin, 2001; Becker, 2015; Petrin, 2018
Dimensional	What configuration of market and political authority structures prove optimal for achieving research funding goals	Focuses not on public research but the publicness of the providers of research (i.e. not sector but mix of political and market structures. Does not otherwise provide prescriptions, other than to note which mix of political and market authority seems to work best for what broad research missions	Not widely familiar; not useful for broadest-level policymaking; brings important insights and prescriptions to institutional arrangements for policy delivery	Bozeman, 1987; Crow and Bozeman, 1987; Crow and Bozeman, 1998; Larédo and Mustar, 2000, 2004; Sanz-Menéndez and Cruz-Castro, 2003; Cruz-Castro et al., 2015; Cruz-Castro and Sanz-Menéndez, 2018; Jongbloed, 2015; Coccia et al., 2015
Public goods	How is economic efficiency best achieved in the provision of goods and services?	Public research is inherently less efficient because of the difficulty and fully recovering investments and profit. Public research should focus on cases of externalities and other market failures	Familiar framework; broad applications; but more idealization than practical; gives limited and simplistic attention to social benefits and costs and their evaluation	Nelson, 1959; Mansfield, 1964; Mueller and Tilton, 1969; Klette et al., 2000; Jones and Williams, 2000; Bleda and Del Rio, 2013; Perez-Sebastian, 2015; Choi and Lee, 2017; Alam et al., 2020
Public values	What are the public values objectives of research activity and how what legal and structural designs best achieve these values?	Agnostic about sector and focuses instead on most effective institutions and partnerships for achieving public values	Intuitive but not broadly familiar (except in earlier concept of "public interest"); operationalization and measurement problematic; strong normative and prescriptive focus; highlights social benefits and costs with economic outcomes viewed as means not ends	Bozeman and Sarewitz, 2005, 2011; Bornmann, 2013; Joly et al., 2015; De Jong et al., 2014; McNie et al., 2016; Bozeman and Youtie, 2017; Molas-Gallart, 2015; D'Este et al., 2018; Booth et al., 2121; Ribeiro and Shapira, 2020; Ciarli and Ráfols, 2019; Matt et al., 2017; Shin and Lee, 2017

Note: * In the case of the "sector" and "public goods" categories the literature is expansive, and the literature cited includes core studies or literature reviews. In the other two categories, "dimensional" and "public value," the illustrations provide a fuller representation of the structure and content of two much smaller literatures.

that an increasing percentage of research grants resources is taken up with administration as opposed to research. We might add to these concerns the fact that there is often little or no connection between the theoretically elegant medical research "solutions" provided and the health objectives they are supposed to advance. Indeed, one study (Youtie et al., 2006) indicated that a substantial percentage of NIH-funding publications in at least one major field of study have little or no impact on practitioners.

The overarching problem in government-sponsored science is that many technological advances resulting from publicly funded research give little or no heed to the fact that there may be substantial economic or social barriers to accessing the innovation. A medical device that costs millions of dollars of capital investment and, thus, requires repayment and amortization, gives little benefit those who cannot afford to pay, or do not have quality private insurance, or do not have adequate government-sponsored insurance. In the US and many other countries, millions of people cannot benefit from innovation because they do not have the required resources. If the NIH doubles its pace of innovation, the increments to public health may be minimal if a substantial part of the population, including many of the least healthy, do not have the wherewithal to take advantage.

ENTER COVID-19

On December 1, 2019, "patient zero" in Wuhan, China was discovered to have disease symptoms not previously observed.[1] Little is known about how he contracted what may be the first human case of the malady that came to be known as COVID-19. The man had not been to the Huanan Seafood Wholesale Market, later thought, with no iron-clad proof, to be a locus of the origins of the transgenic disease. Three weeks later, 27 apparently similar coronavirus-based cases had emerged in Wuhan, with several proving quite serious. By January 4, 2020, the United Nations had announced an "incident management" and China as well as other nations had begun to investigate the disease. A few days later the first case outside China was reported in a small town near Seoul, South Korea. In February, cases were reported throughout Europe, the first death was reported in the US and by March 2020 the US led the world in confirmed cases with 81,321 confirmed infections and more than 1,000 deaths. The year 2020 will always be known for its sobering annual world health statistics, with more than 76 million people sickened by the COVID-19 virus and 1.6 million dead.

By late February 2020 and the World Health Organization said that it expected that no effective vaccine would probably be available for at least 18 months. By April 2020, some 78 companies and research laboratories in 19 nations had begun work on a vaccine (Leroy et al., 2021), with some of the leading pharmaceutical firms in the world pulling out all the stops to develop a viable vaccine at the earliest possible time. In early December 2020, more than six months ahead of early forecasts, the UK became the first country in the world to give emergency approval for use of a COVID-19 vaccine. Other nations, many working together with the World Health Organization and some (e.g. US) following an independent path, soon followed suit. By early March 2022, more than 557 million doses of COVID-19 vaccine had been provided in the sometimes vaccination-averse US. Presently, more than 217 million Americans have been fully vaccinated. More than 11 billion doses of vaccine have been provided throughout the world and 4.47 billion have been fully vaccinated. Given that the two most prominent vaccines, Pfizer and Moderna, show an initial efficacy rate of about 90%, significant headway has been made in the battle against COVID-19.

COVID-19 Medical Research

Arguably, the worldwide research effort aimed at developing and then mass producing and distributing an effective vaccine has been, literally, one of the most impressive feats in the history of science-for-application. However, success has come at a price, not only an enormous cost in terms of research funding but also quite possibly the greatest concentration of human scientific resources and energies in human history. In some cases, success has "succeeded" in highlighting massive problems, including inequality, racism, and social fragmentation, problems long preceding the pandemic but brought into to sharp relief by it. The most straightforward part of the story is also an aspect quite relevant to this chapter's purposes: an account of public spending on research.

According to the US Government Accounting Office (2021), as of March 14, 2021, the Department of Health and Human Services and the Department of Defense have obligated more than $20 billon to the development, manufacture, and distribution of COVID-19 vaccines, with the preponderance of funds being allocated to six pharmaceutical firms – Pfizer ($6.0 billion), Moderna ($5.3 billion), Sanofi ($2.2 billion), Janssen ($2.1 billion), AstraZeneca ($1.6 billion) and Novavax ($1.6 billion) – and has provided another $1.5 billion to companies to help expand production facilities or produce materials such as syringes and glass vials. These enormous expenses remain a fraction of the spending for COVID-19 economic relief programs, reported in March 2022 to be $5.2 trillion (Ballotpedia, 2022).

WHAT IS PUBLIC RESEARCH? ILLUSTRATION FROM COVID-19

In the section above, four "theory lenses" for understanding concepts of public research were presented. Here we examine each of these for distinctive insights into spending on COVID-19 research. We begin with a narrative explaining US policy for investing in vaccine development research.

At the onset of the pandemic the US federal government made the unsurprising decision to support private sector vaccine development. They did this in two ways, providing funds directly for industry R&D and by agreeing to purchase successful vaccines. The emergency nature of the vaccine development policies was suggested in the "Operation Warp Speed" project name, a project rolled out in May 2020 by the Department of Health and Human Services, structured as a collaboration among the Centers for Disease Control and Prevention, the Food and Drug Administration, the NIH and the Department of Defense, with funding provided via the Biomedical Advanced Research and Development Authority (BARDA). Under the Operation Warp Speed aegis, the federal government provided more than $19 million to assist seven private sector pharmaceutical firms in the development of a COVID-19 vaccine. Five of the firms accepted the R&D funding and six of the seven signed advance purchase agreements. Ultimately, three of the vaccines supported by BARDA funding succeeded to an extent that they received emergency use authorizations from the FDA and two others were in phase III clinical trials in late 2020.

The two recipients of the largest amount of BARDA funds, Pfizer and Moderna, were successful in developing effective and widely distributed vaccines. A third, developed by Johnson and Johnson, has been in widespread use, although less so after effectiveness rates were shown to be somewhat lower than the other two. As this chapter is being written, in May 2022, more than 254 million Americans (77%) have been vaccinated with at least one shot (the Johnson and Johnson requires only one) and 65.6% have been fully vaccinated. This conforms closely to the world population, although there are stark differences by country. The highest rates of vaccination have occurred in Middle Eastern countries. At this point, nearly all US citizens have access, at no-cost, to one of three vaccines and there is little growth in the percentage vaccinated because (1) young children are not eligible, (2) many who have had COVID are choosing not to be vaccinated, and, interestingly, (3) vaccination has become at political act, with Republicans and political conservatives sometimes eschewing vaccination as a personal liberty issue. The result of the latter is that states with a higher percentage of Republicans continue to have higher infection and death rates.

At present, the US appears confident in its stock of vaccine and its production agreements, so much so that in June 2021, the Biden Administration announced its intention to provide 500 million vaccine doses to low-income nations. As of March 2022, 475 million doses reportedly had been sent, but world health experts note that many more are needed to address the high incidence of the coronavirus in poorer countries (Wilson and Payne, 2022). Many other nations and NGOs, especially the World Health Organization and the COVAX program for equitable access to vaccines (https://www.who.int/initiatives/act-accelerator/covax), have, likewise, banded together to provide vaccines to nations that otherwise have limited ability to obtain them. Still, the vaccine gap between poor and rich countries remains, as do the case levels. These critical outcomes present somewhat of a tragedy of the commons from the neglected disease issues discussed by Coburn and co-authors (Chapter 10, this *Handbook*), but the cases present interesting comparisons.

PUBLIC FUNDING OF RESEARCH: FOUR PERSPECTIVES

A primary objective of the chapter is to show how different concepts of "public research" can have quite different implications for understanding research performance, research policy, and research objectives. Table 2.2 considers the four "public" perspectives in connection with issues related to COVID-19 research.

Lens: Sector and COVID-19 Research

The key issue in a sector-based view of public research spending is the matter of allocation and amount spent by the public sector, in most respects equivalent to government. The COVID-19 case is anything but routine. Most public sector budgeting, including budgeting for research, is incremental, meaning that allocations for year "T" are the best predictor of allocations for year "$T+1$." However, the incrementalism traditions of public budgeting are traditions not iron clad law. In research, as in most areas of the budget, non-incremental departures, both increases and decreases, occur, typically as a result of massive change in the partisan composition of Congress or a national emergency (White, 2020; Flink and Robinson, 2020). By any standard, the COVID-19 pandemic qualifies as a national emergency, one reflected in the increased US

Table 2.2   *Four foci of public research: COVID-19 research experience*

Theory lens	COVID-19 research funding Q&A	COVID-19 implications for concept of public research	Possible aftermath
Sector	*Q:* What research should be publicly funded and what privately funded? *A:* Urgency set aside usual concerns on increments and base; massive government funding of private research in pharmaceutical industry	Unusually clear delineation of roles, with government as funding agent and industry as provider	Few long-run implications for public research conception
Dimensional	*Q:* What configuration of market and political authority structures prove optimal for achieving research funding goals? *A:* Government provided strong hand in strategic development; funding of private research dominant, but with contracts and performance standards	Limited concern about institutional arrangements owing to clear delineation of roles	Renewed scrutiny of institutional arrangements given range of organizational outcomes
Public goods	*Q:* How is economic efficiency best achieved in the provision of goods and services? *A:* Efficiency concerns minimized due to timing and urgency; market failure issues diminished.	Public goods core assumptions largely ignored owing to traditional role of private sector in vaccine research and manufacture	Not clear. On the one hand, positive role for government exhibited, on the other success of private sector providers
Public values	*Q:* What are the public values objectives of research activity and what legal and structural designs best achieve these values? *A:* Clear-cut, consensus, public values in mission; public failures evident in research outcomes	Public values model paramount with focus on effectiveness of intuitions and desire for partnerships for achieving public values	Public values rise to the fore in times of calamity, but also can make evident public failures

federal budget. Thus, the US federal budget for 2019 was $4.4 trillion but in 2020 it rose to $5.8 trillion, including $2.3 trillion in deficit financing. The pandemic was clearly a primary factor in this non-incremental increase, though the exact size of the "pandemic bill" is not easily determined because it affects nearly every budget category.

Another non-routine element of budgeting, in this case for research, was the budget for COVID-19 vaccine development. While the US typically provides a significant percentage of its research spending to private sector research performers, in this case one private sector performer category is of interest, the pharmaceutical industry. Almost all drugs developed in the US and most other nations are developed by the pharmaceutical industry, typically with their own investment in R&D. The investment is substantial. The typical cost of developing a new drug, including R&D and capital costs, ranges from $1 to 2 billion. In 2019, the industry spent more than $83 billion on R&D, nearly 20% of net revenue. COVID-19 vaccine development departed from the usual proprietary R&D engaged in by the industry.

Regarding the sector model's lens, it seems clear that this perspective gives little insight into COVID-19 vaccine research. The sector perspective focuses chiefly on determining allocation of responsibilities for research performance and, over many years, has developed certain predictable funding norms, including not only incrementalism but also, in research funding, the expectation that government will fund the preponderance of basic research (Salter and Martin, 2001; Pavitt, 2001) and that most development work, excepting only defense and national security, will be funded by the private sector on the expectation that industry has sufficient profit motives to do so (Levin et al., 1987; Golec and Vernon, 2007). In the case of a, literally, worldwide emergency, these norms do not obtain (Barigozzi and Jelovac, 2020).

Lens: Dimensional Publicness and COVID-19 Research

To reiterate, the dimensional publicness concept focuses on the effectiveness of institutional and organizational designs for delivering public goods and services. Unlike public choice and political economy approaches, it is highly pragmatic, with no built in assumptions about the performance capabilities of specific sector or multi-sector arrangements (Bozeman, 1987). The theory has been applied to a number of domains, including not only science and technology (e.g. Crow and Bozeman, 1998; Bozeman, 2013), but also higher education (Lee, 2017), criminal justice "supply chains" (Seepma et al., 2021), mental health (Merritt et al., 2018), recreation (Talmage et al., 2018) and housing and mortgage institutions (Moulton, 2009).

The dimensional publicness concepts seems to have something to contribute to the understanding of "public funding of research" in the context of COVID-19 vaccine development. In the US, government and industry organizations rather quickly came to agreement about institutional and policy designs viewed as optimal for rapid creation, production and deployment of vaccines (Le et al., 2020). This is a clear case of sector boundary spanning and partnership and creation of unique designs motivated in large measure by severe need rather than ideology or theoretical considerations. These arrangements were characterized by high degrees of publicness in funding (i.e. most R&D funding by government), high degrees of privateness in the execution of the research, and a mix of public and private authority in determinations and partnership pertaining to contractual agreements, bonuses and incentives, performance standards, property ownership, and even subsequent easing of regulations. This is a classic dimensional publicness model in the sense that it is motivated chiefly by pragmatic decisions (Corey et al., 2020) about what are the most feasible and effective approaches to accomplishing mission and objectives. Arguably, the dimensional publicness model is particularly useful for understanding rapid and crisis-based policymaking, instances where the usual norms and design arrangements (Sampat and Lichtenberg, 2011) may seem more like strictures than guidelines (Di Minin et al., 2021; Sampat and Shadlen, 2021).

Lens: Public Goods and COVID-19 Research

While public goods approaches to decisionmaking are often paramount, especially when policymakers seek means to ensure efficient and prudential public spending (Boyne, 1996; Stearns and Zywicki, 2009; Kimenyi and Mbaku, 2019), this theoretical lens and its related "new public management" approach (Ferlie et al., 1996; Hammerschmid et al., 2019) are arguably the least helpful interpretation of "public" when considering public research focused on developing COVID-19 vaccines. In the case of vaccine development, clearly the priority was effectiveness but combined with speed (US Government Accounting Office, 2021). In truly urgent cases of policymaking, especially ones with ubiquitous consequences, the usual interest in economic efficiency almost always moves to the background.

The acceleration of COVID-19 vaccine research was only one policy initiative among several aimed at attacking the pandemic. For example, Operation Warp Speed decisionmakers, a public–private partnership initiated by the US government to facilitate and accelerate the development, manufacturing, and distribution of COVID-19 vaccines, therapeutics, and diagnostics, used a portfolio approach selecting vaccine companies to support, optimizing by selecting research approaches using different physical mechanisms (platform technologies) to stimulate immune response. The Operation Warp Speed authorities also worked together to expedite visa approval for international technical and scientific personnel. Similarly, pharmaceutical companies took their own measures, including the unusual step of beginning manufacturing well before clinical trials had authorized distribution (Center for Disease Control and Prevention, 2021). In short, clearly in this emergency context little time was available for contemplating issues of market failure or either theoretical or practical guidelines regarding production and pricing efficiency, issues long deliberated in most policy and development contexts.

Lens: Public Values and COVID-19 Research

A public values lens takes a very different concept of public than the three others presented here. First, whereas the other three perspectives focus strongly on allocation issues or institutional design issues, inputs into desired outcomes, the public values approach, more normative, focuses on whether a public value is achieved (or whether there are demonstrable public failures around which to build and agenda). Research shows that there are only a few "consensual public values" (Jørgensen and Bozeman, 2007; Bozeman, 2019), issues such as the right to sustenance and health, personal freedom, and ability to participate in politics, but also implies that these values transcend efficiency and more pragmatic considerations.

Perhaps the most important difference between the public values lens, a difference that makes it especially apt for addressing a worldwide calamity, is that does not disaggregate processes (research, development, manufacturing, dissemination) because its focus in on the achievement of public values, broadly defined, as opposed to specific steps toward an instrumental objective. Thus, for example, if we take the predominant public value in the COVID-19 case as public health, then the approach gives little concern to the productivity of research or even its cost if it does not, for whatever reason, successfully address the public value objective. Thus, a high-quality vaccine that is not widely distributed is a public failure, an economically efficient pricing structure that deprives many citizens of access is a public failure, and, arguably, political processes that lead to "benefit hoarding" (Bozeman, 2002), such that wealthy nations have high access to vaccine and poor nations have little access are also a public failure (depending in part on the reasons for the disparity).

An important aspect of the public values approach is that in this case "public" does not mean government or political authority or public partnership but is more akin to the meaning of "citizen." Thus, when we consider "public research" in such a normative context we are, essentially, saying "research for the collective good of citizens," and with that concept come various attendant assumptions, such as implications for who finances public research and who performs it.

CONCLUSIONS

Which meaning of "public research" is the most useful? The answer to that question depends upon a variety of prior questions, including, most importantly, what is the ultimate objective of the research? If the objective is enhancing productivity, then one-answer version of "public" may be best; if the answer is assuring economic efficiency, then another concept may be preferred, and, as this chapter has labored to point out, if the objective is "serving the public interest" then a very different concept seems most useful. Related, the best "public" concept may well depend upon perspective. Citizens, policymakers, elected officials, industrial leaders: there are good reasons why these very different clients for "public spending on research" will have different preferred concepts of "public." Nevertheless, it may well be valuable for any stakeholder to reflect long and carefully about the meaning of "public" and "public research." Doing so may provide a fuller conception and richer understanding of the multifarious interests in the support, production and use of research.

NOTE

1. This brief chronology is developed from several sources, including New York Times (2021) and Baraniuk, C. (2021).

REFERENCES

Alam, A., Uddin, M., Yazdifar, H., Shafique, S., and Lartey, T. (2020). R&D investment, firm performance and moderating role of system and safeguard: Evidence from emerging markets. *Journal of Business Research*, *106*, 94–105.

Ballotpedia (2022). Overview of sending during the coronavirus pandemic. Downloaded May 12, 2022 from https://ballotpedia.org/Overview_of_federal_spending_during_the_coronavirus_(COVID-19)_pandemic.

Baraniuk, C. (2021). Covid-19: How the UK vaccine rollout delivered success, so far, *British Medical Journal*, February, 372, n. 421. Downloaded March 7, 2021 from https://www.bmj.com/content/372/bmj.n421.full.

Barigozzi, F., and Jelovac, I. (2020). Research funding and price negotiation for new drugs. *Health Economics*, *29*, 83–96.

Bator, F. M. (1958). The anatomy of market failure. *The Quarterly Journal of Economics*, *72*(3), 351–379.

Becker, B. (2015). Public R&D policies and private R&D investment: A survey of the empirical evidence. *Journal of Economic Surveys*, *29*(5), 917–942.

Birch, K. (2020). Technoscience rent: Toward a theory of rentiership for technoscientific capitalism. *Science, Technology, and Human Values*, *45*(1), 3–33.

Bleda, M., and Del Rio, P. (2013). The market failure and the systemic failure rationales in technological innovation systems. *Research Policy*, *42*(5), 1039–1052.

Booth, A., Reed, A. B., Ponzo, S., Yassaee, A., Aral, M., Plans, D., Labirque, A., and Mohan, D. (2021). Population risk factors for severe disease and mortality in COVID-19: A global systematic review and meta-analysis. *PloS one*, *16*(3), e0247461.

Bornmann, L. (2013). What is societal impact of research and how can it be assessed? A literature survey. *Journal of the American Society for Information Science and Technology*, *64*(2), 217–233.

Bowen, A., and Casadevall, A. (2015). Increasing disparities between resource inputs and outcomes, as measured by certain health deliverables, in biomedical research. *Proceedings of the National Academy of Sciences*, *112*(36), 11335–11340.

Boyne, G. A. (1996). Competition and local government: A public choice perspective. *Urban Studies*, *33*(4–5), 703–721.

Bozeman, B. (1987). *All organizations are public: Bridging public and private organizational theories.* Jossey-Bass.

Bozeman, B. (2002). Public-value failure: When efficient markets may not do. *Public Administration Review*, *62*(2), 145–161.

Bozeman, B. (2007). *Public values and public interest: Counterbalancing economic individualism.* Georgetown University Press.

Bozeman, B. (2013). What organization theorists and public policy researchers can learn from one another: Publicness theory as a case-in-point. *Organization Studies*, *34*(2), 169–188.

Bozeman, B. (2019). Public values: Citizens' perspective. *Public Management Review*, *21*(6), 817–838.

Bozeman, B. (2020). Public value science. *Issues in Science and Technology*, *36*(4), 34–41.

Bozeman, B., and Bretschneider, S. (1994). The "publicness puzzle" in organization theory: A test of alternative explanations of differences between public and private organizations. *Journal of Public Administration Research and Theory*, *4*(2), 197–224.

Bozeman, B., and Sarewitz, D. (2005). Public values and public failure in US science policy. *Science and Public Policy*, *32*(2), 119–136.

Bozeman, B., and Sarewitz, D. (2011). Public value mapping and science policy evaluation. *Minerva*, *49*(1), 1–23.

Bozeman, B., and Youtie, J. (2017). Socio-economic impacts and public value of government-funded research: Lessons from four US National Science Foundation initiatives. *Research Policy*, *46*(8), 1387–1398.

Center for Disease Control and Prevention (2021). Developing COVID-19 vaccines. Downloaded June 2, 2021 from https://www.cdc.gov/coronavirus/2019-ncov/vaccines/distributing/steps-ensure-safety .html.

Chatterjee, J. (2014). Falling through the cracks and bridging the gap – India and USA showing similar trends. *Current Science*, *106*(5), 691–697.

Choi, J., and Lee, J. (2017). Repairing the R&D market failure: Public R&D subsidy and the composition of private R&D. *Research Policy*, *46*(8), 1465–1478.

Ciarli, T., and Ràfols, I. (2019). The relation between research priorities and societal demands: The case of rice. *Research Policy*, *48*(4), 949–967.

Coccia, M., Falavigna, G., and Manello, A. (2015). The impact of hybrid public and market-oriented financing mechanisms on the scientific portfolio and performances of public research labs: A scientometric analysis. *Scientometrics*, *102*(1), 151–168.

Congressional Research Service (2020). *Federal Funding for Research and Development R&D Funding: FY2020.* Downloaded March 1, 2021 from https://fas.org/sgp/crs/misc/R45715.pdf.

Corey, L., Mascola, J. R., Fauci, A. S., and Collins, F. S. (2020). A strategic approach to COVID-19 vaccine R&D. *Science*, *368*(6494), 948–950.

Cowen, T. (1985). Public goods definitions and their institutional context: A critique of public goods theory. *Review of Social Economy*, *43*(1), 53–63.

Crow, M., and Bozeman, B. (1987). R&D laboratory classification and public policy: The effects of environmental context on laboratory behavior. *Research Policy*, *16*(5), 229–258.

Crow, M., and Bozeman, B. (1998). *Limited by design: R&D laboratories in the US national innovation system.* Columbia University Press.

Cruz-Castro, L., and Sanz-Menéndez, L. (2018). Autonomy and authority in public research organisations: Structure and funding factors. *Minerva*, *56*(2), 135–160.

Cruz-Castro, L., Sanz-Menéndez, L., and Martínez, C. (2012). Research centers in transition: Patterns of convergence and diversity. *The Journal of Technology Transfer*, *37*(1), 18–42.

Cruz-Castro, L., Martínez, C., Peñasco, C., and Sanz-Menéndez, L. (2020). The classification of public research organizations: Taxonomical explorations. *Research Evaluation*, *29*(4), 377–391.

D'Este, P., Ramos-Vielba, I., Woolley, R., and Amara, N. (2018). How do researchers generate scientific and societal impacts? Toward an analytical and operational framework. *Science and Public Policy*, *45*(6), 752–763.

De Jong, S., Barker, K., Cox, D., Sveinsdottir, T., and Van den Besselaar, P. (2014). Understanding societal impact through productive interactions: ICT research as a case. *Research Evaluation, 23*(2), 89–102.

Di Minin, A., Dooley, L., Lazzarotti, V., Manzini, R., Mortara, L., and Piccaluga, A. (2021). R&D Management at a time of crisis: What are we learning from the response to the COVID-19 pandemic? *R&D Management, 51*(2), 165.

Etukudoh, N. S., Ejinaka, R. O., Olowu, F. A., Obeta, M. U., Adebowale, O. M., and Udoudoh, M. P. (2020). Coronavirus (COVID-19); Review from a Nigerian perspective. *American Journal of Biomedical Science and Research, 9*(1), https://doi.org/10.34297/AJBSR.2020.09.001347.

Ferlie, E., Fitzgerald, L., and Pettigrew, A. (1996). *The new public management in action.* Oxford University Press.

Flink, C. M., and Robinson, S. E. (2020). Corrective policy reactions: Positive and negative budgetary punctuations. *Journal of Public Policy, 40*(1), 96–115.

Furton, G., and Martin, A. (2019). Beyond market failure and government failure. *Public Choice, 178*(1), 197–216.

Golec, J., and Vernon, J. A. (2007). New estimates of pharmaceutical research and development spending by US-based firms from 1984 to 2003. *Managerial and Decision Economics, 28*(4/5), 481–483.

Grant, J., and Buxton, M. J. (2018). Economic returns to medical research funding. *BMJ Open, 8*(9), e022131.

Hammerschmid, G., Van de Walle, S., Andrews, R., and Mostafa, A. M. S. (2019). New public management reforms in Europe and their effects: Findings from a 20-country top executive survey. *International Review of Administrative Sciences, 85*(3), 399–418.

Hartley, S., McLeod, C., Clifford, M., Jewitt, S., and Ray, C. (2019). A retrospective analysis of responsible innovation for low-technology innovation in the Global South. *Journal of Responsible Innovation, 6*(2), 143–162.

Joly, P. B., Gaunand, A., Colinet, L., Larédo, P., Lemarié, S., and Matt, M. (2015). ASIRPA: A comprehensive theory-based approach to assessing the societal impacts of a research organization. *Research Evaluation, 24*(4), 440–453.

Jones, C. I., and Williams, J. C. (2000). Too much of a good thing? The economics of investment in R&D. *Journal of Economic Growth, 5*(1), 65–85.

Jongbloed, B. (2015). Universities as hybrid organizations: Trends, drivers, and challenges for the European university. *International Studies of Management and Organization, 45*(3), 207–225.

Jørgensen, T. B., and Bozeman, B. (2007). Public values: An inventory. *Administration and society, 39*(3), 354–381.

Joseph, R. A., and Johnston, R. (1985). Market failure and government support for science and technology: Economic theory versus political practice. *Prometheus, 3*(1), 138–155.

Kimenyi, M. S., and Mbaku, J. M. (2019). *Institutions and collective choice in developing countries: Applications of the theory of public choice.* Routledge.

Klette, T. J., Møen, J., and Griliches, Z. (2000). Do subsidies to commercial R&D reduce market failures? Microeconometric evaluation studies. *Research Policy, 29*(4–5), 471–495.

Larédo, P., and Mustar, P. (2004). Public sector research: A growing role in innovation systems. *Minerva, 42*(1), 11–27.

Larédo, P., and Mustar, P. (2000). Laboratory activity profiles: An exploratory approach. *Scientometrics, 47*(3), 515–539.

Le, T. T., Andreadakis, Z., Kumar, A., Román, R. G., Tollefsen, S., Saville, M., and Mayhew, S. (2020). The COVID-19 vaccine development landscape. *National Review of Drug Discovery, 19*(5), 305–306.

Leroy, S., Schmidt, A. M., and Madjar, N. (2021). Working from home during COVID-19: A study of the interruption landscape. *Journal of Applied Psychology, 106*(10), 1448–1465. https://doi.org/10.1037/apl0000972.

Levin, R. C., Klevorick, A. K., Nelson, R. R., Winter, S. G., Gilbert, R., and Griliches, Z. (1987). Appropriating the returns from industrial research and development. *Brookings Papers on Economic Activity, 1987*(3), 783–831.

Mansfield, E. (1964). Industrial research and development expenditures: Determinants, prospects, and relation to size of firm and inventive output. *Journal of Political Economy, 72*(4), 319–340.

Matt, M., Gaunand, A., Joly, P. B., and Colinet, L. (2017). Opening the black box of impact – Ideal-type impact pathways in a public agricultural research organization. *Research Policy*, *46*(1), 207–218.

Mazzucato, M. (2018). Mission-oriented innovation policies: challenges and opportunities. *Industrial and Corporate Change*, *27*(5), 803–815.

McNie, E. C., Parris, A., and Sarewitz, D. (2016). Improving the public value of science: A typology to inform discussion, design and implementation of research. *Research Policy*, *45*(4), 884–895.

Merritt, C. C., Cordell, K., and Farnworth, M. D. (2018). Less is more? Publicness, management strategy, and organizational performance in mental health treatment facilities. *Public Administration Quarterly*, *42*(1), 3–31.

Molas-Gallart, J. (2015). Research evaluation and the assessment of public value. *Arts and Humanities in Higher Education*, *14*(1), 111–126.

Moulton, S. (2009). Putting together the publicness puzzle: A framework for realized publicness. *Public Administration Review*, *69*(5), 889–900.

Mueller, D. C., and Tilton, J. E. (1969). Research and development costs as a barrier to entry. *The Canadian Journal of Economics/Revue canadienne d'Economique*, *2*(4), 570–579.

Nelson, R. R. (1959). The simple economics of basic scientific research. *Journal of Political Economy*, *67*(3), 297–306.

New York Times (2021). A timeline for the coronavirus pandemic, *New York Times*, March 7 2021. Downloaded March, 2020 from https://www.nytimes.com/article/coronavirus-timeline.html.

NIH (2021). *Healthy People 2030 Research Objectives*. Downloaded March 1, 2021 from https://prevention.nih.gov/research-priorities/research-needs-and-gaps/healthy-people-2030-research-objectives.

Organisation for Economic Co-operation and Development (2020). Health Spending. Accessed Sepember 28, 2020.

Pappas, G., Panagopoulou, P., and Akritidis, N. (2009). Reclassifying bioterrorism risk: Are we preparing for the proper pathogens? *Journal of Infection and Public Health*, *2*(2), 55–61.

Pavitt, K. (2001). Public policies to support basic research: What can the rest of the world learn from US theory and practice? (And what they should not learn). *Industrial and Corporate Change*, *10*(3), 761–779.

Perez-Sebastian, F. (2015). Market failure, government inefficiency, and optimal R&D policy. *Economics Letters*, *128*, 43–47.

Petrin, T. (2018). *A literature review on the impact and effectiveness of government support for R&D and innovation*. ISIGrowth.

Randall, A. (1983). The problem of market failure. *Natural Resources Journal*, *23*(1), 131–148.

Ribeiro, B., and Shapira, P. (2020). Private and public values of innovation: A patent analysis of synthetic biology. *Research Policy*, *49*(1), 103875.

Salter, A. J., and Martin, B. R. (2001). The economic benefits of publicly funded basic research: a critical review. *Research Policy*, *30*(3), 509–532.

Sampat, B. N., and Shadlen, K. C. (2021). The COVID-19 Innovation System: Article describes innovations that emerged during the COVID-19 pandemic. *Health Affairs*, *40*(3), 400–409.

Sampat, B. N., and Lichtenberg, F. R. (2011). What are the respective roles of the public and private sectors in pharmaceutical innovation?. *Health Affairs*, *30*(2), 332–339.

Sanz-Menéndez, L., and Cruz-Castro, L. (2003). Coping with environmental pressures: Public research organisations responses to funding crises. *Research Policy*, *32*(8), 1293–1308.

Sarewitz, D. (2010). Double trouble? To throw cash at science is a mistake. *Nature News*, *468*(7321), 135–135.

Scherer, F. M. (1986). *Innovation and growth: Schumpeterian perspectives*. MIT Press.

Seepma, A. P., Van Donk, D. P., and De Blok, C. (2021). On publicness theory and its implications for supply chain integration: The case of criminal justice supply chains. *Journal of Supply Chain Management*, *57*(3), 72–103.

Shin, D. H., and Lee, M. K. (2017). Public value mapping of network neutrality: Public values and net neutrality in Korea. *Telecommunications Policy*, *41*(3), 208–224.

Stearns, M. L., and Zywicki, T. (2009). *Public choice concepts and applications in law*. West Publishing.

Stilgoe, J., Owen, R., and Macnaghten, P. (2013). Developing a framework for responsible innovation. *Research Policy*, *42*(9), 1568–1580.

Talmage, C. A., Anderson, D. M., and Searle, M. S. (2018). Whither recreation and parks? Understanding change in public institutions through a theory of adaptive publicness. *Perspectives on Public Management and Governance, 1*(2), 143–158.

Ulnicane, I. (2016). "Grand Challenges" concept: A return of the "big ideas" in science, technology and innovation policy? *International Journal of Foresight and Innovation Policy, 11*(1–3), 5–21.

US FDA (2020). Coronavirus treatment acceleration program. Downloaded June 1, 2021 from https://www.fda.gov/drugs/coronavirus-covid-19-drugs/coronavirus-treatment-acceleration-program-ctap.

US Government Accounting Office (2021). Operation Warp Speed: Accelerated COVID-19 Vaccine Development Status and Efforts to Address Manufacturing Challenges GAO-21-319, Publicly Released: February 11, 2021. Downloaded June 1, 2021 from https://www.gao.gov/products/gao-21-319.

Uyarra, E., Ribeiro, B., and Dale-Clough, L. (2019). Exploring the normative turn in regional innovation policy: Responsibility and the quest for public value. *European Planning Studies, 27*(12), 2359–2375.

Walker, R. M., and Bozeman, B. (2011). Publicness and organizational performance. *Journal of Public Administration Research and Theory, 21*(suppl 3), i279–i281.

Weimer, D. L., and Vining, A. R. (2017). *Policy analysis: Concepts and practice.* Routledge.

White, J. (2020). (Almost). nothing new under the sun: Why the work of budgeting remains incremental. In *Budgeting, policy, politics* (pp. 111–132). Routledge.

Wilson, M. and Payne, D. (2022). When $5 billion is not enough. *Politico.* March 31, 2022. Downloaded March 31, 2022, from https://www.politico.com/newsletters/global-pulse/2022/03/31/when-5-billion-is-not-enough-00021904.

World Data (2019). Life expectance in nations. Downloaded June 3, 2021 from https://www.worlddata.info/life-expectancy.php#by-population.

Youtie, J., Libaers, D., and Bozeman, B. (2006). Institutionalization of university research centers: the case of the National Cooperative Program in Infertility Research. *Technovation, 26*(9), 1055–1063.

Zerbe Jr, R. O., and McCurdy, H. E. (1999). The failure of market failure. *Journal of Policy Analysis and Management: The Journal of the Association for Public Policy Analysis and Management, 18*(4), 558–578.

Zimmer, C., J. Corum, and S. Wee (2021). Coronavirus vaccine tracker, *New York Times*, March 5 2021. Downloaded March 7, 2020 from https://www.nytimes.com/interactive/2020/science/coronavirus-vaccine-tracker.html.

3. Motivations guiding public research funding in science, technology and innovation (STI) policy: a synthesis[1]

Aixa Y. Alemán-Díaz

INTRODUCTION

The organization of science, technology and innovation (STI) has been 'historically … trapped in a tension between the autonomy of creativity and the politics of purpose' (Borrás, 2012). This persistent controversy has been a key recursive device called upon by scientists or by the state to drive investment in STI. As the share of government involvement in STI has increased over time (Borrás, 2012), public research funding (PRF) has become a means to achieve varied policy goals. These include, for example, promoting research excellence (Dasgupta and David, 1994), efficiency in the use of public funds (Hicks, 2012) and the relevance of research to address and meet societal, economic or other kinds of needs (Larrue et al., 2019; Larrue, 2021). In this context, actors involved in STI policy (Elzinga and Jamison, 1995) and the state (Borrás and Edler, 2020) have been central, especially after World War II. Over time, these actors have either chosen winners, engaged in specific missions to address societal needs, or corrected market or system failures that prevent the growth and disposition of knowledge, technology and innovation (Borrás and Edler, 2020; Edler and Fagerberg, 2017; Martin and Scott, 2000). However, the policy landscape is getting 'more diverse, more complex, and ever more far reaching in its impact on science' (Simon et al., 2019, p. 7). The environment surrounding public research has changed in the last decades, making the underlying motivations of science policy more complex, heterogeneous and hybrid (Borrás, 2012; Elzinga, 2012). In this chapter, motivations refer to the narratives used by various actors to envision what should be achieved through PRF, but also suggesting how it could be achieved.

Changes in the PRF landscape include shifts associated with emerging rationales such as academic capitalism (Slaughter and Rhoades, 2004), new public management (Ferlie et al., 2008; Geuna, 2001; Paradeise et al., 2009), transformative innovation (Schot and Steinmueller, 2018), responsible innovation (Stilgoe et al., 2013), responsible research and innovation (von Schomberg, 2013) and holistic innovation policy (Borrás and Edquist, 2019), to name a few. It has been argued that 'academic capitalism' might threaten the social norms of science and scientific cooperation with adverse long-term effects on the institutions of science (Squazzoni et al., 2013). See, for example, the chapter on academic capitalism (Bégin-Caouette et al., Chapter 20 in this *Handbook*) for a discussion on the types of academic capitalism and a comparison of how policies and their outcomes are tempered by countries' specific context. The diffusion of ideas, like new public management, suggests a retreat of the state and the introduction in the public sector of competitive and corporate practices that have an impact also on research and higher education policies (Ferlie et al., 2008; Paradeise et al., 2009). The changes have also entailed adjustments in the 'social contract for science' from steady support for basic science to economic, social and policy targets influencing its allocation (Guston and Keniston, 1994, 2009; Elzinga and Jamison, 1995) and greater support for applied and user-oriented research at the expense of basic research (Stephan, 2012). Capano (Chapter 5 in this *Handbook*) finds the evolution in the social contract for science 'to a new type of contract based on evaluation and performance (that) can be read as a process through which new ideas (about what publicly funded research should do or should give back to funders) and new instruments (the approaches to use to pursue the new ideas) have been adopted'. It is, therefore, timely to understand the motivations described in the literature that influence modes of governing socio-technical systems and PRF around the world.

The chapter explores the motivations guiding PRF stemming from the tension between autonomy and purpose and aims to synthesize relevant literature describing them. It departs from the notion that these motivations emerge from 'cyclical, socially constructed process(es) of interaction between science and technology, on the one hand, and cultural critique or response, on the other' (Elzinga and Jamison, 1995, p. 575). Changes in the motivations driving PRF have been more gradual and less linear than frequently advocated (Larrue et al., 2019). The motivations in this chapter depart from the triad of curiosity, mission and market motivations, but aim to re-think the mix in light of old and new debates to transform PRF. The more classical triad takes for granted the structure of science–society relationships, but, as I show through the chapter, these structures become insufficient to address new challenges. Therefore, the chapter suggests a slightly different mix of motivations – *creativity, purpose* and *transformation* – and considers them as co-exiting in national PRF environments. This novel taxonomy enables the inclusion of emergent and disparate motivations, alongside more traditional motivations found in the literature.

The *creativity motivation* draws on curiosity based on the principle of 'free research' guided by experimentation and collegial debates. The *purpose motivation* centers around missions that involve the planning and direction of research by the state or scientific knowledge used as a resource for the market. Some argue that 'the post-war visions of "curiosity-driven" research and mission-driven "big" science turned into calculated investments in neoliberal "innovation science"' (Juhl, 2016). Critics also contend that 'we need a more realistic view of the relationship between basic science and technological innovation to frame science and technology policies for a new century' (Stokes, 1997, p. 2); that 'our present understandings and practices of STI policy are not sufficient to address Grand Challenges and set priorities accordingly' (Kuhlmann and Rip, 2014); or that national innovation policies still remain fragmented and are 'not truly systemic' (Borrás and Laatsit, 2019). The *transformation motivation* describes these alternative views of the relationship between science, technology and society found in PRF, as well as more systemic approaches claiming to be more responsive to new societal requirements and expectations. This work extends Elzinga's contribution (Elzinga, 2012), which took a time-based, succession approach to exploring the meta narratives that guide public funding, by exploring the types of funding motivations described in the literature. For more explicit explorations of the connection between policy frames and instruments, see Ulnicane and Capano (Chapters 4 and 5 in this *Handbook*, respectively). While Reale et al., Coburn et al., and Cruz-Castro et al. (Chapters 7, 10, and 14 in this *Handbook*) explore the effects of policy frames in the formulation of specific instruments (i.e. R&D programs, research targeting, and, funding schemes, respectively) to address particular goals.

The motivations described here stem from centuries old discussions about the organization of STI where 'debates about knowledge, ideas, and growth have been central to economic and political thinking in all cultures' (Khan, 2020, p. 347). In these exchanges, Michael Polanyi represents a legendary figure of the curiosity motivation for his support of the autonomy of science, arguing that 'any attempt at guiding scientific research towards a purpose other than its own is an attempt to deflect it from the advancement of science' (Polanyi, 1962). John Desmond Bernal, on the other hand, argued for 'the essential socio-economic function of science, invariably requiring the grand mobilization of knowledge in order to achieve explicitly formulated goals in planned economies' (Borrás, 2012). For Polanyi science exists for science's sake, whereas for Bernal 'usefulness ... was the central objective of the scientific enterprise and the desired end of state support of science' (Pielke, 2014). This usefulness becomes visible in the context of purpose motivations, which expect different actors (e.g. the market or the state) to either benefit or organize for STI. However, some argue that Bernal's early 'revolutionary thinking in the 1930's was ... taken over by the captains of industry and ministers of government in the postwar period ... (resulting in) the weaker (known) Bernalism of planning, programming, people, money and equipment for efficient growth' (Elzinga and Jamison, 1995, p. 573) used as the main legitimation for science policy. Figures like Polanyi (1962), Merton (1973), and Bernal, 'still cast long shadows onto contemporary perceptions of the nature of science and government' (Bimber and Guston, 1995, p. 2). However, more recent motivations stem from observations that challenge 'the assumptions of the Cold War era and the guiding conceptions of the state ... (as well as) the political value and nature of basic research itself' (Elzinga and Jamison, 1995, p. 573). These motivations seek to transform the direction and impact of PRF, as well as its organization.

The directionality between motivations described in academic narratives and policy change can be hard to ascribe. Academic work on science policy 'advance(s) knowledge claims which appear to either anticipate or justify policy interventions ... (while policy documents) refer to or draw upon these academic narratives to justify the science–society interaction they advocate' (Jacob, 2006, p. 432). This chapter does not attribute directionality, but argues that academic and policy narratives co-exist and co-produce themselves. Raising awareness of this quality can support reflection by academics and policy-makers about the normative and practical implications of their positions.

The chapter describes the motivations – *creativity, purpose, and transformation* – and briefly describes how these motivations get inserted and operationalized in the US and in the EU.

PUBLIC RESEARCH FUNDING MOTIVATIONS

The Autonomy of Creativity

The *curiosity motivation* draws on the principle of 'free research' guided by curiosity, experimentation and collegial debates (Beddeleem, 2015). Core ideas associated with this motivation include blind delegation, *laissez-innover*, excellent ('breakthrough') research (Dasgupta and David, 1994), and Mode 1 (Gibbons et al., 1994). Polanyi, for example, envisioned a science that seeks the 'truth for its own sake' and that 'can be accomplished only if it remains free from political, ideological and economical influences' (Hartl, 2012). He further states 'that the pursuit of science by independent self-co-ordinated initiatives assures the most efficient possible organization of scientific progress' (Polanyi, 1962). Polanyi viewed the erosion of the distinction between basic and applied science as 'dangerous arguments for the social responsibility of scientists, central planning of scientific research, and relinquishment of individual freedom' (Nye, 2011, p. 194).

Within the curiosity motivation, Mode 1 knowledge production (Gibbons et al., 1994; Nowotny et al., 2003), defined in opposition to Mode 2 (see Transformation motivation), emerges as part of a two-form explanatory model of knowledge production primarily focused on science and technology but that also has been used to characterize innovation (Kaplinsky, 2011). Mode 1, often associated with the curiosity motivation, is compatible with the linear model of innovation.[2] Gibbons et al. (1994) and Nowotny et al. (2003) emphasized the knowledge that stemmed largely from an academic context and within disciplinary boundaries to demarcate 'sound scientific practice' (Gibbons et al., 1994, p. 167). Mode 1 science conforms 'with traditional knowledge production sites (universities, federal laboratories, industry laboratories), and hierarchical decision making' (Logar, 2011). It prioritizes basic research, often publicly funded and via universities, as 'essential to guarantee the generation of the knowledge and rationales to underpin the flow of innovations required for survival in the global economy' (Gibbons, 2013). Curiosity motivations focus on questions of why, as opposed to questions of how often associated with applied research (Jaffe et al., 2007). Mode 1 is discipline-based and Mode 1 scientists are accountable to one another and their discipline. They seek 'breakthroughs in fundamental science … carried out in typical university laboratories' (Gibbons, 2013, p. 1287). Success in Mode 1 can be defined as 'academic excellence, which is a comprehensive explanation of the world (and of society) on the basis of "basic principles" or "first principles", as is being judged by knowledge producer communities (academic communities structured according to a disciplinary framed peer review system)' (Campbell and Carayannis, 2013, p. 32). Curiosity motivations center on scientists and their needs in the quest to expand knowledge frontiers. They center around an investigator-initiated mechanism, which affords maximum freedom of intellectual inquiry and hinges on the potential of great intellectual payoff, but does not define it. Examples of the types of PRF organizations that support and enable individual researchers in their pursuits can be found in the European Research Council (Benner, 2018b) and the US National Science Foundation (NSF). This motivation was prominent in the arguments for the establishment of the US NSF (Bush, 1945; Stephan, 2015). In the US, philanthropic support, especially targeting specific diseases, was also a source of funding for this type of research (Benner, 2018a). But this kind of science also comes at a considerable cost, as it requires time both on the proposing and reviewing end and may also discourage risk taking' (Stephan, 2012, p. 114). Historically, curiosity motivations have been used 'in opposition to rationales of socialism and centralized steering of scientific agendas' (Elzinga, 2012) and sole investment in this type of science has been seen as insufficient to 'guarantee the technology required to compete in the world economy and meet a full spectrum of societal needs' (Stokes, 1997, p. 58). While curiosity rationales, as we have defined them here, appear 'to count for less in the official policy discourse', they are seen as a form of resistance to in response to management changes in research (Elzinga, 2012).

The Politics of Purpose

The politics of purpose, in this chapter, entail motivations around PRF that are about missions led by the state, aim to achieve value from research, or that explore the nature of purpose when doing science. This is a departure from more classical understandings that view market and mission motivations as distinct. However, these motivations are understood here as bringing together activities that often have clear goals and intention in their conception. They are the effect of a 'transformation within science' away from the politics of autonomy (described elsewhere as a quest for pure science) onto 'science as a source of economic, and by extension, political power' (Jotterand, 2006, p. 659). They also assume that stimulating innovation can be positive because ultimately everyone will benefit from it in some way, for example with the new high-quality jobs that could be generated.

The market motivation refers to the idea that research supports economic growth and creates jobs. It focuses on the goal of achieving economic returns and value from PRF, which goes beyond the traditional view that the market is served indirectly or best through curiosity-driven research. This motivation stems from the rising importance of competition and economic incentives as the main mechanism for the allocation of research (Geuna, 2001; Lepori, 2011; Slaughter and Rhoades, 2004; Teixeira et al., 2004) and responds to policy rationales, such as New Public Management (Christensen and Lægreid, 2001; Ferlie et al., 1996) that encourage the adoption of management practices from the private sector in the public sector. Competition in PRF is expected to lead to increased responsiveness and efficiency (Krücken, 2021; Musselin, 2018). As part of this motivation the entrepreneurial role gets added to the conventional responsibilities of research and education of the university (Thune, 2010). The triple helix framework[3] (Etzkowitz and Leydesdorff, 1995), which is rooted in an evolutionary perspective (Jacob, 2006), tries to explain the emergence of entrepreneurship at universities, along with the infrastructure that promotes it (Jacob, 2006). These changes facilitate the adoption of new roles, such as the commercialization of knowledge and firm formation as part of the university's core mission (Etzkowitz, 1998; Etzkowitz and Leydesdorff, 2001; Jacob, 2006), and focus on turning knowledge into wealth (Jacob, 2006). The triple helix notion has evolved into the quadruple helix, as well as the quintuple helix (Carayannis and Campbell, 2013). The notion of the quadruple helix, for example, was endorsed by the European Commission in its strategy for smart specialization (Foray et al., 2012b). These conditions enable businesses to invest in research and development and collaborate with complementary partners in the production of applications.

Yet competition appears as the source of incremental research, lower epistemic innovation, and an erosion of the academic social fabric (Boudreau et al., 2016; Franssen et al., 2018; Franssen and De Rijcke, 2019; Heinze et al., 2009). It has also been conceptualized as 'multiple competitions' within university governance that generate positive and negative unintended consequences (Krücken, 2021, pp. 173–178). The notion of national innovation systems (Lundvall, 1992), so core to the market motivation, has also been challenged by the 'open, interactive, and globalized nature of much research and innovation activity' (Weber and Truffer, 2017, p. 102). These systems rely on political systems centered around nation-states or nation-state-based political systems (Kuhlmann, 2001), which raises the question of 'whether and to what extent territorially and sectorally delimited innovation systems are still adequate to capture reality' (Weber and Truffer, 2017, p. 102). Other critics of this motivation allude to 'consensus of the literature that reliance on market processes alone will result in underinvestment in research and development, from a social point of view' (Martin and Scott, 2000). The market motivation has also led to performance criteria within university research (Geuna, 2001; Hicks, 2012) that 'has led faculty, and the government agencies that support faculty, to be risk averse ... "Sure bets" are preferred over research agendas with uncertain outcomes' (Stephan, 2012, p. 149). The early focus on innovation as tied to competitiveness at national, regional or sectoral levels has also opened up criticism 'about the contribution of innovation activities to tackling major societal, environmental, and developmental challenges' (Weber and Truffer, 2017, p. 102). But some argue that even with these new challenges the systems-oriented approach to innovation, which emphasized functional and generic aspects needed for growth, can still provide an appropriate guideline for STI policy (Gassler et al., 2007).

The mission motivation, on the other hand, revolves around national or societal interests and involves the planning and direction of research by the state. It involves an active state, often directing, but also collaborating with stakeholders across society to further national strategic goals. Core literature includes old and new mission orientation, grand challenges, and rationales about 'solvable challenges' and 'wicked problems' (e.g. Hicks, 2016; Larrue, 2021; Mazzucato, 2018a). Coburn et al. (Chapter 10 in this *Handbook*) show how research targeting to address societal problems (in their case neglected diseases) can be affected by the way it interacts with existing research evaluation practice. A key characteristic of grand challenges is that they often involve diverse constellations of actors, especially civil society actors (Cagnin et al., 2012; Kuhlmann and Rip, 2018; Ulnicane, 2016; Weber and Rohracher, 2012). But research has found that civil society mostly gets involved as an additional party in constellations with more traditional innovation actors (Howoldt, 2021; Kallerud et al., 2013; Mazzucato, 2018b). These new missions, sometimes called grand challenges, are rationales that travel and get locally adapted, even if in practice the challenge is defined differently (Hicks, 2016).

Old and new mission rationales juxtapose the feats of 'public R&D programs ... (like the) U.S. government-sponsored Manhattan Project or Project Apollo' with new societal missions that extend beyond technical matters and must be co-defined by a large number of stakeholders (Foray et al., 2012a; Modic and Feldman, 2017). In their evolution earlier missions 'were designed, funded, and managed by federal agencies to achieve a specific technological solution for which the government was effectively the sole "customer"'; but new missions offer 'technological solutions to global climate change' to be deployed throughout the world by many different actors with very high investment from the public and private sectors (Mowery et al., 2010, p. 1012). In the space sector, original mission-oriented policies focused 'on clear challenges with identifiable concrete problems and directed by a strong centralized agency', whereas new missions are broadly defined within a 'decentralized innovation systems with mixed top-down and bottom-up problem definition' (Robinson and Mazzucato, 2019, p. 936).

Another idea found in purpose motivations is *dual-purpose knowledge*, which reveals the limitation of describing PRF motivations in terms of curiosity or purpose alone. This assumes clearly defined boundaries between research that claims to pursue fundamental understandings and that which pursues application or to addresses societal challenges. However, research often does not lie clearly within either boundary and some have sought to explain the motivation behind such work. A prime example would be 'Pasteur's research on fermentation (which) simultaneously offered fundamental insights that led to the germ theory of disease and was of immediate practical significance for the French beer and wine industry' (Jaffe et al., 2007, p. 34). Daniel Stokes coined the term 'Pasteur's quadrant' to describe such 'dual purpose' knowledge (Stokes, 1997). In his seminal book, Stokes introduced two fundamental questions – whether research pursues fundamental understanding and whether it considers use. By framing the discussion in the context of these two purposes, Stokes brings to the reader's attention the notion of dual-use or user-inspired research. Dual purpose emerges from criticism of the linear model of innovation that faces off basic science against any consideration of use (Logar, 2011). Such a model makes science and use 'mutually exclusive' because it assumes basic research as the pursuit for fundamental understanding and an activity that is free from use considerations (Logar, 2011). Use-oriented research has also been described as 'playing it safe' and 'not science in its truest sense because science is the process by which we define the unknown' (Stephan, 2012, p. 149). Stokes (1997) did not suggest 'turning the power of basic science to national needs' (p. 151) as a way to displace basic research, but sought to bring together 'scientific integrity' to the use-inspired research that could be used to meet national needs in the US.

The clash between the old mission paradigm or the market ideas and the new societal requirements and expectations gives a foundation to new iterations in which missions are again offered as a solution. The mission motivation is 'not just about throwing funds at problems but doing so in specific ways' (Mazzucato, 2018a). This involves a proactive state that wants to lead and 'business follows', which differs from the old approach in that the state before took a role of 'a fixer of markets' (Mazzucato, 2018a). The scale of the problems sought to target by the new missions is novel (Ulnicane, 2016), but it still draws on more traditional views about the social function of science and PRF. Critics also contend that 'our present understandings and practices of STI policy are not sufficient to address Grand Challenges and set priorities accordingly' (Kuhlmann and Rip, 2014).

Transformation

The transformation motivation implicitly questions the distinctions (e.g. between actors or sectors) found in the previous motivations and fosters 'hybrid' settings for PRF. It often emerges in connection to new purposes, such as the Sustainable Development Goals, that require a fundamental transformation of science–society relationships. The changing context of how scientific knowledge gets produced has enabled new interpretations of the relationship between society, science, and technology, and between the actors that produce, use, and contest them. This motivation acknowledges that purpose or curiosity alone are not always transformative. It signals dissatisfaction with 'business as usual', and seeks to challenge it. The transformation motivation stems from 'frustration of insufficient or slow transformation' that seems to prevent major societal challenges from being eradicated (Borrás and Edler, 2020).

Part of the transformation motivation aims to better account for changes in knowledge production and the new relationships that have developed over time. Mode 2 emerged as part of the puzzle. Mode 2 'calls into question the adequacy of familiar knowledge producing institutions' (Gibbons et al., 1994), including government research institutions. Mode 2 does not mean applied science 'because as yet there is no science to be applied in that context' (Gibbons, 2013, p. 1286). Actors in this mode may come from 'government laboratories, some from industry, and others from social action groups and concerned citizens, perhaps with no particular scientific training at all' (Gibbons, 2013, p. 1286), which is in accord with its transdisciplinary[4] trait. The broadening and hybridization of knowledge production characterizes Mode 2 (Pfotenhauer and Juhl, 2017, p. 90), yet it signals increasing tensions around user involvement and the importance of local context in practice (Hakansta and Jacob, 2016). Collaboration tends to take varied forms, includes 'socially accountable decision making' (Logar, 2011) and exists 'only so long as the problem in hand requires them all' (Gibbons, 2013, p. 1286). Mode 2 has been characterized as a tempting concept but not as a change agent or even good descriptor of social change, questioning whether it is just 'a metaphor, or just a catch phrase?' (Shinn, 2002). The forces described at universities 'are seen as quasi-natural and inevitable' (Pfotenhauer and Juhl, 2017, p. 90). In the case of Mode 2, it highlighted social utility and the organization of knowledge production. The Mode 2 framework[5] suggests an interest in application with an acknowledgment of change in the organization of innovation and research, as well as an expansion in terms of its actors, users and beneficiaries. The changes associated with the transformative motivation seen in universities have also resulted in particular forms of performance-based research funding systems that aim for excellence, but in their execution 'may compromise other important values such as equity or diversity ... (and) will not serve the goal of enhancing the economic relevance of research' (Hicks, 2012, p. 260).

Within this motivation there are also calls for re-visiting existing structures and systems of PRF. Ideas,[6] such as responsible innovation or development, as well as an emphasis on inclusion, diversity, equity and access in STI, emerge as measures to optimise and broaden participation in PRF. Responsible innovation (Stilgoe et al., 2013), responsible research and innovation (von Schomberg, 2013) (also known as RRI), or broader impacts (National Science Foundation, 2014), address the interconnection between PRF, research practices, and the future that is enabled by them. The notions of RRI and broader impacts emerged in a policy context (Davis and Laas, 2013; Flink and Kaldewey, 2018), whereas responsible innovation has more academic roots that connect it to the study of ethical, legal, and social aspects or implications of emerging technologies (Hilgartner, 2018; Swierstra and Rip, 2007; also known as ELSA/ELSI). These distinctions connect the terms to practice and theory in ways that infuse the transformative motivation with different concerns, for example, that these ideas are supposedly too close to 'what politicians want and what gets funded' (Davis and Laas, 2013, p. 966), which runs against assumptions found within the creativity motivation about the expected benefits from the unpredictability of research. A criticism of PRF efforts in this area has been the mismatched expectations between involved actors, e.g. social scientists as 'mediators between nanotechnology and society' instead of being integrated into practices as scientists in their own right (Rip, 2009, p. 666). Also the 'practical barriers and cultural differences' within laboratories represent obstacles to achieving and enacting these ideas within science (van Hove and Wickson, 2017, p. 213). Ample work has explored and questioned the makeup of research landscapes by challenging the indicators used to assess them and calling for more diverse, equitable and inclusive participation. Cruz-Castro et al. (Chapter 17 in this *Handbook*) explore differences in research funding for gender and underrepresented minorities (see also for example Bird and Rhoton, 2021; National Research Council, 2010; Francis et al., 2017; Goulden et al., 2011; Hodgins and O'Connor, 2021; Mcquillan, 2021; Meng and Shapira, 2010; O'Connor, 2020; Otero-Hermida and García-Melón, 2018; Page et al., 2009; Ratele et al., 2019; Shattuck and Cheney, 2020; Smith-Doerr, 2021; Smith-Doerr et al., 2017, 2019; Stirling, 2007). This work infuses the transformation motivation with a sense of self-reflection and change that calls for system overhaul. However, these calls for inclusion, diversity, equity, and access often exist outside existing instruments for PRF or within specific research calls, which prevent them from becoming the norm.

More ambitious visions of transformation acknowledge that policy should give direction and support the generation, use and diffusion of innovations (Borrás and Edler, 2020) as well as call for new arguments to legitimize policy interventions (Weber and Rohracher, 2012). They contest the direction and form of technical change (Irwin, 2006). They acknowledge the interconnections that exist in socio-technical systems and understand that innovation does not always equal social progress and that many technologies fuel persistent environmental and social problems (Schot and Steinmueller, 2018). Optimizing existing institutions and practices is not sufficient to meet challenges, such as those posed by the Sustainable Development Goals (Daniels et al., 2020). The need to restructure scientific research to meet society's needs (Conn et al., 2021) raises questions about the ability of existing coordinating structures to meet this goal (Flagg and Garg, 2021; Fuchs, 2021; McNutt and Crow, 2020; Schot and Steinmueller, 2018). The relationship between inequality and innovation becomes salient in the transformation motivation highlighting the trajectory of high-tech solutions that assume particular infrastructures in place and high purchasing power (Kaplinsky, 2011). These visions also acknowledge that innovation policies remain 'skewed, unfocused and limited' (Borrás and Edquist, 2019, p. 2). The PRF landscape needs a 'more explicit, conscious approach to understand governance conditions' that elicit the transformative change it envisions (Borrás and Edler, 2020). The transformative motivation brings attention to alternative futures and to the co-production of STI with society (Daniels et al., 2020). These visions of systemic change see policy as playing a role in supporting positive societal development and claim that it should be transformative (Foray et al., 2012a; Kuhlmann and Rip, 2018; Schot and Steinmueller, 2018; Weber and Rohracher, 2012). Transformation should be the aim and a complement to policies that target market or system failures in directionality, policy coordination, demand-articulation and reflexivity (Weber and Rohracher, 2012). It calls for a PRF landscape optimized for different incentives (Flagg and Garg, 2021).

The transformation motivation, as presented here, grapples with concerns about the changing relationships within PRF, the need for institutional and structural change in order to engender more equitable and socially responsible knowledge systems, and ends with calls for systemic changes that can better respond to the complex needs of our society. In their quest for transformation, all these ideas embrace complexity differently – by describing it, by calling for new values or holistic responses, or by acknowledging the politics of policy change. But in all the ideas within the transformation motivation we run the risk that 'that complexity is simply "black boxed" and rendered unproblematic' (Flanagan et al., 2011, p. 701).

CONCLUSIONS

Throughout this chapter, we see a gradual move from individual curiosity to systemic explanatory models that aim to connect organization, actors and goals sought through PRF. The politics of purpose, as described here, 'assume[s] that stimulating innovation is positive, (yet) there is no deep engagement with the fact that innovation always represents a certain directionality' (Schot and Steinmueller, 2018, p. 1562). This lack of engagement with the potential negative long-term effects of technology development gave way to more expansive and ambitious motivations that seek to challenge the ideals and governance of PRF. The transformation motivation articulates an increasing attention to PRF as a means to meet societal expectations (Husted et al., 2000) and encompasses 'a modernistic commitment to innovation and global growth … (that) encounters more democratic and inclusive perspectives on the necessity for, and direction of, such change' (Irwin, 2006, p. 317). While this synthesis focused on the motivations found in the literature, I include two text boxes that illuminate their dynamic presence in STI policy beyond academic narratives.

Collaboration emerges as a common thread throughout the motivations described here, especially those about purpose and transformation. For them coordination, for example across actors, sectors and organizations, becomes a necessary condition for success. Yet all the motivations in this chapter depart from a knowledge production system that 'discourages scientists from helping contenders' (Franzoni and Sauermann, 2014, p. 9), while prominently pushing for interdisciplinary research (Simon et al., 2019). In an interdisciplinary or transdisciplinary world, synthesizing the understanding from different disciplinary and practice contexts becomes crucial (Bammer, 2008, p. 877). Therefore, understanding the ideas, expectations and limitations embedded in the motivations informing PRF becomes critical to explain and grasp how they can shake the knowledge production systems in place. The fate of the most ambitious motivations for PRF depends not only on narratives, that for example put a primacy on collaboration, but on actors, actions, and institutions that value, integrate, and invest in them.

In short, the chapter focused on motivations for PRF because they shape choices that policy actors take (e.g. the design of funding schemes), have an effect on the relationships between actors/sectors, and become embedded into policy instruments. As Capano (Chapter 5 in this *Handbook*) explains, the relationship between motivations and instruments runs deep and represents an important source of policy dynamics. Therefore, it is crucial to take a step back and revisit the motivations that inform PRF, i.e. the ideas that shape what actors conceive as possible within them. The motivations in this chapter signal a recurrent concern between scientific inquiry and application, that at times appear as separate, but that seem to blur over time. One major criticism of these academic explanations has been that they have not yet given way to the concrete problems faced by policy-makers (Borrás and Edquist, 2019) because they do not imply a 'one to one mapping between scholarly ideas and policy rationales' (Flanagan et al., 2011, p. 704). However, the chapter shows how the transformation motivation is based on an acknowledgment that society's needs require profound changes to the way we envision, structure, and organize PRF.

NOTES

1. My interest in writing this piece emerged from co-authored research in the *Isomorphic Difference Project: Familiarity and Distinctiveness in National Innovation Policies* project (Independent Research Fund Denmark (grant number 8019-00044B)) presented at the EUSPRI conference in June 2021. I am grateful to Professors Diana Hicks, Benedetto Lepori and Ben Jongbloed, who offered the chance of an in-depth exploration of some ideas from the original paper for this *Handbook*. Their comments and suggestions strengthened this piece. Any errors are my own.

2. This model is often connected to Vannevar Bush (1945) – see e.g. Carayannis and Campbell (2013) – even though 'models of innovation' emerge in a later era (Godin, 2015). Additionally Bush did not propose a 'linear model' explicitly, nor did he pioneer the conceptualization of innovation in a linear way (Pfotenhauer and Juhl, 2017, p. 90).

3. The triple helix framework is presented here as part of the market motivation owing to its strong connection to entrepreneurship and the mix of actors and institutions it seeks to explain. One could also argue that in its construction and application, the triple helix also speaks to the transformation motivation but with the goal of turning research into wealth (Jacob, 2006).

4. 'Strictly speaking, it is neither multidisciplinary nor interdisciplinary because the knowledge elements that enter Mode 2 draw on sources beyond those of any set of disciplines' (Gibbons, 2013, p. 1286).

5.   This framework has seen developments towards Mode 3 knowledge production that acknowledge the existence of national innovation systems but emphasize their global embeddedness (Carayannis et al., 2015).
6.   There are other related ideas that owing to lack of space I did not include, but would be relevant, e.g. inclusive innovation (Agola and Hunter, 2016; Chataway et al., 2014), social innovation (Howaldt et al., 2021; Joly, 2017; Mulgan et al., 2007), grassroots innovation (Gupta, 2012; Smith et al., 2014; Smith and Seyfang, 2013), frugal innovation (Leadbeater, 2014; Radjou and Prabhu, 2014; Ratten, 2019) and innovation for inclusive development (C. U. Daniels et al., 2017; Organisation for Economic Co-operation and Development, 2012).

REFERENCES

Agola, N. O., and Hunter, A. (2016). *Inclusive Innovation for Sustainable Development: Theory and Practice*. Palgrave Macmillan.

Bammer, G. (2008). Enhancing research collaborations: Three key management challenges. *Research Policy*, *37*(5), 875–887. https://doi.org/10.1016/j.respol.2008.03.004.

Beddeleem, M. (2015). *Michael Polanyi: From Academic to Cultural Freedom* (Towards Good Society – 6th Project Meeting, Copenhagen, 9–11 December 2015).

Benner, M. (2018a). Why is there no knowledge policy in the United States? In *The New Global Politics of Science: Knowledge, Markets and the State* (pp. 84–115). Edward Elgar. https://doi.org/10.4337/9781784717179.00010.

Benner, M. (2018b). The European Union: straddling interests and expectations. In *The New Global Politics of Science: Knowledge, Markets and the State* (pp. 116–140). Edward Elgar.

Bimber, B., and Guston, D. H. (1995). Politics by the same means: Government and science in the United States. In S. Jasanoff, G. E. Markle, J. C. Petersen, and T. Pinch (Eds.), *Handbook of Science and Technology Studies, Revised Edition*. SAGE. https://doi.org/http://dx.doi.org/10.4135/9781412990127.n24.

Bird, S. R., and Rhoton, L. A. (2021). Seeing isn't always believing: Gender, academic STEM, and women scientists' perceptions of career opportunities. *Gender and Society*, *35*(3), 422–448. https://doi.org/10.1177/08912432211008814.

Borrás, S. (2012). Three tensions in the governance of science and technology. In D. Levi-Faur (Ed.), *The Oxford Handbook of Governance* (pp. 429–440). Oxford Handbook Online. https://doi.org/10.1093/oxfordhb/9780199560530.013.0030.

Borrás, S., and Edler, J. (2020). The roles of the state in the governance of socio-technical systems ' transformation. *Research Policy*, *49*, 1–9. https://doi.org/10.1016/j.respol.2020.103971.

Borrás, S., and Edquist, C. (2019). *Holistic Innovation Policy: Theoretical Foundations, Policy Problems, and Instrument Choices* (1st edn). Oxford University Press.

Borrás, S., and Laatsit, M. (2019). Towards system oriented innovation policy evaluation? Evidence from EU28 member states. *Research Policy*, *48*, 312–321.

Boudreau, K. J., Guinan, E. C., Lakhani, K. R., and Riedl, C. (2016). Looking across and looking beyond the knowledge frontier: Intellectual distance, novelty, and resource allocation in science. *Management Science*, *62*(10), 2765–2783. https://doi.org/10.1287/mnsc.2015.2285.

Bush, V. (1945). Science, the endless frontier 75th Anniversary edition. Report, reissued by the National Science Foundation. https://doi.org/10.1038/372012a0.

Cagnin, C., Amanatidou, E., and Keenan, M. (2012). Orienting European innovation systems towards grand challenges and the roles that FTA can play. *Science and Public Policy*, *39*(2), 140–152. https://doi.org/10.1093/scipol/scs014.

Campbell, D. F. J., and Carayannis, E. G. (2013). *Epistemic Governance in Higher Education: Quality Enhancement of Universities for Development*. Springer. https://doi.org/10.1007/978-1-4614-4418-3.

Carayannis, E. G., and Campbell, D. F. J. (2013). Mode 3 knowledge production in quadruple helix innovation systems: Quintuple helix and social ecology. In *Encyclopedia of Creativity, Invention, Innovation and Entrepreneurship* (pp. 1293–1298). Springer Science and Business Media. https://doi.org/10.1007/978-1-4614-3858-8.

Carayannis, E. G., Campbell, D. F. J., and Rehman, S. S. (2015). Mode 3 knowledge production: Systems and systems theory, clusters and networks. *Journal of Innovation and Entrepreneurship*, 5(1). https://doi.org/10.1186/s13731-016-0045-9.

Chataway, J., Hanlin, R., and Kaplinsky, R. (2014). Inclusive innovation: An architecture for policy development. *Innovation and Development*, 4(1), 33–54. https://doi.org/10.1080/2157930X.2013.876800.

Christensen, T., and Lægreid, P. (2001). *New Public Management: The Transformation of Ideas and Practice*. Ashgate.

Conn, R. W., Crow, M. M., Friend, C. M., and McNutt, M. (2021). The next 75 years of US science and innovation policy: An introduction. *Issues in Science and Technology*, July. https://issues.org/the-next-75-years-of-us-science-and-innovation-policy-an-introduction/.

Daniels, C., Schot, J., Chataway, J., Ramirez, M., Steinmueller, E., and Kanger, L. (2020). Transformative innovation policy: Insights from Colombia, Finland, Norway, South Africa and Sweden. In M. B. Cele, T. M. Luesche, and A. W. Fadiji (Eds.), *Innovation Policy at the Intersection: Global Debates and Local Experiences* (pp. 9–30). HSRC Press. https://www.hsrcpress.ac.za/books/innovation-policy-at-the-intersection.

Daniels, C. U., Ustyuzhantseva, O., and Yao, W. (2017). Innovation for inclusive development, public policy support and triple helix: perspectives from BRICS. *African Journal of Science, Technology, Innovation and Development*, 9(5), 513–527. https://doi.org/10.1080/20421338.2017.1327923.

Dasgupta, P., and David, P. A. (1994). Towards a new economics of science. *Research Policy*, 23, 487–532.

Davis, M., and Laas, K. (2013). 'Broader Impacts' or 'Responsible Research and Innovation'? A comparison of two criteria for funding research in science and engineering. *Science and Engineering Ethics*, 20(4), 963–983. https://doi.org/10.1007/s11948-013-9480-1.

Edler, J., and Fagerberg, J. (2017). Innovation policy: What, why, and how. *Oxford Review of Economic Policy*, 33(1), 2–23. https://doi.org/10.1093/oxrep/grx001.

Elzinga, A. (2012). Features of the current science policy regime: Viewed in historical perspective. *Science and Public Policy*, 39(4), 416–428. https://doi.org/10.1093/scipol/scs046.

Elzinga, A., and Jamison, A. (1995). Changing policy agendas in science and technology. In S. Jasanoff, G. E. Markle, J. C. Petersen, and T. Pinch (Eds.), *Handbook of Science and Technology Studies, Revised Edition* (pp. 572–597). SAGE.

Etzkowitz, H. (1998). The norms of entrepreneurial science: cognitive effects of the new university–industry linkages. *Research Policy*, 27(8), 823–833. https://doi.org/10.1016/S0048-7333(98)00093-6.

Etzkowitz, H., and Leydesdorff, L. (1995). The triple helix – University–industry–goverment relations: A laboratory for knowledge based economic development. *EASST Review*, 14(1), 14–19.

Etzkowitz, H., and Leydesdorff, L. (2001). *Universities and the Global Knowledge Economy: A Triple Helix of University–Industry–Government Relations*. Continuum.

Ferlie, E., Ashburner, L., Fitzgerald, L., and Pettigrew, A. (1996). *The New Public Management in Action*. Oxford University Press. https://doi.org/10.1093/acprof:oso/9780198289029.001.0001.

Ferlie, E., Musselin, C., and Andresani, G. (2008). The steering of higher education systems: A public management perspective. *Higher Education*, 56(3), 325–348. https://doi.org/10.1007/s10734-008-9125-5.

Flagg, M., and Garg, A. (2021). Science policy from the ground up. *Issues in Science and Technology*, Fall, 51–55. https://doi.org/10.1080/00988157.1975.9977143.

Flanagan, K., Uyarra, E., and Laranja, M. (2011). Reconceptualising the 'policy mix' for innovation. *Research Policy*, 40(5), 702–713. https://doi.org/10.1016/j.respol.2011.02.005.

Flink, T., and Kaldewey, D. (2018). The new production of legitimacy: STI policy discourses beyond the contract metaphor. *Research Policy*, 47(1), 14–22. https://doi.org/10.1016/j.respol.2017.09.008.

Foray, D., Mowery, D. C., and Nelson, R. R. (2012a). Public R&D and social challenges: What lessons from mission R&D programs? *Research Policy*, 41(10), 1697–1702. https://doi.org/10.1016/j.respol.2012.07.011.

Foray, D., Goddard, J., Beldarrain, X. G., Landabaso, M., McCann, P., Morgan, K., Nauwelaers, C., and Ortega-Argilés, R. (2012b). *Guide to Research and Innovation Strategies for Smart Specialization (RIS3)* (issued May). https://doi.org/10.2776/65746.

Francis, B., Archer, L., Moote, J., DeWitt, J., MacLeod, E., and Yeomans, L. (2017). The construction of physics as a quintessentially masculine subject: Young people's perceptions of gender issues in access to physics. *Sex Roles*, 76(3–4), 156–174. https://doi.org/10.1007/s11199-016-0669-z.

Franssen, T., and De Rijcke, S. (2019). The rise of project funding and its effects on the social structure of academia. *The Social Structures of Global Academia*, May, 144–161. https://doi.org/10.4324/9780429465857-9.

Franssen, T., Scholten, W., Hessels, L. K., and de Rijcke, S. (2018). The drawbacks of project funding for epistemic innovation: Comparing institutional affordances and constraints of different types of research funding. *Minerva*, 56(1), 11–33. https://doi.org/10.1007/s11024-017-9338-9.

Franzoni, C., and Sauermann, H. (2014). Crowd science: The organization of scientific research in open collaborative projects. *Research Policy*, 43(1), 1–20. https://doi.org/10.1016/j.respol.2013.07.005.

Fuchs, E. R. H. (2021). What a national technology strategy is – And why the United States needs one. *Issues in Science and Technology*, 9 September. https://issues.org/national-technology-strategy-agency-fuchs/.

Gassler, H., Polt, W., and Rammer, C. (2007). Priority setting in technology policy: Historical developments and recent trends. InTeReg Working Paper Series (No. 36-2007; InTeReg Working Paper). https://www.joanneum.at/fileadmin/user_upload/imported/uploads/tx_publicationlibrary/WP_36_priority_settings.pdf.

Geuna, A. (2001). The changing rationale for European university research funding: Are there negative unintended consequences? *Journal of Economic Issues*, 35(3), 607–632. https://doi.org/10.1080/00213624.2001.11506393.

Gibbons, M. (2013). Mode 1, mode 2, and innovation. In *Encyclopedia of Creativity, Invention, Innovation and Entrepreneurship* (pp. 1285–1292). Springer Science and Business Media. https://doi.org/10.1007/978-1-4614-3858-8.

Gibbons, M., Limoges, C., Nowotny, H., Schwartzman, S., Scott, P., and Trow, M. (1994). *The New Production of Knowledge: The Dynamics of Science and Research in Contemporary Societies*. SAGE. https://doi.org/10.2307/2076669.

Godin, Benoît. (2015). Models of innovation: Why models of innovation are models, or what work is being done in calling them models? *Social Studies of Science*, 45(4), 570–596. https://doi.org/10.1177/0306312715596852.

Goulden, M., Mason, M. A., and Frasch, K. (2011). Keeping women in the science pipeline. *Annals of the American Academy of Political and Social Science*, 638(1), 141–162. https://doi.org/10.1177/0002716211416925.

Gupta, A. K. (2012). Innovations for the poor by the poor. *International Journal of Technological Learning, Innovation and Development*, 5(1–2), 28–39. https://doi.org/10.1504/IJTLID.2012.044875.

Guston, D.H., and Keniston, K. (1994). Updating the social contract for science. *Technology Review*, 97(8), 60. https://link.gale.com/apps/doc/A16391748/AONE?u=cbs&sid=bookmark-AONE&xid=43cfec19.

Guston, D.H., and Keniston, K. (2009). Introduction: The social contract for science. *The Fragile Contract: University Science and the Federal Government* (pp. 1–41). papers://d3978ab5-8702-4bf9-be6f-7c3f6904d049/Paper/p5078.

Hakansta, C., and Jacob, M. (2016). Mode 2 and the tension between excellence and utility: The case of a policy-relevant research field in Sweden. *Minerva (London)*, 54(1), 1–20. https://doi.org/10.1007/s11024-015-9288-z.

Hartl, P. (2012). Michael Polanyi on freedom of science. *Synthesis Philosophica*, 27(2), 307–321.

Heinze, T., Shapira, P., Rogers, J. D., and Senker, J. M. (2009). Organizational and institutional influences on creativity in scientific research. *Research Policy*, 38(4), 610–623. https://doi.org/10.1016/j.respol.2009.01.014.

Hicks, D. (2012). Performance-based university research funding systems. *Research Policy*, 41(2), 251–261. https://doi.org/10.1016/j.respol.2011.09.007.

Hicks, D. (2016). Grand challenges in US science policy attempt policy innovation. *International Journal of Foresight and Innovation Policy*, 11(1), 22–42. https://doi.org/10.1504/IJFIP.2016.078379.

Hilgartner, S. (2018). The Human Genome Project and the legacy of its ethics programs. In S. Gibbon, B. Prainsack, S. Hilgartner, and J. Lamoreaux (Eds.), *Handbook of Genomics, Health and Society* (2nd ed., pp. 123–132). Routledge. https://www.taylorfrancis.com/books/edit/10.4324/9781315451695/

handbook-genomics-health-society-sahra-gibbon-barbara-prainsack-stephen-hilgartner-janelle-lamor
eaux?refId=3e1de873-b8e6-4b22-a99d-40aefd67c951&context=ubx.

Hodgins, M., and O'Connor, P. (2021). Progress, but at the expense of male power? Institutional resistance to gender equality in an Irish university. *Frontiers in Sociology*, 6(July), 1–14. https://doi.org/10
.3389/fsoc.2021.696446.

Howoldt, D. (2021). *Policy Instruments and Policy Mixes for Innovation: Analyzing their relationship to
grand challenges, entreprenership and innovtion caability with natural language processin and latent
variable methods* [Copenhagen Business School]. https://research-api.cbs.dk/ws/portalfiles/portal/
69776002/david_howoldt_phd_series_38_2021.pdf.

Howaldt, J., Kaletka, C., and Schröder, A. (2021). *A Research Agenda for Social Innovation*. Edward
Elgar. https://doi.org/https://doi.org/10.4337/9781789909357.

Husted, K., Mønsted, M., Wenneberg, S. B., and Ernø-Kjølhede, E. (2000). Managing university
research in the triple helix. Department of Management, Politics and Philosophy (MPP) Working
Paper, October (issue 13). https://doi.org/10.3152/147154301781781679.

Irwin, A. (2006). The politics of talk: Coming to terms with the 'new' scientific governance. *Social
Studies of Science*, 36(2), 299–320. https://doi.org/10.1177/0306312706053350.

Jacob, M. (2006). Utilization of social science knowledge in science policy: Systems of innovation, triple
Helix and VINNOVA. *Social Science Information*, 45(3). https://doi.org/10.1177/0539018406066535.

Jaffe, A. B., Lerner, J., and Stern, S. (2007). *Innovation Policy and the Economy*. MIT Press. http://
ebookcentral.proquest.com/lib/kbhnhh-ebooks/detail.action?docID=3338488.

Joly, P.-B. (2017). Beyond the competitiveness framework? Models of innovation revisited. *Journal of
Innovation Economics and Management*, 22(1), 79–96. https://doi.org/10.3917/jie.pr1.0005.

Jotterand, F. (2006). The politicization of science and technology: Its implications for nanotechnology.
Journal of Law, Medicine and Ethics, 34(4), 658–666. https://doi.org/10.1111/j.1748-720X.2006
.00084.x.

Juhl, J. (2016). Innovation science: Between models and machines. *Engineering Studies*, 8(2), 116–139.
https://doi.org/10.1080/19378629.2016.1205593.

Kallerud, E., Amanatidou, E., Upham, P., Nieminen, M., Klitkou, A., Olsen, D. S., Toivanen, M. L.,
Oksanen, J., and Scordato, L. (2013). Dimensions of research and innovation policies to address grand
and global challenges. *The Emergence of Challenge-Driven Priorities in Research and Innovation
Policy*, 1, 1–22.

Kaplinsky, R. (2011). Schumacher meets Schumpeter: Appropriate technology below the radar.
Research Policy, 40(2), 193–203. https://doi.org/10.1016/j.respol.2010.10.003.

Khan, B. Z. (2020). *Inventing Ideas: Patents and Innovation Prizes, and the Knowledge Economy*.
Oxford University Press.

Krücken, G. (2021). Multiple competitions in higher education: A conceptual approach. *Innovation:
Organization and Management*, 23(2), 163–181. https://doi.org/10.1080/14479338.2019.1684652.

Kuhlmann, S. (2001). Future governance of innovation policy in Europe – Three scenarios. *Research
Policy*, 30(6), 953–976. https://doi.org/10.1016/S0048-7333(00)00167-0.

Kuhlmann, S., and Rip, A. (2014). Research policy must rise to a grand challenge. *Research Europe*,
2013, 1–11.

Kuhlmann, S., and Rip, A. (2018). Next-generation innovation policy and grand challenges. *Science and
Public Policy*, 45(4), 448–454.

Larrue, P. (2021). The design and implementation of mission-oriented innovation policies: A systemic
policy approach to address societal challenges. *OECD Science, Technology and Industry Policy
Papers*, 100, 1–22.

Larrue, P., Guellec, D., and Sgard, F. (2019). New trends in public research funding. In *OECD Science,
Technology and Innovation Outlook 2018: Adapting to Technological and Societal Disruption*
(pp. 185–202). https://doi.org/https://doi.org/10.1787/25186167.

Leadbeater, C. (2014). *The Frugal Innovator: Creating Change on a Shoestring Budget*. Palgrave
Macmillan. https://doi.org/10.1057/9781137335371.

Lepori, B. (2011). Coordination modes in public funding systems. *Research Policy*, 40(3), 355–367.
https://doi.org/10.1016/j.respol.2010.10.016.

Logar, N. (2011). Scholarly science policy models and real policy, RSD for SciSIP in US Mission
Agencies. *Policy Sciences*, 44(3), 249–266. https://doi.org/10.1007/s11077-011-9136-4.

Lundvall, B. Å. (1992). *National Systems of Innovation: Toward a Theory of Innovation and Interactive Learning* (2010 Web). Pinters/Anthem Press. https://doi.org/10.7135/UPO9781843318903.

Martin, S., and Scott, J. T. (2000). The nature of innovation market failure and the design of public support for private innovation. *Research Policy*, *29*, 437–447. https://doi.org/10.1016/S0048-7333(99)00084-0.

Mazzucato, M. (2018a). Mission-oriented innovation policies: Challenges and opportunities. *Industrial and Corporate Change*, *27*(5), 803–815. https://doi.org/10.1093/icc/dty034.

Mazzucato, M. (2018b). Mission-oriented research and innovation in the European Union: A problem-solving approach to fuel innovation-led growth. https://doi.org/10.2777/360325.

McNutt, M., and Crow, M. M. (2020). Science institutions for a complex, fast-paced world. *Issues in Science and Technology*, *Winter*, 30–34. https://issues.org/wp-content/uploads/2020/01/McNutt-Crow-Science-Institutions-for-a-Complex-Fast-Paced-World-Winter-2020.pdf.

Mcquillan, J. (2021). Real-life conundrums in the struggle for institutional transformation. *Gender and Society*, *35*(3), 300–329. https://doi.org/10.1177/08912432211013147.

Meng, Y., and Shapira, P. (2010). Women and patenting in nanotechnology: Scale, scope and equity. In S. E. Cozzens and J. M. Wetmore (Eds.), *Nanotechnology and the Challenges of Equity, Equality and Development* (pp. 23–46). Springer. https://doi.org/10.1007/978-90-481-9615-9_2.

Merton, R. K. (1973). *The Sociology of Science: Theoretical and Empirical Investigations* (N. W. Storer (Ed.)). The University of Chicago Press.

Modic, D., and Feldman, M. P. (2017). Mapping the human brain: Comparing the US and EU Grand Challenges. *Science and Public Policy*, *44*(3), 440–449. https://doi.org/10.1093/scipol/scw085.

Mowery, D. C., Nelson, R. R., and Martin, B. R. (2010). Technology policy and global warming: Why new policy models are needed (or why putting new wine in old bottles won't work). *Research Policy*, *39*(8), 1011–1023. https://doi.org/10.1016/j.respol.2010.05.008.

Mulgan, G., Tucker, S., Rushanara, A., and Sanders, B. (2007). Social innovation: What is it, why it matters, and how it can be accelerated. University of Oxford, Young Foundation. https://youngfoundation.org/wp-content/uploads/2012/10/Social-Innovation-what-it-is-why-it-matters-how-it-can-be-accelerated-March-2007.pdf.

Musselin, C. (2018). New forms of competition in higher education. *Socio-Economic Review*, *16*(3), 657–683. https://doi.org/10.1093/SER/MWY033.

National Research Council (2010). Gender differences at critical transitions in the careers of science, engineering, and mathematics faculty. Report. https://doi.org/10.17226/12062.

National Science Foundation. (2014). Perspectives on Broader Impacts (NSF 15-008). https://www.nsf.gov/od/oia/publications/Broader_Impacts.pdf.

Nowotny, H., Scott, P., and Gibbons, M. (2003). Introduction: 'Mode 2' Revisited: The new production of knowledge. *Minerva*, *41*(3, Special Issue: Reflections on the New Production of Knowledge), 179–194.

Nye, M. J. (2011). *Michael Polanyi and his Generation: Origins of the Social Construction of Science.* University of Chicago Press.

O'Connor, P. (2020). Why is it so difficult to reduce gender inequality in male-dominated higher educational organizations? A feminist institutional perspective. *Interdisciplinary Science Reviews*, *45*(2), 207–228. https://doi.org/10.1080/03080188.2020.1737903.

Organisation for Economic Co-operation and Development (2012). *Innovation for Development: A Discussion on the Issues and an Overview of Work of the OECD Directorate for Science, Technology and Industry.* https://www.oecd.org/innovation/inno/50586251.pdf.

Otero-Hermida, P., and García-Melón, M. (2018). Gender equality indicators for research and innovation from a responsible perspective: The case of Spain. *Sustainability*, *10*(9). https://doi.org/10.3390/su10092980.

Page, M., Bailey, L., and Van Delinder, J. (2009). The Blue Blazer Club: Masculine hegemony in science, technology, engineering, and math fields. *Forum on Public Policy Online*, *2009*(2), 1–23.

Paradeise, C., Reale, E., Bleiklie, I., and Ferlie, E. (2009). *University Governance* (C. Paradeise, E. Reale, I. Bleiklie, and E. Ferlie (Eds.)). Springer. https://link.springer.com/book/10.1007/978-1-4020-9515-3.

Pfotenhauer, S. M., and Juhl, J. (2017). Innovation and the political state: Beyond the myth of technologies and markets. In B. Godin and D. Vinck (Eds.), *Critical Studies of Innovation:*

Alternative Approaches to the Pro-Innovation Bias (pp. 68–93). Edward Elgar. https://doi.org/10.4337/9781785367229.00012.

Pielke Jr., R. A. (2014). In retrospect: The social function of science. *Nature (London)*, *507*(7493), 427–428. https://doi.org/10.1038/507427a.

Polanyi, M. (1962). The republic of science. Its political and economic theory. *Minerva*, *I*(1), 54–73. https://doi.org/10.1007/BF01101453.

Radjou, N., and Prabhu, J. (2014). What frugal innovators do. *Harvard Business Review*, 1–7. https://hbr.org/2014/12/what-frugal-innovators-do#:~:text=Frugal innovation is more than,that favors agility over efficiency.

Ratele, K., Verma, R., Cruz, S., and Khan, A. R. (2019). Engaging men to support women in science, medicine, and global health. In *The Lancet*, *393*(10171), 609–610. https://doi.org/10.1016/S0140-6736(19)30031-5.

Ratten, V. (2019). *Frugal Innovation*. Routledge.

Rip, A. (2009). Viewpoint: Futures of ELSA. *European Molecular Biology Organization Reports*, *10*(7), 666–670.

Robinson, D. K. R., and Mazzucato, M. (2019). The evolution of mission-oriented policies: Exploring changing market creating policies in the US and European space sector. *Research Policy*, *48*(4), 936–948. https://doi.org/10.1016/j.respol.2018.10.005.

Schot, J., and Steinmueller, W. E. (2018). Three frames for innovation policy: R&D, systems of innovation and transformative change. *Research Policy*, *47*(9), 1554–1567. https://doi.org/10.1016/j.respol.2018.08.011.

Shattuck, S., and Cheney, I. (2020). *Picture a Scientist* (I. Cheney, S. Shattuck, and M. Pottle (Eds.)). Film Platform. https://d3crmev290s45i.cloudfront.net/content/1010999xxx/1010999569/1010999569-size-exact-230x325.jpg.

Shinn, T. (2002). The Triple Helix and new production of knowledge: Prepackaged thinking on science and technology. *Social Studies of Science*, *32*(4), 599–614. https://doi.org/10.1177/030631202128967271.

Simon, D., Kuhlmann, S., Stamm, J., and Canzler, W. (2019). Introduction: Science and public policy – relations in flux. In D. Simon, S. Kuhlmann, J. Stamm, and W. Canzler (Eds.), *Handbook on Science and Public Policy* (pp. 1–10). Edward Elgar.

Slaughter, S., and Rhoades, G. (2004). *Academic Capitalism and the New Economy: Markets, State, and Higher Education*. Johns Hopkins University Press.

Smith, A., and Seyfang, G. (2013). Constructing grassroots innovations for sustainability. *Global Environmental Change*, *23*(5), 827–829. https://doi.org/10.1016/j.gloenvcha.2013.07.003.

Smith, A., Fressoli, M., and Thomas, H. (2014). Grassroots innovation movements: challenges and contributions. *Journal of Cleaner Production*, *63*, 114–124. https://doi.org/10.1016/j.jclepro.2012.12.025.

Smith-Doerr, L. (2021). Colleges should research DEI on their own campuses (opinion). *Inside Higher Ed*. https://www.insidehighered.com/print/views/2021/09/15/colleges-should-research-dei-their-own-campuses-opinion.

Smith-Doerr, L., Alegria, S. N., and Sacco, T. (2017). How diversity matters in the US science and engineering workforce: A critical review considering integration in teams, fields, and organizational contexts. *Engaging Science, Technology, and Society*, *3*, 139. https://doi.org/10.17351/ests2017.142.

Smith-Doerr, L., Alegria, S. N., Fealing, K. H., Fitzpatrick, D., and Tomaskovic-Devey, D. (2019). Gender pay gaps in U.S. federal science agencies: An organizational approach. *American Journal of Sociology*, *125*(2), 534–576. https://doi.org/10.1086/705514.

Squazzoni, F., Bravo, G., and Takács, K. (2013). Does incentive provision increase the quality of peer review? An experimental study. *Research Policy*, *42*(1), 287–294. https://doi.org/10.1016/j.respol.2012.04.014.

Stephan, P. (2015). The endless frontier: Reaping what Bush sowed? In A. B. Jaffe and B. F. Jones (Eds.), *The Changing Frontier: Rethinking Science and Innovation Policy* (National B, Issue July, pp. 321–366). University of Chicago Press. http://www.nber.org/papers/w19687.pdf.

Stephan, P. E. (2012). *How Economics Shapes Science*. Harvard University Press.

Stilgoe, J., Owen, R., and Macnaghten, P. (2013). Developing a framework for responsible innovation. *Research Policy*, *42*(9), 1568–1580.

Stirling, A. (2007). A general framework for analysing diversity in science, technology and society. *Journal of the Royal Society Interface*, *4*(15), 707–719. https://doi.org/10.1098/rsif.2007.0213.

Stokes, D. E. (1997). *Pasteur's Quadrant: Basic Science and Technological Innovation*. Brookings Institution.

Swierstra, T., and Rip, A. (2007). Nano-ethics as NEST-ethics: Patterns of moral argumentation about new and emerging science and technology. *NanoEthics*, *1*(1), 3–20. https://doi.org/10.1007/s11569 -007-0005-8.

Teixeira, P., Jongbloed, B. B., Dill, D. D., and Amaral, A. (2004). *Markets in Higher Education Rhetoric or Reality?* (1st ed.). Springer. https://doi.org/10.1007/1-4020-2835-0.

Thune, T. (2010). The training of 'Triple Helix workers'? Doctoral students in university–industry– government collaborations. *Minerva*, *48*(4), 463–483. https://doi.org/10.1007/s11024-010-9158-7.

Ulnicane, I. (2016). 'Grand Challenges' concept: a return of the 'big ideas' in science, technology and innovation policy? *International Journal of Foresight and Innovation Policy*, *11*(1–3), 5–21. https:// doi.org/10.1504/IJFIP.2016.078378.

van Hove, L., and Wickson, F. (2017). Responsible research is not good science: Divergences inhibiting the enactment of RRI in nanosafety. *NanoEthics*, *11*(3), 213–228. https://doi.org/10.1007/s11569-017 -0306-5.

von Schomberg, R. (2013). *A Vision of Responsible Research and Innovation* (pp. 51–74). John Wiley & Sons. https://doi.org/10.1002/9781118551424.ch3.

Weber, K. M., and Rohracher, H. (2012). Legitimizing research, technology and innovation policies for transformative change: Combining insights from innovation systems and multi-level perspective in a comprehensive 'failures' framework. *Research Policy*, *41*(6), 1037–1047. https://doi.org/10.1016/j .respol.2011.10.015.

Weber, K. M., and Truffer, B. (2017). Moving innovation systems research to the next level: Towards an integrative agenda. *Oxford Review of Economic Policy*, *33*(1), 101–121. https://doi.org/10.1093/ oxrep/grx002.

4. Politics of public research funding: the case of the European Union[1]

Inga Ulnicane

'... Research policy has become of one of the EU's core instruments for advancing its policies, promoting European integration, and achieving change. It has won the support of researchers, both in Europe and beyond, gained prestige, and found a solid place on the EU political agenda. With its extensive programs and significant funding, it has transformed the European research landscape for good. However, to remain relevant, the EU research policy needs to be tailored to serve the most compelling needs of the European societies. If designed right, it can be a powerful force, enabling critical and truly transformative effort for which none of the individual member states would be capable alone.'
(Mitzner, 2020, p. 276)

INTRODUCTION: EU RESEARCH POLICY AS A SUCCESS STORY?

While in developed countries research policy and funding tend to be predominantly decided at national level, there are a number of emerging international science policy and funding initiatives. Such initiatives are particularly relevant in the area of research because the scientific community has a long-standing tradition of collaborating across borders (Kastenhofer and Molyneux-Hodgson, 2021; Nedeva, 2013). So far emerging international research policy and funding initiatives tend to be small and fragmented, with the European Union (EU) being the major exception.

Since the 1980s, the EU research policy has experienced major growth in terms of an increase in EU-level competencies, funds, initiatives and instruments. Over the past 40 years, the EU research funding programme, known as the European Union Framework Programme (EU FP), has grown considerably from 3 billion euros allocated for the first EU FP for research and development (1984–1987) to almost 100 billion euros assigned for the current ninth EU FP (2021–2027), known as Horizon Europe (European Commission, 2021). Moreover, research at the EU level is funded not only through the EU FPs but also through other programmes, in particular, the Structural Funds for regional development and the recently launched European Defence Fund for defence research. The EU research policy has become the third largest item on the EU budget after agriculture and structural funds (Ulnicane, 2016a). Research policy is seen as a success story of European integration where it represents 'an area of sustained growth and impact' (Mitzner, 2020, p. 1).

How to explain the establishment and continuous expansion of EU research policy as a major example of international research policy and funding? This chapter examines this question by applying a constructivist lens of policy framing that in particular considers political and social aspects of policy design (Rein and Schon, 1993, 1996; Schon and Rein, 1994). A policy framing approach focuses on how in policy practice, policy stories influence the shaping of laws, regulations, allocation decisions, institutional mechanisms and incentives.

Policy frames, which integrate facts, values, theories and interests, help to structure and inform policy debates and practice, which are situated in a specific political and historical context.

Examining research policy through the lens of policy frames helps to uncover political and social aspects of designing research policy and funding programmes. Thus, rather than perceiving design of research funding programmes as purely technocratic activity driven by increasingly questioned economic ideas such as market failure, government failure and public goods (Bozeman, Chapter 2 in this *Handbook*; Mazzucato, 2021), this chapter uses a policy framing lens to examine political and social aspects of designing research policy and funding in a specific historical context. The idea that research investments can be seen as 'a continuation of politics by other means' (Elzinga, 2012, p. 416) helps to investigate the case of the EU, where the establishment and expansion of research policy and funding have been part of political European integration process. Thus, this chapter examines the role of policy framing in structuring the design of EU research policy and funding.

The chapter draws on an extensive and growing but fragmented literature on EU research policy and funding. Typically, this literature originating from various disciplines including political science, history and economics focuses on specific EU initiatives and funding instruments. This chapter integrates this disperse literature to examine the role of framing in the establishment and growth of EU research policy.

This chapter proceeds as follows: first, an overview of the establishment and growth of EU research policy is provided; second, the conceptual lens of policy frames and their use in research policy are introduced; third, various frames of EU research policy and their role in the growth of this policy area are examined; and finally, key findings are discussed.

ESTABLISHMENT AND GROWTH OF EU RESEARCH POLICY

Today the EU's research funding programme is largely taken for granted. However, in the early days of European political and economic integration in the 1950s, the establishment of EU research policy was far from obvious. Back then, almost all decisions about research and its funding remained at national level. To understand the contested origins of EU research policy (Mitzner, 2020), it is important to pay close attention to the political and historical context of European integration.

The establishment and growth of EU research policy is intertwined with the European integration process. Broadening, deepening and expansion of European integration provided opportunities for the launch and growth of new initiatives and programmes in the area of research. New EU treaties, competencies, enlargements and political priorities shaped the evolution of EU research policy. Since the initial Treaties on European integration in the 1950s, research policy has emerged and expanded gradually (see Table 4.1). To introduce the political and historical context of the establishment and expansion of EU research policy, four key developments are presented here: (1) mixed beginnings within and outside the European Communities 1950s–1970s; (2) establishment and expansion of EU research funding programme since the 1980s; (3) establishment and expansion of the EU legal competencies in area of research; and (4) expansion of new types of instruments in 2000s.

Table 4.1   *Key milestones in history of EU research policy*

Year	Launch of milestones in research policy	Initiative
1950s–1970s	Mix of initiatives within and outside the European Communities framework	Euratom (European Atomic Energy Community) Treaty
1984	EU research funding	Launch of the Framework Programme
1987	EU competence in the area of research	Introduction of legal competence in research in the Single European Act
2000	New types of instruments	Launch of the European Research Area

Source: Own compilation.

Mixed Beginnings Within and Outside of the European Communities, 1950s–1970s

The first decades of European integration in the 1950s in the area of research can be characterized by a mix of limited research policy within the newly launched European Communities (as predecessors of the European Union were known), and a number of ad hoc intergovernmental initiatives outside the European Communities framework.

While in the field of research there is a long tradition of international cooperation at the level of scientific community (Kastenhofer and Molyneux-Hodgson, 2021) and integration in terms of technological infrastructures (Misa and Schot, 2005), the initial Treaties on European integration in the 1950s paid little attention to research policy.[2] The exception was the Euratom Treaty on the European Atomic Energy Community in 1957 that among other things aimed to promote research in the field of nuclear energy. Experience of the Euratom provided an important legacy for future development of EU research policy (Mitzner, 2020). The 1960s and 1970s also saw establishment of the first institutions in the field of research such as the Directorate General for Research at the Commission and the committee of member state and Commission representatives known as PREST (Politique de la Recherche Scientifique et Technique) and later as CREST (Comité de la Recherche Scientifique et Technique) to advise the Council of Ministers and the Commission.

However, from the 1950s until the 1970s most joint European cooperation initiatives in the field of research took place outside the Treaties (Cramer, 2020; Cramer and Hallonsten, 2020; Krige, 2003; Papon, 2009). Such intergovernmental research initiatives included the establishment of large-scale research facilities such as the European Organization of Nuclear Research CERN in 1954, the European Southern Observatory in 1962, and the European Molecular Biology Laboratory in 1974 (Ulnicane, 2020). The first joint research funding initiatives also were launched as cooperation among national governments with major examples being the European Cooperation in Science and Technology COST in 1971 and the European Science Foundation in 1974.

Important reasons for this initial cooperation taking place outside the Treaties were: first, a lack of legal competencies in the area research policy in the initial Treaties (see above), and second, initially a small number of member states of the European Community (EC)[3] (six in the 1950s and the 1960s, and nine from 1973[4]), while these intergovernmental initiatives typically brought together 10 or more countries. Although these initiatives were launched outside the Treaties, the European Commission and the Council of Ministers have been involved in negotiations preceding some of these initiatives, over the years have established cooperation with them, and also later developed new EU policy frameworks for such cooperation, for example, for European Research Infrastructures (Ulnicane, 2022).

Launch and Expansion of European-level Research Funding

Important changes took place in the 1980s when 'research became a full-fledged EC policy with sizable budgets, truly ambitious programs, and a more strategic approach' (Mitzner, 2020, p. 231) bringing together the various plans and scattered initiatives of the previous twenty years (Mitzner, 2020, p. 261). A major milestone was the launch of the EU FP for funding research and innovation in 1984. As mentioned in the introduction, over the past 40 years the amount of funding allocated to multi-annual FPs has increased considerably. While the subsequent FPs were typically known by their numbers from FP1 (1984) until FP7 (2007–2013), the two most recent programmes are known as Horizon 2020 (2014–2020) and Horizon Europe (2021–2027). The Horizon 2020 amounted to approximately 8% of the EU multi-annual budget for 2014–2020 (Ulnicane, 2016a). Participation in FPs is open not only to the EU member states but also to non-EU countries (Cavallaro and Lepori, 2021; European Commission, 2020). In Horizon 2020, 16 associated countries participated fully or partially (Ulnicane, 2020).

The expansion of EU FPs has involved the launch of new funding programmes and instruments. A prominent example of a new FP funding instrument has been the launch of the European Research Council (ERC) in 2007 to fund investigator driven blue-sky research (König, 2017; Nedeva, 2013; Wedlin and Nedeva, 2015).

In addition to the EU FP, the EU also funds research from a number of other programmes. In the current EU multi-annual budget 2021–2027, funding for research, innovation and technology features prominently including within the post-Covid recovery agenda Next Generation Europe (European Commission, 2020). Research and innovation in less developed regions are supported by the EU Cohesion Policy and Structural Funds (European Commission, 2020; Sharp, 1998). In 2017, the EU set up the European Defence Fund to fund defence research (Calcara, Csernatoni, and Lavalée, 2020). While the EU FP funds research with exclusive focus on civilian applications, the new European Defence Fund is a unique example of international funding for defence research, which traditionally has been seen as a highly sensitive area of national sovereignty. Different EU research funding programmes have different allocation models. If the EU FP funding is allocated competitively to research projects at EU level, then the Structural Funds are allocated to regions which then have their own funding allocation models.

In EU member states with more developed research systems the majority of public research funding is allocated at the national level, and EU programmes provide some additional funds. For example, during 2007–2013, the FP7 funds typically amounted to approximately 10–20% of government support for research and development (R&D) in the EU member states (Veugelers, 2014). FP funding has played an important role in facilitating international research collaborations in Europe (Borras, 2019). During the same time, the EU Structural Funds' contribution to research and development amounted to just 1–3% of government support in the most developed national research systems in Europe such as Sweden, Finland and Denmark, while they constituted over 50% of government support for R&D in East European member states such as Slovenia and Hungary (Veugelers, 2014). Against this background, the European Commission has repeatedly emphasized the limits of EU funding for research and innovation (R&I) and the continuous importance of national funding reminding that:

> Horizon Europe and other relevant programmes under the EU budget alone, such as Cohesion Policy or Next Generation EU, would not be enough to fund the R&I needed for the green and digital transitions. In order to bring about a real positive change, this must be complemented by investments from Member States. These efforts combined should crowd in significant private investment to ensure ownership and quality of results. (European Commission, 2020, p. 6)

Establishment and Expansion of EU Competence in the Field of Research

If the initial Treaties on the European Communities in the 1950s included hardly any competencies in research policy (except the Euratom), then soon after the launch of the FP in 1984 the Community competence for research policy was introduced in the Single European Act (SEA) that came into force in 1987.[5] Although this official introduction of the EC competence in research was legally important, Veera Mitzner points out that 'it was more about reaffirmation of established practices rather than creating truly new ones' (Mitzner, 2020, p. 246). The initially restricted supporting competence[6] in this area introduced in the SEA was gradually expanded in the subsequent Treaties (Mitzner, 2020, p. 264). Finally, the most recent Lisbon Treaty that came into force in 2009 introduced a shared competence in this area. Article 179 of the Treaty on Functioning of the EU defines the aim of EU research policy as follows:

> The Union shall have the objective of strengthening its scientific and technological bases by achieving a European research area in which researchers, scientific knowledge and technology circulate freely, and encouraging it to become more competitive, including in its industry, while promoting all the research activities deemed necessary by virtue of other Chapters of the Treaties.

New Types of Policy Instruments

The Treaty mentions the European Research Area (ERA) initiative that was launched by the European Commission in 2000 and has been portrayed as a new step towards deepening European integration in research (Borras, 2003; Chou and Gornitzka, 2014; Delanghe, Muldur and Soete, 2009; Edler, Kuhlmann and Behrens, 2003; Prange-Gstohl, 2010; Ulnicane, 2015). While the main type of policy instruments in EU research policy has been funding and dedicated funding instruments have been launched in subsequent FPs to implement the ERA, this initiative also introduced a new type of instrument in this policy area, namely, the Open Method of Coordination. The Open Method of Coordination is aimed at facilitating coordination among EU member states by setting joint targets as well as identifying, sharing and learning from good practices. The main example of the Open Method of Coordination in research policy is the so called 3% target that aims to achieve that national R&D funding is increased to 3% of gross domestic product (GDP). However, this target has been criticized for focusing only on inputs rather than on how research funding is spent. Moreover, its usefulness and efficiency have been questioned as almost 20 years after setting this target in 2002, it has still not been achieved in many EU countries (Borras, 2019; Ulnicane, 2016a) and in 2018 on average the EU countries were investing 2.19% of GDP in R&D (European Commission, 2020). Thus, new objectives and instruments introduced by the ERA initiative are closely connected to funding either by influencing design of the FPs or by aiming to influence the amount of national research funding.

To summarize, while in the early days of European integration in the 1950s there was hardly any indication of potential EU research policy, since the 1980s the EU funding, competencies and a range of instruments in area of research policy have been established and grown considerably. How to explain this emergence and growth of EU research policy? What role has policy framing played in it?

A CONCEPTUAL LENS: FRAMES IN RESEARCH POLICY

The approach of policy framing (Rein and Schon, 1993, 1996; Schon and Rein, 1994) is a fruitful way to examine political and social dynamics of the growth and evolution of EU research policy and funding. Policy frames are 'diagnostic/prescriptive stories that tell, within a given issue terrain, what needs fixing and how it might be fixed' (Rein and Schon, 1996, p. 89). According to Martin Rein and Donald Schon (1993),

> framing is a way of selecting, organizing, interpreting, and making sense of a complex reality to provide guideposts for knowing, analysing, persuading, and acting. A frame is a perspective from which an amorphous, ill-defined, problematic situation can be made sense of and acted on. (Rein and Schon, 1993, p. 146)

In such frames 'facts, values, theories, and interests are integrated' (Rein and Schon, 1993, p. 145). Rein and Schon distinguish between two closely connected types of frames – rhetorical and action. According to them, 'rhetorical frames are constructed from the policy-relevant texts that play important roles in policy discourse, where the context is one of debate, persuasion, or justification' (Rein and Schon, 1996, p. 90), while 'action frames are constructed from the evidence provided by observation of patterns of action inherent in the practice of policy practitioners' (Rein and Schon, 1996, p. 91).

They associate policy frames with public controversies and pluralism, as 'in any given issue terrain, there are almost always a variety of frames competing for both meaning and resources', where 'the contest over meaning gives legitimacy to the claim for economic and social resources' (Rein and Schon, 1996, p. 95). According to Schon and Rein, these situated policy controversies with their competing frames structure policy debates and practices and shape the design of policies (Schon and Rein, 1994; see also Capano, Chapter 5 in this *Handbook*). For them, design of policy is a social and political process involving divergent interests and powers of actors. In their approach to policy design, Schon and Rein emphasize interaction of multiple designers, redesign in use and shifting contexts. Thus, this constructivist approach offers an insightful way to analyse research policy frames and their influence on the design of EU research policy and funding.

The concept of policy frames as well as related notions of policy paradigms, discourses, narratives, rationales, motivations, periodizations and generations has been productively applied to analyse evolution, growth and changes in science, technology and innovation policy within and beyond the EU (Alemán-Díaz, Chapter 3 in this *Handbook*; Borras, 2003; Boekholt, 2010; Diercks, Larsen and Steward, 2019; Elzinga, 2012; Mitzner, 2020; Ulnicane, 2015). Evolution and international diffusion of science, technology and innovation policy frames have been facilitated by epistemic communities of experts and policy-makers collaborating in international forums such as the Organisation for Economic Co-operation and Development and the EU. Typical evolution of policy frames are characterized by moving from science, technology and innovation contributing to economic objectives towards their role in addressing societal issues in areas such as health, environment and energy. An example here would be the recent shift towards a transformative innovation policy paradigm. This shift includes a move from a focus on economic competitiveness and only positive outcomes of innovation towards highlighting the relevance of science and technology for other objectives and policy domains (e.g. health, environment) as well as acknowledging both positive and negative outcomes of innovation, namely, that new technologies can also have harmful effects on health, safety and environment (Diercks et al., 2019).

This shift from a mostly economic focus towards broader societal challenges is sometimes described as a normative turn (Diercks et al., 2019) emphasizing values and norms underpinning the societal challenges agenda. However, such association of societal challenges with normative turn implies that previous focus on economic growth and competitiveness is value free and purely technocratic. It would be important to recognize normative underpinnings of all frames admitting that the traditional economic focus of research policy is also highly normative, prioritizing values of economic growth and competitiveness, which in the current situation of climate crisis are increasingly questioned.

However, the evolution of science, technology and innovation policy frames should not be seen as a simple linear development from narrow to broader objectives and understandings. It is rather a process of path dependence and the reinvention of ideas characterized by 'the continuation and deepening of old issues in new forms' (Elzinga, 2012, p. 426). Instead of being a rational process of continuous improvement, changes in science, technology and innovation policy are rather a result of many complex socially, politically and economically embedded factors (Borras, 2003). This is a highly relevant insight also for examining the development of EU research policy.

EXPANSION OF EU POLICY FRAMES AND FUNDING PROGRAMME

What are the dominant EU research policy frames and what role have they played in the establishment and expansion of EU funding for research? The two recent EU Framework Programmes have been designed according to the three main policy frames of economic competitiveness, scientific excellence, and societal challenges. The Horizon 2020 programme (2014–2020) was organized according to the three pillars of excellent science, societal challenges and industrial competitiveness. The current Horizon Europe programme (2021–2027) has three slightly revised main priorities of excellent science, global challenges and European industrial competitiveness, and innovative Europe (European Commission, 2021). More than half (53.5 billion euros) of Horizon Europe's almost 97 billion euros budget is allocated to the global challenges and European industrial competitiveness priority, followed by 25 billion euros earmarked for excellent science and 13.5 billion euros planned for innovative Europe (European Commission, 2021). Funds are also allocated for widening participation and strengthening the ERA (3.3 billion euros) and Euratom (1.3 billion euros) (European Commission, 2021).

What are the key features of these three dominant frames in the recent FPs? The first frame of the economic competitiveness focuses on the role of EU research policy in contributing to economic growth and closing the technology gap with the US and Asia (Mitzner, 2020). The second frame of scientific excellence highlights the EU's attempts to fund investigator-driven 'blue sky' fundamental research (König, 2017; Nedeva, 2013; Wedlin and Nedeva, 2015). The third frame of societal challenges (Ulnicane, 2016b) includes joint activities that aim to contribute to major societal issues and achieving the United Nations' Sustainable Development Goals (Mazzucato, 2021). While the economic competitiveness has been a dominant frame facilitating the emergence and expansion of EU research policy since the early days of European integration, the other two – scientific excellence and societal challenges – frames have acquired prominent positions and resources in the past 15 years (see information on Horizon 2020 and Horizon Europe above).

These three frames draw on old and new ideas in European integration and science, technology and innovation policy and contribute to further European integration in this area. While similar frames can also be found in national and international research policy (Alemán-Díaz, Chapter 3 in this *Handbook*; Diercks et al., 2019), a unique feature of EU research policy is that here the framing of diagnosis and prescription is related to European integration and cooperation.

Table 4.2 summarizes these three dominant frames focusing on their background ideas, diagnosis of the problems and corresponding prescriptions for tackling them. Below, each of these frames and their roles in EU research policy are explained in more detail examining how they have emerged and developed in particular political and historical context, what ideas, beliefs and values they entail, and how they have shaped EU research policy and funding.

Table 4.2   *Dominant frames in EU research policy*

Frame	Background ideas	Diagnosis	Prescription
Economic competitiveness	Research as a source of economic growth; technological gap between EU and others – US, Japan, China	EU is lagging behind because it is too fragmented and invests too little in R&I	EU will be more economically prosperous and internationally competitive if it has EU-level competencies and initiatives in research; coordinates and cooperates more
Scientific excellence	'Republic of Science' (Polanyi, 1962), academic freedom, self-governance of scientific community	Scientific elite dissatisfied with perceived quality, applied orientation and top-down nature of FPs	EU supports investigator-driven fundamental research allocated competitively on EU level based on scientific excellence
Societal challenges	Societal function of research (Bernal 1939), social relevance	Research has to address major societal challenges that require efforts beyond national capacity	Joint EU activities to address Grand Societal Challenges and UN SDGs

Economic Competitiveness

The economic competitiveness frame is a long-standing driver behind the establishment and expansion of EU research policy (Mitzner, 2020). According to this frame, research is seen as a major contributor to economic growth and productivity which are considered to be desirable political goals. In this context, research becomes a key ingredient of the discourse of international economic competitiveness. Economic competitiveness discourse has been popular around the world including in the US, which have experienced their own concerns about a Japanese 'threat' in the 1980s and more recently about China's growth (O'Mara, 2019). While this international economic competitiveness narrative has been criticized, pointing out that countries do not compete like companies and international economy is not a zero-sum game (Krugman, 1994), it continues to dominate policy and media discussions.

In Europe, the economic competitiveness discourse has focused on the EU's standing vis-à-vis major global powers such as the US and Asian countries. One of the key concerns in this discourse has been the technology gap, where Europe is portrayed as lagging behind other global powers. The typical diagnosis for this gap is that Europe is too fragmented and is not investing enough in research and innovation. Accordingly, the prescription has been that in order to be competitive and catch up with other countries, Europe should cooperate and coordinate more, and have the necessary legal competencies and ambitious initiatives in this area. Mitzner (2020) explains the historical role of the technology gap narrative in the establishment of EU research policy as follows:

> the gap became a political imperative in European integration. The basic argument was straightforward: science had expanded exponentially and now required resources that not even the largest European states could provide on their own. In the world of 'big science,' national efforts remained too fragmented and insufficient, while European firms lacked the critical scope to successfully face global competition. So, for the promoters of integration, the problem of the gap was first and foremost a problem of a scale. The American advantage not only stemmed from generous government spending, but also from the sheer size of the country and its powerful companies, which were big enough to undertake large scale research and enter large markets. [...] this argument was adopted by a number of politicians, public officials, and other actors promoting a 'common research policy' within the framework of the European Community. (Mitzner, 2020, pp. 49–50)

The policy frame of economic competitiveness and technology gap demonstrates a strong continuity from early discussions about the need to establish a European research policy in the 1960s (Mitzner, 2020) until the most recent EU research policy documents (European Commission, 2020). In the 1960s, focus on the utilitarian idea of research as a contributor to economic growth was important owing to the then rather limited competencies of the European Community that were largely focusing on promoting economic cooperation and prosperity. Framing research as essential for economic growth and competitiveness allowed the consideration of European activities in the area in times when there was no European research policy. Ideas of European cooperation in research as a way to increase economic competitiveness and to close the technology gap provided an important rationale for launching European funding and establishing legal competencies in the area of research in the 1980s. If in the 1960s early discussions about European research policy were fuelled by fears about lagging behind the US, then the launch of the major milestones of European research policy in the 1980s were accompanied also by new worries about Japanese domination in new technologies (Mitzner, 2020; Sandholtz, 1992).

The economic competitiveness and technology gap discourse was also at the core of launching the ERA initiative in 2000. It was framed in terms of the urgent need for joint action to improve Europe's competitive position and close the gap with the US and Japan, in particular in areas some of which have been of concern already since the 1960s (Mitzner, 2020) such as public and private expenditure on research and development, employment of researchers in industry and trade in high-tech products (Ulnicane, 2015). To address the usual 'suspects' behind the gap, such as the lack of coordination and investment, the ERA initiative suggested policy coordination measures and in 2002 declared the so-called '3% target' of national research and development funding reaching 3% of GDP to catch up with the US and Japan. The EU has recently reaffirmed the aim to achieve the 3% target, even though in the past 20 years progress towards this controversial target (Borras, 2019; Ulnicane, 2015, 2016a) has been limited and the R&D funding level in Europe still lags behind the US, Japan, South Korea and China (European Commission, 2020). The economic competitiveness rationale for EU research coordination and cooperation in the early years of the ERA was reinforced by its close links to the EU's Lisbon strategy also launched in 2000 and aiming to make the EU the most competitive knowledge-based economy by 2010 (Ulnicane, 2015).

While the ambitious goal of the Lisbon strategy was never achieved, the discourse of economic competitiveness has continued to dominate EU policies, including in the area of research. It was prevalent during the post-2008 financial crisis recovery when the EU policy presented research and innovation as sources of renewed economic growth (Ulnicane, 2016a). In times of austerity, the EU increased its funding for research seeing that as a source of economic growth and competitiveness vis-à-vis the US, Japan and China. Similarly, recent EU policy documents present research not only as a part of the post-Covid recovery but also as a crucial ingredient for the agenda to close the persistant technological gap with other major powers (European Commission, 2020).

The continuity of the economic competitiveness and technological gap frame in EU research policy is remarkable. Already over some 60 years it has served as a major driving force for the establishment and continuous expansion of EU research policy.

While in the past 20 years two additional frames of scientific excellence and societal challenges have emerged and facilitated further expansion of EU research policy, this traditional frame of economic competitiveness and technology gap still has a strong presence in today's policy-making in the area of EU research.

Scientific Excellence

In addition to the traditionally dominant frame of economic competitiveness in EU research policy, the discourse of scientific excellence gained support in the early years of the 21st century. Largely promoted by the scientific elite, this policy frame draws on ideas about the importance of self-governance, autonomy and independence of the scientific community that have been well known since Michael Polanyi's work on the Republic of Science (1962). The scientific excellence frame in EU research policy largely evolved during the discussions that preceded establishment of the ERC in 2007 as the main instrument to fund excellent science at the EU level (König, 2017; Nedeva, 2013).

Discussions before the establishment of the ERC identified a number of shortcomings in EU research that needed to be fixed. The European scientific elite was dissatisfied with the FPs owing to their perceived quality issues, top-down organization and applied nature (Luukkonen, 2014). The well-known discourse of the European paradox was challenged. If traditionally it was claimed that Europe was good at fundamental science but weak in application, then it was increasingly argued that Europe was lagging behind also in fundamental science (Wedlin and Nedeva, 2015).

As a prescription to these problems, ideas for the ERC were developed to support EU-wide competition for investigator driven risky and novel 'frontier research' based on the sole criterion of scientific excellence. This included revisiting ideas about 'European added value'. If previously added value of EU policy and funding was seen in cooperation and coordination, then now it was extended to include Europe-wide competition as well (Wedlin and Nedeva, 2015). Ideas about the ERC as an autonomous governance body where the scientific elite decides funding allocation independently from policy considerations were developed by learning from the experiences of the US National Science Foundation and the intergovernmental European Science Foundation (König, 2017; Nedeva, 2013). Thus, also in the scientific excellence frame we see a number of elements of international comparison and global positioning of EU research play an important role. Huge and highly competitive investigator-driven ERC grants for blue-sky research have quickly become popular among the scientific elite, and the ERC has been presented as a success story of EU research policy.

Although the ERC has constituted the core of the excellent science priority in Horizon 2020 and Horizon Europe programmes, this priority has also included some other actions. The Marie Sklodowska-Curie Actions providing funding for individual mobility grants and research training networks fit with the main features of the scientific excellence frame such as scientific freedom and EU-wide competition based on the criterion of scientific quality. Other activities funded under this priority – research infrastructures and Future and Emerging Technology Flagships (discontinued in Horizon Europe programme) – are expected to contribute not only to scientific excellence but also to societal challenges and economic competitiveness (European Commission, 2020; Ulnicane, 2020).

What is common to all scientific excellence funding schemes is a strong presence of and support from the scientific community or more narrowly scientific elite. If the traditional frame of economic competitiveness has at least initially been largely promoted by policy-makers and industry representatives, the more recent emergence of the scientific excellence frame in EU has been co-shaped by the scientific community as one of the main stakeholders of expanding EU research policy.

The scientific excellence frame is largely about supporting fundamental research and academic freedom, which are some of the most traditional characteristics of research policy (Elzinga, 2012). However, in EU research policy this frame emerged relatively late. It took more than 20 years from the launch of the FP to the establishment of ERC. Historically, the idea that there should be support for fundamental research at the EU level was far from obvious. From the original focus on economic integration in Europe, research policy initially emerged to support Europe-wide cooperation for global economic competitiveness and closing the technology gap with other major global powers. Accordingly, support for fundamental research was left for national research funding at the member-state level. The relatively recent EU support for fundamental research emerged owing to a novel excellent science frame challenging established notions and highlighting that the EU is lagging behind not only in technology but also in science and to address this gap the EU research funding should not only support cooperation but also the EU-wide competition for individual investigator-led grants.

Societal Challenges

Interestingly, in the early 21st century in parallel to the emergence of excellent science frame in EU research policy, a completely opposite frame of societal challenges started to develop as well. If the excellent science frame focuses on fundamental research and academic freedom, then the societal challenges frame highlights the need for science to address societal needs and develop according to societal values. This tension between academic freedom and societal relevance has been well known since the so-called Bernal–Polanyi debate where the former argued for social function of science (Bernal, 1939), while according to the latter any interference in the self-governing Republic of Science is potentially harmful for scientific enquiry (Polanyi, 1962).

While the idea that science has to address human needs has a long history (Bernal, 1939), it gained particular prominence in research policy in the early 21st century when the societal challenges frame became popular around the world. Societal challenges, also known as Grand Challenges and global challenges, typically focus on major social issues in areas such as environment, health and energy through cross-disciplinary and cross-sectoral collaborations (Diercks et al., 2019; Ulnicane, 2016b). Although the concept of Grand Societal Challenges has been widely used around the world (Hicks, 2016), a unique feature of its framing in EU policy is that the formulation of problems and solutions is related to European cooperation, namely, societal challenges cannot be tackled by individual nations, they require European cooperation, and EU-level funding is provided to address them (Ulnicane, 2016b).

The concept of societal challenges became part of the EU research policy rhetoric in 2007 when the ERA Green Paper highlighted that EU research policy should be deeply rooted in European society and support sustainable development in the fields of major public concern such as health, energy and climate change (European Commission, 2007). To optimise EU research policy, this document called for the systemic identification of major societal challenges relevant to many countries and requiring research efforts beyond national capacity. To address such common societal challenges, the Green Paper suggested European research cooperation involving stakeholders and citizens.

Additional impetus for using the Grand Challenges concept in EU research policy came from the ERA expert group report (ERA Expert Group, 2008), which followed the Green Paper and argued that the Grand Challenges concept can provide the content dimension for the ERA as well as help to increase support and funding for European research. In the context of the ERA expert group recommendations, the Grand Challenges concept had a role in moving EU research policy beyond a focus on deficit (e.g. fragmentation and lack of coordination) towards opportunities to jointly tackle Grand Challenges of climate change, food and energy security. The experts suggested that the focus on Grand Challenges would help to capture public and political imagination and thus play an instrumental role in shifting EU budget allocations towards research. This is an interesting example of explicitly using a particular frame in a highly strategic manner to advocate for the increase in EU research funding.

The major support for Grand Challenges was announced in the Lund Declaration 'Europe must focus on the grand challenges of our time' adopted during the Swedish Presidency of the Council of the EU in 2009 (Lund Declaration, 2009). The Lund Declaration called for moving away from rigid thematic approaches towards research priorities based on Grand Challenges in areas such as global warming, tightening supplies of energy, water and food, ageing societies, public health, pandemics and security. The Lund Declaration played a key role in the preparation of Horizon 2020, where societal challenges were one of the three priorities. Within this priority, funding was allocated to seven broad societal challenges from health and food security to climate action and secure, clean and efficient energy. These challenges were addressed through a number of instruments supporting large-scale cross-sectoral cooperation such as Joint programming initiatives and European Innovation Partnerships (Ulnicane, 2016b).

In the current Horizon Europe programme the global challenges priority is implemented through the missions-approach. The development of the missions-approach in the Horizon Europe has been led by economist Mariana Mazzucato who sees missions as moonshots similar to the Apollo programme launched by the US government to put a man on the moon (Mazzucato, 2021). According to her, missions are bold societal goals which can be achieved by collaboration on a large scale between public and private entities. This has important implications for the role of public policy in supporting research. Rather than correcting market failures, mission-oriented research policy is expected to have a more active role in shaping markets, making risky investments and setting direction for research towards achieving societal goals (Mazzucato, 2021).

In Horizon Europe, missions have been defined in five areas: first, cancer; second, adaptation to climate change including societal transformation; third, healthy oceans, seas, coastal and inland waters; fourth, climate-neutral and smart cities; and fifth, soil health and food (European Commission, 2021). It is expected that tackling these missions will contribute to the goals of major EU and global initiatives, such as the European Green Deal and the UN SDGs.

Thus, the key focus of recent EU policies to address societal challenges, missions and Sustainable Development Goals is on shaping research towards societal goals and values (see also Bozeman, Chapter 2 in this *Handbook*). In EU research policy this orientation towards societal values and broad societal benefits of research has been further enhanced by supporting approaches such as Responsible Research and Innovation and Open Science that aim to put societal needs at the core of research (Owen et al., 2021).

Beyond the Framework Programmes: Other EU Research Policy Frames

While the three main above discussed frames dominate the recent EU FPs, some further frames can also be encountered, in particular in relation to other EU funding programmes for research. Two frames of cohesion and defence are briefly discussed here.

First, in the shadow of the global competitiveness discourse and concerns about Europe catching up with other major powers, a very different frame concerning huge differences in research performance among EU member states has developed (Sharp, 1998). With the EU enlargements to southern and eastern Europe, the narrative of weaker national research systems catching up with western and northern countries has become more important. The main instrument to enhance internal cohesion has been EU regional funds allocating resources for research capacity building within less developed regions. Some funding for this purpose has also been allocated within the FPs such as in the widening participation and strengthening ERA package in the current Horizon Europe programme (European Commission, 2021). Additionally, the EU also provides expert advice and support for reforming national research systems. Despite the variety of EU support instruments for weaker research systems over decades, important differences in policies and performance persist (European Commission, 2020; Ulnicane, 2016a).

Second, in recent years a new EU research funding frame has emerged outside the EU FP, which facilitated the launch of the European Defence Fund in 2017 to fund EU defence research (Calcara et al., 2020). The emergence of the EU-level funding for defence research was supported by the discourse that the EU is too fragmented to address new security threats and challenges, and therefore joint EU defence research is needed. Considering that traditionally defence research has been perceived as a highly sensitive area of national sovereignty, the launch of the European Defence Fund is a recent example of EU research funding expanding further into areas that have previously been sole responsibility of the member states. It remains to be seen if and how the newly launched European Defence Fund with its explicit focus on defence research will interact with the FPs that only fund research with an exclusive focus on civil applications. Interestingly, a recent major document on EU research policy (European Commission, 2020) does not even mention defence research, leaving open questions about the relationships between different EU research funding programmes.

Thus, since the 1980s a number of major and minor policy frames have facilitated expansion of EU research funding within and beyond the FPs and the launch of new EU programmes and instruments gradually moving into areas that have traditionally been perceived as the realm of national government funding from investigator-driven fundamental research to joint defence research. It remains to be seen how recent changes in EU politics, e.g. a major revision of EU energy and defence policies in early 2022 after the Russian invasion in Ukraine, will affect future development on EU research policy and funding.

CONCLUSIONS

This chapter has demonstrated how since the 1950s EU research policy as a key example of international research funding has gradually emerged and expanded in terms of funds, competencies and policy instruments. Its emergence and expansion have been facilitated by certain policy frames which have been shaped by broader political, economic and social processes within and beyond Europe. Most prominent among these policy frames has been the economic competitiveness and technological gap narrative that has portrayed research as a source of economic growth and highlighted that Europe has been lagging behind other major powers such as the US and Asian countries. To facilitate research contributing to economic growth and closing the gap, European policy, cooperation and coordination have been promoted as the main prescription. More recently two other major frames of scientific excellence and societal challenges have facilitated further expansion of EU research policy. These three major policy frames have guided the design of recent FPs.

While similar frames of economic competitiveness, scientific excellence and societal challenges can be also found at national level, a unique feature of EU research policy is the claim that they cannot be properly addressed at the level of individual member states and therefore EU-level cooperation, coordination and competition is needed. If some accounts of the development of science policy focus on common features across countries and regions (Alemán-Díaz, Chapter 3 in this *Handbook*; Elzinga, 2012), then this chapter demonstrates the importance of historical and political context. For example, while academic freedom and the science–national defence link are typically seen as traditional and long-standing features of research policy (Elzinga, 2012), then in the case of the EU they started to play the role relatively recently owing to the expansion of European integration to new areas.

As can be expected on the basis of the policy frames literature, some competition over meaning, legitimacy and resources can be seen among these three main frames of economic competitiveness, scientific excellence and societal challenges. However, continuous expansion of policy and increased funds allocated to recent FPs have also alleviated this competition among the various frames in EU research policy, ensuring that each frame and related stakeholders promoting them get substantial funding. At the same time, designing the FPs according to the three main policy frames has also led to a certain fragmentation in policy practice and academic research, where specific academic and policy communities focus on a certain frame – be it scientific excellence or mission-oriented policy – with little cross-fertilization and focus on interaction across different frames.

The question asked at the beginning of this chapter about EU research policy as a success story is not easy to answer. As argued by Mitzner (2020), continuous expansion and impact of EU research policy can be seen as a success story. At the same time, more questionable is the success of EU research policy trying to pursue more or less controversial aims, targets and indicators such as catching up with US and Asian countries, cohesion among EU counties and the increase of national research funding to 3% of GDP. The question of what counts as success in international research funding remains open and invites further public debates and scientific investigation, including about norms and values underpinning not only the recent societal challenges frame but also more traditional economic competitiveness discourse. One direction for such debates and investigation is suggested in the introductory quote to this chapter that highlights the need for EU research policy to be a transformative effort serving the needs of the European societies, which are also open to the debate.

This chapter has highlighted the role of politics in public research funding. While often perceived as highly technocratic area, this chapter demonstrates how political priorities, values, norms and interests have been shaping EU research policy and funding. Political priorities of European integration and their change over time – from initial focus on peace project and economic cooperation to more recent prioritization of sustainability and emergence of defence cooperation – have had a direct impact on the way EU research policy and funding have been established and evolved over time, exemplifying how research investments play their political role being 'a continuation of politics by other means' (Elzinga, 2012, p. 416).

NOTES

1. This research has benefited from comments on earlier versions presented at the 2021 virtual conferences of Eu-SPRI (European Forum for Studies of Policies for Research and Innovation) and UACES (Academic association for Contemporary European Studies).
2. On history of European integration see here https://europa.eu/european-union/about-eu/history_en Accessed 9 August 2021.
3. Referring to the development before the Maastricht Treaty adopted in 1992 that established the European Union, the term 'European Community' is used. On history of European integration see here https://europa.eu/european-union/about-eu/history_en Accessed 9 August 2021.
4. On the history of EU enlargements see https://ec.europa.eu/neighbourhood-enlargement/policy/from-6-to-27-members_en Accessed 2 August 2021.
5. On history of EU Treaties see https://europa.eu/european-union/law/treaties_en Accessed 2 August 2021.
6. The EU has the three main types of competencies: exclusive, shared and supporting. They refer to the division of competencies between the EU and its member states. The Single European Act that came into the force in 1987 conferred the Community supporting competence in area of research which meant that the Community could only support, coordinate or complement the action of the member states in this area. Since the Lisbon Treaty that came into force in 2009, the EU has a shared competence for research which means that both the EU and its member states are able to legislate and adopt legally binding texts. Available from https://eur-lex.europa.eu/legal-content/EN/TXT/?uri=LEGISSUM%3Aai0020 Accessed 2 August 2021.

REFERENCES

Bernal, J.D. (1939). *The Social Function of Science*. The MIT Press.

Boekholt, P. (2010). The evolution of innovation paradigms and their influence on research, technological development and innovation policy instruments. In Smits, R.E., Kuhlmann, S., and Shapira, P. (Eds) *The Theory and Practice of Innovation Policy. An International Research Handbook* (pp. 333–359). Edward Elgar.

Borras, S. (2003). *The Innovation Policy of the European Union. From Government to Governance*. Edward Elgar.

Borras, S. (2019). Changes in European research and innovation governance: coordination effect and membership effects. In Simon, D., Kuhlmann, S., Stamm, J., and Canzler, W. (Eds) *Handbook on Science and Public Policy* (pp. 401–418). Edward Elgar.

Calcara, A., Csernatoni, R., and Lavalée, C. (Eds) (2020). *Emerging Security Technologies and EU Governance: Actors, Practices and Processes*. Routledge.

Cavallaro, M., and Lepori, B. (2021). Institutional barriers to participation in EU framework programs: Contrasting the Swiss and UK cases. *Scientometrics*, 126(2), 1311–1328.

Chou, M.-H., and Gornitzka, A. (Eds) (2014). *Building the Knowledge Economy in Europe. New Constellations in European Research and Higher Education Governance*. Edward Elgar.

Cramer, K. C. (2020). *A Political History of Big Science in Europe. The Other Europe*. Palgrave Macmillan.

Cramer, K. C., and O. Hallonsten (Eds) (2020). *Big Science and Research Infrastructures in Europe*. Edward Elgar.

Delanghe, H., Muldur, U., and Soete, L. (Eds) (2009). *European Science and Technology Policy: Towards Integration or Fragmentation?* Edward Elgar.

Diercks, G., Larsen, H., and Steward, F. (2019). Transformative innovation policy: Addressing variety in an emerging policy paradigm. *Research Policy*, 48(4), 880–894.

Edler, J., Kuhlmann, S., and Behrens, M. (Eds) (2003). *Changing Governance of Research and Technology Policy: The European Research Area*. Edward Elgar.

Elzinga, A. (2012). Features of the current science policy regime: Viewed in historical perspective. *Science and Public Policy*, 39(4), 416–428.

ERA Expert Group (2008). *Challenging Europe's Research: Rationales for the European Research Area (ERA)*. Report.

European Commission (2007). *The European Research Area: New Perspectives*. Green Paper. 04.04.2007. COM(2007) 161.

European Commission (2020). *A new ERA for Research and Innovation*. Communication. 30.9.2020. COM(2020) 628.

European Commission (2021). Horizon Europe. Available from https://ec.europa.eu/info/research-and -innovation/funding/funding-opportunities/funding-programmes-and-open-calls/horizon-europe_en Last accessed: 22 June 2021.

Hicks, D. (2016). Grand challenges in US science policy attempt policy innovation. *International Journal of Foresight and Innovation Policy*, 11(1–3), 22–42.

Kastenhofer, K., and Molyneux-Hodgson, S. (2021). *Community and Identity in Contemporary Technosciences*. Sociology of Sciences Yearbook, Vol. 31. Springer.

König, T. (2017). *The European Research Council*. Polity.

Krige, J. (2003). The politics of European scientific collaboration. In Krige, J. and Pestre, D. (Eds) *Companion to Science in the Twentieth Century* (pp. 897–918). Routledge.

Krugman, P. (1994). Competitiveness: A dangerous obsession. *Foreign Affairs*, 73(2), 28–44.

Lund Declaration (2009). Europe must focus on the grand challenges of our time. The Lund Conference 'New Worlds – New Solutions', July.

Luukkonen, T. (2014). The European Research Council and the European Research Funding Landscape. *Science and Public Policy*, 41(1), 29–43.

Mazzucato, M. (2021). *Mission Economy: A Moonshot Guide to Changing Capitalism*. Allen Lane.

Misa, T. J., and Schot, J. (2005). Inventing Europe: Technology and the hidden integration of Europe. *History and Technology*, 21(1), 1–19.

Mitzner, V. (2020). *European Union Research Policy. Contested Origins*. Palgrave Macmillan.

Nedeva, M. (2013). Between the global and the national: Organising European Science. *Research Policy*, 42, 220–230.

O'Mara, M. (2019). *The Code: Silicon Valley and the Remaking of America*. Penguin Press.

Owen, R., von Schomberg, R., and Macnaghten, P. (2021). An unfinished journey? Reflections on a decade of responsible research and innovation. *Journal of Responsible Innovation*, 8(2), 217–233.

Papon, P. (2009). Intergovernmental cooperation in the making of European research. In Delanghe, H., Muldur, U., and Soete, L. (Eds) *European Science and Technology Policy: Towards Integration or Fragmentation?* (pp. 24–43). Edward Elgar.

Polanyi, M. (1962). The Republic of Science. Its political and economic theory. *Minerva*, 1(1), 54–73.

Prange-Gstohl, H. (Ed) (2010). *International Science and Technology Cooperation in a Globalized World. The External Dimension of the European Research Area*. Edward Elgar.

Rein, M., and Schon, D. (1993). Reframing Policy Discourse. In Fischer, F., and Forester, J. (Eds) *The Argumentative Turn in Policy Analysis and Planning* (pp. 145–166). UCL Press.

Rein, M., and Schon, D. (1996). Frame-critical policy analysis and frame-reflective policy practice. *Knowledge and Policy: The International Journal of Knowledge Transfer and Utilization*, 9(1), 85–104.

Sandholtz, W. (1992). ESPRIT and the politics of international collective action. *Journal of Common Market Studies*, XXX(1), 1–21.

Schon, D., and Rein, M. (1994). *Frame Reflection: Toward the Resolution of Intractable Policy Controversies*. Basic Books.

Sharp, M. (1998). Competitiveness and cohesion – are the two compatible? *Research Policy*, 27, 569–588.

Ulnicane, I. (2015). Broadening aims and building support in science, technology and innovation policy: The case of the European Research Area. *Journal of Contemporary European Research*, 11(1), 31–49.

Ulnicane, I. (2016a). Research and innovation as sources of renewed growth? EU policy responses to the crisis. *Journal of European Integration*, 38(3), 327–341.

Ulnicane, I. (2016b). 'Grand challenges' concept: A return of the 'big ideas' in science, technology and innovation policy? *International Journal of Foresight and Innovation Policy*, 11(1–3), 5–21.

Ulnicane, I. (2020). Ever-changing big science and research infrastructures: Evolving European Union policy. In Cramer, K. and Hallonsten, O. (Eds) *Big Science and Research Infrastructures in Europe* (pp. 76–100). Edward Elgar.

Ulnicane, I. (2022). Introduction – Technologies and European integrations. In Hoerber, T., Cabras, I., and Weber, G. (Eds) *Routledge Handbook of European Integrations* (pp. 199–207). Routledge.

Veugelers, R. (2014). *Undercutting the Future? European Research Spending in Times of Fiscal Consolidation*. Bruegel Policy Contribution, Issue 2014/06.

Wedlin, L., and Nedeva, M. (2015). *Towards European Science: Dynamics and Policy of Evolving European Research Space*. Edward Elgar.

PART II

POLICY MIXES IN PUBLIC RESEARCH FUNDING: LAYERING AND COMPLEXITY

5. Ideas and instruments in public research funding

Giliberto Capano

5.1   INTRODUCTION

Public research funding (PRF) should be allocated in one way or in another. This happens through specific policies in which the choice of how to allocate public funding depends on two main components: the underlying ideas, in terms of beliefs regarding goals and how to reach them, and the types of instruments adopted, which are intended to be effective in reaching the expected goals. Thus, to better understand how PRF evolves over time and how it works, it is analytically relevant to analyse PRF based on both an ideational and an instrumental perspective. The ideational perspective can better indicate why PRF instruments are chosen, while an instrumental perspective can better indicate how PRF is organized and whether and how it is truly as effective as expected. Furthermore, by linking ideational and instrumental analyses, the world of PRF can be better presented because it is possible to understand the reciprocal influence between ideas and instruments. It is not necessarily the case, as the institutional perspective teaches us, that ideas come before instruments.

To address this theme, the chapter is structured as follows. In Section 5.2, an overview of the literature on ideas and instruments in public policy is presented. In Section 5.3, PRF is analysed from an ideational perspective, while in Section 5.4, the analysis is performed from an instrumental perspective. Section 5.5 shows how, over time, PRF systems develop as mixes of ideas and instruments that are not necessarily consistent or coherent.

5.2   POLICY IDEAS AND POLICY INSTRUMENTS: AN OVERVIEW

5.2.1   Policy Instruments: What Are They Truly?

The policy instrument approach represents one of the most frequently adopted perspectives in public policy because radical shifts in governing have led to a governance turn in policy research (Salamon 1981, 2002; Salamon and Lund 1989; Eliadis et al. 2005). Salamon's call for an instrument-oriented approach to overcome the shortcomings of implementation research (1981) and to deal with the "massive proliferation" of public action tools (Salamon and Lund 1989: 3) has widely resonated across the field, and policy instruments have become a significant focus of research on the policymaking process. However, why have instruments become so analytically relevant? The simple answer is that instruments are the way in which "things get done" in public policy. According to the most frequently cited definitions, policy instruments are "an identifiable method through which collective action is structured to address a public problem" (Salamon 2002: 19), "a set of techniques by which governmental authorities wield their power in attempting to ensure support and affect or prevent social change" (Vedung 1998: 21), or the means that governments use "to deliberately affect the nature, types, quantities and distribution of the goods and services provided in a society" (Howlett 2000: 415). Overall, what governments do when they design policies is they work with policy instruments, and what interest groups want is for some specific instruments to be adopted. Therefore, policy instruments have become pillars of public policy analysis both when the focus is on the characteristics of policymaking, policy dynamics and governance shifts and when the focus is on policy design. To analyse policy instruments, there is a long-lasting tradition in public policy that has tried to classify them based on specific analytical dimensions (Capano and Engeli 2022): from coercion (Vedung 1998) to behavioural assumptions (Ingram and Schneider 1990) to governmental resources (Hood 1983). This distinction is important because what instruments are assumed to do in the reality of policymaking depends on their conceptualization. The same policy instrument, for example, performance-based funding, can be considered to impact reality based on the way in which it is theoretically defined. Thus, for example, performance-based funding can be defined as an economic instrument based on the classification of Vedung, as an incentive based on the typology of Ingram and Schneider and as a treasury-based tool according to Hood.

Furthermore, policy instruments vary based on the theoretical perspective through which they are conceptualized. According to Hood (2007), three approaches can be extracted from the literature: the "instrumental perspective", the "political perspective" and the "institutionalist perspective". From the "instrumental perspective", policy instruments are seen as external to the policy process and are rationally chosen by policy actors based on their preferences and contextual constraints. Such a perspective is "neutral" with regard to the choice of policy instruments (i.e. the best instruments are chosen based on the specific context), as it postulates that each instrument has specific "objective" features that ensure specific, coherent effects to produce the expected change (Campbell et al. 2004; May et al. 2005). According to this perspective, for example, the choice of introducing a national research assessment would be taken because it was conceived as the best "technical" solution to increase the quality and the public value of research.

Seen from the "political perspective" (Linder and Peters 1989, 1998), policy instruments are an endogenous part of the policy process. As a result of political interaction, policy actors choose the instruments as frameworks through which to interpret policy problems and not because such instruments are neutral. The choice of instruments is based not on a simple, neutral/instrumental rationale (the pursuit of optimality or effectiveness) but on the underlying political interaction governing how reality is constructed. According to this perspective, a national research assessment would be chosen not because it was considered the best technical solution but because the policy instruments better fit the political condition of the moment and clearly send a political message to the public and to the policy target (the research institutions and universities)

Finally, the "institutionalist" perspective (Salamon 2002) states that policy instruments should be treated as "institutions", that is, either as a set of organized rules and standard operating procedures playing a partly independent role in political life (March and Olsen 2006) or as a set of social and political values and, as such, as potential carriers of meanings and values that contribute to the construction of reality (Lascoumes and Le Galés 2004, 2007). By considering policy instruments as institutions, it is theoretically possible to free instruments from policy goals (i.e. release them from their taken-for-granted relationship). Considered as institutions, instruments exist without any clearly defined goals and (like all institutions) enjoy an independent existence (that is, independent from the original ideas that caused their adoption in the policy setting). According to this perspective, at a certain point, after having been adopted, a national research assessment becomes independent from the policy context, and it becomes institutionalized because it is perceived to have *a value per se* and because it is considered a bearer of certain ideas (such as competition, excellence and institutional accountability).

5.2.2   Policy Ideas: Normative and Cognitive Dimensions

Over the last three decades, the role played by ideas in politics and public policy has come to be taken seriously (Stone 1989; Hall 1993; Campbell 2002; Béland and Cox 2011; Hogan and Howlett 2015). A large number of different notions have emerged in the course of the intense debates on how to conceptualize the ideational dimension. Policy ideas, paradigms, belief systems, discourses and frames are among the words most frequently used to grasp the ideational dimension of public policy.

When focusing on policy ideas, the most fundamental conceptual distinction made in the literature integrating the ideational dimension into public policy discussions is that between the "*cognitive*" and the "*normative*" dimensions. In fact, when we talk about "ideas" or, in particular, about "*policy ideas*", we usually refer only to the *cognitive* dimension. The following definition of ideas makes this point clear. Policy ideas are a "programmatic set of statements of cause and effect concerning specific policy problems together with a policy theory or method for influencing these causal relationships" (Hemerijck and Kersbergen 1999: 177). In this sense, policy ideas mean concepts or theories about how the world might work and how we should act in policymaking to solve policy problems. Cognitive definitions of policy ideas usually do not mention instruments explicitly, but it is clear – given that instruments should be the means of influencing causal relations in the world – that a concept of ideas should also present ways and means of solving policy problems and, hence, which instruments to use. Therefore, instruments follow from knowledge and expectations about causality.

Without an "idea" about what to expect when we act, actors cannot intervene. However, this point is not sufficient to explain policy "choice". The second crucial "evaluative" dimension here is the "*norms and values*" that motivate actors. They tell actors what they should and should not do. Value systems permit or prohibit different actions (and instruments) and may even have an influence on what kind of causal theory or policy idea may circulate among policy actors. This can also work the other way around: causal theories that contradict certain value systems can contribute to an adjustment of such values in the long run.

In this sense, both dimensions are probably not independent from each other and can be treated as analytically autonomous "ideational" dimensions. Both have the same effect on policy choice: they reduce complexity for actors, and hence, they simplify options. However, for policy instruments, the two dimensions work differently: as noted above, policy ideas lead to the choice of instruments on the basis of cognitive beliefs about causality (thus, for example, a national research assessment can be considered a reliable cause of improving the quality of research). Norms influence what kind of actions and instruments may be preferred or not used at all, even if they make sense cognitively. Here, norms and values act as filters on the choice of instruments. Thus, for example, the choice to introduce a national research assessment would depend not on its cognitive component (which tells whether and how it can work), but on the prevailing values with respect to the role and the public value of research and of the organizations in charge of delivering it.

In the literature, although one often finds this analytical distinction, the two dimensions are usually clustered together and become part of a "paradigm" (Hall 1993), a "belief system" (Sabatier 1993; Sabatier and Jenkins Smith 1999) or a policy frame (Surel 2000).

For example, policy paradigms and the "overarching set of ideas" entailed within the paradigm "specify how the problems facing (decision-makers) are to be perceived, which goals must be attained through policy and what sort of techniques can be used to reach those goals" (Hall 1992: 91). A paradigm supplies coherence, as it "interlocks" the different matters in a coherent way (ibid.). As Hall explains in another article (Hall 1993: 279), it is "Gestalt"-like, a framework that serves to interpret policy problems and that gives a selection process at hand to take action. This selection process is based on "ideas and standards" that specify "not only the goals of policy and *the kind of instruments* that can be used to attain them but also the very nature of the problems they are meant to be addressing" (ibid.). The notion of a *framework* suggests a relative coherence of the elements constituting the framework. At the same time, it is a device that reduces complexity, as a framework can be seen as a certain interpretation of reality (based on its constituent elements) that thus excludes other frameworks or interpretations. Frameworks are inherently selective.

Sabatier and Jenkin-Smith's belief system concept includes fundamental beliefs about the world, norms and principles, and concepts of causal relations. These components constitute the three well-known levels of the belief system: the "*deep core*", which is the most fundamental level of "ontological and normative beliefs"; the "*policy core*", which represents "normative commitments (and 'fundamental value priorities') and causal perceptions across an entire policy domain or subsystem"; and "*secondary aspects*", which are a "large set of narrower (…) beliefs concerning the seriousness of the problem or the relative importance of various causal factors in specific locales, policy preferences regarding desirable regulations (…), the design of specific institutions" (Sabatier and Jenkins-Smith 1999: 121–122). Belief systems are at the base of policymakers' strategies when they are confronted with policy problems. Policy instruments are part of these strategies and follow logically – although this point is not explicitly discussed by Sabatier and Jenkins-Smith – from evaluation and cognition. They are the means of realizing the objectives that actors have, given their belief systems. Additionally, one can deduce that instruments can change relatively easily if "secondary aspects" in belief systems are contested and new strategies for dealing with problems evolve. The authors stress that such adaptation of secondary aspects (and, more seldom, of the policy core) is part of a "learning process" that results from "experience and/or new information and that (is) concerned with the attainment or revision of policy objectives".

Additionally, in the notion of a "policy frame", the main idea is that actions are guided by a selection process that helps to make sense of what happens in the world. The frame concept links the evaluative and cognitive dimensions. This linkage appears most obviously in Surel's definition (Surel 2000: 496): a policy frame is a "coherent system of normative and cognitive elements which define, in a given field, 'world views', mechanisms of identity formation, principles of actions, as well as methodological prescriptions and practices for actors subscribing to the same frame". Like belief systems and paradigms, frames are tasked with reducing complexity; thus, they help actors choose. They "can constrain action by directing attention to particular elements or issues, diverting it from others, and thereby defining boundaries between acceptable and unacceptable choices"; policy frames also enable action by "redefining or reshaping definitions of problems and generating new strategies for action" (Bhatia and Coleman 2003: 716–717). They favour "a particular causal story that explains how the problem came to be, assigns blame for it, and identifies the goals or expectations to be pursued in solving the problem. Finally, a policy frame influences perceptions of which actors have legitimacy to address the problem" (ibid. 717–718).

All these notions are similar in the sense that they integrate the cognitive and normative dimensions, stress the collective aspect of the ideational dimension (that beliefs, world views, etc., are "shared" among a group of people) and assume a certain "coherence" in the representation of the world within these ideational notions. What emerges from the literature, then, is that both the dimensions of ideas – the normative and the cognitive – are embedded in the policy process in different ways, with the expectation that the normative dimension is the most difficult to change over time, while the cognitive dimension is the place for change exactly because it is based on the assessment of cause–effect relations.

This short examination of the conceptualization of ideas clearly shows how their role can be very differentiated in the policy process when instruments are at stake. In fact, the copresence of both a cognitive and a normative dimension in any idea or set of ideas means that real choices of policy instruments always must find an equilibrium between them. Furthermore, this equilibrium cannot be predicted because it depends on many contextual factors and on the motivation of the policy actors involved.

5.2.3   Ideas and Instruments: A Multifaceted Linkage

What emerges from this brief literature review is that under ideational approaches, instruments are seen as part of a coherent framework of ideas in which they have a dependent role or in which they are determined by objectives that themselves are the result of certain value systems, cognitive beliefs and (exogenous) interests. Instruments are "means" linked to objectives in a functional way (they serve to achieve the objectives that actors hold). In other words, instruments "follow ideas". Here, however, the instrument literature has gone a step further: the political approach has underlined how instruments are embedded in the political context and how their meaning and consequent choices thus depend on the characteristics of the political dynamics. The institutionalist approach stresses that ideas may become dependent on instruments because, as "institutions", instruments give values to the ideas they support (Kassim and Le Galès 2010; Capano and Lippi 2017; Dale 2018; Verger et al. 2019). Another interesting point is that under this approach, instruments can be considered values, i.e. emotional sources of an ideational policy system (Durnova and Hejzlarova 2018). Furthermore, it has been noted how policy instruments can become the glue of specific constituencies (composed of consultants, governmental officials and experts) that, by sharing a deep preference for a specific policy instrument, use these instruments for chasing problems regardless of policy context (Voß and Simons 2014; Béland and Howlett 2016; Foli et al. 2018).

The implication is that in every policy field, the linkage between ideas and policy instruments is not linear or unidirectional. Ideas are carriers of specific policy instruments. However, this linkage is not necessarily based on a cognitive reason (that founds the preference for specific instruments on empirical evidence); it can also be driven by normative assumptions (through which a specific instrument is chosen because it is considered coherent with the values supported by the ideas). On the other hand, policy instruments are not only "objective" tools for reaching a specific policy outcome. They can also be independent factors that, by becoming institutionalized, shape the ideational frame in a specific policy context and become values to be maintained.

5.3   THE RISE OF THE EVALUATIVE PARADIGM OF PRF: COMPETITION, PERFORMANCE MEASUREMENT, AND EXCELLENCE

When focusing on ideas about PRF, the point of departure of any kind of reflection is the developments that have happened in recent decades, when the historically prevailing set of tools adopted for allocating PRF (mainly either direct input allocation or competitive project funding that covered a small part of the overall allocated budget) has undergone a structural redesign over time towards a more differentiated system based on the evaluation of outputs and, in some cases, on outcomes (Jongbloed and Lepori 2015). These changes can be linked to the interaction between general and sector-specific dynamics (with respect to the field of public research). General dynamics refer to the general diffusive trend that has led to the rise of the so-called "neo-liberal age" as the point of reference of most of the reforms adopted in many policy sectors (and thus also in research policy). According to the neo-liberal doctrine, market-driven policy instruments, managerialism, privatization, competition and evaluation have had a central role in reforming and governing public policies (Campbell and Pedersen 2001; Thatcher and Schmidt 2013; Springer et al. 2016). This general shift has taken various shapes in terms of ideas that have become hegemonic, and very often, these ideas have been summarized under the label of new public management (NPM) (Pollitt and Boukaert 2017). While NPM cannot be considered a coherent frame (Hood 1991), it represents, however, a synthetic definition of the huge adoption of hegemonic ideas – such as marketization, competition and managerialization – that have driven the adoption of policy instruments accordingly. However, it must be underlined that NPM is more than a paradigm; it is a kind of box containing ideas and instruments from which policymakers can extract what is more interesting for them or what is more useful in a specific context. This means that the same idea could be used for different policy goals; for example, competition can be adopted by those who assume that marketization of policies by definition ensures better trade-offs but also by those who pursue a higher contribution of research to the development of society.

Sector-specific dynamics refer to the evolution of state (and the related society) and science relationships (Whitley and Glaser 2007; Elzinga 2012) and the development of what has been called academic capitalism (Slaughter and Rhoades 2004). The sector-specific dynamics have driven to change the equilibrium between the internal narratives that, as underlined by Alemán-Díaz (Chapter 3 in this *Handbook*), are the motivations that activate research processes. The evolution of the relationship between the world of science and the external world has decreased the relevance of "creativity" (the free, curiosity-driven type of research) while increasing the significance of the narrative based on "purpose" and thus on the role of knowledge as a fundamental resource for developing the economy. At the same time, there is a third narrative that is emerging that is based on "transformative" motivation or the idea that research should have a more systemic impact in terms of meeting not only economic expectations but also the most relevant societal needs and structural challenges. This third narrative also echoes the public value perspective presented by Bozeman in his chapter (Chapter 2 in this *Handbook*).

These dynamics have been forced to interact owing to globalization and increasing international competition, requiring governments to ask more of public research organizations. This process has been contextually driven by each country's model of capitalism (as clearly shown by Bégin-Caouette et al., Chapter 20 in this *Handbook*). As a result, according to Elzinga (2012: 417), the relationship between the state and science has fallen in a period of accountability, which has "coincided with the final loss of science policy's special status and it becoming definitively subjected to the same logic as other policies as evidenced in the entry of new public management (NPM) into academe". Thus, overall, increasing international competition has changed the relationship between the state and science according to national policy legacies (in terms of academic structures and culture) and political–economic characteristics. This process of change has found, in an emerging and apparently commonly shared paradigm, the ideational dimension of the policy solution to hold public research organizations and universities more accountable and more constrained towards producing socioeconomically valuable research. Thus, this process of change has driven a common frame based on three main ideas with respect to PRF: competition, performance funding and excellence. Considered together, these three ideas compose what I define, following the concept of evaluative state proposed by Guy Neave (2012), as the "evaluative paradigm".

It should be noted that the evaluative paradigm could be considered as potentially coherent not only to push research towards emphasizing the purpose and thus to produce results useful for the economic needs of a society (according to a market oriented perspective), but also to be congruent with the motives of transformation and thus to generate "research for the collective good of citizens" (Bozeman, Chapter 2 in this *Handbook*). This potential polyvalence of the evaluative paradigm (and of its three main ideational components) could appear contradictory, but at the same time, it shows how the same ideas can be framed in different ways and thus, in the case of PRF, not only in terms of the NPM paradigm but also in terms of transformative motivation/public value.

This evaluative paradigm is characterized by a significant shift in the normative core of the relationship between the state/society and universities/public research organizations: the latter are no longer considered a *value per se* that can independently reach goals relevant to society on the basis of a trustful relationship with the lender (the state) (Sörlin 2007). This shift partially cancelled the "old social contract for science" (van der Meulen 2003; Guston 2009), which was hegemonic. Governments have started to consider that universities and public research organizations need to be steered differently to ensure that societal goals can be reached in a more effective way. In fact, as Whitley (2010: 3) notes, "the state and other collective actors have become more proactive in seeking to steer the direction of academic research through the implementation of formal science policies and the incorporation of public policy goals into funding agencies' evaluation criteria". Thus, the governance of public research systems has slowly but firmly shifted towards a system of rules consciously designed to increase competition in research and thus has focused on performance measurement as the focal principle on which this shift can be steered. Block grant funding, both for universities and national research centres, has been decreasing: this has meant a clear emergence of performance funding, project funding and public policy use-driven funding as the pillars of the new arrangements of national research systems. Furthermore, the search for external private funding has been incentivized through specific research programmes designed to increase the public–industry partnership.

Importantly, however, the adoption of performance funding and competition as the main ideational resources to design the instrumentation of PRF has not meant the real adoption of a common template. Therefore, this change means that the final result is not convergence but different interpretations of the same general recipe that have driven different implementations of the evaluative paradigm. Thus, from a comparative perspective, the evaluative paradigm has not been implemented in a homogenous way; rather, it has been diluted based on national traditions (Capano and Pritoni 2018, 2020) and according to ways to increase competition and the relevance of performance funding. For example, in the general dynamics that have pushed for the use of competition and performance funding, there are countries that have introduced strong systems of performance evaluation based on periodic assessment of institutional research. However, among these countries, only a few link recurrent assessment to performance funding: Australia, Belgium, Hong Kong, Italy, Norway, the Slovak Republic, Spain, New Zealand, and the UK. Among them, two countries allocate a significant portion of public funding to universities (and public research organizations in the case of Italy) on the basis of national research assessment: Italy (30% in 2021) and the UK (approximately 50% of the direct public grant).

Thus, the rise of the evaluative paradigm has been characterized by a nationally differentiated way through which performance measurement and competition have been implemented. In many cases, the idea of competition has not been relevant, while the performance measurement has been considered essential to frame policies to redirect the attention of public research organizations towards societal needs (thus increasing their social accountability). For example, performance measurement in France was introduced as a frame to support the contractualization between the ministry and the universities, without any attention to competition, while in the UK, performance measurement was mainly introduced with a research exercise through which universities compete to obtain substantial institutional funding. Furthermore, especially in continental Europe, ideas of performance funding have been adopted to incrementally change annual institutional funding to move away from historically based block funding and towards competitive research funding administered by national academic committees. The rise of the evaluative paradigm drove a change in the allocation rules of public funding based on the idea that institutions should focus on outputs, not only in teaching but also in research. From this perspective, performance measurement was considered a tool for ensuring social accountability more than a tool for pushing competitiveness.

In the UK, however, performance measurement and competition are interlinked on the basis of the assumption that what is at stake can directly activate competition, which should improve systemic performance. The UK has been suddenly and unexpectedly followed in this path by Italy, a country with a completely different policy legacy that has adopted a very competitive and financially impactful national research assessment.

This differentiation in the logics of performance measurement and competition should be taken into account because they can have different trajectories and relevance in different contexts. However, the rise and institutionalization of the evaluative paradigm for allocating PRF has been a long process that has made performance measurement a pivotal ideational reference of the new paradigm. This means that the triad of performance measurement as an inescapable idea for assigning PRF has circumscribed the meaning of PRF itself. In other words, it is now considered fair and appropriate to distribute public money for research only through some type of measurement. Competition can vary, according to the type of instrument adopted for funding, but no money can be attributed without some kind of measurement.

This ideational shift has also been nurtured by the rhetoric of excellence as a narrative to push the behaviour of researchers and institutions based on a value that can be considered the "holy grail of academic life" (Lamont 2009: 1). Excellence has been used as the parameter of reference in every policy design, and thus, policymakers have adopted one of the constitutive values of the academic world, even though it very often means different things in different disciplines and institutional contexts, as one core goal of the ideational shift together with the need for a major commitment to social values (Moore et al. 2017). Excellence has arrived third after performance funding and competition in characterizing the evaluative paradigm, but now it is not only embedded in the public discourse of research funding but also frames many governmental policy initiatives programmatically committed to increasing the excellence of the national research systems (OECD 2014; Cremonini, Horlings, and Hessels 2017; Hellström 2018; Borlaug and Langfeldt 2020). From this point of view, it is the idea of excellence that has increased the relevance of the idea of competition. In fact, while performance measurement does not necessarily need to be paired by competition – and when this happens, it depends on the more general ideological vision of policymakers – the idea of excellence necessarily has to be accompanied by the idea of competition. Furthermore, the increasing relevance of the idea of excellence in research has driven many efforts to search for indicators of performance measurement (Tijssen 2003; Sørensen et al. 2016), thus reinforcing the pivotal role of performance measurement.

This ideational shift has undergone institutionalization, and the evaluative paradigm has become hegemonic in PRF, although through different interpretations can be more or less market-oriented or more or less public value-oriented. Furthermore, it must be underlined that performance measurement, competition and excellence in PRF have been mixed together in different ways based on the characteristics of national reforms. Thus, these three "new" ideas have been included based on the national redesign of the governance of research and socioeconomic priorities. This means that their meaning can vary from country to country, and thus the rise of the evaluative paradigm in PRF can be considered a general trend, but it cannot be read as a direct driver of the cross-country homogenization of the concrete set of adopted instruments.

5.4 AN INSTRUMENTAL PERSPECTIVE ON PUBLIC RESEARCH FUNDING IN THE EVALUATIVE ERA

5.4.1 Assessing the Varieties of Instruments of PRF According to the Evaluative Paradigm

If this progressive shift towards the evaluative paradigm as a core frame of funding public research is the general ideational landscape, the ways in which the new paradigm has been implemented have differed in terms of how instruments have been conceptualized, designed and operationalized.

Drawing from the literature on policy instruments in PRF (Hicks 2012; Zacharewicz et al. 2019; Lepori et al. 2007, 2018; Lepori 2011; Jongbloed and Vossensteyn 2016), the modes of PRF can be divided into two types: institutional funding and project funding. Each of these two modes can be implemented based on different delivery organizations and measurement

Table 5.1   *Instrumentation of PRF*

Modes of research funding	Instruments of allocation	Delivery organizations	Performance measurement techniques
Institutional funding	Historical allocation	Ministries	Historically inherited
	Competitive bids	National agencies	Qualitative assessment of proposals + quantitative indicators
	Negotiated allocation		
	Funding formula		Output indicators (PhD students, publications, patents, external funding):
			• *input*-based (type of research, staff posts, income from research, etc.)
			• *output*-based (PhD graduates, patents, types of publications)
			• *outcome*-based/research performance (bibliometric indicators or national research assessment based on informed peer review or pure peer review)
Project funding	Investigator driven	Research councils	Informed peer review (reputation of the principal investigator (PI) and bibliometric data)
	Strategic	National agencies	
		Ministerial committees	Pure peer review
			Qualitative assessment (scientific relevance, social relevance, technological relevance)

techniques (for a more detailed analysis, see Reale et al., Chapter 7 in this *Handbook*). Table 5.1 summarizes these characteristics.

How are these policy instruments related to the evaluative paradigm, and above all, how can the ideational components of this paradigm be more or less present in the various instruments? These questions emerge immediately from this table because it presents a significant variety of instruments and measurement methods through which the ideas composing the evaluative paradigm can be instrumentally operationalized.

Instruments of institutional funding can be distinguished based on the type of allocation: historical, competitive bids, negotiated and a funding formula. The delivery organization can be either the ministry in charge of higher education and research or a specific agency. The measurement techniques for allocation can be very different based on the type of instrument adopted. For example, it must be underlined that when PRF is allocated through a funding formula in which most of the public funding is given to public research institutions and universities, the measurement technique can vary based on input-based, output-based, and outcome-based indicators. Here, the measurement of outcomes can also be operationalized through a national research assessment as observed in various countries (including Italy, the UK, Australia, Hong Kong and Poland).

Interestingly, PRF through institutional funding can be allocated without any kind of performance measurement (such as when it is anchored to historical mechanisms) or based on either ex ante or ex post evaluation performance (Auranen and Nieminen 2010). For example, competitive bids (such as those that allow the establishment of centres of excellence or that award the best departments, such as in Italy, or the best institutional development projects, such as the Excellence Initiative in Germany) are based on ex ante evaluation because the assessment criteria are the perceived quality of the research potential. However, the measurement technique can be very different: for example, in the case of the German Excellence Initiative, the assessment is done only on the potential of the institutional project, while in the Italian case, the best departments are selected according not only to the quality of the institutional project but also (two/thirds of the score) on the basis of the performance in the last national research exercise. This comparison shows how excellence through competition can be operationalized in different ways: it can be based mainly on assessing potential performance in the future or it can be pursued mainly on prizing past performance.

Additionally, negotiated contracts are based on ex ante evaluation, and thus, there is no real room for competition or excellence. However, there is room to find an agreement on the diversification and profiling of institutional activities (and thus also of those linked to research) that can be used by policymakers to push towards research more responsive to contextual socioeconomic needs.

The other type of institutional funding (formula funding) involves mainly ex post evaluation measurements (de Boer et al. 2015); thus, these instruments cannot be considered proactive in terms of truly pushing towards competition and excellence.

The project funding types can be divided between investigator-driven research and strategic research. Here, organizational delivery can work not only through governmental organizations and agencies but also through academic committees and groups. In this respect, peer review is a dominant technique, although it can be complemented by other criteria, such as bibliometrics, academic reputation, and potential social and technological relevance. The project funding instrumentation has progressively become the most widely adopted technique to implement the ideas of excellence and competition. Investigator-driven funding in most countries is characterized by high competition and by an institutionalized commitment of funders to push for excellent projects capable of proposing breakthrough research. Strategic project funding is the instrument adopted to push researchers to focus on those who are considered the main socioeconomic priorities and societal challenges (Lepori et al. 2007). Additionally, this instrument can be considered ambiguous from the ideational point of view. In fact, while it clearly can be considered a result of the shift towards the evaluative paradigm, it cannot necessarily be interpreted as a tool for the marketization and commercialization of research because it can also be adopted as a tool for pursuing public value-oriented research.

Thus, the actual set of policy instruments at the disposal of policymakers in regard to PRF appears to be an expression of the progressive inclusion of the new ideas in the actual paradigm. In fact, the ideational shift in PRF is clearly represented in the actual set of policy instruments, which implies the inclusion of new instruments. The old PRF system, characterized by a significant separation between public research organizations and universities and thus more academically oriented and creatively driven in its research choices and dynamics, used instruments such as the old standby of institutional funding allocation (based on historical criteria) and by investigator-driven projects (not necessarily very competitive). The new PRF system, through a continuous process of layering (Aagard 2017; Capano 2019), has ideationally shifted towards the evaluative paradigm. This progressive ideational shift has pushed towards the inclusion in institutional funding allocation first of all of instruments and methods coherent with performance measurement (such as quantitative analysis of outputs and outcomes and formula funding) and subsequently of instruments depending on the ideas of competition and excellence (competitive bids, negotiated agreements and performance-based formulas). Finally, regarding the project funding, strategic project instrumentation has become significantly more relevant (Lepori et al. 2007).

This means that, over time, there has been a progressive ideational hybridization of PRF and thus an institutionalization of policy mixes as the instrumental dimension of it.

This hybridization is due precisely to the fact that policymakers, owing to the prevalence of the evaluative paradigm, have started to have a larger set of instruments and techniques at their disposal (Hicks 2012; Lepori et al. 2007, 2018; Langfeldt and Scordato 2016; Zacharewicz et al. 2019). This variety allows policymakers to choose according to their goals and the contexts in which they act. Thus, we can expect the relations between ideas and instruments to be modelled differently by policymakers according to the perspectives they adopt.

5.4.2   Assessing the Varieties of Instruments of PRF: Instrumental, Political and Institutional Perspectives

Thus, this variety of instruments at policymakers' disposal, with their ideational content, can be read according to the three analytical perspectives summarized above.

From the instrumental perspective, it can be considered an objective toolbox that policymakers have at their disposal to intervene in reality. Based on their goals, policymakers can choose the type of instrument and related technique that appear to fit the goal itself. This perspective, however, is clearly too optimistic because policymakers very often do not have a clear goal in mind as long as they can show that they are doing something to increase the accountability of research organizations.

According to the political perspective, the variety of policy instruments at the disposal of policymakers does not drive their choice but simply represents a toolbox based on which policymakers interpret their actual problem. This means that instruments are used not only as instruments but also as carriers of a meaning that is constructed by the policymakers themselves. For example, policymakers can decide to choose various ways to implement the evaluative paradigm based on the actual political equilibrium and the strength of the policy stakeholders. From this perspective, the different types of instruments at their disposal allow policymakers to construct the "meaning" that they consider useful (from the political and/ or the policy perspective) at a specific historical moment based on emerging problems, their general ideas regarding the role of the state and their perception of the role of public research organizations. From this perspective, policy instruments are equifinal for policymakers, and they are chosen based on their capacity to meet the political needs of the moment. Thus, for example, negotiated allocation can be adopted as a first step in implementing an evaluative policy or can be chosen after some output indicators introduced into the funding formula have not demonstrated sufficient success. Alternatively, competitive bids for excellence can be considered tools for awarding past performance and, thus, for showing attention to the rhetoric of excellence (as Italy did with the programme to fund the best departments launched in 2016), or they can be considered tools for investing resources in the future (as in the case of the German excellence initiative that started in 2006, which aimed to increase the quality of higher education and to push institutions to collaborate with each other). Finally, a national research exercise can be used in different ways based on the political perspective of instruments: as an informational tool promoting learning and transparency, as in Australia and Norway (where this assessment has a small financial impact), or as the main technique for allocating public funding based on performance assessments (as in the UK and Italy). Interestingly, the same measurement technique can be adopted based on different meanings that are politically constructed. Here, instruments become labels whose ideational content is assigned based on the political context.

From the institutional perspective, PRF policy instruments and techniques can truly show the capacity to become independent from the original meaning that was attributed to them when chosen by policymakers and thus institutionalized. This means that, for example, they can continue to exist even though they have not shown the capacity to reach the expected goals simply because they have become routines or values for many stakeholders. From this perspective, for example, we could expect that national research exercises could persist over time, even if they do not show the capacity to boost competition or show unintended effects (such as a greater quantity of lower quality output; Larivière and Costas 2016), because they become the legacy of the past or have become representative of a political value (such as meritocracy).

5.4.3   Instruments of PRF Become More Sophisticated Over Time

The institutionalization of the instrumentation adopted in PRF is also helped by the process through which its level of technical sophistication continuously increases. The implementation of policy instruments for allocating public funding undergoes a process of evolution over time in terms of technical evolution (Reale and Seeber 2013). This means that when a specific type of instrument is adopted, not only can it persist over time, but it is also subject to continuous technical adjustment and becomes increasingly detailed and sophisticated. This is the case with funding formulas, which can adopt different types of output indicators that can become increasingly detailed based on the capacity to collect and process data (for example, regarding the citational impact of publications). This can also be the case with negotiated allocation, which can become very multifaceted, or with national research exercises, which have been developed by including other subjects of assessment (not only the quality of research but also socioeconomic impact and public engagement).

This process through which the sophistication of technical measurements continuously increases can impact the evolution of national strategies of PRF in regard to relations between ideas and instruments. In fact, the more sophisticated an instrument becomes, the more it becomes independent and thus capable of structuring the behaviour of the target (and of the evaluators) to the point that it becomes the main driver of evaluation (and, thus, of performance) in a specific context. Thus, the instrument becomes the idea, or even better, it defines what the idea means in practice. Consequently, instruments become carriers of meanings and certify what the prevailing values are. Thus, the relationship between ideas and instruments is completely overturned.

5.5   IDEAS, INSTRUMENTS AND THE DAMNATION OF POLICY MIXES

From the discussion above, it emerges that the relation between ideas and instruments in PRF is less simple than expected. Ideas matter but only in the sense that there are general points of reference for political and policy discussions. They can be fundamental for designing general policy trends, but when they have to be operationalized, they encounter two main problems. The first is that existing ideas cannot simply be abandoned. The idea of performance measurement, for example, had to reconcile with the previous idea that researchers (especially academics) had the absolute freedom to do their research according their interests and without any type of constraint (time or obligation to publish). Competition and excellence had to deal with the previous dominant ideas, which held that academics and researchers were equal because they were focused on an intellectual commitment assigned a high moral value (to perform research). The prioritizing of societal goals had to resolve the previous value of academic freedom to choose research topics. Thus, while being placed on the agenda against older ideas, new PRF ideas must be settled in the pre-existing context. They are layered. Clearly, this process of ideational layering changes the characteristics of the existing frame/paradigm/belief system. New ideas can become predominant, while older ideas are still there and can have supporters. This process creates an ideational mix that it is coupled to an instrument mix because the emergence of new ideas is accompanied by the adoption of new policy instruments. This process of continuous layering of both ideas and instruments also makes the field of PRF characterized by "policy mixes" that, as underlined by the public policy literature, are composed of different instruments and ideas that belong to different frames and that have been settled over time (Kern and Howlett 2009; Rogge and Reichardt 2016; Rayner et al. 2017; Kern et al. 2019). These mixes are not consistent or coherent (Bressers and O'Toole 2005), and thus, it is unlikely that implementation can represent a pure frame or paradigm. As a mix of different ideas and instruments, PRF systems represent a challenge for both scholars and policymakers. Scholars must take into account the intrinsically mixed nature of PRF systems to better understand how they work and why they very often do not work as expected. All too often, only some ideational or instrumental dimensions are considered, as shown by all the studies emphasizing the evaluative turn in PRF, and this does not help in grasping how the new ideas and instruments merge with the oldest ones and how these interactions can produce paradigmatic mixes in single instruments (thus driving unexpected effects). Furthermore, we should pay attention to the fact that the copresence of old and new ideas and instruments represents a fundamental source of policy dynamics in terms of the ideational battle among different stakeholders and policy actors. Finally, as sketched out by the above analysis, when focusing on the link between ideas and instruments in PRF, it is important to avoid extreme interpretations. Overall, the rise of the evaluative paradigm does not represent the triumph of marketization and of the neoliberal vision of public research but a common framing about how public research should be funded. This frame can be used both for marketizing and commercialising research and for pushing it to focus on public values and societal needs. The way forward is not to be found in the paradigm but in the way the policymakers use it.

REFERENCES

Aagaard, K. (2017) The evolution of a national research funding system: Transformative change through layering and displacement. *Minerva*, 55(6), 1–19.

Auranen, O. and Nieminen, M. (2010). University research funding and publication performance – An international comparison. *Research Policy*, 39(6), 822–834.

Béland, D. and Cox, R. H. (eds.) (2011). *Ideas and Politics in Social Science Research*. Oxford: Oxford University Press.

Béland, D. and Howlett, M. (2016). How solutions chase problems: Instrument constituencies in the policy process. *Governance*, 29(3), 393–409.

Bhatia, V. and Coleman, W. D. (2003). Ideas and discourse: Reform and resistance in the Canadian and German health systems. *Canadian Journal of Political Science*, 36(4), 715–739.

Borlaug, S. and Langfeldt, L. (2020). One model fits all? How centres of excellence affect research organisation and practices in the humanities. *Studies in Higher Education*, 45(8), 1746–1757.

Bressers, H. T. A. and O'Toole, L. J. (2005). Instrument selection and implementation in a networked context. In E. Pearl, M. M Hill and M. Howlett (eds.), *Designing Government: From Instruments to Governance*. Montreal: McGill–Queen's University Press, pp. 132–153.

Campbell, J. L. (2002). Ideas, Politics and Public Policy. *Annual Review of Sociology*, 28, 21–38.

Campbell, J. L. and Pedersen, O. (eds.) (2001). *The Rise of Neoliberalism and Institutional Analysis*. Princeton, NJ: Princeton University Press.

Campbell, R. M., Johnson, R. M., and Larson, E. H. (2004). Prices, devices, people, or rules: The relative effectiveness of policy instruments in water conservation. *Review of Policy Research*, 21(5), 637–662.

Capano, G. (2019) Reconceptualizing layering. From mode of institutional change to mode of institutional design: Types and outputs. *Public Administration*, 97(3), 590–604.

Capano, G. and Engeli, I. (2022). Using instrument typologies in comparative research: Conceptual and methodological trade-offs. *Journal of Comparative Policy Analysis*, 24(2), 99–116.

Capano, G. and Lippi, A. (2017). How policy instruments are chosen: Selecting between legitimacy and instrumentality, *Policy Sciences*, 50(2), 269–293.

Capano, G. and Pritoni, A. (2018). Varieties of hybrid systemic governance in European higher education. *Higher Education Quarterly*, 73(1), 10–28.

Capano, G. and Pritoni, A. (2020). What really happens in higher education governance? Trajectories of adopted policy instruments in higher education over time in 16 European Countries. *Higher Education*, 80(5), 989–1010.

Cremonini, L., Horlings E., and Hessels, L. K. (2017). Different recipes for the same dish: Comparing policies for scientific excellence across different countries. *Science and Public Policy*, 45(2), 232–245.

Dale, R. (2018). Global education policy: Creating different constituencies of interest and different modes of valorisation. In A. Verger, H. K. Altinyelken, and M. Novelli (eds.), *Global Education Policy and International Development: New Agendas, Issues and Policies*. New York: Bloomsbury, pp. 289–298.

de Boer, H., Jongbloed, B. et al. (2015). *Performance-based Funding and Performance Agreements in Fourteen Higher Education Systems*. The Hague: Ministry of Education, Culture and Science.

Durnova, A., and Hejzlarova, E. (2018). Framing policy designs through contradictory emotions: The case of Czech single mothers. *Public Policy and Administration*, 33(4), 409–427.

Eliadis, P., Hill, M. et al. (eds.) (2005). *Designing Government. From Instruments to Governance*. Montreal: McGill–Queen's University Press.

Elzinga, A. (2012) Features of the current science policy regime: Viewed in historical perspective. *Science and Public Policy*, 39(4), 416–428.

Foli, R., Béland, D., and Fenwick, T. B. (2018). How instrument constituencies shape policy transfer: A case study from Ghana. *Policy and Society*, 37(1), 108–124.

Guston, R. (2009). *Between Politics and Science*. Cambridge: Cambridge University Press.

Hall, P. A. (1992). The movement from Keynesianism to monetarism: Institutionalanalysis and British economic policy in the 1970s. In S. Steinmo, K. Thelen and F. Longstreth (eds.), *Structuring Politics. Historical Institutionalism in Comparative Analysis*. Cambridge, MA: Cambridge University Press, pp. 90–113.

Hall, P. A. (1993). Policy paradigms, social learning, and the state. The case of economic policymaking in Britain. *Comparative Politics*, 25(3), 275–296.

Hellström, T. (2018). Centres of excellence and capacity building: From strategy to impact. *Science and Public Policy*, 45(3), 543–552.

Hemerijck, A. and Kersbergen, K. v. (1999). Negotiated change: Institutional and policy learning in tightly coupled welfare states. In D. Braun and A. Busch (eds.), *Public Policy and Polictical Ideas*. Cheltenham: Edward Elgar, pp. 168–188 (p. 177).

Hicks, D. (2012). Performance-based university research funding systems. *Research Policy*, 41(2), 251–261.

Hogan, J. and Howlett, M. (eds.) (2015). *Policy Paradigms in Theory and Practice Discourses, Ideas and Anomalies in Public Policy Dynamics*. London: Palgrave

Hood, C. (1983). *The Tools of Government*. London: Macmillan.

Hood, C. (1991). A public management for all seasons? *Public Administration*, 69(1), 3–19.

Hood, C. (2007). Intellectual obsolescence and intellectual makeovers: Reflections on the tools of government after two decades. *Governance*, 20(1), 127–144.

Howlett, M. (2000). Managing the "hollow state": Procedural policy instruments and modern governance. *Canadian Public Administration*, 43(4), 412–431.

Ingram, H. and Schneider, A. (1990). The behavioral assumptions of policy tools. *The Journal of Politics*, 52 (2), 510–529.

Jongbloed, B. and Lepori, B. (2015). The funding of research in higher education: Mixed models and mixed results. In J. Huisman, H. de Boer, D. D. Dill, and M. Souto-Otero (eds.), *The Palgrave International Handbook of Higher Education Policy and Governance*. London: Palgrave, pp. 439–462.

Jongbloed, B. and Vossensteyn, H. (2016). University funding and student funding: International comparisons. *Oxford Review of Economic Policy*, 32(4), 576–595.

Kassim, K. and Le Galès, P. (2010). Exploring governance in a multi-level polity: A policy instruments approach. *West European Politics*, 33(2), 1–21.

Kern, F. and Howlett, M. (2009). Implementing transition management as policy reforms: A case study of the Dutch energy sector. *Policy Sciences*, 42(3), 391–408.

Kern, F., Rogge, K. S., and Howlett, M. (2019). Policy mixes for sustainability transitions: New approaches and insights through bridging innovation and policy studies. *Research Policy*, 48(1), article 103832.

Lamont, M. (2009). *How Professors Think: Inside the Curious World of Academic Judgment*. Cambridge, MA: Harvard University Press.

Langfeldt, L. and Scordato, L. (2016). *Efficiency and Flexibility in Research Funding. A Comparative Study of Funding Instruments and Review Criteria*. Oslo: Nordic Institute for Studies in Innovation, Research and Education.

Larivière V., and Costas R. (2016). How many is too many? On the relationship between research productivity and impact. *PLoS ONE*, 11(9), e0162709.

Lascoumes, P. and Le Galès, P. (eds.) (2004). *Gouverner par les instruments*. Paris: Presse Presse de la Fondation Nationale des Sciences Politiques.

Lascoumes, P. and Le Galès, P. (2007). Introduction: Understanding public policy through its instruments? From the nature of instruments to the sociology of public policy instrumentation. *Governance*, 20(1), 1–21.

Lepori, B. (2011). Coordination modes in public funding systems. *Research Policy*, 40(3), 355–367.

Lepori, B., van den Besselaar, P., Dinges, M., Poti, B., Reale, E., Slipersaeter, S., Theves, J., and van der Meulen, B. (2007). Comparing the evolution of national research policies: What patterns of change? *Science and Public Policy*, 34(3), 372–388.

Lepori, B., Reale, E., and Spinello, A. O. (2018). Conceptualizing and measuring performance orientation of research funding systems. *Research Evaluation*, 27(2), 171–183.

Linder, S. H. and Peters, B. G. (1989). Instruments of government: Perceptions and contexts. *Journal of Public Policy*, 9(1), 35–58.

Linder, S. H. and Peters, B. G. (1998). The study of policy instruments: Four schools of thought. In: B. G. Peters and F. K. M. v. Nispen (eds.), *Public Policy Instruments. Evaluating the Tools of Public Administration*. Cheltenham: Edward Elgar, pp. 33–45.

March, J. G. and Olsen, J. P. (2006). Elaborating the "New Institutionalism". In: R. A. W. Rhodes, S. Binder and B. Rockman (eds.), *The Oxford Handbook of Political Institutions*. Oxford: Oxford University Press, pp. 3–20.

May, P. J., Jones, B. D., Beem, B. E., Neff-Sharum, E. A., and Poague, M. K. (2005). Policy coherence and component driven policy making: Arctic policy in Canada and the United States. *Policy Studies Journal*, 33(1), 37–63.

Moore, S., Neylon, C., Paul Eve, M. et al. (2017). "Excellence R Us": University research and the fetishisation of excellence. *Palgrave Communications*, 3, 16105.

Neave, G. (2012). *The Evaluative State, Institutional Autonomy and Re-engineering Higher Education in Western Europe*. London: Palgrave.

OECD (2014). *Promoting Research Excellence: New Approaches to Funding*. Paris: OECD Publishing.

Pollitt, C. and Bouckaert, G. (2017). *Public Management Reform: A Comparative Analysis-into the Age of Austerity*. Oxford: Oxford University Press.

Rayner, J., Howlett, M., and Wellstead, A. (2017). Policy mixes and their alignment over time: Patching and stretching in the oil sands reclamation regime in Alberta, Canada. *Environmental Policy and Governance*, 27(4), 472–483.

Reale, E. and Seeber, M. (2013). Instruments as empirical evidence for the analysis of Higher Education policies. *Higher Education*, 65(2), 135–151.

Rogge, K. S. and Reichardt, K. (2016). Policy mixes for sustainability transitions: An extended concept and framework for analysis. *Research Policy*, 45, 1620–1635.

Sabatier, P. A. (1993). Policy change over a decade or more. In: P. Sabatier and H. Jenkins-Smith (eds.), *Policy Change and Learning: An Advocacy Coalition Approach*. Boulder, CO: Westview Press, pp. 13–39.

Sabatier, P. A. and Jenkins-Smith, H. C. (1999). The advocacy coalition framework. An assessment. In: P. A. Sabatier (ed.), *Theories of the Policy Process*. Boulder, CO: Westview Press, pp. 117–166.

Salamon, L. M. (1981). Rethinking public management: Third party government and the changing forms of government action. *Public Policy*, 29(3), 255–275.

Salamon, L. M. (ed.) (2002). *The Tools of Government. A Guide to the New Governance*. Oxford: Oxford University Press.

Salamon, L. M. and Lund, M. S. (1989). *Beyond Privatization: The Tools of Government Action*. Washington, DC: The Urban Institute Press.

Slaughter, S. and Rhoades, G. (2004) *Academic Capitalism and the New Economy: Markets, State, and Higher Education*. Baltimore, MD: Johns Hopkins University Press.

Sörlin, S. (2007). Funding diversity: Performance-based funding regimes as drivers of differentiation in higher education systems. *Higher Education Policy*, 20(4), 413–440.

Sørensen, M., Bloch, C., and Young, M. (2016). Excellence in the knowledge-based economy: From scientific to research excellence. *European Journal of Higher Education*, 6(3), 217–236.

Springer, S., Birch, K., and MacLeavy, J. (eds.) (2016). *Handbook of Neoliberalism*. London: Routledge.

Stone, D. A. (1989). Causal stories and the formation of policy agendas. *Political Science Quarterly*, 104(2), 281–300.

Surel, Y. (2000). The role of cognitive and normative frames in policy-making. *Journal of European Public Policy*, 7(4), 495–512.

Thatcher, M. and Schmidt, V. A. (2013). Conclusion: Explaining the resilience of neo-liberalism and possible pathways out. In: V. A. Schmidt and M. Thatcher (eds.), *Resilient Liberalism in Europe's Political Economy*. Cambridge: Cambridge University Press, pp. 403–431.

Tijssen, R. (2003). Scoreboards of research excellence. *Research Evaluation*, 12(2), 91–103.

van der Meulen, B. (2003). New roles and strategies of a research council: Intermediation of the principal–agent relationship. *Science and Public Policy*, 30(3), 323–336.

Vedung, E. (1998). Policy instruments: Typologies and theories. In M. Bemelmans-Videc, R. C. Rist and E. Vedung (eds.), *Carrots, Sticks, and Sermons: Policy Instruments and their Evaluation*. New Brunswick, NJ: Transaction, pp. 21–58.

Verger, A., Fontdevila, C., and Parcerisa, L. (2019). Reforming governance through policy instruments: How and to what extent standards, tests and accountability in education spread worldwide. *Discourse: Studies in the Cultural Politics of Education*, 40(2), 248–270.

Whitley, R. and Gläser, J. (eds.) (2007). *The Changing Governance of the Sciences. The Advent of Research Evaluation Systems*. Dordrecht: Springer.

Whitley, R. (2010). Reconfiguring the public sciences: The impact of governance changes on authority and innovation in public science systems. In R. Whitley, J. Gläser and J. Engwall (eds.) *Reconfigruing Knowledge Production*. Oxford: Oxford University Press, pp. 3–50.

Voß, J. P. and Simons, A. (2014). Instrument constituencies and the supply side of policy innovation: the social life of emissions trading. *Environmental Politics*, 23(5), 735–754.

Zacharewicz, T., Lepori, B., Reale, E., and Jonkers, K. (2019). Performance-based research funding in EU Member States – A comparative assessment. *Science and Public Policy*, 46(1), 105–115.

6. Performance-based research funding and its impacts on research organizations

Gunnar Sivertsen

6.1 INTRODUCTION

Performance-based research funding systems (PBFS) allocate direct institutional funding to universities and other public research organizations based on an assessment of their research. They appear in three main types: evaluation-based funding, indicator-based funding and funding contingent on performance agreements. Combinations are possible. PBFS add an element of competition to direct institutional funding which comes in addition to the contest for indirect external project funding awarded by research councils and other funding organizations.

Many countries have implemented PBFS for direct funding of higher education institutions at the national or regional level. The systems may seem similar across countries, but they are never the same and they are modified all the time. PBFS differ because they are anchored in the local traditions and mechanisms of state budgeting and embedded in the local negotiations about priorities and developments in the higher education sector. They are dynamic because they are continuously contested and thereby often adjusted. Countries also mutually learn from each other and inspire changes in their PBFS. The systems are conservative as well. Once implemented, they become games with rules and specific terminologies and infrastructures that are difficult to change. Also, they need to be predictable because they influence budgets and the spending of tax revenues on the funding side. They also need to ensure some stability of budgets at the institutions.

The purpose of this chapter is to discuss potential problems with PBFS and their possible solutions from the perspective of universities and other research organizations that are exposed to PBFS. The argument will be that the potential problems with PBFS depend on three factors: (1) the type and design of the system; (2) the strength of its influence on funding and reputation; and (3) the involvement of the funded organizations in collaboration about the design, implementation, management and evaluation of the system.

The type and design of the PBFS are often discussed as the most important factors, e.g. in the debate in the UK about the evaluation-based versus the indicator-based alternatives (Taylor, 2011; Geuna and Piolatto, 2016; Wilsdon et al., 2015; Sivertsen, 2017; Harzing, 2018). This chapter will show that all three major types have pros and cons, and that any preference depends on whether the PBFS is expected to serve other purposes in addition to funding allocation.

The second factor, the strength of the influence on funding and reputation, is less recognized. The validity of the methods for evaluation may be reduced because evaluees and evaluators fear negative outcomes. Qualitative information about strengths and weaknesses can become vague, generally positive and less reliable. Documentation and statistics may become selective, and indicators can turn into displaced goals. The paradox is that, to reach the aims of a PBFS more effectively, their effects on funding and reputation should be minimized.

The third factor, involvement of the funded organizations, is easy to underestimate as well. The autonomy and influence of universities does not include the funding itself, which is the sole responsibility of governments on behalf of society. Governments may execute this responsibility by designing and implementing a funding mechanism that expresses their expectations and ambitions (often the core ideas of New Public Management) through a PBFS. Why should the funded organizations be involved at all in this political task? Collaboration is favourable because experience shows that the outcome of a PBFS also depends on the degree of alignment between the external expectations and financial incentives that are built into the PBFS at the system level and the internal values, aims and incentive structures at the level of universities. This domain of possible tensions and dilemmas is also covered – within an agency theory framework – in Chapter 12 by Jussi Kivistö and Charles Mathies in this book. The two chapters thereby supplement each other.

The discussion in this chapter is based on the author's experiences with the designs, implementations, developments and discussions of PBFS in 26 countries. In some cases, the experience comes from being formally involved in providing advice to individual countries (Australia, the Czech Republic, Denmark, Finland, Flanders in Belgium, Norway and Sweden). In another context (Debackere et al., 2018), advice was provided for a partially overlapping group of countries hosted by the European Commission to seek mutual learning about PBFS (Armenia, Austria, Croatia, the Czech Republic, Estonia, Italy, Moldova, Norway, Portugal, Slovenia, Spain, Sweden and Turkey). Other countries have asked for contributions to meetings about aspects or principles of their evaluation and funding systems (Argentina, China, Germany, Iceland, Morocco, New Zealand, Poland, South Africa and the UK). Most of these countries will not be mentioned directly in this chapter, and the discussion will only refer to public documents.

The chapter starts with defining PBFS and its three main types: evaluation-based funding, indicator-based funding and funding contingent on performance agreements. Possible problems and solutions are then discussed in relation to the three determining factors mentioned above: type and design; influence on funding and reputation; and involvement of the funded organizations.

6.2   DEFINITION AND MAIN TYPES OF PBFS

Hicks (2012) provided a definition of PBFS which she characterized as narrow, but it has proved useful in several subsequent studies:

> Performance-based research funding systems (PBFS) are national systems of research output evaluation used to distribute research funding to universities.

This definition was based on the specifications given by the OECD as they commissioned her first overview of PBFS (Hicks, 2010): The systems should be *national*, the *research* must be evaluated, it must be done *ex post*, and the funding of the universities must at least partly *depend on the results of the evaluation*. Hicks' definition is also used in overviews of PBFS by Jonkers and Zacharewicz (2016), Sivertsen (2017) and Zacharewicz et al. (2019). I will use it here as well although 'output evaluation' mainly describes the evaluation-based type of PBFS. The term is perhaps too narrow for what is assessed by performance agreements and indicator-based systems, as we shall see below. Also, indicator-based systems are intended for funding allocation only and not regarded as proper evaluation.

Hicks (2012) classifies major types of PBFS by their methods. Some systems apply 'peer review or peer review informed by metrics', and these systems usually focus on individuals, departments or fields of research as the unit of evaluation. Evaluation usually takes place at intervals of several years. Other systems apply 'indicators based on paper counts or indicators based on both papers and citations'. Indicator-based assessments are usually performed annually and focused on the university as the unit of evaluation.

Sivertsen (2017) provides a similar classification of major types of PBFS but takes into consideration that indicator-based systems may go beyond paper and citation counts (bibliometrics) and apply other indicators reflecting research activities. Zacharewicz et al. (2019) go further in the same direction and specify several indicators that may be used instead of or as a supplement to bibliometric indicators: patents, external project funding revenues, revenues from contract research, quantifications of knowledge transfer activities and spin-off companies, internationalization indicators and diversity measures such as the gender composition of staff. They also add indicators related to educational activities. This is an important addition because several countries *combine* research and education in their PBFS while some countries only apply performance-based funding for the educational activities.

In a further attempt to classify the PBFS of member states of the European Union, Zacharewicz et al. (2019) make a main distinction between 'countries which base their funding allocation formula on quantitative metrics-based assessments' and 'countries which base their funding allocation formulae on peer review-based assessment exercises'. They provide a detailed overview of different practices and indicators that are used within each major type.

One of these practices is performance agreements (PAs) signed between funding authorities and individual universities or colleges. PAs have become widespread in the governance of universities and sometimes include research performance (de Boer et al., 2015; Jonkers and Zacharewitz, 2016). Jongbloed et al. (2018) describe the purposes and functioning of PAs in depth and argue that they have emerged as a distinct form of PBFS in higher education systems. PAs differ from the evaluation-based and indicator-based types by being forward-looking and able to reflect different purposes and ambitions within a heterogenous sector of higher education institutions. These purposes and ambitions may be represented in a broad array of goals and indicators in the performance agreement. A PA usually includes a financial penalty or sanction if objectives are not achieved, which makes it a type of PBFS.

The proliferation of performance agreements in Europe is confirmed in the overview provided by Zacharewicz et al. (2019), which shows that PAs with a research component are present in five European countries among which Austria and the Netherlands otherwise only apply performance-based funding of education. As we shall see in the next section of the chapter, it can be useful to regard PAs as a distinctive approach to PBFS. This chapter therefore distinguishes between three major types of approaches to PBFS (with possible combinations):

1. *Evaluation-based.* Examples: Czech Republic, France, Italy, Latvia, New Zealand, Portugal, UK.

2. *Indicator-based.* Examples: Belgium, Croatia, Denmark, Estonia, Finland, Germany (at the level of federated states), Norway, Poland, Slovakia, Sweden.
3. *Performance Agreements.* Examples: Austria, Denmark, Estonia, Finland, Netherlands, Switzerland.

The examples are based on the overviews provided by Zacharewicz et al. (2019) with the addition of information from Jonkers and Zacharewitz (2016), Dohmen (2016) and Kulczycki et al. (2017). As the following discussion will show, all three types have strengths and weaknesses.

In a review of 354 pieces of literature on the topic of PBFS, Thomas et al. (2020) find almost a third discussing the pros and cons of different types and designs of PBFS. The majority of these discuss the costs and effects of evaluation-based versus indicator-based systems, some advocating one or the other, some advocating combinations. The pros and cons of different approaches to PBFS is also a topic of the overviews referred to above. Hicks (2010) summarizes that peer review is met with less scepticism than metrics by the academic community, but indicator-based approaches can be less costly and performed more regularly. Jonkers and Zacharewitz (2016), with an extended discussion in Zacharewicz et al. (2019), emphasize the strengths of peer review: it is based on specialised knowledge of the scientific field and it can identify unquantifiable aspects such as novelty and understand the research in context. They also point out possible problems other than the practical: there can be a lack of transparency, and peer review can be conservative and favour mainstream research. Indicator-based solutions, on the other hand, may be less costly and intrusive, but the methodology can be biased against certain fields of research and their publishing practices, and the sole use or abuse of bibliometric indicators can create perverse incentives.

Most of the discussions of the pros and cons of different types and designs of PBFS take the perspective of best practice in *research evaluation*. However, in PBFS, evaluation is only one of several available methods to achieve fairness and legitimacy in funding allocation. Evaluation was first introduced as a method for PBFS in the UK in 1986. The purpose at that time was clearly funding allocation: to avoid cutbacks in the places that least deserved it. Well-established methods in competitive grant allocation were borrowed to serve the new purpose. The University Grants Committee required that the departments submit statements of their research along with five selected research outputs in 37 subject areas. The documentation was then rated as 'outstanding', 'above average', 'average' or 'below average', just as in competitive grant allocation. In 2021, on the front page of REF2021, the original allocation method became the main purpose: The Research Excellence Framework is 'the system for assessing the quality of research in UK higher education institutions'. With evaluation as the main purpose, peer review may be considered preferable over metrics, as in the recommendation for the REF stated by *The Metric Tide* report (Wilsdon et al., 2015):

> Metrics should support, not supplant, expert judgement. Peer review is not perfect, but it is the least worst form of academic governance we have, and should remain the primary basis for assessing research papers, proposals and individuals, and for national assessment exercises like the REF.

In practice, this recommendation is not against having an indicator-based PBFS. Countries such as the Netherlands and Norway run national research evaluation systems based on peer review that are detached from funding, and they have indicator-based PBFS that run separately (Sivertsen, 2017).

We conclude so far that there is no general rule that an evaluation-based system is preferable over an indicator-based system. The connection to funding allocation imposes several limitations on both types (see also next section). Both become quantitative when translated to a funding formula, and both demand comparability among different research organizations and may therefore promote homogeneity. If there is a wish to preserve diversity in the higher education sector, a third and less discussed alternative, performance agreements, might be preferable.

With reference to evaluations of the experience with performance agreements in the Netherlands, Jongbloed et al. (2018) summarize the pros and cons of this alternative. Both the funding and funded sides may agree that these arrangements can underpin more attention to the diversity of profiles in the higher education sector than other funding arrangements allow for. They can improve the dialogue between stakeholders on both sides and provide increased transparency and accountability owing to the setting of targets and use of indicators. The dialogue also allows for telling the 'story behind the numbers'. Drawbacks may be a possible decline in institutional autonomy, an additional bureaucracy owing to the emphasis on uniform indicators and the possible financial penalty for not achieving goals that are partly beyond the influence of the funded organizations. Also, the core indicators may contribute to unintended effects.

6.3   PROS AND CONS OF DIFFERENT TYPES FROM THE PERSPECTIVE OF RESEARCHERS

We have seen above that all types of PBFS may have problems. This conclusion is in line with this author's observations from many countries among which one, Denmark, will provide an example of how the pros and cons of the major types of PBFS are viewed from the perspective of researchers in different fields of research.

Denmark introduced an indicator-based PBFS with weak effects on funding and reputation in 1997. Most of the direct funding for research at the universities is based on historical distributions. Only 13 per cent is performance-based and related to four indicators according to the so-called '45–20–25–10' model: educational statistics (to support research-based education, 45 per cent), external funding revenues (20 per cent), a bibliometric indicator (25 per cent) and PhD production (10 per cent).

The PBFS was seldom debated until 2009. Then, inspired by Norway, the more controversial bibliometric indicator was introduced (Aagaard, 2018). This indicator represents research activity by considering the total annual output of peer-reviewed research publications across all fields including the social sciences and humanities. It can do so by not only building on international data sources such as Scopus or Web of Science, but also on metadata registered in local research information systems. Finland (Pölönen, 2018) and Norway (Sivertsen, 2018) have a similar indicator in their PBFS while Swedish universities use the Norwegian variant for internal purposes (Hammarfelt, 2018).

Reflecting the controversies over the bibliometric indicator, the Danish Ministry of Higher Education and Science in 2018 appointed an expert group to provide a report that could help them redesign the existing approach to PBFS to better identify and promote research quality.

The final report (Gornitzka et al., 2019) discussed the pros and cons of four solutions without prioritizing them:

1. a modified publication indicator, extended with citations where relevant for the field of research;
2. performance agreements;
3. evaluation-based PBFS;
4. a combination of the first and second alternative.

After the report was published, the Ministry hosted a one-day national meeting with representatives of the most prominent researchers in all fields at all universities. They were nominated by Universities Denmark, the Danish Rectors' Conference. The discussion among them took place in group meetings for each of four major areas of research (humanities, social sciences, natural sciences and engineering, and medical and health sciences) after which they reported to the plenary. A summary is publicly available in Danish.[1]

The humanities said that they preferred to keep the publication indicator as it was. The indicator had enhanced the quality of research in their fields. Also, citations are either inapplicable or incomparable in the humanities and may distort behaviour. *The social sciences* said they would welcome the extension of the publication indicator with citations if the publication indicator was still included. Some fields in the social sciences are mainly nationally oriented. *The natural sciences and engineering* said they approved of adding citations but reminded of the complexity of field-normalizing citation impact to produce robust indicators. *The health sciences* said citation indicators are well established in their fields. The bibliometrics of the PBFS would be easier to recognize from their own practices if citations were included.

Regarding performance agreements, *the humanities* said this solution would transfer the responsibility for good quality performance from the individual to the organizational level, which would be a gain. The use of the bibliometric indicator at the individual level would pass away. On the other hand, this solution might reduce autonomy and reintroduce political steering. It could result in gaming and creative writing of performance reports. National comparisons as well as the involvement of the disciplines in the PBFS could go away.

A more forward-looking PBFS with performance agreements appealed to the *social sciences*, but the challenges would be bureaucracy and window-dressing. *The natural sciences and engineering* also found a forward-looking PBFS based on performance agreements desirable if it would not lead to detailed ministerial steering and become resource-demanding on the side of the universities. *The health sciences* could also identify with performance agreements as a solution. Prospective orientation, dialogue and formative evaluations to learn from are all good. However, it seemed unclear how relevance, societal impact and research-based education would be covered.

To *the humanities*, an evaluation-based PBFS could be preferable from one perspective: while the government would define research quality in performance agreements, academic communities would do so with peer review. However, this alternative would be too costly compared with the marginal reallocation effects of the existing system. Also, it can be difficult to nominate unbiased peers to panels in some fields of the humanities where mainly Danish or other Nordic researchers contribute. Peer review might increase the focus on individual performances even more than the bibliometric indicator does.

The social sciences found the evaluation-based alternative with peer-review expensive, and it might give arbitrary and incomparable results. According to *the natural sciences and engineering*, the strength of an evaluation-based PBFS would be that it can identify research quality at the units of research performance. A problem might be to make consistent comparisons across units and to defend the costs of running the exercise. The view of *the health sciences* was that the strength of an evaluation-based PBFS might be to create a comparison of research quality. However, the funding consequences could diminish the learning outcomes. There would also be a concentrated focus on research separated from other institutional missions such as education.

The fourth solution with a combination of performance agreements and indicators did not find support in *the humanities*: it would increase complexity and the lack of transparency and autonomy. The role of the publication indicator, which is simple, transparent and not influenced by policy, would be reduced. *The social sciences* also said the modified indicator-based approach alone would be the least problematic solution. *The natural sciences and engineering* said combining indicators and performance agreements would represent the same pros and cons as with each of them. *The health sciences* were afraid that the publication indicator with its extension to citations would disappear with the introduction of performance agreements.

The Danish government recently decided to cease using the bibliometric indicator as of 2022 with no replacement. The indicator-based PBFS is retained with the three other indicators of education, external funding revenues and PhD production. The design is changed, not the type.

We have seen that no type of PBFS stands out as clearly preferable from the point of view of the researchers in the main areas of research. All types have their pros and cons, also according to the literature we reviewed.

6.4   THE PARADOX OF PERFORMANCE-BASED FUNDING IN EVALUATION-BASED SYSTEMS

The type and design of a PBFS are often discussed as important for how it works. We used the discussion about the REF in the UK as an example in Section 6.2 above. According to this author's experiences with discussions about PBFS in several countries, the strength of the influence of the system on funding and reputation can be just as important as the type of system. In the Danish example above, the researchers' considerations about possible negative effects were expressed in a relaxed discussion of pros and cons in which the idea of the PBFS itself was not questioned. I have witnessed much more heated discussions in other countries where the PBFS is more decisive for funding and reputation.

To measure the strength of the influence of a PBFS, Zacharewicz et al. (2019) provided an important innovation in international overviews of such systems by using country-level economic statistics on public spending for research to estimate the relative influence of the PBFS on the total economy of the universities in each country. The influence partly depends on the balance between direct institutional funding and external competitive project funding, partly also on the proportion of the direct funding for research that is influenced by the PBFS. Some countries allocate almost all of the direct funding according to the outcomes of the PBFS while other countries have introduced PBFS with only light economic consequences.

To take two examples provided by Zacharewicz et al. (2019), universities in the UK were 35 per cent dependent on institutional funding versus external funding while universities in Norway were 60 per cent dependent on institutional funding. Even so, the universities in the UK are more dependent the outcomes of the PBFS (on average 20 per cent of their total revenues) than universities in Norway (7 per cent) because most of the direct funding in Norway is based on the so-called 'historical' distribution of funding and not related to performance.

The PBFS of the UK is known to receive a lot of attention and create much debate at the universities (Butler, 2010; Thomas et al., 2020). The same is true for the PBFS in Norway (Sivertsen, 2018), indicating that even small effects on funding and reputation can represent strong ways of steering. According to Hicks (2012), small effects on funding can still have a strong influence because public judgements about the relative prestige of an institution also matter. Universities compete for recognition, not only for funding.

The general problem is that PBFS may disturb or undermine their own aims and methods by being connected to funding and reputation. Evaluations are usually meant to be formative, to inform about strengths and weaknesses and provide a basis for improvement. When connected to funding, evaluations (direct or related to contracts) may become less reliable and informative. Qualitative information about strengths and weaknesses can become vague and generally positive. Similarly, statistics should provide information and indicators should provide benchmarks as a basis for strategic development. When connected to funding, they may instead narrow the focus of the organization and become displaced goals.

The paradox is that to reach the aims of a PBFS more effectively, the consequences for funding and reputation should probably be minimized. To what extent?

Speaking from experience, a reallocation of less than 10 per cent of the total budget for direct funding of research at a country's universities, influencing less than 1 per cent of the budget margin per institution, is more than enough to steer internal priorities and behaviour at universities in the direction of the incentives. At the same time, there is a risk of losing the reliability of formative information for strategic development.

As an experiment, one could ask: what would be the outcome if the evaluation exercise did not affect funding and reputation? Would the evaluation make no change at all or inspire profound changes in an institution's ability to promote research quality? It is not easy to find evidence that answers these questions, but the cases of Australia and of Uppsala University in Sweden are helpful.

The Australian periodical research evaluation exercise, Excellence in Research Australia (ERA), ran as a PBFS in two rounds until 2012, after which it was disconnected from university funding in the third round in 2018. The rating of universities now only influences their reputation but still receives much attention. The evaluators also seem to have cared about their reputation. The average rating has increased from round to round (Australian Research Council, 2021). The example shows that recognition can be just as important as funding.

The example also shows that PBFS can be conservative, as indicated in the introduction. The ERA still uses a summative methodology with strict criteria for comparability and evidence from past performances. The main result of the exercise continues to be a rating of the universities on a scale of excellence in each field of research. With this rating, the universities are expected to improve their performance because they care about their external reputation, not because the evaluation provides information and learning for their strategic development. The exercise is thereby 'indirectly formative' according to the documentation.

To be directly formative and provide information and learning for improvement, the ERA would need a fundamental change. A definition of the practices and purpose of formative organizational evaluation is available from *BetterEvaluation*, a global not-for-profit organization working to improve the practices worldwide, in the document 'Evaluating the Performance of an Organisation' (BetterEvaluation, n.d.):

An organisational assessment is a systematic process for obtaining valid information about the performance of an organisation and the factors that affect performance. It differs from other types of evaluations because the assessment focuses on the organisation as the primary unit of analysis. Organisations are constantly trying to adapt, survive, perform, and influence. However, they are not always successful. To better understand what they can or should change to improve their ability to perform, organisations can conduct organisational assessments.

This definition can be contrasted with the continuing practices of the ERA in Australia, as described above, and two self-initiated evaluations organized by Uppsala University of Sweden in in 2007 and 2011, both of them with effects on internal resource allocation. However, in 2017, Uppsala University changed the game completely and introduced formative organizational evaluation without resource allocation. As we shall see, the definition of formative evaluation above became applicable. The example thereby answers the question: would the evaluation make no change at all or inspire profound changes in an institution's ability to promote research quality? The limitation of the example is still that it does not represent a governmental PBFS.

The main title of the three evaluation reports (Uppsala University, 2007, 2011, 2017) was always *Quality and Renewal*. The subtitle of the first two reports was *An overall evaluation of research at Uppsala University*. It changed to *Research Environment Evaluation at Uppsala University* in 2017, thereby reflecting the change from summative evaluation with internal resource allocation to formative organizational evaluation for learning.

The purposes of the evaluation in 2007 were expressed as both summative and formative, 'to identify strong research and interesting opportunities for renewal', but summative evaluation methods dominated because resource allocation was the expected outcome. International disciplinary panels performed site visits and reviewed a package of information per department/ unit: self-assessments with lists of representative publications, a document presenting numbers of different research-related activities, and a document with facts and figures related to personnel, economy, dissertations and publications. The panels were asked to make a general assessment of the department/unit and comment on the quality of research, the research environment and infrastructure, the networks and collaborations, opportunities for renewal and emerging science, and actions for successful development. On this basis, the panels were recommended to conclude with these ratings: 'Top quality or world leading; Internationally high standard; Internationally recognized standard; Acceptable standard'. The methods were repeated in 2014 except that the possible rating of 'Insufficient' was added. Now, the panels were also asked to comment on the effects of the evaluation in 2007.

The outcomes of the evaluations in 2007 and 2014 were also dominated by summative evaluation with no general advice to the university or its faculties. Evaluative statements were reported per panel and unit of assessment. These statements tended to be general and positive: 'It is important that the faculty and students should have a teaching load that leaves plenty of time for research'. 'The chair holder has a good research and publication record'. 'The institute as a whole is regarded by the panel as having an internationally high standard'. 'We note with satisfaction the positive working environment and conditions for doctoral students'. Ratings influenced the internal reallocation of resources. Not unexpectedly, the ratings were overall higher in 2011 than in 2007.

In advance of the third evaluation at Uppsala University in 2017, an internal commission performed interviews with key persons and extensive consultations with various bodies of the university. Out of this process came a clear recommendation that the next evaluation should be 'more forward-oriented and focus on preconditions for and processes underpinning high quality research, rather than assessing research quality as such'. Following this recommendation, the third evaluation started with an internet-based survey in which around 3,700 active researchers at Uppsala University shared their perceptions of and opinions on their local research environments at the University. The researchers were not asked about their contributions to the university's performance. They were asked about how the university contributed to their performance and how it could improve in doing so.

The evaluation in 2017 involved 132 experts from 18 countries serving in 19 different panels. Each panel consisted of six to eight experts, including a chair, a Swedish panellist from another university (to bring knowledge of the Swedish context), and a 'researcher on research' panellist (to contribute with scientifically based knowledge about research environments). The evaluation was informed by self-evaluations, the survey results, bibliometric analyses and a basic fact sheet. In advance, for writing the self-evaluations, the units were provided with the survey results, the bibliometric analysis and the basic data sheet. They were encouraged to provide constructive and critical self-reflection and to attach other documents if they wished. The complete material was shared with the panels ahead of their site visits. Panels were asked to be 'critical friends' who could assess organizational strengths and weaknesses and make recommendations for strategic development. This time, they were not asked to rate the units.

The outcome of the evaluation in 2017 was a much larger number of specific and consequential recommendations for organizational progress than the earlier evaluations had provided. This time, the evaluation also spoke to the university as a whole, not only its departments. It concluded that (Uppsala University, 2017, p. 12):

> a number of areas have been identified where action is needed if Uppsala University is to take steps towards reaching its full potential. These relate to: quality culture and control, leadership and strategic renewal, talent attraction and retention, international milieu, external collaboration and outreach, research-teaching linkages, and organisation and infrastructure. Two actions emerge as especially critical and urgent and should therefore be highlighted as university-wide priorities: the strengthening of the academic leadership's capacity for strategic renewal, and the further development of career paths and career support.

It seems evident that a national PBFS-related evaluation system cannot provide a similar useful outcome for each of the universities. The need for strict criteria for the comparability of evidence of past performance makes it difficult to provide specific forward-looking advice, and the risk of losing funding and recognition inhibits the sincerity of both the self-assessment and the external assessment. This effect is probably stronger the more consequential the PBFS is.

The analysis above is relevant mainly for PBFS that are evaluation-based or related to performance agreements with qualitative goals. It leads to the paradox that to reach the aims of a PBFS more effectively, the consequences for funding and reputation should probably be minimized. Arnold et al. (2018) compare some countries and find that the UK is unusual in that a large proportion of institutional funding is determined by the PBFS.

6.5   THE PARADOX OF PERFORMANCE-BASED FUNDING IN INDICATOR-BASED SYSTEMS

For indicator-based PBFS and the use of indicators in performance agreements, the paradox of performance-based funding is often referred to as 'Goodhart's law': When a measure becomes a target, it ceases to be a good measure. The British economist Charles Goodhart's (1975) own expression was: 'Any observed statistical regularity will tend to collapse once pressure is placed upon it for control purposes'.

Although this sentence seems reasonable as an expression of what happens when indicators are introduced in the context of a PBFS, Goodhart's law has not been confirmed in studies of effects of PBFS. In an early overview, Butler (2010) noted that the literature 'is full of words like "likely", "potential", and "possible" without much evidence'. The most complete and recent comparative overview of PBFS in Europe (Zacharewicz et al., 2019) finds that there is an 'absence of an assessment of the impact of the different types of performance-based funding systems'. Thomas et al. (2020) observes that one fourth of the literature on PBFS comprises studies about their possible effects that, taken together, are inconclusive.

The reason for this continued absence of conclusive evidence of effects is probably the complexity of the task (Auranen and Nieminen, 2010; Hicks, 2012; Hammarfelt and de Rijcke, 2015; de Rijcke et al., 2016; Gläser and Laudel, 2016; Aagaard and Schneider, 2017). PBFS differ widely among countries by type, local design and the degree of economic incentives, and they constantly change. More importantly, it is difficult to isolate the incentives and value systems created by a local PBFS from other influences. Observable changes in performance may be the effects of other funding and evaluation arrangements. Particularly influential are the highly competitive national or international sources of external funding. There are, however, some studies showing that bibliometric indicators introduced with PBFS can influence publication patterns at universities. Such studies are reviewed in Chapter 12 by Jussi Kivistö and Charles Mathies in this book.

To illustrate that indicator-based PBFS with only small economic effects might not follow Goodhart's law, two Scandinavian examples are useful. The Danish researcher Kaare Aagaard (2015) studied the influence on local management and publication practices of the bibliometric indicator used in the Norwegian PBFS. He arrived at the physical metaphor of 'trickling down' to describe how the national system impacted local decisions and behaviour. However, the study showed that the local use of the indicator varied considerably, not only across institutions and fields of research, but also within institutions, between different faculties and even between individual departments within the same faculty. There was nothing similar to a physical law at work, perhaps because the bibliometric indicator in Norway only reallocates less than 2 per cent of the funding.

The Swedish PBFS is since 2009 partly based on bibliometric indicators with data from Web of Science, again only with a light-touch effect on funding. Hammarfelt et al. (2016) studied possible local effects at Swedish universities and used Aagaard's physical metaphor in their conclusion: 'Our study clearly shows how measures and incentives on a national level trickle down and influence decisions on lower levels'. However, their study showed that many Swedish universities were *not* using the Web of Science-based indicators of the Swedish PBFS. They used the more inclusive bibliometric indicator in Norway's PBFS. Leaders and organizations in academia can be self-determined and take other decisions than following weak funding incentives. This is also shown by Edlund and Wedlin (2017) in a study from the

Faculty of Social Sciences at Uppsala University. The Norwegian indicator was chosen there because it suited local needs better than the indicators based on Web of Science that had been introduced at the national level.

The Swedish example of local self-governance indicates that it may be difficult to distinguish between intended and unintended effects of PBFS with weak implementations. Instead, one could say that any introduced indicator may have constitutive effects by defining new possibilities and problems wherever it is used (Dahler-Larsen, 2014). In this perspective, the introduction of the Swedish PBFS may have paved the way for local use of the Norwegian indicator as a compromise between national incentives and local utility. A stronger PBFS implementation would probably have resulted in a conflict rather than a compromise. Before Sweden's PBFS was implemented in 2009, the Swedish deans of the social sciences and humanities collectively protested against the Web of Science-based PBFS in a letter on the 29th of September 2008 to the Ministry of Education. They proposed the more inclusive Norwegian indicator as a less harmful alternative.

Anyhow, PBFS are compromises between aims and methods. Strong effects on funding and reputation weaken the validity and usefulness of the methods. The same was observed by Diana Hicks (2012) in her overview of PBFS 10 years ago: the aims of a PBFS seem more effectively achieved with weak consequences. By minimizing the influence on the economy and reputation of the universities, the PBFS can be more useful to them, and adverse effects may be reduced.

It should be possible to limit the direct consequences of PBFS in practice. Just as the Leiden Manifesto (Hicks et al., 2015) reminds that 'assessors must not be tempted to cede decision-making to the numbers', policy making for higher education and research should not be replaced by funding formulas. Prioritizing by decision is legitimate.

6.6   GOVERNANCE BY COLLABORATION TO SUPPORT VALUE CREATION

In addition to the type, design and strength of the PBFS, the validity of the methods and the usefulness for universities also depend on a third factor, collaboration between the funder and the funded on the design and organization of the PBFS. This is a question of governance on the funding side. Hicks (2012) observed that Public Value Management (Stoker, 2006) could be a more appropriate governance model for PBFS than New Public Management. The implication would be that PBFS should be developed and implemented in close collaboration with the universities and support them in creating the public values of a university.

PBFS emerged with the era of New Public Management (NPM) and are motivated by some of the core ideas: less central steering combined with required accountability, performance and outcome measurement, and increased efficiency through competition. If we add the aim of increasing research quality, the core ideas of NPM are often reflected in official motivations for PBFS. As an example, the official motivation for PBFS at the European level is to establish 'more effective national research systems – including increased competition within national borders and sustained or greater investment in research', as expressed by the European Commission (2012) in a communication with guidelines for *A Reinforced European Research Area Partnership for Excellence and Growth*. The optimism in this statement about what PBFS can achieve is characteristic for NPM and understandable from the perspective of the funder. We will take the perspective of the funder for once in this chapter before returning to the perspective of the research organizations in the conclusion.

In many countries, PBFS evidently serve more purposes than the core NPM idea of efficiency through competition. The systems create statistical overview and insight into research activities, they make the funding allocation criteria fairer and more transparent, and they reinforce the willingness of governments to sustain or increase funding of the higher education sector. These purposes will not disappear in a societal sector of increasing importance and expenses. The ages before NPM and PBFS were different. Higher education was for the few and research was performed by an elite with close relations to government. Lobbyism, not equity, was the funding mechanism. NPM now allows for connecting funding to explicit ambitions and targets for large public investments in research. Against this background, it is understandable that several countries have seen their parliaments unanimously agree on continuing their PBFS despite critical voices from academia. PBFS seem to be the preferable way of funding and steering an otherwise autonomous sector of society.

From an NPM perspective, it seems obvious that the design and use of the PBFS should be the sole responsibility of the funder. However, as shown in the chapter by Jussi Kivistö and Charles Mathies in this book, experience shows that the outcome of a PBFS also depends on the degree of alignment between the external expectations and financial incentives that are built into the PBFS on the funding side, and the internal values, aims and incentive structures that are at work on the funded side. To achieve such an alignment, collaboration could be preferable with Public Value Management (Stoker, 2006) as the governance model.

The aim of the collaboration would be to make the PBFS support the institutions to create and maintain the public values of universities. A typical NPM aim such as 'more effective national research systems' in the above cited example could then be translated to for example 'more support for the characteristic and unique forms of societal value creation at universities'. The aim of 'increased competition within national borders' could be replaced by 'increased collaboration among universities and with society in creating these values'. The efficiency of the universities in producing outputs and impacts would probably not decrease. There is pressure to be compared and compete in all other funding sources in the research system.

Among the 26 countries that this chapter is built on experiences with, several include collaboration between the government and the universities in the design and organization of the PBFS. We have already seen that Denmark involved the universities and their researchers in discussions of the type and design of the PBFS. A few other examples will suffice.

Australia and the UK run consultation processes with the universities before each round of the exercise, and their systems are redesigned accordingly. The UK has also invited independent and openly published reports with assessments and recommendations for further development of the system (Wilsdon et al., 2015; Stern, 2016; Arnold et al., 2018). In 2014–15, the Czech Republic organized a redesign of the PBFS in which the government let the universities and their most prominent researchers take the main responsibility for the process (Mahieu et al., 2015). International expertise was provided to aid the process. Also in 2014–15, after six years with an indicator-based approach to PBFS, the Swedish government designed a PBFS inspired by the evaluation-based Research Excellence Framework in the UK. The new model, named FOKUS (Swedish Research Council, 2015), ended up being rejected by the Swedish universities, partly for reasons of cost, but also because the universities were concerned about their institutional autonomy and wanted to organize the research evaluations themselves

(Swedish Government, 2016). The government respected the opinion of the universities and did not implement the new model.

A few countries have imposed PBFS with strong consequences for the universities without collaboration. A combination of conflicts, gaming, resignation and loss of dialogue between the funder and the funded is usually the outcome. Collaboration is the third of three factors that are important to consider whenever problems arise with PBFS.

6.7   CONCLUSIONS

This chapter has discussed potential problems with PBFS and their possible solutions, mainly from the perspective of the funded organizations, but also from the perspective of funders. Three factors are important:

- The type and design of a PBFS is important, but there is no ideal solution that solves the problems. All three major types have pros and cons: evaluation-based, indicator-based and funding contingent on performance agreements. How they are designed is the more important question, and any preference of type depends on whether the PBFS is expected to serve other purposes in addition to funding allocation.
- PBFS easily become compromises between aims and methods, which is what I have named the paradox of performance-based funding. The validity of the methods, and thereby the usefulness of PBFS, may be reduced when performance assessment or measurement is connected to funding. Minimizing their effects on funding and reputation may support the achievement of their aims. The effects on funding depend on the proportion of the direct funding that is performance-based and the role of direct funding versus competitive external funding for the strategic development of the institutions. A reallocation of less than 10 per cent of the total budget for direct institutional funding of research at a country's universities, influencing less than 1 per cent of the budget margin per institution, is more than enough to receive attention and steer internal priorities and behaviour.
- Governance is important. The usual focus in New Public Management on comparability and competition to achieve efficiency might be counterproductive. The funded organizations should be involved in collaboration about the design, implementation, management and evaluation of the system. External expectations and financial incentives need to be aligned with characteristic forms of public value creation at universities.

Together, these three factors could easily serve as arguments for the termination of PBFS. However, there are strong arguments on the funder's side for keeping the systems. PBFS communicate society's expectations to a sector of increasing societal importance. They may also create overview and external insight into the activities and provide fairer and more transparent funding allocation criteria, thereby serving purposes beyond the aims of New Public Management.

The way forward is probably to achieve such aims by minimizing the effects of PBFS on funding and reputation and by developing them further in close collaboration with the universities. To support such development, research on PBFS could focus less on types of PRFS and their adverse effects and more constructively on the paradox of performance-based funding and what is gained for formative purposes by reducing their effects.

NOTE

1.   This author was present at the meeting. The minutes have been published in Danish: https://
    ufm.dk/forskning-og-innovation/statistik-og-analyser/den-bibliometriske-forskningsindikator/
    organisering/fagligt-udvalg/modereferater/referat-af-bfi-stormode-for-faggruppeformaend-den-2
    -maj-2019.

REFERENCES

Aagaard, K. (2015). How incentives trickle down: Local use of a national bibliometric indicator system. *Science and Public Policy*, 42, 725–737.

Aagaard, K. (2018). Performance-based research funding in Denmark: The adoption and translation of the Norwegian model. *Journal of Data and Information Science*, 3(4), 20–30.

Aagaard, K., and Schneider, J.W. (2017). Some considerations about causes and effects in studies of performance-based research funding systems. *Journal of Informetrics*, 11(3), 923–926.

Arnold, E., Simmonds, P., Farla, K., Kolarz, P., Mahieu, B., and Nielsen, K. (2018). *Review of the Research Excellence Framework. Evidence Report*. Brighton: Technopolis Group.

Auranen, O., and Nieminen, M. (2010). University research funding and publication performance – An international comparison. *Research Policy*, 39(6), 822–834.

Australian Research Council (2021). *ERA EI Review Final Report 2020–2021*. Canberra: Commonwealth of Australia.

BetterEvaluation (n.d.). *Evaluating the Performance of an Organisation*. Retrieved May 7, 2021, from https://www.betterevaluation.org/en/theme/organisational_performance.

Butler, L. (2010). Impacts of performance-based research funding systems: A review of the concerns and the evidence. In: *Performance-based Funding for Public Research in Tertiary Education Institutions: Workshop Proceedings*. OECD Publishing.

Dahler-Larsen, P. (2014). Constitutive effects of performance indicators: Getting beyond unintended consequences. *Public Management Review*, 16(7), 969–986.

de Boer, H.F., Jongbloed, B., Benneworth, P., Cremonini, L., Kolster, R., Kottmann, A., Lemmens-Krug, K., and Vossensteyn, H. (2015). *Performance-based Funding and Performance Agreements in Fourteen Higher Education Systems – Report for the Ministry of Education, Culture and Science*. Enschede: CHEPS, University of Twente.

de Rijcke, S., Wouters, P.F, Rushforth, A.D., Franssen, T.P., and Hammarfelt, B. (2016). Evaluation practices and effects of indicator use – A literature review. *Research Evaluation*, 25(2), 161–169.

Dohmen, D. (2016). Performance-based funding of universities in Germany – An empirical analysis. In: José Manuel Cordero Ferrera, J.M.C., and Rodríguez, S.R (eds.), *Investigaciones de Economía de la Educación* (Vol. 11, pp. 111–132). Asociación Economía de la Educación.

Debackere, K., Arnold, E., Sivertsen, G., Spaapen, J., and Sturn, D. (2018). *Mutual Learning Exercise: Performance-based funding of university research: Horizon 2020 Policy Support Facility, Summary Report*. European Commission.

Edlund, P., and Wedlin, L. (2017). Den kom flygande genom fönstret. Införandet av ett mätsystem för resursfördelning till forskning. In: Wedlin, L., and Pallas, H. *Det ostyrda universitetet: Perspektiv på styrning, autonomi och reform av svenska lärosäten* (pp. 216–243). Göteborg: Makadam Förlag.

European Commission (2012). Communication from the Commission to the European Parliament, the Council, the European Economic and Social Committee and the Committee of the Regions. A Reinforced European Research Area Partnership for Excellence and Growth.

Geuna A., and Piolatto M. (2016). Research assessment in the UK and Italy: Costly and difficult, but probably worth it (at least for a while). *Research Policy*, 45(1), 260–271.

Gläser, J., and Laudel, G. (2016). Governing science: How science policy shapes research content. *European Journal of Sociology*, 57(1), 117–168.

Goodhart, C. (1975). Problems of monetary management: The U.K. experience. *Papers in Monetary Economics, 1*. Sydney: Reserve Bank of Australia.

Gornitzka, Å., Hansen, H.F., Hesthaven, J.S., Schneider, J.W., and Sivertsen, G. (2019). *Fremtidssikring af forskningskvalitet. Ekspertudvalget for resultatbaseret fordeling af basismidler til forskning.* Copenhagen: Ministry of Science and Education.

Hammarfelt, B. (2018). Taking comfort in points: The appeal of the Norwegian model in Sweden. *Journal of Data and Information Science,* 3(4), 85–95.

Hammarfelt, B., and de Rijcke, S. (2015). Accountability in context: Effects of research evaluation systems on publication practices, disciplinary norms, and individual working routines in the faculty of Arts at Uppsala University. *Research Evaluation,* 24(1), 63–77.

Hammarfelt, B., Nelhans, G., Eklund, P., and Åström, F. (2016). The heterogeneous landscape of bibliometric indicators: Evaluating models for allocating resources at Swedish universities. *Research Evaluation,* 25(3), 292–305.

Harzing, A.W. (2018). Running the REF on a rainy Sunday afternoon: Can we exchange peer review for metrics? *STI 2018 Conference Proceedings,* pp. 339–345.

Hicks, D. (2010). Overview of models of performance-based research funding systems. In: *Performance-based Funding for Public Research in Tertiary Education Institutions: Workshop Proceedings.* OECD Publishing.

Hicks, D. (2012). Performance-based university research funding systems. *Research Policy,* 41(2), 251–261.

Hicks, D., Wouters, P., Waltman, L., De Rijcke, S., and Rafols, I. (2015). Bibliometrics: The Leiden Manifesto for research metrics. *Nature News,* 520(7548), 429–431.

Jongbloed, B., Kaiser, F., van Vught, D.F., and Westerheijden, A. (2018). Performance agreements in higher education: A new approach to higher education funding. In: Curaj, A., Deca, L., and Pricopie, R. (eds), *European Higher Education Area: The Impact of Past and Future Policies.* Cham: Springer.

Jonkers, K., and Zacharewicz, T. (2016). *Research Performance Based Funding Systems: A Comparative Assessment.* EUR 27837. Luxembourg: Publications Office of the European Union.

Kulczycki, E., Korzeń, M., and Korytkowski, P. (2017). Toward an excellence-based research funding system: Evidence from Poland, *Journal of Informetrics,* 11(1), 282–298.

Mahieu, B., Dvorák, J., Chudlarský, T., Sivertsen, G., and Vondrák, T. (2015). *R&D Evaluation Methodology and Funding Principles. Final report 3: The Small Pilot Evaluation and the Use of the RD&I Information System for Evaluation.* Brighton: Technopolis Group.

Pölönen, J. (2018). Applications of, and experiences with, the Norwegian model in Finland. *Journal of Data and Information Science,* 3(4), 31–44.

Sivertsen, G. (2017). Unique, but still best practice? The Research Excellence Framework (REF) from an international perspective. *Palgrave Communications,* 3, 17078.

Sivertsen, G. (2018). The Norwegian model in Norway. *Journal of Data and Information Science,* 3(4), 2–18.

Stern, N. (2016). *Research Excellence Framework (REF) Review: Building on Success and Learning from Experience.* Ref: IND/16/9. Department for Business, Energy and Industrial Strategy.

Stoker, G. (2006). Public value management: A new narrative for networked governance? *The American Review of Public Administration,* 36, 41–57.

Swedish Government (2016). Regeringens Proposition 2016/17:50. Kunskap i samverkan – för samhällets utmaningar och stärkt konkurrenskraft.

Swedish Research Council (2015). *Research Quality Evaluation in Sweden – Fokus: Report of a Government Commission regarding a Model for Resource Allocation to Universities and University Colleges Involving Peer Review of the Quality and Relevance of Research.* Swedish Research Council: Stockholm.

Taylor, J. (2011). The assessment of research quality in UK universities: Peer review or metrics? *British Journal of Management,* 22(2), 202–217.

Thomas, D.A., Nedeva, M., Tirado, M.M., and Jacob, M. (2020). Changing research on research valuation: A critical literature review to revisit the agenda. *Research Evaluation,* 29(3), 275–288.

Uppsala University (2007). Quality and renewal 2007. An overall evaluation of research at Uppsala University 2006/2007. http://uu.diva-portal.org/smash/get/diva2:43034/FULLTEXT01.pdf.

Uppsala University (2011). Quality and renewal 2011. An overall evaluation of research at Uppsala University 2010/2011. http://uu.diva-portal.org/smash/get/diva2:461235/FULLTEXT01.pdf.

Uppsala University (2017). Quality and renewal 2017. Research environment evaluation at Uppsala University. https://uu.diva-portal.org/smash/get/diva2:1153914/FULLTEXT01.pdf.

Wilsdon, J., Allen, L., Belfiore, E., Campbell, P., Curry, S., Hill, S. Jones, R., Kain, R., Kerridge, S., Thelwall, M., Tinkler, J., Viney, I., Wouters, P., Hill, J., and Johnson, B. (2015). *The Metric Tide: Report of the Independent Review of the Role of Metrics in Research Assessment and Management.* 10.13140/RG.2.1.4929.1363.

Zacharewicz, T., Lepori, B., Reale, E., and Jonkers, K. (2019). Performance-based research funding in EU Member States – A comparative assessment. *Science and Public Policy*, 46(1), 2019, 105–115.

7. R&D programs as instruments for governmental R&D funding policy

Emanuela Reale, Magnus Gulbrandsen and Thomas Scherngell

7.1   INTRODUCTION

The emergence of competition in funding for research and development (R&D) is based on long-term changes in trajectories and rationales for governmental R&D support. Starting from the 1970s, governmental R&D funding was deeply transformed in European countries, and a project-based mode of allocation became more dominant. This had two main reasons. First, the stagnation of the volume of public research funding induced more selective modes of allocation. Second, new policy rationales about efficient use of public resources emphasized competitive allocation as a means to increase the quality, efficiency, and effectiveness of research systems (Lepori et al., 2007). More fundamentally, R&D programs are long-term means of the government pursuing strategic goals such as increasing excellence of the research system or reinforcing the collaboration between public and private research performers. The organization of R&D programs is at the core of both project-based and competitive funding.

The aim of this chapter is to give an overview of the main theoretical underpinnings and advancements concerning R&D programs as instruments of governmental R&D policy. Programs are meso-level instruments that serve several purposes, such as directing R&D efforts towards specific societal challenges or knowledge domains. They act as coordinating mechanisms, usually for clusters of R&D projects to improve their quality and productivity. Two questions drive our exploration: what is the role of programs in government funding of R&D? How can we understand programs theoretically and device frameworks for empirically observing them in order to support and advance underlying theoretical considerations? The chapter illustrates the diversity and the complex nature of R&D programs, as well as strategies and objectives they reveal, the actors implementing the programs, and the modes of implementation. It also develops new conceptual framings based on this theoretical review informed by data and infrastructure examples.

The chapter primarily focuses on government programs for R&D funding to academic research, mainly performed by universities and non-higher education public research organizations, in some cases in collaboration with the private sector. Such governmental R&D funding may address different topics, and it is possibly oriented at solving societal challenges and needs with varying degrees of specific objectives, and rarely oriented at blue skies or curiosity-driven research only. It does include investigator-driven grant schemes and not only thematically oriented programs. R&D programs may foresee innovation activities found under labels like pre-competitive research, but this chapter does not discuss instruments per se related to innovation policy devoted to supporting firms' capabilities to introduce new products in the market and similar.

Section 7.2 presents a fundamental narrative about how programs have emerged and what a governmental R&D funding program is. We discuss different notions of programs in national and supra-national contexts, as well as differences that are linked to sectoral and funding perspectives. By reviewing the literature, Section 7.3 presents the multifaceted problems of R&D funding programs focusing on the features that are essential for their understanding, mobilizing the most important theoretical perspectives to this aim. In addition, it discusses some relevant issues of the current evolution of programs as policy instruments, namely modes of coordination, policy mixes, hybridity of R&D programs, and the portfolio perspective. Moreover, it provides a few examples of research endeavors trying to empirically observe characteristics of R&D funding programs. The chapter ends with a critical assessment of gaps in the theoretical perspectives on R&D programs and future research directions dealing with open issues (Section 7.4).

7.2   R&D FUNDING PROGRAMS: ORIGINS AND DEFINITION

Defining the peculiar nature of a R&D funding program is difficult. In the context of R&D funding systems, programs have been described as meso-level instruments that distribute project funding (Lepori et al., 2017) to research groups on a regular and systematic basis. The program design explicates the aim and scope of the actions, the expected results and the impact foreseen. Also, it indicates the R&D projects' funding streams like grants, projects, contracts and funding to networks that are devoted to put into action the chosen aims and goals. For instance, the *Excellence Initiative* in Germany is a large program pursuing the improvement of the quality and international standing of the German universities. The program is articulated into different project-funding streams (graduate schools for early career researchers, clusters of excellence, universities of excellence) to the performers on the base of competitive calls. Another example is *FIRST* in Italy, a program to sustain firms' investment in R&D, which is articulated in four project funding lines: international research project funding, social innovation, spin offs from research and strategic research projects.

This definition has two main implications. First, R&D programs involve several functions and manage several processes. The main ones are: (a) the construction of an explicit mission statement, including the goals to be reached; (b) the identification of scientific priorities and of the type and mode of research expected; (c) procedures and rules for submitting proposals, as well as for their evaluation and selection; and (d) a dedicated budget and procedures for contract management, including monitoring and reporting. Programs have different goals, whose attainment might involve different research fields or combinations thereof.

Second, R&D programs can be designed by a research funding organization/agency (RFO) or jointly by two or more funding agencies that mediate between the state and the performing sector. Therefore, programs may vary according to the missions attributed to the funding agencies involved and the policy objectives they must address, and to the policy space of the funding agency following government delegation (Braun, 2006b). Different national contexts have different funding traditions influencing the way in which programs are formulated, the rules and the organizational logics of their management, the fields and beneficiaries addressed, and the regulations affecting the selection and the evaluation processes. In this respect, governmental R&D funding programs differ from targeted funding or project funding since they delineate the content of public policy and the preferences of the actors involved in design and implementation. Governmental R&D funding programs are clearly visible from the 1970s or in some countries from the 1980s. During these decades the relationships between science and society, represented through the metaphor of a contract, changed. Before the 1970s, the contract foresaw a clear division of tasks between the two parties: the government (as representative of the society) supplied money, while the scientific community provided knowledge, retaining the power to decide the research agenda, methods and tools to guarantee integrity and social benefits (Guston, 1996). Government maintained the right to decide the level of funding without posing limitations to the autonomy of science (van der Meulen, 1998). Increasingly, this contract came under critique and scrutiny (Weinberg, 1974; Jasanoff, 1987), captured by a new ideal that public funding of research should lead to "socially robust knowledge". This knowledge more explicitly and directly addresses societal needs, seeking to find solutions to emerging problems through the collaborative effort of different actors under a new trans-disciplinary perspective (Gibbons et al., 1994; Martin, 2003). Early efforts and programs often had broad goals where the societal need served as an umbrella for regular academic research, thus bringing together related research activities from different research-performing organizations, providing in some cases advantages of additional resources and opportunities for collaboration, with a soft directional steering of research (Mathisen, 1996). At the supranational level, the EU framework programs started in the 1980s fit into this category with their thematic priorities based on negotiations between civil servants and various societal interest groups.

The proliferation of governmental program funding is tied to this fundamental shift in the framing of science policy rationales, moving from a block funding perspective to a goal-oriented one. The emergence of large programs devoted to sustaining research on the frontier of technological innovation (Laredo and Mustar, 2002; Senker, 2006) was one consequence of this new orientation. Another was changing patterns of funding allocation to research performers, emphasizing competitive project-based funding (Lepori et al., 2007; Thèves et al., 2007) that sought higher quality research outputs and positive effects on economic and social growth, by addressing political problems or technological innovation. In this respect, funding became an instrument to steer the research and innovation system by orienting activities and results toward pre-determined goals. New funding agencies were established for this purpose, and many thematically bound programs emerged in funding organizations whose mission was to provide competitive funding for specific scientific disciplines.

National political and economic strategies drove many of the mentioned changes, but a key role was also played by European funding to R&D, mainly through the European Framework Programs, which largely modified both the constellations of actors involved and the design of the programs (Geuna, 2001; Delanghe et al., 2009). The European Union played a major role translating policy frames that had been shaped within and beyond Europe into R&D funding programs (Ulnicane, Chapter 4 in this *Handbook*). The transformation of the organization of research funding moved from the rationale of complementarity between the national level and the European level, to a new rationale of competition for funding by launching programs toward the building of "European Science" (Edler et al., 2003; Nedeva and Wedlin, 2015; Braun, 2017; Scherngell and Lata, 2013).

In the new century, further developments at the European policy level pushed for more decisive action toward providing science-based solutions to societal needs. The rhetoric of R&D policy outlined the importance of committed research efforts to find solutions for the so-called Societal Grand Challenges (Kuhlman and Rip, 2018), the importance of research instruments for sustaining the development and the use of Key Enabling Technologies (Martin, 2016), and the strong directionality recommended for research and innovation policy toward the achievement of Sustainable Development Goals (OECD, 2018). New concepts from scholars in the field of science, technology and innovation studies have emerged in parallel with and as a response to the new policy narratives. These include conceptualizations of transformative innovation processes (Schot and Steinmueller, 2018), new attitudes, societal values and practices in the realm of R&D policy (Kaldewey, 2018), and the need for action aimed at stimulating a more entrepreneurial state driving efforts toward mission-oriented R&D policies (Foray et al., 2011; Mazzucato, 2018). All these developments have major implications for both the organization and scope of governmental R&D programs. For example, instances of inter-disciplinarity as well as public and private collaboration have been put forward as means to translate research efforts into concrete solutions for the economy and society.

The main argument of this section is that the emergence of programs in R&D policy represents the merger of two long-standing characteristics of the research system. First, *thematic priorities* were earlier found in the support for specialized research centers and institutes targeting specific technologies, industry sectors or policy areas. Second, *independent RFOs were established* in most countries in the first five to six decades of the 20th century, allocating funding through *competition* based on expert reviews.

7.3   UNDERSTANDING R&D FUNDING PROGRAMS

Here we present some theoretical approaches that have been used to characterize and understand governmental R&D funding programs. This is strongly related to the conceptualization of the relationship between government and science, since programs are policy means of steering the research performer toward the realization of specific public aims. Programs are therefore tied to RFOs that play a major role in defining the characteristics of programs.

7.3.1   Theoretical Approaches for Analyzing Governmental R&D Programs

One stream of literature conceptualizes the relationship between government and science as a principal–agent game or relationship (Guston, 1996). Here, government acts as the principal, which hands over resources, often in a contractual relationship, to agents, the research performers, for the purpose of reaching certain goals that the principal cannot reach on its own. Van der Meulen (1998) and other colleagues (Braun, 1993, 2017) elaborate on the characteristics of this relationship in R&D policy. Central aspects are information asymmetry between the principal and the agents (principals often do not know the best suited agent for a specific purpose), moral hazard in the implementation of the research (agents have goals that may contrast with those of the principal), and path dependency as factors affecting the tendency toward stabilization of the funding system. Principal–agent theory as an analytical tool in R&D policy has been elaborated not as a bilateral game between government and science, but as a multi-actor game. This game involves not only several agents, but also different principals, making up a trilateral relationship between governments, science and the RFOs as intermediaries (Klerkx and Leeuwis, 2008).

Following principal–agent theory, R&D funding programs ensure that agents (the research performers) engage with the principals' (the RFOs) goals and priorities. Programs are designed by RFOs based on a specific delegation from the government, which is why they are often conceptualized as intermediaries between the principal and the agents (van der Meulen, 2003; Kivistö and Mathies, Chapter 12 in this *Handbook*). However, programs require the involvement of research agents that are willing to participate, and their contributions need to fulfil certain quality criteria while addressing the principals' goals. It means that the steering capability of the programs under principal–agent theory is circumscribed by: (a) the existence of research expertise to achieve the given aim; (b) the willingness of agents to engage in the program; (c) the ability of the principal to select the most appropriate agent for the work; and (d) the ability of the principal to monitor and follow up funding. It has been found that "researchers' willingness to respond to top-down programming initiatives depends, to some extent, on the relation between that program and their own ambitions, their relative hunger for means of support, their chances of getting funding from other sources, and so forth" (Shove, 2003: 376).

Another approach is to consider programs as government policy instruments. Lascoumes and Le Galès (2007) depict instruments as institutions that enable a policy to be operative and that organize the relationship between the public power and the recipients, according to the representations (goals) and meanings (values) that they incorporate. This means that instruments incorporate a theory of the relationship between government and governed institutions, and that they are not neutral; they keep memory of the policies that created them and they are vehicles of specific values. Using this theoretical perspective to conceptualize R&D programs has some implications:

- Programs can generate effects that are not connected to their original goals; these unintended effects can modify the goals and eventually distort them, creating stable ideas.
- As institutions, programs tend to persist through time, and they usually change incrementally through additions and changes rather than radical breakthroughs. Because of the persistence through time, and implementation inertia, RFOs generally build initiatives on existing programs by adapting them to the new policies, while only in rare cases removing or substituting the whole scheme (Hood, 1986).
- Changes in programs do not necessarily imply shifts in policy goals. However, programs can be modified or substituted by others judged to be more effective, but modifications in the instruments themselves can modify the goals as well. In both cases, changes compel the actors to adapt; in this sense programs may be vectors of change and stability at the same time.

This highlights the problem of how policies balance elements of continuity and change (Pierson, 1993). Some authors have used concepts from policy feedback theory to understand how the institutionalization of some programs creates ideas informing other policies (e.g. the positive effects of broadening competition for funding, Wang et al., 2018) as well as values and beliefs that stabilize a given problem in the policy frame (e.g. the legitimate interest to shift R&D programs to goals addressing societal grand challenges).

A crucial element in the analysis of programs as policy instruments is the autonomy that programs leave to the actors – how the instrument changes the actors' policy spaces (Braun, 2006a). For instance, shaping objectives about performance (efficiency related to management and results) can be implemented through compulsory rules, standards or guidelines. Recipients of program funding have varying room to maneuver and possibility to create spaces for action. Moreover, it is important to consider path dependency effects (North, 1990) whereby program characteristics may affect both current and future choices and opportunities. Finally, it is worth recalling the role that ideas play in the design and implementation of policy instruments – including programs (Capano, Chapter 5 in this *Handbook*), and the motivations guiding public research funding to find solutions to more complex realities and demands. Alemán Díaz (Chapter 3 in this *Handbook*) highlights the presence of three motivations – creativity, purpose, and transformation, which center respectively on (a) preserving the principle of free research in the choice of research topics to address, (b) improving the steering capability of the government to the research performers toward mission research and (c) raising the responsiveness of the science system toward emerging societal needs.

In sum, the principal–agent and instrument perspectives see programs as instruments of governmental R&D funding policy, located at the meso level between politics and research performers (Reale and Seeber, 2013). Programs can be articulated as one single instrument or as a combination (or mix) of different instruments, involving aspects such as regulation, communication and expert groups that aim to steer research (Flanagan et al., 2011; Kern et al., 2019) to achieve intended policy goals (Martin, 2016). Programs can also combine different organizational logics in their design, for example logics of hierarchical governance with logics of steering from a distance (Capano and Pritoni, 2019). Finally, R&D programs can in principle be characterized using existing typologies of policy instruments (Vedung, 2007; Howlett, 2005; Martin, 2016; Peters, 2005). This has not been fully exploited in the literature, although there are some recent works trying to explore this possibility (Capano et al., 2020; Lepori and Reale, 2019). Finally, it is worth mentioning that the two theoretical approaches presented in the section correspond to different (complementary) facets of the same process. Principal–agent theory is in fact one of the possible action mechanisms of public policies and programs are instruments of public policy largely working through delegation, which is indeed at the core of new public governance (Salamon, 2002).

7.3.2   The Organizational Dimension

We have seen that diversity is a structural feature of governmental R&D programs. The "program" concept is fluid and non-homogeneous, given the multiplicity of actors involved with different objectives, logics, preferences – including the government levels where they are formulated. Even the wording – programs – can differ between countries, because of variations in sectors, funding context and policy history.

The diversity characterizing R&D programs strongly depends on the organizational characteristics and policy space of RFOs managing them (Braun, 1998; Potì and Reale, 2007). Programs are complex objects that coordinate existing and emerging ideas about policy (knowledge and expectations about causality; see Capano, Chapter 5 in this *Handbook*) and norms (preferences on how policy should be enacted on the base of past experiences, policy legacies and administrative traditions, cf. Hood, 1986 and Verhoest et al., 2009). RFOs are key policy actors designing, administering and managing programs according to their own mission, objectives, strategies and traditions of research funding. Programs may be funded from a combination of different policy areas and related ministries, which gives the RFOs a role in setting up new and combined goals (Braun, 1998). The Austrian Climate and Energy Fund funding energy-related research projects is an example that can be put in context in that respect.[1]

As mentioned, RFOs have been conceptualized as mediators between the government and the research performers, and their policy spaces are shaped by the proximity between the policy level and the science community (Braun, 2006b). The intermediary approach focuses the interest on the capability of the RFOs to solve the tensions between the state and the research community (Braun, 2003) where R&D programs are concerned. For instance, Gulbrandsen (2005) argues that research councils' setting up of strategies, procedures and R&D programs is characterized by fundamental tensions, seen as problems of balancing different options in research funding. RFOs therefore can be characterized based on their position vis-à-vis the state (e.g. their capacity of autonomous decision-making), and the intermediary role they play between governors and the research community (van den Meulen, 2003), the functions they fulfil in the public research funding and the influence they might have in the cognitive development of science (Braun, 1998). It is important to recall that RFOs shape the procedural and organizational dimensions in the program delivery package (Howlett, 2009), for instance by designing the selection procedures of the beneficiaries and the goal of the program, which allows them to understand the underlying logics or policy frames of the instrument.

In sum, RFOs are important actors for shaping horizontal or vertical specialization of the national research funding system (Lepori, 2011) and the degree of control from the government. RFOs need to find an effective balance between different options in research funding programs: basic vs applied research, steering of the system toward achieving pre-determined objectives vs aggregation for a socially constructed research agenda, disciplinary vs cross disciplinary research, authority distribution between researchers and users or stakeholders, and types of reviewing and monitoring (Gulbrandsen, 2005).

7.3.3   The Main Dimensions of R&D Programs

Following Nedeva (2013), programs can be tied to two central dimensions. The first one is organizational because programs are found at the intersection of the international arena of the research field in question and the local research space shaped by the actors and unique context of a particular country, region or sector. This interaction leads to different considerations about what "good research" may mean for a specific program, which will be based on combinations of criteria derived from research fields and societal sectors or spaces. Langfeldt and colleagues (2020) name this a balance between F-type (research fields) and S-type (societal spaces) criteria. Programs can therefore be seen as instruments to manage tensions between these sources of normative expectations to research.

The second dimension important to understand programs is what kind of R&D activities they give priority to, which may be called their *scope*. A traditional distinction from the R&D statistics is between different types of knowledge production (basic and applied research, development work), but this can also be extended to how programs identify relevant participants and wider stakeholders. As such, the scope can be narrow, if a program targets primarily one type of knowledge production and related knowledge producers, or broad, when the objectives of the program require or allow for wider participation and activities. For example, the European Research Council's programs could be defined as narrow (focused on excellent basic research) and organized towards F-type quality criteria. The scope may be determined by the funding organization itself or by a ministry in its allocation to an RFO.

We propose some stylized characteristics of R&D programs based on their scope and organizational emphasis, relating in a 2 × 2 matrix of these two dimensions to differing thematic goals, research goals and research-performing organizations' objectives (Table 7.1). In this way, the analysis of programs as a means to coordinate ideas and norms can be operationalized through various descriptors to empirically classify and study R&D programs. For instance, such a classification may be used as a heuristic to investigate the portfolios of RFOs or to analyze changes in instruments over time. Relevant descriptors need to be based on the type of program under investigation and its wider national, sectoral and knowledge production context. Also, this classification can be used to study the characteristic of the RFOs themselves on the basis of the choices they made in program design and implementation, and to highlight instances of hybridization in the public funding systems (see Section 7.3.4).

The classification has limitations not least because the fields/societal space distinction can be unclear in many cases, and because the terms used to describe activities can be heterogeneous or contested. Consequently, this also raises challenges for the empirical observation of R&D programs, but empirical insights are increasingly needed, not only for underlining and potentially adapting the conceptualization of programs, but also in a policy evaluation context. Indeed, we do observe an increasing interest in improving the empirical foundations for understanding instruments for governmental R&D and their diversity. For instance, the STIP Compass (OECD, 2021) collects data based on a comprehensive survey, intended to characterize different policy instruments, including R&D programs, in particular in terms of the policy issues that are addressed, such as public research, business or service innovation, and knowledge transfer (e.g. science-industry programs), but also issues like societal challenges and governance modes.[2]

Figure 7.1 provides an illustrative example visualization of R&D policy instruments implemented by the EU member states (current instruments, status 2019). It underlines the heterogenous and diverse character of R&D programs and underlying instruments, indicating the frequency of instruments assigned to different classes (darker shades imply higher numbers of instruments in the specific category), as well as different budget ranges associated which each instrument. It can be seen that R&D funding related to grants for business R&D and innovation and project grants for public research are the most frequent R&D policy instruments used by the EU member states in the highest budget range (more than 500Mio EUR). Not only this simple example, but also related literature using STIP data (see e.g. Borowiecki and Paunov, 2018) underline the increasingly diverse composition of institutions and mechanisms of policy initiatives and related instruments.

However, the illustration put forward in Figure 7.1 underlines the difficulties and challenges for the systematic collection of data on R&D programs, related to conceptual ambiguities, but also data collection challenges and the classification of collected data programs in terms of their characteristics. Therefore, next to STIP, other research efforts are still in progress. For instance, recent endeavors have tried to get a more systematic empirical overview on instruments from a systemic perspective, e.g. by collecting evidence on rationales, legitimation and orientation of R&D funding. One example is the PREF study on national public research funding (Reale, 2017; Lepori et al., 2018; Primeri et al., 2014; Zacharewicz et al., 2019), which has put strong emphasis on the identification of funding themes, fields and the types of allocation (in particular competitive project-based R&D programs vs institutional funding), comparing countries in terms of their funding focus on societal challenges between 2008 and 2014. New initiatives currently under development[3] aim to deepen empirical foundations in that direction, experimenting with the usage of text mining methods to characterize R&D

Table 7.1   *Central characteristics of governmental R&D programs*

Some characteristics of programs		R&D activity/knowledge production scope	
		Narrow	Broad
Organizational emphasis	Science fields (F-type)	• Programs that target established scientific fields or disciplines (physics, biomedicine, etc.). • Activities will mainly be basic research. • Main participants will be found in academia and some research institutes.	• Programs that target an emerging area with scientific promise. • Activities: basic and applied research, education/capacity building. • Participants: academia, research institutes, some firms.
	Society (S-type)	• Programs that target wide areas like oceans, food, energy, maybe with reference to the UN Sustainable Development Goals and similar. • Activities: basic and to some extent applied research. • Participants: different types of academic organizations and research institutes.	• Programs that target specific societal problems and challenges. • Activities: whole R&D spectrum including innovation. • Participants: applied research organizations, firms, hospitals, public actors, civil society organizations.

Source: Authors' own elaboration.

funding instruments more systematically, e.g. in terms of their relevance for Sustainable Development Goals.

7.3.4   Changing Configurations of Program Coordination Mixes and Portfolio

So far, we have presented R&D programs as characteristics tied to organizational and knowledge production priorities and goals, in an overall context where programs represent contractual mechanisms for selection and delegation. However, programs do not work in isolation but are parts of wider policy mixes and contain contrasts and combinations that may give them a hybrid rather than a uniform set of characteristics. The increased fragmentation of policy landscapes of R&D funding with multiple goals, strategies and agencies has been highlighted as a source of scarce coordination, weakening the steering capability of programs as incentives for pushing researchers toward a given goal, such as efficiently addressing societal challenges (Larrue et al., 2018). The literature points out some theoretical knowledge gaps as to coordination of funding programs and new directions of analysis to deepening the structure of policy mixes, the type of hybridity affecting the program design and the possibility of adopting a portfolio approach.

Policy mixes refer to the interactions between instruments in different areas. Mixes might evolve over time in ways that may deviate from original goals, like the process for individual instruments described earlier. Also, a large variation in the way in which a given RFO combines different instruments at work is visible between and within countries, between and within RFOs (Braun, 2006a). Flanagan et al. (2011) propose a conceptualization for policy mixes looking at dimensions in which the interactions between instruments can occur: across policy spaces, governance spaces, geographical spaces and time, and interactions between different instruments and across different dimensions of the same instruments. Tensions between instruments can rise from conflicts between policy rationales and goals, and from

Source: EC-OECD (2020), STIP Compass International Database on STI Policies, https://stip.oecd.org.

Figure 7.1   *R&D policy instruments used by the EU member states (STIP Compass 2019)*

implementation approaches, thus setting conditions for the success or failure of a given R&D funding policy (Kern et al., 2019; Edmondson et al., 2019).

A related conceptualization looks at the evolving *hybridity in the formulation of funding programs*, which is portrayed as *combinations* of different logics inside one program or in the management of programs following different logics. Capano and Pritoni (2019) outline that policy instruments like R&D programs incorporate and combine in various way the traditional principles of coordination – hierarchy, market and networks. In this context, hybridity can occur through compromising, which means incorporating elements of conflicting logics within the same program. In R&D funding program design, hybridity might affect the organizational logics by mixing features related to both fields and society goals, and the allocation criteria and target group addressed.

Polzer and Höllerer (2016) distinguish between two ways of compromising, namely blending and layering. Blending implies generating new practices in which the original logics are joined together and cannot be separated; in funding programs this might emerge when different allocation criteria are combined, such as societal relevance and academic quality. Layering is the juxtaposition of elements introduced on top of pre-existing ones over time (Capano and Pritoni, 2019). For R&D funding programs this might be the presence within the same instrument of one competitive and one non-competitive component. A related hybridization concept is compartmentalization, which is used to analyze settings where different logics coexist (Skelker and Smith, 2015) either in distinct sub-programs or in the profiles of multiple RFOs. The goal of compartmentalization is to avoid conflicts between logics, but it can at the same time generate coordinating issues between potentially inconsistent instruments (Braun, 2008). We can find several examples of programs promoted by research councils of European countries that fit to the mentioned characteristics, namely R&D funding schemes with very different logics and high coordination efforts (Reale et al., 2021).

Hybridity in R&D funding programs is still largely unexplored (Gulbrandsen, 2011; Gulbrandsen et al., 2015). Capano and Pritoni (2019) identify three ideal modes of hybrid systemic governance of higher education in Europe, namely performance-based, re-regulated and goal oriented. Lepori et al. (2014) demonstrate that national programs aimed at funding transnational research blended three ideal type logics – integration, cooperation and collaboration – allowing the design of programs fitting the interests of the actors involved, like funding agencies and national or supranational actors. Other efforts are under development to understand how hybridity is concretely implemented in the funding program formulation, and how hybridization produces combinations of different logics within the same program or in the setup of new programs. In this respect, one major gap is about understanding the effects – positive or negative – that different types of hybridity can produce, and to explain how policy strategies are put into action by programs following complex mixes of incoherent ideas and values. Thus, a relevant research question can be: do hybrid funding programmes work? What do they achieve that is not achieved in other types of funding of non-hybrid nature?

Finally, it is worth recalling a third approach to study the coordination of R&D programs, which assumes that programs are in some settings increasingly put into a sort of *portfolio perspective* (Bozeman and Rogers, 2001) "in order to fulfil a widening set of objectives, from scientific excellence and economic relevance to contributing to a variety of societal challenges (inclusiveness, gender diversity, sustainability, etc.)" (Larrue et al., 2018). One may think of a program as a portfolio in itself (of projects) or think of sets of programs as a portfolio to address a scientific and/or societal need, whose management is characterized by the maximization of the value with respect to the intended achievements, the balance between different programs at stake, the coherence with the strategic goals and the capability to maintain alive the right number of programs with respect to the available resources. A portfolio perspective and portfolio governance emphasize reducing risk and uncertainties, but may also be seen as a means to increase the chances of radical originality/innovation or as a means of coordination (Wallace and Rafols, 2015). Despite the different aims of the analyses, there is a link between a portfolio perspective and the policy mix perspective in the sense that both highlight the evolutionary and complex nature of interplays between many actors and entities.

In this section we have aimed for a comprehensive overview of central theoretical frameworks that have been or can be used for analyzing R&D programs. Some frameworks derive from theories about the relationship between science and society, others take RFOs or the programs and funding instruments themselves as the starting point, or the relationship between instruments in a wider policy or funding context. Theoretical frameworks have emerged in tandem with new trends in R&D funding, highlighting the need also for studying programs from a longer-term and longitudinal perspective, and to understand how far transformative effects related to the implementation of R&D programs goes with internal transformation of the research process itself (Bührer, Seus, and Walz, Chapter 9 in this *Handbook*). Lastly, an interesting approach is to study funding programs by looking at configurations, trials, and amalgamations as suggested by Thomas and Ramos-Vielba in Chapter 15 of this *Handbook*.

7.4   CONCLUDING REMARKS

Governmental R&D funding programs have been under ongoing transformation over the past decades, both in terms of organizational emphasis and scope. This chapter has shed some light on the main theoretical underpinnings and advancements dealing with R&D programs as instruments of governmental R&D policy, and on their changing natures. It has sought to provide a comprehensive discussion and illustration of the increasing diversity and complexity of such programs, including multi-faceted strategies followed by an increasingly diverse set of engaging actors, in particular research funding organizations. Recent endeavors to empirically characterize R&D programs in a more systematic and robust manner to underline and advance theoretical considerations have been highlighted, including related challenges and problems for data availability.

A fundamental perspective is that an R&D program is a funding instrument for attaining specific goals by establishing procedures for the selection and management of a portfolio of projects. These programs can target academic or societal goals, and they can target academic knowledge producers or a broader set of recipients – or more hybrid and complex mixes of these. Furthermore, programs can fruitfully be seen as part of wider policy contexts and historical trajectories and the specificities of national, regional and sectoral settings.

As such, a main point of the chapter has been to illustrate the diversity and the complex nature of R&D programs, as well as the manifold strategies and objectives they reveal, the actors implementing the programs and the modes of implementation. We propose a conceptual characterization of R&D programs in terms of their *scope* and *organizational* emphasis, relating these two dimensions to differing underlying thematic goals, research goals and research-performing organization objectives. A second important point put forward has been to discuss new conceptual and theoretical framings of R&D programs. Some frameworks derive from theories about the relationship between science and society, others take RFOs or the programs and funding instruments themselves as the starting point, or the relationship between instruments in a wider policy or funding context. Of course, some gaps emerge in the study of government public R&D funding. One concerns the ideational dimension of governmental R&D programs and how they are put into action. On the one hand, the distance between the original goal and aim of the policy makers and the actual formulation of the instruments by the RFO has not been sufficiently empirically studied, including factors affecting the translation process of policy rationales in the instruments. On the other hand, the evidence about how the opportunities provided by the funding programs have been understood by the performers and then translated into research projects is still limited. Therefore, the capability of governmental funding programs to steer public research remains largely unknown.

Several developments can be outlined for R&D funding programs, which might be a source of new research avenues. First, the recent emphasis on mission-oriented policies to address Grand Challenges and Sustainable Development Goals (see Section 7.2), can result in a stronger and more pervasive focus and control toward the achievement of policy goals. This development might be further reinforced by the new awareness about the social responsibility of the scholars' community and the need to produce an impact, thus contributing to solving societal problems. Does this lead to an increasing strategic and organizational diversity of R&D funding programs?

Second, we can envisage a strong influence from the Covid-19 pandemic on R&D funding programs, which will probably be a source of central research themes in the coming years, including learning from widespread pandemic-oriented R&D programs that were set up quickly in 2020. It is not clear whether this may induce pendulum swings between the different scopes and logics described in this chapter, and whether it implies new forms of programs or a clearer division of labor between different RFOs.

Third, there is a large potential with new empirical data to contribute to the discussion on effects of R&D funding mechanisms on research performance and impact, even if impact fundamentally rests on characteristics beyond the funding program itself. As such, studies of impact may put R&D programs in a wider science–society setting, which can be a source of fruitful new research questions that can be addressed through new data available and their combinations.

NOTES

1. https://www.bmk.gv.at/en/topics/climate-environment/climate-protection/climate-energy-fund .html, last accessed 9 March 2022.
2. The Compass currently covers more than 7000 policy instruments, initiated across 50+ countries over the past four decades, with the instruments being attributed to five main categories according to their main function (governance, direct financial support, indirect financial support, collaborative infrastructures, guidance, and regulation), and more detailed 28 subcategories (EC-OECD, 2020). Its relevance has been underlined by the production of cross-country comparisons of national R&D policy programs (Borowiecki and Paunov, 2018; Guimón and Paunov, 2019; Capano et al., 2020). Other recent initiatives have tried to shift emphasis from survey-based to a more statistically and quantitative driven collection of data on R&D policy programs – directly collected from national statistical offices or even RFOs – to enable more meaningful cross-country comparisons or indicators production. Moreover, data science and semantic technologies inspired approaches are increasingly considered in the collection or the classification of programs in terms of their thematic orientations (e.g. societal challenges, Sustainable Development Goals).
3. One example is the European dataset of public R&D funding instruments (EFIL) that is currently under development as one main part of the RISIS infrastructure for Science and Innovation Policy Studies (risis2.eu).

REFERENCES

Borowiecki, M., and Paunov, C. (2018). *How is Research Policy Across the OECD Organised? Insights from a New Policy Database.* OECD, Paris.

Bozeman, B., and Rogers, J. (2001). Strategic management of government-sponsored R&D portfolios. *Environment and Planning C: Politics and Space*, 19(3), 413–442.

Braun, D. (1993). Who governs intermediary agencies? Principal–agent relations in research policy-making. *Journal of Public Policy*, 13(2), 135–162.

Braun, D. (1998). The role of funding agencies in the cognitive development of science. *Research Policy*, 27, 807–821.

Braun, D. (2003). Lasting tensions in research policy-making – A delegation problem. *Science and Public Policy*, 30(5) 309–321.

Braun, D. (2006a). The mix of policy rationales in science and technology policy. *Melbourne Journal of Politics*, 31, 8–35.

Braun, D. (2006b). Delegation in the distributive policy arena. The case of research policy. In: Braun, D., and Gilardi F. (Eds.), *Delegation in Contemporary Democracies*. Routledge, Abingdon, 146–170.

Braun, D. (2008). Organizing the political coordination of knowledge and innovation policies. *Science and Public Policy*, 35(4) 227–239.

Braun, D. (2017). Funding agencies and political intervention – A re-assessment of principal–agent relationships in the funding of basic research. Working Paper, University of Lausanne.

Capano, G., and Pritoni, A. (2019). Varieties of hybrid systemic governance in European higher education. *Higher Education Quarterly*, 73(1), 10–28.

Capano, G., Pritoni, A., and Vicentini, G. (2020). Do policy instruments matter? Governments' choice of policy mix and higher education performance in Western Europe. *Journal of Public Policy*, 40(3), 375–401.

Delanghe, H., Sloan, B., and Muldur, U. (2009). Transnational collaboration in public research funding and publicly supported research in Europe. In: Delanghe H., Muldur U., and Soete L. (Eds.), *European Science and Technology Policy: Towards Integration or Fragmentation?* Edward Elgar, London, 175–190.

EC-OECD (2020). STIP Compass Taxonomies Describing STI Policy data, edition 2019. https://stip.oecd.org.

Edler, J., Kuhlmann, S., and Behrens, T. (2003). *The Changing Governance of Research and Technology: The European Research Area.* Edward Elgar, Cheltenham.

Edmondson, D.I., Kern, F., and Rogge, K.S. (2019). The co-evolution of policy mixes and socio-technical systems: Toward a conceptual framework of policy mix feedback in sustainable transition. *Research Policy*, 48, 103555.

Flanagan, K., Uyarra, E., and Laranja, M. (2011). Reconceptualising the "policy mix" for innovation. *Research Policy*, 40, 702–713.

Foray, D., Mowery, D.C., and Nelson, R.R. (2012). Public R&D and social challenges: What lessons from mission R&D programs? *Research Policy*, 41, 1697–1702.

Geuna, A. (2001). The changing rationale for European university research funding: Are there negative unintended consequences? *Journal of Economic Issues*, 35(3), 607–632.

Gibbons, M., Limoges, C., Nowotny, H., Schwartzman, S., Scott, P., and Trow, M. (1994). *The New Production of Knowledge. The Dynamics of Science and Research in Contemporary Society.* SAGE, London.

Guimón, J., and Paunov, C. (2019). *Science–Industry Knowledge Exchange: A Mapping of Policy Instruments and their Interactions.* OECD, Paris.

Gulbrandsen, M. (2005). Tensions in the research council-research community relationship. *Science and Public Policy*, 32(3), 199–209.

Gulbrandsen, M. (2011). Research institutes as hybrid organizations: Central challenges to their legitimacy. *Policy Science*, 44, 215–230.

Gulbrandsen, M., Thune, T., Brorstad Borlaug, S., and Hanson, J. (2015). Emerging hybrid practices in public–private research centres. *Public Administration*, 93(2), 363–379.

Guston, D.H. (1996). Principal–agent theory and the structure of science policy. *Science and Public Policy*, 23, 229–240.

Heinze, T. (2008). How to sponsor ground-breaking research: A comparison of funding schemes. *Science and Public Policy*, 35, 802–818.

Hood, C. (1986). *The Tools of Government*. Chatham House, London.

Howlett, M. (2005). What is a policy instrument? Tool mixes and implementation styles. In: Eliadis, P., Hill, M., and Howlett, M. (Eds.), *Designing Government: From Instruments to Governance*. McGill–Queens University Press, Montreal, 31–50.

Howlett, M. (2009). Governance modes, policy regimes and operational plans: A multi-level nested model of policy instrument choice and policy design. *Policy Sciences*, 42(1), 73–89.

Jasanoff, S.S. (1987). Contested boundaries in policy-relevant science. *Social Studies of Science*, 17, 195–230.

Kaldeway, D. (2018). The grand challenge discourse: Transforming identity work in science and science policy. *Minerva*, 56, 161–182.

Kern, F., Rogge, K.S., and Howlett, M. (2019). Policy mixes for sustainability transitions: New approaches and insights through bridging innovation and policy studies. *Research Policy*, 48, 103832.

Klerkx, L., and Leeuwis, C. (2008). Delegation of authority in Research funding to networks: Experiences with a multiple goal boundary organization. *Science and Public Policy*, 35(3), 183–196.

Kuhlman, S., and Rip, A. (2018). Next generation innovation policy and grand challenges. *Science and Public Policy*, 45(4), 448–454.

Langfeldt, L., Nedeva, M., Sorlin, S., and Thomas, D.A. (2020). Co-existing notions of research quality: A framework to study context-specific understandings of good research. *Minerva*, 58, 115–137.

Laredo, P., and Mustar, P. (2002). Innovation and research policy in France (1980–2000) or the disappearance of the Colbertist state. *Research Policy*, 31(1), 55–72.

Larrue, P., Guellec, D., and Sgard, F. (2018). *New Trends in Public Research Funding*. OECD STI Outlook 2019. OECD, Paris.

Lascoumes, P., and Les Gàles, P. (2007). Introduction: Understanding public policy through its instruments – From the nature of instruments to the sociology of public policy instrumentation. *Governance*, 20(1), 1–21.

Lepori, B. (2011). Coordination modes in public funding systems. *Research Policy*, 40, 355–367.

Lepori, B., and Reale, E. (2019). The changing governance of research systems. Agencification and organizational differentiation in research funding organizations. In: *Handbook on Science and Public Policy*. Edward Elgar, Cheltenham, 448–463.

Lepori, B., Dinges, M., Potì, B., Reale, E., Slipersaeter, S., Theves, J., and Van den Besselaar,P. (2007). Comparing the evolution of national research policies: What patterns of change? *Science and Public Policy*, 34(6), 372–388.

Lepori, B., Reale, E., and Laredo, P. (2014). Logics of integration and actors' strategies in European Joint Programs. *Research Policy*, 43, 391–402.

Lepori, B., Reale, E., and Spinello, A.O. (2018). Conceptualizing and measuring performance orientation of research funding systems. *Research Evaluation*, 27(3), 171–183.

Martin, B. (2003). *Science and Innovation. Rethinking the Rationales for Funding and Governance*. Edward Elgar, Cheltenham.

Martin, B. (2016). R&D policy instruments. A critical review of what we do and don't know. *Industry and Innovation*, 23(2), 157–176.

Mathisen, W.C. (1996). Research priority areas and R&D programmes in Norway. *Science and Public Policy*, 23(4), 251–260.

Mazzucato, M. (2018). Mission-oriented innovation policies: Challenges and opportunities. *Industrial and Corporate Change*, 27, 803–815.

Nedeva, M. (2013). Between the global and the national: Organising European science. *Research Policy*, 42, 220–230.

Nedeva, M., and Wedlin, L. (2015). From "Science in Europe" to "European Science". In: Wdlin, L., and Nedeva, M. (Eds.), *Towards European Science. Dynamics and Policy of an Evolving European Research Space*. Edward Elgar, Cheltenham.

North, D.C. (1990). *Institutions, Institutional Change and Economic Performance*. Cambridge University Press, Cambridge.

OECD (2018). Effective operation of competitive research funding systems. Policy Paper no. 57.

OECD (2021). What is STIP Compass? Available from https://stip.oecd.org/About.html, retrieved May 7 2021.

Peters, B.G. (2005). Policy instruments and policy capacity. In: Painter M., and Pierre J. (Eds.), *Challenges to State Policy Capacity*. Palgrave Macmillan, London.

Pierson, P. (1993). When effect becomes Cause: Policy feedback and policy change. *World Politics*, 45(4), 595–628.

Polzer, M., and Höllerer, S. (2016). Institutional hybridity in public sector reform: Replacement, blending, or layering of administrative paradigms. In *How Institutions Matter!* Emerald, Bingley, 69–99.

Potì, B., and Reale, E. (2007), Changing allocation models for public research funding: An empirical exploration based on project funding data, *Science and Public Policy*, 34, 417–430.

Primeri, E., Reale, E. et al. (2014), Measuring the opening of national R&D programs: What indicators for what purposes? *Research Evaluation*, 23(4), 312–326.

Reale, E. (2017). Analysis of National Public Research Funding – PREF. Final Report. JRC Technical Report. Publications Office of the European Union, Luxembourg, 190–198; doi: 10(19140).

Reale, E., and Seeber, M. (2013). Instruments as empirical evidence for the analysis of higher education policies. *Higher Education*, 65, 135–151.

Reale, E., Spinello, A., and Zinilli, A. (2021). The diversity of policy instruments for public R&D funding: The role of research councils. ECPR General Conference, 31 August to 3 September, https://ecpr.eu/Events/Event/PaperDetails/57946.

Salamon, L. (2002). *The Tools of Government: A Guide to the New Governance*. Oxford University Press, Oxford.

Senker, J. (2006). Reflections on the transformations of European Public Sector Research. *Innovation The European Journal of Social Science Research*, 19(1), 67–77.

Scherngell, T., and Lata, R. (2013). Towards an integrated European Research Area? Findings from Eigenvector spatially filtered spatial interaction models using European Framework Programme data. *Papers in Regional Science*, 92(3), 555–577.

Schot, J., and Steinmueller, E. (2018). Three frames for innovation policy: R&D, systems of innovation and transformative change. *Research Policy*, 47(9), 1554–1567.

Shove, E. (2003). Principals, agents and R&D programmes. *Science and Public Policy*, 30(5), 371–381.

Skelcher, C., and Smith, S.R. (2015). Theorizing hybridity: Institutional logics, complex organizations, and actor identities: The case of nonprofits. *Public Administration*, 93(2), 433–448.

Thèves, J., Lepori, B., and Larédo, P. (2007). Changing patterns of public research funding in France. *Science and Public Policy*, 34, 389–399.

van der Meulen, B. (1998), Science policies as principal–agent games: Institutionalization and path dependency in the relation between government and science. *Research Policy*, 27, 397–414.

van der Meulen, B. (2003). New roles and strategies of a research council: Intermediation of the principal–agent relationship. *Science and Public Policy*, 30(5), 323–336.

Vedung, E. (2007). Policy instruments: Typologies and theories. In Bemelmans-Videc, M., Rist, R.C., and Vedung, E. (eds.), *Sticks Carrots and Sermons. Policy Instruments and Their Evaluation*. Transaction, New Brunswick, NJ, 21–58.

Verhoest, K., Roness, P.G., Verschure, B., Rubecksen, K., and Carhaigh, M.M. (2009). *Autonomy and Control in State Agencies*. Palgrave Macmillan, Basingstoke.

Wallace, M.L., and Rafols, I. (2015). Research portfolio analysis in science policy: Moving from financial returns to societal benefits. *Minerva*, 53, 89–115.

Wang, J., Lee, Y., and Walsh, J.P. (2018). Funding model and creativity in science: Competitive versus block funding and status contingency effects. *Research Policy*, 47(6), 1070–1083.

Weinberg, A.M (1974). Science and trans-science. *Minerva*, 10(2), 209–222.

Zacharewicz, T., Lepori, B., Reale, E., and Jonkers, K. (2019). Performance-based research funding in EU Member States – A comparative assessment. *Science and Public Policy*, 46(1), 105–115.

8. Size matters! On the implications of increasing the size of research grants

Carter Bloch, Alexander Kladakis and Mads P. Sørensen

INTRODUCTION

In recent years, growing attention has been placed on inequality in science. While the science system has always been characterised by a high degree of stratification (Price, 1963; Merton, 1968; Cole and Cole, 1973), recent studies indicate a strengthening of trends towards concentration of resources, rewards and recognition (Ma et al., 2015; Mongeon et al., 2016; Aagaard et al., 2020; Katz and Matter, 2020; Nielsen and Andersen, 2021). Developments over time, with increased reliance on competitive funding and declining success rates, can impact researchers' strategies for conducting research and obtaining funding (see Laudel, Chapter 16 in this *Handbook*). Competition is thus undergoing change along with funding conditions, where funding practices also act to shape understandings of competition (see Arora-Jonsson et al., Chapter 11 in this *Handbook*).

Recent studies document an intensification in funding inequality and concentration in global science (see e.g. Larivière, 2010; Bol et al., 2018; Katz and Matter, 2020). Policies play a key role in these developments, particularly through the design of funding instruments, where a focus on larger research grants can contribute to resource concentration. The distribution of funding has repercussions for the science system at all levels, from individual researchers to institutions, regions, and disciplines (e.g., Fortin and Currie, 2013; Bol et al., 2018; Madsen and Aagaard, 2020). This raises issues concerning the consequences of increased concentration of research funding.

Motivated by this recent surge in studies addressing the concentration of funding and its consequences, this chapter will explore how the trends, rationales and implications of increases in the size of grants have developed in recent years. The purpose of the chapter is to provide an overview of the potential positive and negative impacts of increases in the size of research funding and existing evidence on the role of size. With further evidence, the chapter extends an earlier paper (Bloch and Sørensen, 2015), in which we examined the role of size in competitive research funding for individual and project grants. First, we examine the potential implications of trends towards increasing grant sizes and larger grant forms. Next, we synthesise the rationales behind these trends and discuss the implications of more recent developments. Finally, we take a closer look at recent empirical examples of increases in the average size of grants. Government R&D programmes are very diverse and complex, with many steps from policy to instruments, and with a variety of objectives (see also Reale et al., Chapter 7 in this *Handbook*). This complexity is also visible in the plethora of different funding configurations of researchers. In this *Handbook*, Thomas and Ramos-Vielba (Chapter 15) explore how research and impacts are influenced by the interplay of funding strands among collaborative researchers.

Despite a general lack of accessible data on developments in the size of grants across countries, Bloch and Sørensen (2015) found several indications of increases in funding size, but also cases where increases had not taken place. Based on a review of the literature, we identified a number of rationales behind larger grant forms, spanning from large individual or project grants to research centres. These included economies of scale in research and redistribution of resources towards top researchers as a means to increase scientific productivity and the likelihood of fostering pathbreaking research. However, these rationales should be contrasted with potential negative effects of increases in the size of grants, and the concentration of funding among a smaller number of researchers.

In recent years, the issue of funding concentration and its implications has received growing attention with results indicating that concentration and inequality in research are intensifying (Aagaard et al., 2020; Nielsen and Andersen, 2021; Bol et al., 2018; Petersen and Penner, 2014; Madsen and Aagaard, 2020). The possible ramifications of such patterns can be particularly severe for early career researchers (see e.g. Melkers, Woolley and Kreth, Chapter 18 in this *Handbook* on the relation between research funding and careers).

Research grants can take on many forms. In this chapter we focus on three stylised forms. The first is standard research project grants, which typically can range from 100,000 to 300,000 USD. The second is larger grant forms, in particular individual grants with larger amounts and often longer durations. The third form is research centre grants.

The chapter is structured in the following way. First, we examine international *trends* towards increased funding sizes. We look at empirical examples of developments in the average size of existing grants – from a range of different countries – as well as shifts in the allocation of external funding to larger grant forms. Our focus is on individual and project grants or centre grants, as opposed to block grants to universities. Second, we look at the *rationales* behind more recent developments and survey the literature from before and after 2015 when our original paper was published. We present the arguments pro and contra increased grant sizes and subsume arguments under seven overall but closely related categories: Efficiency/productivity, Administration, Excellence, Matthew-effects, Socioeconomic impact, Epistemic impact, and Equity. Third, we review evidence on the *impact* of increased funding sizes. Finally, we offer a brief conclusion.

TRENDS TOWARDS INCREASED FUNDING SIZES AND LARGER GRANT FORMS

Research funding systems have undergone major changes in the last decades. Worldwide there has been a shift away from a national trust-based system of funding towards a more performance-based system. Within the new performance-based system, Sörlin (2007, p. 426) points to a number contemporary trends, such as increased project-based funding, new laws for tax deductible contributions towards university research, and the expanding role of research in industry and broader society, that have fuelled the rise of academic superstars and a resulting 'winner takes all' trend in funding. A further potential implication of these trends is a concentration of funding in larger project grants and other, larger grant forms, such as large individual fellowships or research centres, partly at the expense of individual and smaller grants.

Our previous study (Bloch and Sørensen, 2015) was complicated by data limitations on basic grant characteristics such as average grant size. However, we generally found a trend towards significant increases in the size of grants in many countries, although with notable exceptions. For this chapter, we have collected additional data on funding and grant sizes across a range of funding organisations in a number of countries. Our analysis shows that the trend still exists in a number of countries, with continued increases in grant sizes in, for example, Denmark, Switzerland and the UK. However, average funding sizes have remained at more stable levels for many other countries and funding organisations over the past decade.

The development of the research funding system in Denmark provides an illustrative example of the trend towards increases in grant sizes. Over the course of the past two to three decades, the Danish funding system has experienced significant increases in larger grant forms, such as e.g. centres of excellence funded by the Danish National Research Foundation, along with a general increase in the size of individual project grants. For the period 2015–2020, the average size of centre grants from the Danish National Research Foundation was around 62.5 million DKK (approx. 10 million USD). In 2001, 65% of all project grants from the Council for Independent Research were below 1 million DKK (approx. 170,000 USD), while 19% of grants were above 1.5 million DKK (approx. 260,000 USD) (Bloch et al., 2011). In 2009, the share of small grants for less than 1 million DKK had dropped to 16%, while the share of project grants for more than 1.5 million DKK had increased to 70%. In the period 2001–2019, the average size of project grants had increased from 1.0 to 3.2 million DKK, an increase of 313% (237% in real terms). One consequence of this development has been that the success rate dropped from 28% in 2001 to 12% in 2009. Since then, it has remained relatively low and was at 15% in 2019.

When examining the six most prominent grant types from the Norwegian Research Council, we found that the average grant size has increased by 48% from 2011 to 2020 (from 1.47 million NOK to 2.18 million NOK).[1] Average grant sizes have also increased at the Swiss National Science Foundation (SNSF). Grants at the SNSF are grouped into four categories (Projects, Careers, Programmes and Infrastructure), and all types have increased in average size during the period from 2005 to 2020. For example, the average grant size for Projects increased from 238,000 CHF in 2005 to 534,000 CHF in 2020.[2]

Ma et al. (2015) study developments in the distribution of research funding from the UK Engineering and Physical Sciences Research Council over a period from 1985 to 2013. They find large increases in the total amount of grant money available in the system and in the number of grants allocated. Moreover, they find a substantial increase in the average size of grants during the period studied (from around 200,000 GBP to more than 600,000 GBP).

At the National Science Foundation (NSF) in the US there was a 41% increase (in current dollars) from 2000 to 2005 in the annual mean award size provided by the NSF, from $101,200 to $142,600 per year (NSF, 2007, pp. 4–5) This increase in the size of awards was motivated by the wish to 'increase productivity by minimising the time PIs (principle investigators) would spend writing multiple proposals and managing administrative tasks, providing increased stability for supporting graduate students, and facilitating collaborations to address particularly complex issues' (NSF, 2007, p. 5). However, in more recent years, average grant sizes at the NSF have remained at a stable level, with increases similar to inflation rates. From 2012 to 2022, average grant sizes rose by 9% from 164,700 USD to 179,900 USD.[3]

If we turn to the National Institutes of Health in the US (NIH), the average grant size has increased by 15% in nominal terms during the period from 2014 to 2020,[4] which is similar to the increase in prices (the GDP deflator index for the USA increased by around 11% over the same period). The NIH also funds larger research centres, although funding devoted to these centres has decreased in relative terms. In all, the NIH awarded 8.3 times more funding for individual research projects than research centres in 1995, increasing to 10.9 in 2017.[5]

In Bloch and Sørensen (2015), we found that grant sizes for independent research projects (Discovery Projects) from the Australian Research Council (ARC) had not increased in recent years, though new and larger funding instruments had been introduced. These include Centres of Excellence schemes and the Future Fellowship funding programmes, which were introduced in 2008 to attract and maintain top researchers in Australia. The average size of these new and larger funding constructions was around double the size of that for Discovery Project grants and accounted for around 15% of total ARC grant funding in 2011. Funding sizes have generally remained similar in the more recent period from 2013 to 2020. Average sizes of the three grant types (Discovery project, Future Fellowships and Centres of Excellence) have more or less followed inflation rates, although the share of overall funding devoted to Future Fellowships declined by 40% from 2013 to 2020.[6]

In Japan, Shibayama (2011) finds that a shift took place during the period from 1976 to 2005, from small grants (< 10 million JPY) to large grants (> 100 million JPY). In 1976–1980, 66% of funding went to small grants and none to large grants, while shares of small grants fell to 32% in 2001–2005 and up to around 20% for large grants. However, the average size of smaller project grants fell from 2005 to 2011.

Excellence initiatives have been launched in a number of countries, in some cases taking up a fair share of total public research funds. In the Nordic countries relatively comprehensive Centre of Excellence (CoE) schemes have been introduced in Denmark, Finland, Norway, and Sweden over the past 20 years (Aksnes et al., 2012). In Germany, Excellence Initiatives were launched in 2005, with a budget of €1.9 billion ($2.5 billion) (DFG, 2013). Here, 10.2% of the total budget or 747.5 million EUR (977 million USD) was spent on Clusters of Excellence funding from 2008 to 2010. This share has remained fairly constant from 2010 to 2020. The Excellence initiative led to an increase in the relative share of funding devoted to larger grant forms. The share of individual research grants went down from 39.9% in the period 1999–2001 to 28.7% in the period from 2008–2010 (DFG, 2003, p. 27; DFG, 2012, p. 37). In the period since 2010, the share of funding devoted to individual research grants has risen to around 33% in 2019.[7]

RATIONALES FOR AND AGAINST INCREASED GRANT SIZES

As was the case in 2015 (Bloch and Sørensen, 2015), the evidence based on the examples provided in the previous section is mixed. While an increase in the size of standard research project grants can be documented for a number of national science systems, the picture is not uniform in all the countries examined. As evidenced, increasing emphasis has in more recent decades been placed on much larger grant forms, such as Centres of Excellence. In the following, we explore in detail the rationales for and against such increases in funding size and subsume arguments under seven analytical categories: Efficiency/Productivity, Administration, Excellence, Matthew effects, Socioeconomic impact, Epistemic effects, and Equity.

While we for purposes of clarity, view it as helpful to present these seven types of implications as analytically separate, they are in reality intricately intertwined. For example, arguments tied to 'administrative costs' are closely connected to 'efficiency and productivity'.

Similarly, 'excellence'-related arguments and arguments tied to social mechanisms such as that of 'the Matthew effect' also share common traits. For all seven categories, an overview of the arguments for and against increased grant sizes is shown in Table 8.1. For the most part, these arguments are relevant for all three grant forms considered here (i.e. project grants, large individual grants and centre grants), although some arguments are tied to centre grants specifically.

Efficiency/Productivity

Under the broad category of Efficiency and productivity, we find the argument that an increase in the size of research grants allows for the critical mass necessary to promote and achieve scientific excellence. According to this logic of argumentation, scientific production, impact and performance are believed to scale with an increase in the size of research grants (Bonaccorsi and Daraio, 2005; Bloch and Sørensen, 2015; Bloch et al., 2016; Hellström et al., 2017). Moreover, large grants are also thought to allow for the creation of critical mass in terms of equipment, infrastructure, intellectual capacity and expertise that can enhance research performance (Breschi and Malerba, 2011; Bloch et al., 2016; Aagaard et al., 2020). A commonly held notion here is that bigger is simply better (Bonaccorsi and Daraio, 2005). According to this strand of argumentation, funding should be distributed in large grants to avoid the dilution of resources, optimise the use of productive resources and in turn increase productivity (von Tunzelmann et al., 2003; Bonaccorsi and Daraio, 2005; Hicks and Katz, 2011; Vaesen and Katzav, 2017).

However, as found in the literature, several contributions suggest that an increase in the size of research funding may in fact lead to diseconomies of scale (Johnston, 1994; von Tunzelmann et al., 2003; Bloch et al., 2016). Several studies find that there may be economies of scale for grants up until a certain threshold level after which decreasing returns set in (Bonaccorsi and Daraio, 2005; Nag et al., 2013; Bloch et al., 2016). Similarly, studies point to decreasing marginal returns – a stagnation in the productivity and citation impact of research – with grants above a certain level (Breschi and Malerba, 2011; Berg, 2012; Fortin and Currie, 2013; Bloch and Sørensen, 2015; Doyle et al., 2015; Lorsch, 2015; Bloch et al., 2016; Mongeon et al., 2016; Wahls, 2018a, 2018b). As Breschi and Malerba (2011) remark, one consequence of the excessive focus, in recent years, on achieving critical mass has been the formation of 'too large' projects and research consortia as well as the artificial enlargement of partnerships well beyond optimal levels of efficiency and productivity.

A number of empirical studies suggest that spreading out grants on more researchers at moderate funding levels is a better funding strategy, on average yielding more high-impact articles than handing out big grants to a lower number of researchers (Lorsch, 2015; Fortin and Currie, 2013; Mongeon et al., 2016). Another central efficiency-related argument in favour of resource dispersal is that the excess size of research projects and grants can lead to fragmentation and problems with coordination within large research teams and consortia (Alberts, 1985; Breschi and Malerba, 2011; Nag et al., 2013).

Administration

Connected to discussions of efficiency and productivity are also arguments related to administration and bureaucracy. Here, a key argument for distributing funding in fewer and bigger

Table 8.1   Rationales behind increased grant sizes

Topics	Arguments in favour of increased grant sizes	Arguments against increased grant sizes
Efficiency/ productivity	• Economies of scale: scale return in performance/ productivity with an increase in grant size • Optimal use of resources – avoiding dilution of resources • Critical mass in terms of pooling of intellectual capacity, equipment and research infrastructure • 'Bigger is better': grants and research units should be large in order to increase productivity	• Diseconomies of scale: decreasing returns to research with an increase in grant size • Decreasing marginal returns: grants above a certain size result in diminishing marginal returns measured as scientific production and impact • Focus on achieving critical mass has been excessive resulting in artificially large research grants, projects, teams and consortia • Excess size of research grants leading to fragmentation and problems with coordination within large research groups and consortia • Productivity and performance can be enhanced via support for smaller and medium-sized grants
Administration	• Lower assessment costs and smaller administrative burden • Allocation of funding in smaller grants requires extra scrutiny, is more costly and adds to the administrative burden	• *Centres:* excess size of research projects may lead to cumbersome levels of administration, coordination and problems with management within large teams, centres and consortia • *Centres:* may turn good scientists into 'science managers' using most of their time on administration
Excellence	• Large-scale funding will maximise scientific impact and the likelihood of making new discoveries • Resource stability that can facilitate autonomy, the pursuit of novel ideas, and riskier research • Excellence schemes are expected to generate critical mass, the pooling of resources and expertise, facilitate interdisciplinarity, research training and international visibility	• Spreading research resources across many scientists through smaller grants may result in more value for money in terms of high-impact articles • *Centres:* the system still incentivises centre grant recipients to apply for further funds, which in turn puts pressure on other non-grant-holding researchers and the system as a whole
Matthew effects	• Larger grants intensify and accelerate the concentration of research resources on successful groups and scientists • Social mechanisms in science and funding policies act to limit too unequal distributions of funding	• The winning of an early career grant – and not merit in itself – improves the chances of later funding and career success. Large grants magnify this process • Failure to win an early career grant will diminish chances of getting funding at a later stage and even discourage future participation in funding competitions
Socioeconomic impact	• *Centres:* large-scale funding directly or indirectly promotes industry–science collaboration, thereby strengthening the impact of research on innovation and international competitiveness • *Centres:* by building strong research centres within areas deemed of strategic economic importance, research is directed towards economic goals and enhances the quality of research within selected areas	• Little evidence for increased scientific productivity through concentration of resources in larger grants • Consortium and centre grants can get too big, leading to decreasing productivity

Topics	Arguments in favour of increased grant sizes	Arguments against increased grant sizes
Epistemic effects	• Facilitates research capacity and stimulates scientific development and advances • *Centres and large individual grants:* large-scale funding schemes such as centres of excellence or large individual grants allow for resource availability, stability and flexibility to pursue 'high-risk/high-gain research'	• More grantees will increase the number of experiments and thereby the likelihood of scientific breakthroughs • Increasing the number of grant holders reduces the risk of accumulated failure and provides better conditions for risk-taking • Increasing the number of grant holders and funded areas increases the diversity of fields of research and the range of opportunities available to students and researchers
Equity	• Funding should follow performance – the best performers should have more and larger grants • Spreading funding in smaller grants and on more researchers leads to the dilution of resources and funding bodies renouncing their control over the course of science	• Need for more fair distribution of resources among qualified researchers, through more and smaller grants

grant portions is the smaller administrative burden and assessment costs per funded unit (Johnston, 1994; Berg, 2012; Dimke et al., 2019). Berg (2012) describes how policies in the NIH aimed at capping funding per principal investigator and reducing resource concentration met criticism for adding to the administrative burden. According to the critique, the allocation of funding in smaller grants would require extra scrutiny and additional resources for lengthy peer-review evaluation procedures.

On the other hand, a key argument against resource concentration is that excess size of consortium and network grants can lead to cumbersome levels of administration, coordination and problems with management of partners (Alberts, 1985; Breschi and Malerba, 2011; Nag et al., 2013; Kimble et al., 2015). Alberts (1985) early on pointed out that concentration of funding may turn group leaders in big research teams into 'science managers' who spend nearly all their time on grant writing, science administration, and organisational matters, leaving little time for doing actual research and mentoring students and junior staff (see also Kimble et al., 2015).

Excellence

While the main rationale for the concentration of funding for many years has centred around achieving benefits related to critical mass and economies of scale (Johnston, 1994), focus has in more recent decades shifted towards excellence (Sørensen et al., 2016) and the concentration of funding among top researchers, both to increase production of high-quality research and to enhance conditions for the generation of scientific breakthroughs. Here, the main rationale is that the best researchers are the most productive, with the greatest potential to produce high-quality research and groundbreaking results (Hicks and Katz, 2011). Hence, the most efficient allocation of resources is to provide the very best with optimal material conditions for conducting research.

The increasing attention on excellence has globally resulted in a number of excellence funding schemes, primarily aimed at providing financial support for the setting up of so-called Centres of Excellence. If we consider the rationales for investing in large-scale CoE schemes, the arguments revolve around the maximisation of productivity, scientific impact, and providing optimal conditions for making new discoveries (Ida and Fukuzawa, 2013; Bloch et al., 2016). Another argument in favour of CoE schemes is that large-scale centre grants provide researchers with resource stability in terms of long-term generous funding that can facilitate autonomy, the pursuit of novel ideas, and riskier research (Hellström et al., 2017).

Among the arguments against the 'excellence'-agenda in science, and in line with the rationale that resource concentration may lead to inefficiencies of scale, Breschi and Malerba (2011) suggest that sustaining excellence may be more difficult with an increase in the size of projects and consortia. In other words, funding strategies targeting diversity, i.e., spreading research resources on many smaller grants and scientists, is according to this line of reasoning expected to yield more value for money in terms of high-impact articles than pursuing funding policies aimed at achieving excellence by way of concentrating resources among the few (Fortin and Currie, 2013). Finally, while excellence schemes were initially put in place to free the most capable researchers from the arduous task of writing grant applications, the system still incentivises centre grant recipients to apply for further funds, which in turn puts pressure on other non-grant holding researchers and the system as a whole (Sandström et al., 2010).

Matthew Effects

Scientific productivity and access to research resources is unevenly distributed among researchers (Stephan, 1996; Hicks and Katz, 2011). While some of these dissimilarities undoubtedly have to do with individual level variations in talent, effort and efficiency, differences in productivity and achievement cannot solely be explained by ability, hard work and motivation, but must also be understood as 'cumulative advantage' and the ability to leverage past successes (Stephan, 1996). As a process of social selection, the Matthew effect intensifies and accelerates the concentration of research resources on successful groups and scientists (Merton, 1968; Franssen and de Rijcke, 2019; Katz and Matter, 2020). However, it is suggested that there are limits to cumulative advantage and that various social mechanisms in science act to limit too unequal distributions of funding (Bloch et al., 2016). Moreover, policies put in place by funding agencies such as NIH that try to reduce funding for well-off investigators seem to suggest that reverse Matthew effects might work to curb tendencies toward uncontrolled resource concentration (Berg, 2012).

There are however undeniable and well-documented negative effects of the Matthew effect, as it sets in motion processes of cumulative advantage where the winning of an early career grant significantly improves the chances of later funding and career success, while non-winners do not reap the same career benefits (Bol et al., 2018). Whereas early funding success will promote continued participation in the competition for funding, early career failure to win a grant will discourage future participation in funding competitions (Bol et al., 2018, p. 4887). The handing out of larger grants will magnify this process. In addition, it has been pointed out that the Matthew effect as a social mechanism undermines meritocracy in science as researchers who have been fortunate to begin with benefit from self-perpetuating processes of accumulative advantage, while similarly talented but less fortunate early career scholars do not (Bol et al., 2018).

Socioeconomic Impact

A core socioeconomic argument for large scale funding is that it directly or indirectly promotes industry–science collaboration and thereby strengthens the impact of research on innovation and international competitiveness (Bonaccorsi and Daraio, 2005; Rogers et al., 2012). Strong research centres located in areas of strategic economic importance can help to direct research towards societal goals and to enhance the quality of research within these areas.

In their study, Bonaccorsi and Daraio (2005) examine whether the creation of large research organisations such as the French National Centre for Scientific Research and the French National Institute of Health and Medical Research enhances scientific productivity. This might be expected due to proximity, i.e. that bigger units facilitate personal interaction, face-to-face communication, transmission of tacit knowledge etc. – or a reduction of costs caused by agglomeration. However, based on a study of the French National Institute of Health and Medical Research in France and Italian National Research Council in Italy, Bonaccorsi and Daraio (2005) do not find evidence supporting the idea that a concentration of resources into larger institutes will lead to an upsurge in scientific productivity. This conclusion is supported by Breschi and Malerba's (2011) findings. Examining the scientific productivity effects of the European Union's 6th framework programme, they find that grants and consortia can get too big. According to them, scientific productivity increases up to a certain point when consortia grow in size – beyond this point decreasing marginal returns can be observed.

Epistemic Effects

Another line of argumentation identified in the literature is concerned with the epistemic effects of funding policies either targeting 'selectivity' or 'diversity'. Studies that high-light benefits associated with an increase in grant size point to resource concentration as a way to achieve certain positive epistemic effects (Hellström et al., 2017). For instance, it is assumed that concentration of resources in large centres or units can facilitate research capacity and stimulate scientific development and advances (Hellström et al., 2017). The argument here is that selectivity in the distribution of funding will secure enough resources for the most capable and productive scientists, who also have the greatest potential to produce path-breaking research results (Hicks and Katz, 2011; Bloch and Sørensen, 2015; Aagaard et al., 2020). Another argument for focusing effort through concentration of research funds is that large-scale funding schemes such as centres of excellence allow for resource availability, stability and flexibility to pursue 'high-risk/high-gain research' (Hellström et al., 2017).

On the other hand, if each grantee is seen as an experiment, many grantees will increase the number of experiments and thereby the likelihood of scientific breakthroughs. A funding strategy aimed at selectivity or concentration, i.e. handing out large grants to a smaller number of investigators, is perceived as risky because it reduces the number of experiments (Fortin and Currie, 2013; Bloch and Sørensen, 2015; Aagaard et al., 2020). Therefore, one of the most frequent arguments in favour of funding strategies aimed at diversity is that spreading out smaller grants on a larger number of researchers and thereby supporting a greater number of investigators at moderate funding levels spreads risk and provides better conditions for risk-taking. This again increases the potential for transformative research and the chances of scientific breakthroughs (Lorsch, 2015; Kimble et al., 2015; Aagaard et al., 2020).

Another advantage of diversifying research investments is that making more small and medium-sized grants available to a larger pool of researchers increases the diversity of fields of research and the range of opportunities available to PhD students and researchers (von Tunzelmann et al., 2003; Dimke et al., 2019; Aagaard et al., 2020).

Equity

Resource concentration has an adverse effect on equity in science. Equity can be enhanced by distributing research funds more evenly to 'support economic development, strengthen research and enhance diversity and participation in the research enterprise' (Hicks and Katz, 2011, p. 143).

On the other hand, if funding distributions are too heavily informed by equity considerations the best researchers might lose incentives for applying (Hicks and Katz, 2011). Along the lines of this argument, decision makers do not dare to match resource allocation with the extremely unequal distribution of research performance due to an inequality aversion inherent in the science system (Hicks and Katz, 2011). Another critique levelled at egalitarian funding schemes is that such practices could lead to the dilution of resources and funding bodies renouncing their control over the course of science (Hicks and Katz, 2011).

Also, gender imbalances in research have received increasing attention, prompting the examination of potential sources of gender bias in peer review and other forms of scientific assessment (Addis, 2010; European Commission, 2008). Given that gender imbalances are greatest for the highest academic positions, such as professorships, concerns can be raised that a growing focus on large research initiatives such as centres will exacerbate existing gender inequalities (Sandström et al., 2010; Aksnes et al., 2012; DFG, 2012).

EMPIRICAL EVIDENCE ON GRANT SIZE AND PERFORMANCE

Empirical evidence on the impact of project size for grants is fairly limited, though a larger number of analyses have been conducted that are related to the topic. This includes for example analyses of the role of group size (Von Tunzelmann et al., 2003; Johnston, 1994; University Alliance, 2011; Seglen and Aksnes, 2000), of funding acknowledgements (Rigby and Julian, 2014), of large research centres (Sandström et al., 2010; Aksnes et al., 2012; Rogers et al., 2012; Ida and Fukuzawa, 2013; Bloch et al., 2016), and of total funds per researcher (Ma et al., 2015; Mongeon et al., 2016; Katz and Matter, 2017; Shibayama, 2011).

Several studies have examined the role of large research centres, and while these analyses are relevant to the issue of grant size, they do not provide direct evidence on the relation between grant size and performance (see for instance Sandström et al., 2010; Aksnes et al., 2012; Rogers et al., 2012; Ida and Fukuzawa, 2013; and Bloch et al., 2016).

A limited number of studies have looked specifically at the relation between grant size and research performance. In some cases, the studies have only measured productivity in terms of number of publications, though most have considered both productivity and some measure of scientific impact, either journal impact, citation impact or the number of highly cited articles. The general result from these studies is that while both the number of publications and citation impact typically increase with grant size, there are decreasing marginal returns. Measured per dollar spent, these few studies generally find that both publications and impact are decreasing in grant size. However, as indicated by the description below, evidence is limited and based on varying methods. These range from analysis based on survey and qualitative interview responses to statistical analysis of the relation between grant size and different output measures.

Among the limited number of analyses that look specifically at the role of size for research grants, an example is an NIH analysis of the scientific productivity of researchers funded by grants from the NIH National Institute of General Medical Sciences for 2006 (Wadman, 2010). The statistical analysis compares the number of publications with grant amounts, finding that the median number of publications was highest for medium sized grants, peaking at around 750,000 USD. However, in terms of publications per dollar spent, the smallest grants at around 250,000 USD had the highest productivity. The analysis, however, does not look into other performance measures such as citation impacts, nor does it account for factors such as experience, discipline or prior funding.

Two other studies, the first for the NSF and the second for the Danish Council for Independent Research, look in more detail at the role of size for project grants. The NSF commissioned a study on precisely this topic, on principal investigators' (PI) perceptions concerning grant size and duration. The study relies solely on a survey of PIs perceptions and thus did not measure impact on scientific productivity (Ballou et al., 2002). The study covered all PIs for the fiscal year 2001 (in all 4,989). Grant sizes were small to medium sized, with roughly a third each under 162,000 USD, between 162,000 and 330,000 USD, and over 330,000 USD. Respondents noted limitations owing to both amount and length, citing time spent writing proposals and lack of continuity as key reasons why grant size and duration should be increased. However, taking funding constraints into consideration, there is a trade-off between size and success rates, i.e., the larger the grants, the smaller the number of researchers that can receive them. If forced to choose between increasing the amount only, the duration only, or the number of awards, 40% of PIs chose amounts, 24% length and the remaining 36% the number of awards.

A study of grants from the Danish Council for Independent Research covered project grants of a similar size as those for NSF, focusing on a broad range of impacts, both qualitative and quantitative (Bloch et al., 2011; Bloch et al., 2014). Bibliometric analysis on a matched sample of PIs and rejected applicants indicated that PIs for larger projects (over 160,000 USD) had both a higher number of publications and citation rates before and after the grant period, and also a larger increase in productivity over the period. In contrast, survey responses on the number of publications for projects as a whole suggested that the average number of peer-reviewed articles per 100,000 USD granted was substantially higher for small projects (under 160,000 USD), more than double that for larger projects in four out of five main fields. It was not possible to confirm this result via funding acknowledgements or project reporting. Smaller grants were predominantly awarded to early career researchers, and according to interviews with them were used to kick-start their careers and establish them in academia (Degn et al., 2011). The increase in number of publications from these grants was therefore not related to smaller grants benefitting from work previously carried out on bigger grants.

Similar to developments in Denmark, Fortin and Currie (2013) note a shift in funding practice at the National Science and Engineering Research Center in Canada from awarding a large number of small grants to a focus on a smaller number of large grants. Motivated by this change, they use regression analysis to examine the relation between grant size and four indicators across different disciplines: number of publications, number of citations, most cited articles and number of highly cited articles. For all four measures, they find that performance is increasing with grant size, but with diminishing returns, particularly for impact. Hence, the authors find that both publications and citations per dollar funded are decreasing with grant size.

Danthi et al. (2014) compare NIH grants that were allocated as part of the regular budget ('de novo R01 grants') of the NIH with grants that were distributed through the same programme, but through funding provided by the American Recovery and Reinvestment Act (ARRA). ARRA-funded grants were from the same NIH programme, but were smaller, of a shorter duration and had fared less well in peer review (i.e. they would not have received funding without the additional ARRA funds). Hence, this offers both an opportunity to examine the role of grant size through statistical comparison of the two grants and the effectiveness of peer review in selecting the best projects. Citation impact for each grant was normalised by subject, article type and year of publication. Multivariable linear regression models controlled for a number of factors, including peer-review grant percentile ranking, grant size, project duration, involvement of vertebrate animals and human research subjects, and the performance of a clinical trial, early-stage/new-investigator status, prior NIH funding, and number of prior NIH grants. The study finds that the number of articles and impact per dollar awarded were comparable for the two groups of grants.

Lauer et al. (2015) analyses the bibliometric outcomes of de novo cardiovascular R01 grants funded by the National Heart, Lung, and Blood Institute of the NIH between 1980 and 2011. The authors find that the number of top 10% highly cited articles per million USD is increasing in award size, but the coefficient of this increase is much less than 1.

The National Natural Science Foundation of China made a significant change in their funding practices, with large increases in both the size and duration of its grants. Increases varied across fields, for example with 70% increases in average grant size within Chemistry but much smaller increases within the Medical Sciences. Hu (2020) examines the effects of this change on several performance indicators (number of publications, journal impact-weighted publications, number of citations and highest journal impact of publications), controlling for factors such as field, affiliation, age and number of previous grants. Hu (2020) finds large positive effects for the number of publications but smaller effects for impact. However, even for publications, it is unclear whether the results imply increasing or decreasing returns to grant size. Furthermore, Hu (2020) finds that effects are by far the largest for first-time grantees or for researchers with a single previous grant, and smaller or even negative for multiple grant holders.

CONCLUSION

In this chapter, we have examined the role of size for research funding grants, both recent trends and the potential implications of increases in grant size. This study is motivated by a number of indications of increased concentration of research funding, and also by cases of significant increases in average grant sizes in the last 20 years, such as in Denmark. These trends are, however, not present in all cases, with a number of examples of countries or funding organisations where the average size of project grants has remained relatively constant in real terms. It would be interesting to take advantage of this variation to examine whether increases in grant size have improved outcomes in those funding organisations where such changes have taken place.

Above, we also explored arguments for and against increasing the size of grants, placed under seven interrelated categories: Efficiency/Productivity, Administration, Excellence, Matthew effects, Epistemic effects, Socioeconomic impact, and Equity. Efficiency or productivity-related arguments centre around ideas that a critical mass in terms of project size is needed to achieve scientific excellence and that advantages can be reaped in terms of economies of scale to research. Administrative costs are argued to make small grants too costly, although on the other hand, very large grants can require great effort to coordinate and administer.

Excellence arguments focus both on the rationale that the best researchers should have ample funding in order to achieve scientific breakthroughs, and that large grants are more likely to produce novel results. Parallel arguments are made for socioeconomic impacts, namely that large grants are more likely to produce advances that can foster innovation. Large grants are argued to intensify Matthew effects, i.e., the concentration of resources among a smaller group of successful scientists. This has been argued to be both positive as an allocation mechanism and negative as it reinforces unequal distributions of research funding – short term as well as long term.

Grant size has also been linked to epistemic effects, where large grants can be seen as better facilitating epistemic changes in research approaches. However, concentration of funding is also argued to reduce diversity in research. The peer review process has been shown to be imperfect in identifying the most promising projects and also to be subject to a number of biases, both of which can be seen as arguments for greater spreading of funding in smaller grants. Resource concentration has an adverse effect on equity in science, which can be argued to have detrimental repercussions for the science system as a whole.

Empirical analysis of the relation between grant size and research outcomes is somewhat limited. However, existing empirical evidence suggests that there are diminishing returns to grant size, measured for example in terms of number of publications, citation impact and number of highly cited papers. Basic statistical analysis comparing grant size with research outcomes shows a fairly clear pattern of decreasing returns, and qualitative interviews illustrate in particular the importance of small grants for early career researchers. However, less work has been done to control for factors that are related to research outcomes, such as research experience and prior funding and performance.

While a number of positive potential implications of increasing the size of research grants can be found, there may also be a number of adverse effects. Given this, in our view, the lack of evidence that supports positive benefits of a strong shift to larger grants and the increasing inequality in science raise questions on the merits of increased grant size. This issue should also be seen in the context of a science system with increasing competition and a growing number of early career researchers in temporary positions. Increased concentration can be seen both as a result of funding policies and as a factor that increases tensions. Efforts to restrict the number of grants per researcher, to offer smaller size grants or lotteries to reduce costs and mediate peer review biases can help to counter these developments (Adam, 2019; Fang and Casadevall, 2016; Vaesen and Katzav, 2017). In addition, more knowledge is needed both on the relation between grant size and other funding characteristics and research outcomes, and on the consequences of changes in funding landscapes for research conditions and research careers at a systemic level.

NOTES

1. https://www.forskningsradet.no/en/statistics-and-evaluations/statistics-and-evaluations/the-
    -research-councils-statistics/ (accessed 08/05/21). Total inflation for the entire period was 21%.
2. https://data.snf.ch/key-figures (accessed 11/05/21). Overall inflation for the entire period was 2.2%.
3. https://www.nsf.gov/about/budget/fy2020/pdf/04_fy2020.pdf (accessed 08/05/21).
4. https://reporter.nih.gov/search/_KEMtbKkc0iOZVjjoNiIFw/projects/chart (accessed 08/05/21).
5. https://report.nih.gov/fundingfacts/fundingfacts.aspx (accessed 11/05/21).
6. https://rms.arc.gov.au/RMS/Report/Download/Report/a3f6be6e-33f7-4fb5-98a6-7526aaa184cf/
    218; https://www.transparency.gov.au/annual-reports/australian-research-council/reporting-year/
    2018-2019-38 (both accessed 11/05/21).
7. https://www.dfg.de/download/pdf/dfg_im_profil/geschaeftsstelle/publikationen/dfg_jb2019.pdf
    (p. 198) (accessed 11/05/21).

REFERENCES

Aagaard, K., Kladakis, A., and M. W. Nielsen (2020). Concentration or dispersal of research funding? *Quantitative Science Studies*, *1*, 117–149.

Adam, D. (2019). Science funders gamble on grant lotteries. *Nature*, *575*(7785), 574–575.

Addis, E. (2010). Meta-analysis of gender and science research: Topic report – Gender and Scientific Excellence. www.genderandscience.org.

Aksnes, D., Benner, M., Borlaug, S.B., Hansen, H.F., Kallerud, E., Kristiansen, E., Langfeldt, L., Pelkonen, A., and Sivertsen, G. (2012). Centres of Excellence in the Nordic countries. NIFU Working Paper 4/2012.

Alberts, B. M. (1985). Limits to growth: in biology, small science is good science. *Cell*, *41*(2), 337–338. https://doi.org/10.1016/S0092-8674(85)80001-5.

Ballou, J., Mishkind, M., Mooney, G., and van Kammen, W. (2002). National science foundation report on efficiency of grant size and duration. National Science Foundation, Chief Budget and Systems, Operations and Budget Branch, Arlington, VA.

Berg, J. M. (2012). Well-funded investigators should receive extra scrutiny. *Nature*, *489*(7415), 203–203. https://doi.org/10.1038/489203a.

Bloch, C., and Sørensen, M. P. (2015). The size of research funding: Trends and implications. *Science and Public Policy*, *42*, 30–43. https://doi.org/10.1093/scipol/scu019.

Bloch, C., Sørensen, M. P., and Ravn, T. (2011). Evaluation of Research Project Grants of the Danish Council for Independent Research – Main report. Copenhagen: Danish Agency for Science, Technology and Innovation (in Danish).

Bloch, C., Sørensen, M. P., Graversen, E. K., Schneider, J. W., Schmidt, E. K., Aagaard, K., and Mejlgaard, N., (2014). Developing a methodology to assess the impact of research grant funding: A mixed methods approach. *Evaluation and Program Planning*, *43*, 105–117.

Bloch, C., Schneider, J. W., and Sinkjær, T. (2016). Size, accumulation and performance for research grants: Examining the role of size for centres of excellence. *PLoS One*, *11*, e0147726. https://doi.org/10.1371/journal.pone.0147726.

Bol, T., de Vaan, M., and van de Rijt, A. (2018). The Matthew effect in science funding. *Proceedings of the National Academy of Sciences of the United States of America*, *115*(19), 4887–4890. https://doi.org/10.1073/pnas.1719557115.

Bonaccorsi, A., and Daraio, C. (2005). Exploring size and agglomeration effects on public research productivity. *Scientometrics*, *63*, 87–120. https://doi.org/10.1007/s11192-005-0205-3.

Breschi, S., and Malerba, F. (2011). Assessing the scientific and technological output of EU Framework 16 Programmes: Evidence from the FP6 projects in the ICT field. *Scientometrics*, *88*, 239–257. https://doi.org/10.1007/s11192-011-0378-x.

Cole, J. R., and Cole, S. (1973). *Social Stratification in Science*. Chicago, IL: University of Chicago Press.

Danthi, N., Wu, C. O., Shi, P., and Lauer, M. (2014). Percentile ranking and citation impact of a large cohort of National Heart, Lung, and Blood Institute–funded cardiovascular R01 grants. *Circulation Research, 114*(4), 600–606.

Degn, L., Faber, S. T., and Ravn, T. (2011). Delrapport 3: Case-/interviewundersøgelsen, Evaluering af virkemidlet forskningsprojekter [Sub-report 3: Case and Interview study for the Evcaluation of the instrument Research projects]. Danish Centre for Studies in Research and Research Policy, Aarhus University. https://ufm.dk/publikationer/2011/filer-2011/3-interviewundersoegelsen.pdf.

DFG (Deutsche Forschungsgemeinschaft/German Research Foundation) (2003). Funding Ranking 2003. Institutions – Regions – Networks. DFG Approvals and Other Basic Data on Publicly Funded Research. Bonn: Deutsche Forschungsgemeinschaft. http://www.dfg.de/download/pdf/dfg_im_profil/evaluation_statistik/ranking/archiv/dfg_funding_ranki ng_2003.pdf.

DFG (Deutsche Forschungsgemeinschaft/German Research Foundation) (2012). Förderatlas 2012. Kennzahlen zur öffentlich finanzierten Forschung in Deutschland. Bonn: Deutsche Forschungs-gemeinschaft. http://www.dfg.de/download/pdf/dfg_im_profil/evaluation_statistik/foerderatlas/dfg-foerderatlas_2012.pdf.

DFG (Deutsche Forschungsgemeinschaft/German Research Foundation) (2013). DFG Video Portal on the Excellence Initiative. http://www.excellence-initiative.com/excellence-initiative.

Dimke, H., Norn, M. T., Christiansen, P. M., Wohlert, J., and Zinner, N. T. (2019). Most scientists prefer small and mid-sized research grants. *Nature Human Behaviour, 3*, 765–767.

Doyle, J. M., Quinn, K., Bodenstein, Y. A., Wu, C. O., Danthi, N., and Lauer, M. S. (2015). Association of percentile ranking with citation impact and productivity in a large cohort of de novo NIMH-funded R01 grants. *Molecular Psychiatry, 20*(9), 1030–1036. https://doi.org/10.1038/mp.2015.71.

European Commission (2008). *The Gender Challenge in Research Funding. Assessing the European National Scenes.* Luxembourg: Office for Official Publications of the European Communities.

Fang, F. C., and Casadevall, A. (2016). Research funding: The case for a modified lottery. *MBio, 7*(2), e00422–16. https://doi.org/10.1128/mBio.00422-16.

Fortin, J.-M., and Currie, D. J. (2013). Big science vs. little science: How scientific impact scales with funding. *PLoS One*, 8(6), e65263. https://doi.org/10.1371/journal.pone.0065263.

Franssen, T. and De Rijcke, S. (2019). The rise of project funding and its effects on the social structure of academia. In: Cannizzo, F., and Osbaldiston, N. (Eds.), *The Social Structures of Global Academia*. London: Routledge.

Hellström, T., Jabrane, L., and Brattström, E. (2017). Center of excellence funding: Connecting organizational capacities and epistemic effects. *Research Evaluation, 27*, 73–81. https://doi.org/10.1093/reseval/rvx043.

Hicks, D., and Katz, J. S. (2011). Equity and excellence in research funding. *Minerva, 49*, 137–151. https://doi.org/10.2307/43548599.

Hu, A. G. (2020). Public funding and the ascent of Chinese science: Evidence from the National Natural Science Foundation of China. *Research Policy, 49*(5), 103983.

Ida, T., and Fukuzawa, N. (2013). Effects of large-scale research funding programs: a Japanese case study. *Scientometrics, 94*(3), 1253–1273. https://doi.org/10.1007/s11192-012-0841-3.

Johnston, R. (1994). Effects of resource concentration on research performance. *Higher Education, 28*(1), 25–37. https://doi.org/10.1007/BF01383570.

Katz, Y., and Matter, U. (2017). On the biomedical elite: Inequality and stasis in scientific knowledge production. Berkman Klein Center Research Publication, 2017-5.

Katz, Y., and Matter, U. (2020). Metrics of inequality: The concentration of resources in the U.S. biomedical elite. *Science as Culture, 29*(4), 475–502. https://doi.org/10.1080/09505431.2019.1694882.

Kimble, J., Bement, W. M., Chang, Q., Cox, B. L., Drinkwater, N. R., Gourse, R. L., … Seidel, H. S. (2015). Strategies from UW-Madison for rescuing biomedical research in the US. *ELife, 4*, e09305. https://doi.org/10.7554/eLife.09305.

Larivière, V., Macaluso, B., Archambault, É., and Gingras, Y. (2010). Which scientific elites? On the concentration of research funds, publications and citations. *Research Evaluation, 19*(1), 45–53.

Lauer, M. S., Danthi, N. S., Kaltman, J., and Wu, C. (2015). Predicting productivity returns on investment: thirty years of peer review, grant funding, and publication of highly cited papers at the National Heart, Lung, and Blood Institute. *Circulation Research, 117*(3), 239–243.

Lorsch, J. R. (2015). Maximizing the return on taxpayers' investments in fundamental biomedical research. *Molecular Biology of the Cell, 26*(9), 1578–1582. https://doi.org/10.1091/mbc.e14-06-1163.

Ma, A., Mondragón, R. J., and Latora, V. (2015). Anatomy of funded research in science. *Proceedings of the National Academy of Sciences, 112*(48), 14760–14765.

Madsen, E. B., and Aagaard, K. (2020). Concentration of Danish research funding on individual researchers and research topics: Patterns and potential drivers. *Quantitative Science Studies, 1*(3), 1159–1181.

Merton, R. K. (1968). The Matthew effect in science. *Science, 159*(3810), 56–63.

Mongeon, P., Brodeur, C., Beaudry, C., and Larivière, V. (2016). Concentration of research funding leads to decreasing marginal returns. *Research Evaluation, 25*(4), rvw007. https://doi.org/10.1093/reseval/rvw007.

Nag, S., Yang, H., Buccola, S., and Ervin, D. (2013). Productivity and financial support in academic bioscience. *Applied Economics, 45*(19), 2817–2826. https://doi.org/10.1080/00036846.2012.676737.

National Science Foundation (NSF) (2007). Impact of Proposal and Award Management Mechanisms. Final Report, NSF 07-45, 1 August.

Nielsen, M. W., and Andersen, J. P. (2021). Global citation inequality is on the rise. *Proceedings of the National Academy of Sciences, 118*(7).

Petersen, A. M., and Penner, O. (2014). Inequality and cumulative advantage in science careers: A case study of high-impact journals. *EPJ Data Science, 3*, 1–25.

Price, D., and De Solla, J. (1963). *Little Science, Big Science.* New York: Columbia University Press. https://doi.org/10.7312/pric91844.

Rigby, J., and Julian, K. (2014). On the horns of a dilemma: does more funding for research lead to more research or a waste of resources that calls for optimization of researcher portfolios? An analysis using funding acknowledgement data. *Scientometrics.* https://doi.org/101:1067-1075. 10.1007/s11192-014-1259-x.

Rogers, J., Youtie, J., and Luciano, K. (2012). Program-level assessment of research centers: Contribution of Nanoscale Science and Engineering Centers to US Nanotechnology National Initiative goals. *Research Evaluation, 21*, 368–380.

Sandström, U., Wold, A., Jordansson, B., Ohlsson, B., and Smedberg, Å. (2010). Hans Excellens: om miljardsatsningarna på starka forskningsmiljöer. Stockholm.

Seglen, P. O., and Aksnes, D. W. (2000). Scientific productivity and group size: A bibliometric analysis of Norwegian microbiological research. *Scientometrics, 49*(1), 125–143.

Shibayama, S. (2011). Distribution of academic research funds: A case of Japanese national research grant. *Scientometrics, 88*(1), 43–60.

Sörlin, S. (2007). Funding diversity: Performance-based funding regimes as drivers of differentiation in higher education systems. *Higher Education Policy, 20*, 413–440.

Stephan, P. (1996). The economics of science. *Journal of Economic Literature, 34*, 1199–1235.

Sørensen, M. P., Bloch, C., and Young, M. (2016). Excellence in the knowledge-based economy: From scientific to research excellence. *European Journal of Higher Education, 6*(3), 217–236.

University Alliance (2011). *Funding Research Excellence: Research Group Size, Critical Mass and Performance. Report Prepared By Evidence.* London: University Alliance.

Vaesen, K., and Katzav J. (2017). How much would each researcher receive if competitive government research funding were distributed equally among researchers? *PLoS ONE, 12*(9), e0183967. https://doi.org/10.1371/journal.pone.0183967.

von Tunzelmann, N., Ranga, M., Martin, B., and Geuna, A. (2003). The effects of size on research performance: A SPRU review. Report prepared for the Office of Science and Technology, Department of Trade and Industry.

Wadman, M. (2010). Study says middle sized labs do best. *Nature, 468*, 356–357.

Wahls, W. P. (2018a). High cost of bias: Diminishing marginal returns on NIH grant funding to institutions. https://doi.org/10.1101/367847.

Wahls, W. P. (2018b). The NIH must reduce disparities in funding to maximize its return on investments from taxpayers. eLife; 7:e34965. https://doi.org/10.7554/eLife.34965.

9. Potentials and limitations of program-based research funding for the transformation of research systems

Susanne Bührer, Sarah Seus and Rainer Walz

9.1 INTRODUCTION

The aim of this chapter is to analyze the opportunities and limitations of program funding for the transformation of science systems. In recent years, various societal drivers have increased the pressure on the science system to legitimize the use of public funds. It is no longer sufficient to achieve goals intrinsic to research, such as contributing to the development of theory and methods or achieving knowledge gains. Furthermore, the contribution that research makes to solving problems matters, especially in the area of major societal challenges. This debate is strongly linked to keywords such as Sustainable Development Goals, Societal Impacts, the "New social contract of science", the mission and transformation orientation of research policy, the public value of research, next generation metrics as well as different policy frames that shape research and research funding (see also Ulnicane, Chapter 4 and Alemán-Díaz, Chapter 3 in this *Handbook*). All these keywords revolve around the questions of (1) what are legitimate expectations of science and its role in the innovation system, (2) how would internal structures and processes in the science sector need to change in order to meet external expectations, and (3) what can public research funding concretely offer to foster change. In our chapter, we focus on the question of what public program funding, in particular, can realistically contribute to initiating, shaping, accompanying, or accelerating the change processes outlined above.

The chapter is structured as follows: in the following section, we critically review the existing literature on transformative research and corresponding research funding approaches, using sustainability research as an example. The concept of (conflicting) policy frames (see also Ulnicane, Chapter 4 and Alemán-Díaz, Chapter 3 in this *Handbook*) offers a helpful lens through which these transformative changes can be described, namely the "republic of science" (Polanyi 1962) versus "the societal function of research" (Bernal 1939; cited from Ulnicane, Chapter 4 in this *Handbook*). In the third section, we describe the role of research funding for enabling but also changing research processes, before we present the German funding framework to promote sustainability research (FONA) as an empirical illustration, in Section 9.4. The chapter ends with a critical assessment of gaps and future research directions.

9.2 THE SCIENCE TRANSFORMATION DEBATE

In recent years, the concept of mission orientation has become increasingly important in research and innovation (R&I) policy and funding. Missions, which can be understood as a goal-oriented operationalization of the so-called "grand societal challenges", are characterized by their pronounced cross-cutting nature, cross-sectoral and interlocking interdependencies, broad time horizons, and high socio-economic and socio-cultural depths of intervention. It is emphasized that there can be no optimal shape of mission, but that each challenge requires a tailored form (Mazzucato 2018). The characteristics of impactful missions are considered to be having appropriate granularity and being ambitious and inspiring, and at the same time having realistic and measurable goals, as well as openness to different ways of solving problems (ibid.). Translating these elements into concrete research and innovation policy measures and governance presents numerous challenges. One of these is that the missions should not be seen as a continuation of conventional routines for setting research and innovation policy priorities and modifying or further developing existing funding programs. Rather, owing to the transformative nature of missions, it will be necessary to embed the design of research, technology and innovation policy (RTI policy) much more strongly than in the past in processes of social change and to relate it to these processes (Kuhlmann and Rip 2018). Much mission-oriented innovation policy focuses on sustainability, and the Sustainable Development Goals (SDG) inspire research agendas (Mazzucato and Semiuk 2017, Kaldewey 2018). The environmental externalities generated by sustainability challenges (Rennings 2000) add an additional justification for publicly financed research for sustainability to the classic knowledge externality and market failure argument for knowledge production.

In parallel, a debate has been emerging which links an increased focus on societal challenges with fundamental changes in research processes. There are various interrelated strands of argument, which point toward fundamental changes in the research process. The increasing complexity of societal problems and challenges has led to a debate about the necessity of new forms of knowledge production (Nowotny et al. 2003, Etzkowitz and Leydesdorff 2000). This has been taken up by the debate about a transformative science in order to open up to society (Schneidewind et al. 2016, Scholz 2017, Shelley-Egan et al. 2020, Grunwald et al. 2020). These authors see a scientific paradigm shift evolving: the "classical", "normal", "Mode 1" science is characterized by research questions defined primarily in an academic context, disciplinary orientation, quality control exclusively on the basis of criteria inherent to science, and knowledge production without considering the context of use. In contrast, the new "post-normal science", "Mode 2", is characterized by a much stronger need for interdisciplinarity, interaction between research systems and society, and stronger reflection processes (see Nowotny et al. 2003, Frederichs 1999, Gibbons et al. 1994, Weingart 1997).

Closely related to increasing demands of science are expectations that science should cooperate more with societal actors and implement more inter- and transdisciplinarity as well as problem and application orientation (see e.g. Renn 2019, Müller-Christ 2017).[1] A strengthened and improved relationship between science and society is also at the core of the concept of "Responsible Research and Innovation" (RRI), which aims to embed responsibility as a core value in research and innovation processes and cultures (European Commission 2014, Lindner et al. 2016, Bogner et al. 2015). Generally speaking, RRI intends to create a new and improved relationship between science and society. The EU Commission defines RRI as "a process where all societal actors (researchers, citizens, policy makers, businesses) work together during the whole R&I process in order to align R&I outcomes to the values, needs and expectations of European society" (von Schomberg 2013). RRI has also been defined as "a transparent, interactive process in which societal actors and innovators become mutually responsive to each other with a view on the ethical acceptability, sustainability and societal desirability of the innovation process and its marketable products" (Call FP7-SiS-2012-1 n.d.). Scholars like Stilgoe et al. (2013) emphasize four integrated dimensions that characterize responsible research and innovation: anticipation, reflexivity, inclusion, and responsiveness.[2]

One of the most prominent examples of such a paradigm change is sustainability research. The emergence of the new field of sustainability research dates back to the turn of the century, as indicated by landmark publications such as Kates et al. (2001), and high-level conferences such as the World Congress "Challenges of the Earth 2001" (Komiyama and Takeuchi 2006, Gochin and Zaman 2010). The elements connecting sustainability research to the paradigm shift outlined above are twofold: first it is the alignment of scientific research production to societal problems in order to contribute to societal transformation processes; secondly, it is the way that research is conducted (Komiyama and Takeuchi 2006, Gallopin et al. 2001). Research for sustainability aims at providing solutions for existing societal (grand) challenges such as mitigation of and adaptation to climate change, or the protection of natural resources. Hence the usability and transferability of research results into non-academic settings is a core component of sustainability research. This implies changes in the research processes themselves: sustainability science aims at transcending disciplinary boundaries by uniting different scientific disciplines around a problem (interdisciplinarity), and the results of Schoolman et al. (2011) and Lam et al. (2014) indicate that it indeed is moving in this direction. There are several reasons for the importance of interdisciplinary principles for sustainability research: sustainability research is about contributing to solving complex problems. Disciplinary boundaries, however, do not necessarily follow the structure of knowledge necessary for coming up with solutions. Kaufmann and Cleveland (1995) point toward the interdisciplinary nature of sustainability per se, linking natural, economic and social dimensions. According to Newell (2001), complexity is a key justification for an interdisciplinary approach. The different interwoven dimensions of sustainability increase the complexity of the problem. The plurality of values and norms involved furthermore increases complexity, and calls for a holistic view associated with transdisciplinarity and Mode 2 type research (Hirsch et al. 2006, Newig et al. 2019, Lang et al. 2012). Furthermore, sustainability also includes an international perspective and especially takes into consideration implications of the research in countries of the global South. It involves stakeholders in those countries with regard to development issues (Kates 2011), but also with regard to being affected by global changes such as climate change (internationality). In sum, sustainability research adopts a systemic perspective of the research object and takes into consideration the different impacts that research can have beyond the scientific community. This is supported by a survey by Daedlow et al. (2016) that underlines that sustainability research is seen to be increasingly more embedded, self-reflective and co-productive, and there is an acknowledged need for a more inter- and transdisciplinary focus, as well as problem and application orientation.[3]

The nature of sustainability research has also led to calls for specially tailored research programs. The rationale for this seems to be clear: sustainability research emphasizes the outcome of research for society, thus producing "public value",[4] and pushes for research processes which run counter to the traditional, discipline-oriented research program. Thus, within traditional research programs, which put emphasis on academic outcomes only, sustainability-oriented research is disadvantaged in comparison with more traditional forms of research.

Increasingly, research programs are put forward that state impacts on sustainability as an explicit goal, such as the European Framework Programme (e.g. Horizon 2020, Horizon

Table 9.1   *Overview of strategic research funding programs*[a]

	FONA (DE)[b]	SRFI (FI)[c]	FORMAS (SE)[d]
Start date	Since 2005	Since 2015	Since 2000
Budget	ca. 370 million euros per year (total expenses 2005–2018 = €5 billion)	€56 million granted funding per year	€170 million (1.8 billion Swedish kronor) per year
Funding instruments	*Project* funding (single, cooperation junior research groups) and *structural* funding (infrastructures, others like the IPCC secretariat)	Provides funding to long-term multidisciplinary *research* that seeks solutions to the challenges facing Finnish society	Targeted calls (national research program, two-thirds of the budget) and researcher initiated calls (one-third of the budget) for research projects
Interdisciplinarity	Required as a so-called system characteristic	Multidisciplinary research consortia are required	Stimulates activities aiming at cross-sectoral and interdisciplinary approaches
Transdisciplinarity	Required as a so-called system characteristic in several specific program lines	Emphasis on active interaction and engagement with users and beneficiaries of research	Strengthening collaborations between those performing the research, those funding the research and stakeholders in society
Prioritized research problems	Clear focus on promoting research for sustainability and sustainable development	General focus on research that addresses the grand challenges, where sustainability-related topics are at the core, especially in the current programs	Sustainable development, with a particular emphasis on environment, agricultural sciences and spatial planning
User-oriented outputs	Science and technology transfer is again a so-called system characteristic and an important selection criterion for collaborative projects	See above, transdisciplinarity, SFRI requires active collaboration between those who produce research knowledge and those who use it	Particular emphasis is given to science communication and strengthening collaboration between researchers, research funders and societal actors

Notes:
[a] The rows follow the four characteristics for societal targeted research developed by Ramos-Vielba et al. (2022), with added information on the start date and average budget.
[b] See Bührer et al. (2020a).
[c] https://www.aka.fi/en/research-funding/funding-opportunities-at-a-glance/funding-for-strategic-research/.
[d] https://www.formas.se/en/.

Europe), but also national programs for example the German Framework Programme for Sustainability Research (FONA), the Finnish Strategic Research Funding Instrument (SRFI) and the research funded by the Swedish FORMAS.[5] Table 9.1 shows the main characteristics of the mentioned funding program.

All three programs have in common that the research they fund shall contribute to solving urgent societal challenges and that inter-, multi-, and/or transdisciplinary research is required. The three programs pursue overarching strategic goals and are endowed with substantial funds. The funded research should also be clearly oriented toward the needs of future users, i.e. there is a clear requirement to produce useful results outside the realm of science. However, the programs also show several differences. In addition to obvious ones such as the start date of the program and the available budgets, the three examples differ in terms of the content priorities they pursue. While FONA and FORMAS clearly focus on sustainability, SFRI is slightly broader in content and generally prioritizes the major challenges, with sustainability also playing a central role. Additionally, FORMAS places a special emphasis on science communication and policy analysis. FONA, on the other hand, shows the broadest policy mix, since it supports not only collaborative projects between science, business and, in some cases, also other actors from civil society or municipalities, but also large-scale infrastructures, service activities and junior research groups.

9.3   MAIN CHALLENGES IN TRANSFORMING RESEARCH THROUGH PUBLIC FUNDING

Since the 1990s, a reorientation in the relationship between the state and science has taken place in numerous (Western) European countries, which can be summarized by the phrase New Public Management. In essence, this means that the state reduces its (operational) control over public research institutions and grants them more autonomy in their decisions, but in return expects performance to increase (Ferlie et al. 1996). In the course of these changes in governance between scientific institutions and the state, various mechanisms were introduced, like global budgeting, performance-oriented resource allocation and goal agreements. The introduction of New Public Management also led to an increasing relevance of competition and performance-oriented funding, either as part of institutional funding or through an increasing importance of competitive third-party funds (Hicks 2012, Geuna 2001, Jongbloed and Vossensteyn 2001, Jongbloed and Lepori 2015).[6]

Research institutions, like all other organizations, need a range of resources to carry out their missions. In addition to infrastructure and human resources, these are primarily financial resources. In essence, the funding modalities of research performing organizations can be traced back to two basic pillars: (1) *institutional funding* and (2) *project funding*.[7] It is worth noting, however, that institutional funding is also (increasingly) based on performance criteria or at least dependent on different criteria that serve the organizations' strategic goals. Thus the traditional distinction between competitive and institutional funding does not sufficiently reflect the current funding systems (Larrue et al. 2018).[8] However, current practices of assessing the performance of research still almost exclusively rely on criteria inherent to science, and here in particular on peer-reviewed publications in high-ranked journals and subsequent citations. This happens despite a growing trend to question this approach, known under headings like the "metric tide", i.e. the increasingly critical voices from academia on the question of how excellence is measured (Wilsdon et al. 2015, Hicks et al. 2015, Declaration on Research Assessment, 2012, https://sfdora.org/read/).

For the other strand of public research funding, project-based and in particular applied research funding, the following observation can be made: between 1970 and mid-2000, the share of *project funding* steadily increased in the overall public research allocation (Lepori and Jongbloed 2018, Lepori et al. 2007, Larrue et al. 2018).[9] In European countries, it constituted the second main channel of public funding for research funding (Lepori et al. 2007). However, there are significant differences between countries as regards the overall importance and share of performance-oriented funding (Jongbloed and Lepori 2015). The share of project funding varies highly, depending on the countries and can go from 5 to 92%; the majority of European countries seems to have levelled in the past years between 25 and 50% of project funding (OECD 2018, Jonkers und Zacharewicz 2016). Since mid-2000, however, the share of research funding channelled through projects is no longer increasing (Larrue et al. 2018).

For project funding, often also labeled as competitive funding, it has always been clear that certain objectives are linked to it. Thus, competitive project funding is by nature targeted to specific pre-defined objectives. While these objectives were in the past primarily linked to promoting scientific excellence (pushing knowledge frontiers further), qualifying junior researchers or strengthening the research system, the past years have seen a fanning out of goals to which research programs should contribute (see also Reale et al., Chapter 7 in this *Handbook*). As shown in a survey of 75 competitive funding schemes conducted in 2018, research programs no longer have a sole focus on scientific excellence, but are asked to provide results that go beyond the research system and generate profit to non-scientific stakeholders. Approximately one-third of the analyzed funding schemes state as objectives "Responding to societal challenges" and/or "economic competitiveness"[10] (OECD 2018).

After the move toward performance-based funding, we see a second wave of changes toward funding for societal goals gearing up, so far visible only in project-based funding. Clearly it is easier to redirect rather short-lived specific research projects toward new goals than to change existing institutions. Indeed we assume that under the conditions of New Public Management, i.e. a high degree of autonomy of research performing organizations with regard to their internal structures, processes and incentive systems, it is comparatively difficult for externally set incentives to have a sufficient impact on the organization. This is especially true when there are conflicting goals: as mentioned above, internal performance systems are still largely geared toward conventional bibliometric indicators and take only limited account of the special features of transdisciplinary or interdisciplinary research (Wilsdon et al. 2015, Geuna and Piolatto 2016).

The premise of our following reflections is that the greater the importance of institutional funding for the organization is and the more strongly science-inherent performance-based funding elements are applied there, the more difficult it will be to induce institutional change toward a greater alignment of science with societal needs. This applies in particular to sustainability research, which is characterized by its strong transfer orientation as well as transdisciplinarity and interdisciplinarity. These are all important features for achieving the translation work called for in the sustainability debate, also known as "boundary work" (Cash et al. 2003). There is a further aspect: careers in the science system are still often disciplinary and based on conventional scientific criteria. More recent requirements such as the exchange with society, the "third mission", an extended impact orientation and interdisciplinarity are hardly defined as selection criteria for, as an example, the appointment to a professorship position. This is a further hindrance toward a transformative change of research systems (see Jaeger-Erben et al. 2018, Haider et al. 2018, Zucker 2012, Ruppert-Winkel et al. 2015, Pfirman and Martin 2017, Rhoten and Parker 2004). However, as Laudel points out (Chapter 16 in this *Handbook*), no convincing theory yet exists about how to link the macro-level of the research funding landscape with the individual strategies at the micro-level of individual researchers.

The difficulty of initiating transformational changes within institutions supports a strategy starting with program-based funding. Indeed the survey results mentioned above indicate that program-based funding increasingly addresses societal goals explicitly. However, we also argue that focusing on a societal research topic is not sufficient for the transformation of the science system – it has to be accompanied by changes in the research process as well. Thus, we see the following questions arising:

- Do we see indications that the change toward focusing research on societal challenges in project-based research funding is also accompanied by a change in the research process?
- How effective can research funding programs that address societal challenges be in changing the research system as such? Are, for example, particular boundary organizations (Cash et al. 2003) necessary or can the required change also be implemented in the existing research performing organizations?
- How are potential shifts in research processes fostered by program-based funding perceived by the research performing organizations given the existing incentive framework they are subject to?

Tackling these questions will be an important part of research on transforming future research systems.

9.4 EMPIRICAL ILLUSTRATION – THE GERMAN FRAMEWORK PROGRAM FOR SUSTAINABILITY RESEARCH FONA

In the following, we examine the German framework program for sustainability (FONA), of the German Federal Ministry for Education and Research (BMBF), established in 2005, as an empirical example of how public funding can – or cannot – promote a shift in research toward more sustainability. FONA has disbursed €5 billion as of 2018. This example provides a suitable illustration of the possibilities, but also the limitations, of program-based public research funding to transform a science system, for the following reasons: (1) the selected funding instrument has a comparatively long history (whereas such a long-lasting and comprehensive program approach is not yet known from other countries), which allows us to study long-term change; (2) substantial funding is available; (3) the funding instrument is ambitious and aims to contribute to fundamental change in science, business and society; (4) with the focus on sustainability research, a type of research is promoted that genuinely deals with system transformations; and (5) the FONA program has been thoroughly evaluated, whereas other programs have not. The Swedish FORMAS, for example, just launched a survey exploring whether FORMAS fulfils its missions and goals[11] and the Finnish Strategic Research Funding Instrument announced the availability of evaluation results for summer 2021, the respective report being only available in Finnish.[12]

For a better understanding of what follows, it is worth mentioning that research funding in Germany is divided between the Federal government and the Federal states. The latter are primarily responsible for the basic funding of the higher education institutions, whereas the Federal government mainly supports non-university research, research infrastructures and program-oriented research. Owing to this shared responsibility, the hurdles to reaching a common understanding of the policy frames to be pursued and the research funding priorities derived from them are particularly high (the key phrase being no dominant actor; Hinze 2015). If we look at Federal spending on research and development by funding type, the amount for project funding and departmental research was between €6.3 and 7.6 billion, and for institutional funding between €5.3 and 8 billion between 2010 and 2018.[13] By way of comparison,

FONA accounted for just under €6 billion in the period 2005–2018. The Federal government's spending on research and development by funding area in 2019 also shows the great importance of the thematic area of climate, environment and sustainability, which ranks fourth in terms of spending (ibid.). If we compare the FONA expenditures with the funding volume available to the German research foundation, the central funding body for basic research in Germany, almost three times as much funding is available for the period 2005–2018[14] (€14 billion), but this is distributed across all disciplines.

Within Germany, the debate about sustainability science was preceded by a debate about environmental research from a systemic perspective (see for example Daschkeit and Schröder 1998), on which FONA could draw. Two important additional aspects played a key role in dedicating FONA to sustainability research. First, the framework research concept of the German BMBF called for directing the traditional environmental research program of the BMBF much more strongly toward innovation and impact. Second, Germany had introduced a sustainability strategy in 2002, which further drove environmental research toward sustainability research. Thus, FONA's main goals are twofold: (1) promote research for sustainability and strengthening research for sustainability in Germany and thus (implicitly) also induce a change in the research process toward more inter- and transdisciplinarity; and (2) produce research results that are relevant to society and that contribute to solving societal challenges. With the FONA framework, the BMBF focused on a type of research that was not only oriented toward pure knowledge generation or the generation of innovations as such, but that was also explicitly oriented toward global challenges and included the perspectives of diverse societal stakeholders. FONA-funded research projects should be interdisciplinary and transdisciplinary and take up a systemic perspective. Research outputs should not only fulfil scientific excellence criteria but also be useful for non-scientific stakeholders. In short, FONA intends to promote changes which fit into a larger transformation perspective of the German science system. Its policy mix of instruments therefore not only focuses on funding collaborative projects, but also funds junior research groups, infrastructure and international networks and other research-coordinating activities.[15] FONA thus also fulfils the four criteria for research funding oriented toward societal goals identified by Ramos-Vielba et al. (2022; see Table 9.1 and Section 9.2).

The main results of a program evaluation conducted between 2018 and 2020 (Bührer et al. 2020a, b) were that FONA has been successful with regard to initiating first steps toward changes within the German science system by explicitly strengthening interdisciplinary and transdisciplinary research approaches, by enriching the research landscape through funding the emergence of new departments and by integrating new elements into the training schemes for young researchers.

For universities and non-university research institutions, FONA is first and foremost a relevant source of third-party funding which, owing to the relatively long project durations, has a positive significance for the thematic development as well as the training and career prospects of young scientists. In several interviews, the funding was described as indispensable for the thematic orientation of the chair or institute, which made this type of research possible in the first place in terms of content and structure, especially at smaller chairs. FONA results are also used in teaching and make it possible to write theses that are relevant to practice, sometimes in cooperation with practitioners. In particular, the junior research groups offer young scientists the opportunity to establish their own networks early in their careers, which are not limited to their specialist communities.

It was also emphasized in the interviews that FONA has increased the legitimacy of sustainability research in the research institutions. At the beginning of FONA, scientists conducting sustainability research would often have been seen as loners in a niche and not taken very seriously. The third-party funding associated with FONA, but also the continuity of the program, would have changed this thoroughly. Strategy development in universities and non-university research does not follow individual federal programs, but is integrated into institute-specific or cross-institutional strategies (e.g. research areas of the Helmholtz Association of German Research Centers (HGF), performance and target agreements of universities). Projects from the FONA program often form a central element of third-party funding here – in individual research areas or disciplines. In the HGF, these have a predominantly complementary function to the internal program oriented funding; for university research, third-party funding per se is of greater importance. On the one hand, this is because it enables research on a larger scale, and on the other hand, because third-party funding, along with publications, continues to be the central currency for reputational gains. These reputational gains also allow the topic of sustainability research to gain broader recognition compared with traditional research areas.

For scientific institutions, strategic effects often arise only downstream, since FONA is integrated into existing institute and university funding as a component of externally funded research. At the HGF, overarching strategy issues are developed within the framework of the internal overall strategy (program-oriented research) and at the level of the research areas, explicitly incorporating concepts such as the Grand Challenges. Thus, objectives can partly overlap with topics, focal points and programs of FONA, but a medium- and long-term orientation can only be based on budgetary funds and not on third-party funds to be acquired in the future. For universities as a whole, strategic effects of FONA participation can be seen primarily in the strengthening of interdisciplinary cooperation within the university and beyond institutional boundaries. At the same time, funded departments and participating staff units gain opportunities to give the topic of sustainability greater visibility and relevance in the perception of university management, administration, other departments and teaching.

For universities, FONA also stands alongside other funding as an important source of third-party funding. As the acquisition of third-party funding is becoming increasingly important for both the quality and the scope of research at universities, the program fits into university strategies. As a renowned source of third-party funding, FONA can strengthen the relevance of sustainability-oriented chairs and research groups at the respective universities. Staff units benefit from additional funding and projects that increase the visibility and relevance of the topic of sustainability among university management. In some cases, research is also embedded in a larger context of activities, which includes, for example, the preparation of sustainability reports. The longer project durations compared with other funding programs make it possible to build up more constant networks within and outside the universities. These durations were also perceived as positive for the training of young researchers. Overall, there has been a considerable number of new research groups and chairs established at the university level. Non-university research institutions also considerably expanded their activities in the field of sustainability science, even to the extent of new institutes being founded that focus on sustainability research. The evaluation showed that these new organizational structures heavily relied on FONA funding. Thus, FONA has provided impetus for changes toward sustainability, in particular in making sustainability research an established scientific topic both within universities and non-university research organizations.

Additionally, interdisciplinary collaboration[16] was very high in FONA projects. In 75% of the projects surveyed, more than two disciplines worked together. In about a quarter of the projects, engineering and natural scientists worked together with humanities, social and cultural scientists. The cooperation in the interdisciplinary consortia was rated very positively by the project leaders interviewed. Obstacles such as communication and organizational problems within the project team were present, but not dominant. However, further findings indicated that the joint formulation and processing of research questions still has a clear potential for expansion. Additionally, especially in the case of interdisciplinary collaborations between natural and engineering sciences and social scientists, the focus was still strongly on disciplinary scientific exploitation. Following the distinction between multi- and interdisciplinarity as defined by Goschin and Zaman (2010), one explanation of this evidence might be that perhaps many projects remained in a multidisciplinary stage of collaboration and were not moving toward a more intensive interdisciplinarity. A second explanation might be that many journals still reflect a disciplinary pattern. Researchers from FONA might react by publishing their results in a distinctly disciplinary manner in order to adapt to that pressure. A third reason might be that an academic career quite often requires publishing predominantly in journals which are highly ranked in disciplinary journal lists. Clearly the disciplinary structure of academia was particularly inhibiting for young researchers who strive for a scientific qualification (doctorate) or establishment in the science system (post-doctoral thesis/professorial chair). A classic disciplinary profile is still assumed for this. The additional qualifications that result from interdisciplinary cooperation are still not (sufficiently) valued for a career in the German research system, especially the appointment to a professorship.

The strong involvement of practice partners in projects has proved the transdisciplinary character of FONA.[17] The evaluation found that about 40% of the funded FONA projects had been transdisciplinary cooperation in the narrower sense,[18] i.e. cooperation that includes societal stakeholders and public administration in addition to science and/or business. With the FONA funding transdisciplinary research could be funded in its infancy and it is to the BMBF's credit that it was one of the first to fund this type of research in Germany. However, it also became clear that not all of the three phases of transdisciplinary research we referred to above (see Lang et al. 2012) were equally taken up.

Summing up the evidence, the following conclusions for FONA emerge:

- We see clear indications that the change toward focusing research on sustainability in FONA is also accompanied by a change in the research process toward inter- and transdisciplinarity.
- At the same time, the existing traditional excellence criteria set was also successful: the scientists funded by FONA meet the classical requirements for publication output (measured as the number of publications and citations). This can be interpreted in such a way that FONA was able to increase the acceptance of sustainability science not only because of welcome additional research funding, but also because it is committed to and partially fulfilled the existing criteria for success (in publications). In this respect, sustainability science is incorporated into the established science system as an incremental innovation. This suggests that any future funding strategy must take into account that research that addresses grand challenges in particular must be excellent in its own right and fulfil the traditional criteria for scientific excellence, too.

The potential shifts in research processes fostered by project-based funding were perceived by the research-performing organizations according to the existing incentive framework they are subject to: sustainability research had been able to acquire substantial research funds and come up with peer reviewed publications. Thus, it is a growing niche, which has gained some acceptance within the dominant science regime. However, it has not been able to transform the science system as such. Thus, there is still the need to foster additional structural change within the research system. This need is also addressed by FONA. With the FONA-funded initiative "Sustainability in Science",[19] an exchange platform has been created to foster the dialogue on sustainability with and between researchers, administrative staff in research organizations, students and stakeholders outside research and development projects that aim at a sustainable transformation of research organizations.[20] Finally, this is also one of the central characteristics of FONA in comparison with other European research programs, which also aim to strengthen inter- and transdisciplinary sustainability research, but only offer project funding and no funding instruments that support additional structural change.

9.5 CRITICAL ASSESSMENT OF GAPS AND FUTURE RESEARCH DIRECTION

In view of the prevailing paradigm of science, according to which research is most efficient when conducted primarily according to rules developed by science itself (following the policy frame of the "Republic of Science"), it is unrealistic to assume that program or project funding, as extensive and attractive as it may be, can bring about change within a few years. Our case study from Germany has also shown that even a long-term and ambitious funding program can at best provide an impetus in the direction of a system change.

In particular, the evaluation of FONA has identified an area of tension between sustainability research as a symbol for new modes of doing research, which demand impact orientation and inter- and transdisciplinarity, and the conditions for establishing young scientists in the science system. This is where the influence of program-based research funding to transform research systems reaches its limits. On the other hand, with an explicit strategic orientation and ambitious objectives to stimulate transformation, even programs can trigger a debate on another level, in our example the emphasis on "sustainability in science" with strong implications for the design of research processes in research performing organizations outside the higher education sector. Insofar as FONA establishes a niche within the science system, this changes the political economy and the levels of discourse: society's claim on science, which is not shared by all scientific stakeholders, becomes a claim by society together with parts of the science sector.

Furthermore, a Swedish study on the quality and impact of research in political science in Sweden has recently shown that there is a strong link between high scientific quality and impact (Swedish Research Council 2021). Further evidence of that kind is needed to build bridges between the different policy frames and to demonstrate that there is more convergence than contradiction between the "Republic of Science" and the societal function of research. However, there is a lack of systematic empirical studies that investigate on an empirical level whether, and to what extent, trade-offs occur between traditional scientific output and more effectiveness-oriented, inter- and transdisciplinary research. Thus, further research is needed to answer questions like: what are the building blocks for adapting science-inherent strategies and processes to allow more openness for sustainable and responsible research; and how can the coupling of excellence and relevance be empirically investigated (control group comparisons in the direction of scientific and societal impacts)?

Project funding should continue these activities and also expand them in a targeted manner to include aspects of reflection on the effects of one's own research and on the establishment of a quality standard for good interdisciplinary and transdisciplinary research. The application of a framework for reflection, as developed in the FONA-funded LENA project (cf. Helming et al. 2016, Ferretti et al. 2016, Fraunhofer-Gesellschaft et al. 2016), could also lead to greater attention being paid to the effectiveness of one's own research already during the research process, and the achievement of impact not being projected solely onto a transfer phase that takes place after the actual research.

The criteria used to assess the quality of research are of particular importance to solve the tension between disciplinary and interdisciplinary research, as described at the beginning. If interdisciplinarity and transdisciplinarity were regarded as important components of high-quality research, this would also have an impact on career opportunities and evaluation criteria in science. This argument is in line with the ongoing discussions on research quality, as mentioned above. Yet even if the question of the "impact of science" and its measurability is meanwhile very high on the agenda, further research is needed on how evaluation research and practice could contribute to overcome the hindrances toward transformative change within the research system by strengthening, for example, the perspective on the social outcomes of research.

However, some lessons learned can be derived from FONA's overall program design to become effective toward sustainability: (1) the embedding of funding in an overarching strategic framework that is compatible with existing policy strategies; (2) a long-term orientation combined with substantial funds; (3) the policy mix with its variety of funding instruments; and (4) the involvement of various actors from the quadruple helix in the program design but also the implementation of the research.

9.6   CONCLUSIONS

Even a huge research program in terms of funding projects remains only a part of research policy. Transformation cannot be expected from individual project-based programs, but they change the conditions for further policies. Further steps will be taken to enlarge the specific mode of research processes toward other public research instruments such as institutional funding.

Here, the funding bodies would have to communicate their expectations even more clearly and transparently. Above all, they also have to make sufficient funds available to support the respective processes of change. Bottom-up buy-in supports the acceptance of change, as well as top-management commitment. Furthermore, participation and inclusion of the scientific staff raises awareness for the benefits associated with transformation, gains more acceptance and increases the motivation to join, while decreasing resistance.

An adaptation of the science system on all levels is needed, which involves a shift in mind set and also in the practices of individual researchers, the commitment of the research performing organizations including an altered orientation toward the impact of science, the need to overcome the still existing disincentives to interdisciplinary and transdisciplinary work and finally a new "Leitbild" for excellent research, which accounts for the need to direct research toward global challenges without compromising academic rigour.

NOTES

1. Potential unintended consequences of such a shift towards application and impact orientation are discussed in Coburn et al., Chapter 10 in this *Handbook*.
2. A further important strand of the debate in this context revolves around the creation of public value, see among others Bozeman, Chapter 2 in this *Handbook*.
3. Methodological reflections have led to a set of eight criteria, which sustainability research in general should follow (Feretti et al. 2016, Helming et al. 2016), and which have been adopted by the German non-university research organizations (Fraunhofer Gesellschaft et al. 2016).
4. A comprehensive analysis of the meaning of "public" in public research is delivered by Bozeman, Chapter 2 in this *Handbook*.
5. Further funding programs and strategies like the German High-Tech-Strategy, the Swedish Challenge Driven Innovation Programme, the Swiss National Research Programme and the Dutch long-term, interdisciplinary and transdisciplinary research along Dutch Research Agenda (Nationale Wetenschapsagenda) routes by consortia can be perceived as mission-orientated programs but have a broader thematic scope and target groups than the three programs shown in Table 9.1.
6. It should be noted, however, that it is rather contested whether the introduction of New Public Management leads to an improved performance (Auranen and Nieminen 2010, Jongbloed and Vossensteyn 2016, Jongbloed and Lepori 2015, Schubert 2009).
7. There are numerous – and more sophisticated – approaches to illustrate differences in the funding modalities of the public research sector, see for example Lepori et al. 2007, Auranen and Nieminen 2010, Jongbloed 2010, Lepori 2011), but this simplified understanding seems to be purposeful for this chapter.
8. Larrue et al. (2018) therefore propose a new conceptual framework to classify research funding instruments that take the policy context into account and thus acknowledge the increasing relevance of the policy frame that emphasizes the social function of research.
9. A high proportion of third-party funding can have advantages and disadvantages, for example increased transparency and accountability, increased relevance to the research agency objectives, promotion of institutional diversity, better research outputs as well as research community profits on the one hand but also emphasis on short-term, low-risk research, negative career effects, disincentives for collaboration, bureaucracy, bias through peer review process, and a lack of long-term planning for staff/infrastructure as disadvantages (OECD 2018). Further criticism has been articulated by several scholars, emphasizing the risk of the "Matthew principle", i.e. awarding only those who were already strong in the past (Viner et al. 2004), by favoring a certain kind of short-term-oriented mainstream research (Laudel 2006) and by weakening the strategic possibilities of the research performing organizations (Bleiklie et al. 2001).
10. The particular role of program managers at funding agencies and thus the grant-making process in fostering change is analyzed by Arnott (2021). The author describes "these actors as potentially de factor makers of research policy" (p. 8), thus underlining the important influence of program funding in promoting new types of research.
11. https://formas.se/en/start-page/archive/news/news/2021-07-22-focus-survey-on-formas.html, retrieved at 10 January 2022.
12. https://www.aka.fi/globalassets/3-stn/1-strateginen-tutkimus/tiedon-kayttajalle/tietoaineistot/yhteiskunnallisen-vaikuttavuuden-arviointi---strategisen-tutkimuksen-ohjelmat-2016-2019.pdf.
13. https://www.bundesbericht-forschung-innovation.de/de/Abbildungen-und-Tabellen-1713.html.
14. https://www.datenportal.bmbf.de/portal/de/Tabelle-1.1.7.html.
15. The majority (over 70%) of financed research projects or project-related research groups (e.g. junior research groups) receive approximately 20% of funding-financed research infrastructure. A third of the FONA funding went to universities while non-university research organizations received approximately 44% of funding.

16. Interdisciplinary collaborative projects are defined as those that bring together people from different scientific disciplines around a research question, according to the definition of van den Besselaar and Heimericks, who see interdisciplinarity as a deviation from the normal state of a discipline by using new theories, concepts and methods to answer a research question (van den Besselaar und Heimeriks 2001).
17. The BMBF has opted for a definition of transdisciplinary research that is especially used in the German-speaking sustainability research community. It builds on the following three characteristics: (1) research on socially relevant topics; (2) use of paradigms that are cross-disciplinary; and (3) the inclusion of non-scientific actors (participatory research) (Pohl 2010).
18. As R&I activities can also be performed in companies, the FONA evaluation decided to exclude collaboration between scientific and industry actors in the analysis of transdisciplinary activities.
19. https://www.fona.de/de/ueber-fona/nachhaltigkeit-in-der-wissenschaft-sisi.php.
20. In particular three projects are explicitly directed toward a structural change within the science system and aim at involving different actors of the German research landscape: (1) LeNa (Sustainability Management in non-university research organizations); (2) "Hoch-N" (Sustainability at Universities), a network of 11 German universities exploring the topic of sustainability management and reporting for university; and (3) "LeNa Shape", aiming at exploring whether societal responsible research changes research processes with regards to its quality and impacts and effects on researchers and raising the question of what the need for a transformation of research means for the definitions of the quality of research.

REFERENCES

Arnott, J. C. (2021). Pens and purse strings: Exploring the opportunities and limits to funding actionable sustainability science. *Research Policy*, 50, 104362.
Auranen, O.; Nieminen M. (2010). University research funding and publication performance – An international comparison. *Research Policy*, 39, 822–834.
Bernal, J. D. (1939). *The Social Function of Science*. Cambridge, MA: The MIT Press.
Bleiklie, I.; Enders, J.; Lepori, B.; Musselin, C. (2011). New public management, network governance and the university as a changing professional organization. In: Christensen, T.; Laegreid, P. (Eds.): *The Ashgate Research Companion to New Public Management*, pp. 161–176. Aldershot: Ashgate.
Bogner, A.; Decker, M.; Sotoudeh, M. (Eds.) (2015). *Responsible Innovation. Neue Impulse für die Technikfolgenabschätzung?* Baden-Baden: Nomos.
Bührer, S.; Walz, R.; Seus, S.; Astor, M.; Stehnken, T.; Malik, F. (2020a). *Evaluation der BMBF-Rahmenprogram Forschung für die Nachhaltigkeit FONA 1 (2005–2009) & Forschung für Nachhaltige Entwicklungen FONA 2 (2010–2014)*. Karlsruhe/Berlin: Abschlussbericht.
Bührer, S.; Sarah S.; Walz, R.; Neumann, M.; Astor, M.; Malik, F: (2020b). *Ergebnisse aus der Diskursfortsetzung zum zukünftigen FONA*. Karlsruhe/Berlin: Abschlussbericht.
Call FP7-SiS-2012-1 (n.d.). Topic SiS.2012.1.1.1-1: Governance frameworks for Responsible Research and Innovation (RRI).
Cash, D. W.; Clark, W. C.; Alcock, F.; Dickson, N. M.; Eckley, N.; Guston, D. H.; Jäger, J.; Mitchell, R. B. (2003). Knowledge systems for sustainable development. *Proceedings of the national academy of sciences*, 100(14), 8086–8091.
Daedlow, K.; Podhora, A.; Winkelmann, M.; Kopfmüller, J.; Walz, R.; Helming, K. (2016). Socially responsible research for sustainable transformation: An integrated assessment framework. *Current Opinion in Environmental Sustainability*, 23, 1–11.
Daschkeit, A.; Schröder, W. (Eds.) (1998): *Umweltforschung quergedacht. Perspektiven integrativer Umweltforschung und -lehre*. Berlin: Springer.
Etzkowitz, H.; Leydesdorff, L. (2000). The dynamics of innovation: From National Systems and "Mode 2" to a Triple Helix of university–industry–government relations. *Research Policy*, 29, 109–123.
European Commission (2014). *Responsible Research and Innovation – Europe's Ability to Respond to Societal Challenges*. Brussels.

Ferlie, E.; Ashburner, L.; Fitzgerald L.; Pettigrew, A. (1996). *The New Public Management in Action.* Oxford: Oxford University Press.

Ferretti, J.; Daedlow, K.; Kopfmüller, J.; Winkelmann, M.; Podhora, A.; Walz, R.; Bertling, J.; Helming, K. (2016). *Reflexionsrahmen für Forschen in gesellschaftlicher Verantwortung. BMBF-Projekt "LeNa – Nachhaltigkeitsmanagement in außeruniversitären Forschungsorganisationen".* Berlin.

Fraunhofer-Gesellschaft; Helmholtz-Gemeinschaft; Leibniz-Gemeinschaft (2016). Nachhaltigkeits-management in außeruniversitären Forschungsorganisationen. Handreichung. https://www.nach haltig-forschen.de/fileadmin/user_upload/LeNa-Handreichung_final.pdf.

Frederichs, G. (1999). Der Wandel der Wissenschaft. *TATuP – Zeitschrift für Technikfolgenabschätzung in Theorie und Praxis*, 8(3/4), 16–25.

Gallopin, G. C.; Funtowicz, S.; O'Connor, M.; Ravetz, J. (2001). Science for the twenty-first century: from social contract to the scientific core. *International Social Sciences Journal*, 53, 219–229.

Geuna, A. (2001). The changing rationale for European university research funding: Are there negative unintended consequences? *Journal of Economic Issues*, 35, 607–632.

Geuna, A.; Piolatto, M. (2016). Research assessment in the UK and Italy: Costly and difficult, but probably worth it (at least for a while). *Research Policy*, 45, 260–271.

Gibbons, M.; Limoges, C.; Nowotny, H.; Schwartzman, S.; Scott, P.; Trow, M. (1994). *The New Production of Knowledge: The Dynamics of Science and Research in Contemporary Societies.* London: Sage.

Goschin, Z.; Zaman, G. (2010). Multidisciplinarity, interdisciplinarity and transdisciplinarity: Theoretical approaches and implications for the strategy of post-crisis sustainable development. *Theoretical and Applied Economics*, 17(12), 5–20.

Grunwald, A.; Schäfer, M.; Bergmann, M. (2020). Neue Formate transdisziplinärer Forschung. Ausdifferenzierte Brücken zwischen Wissenschaft und Praxis. *Gaia*, 29(2), 106–114.

Haider, L. J.; Hentati-Sundberg, J.; Giusti, M.; Goodness, J.; Hamann, M.; Masterson, V. A. et al. (2018). The undisciplinary journey: Early-career perspectives in sustainability science. *Sustainability Science*, 13(1), 191–204.

Helming, K.; Ferretti, J.; Daedlow, K.; Podhora, A.; Kopfmüller, J.; Winkelmann, M.; Bertling, J.; Walz, R. (2016). Forschen für nachhaltige Entwicklung. Kriterien für gesellschaftlich verantwortliche Forschungsprozesse. *GAIA* 25(3), 161–165.

Hicks, D. (2012): Performance-based university research funding systems. *Research Policy*, 41, 251–261.

Hicks, D.; Wouters, P.; Waltman, L.; de Rijcke, S.; Rafols, I. (2015). Bibliometrics: The Leiden Manifesto for research metrics. *Nature Comment*, 520, 429–431.

Hinze S. (2015). Forschungsförderung und ihre Finanzierung. In: Simon D.; Knie A.; Hornbostel S. (Eds.): *Handbuch Wissenschaftspolitik*, pp. 413–428. Wiesbaden: Springer NachschlageWissen.

Hirsch, H. G.; Bradley, D.; Pohl, C.; Rist, S.; Wiesmann, U. (2006). Implications of transdisciplinarity for sustainability research. Ecological Economics, 60(1), 119–128.

Jaeger-Erben, M.; Kramm, J.; Sonnberger, M.; Völker, C.; Albert, C.; Graf, A.; Hermans, K.; Lange, S.; Santarius, T.; Schröter, B.; Sievers-Glotzbach, S.; Winzer; J: (2018). Building capacities for trans-disciplinary research. Challenges and recommendations for early-career researchers. *GAIA*, 27(4), 379–386.

Jongbloed, B. W. A. (2010). *Funding Higher Education: A View Across Europe.* Brussels: ESMU.

Jongbloed, B.; Lepori B. (2015). The Funding of research in higher education: Mixed models and mixed results. In: Huisman, J.; de Boer, H.; Dill, D. D.; Souto-Otero, M. (Eds.): *The Palgrave International Handbook of Higher Education Policy and Governance.* London: Palgrave Macmillan.

Jongbloed, B.; Vossensteyn, H. (2001). Keeping up performances: An international survey of performance-based funding in higher education. *Journal of Higher Education Policy and Management*, 23(2), 1.

Jonkers, K.; Zacharewicz, T. (2016). *Research Performance Based Funding Systems: A Comparative Assessment.* Luxembourg: European Commission. Publications Office of the European Union.

Kaldewey, D. (2018). The grand challenges discourse. Transforming identity work in science and science policy. *Minerva*, 56(2), 161–182.

Kates, R. W. (2011). What kind of a science is sustainability science? *PNAS*, 108(49), 19449–19450.

Kates, R. W.; Clark, W. C.; Corell, R.; Hall, J. M.; Jaeger, C. C.; Lowe, I.; McCarthy, J. J.; Schellnhuber, H.-J.; Bolin, B.; Dickson, N. M.; Faucheux, S.; Gallopin, G. C.; Grübler, A.; Huntley, B.; Jaeger, J.; Jodha, N. S.; Kasperson, R. E.; Mabogunje, A.; Matson, P.; Mooney, H.; Moore B, III.; O'Riordan, T.; Svedin, U. (2001). Sustainability science. *Science*, 292(5517), 641–642.

Kaufmann, R. K.; Cleveland, C. J. (1995). Measuring sustainability: Needed – An interdisciplinary approach to an interdisciplinary concept. *Ecological Economics*, 15, 109–112.

Komiyama H.; Takeuchi K. (2006). Sustainability science: Building a new discipline. *Sustainability Science*, 1, 1–6.

Kuhlmann, S.; Rip, A. (2018). Next generation innovation policy and grand challenges. *Science and Public Policy*, 45, 448–454.

Lam, J. C. K.; Walker, R. M.; Hills, P. (2014). Interdisciplinarity in sustainability studies: A Review. *Sustainable Development*, 22(3), 158–176.

Lang, D. J.; Wiek, A.; Bergmann, M.; Swilling, M.; Thomas, C. J. (2012): Transdisciplinary research in sustainability science: Practice, principles, and challenges. *Sustainability Science*, 7, 25–43.

Larrue, P.; Guellec, D.; Sgard, F. (2018). New trends in public research funding. In: OECD (Ed.): *OECD Science, Technology and Innovation Outlook 2018. Adapting to Technological and Societal Disruption*, 12th ed., pp. 185–204. Paris: OECD.

Laudel, G. (2006). The art of getting funded: How scientists adapt to their funding conditions. *Science and Public Policy*, 33(7), 489–504.

Lepori, B. (2011). Coordination modes in public funding systems. *Research Policy*, 40, 355–367.

Lepori, B.; Jongbloed, B. (2018). National resource allocation decisions in higher education: Objectives and dilemmas. In: Cantwell, B.; Coates, H.; King, R. (Eds.): *Handbook on the Politics of Higher Education*, pp. 211–228. Cheltenham: Edward Elgar.

Lepori, B.; van den Besselaar, P.; Dinges, M.; Potì, B.; Reale, E.; Slipersæter, S.; Thèves, J.; van der Meulen, B. (2007). Comparing the evolution of national research policies: what patterns of change? *Science and Public Policy*, 34(6), 372–388.

Lindner, R.; Goos, K.; Güth, S.; Som, O.; Schröder, T. (2016): "Responsible Research and Innovation" als Ansatz für die Forschungs-, Technologie- und Innovationspolitik – Hintergründe und Entwicklungen. TAB Hintergrund Papier No. 22. Berlin.

Mazzucato, M. (2018). Mission-oriented innovation policies: challenges and opportunities. *Industrial and Corporate Change*, 27(5), 803–815.

Mazzucato, M.; Semieniuk, G. (2017). Public financing of innovation: New questions. *Oxford Review of Economic Policy*, 33(1), 24–48.

Müller-Christ, G. (2017). Nachhaltigkeitsforschung in einer transzendenten Entwicklung des Hochschulsystems – ein Ordnungsangebot für Innovation. In: Leal, W. F. (Ed.): *Innovation in der Nachhaltigkeitsforschung. Ein Beitrag zur Umsetzung der UNO Nachhaltigkeitsziele*. Theorie und Praxis der Nachhaltigkeit, 161–180. Berlin: Springer Spektrum.

Newell (2001). A theory of interdisciplinary studies. *Issues in Integrative Studies*, 19, 1–25.

Newig, J.; Jahn, S.; Lang, D. J.; Kahle, J.; Bergmann, M. (2019). Linking modes of research to their scientific and societal outcomes. Evidence from 81 sustainability-oriented research projects. *Environmental Science & Policy*, 101, 147–155.

Nowotny, H.; Scott, P.; Gibbons, M. (2003). Mode 2 revisited: The new production of knowledge. *Minerva*, 41, 179–194.

OECD (2018). *Effective Operation of Competitive Research Funding Systems*. OECD Science, Technology and Industry Policy Papers, 57, https://www.oecd-ilibrary.org/industry-and-services/effective-operation-of-competitive-research-funding-systems_2ae8c0dc-en.

Pfirman, S.; Martin, P. J. S. (2017). Facilitating interdisciplinary scholars. In: Rodeman, R. F., Thompson Klein, J.; Pacheco, R. C. (Eds.): *The Oxford Handbook of Interdisciplinarity*, 2nd ed., pp. 387–403. Oxford: Oxford University Press.

Pohl, C. (2010). From transdisciplinarity to transdisciplinary research. *Transdisciplinary Journal of Engineering & Science*, 1, 65–73.

Polanyi, M. (1962). The Republic of Science. Its political and economic theory. *Minerva* 1(1), 54–73.

Ramos-Vielba, I.; Thomas, D. A.; Aagaard, K. (2022). Societal targeting in researcher funding: An exploratory approach. *Research Evaluation*, 31(2), 202–213.

Renn, O. (2019). Die Rolle(n) transdisziplinärer Wissenschaft bei konfliktgeladenen Transformations-prozessen. *GAIA*, 28(1), 44–51.

Rennings, K. (2000) Redefining Innovation – Eco-innovation research and the contribution from ecological economics. *Ecological Economics*, 32, 319–332. https://doi.org/10.1016/S0921-8009(99)00112-3

Rhoten, D.; Parker, A. (2004). Education: Risks and rewards of an interdisciplinary research path. *Science*, 306(5704), 2046.

Ruppert-Winkel, C. et al. (2015). Characteristics, emerging needs, and challenges of transdisciplinary sustainability science: Experiences from the German social–ecological research program. *Ecology and Society*, 20(3), art. 13.

Schneidewind, U.; Singer-Brodowski, M.; Augenstein, K. (2016). Transformative science for sustainability transitions. In: Brauch, H. G.; Spring, U. O.; Grin, J.; Scheffran, J. (Eds.): *Handbook on Sustainability Transition and Sustainable Peace*, pp. 123–136. Heidelberg: Springer.

Scholz, R. (2017). The normative dimension in transdisciplinarity, transition management, and transformation sciences: New roles of science and universities in sustainable transitioning. *Sustainability*, 9(6), 991.

Schoolman, E. D.; Guest, J. S.; Bush, K. F.; Bell, A. R. (2012). How interdisciplinary is sustainability research? Analyzing the structure of an emerging scientific field. *Sustainability Science*, 7(1), 67–80.

Schubert, T. (2009). Empirical observations on New Public Management to increase efficiency in public research – Boon or bane? *Research Policy*, 38, 1225–1234.

Shelley-Egan, C.; Gjefsen, M. D.; Nydal, R. (2020). Consolidating RRI and open science: Understanding the potential for transformative change. *Life Sciences, Society and Policy*, 16(1), 7.

Stilgoe, J.; Owen, R.; Macnagthen, P. (2013). Developing a framework for responsible innovation. *Research Policy*, 42, 1568–1580.

Swedish Research Council (2021). Quality and impact of research in political science in Sweden. A pilot evaluation. https://www.vr.se/english/analysis/reports/our-reports/2021-09-07-quality-and-impact-of-research-in-political-science-in-sweden.html.

van den Besselaar, P.; Heimeriks, G. (2001). Disciplinary, multidisciplinary, interdisciplinary – Concepts and indicators. *8th Conference on Scientometrics and Informetrics*, Sydney.

Viner, N.; Powell, P.; Green, R. (2004). Institutionalized biases in the award of research grants: A preliminary analysis revisiting the principle of accumulative advantage. *Research Policy*, 33(3), 443–454.

von Schomberg, R. (2013). A vision of responsible innovation. In: Owen, R.; Bessant, J.; Heintz, M. (Eds.): *Responsible Innovation: Opening up Dialogue and Debate*. Chichester: Wiley.

Weingart, P. (1997). Neue Formen der Wissensproduktion: Fakt, Fiktion und Mode. Institut für Wissenschafts- und Technikforschung, Univ. Bielefeld, IWT Paper 15. Bielefeld.

Wilsdon, J.; Allen, L.; Belfiore, E.; Campbell, P.; Curry, S.; Hill, S. et al. (2015). The Metric Tide: Report of the Independent Review of the Role of Metrics in Research Assessment and Management, https://www.ukri.org/publications/review-of-metrics-in-research-assessment-and-management/.

Zucker, D. (2012). Developing your career in an age of team science. *Journal of Investigative Medicine*, 60(5), 779–784.

10. Targeting research to address societal needs: what can we learn from 30 years of targeting neglected diseases?

Josie Coburn, Ohid Yaqub and Joanna Chataway

10.1 INTRODUCTION

Over the last half century, there has been wide appreciation for the role of research in stimulating innovation, supporting economic growth and improving health. Recognising the diffused effects of research has provided justification for public funding of research, and rationales for increases in the scale of that public funding (Arrow, 1962; Bush, 1945; Nelson, 1959).

Whilst funding for biomedical research has seen remarkable growth, that growth has recently slowed down and *research targeting* – the notion of setting priority areas to address with research – has taken on greater importance. Across the world, research targeting is on the rise, not just in biomedical research but in scientific research more generally. Appetite for targeting publicly funded research and steering its direction towards addressing specific social goals is growing (Kuhlmann and Rip, 2019; Sarewitz, 1996; Stirling, 2009).

There has been increasing attention on the direction of scientific and technical change for addressing some of society's most complex and urgent problems, ranging from mitigating climate change to meeting the Sustainable Development Goals, from pandemics to other Grand Challenges (Lund Declaration, 2009). Conceptual and policy efforts have taken the form of a 'developmental state' (Block, 2008; Fuchs, 2010), calls for 'responsible research and innovation' (Stilgoe et al., 2013), 'mission-oriented' research (Foray et al., 2012; Mazzucato, 2018; Sampat, 2012), and 'transformative innovation' (Schot and Steinmueller, 2018).

This shift in science policy efforts also relates to different meanings of 'public' in public research; to the conceptualisation of R&D programs as policy levers for steering researchers towards delivering public aims; and to the relationship between public research funding and the need to transform research systems to address complex challenges such as sustainability (see Bozeman's, Reale et al.'s and Bührer et al.'s chapters respectively, Chapters 2, 7 and 9 in this *Handbook*).

To learn more about targeting publicly funded research, we examine 'neglected diseases' as an extreme case of a societal need, for which there has been a clear market failure that justifies publicly funded research, and a clear track record where targeted R&D investment has been sustained over time. The term 'neglected diseases' was first used in the late 1970s with the launch of a network of laboratories devoted to researching the 'great neglected diseases of mankind' (Keating, 2014; Molyneux et al., 2021). However, it was not until the late 1990s – when neglected diseases were widely characterised as a misalignment between research priorities and societal needs (CHRD, 1990) – that they became more generally recognised as a problem.

Whilst this helped to direct attention towards funding for R&D as a way to redress the misalignment, there may have been some unintended consequences, particularly for health system strengthening and research capacity building. Additionally, the difficulty of evaluating such efforts, compared with the relative ease of evaluating more targeted research, may contribute to a 'tragedy of the evaluation commons', where wide remit priorities are overlooked despite their usefulness to multiple stakeholders.

The evolution of neglected diseases, as its own distinct category of research, illustrates some of the dynamics and tensions associated with the targeting of public research funding. These forces may also be playing a role in less conspicuous cases of misalignment between scientific research and societal needs.

The challenges of targeting and evaluating research in this extreme case may well be a subset of a more general phenomenon. As such, the promises and pitfalls of targeting R&D towards neglected diseases should be of broader interest to research policy scholars.

Section 10.2 provides a brief history of how the case for addressing neglected diseases with targeted research was developed. Section 10.3 examines some unintended consequences. Section 10.4 discusses how research evaluation can lock-in further research targeting. Section 10.5 concludes that targeted research efforts may leave behind other complementary investments, which does not necessarily reflect their lower priority but may instead indicate greater evaluation complexity.

10.2   A HISTORICAL AND CONCEPTUAL ACCOUNT OF NEGLECTED DISEASES

Public research funds targeting neglected diseases have increased from an estimated 1 billion USD in 1986 (CHRD, 1990) to 2.6 billion USD in 2019 (Policy Cures Research, 2020). Whilst the doubling in research funding for neglected diseases is remarkable in itself, focusing only on its growth takes neglected diseases largely as a given in terms of what they are, and the range of ways in which they might be addressed. Here, we describe how neglected diseases as a category was developed, how it became characterised as a misalignment in the research system, and how that conceptualisation came to dominate wider global health policy.

The conceptualisation of neglected diseases and attempts to address them have co-evolved over time. In the 1970s, post-war development organisations (e.g. WHO, Rockefeller Foundation) grew increasingly concerned that the health advances seen in the developed world could not be transferred to developing country contexts, and focused their efforts on the need for 'appropriate' technologies (Mahoney and Morel, 2006).[1]

In 1990, the Commission on Health Research for Development (CHRD) published an influential report, which highlighted a severe lack of R&D funding devoted to addressing the health problems of developing countries compared with those of industrialised countries (CHRD, 1990). This was later referred to as the '10/90 Gap' because less than 10% of health research funding was devoted to diseases which caused 90% of global disease burden (GFHR, 2000; MSF, 2001).

To address the 10/90 Gap, the CHRD report proposed: national research, especially in developing countries; international collaboration between scientists to address global challenges; building research capabilities to address developing country problems; and improving international arrangements for monitoring, assessing and promoting the health problems of developing countries (CHRD, 1990). Notably, increasing targeted research funding could be considered as only one of the possible implications of the report's findings.

Another prominent report reinforced the view of illness in the developing world as an economic problem that warranted policy intervention and proposed increasing government spending on health (World Bank, 1993). It argued for more scientific research, but with the proviso that a higher proportion of both international and national research support should be directed towards the needs of developing countries such as epidemiology, preventive medicine, the development of childhood vaccines and inexpensive medical technologies, and research to generate local solutions to local problems.

The World Bank report also introduced the disability-adjusted life year (DALY), combining mortality and morbidity into a single measure, which could then be used to compare national, regional, and global disease burdens (Chen et al., 2015). Along with the ability to draw on science and technology statistics (first standardised in 1963 with the introduction of the OECD Frascati Manual; Godin, 2005), DALYs made it possible to view diseases in terms of how much R&D funding they received relative to the burden of disease they caused. This allowed advocates and analysts to compare diseases directly and observe that some fare better than others in research funding allocations (Gross et al., 1999).

These and other high-level reports (WHO, 1996, 1999), alongside advocacy efforts that exploited the ability to compare diseases in terms of research funding and burden of disease, began to build momentum for addressing the health problems of developing countries, and in particular for addressing them by investing in R&D. These efforts served to conceptualise the challenge of neglected diseases principally as a problem of R&D shortfall. Moreover, the R&D shortfall had an obvious culprit: market failure.

The *rationales* for targeting neglected diseases were thought to reside largely in the public sector, but there was a recognition that many *capabilities* for addressing neglected diseases were largely in the private sector. By the early 2000s, there was a growing perception that public–private partnerships could offer institutional solutions (Chataway and Smith, 2006). A sub-type of the public–private partnership known as the product development partnership (PDP) arrived with the emergence of new global health actors such as the Bill and Melinda Gates Foundation. Notable examples are the International AIDS Vaccine Initiative, and the Medicines for Malaria Venture (Chataway et al., 2007; Hoogstraaten et al., 2020).[2]

PDPs began to develop their own unique capabilities (knowledge brokering and integration) for addressing the *innovation system failures* associated with neglected diseases and not just the *market failures* (Chataway et al., 2007). As such, PDPs have been characterised as 'organisational experiments' and 'social technologies' (Chataway et al., 2010) that 'drive product development for neglected diseases' (Hanson et al., 2012). In this PDP model, not only is a disease targeted, but the way of targeting it (i.e. the product) is also specified, focusing on largely technology-intensive solutions.

The development of the neglected disease category first (and foremost) attracted attention to what was previously neglected, and secondly framed the problem principally as a shortfall of R&D investment. The category also set in motion the development of new institutional forms to address the problem and created a demand for better data and analyses to support funders who might want to invest in neglected diseases.

With improvements in the availability of data,[3] a new body of literature emerged highlighting misalignments between biomedical research and societal needs (Viergever, 2013). One of the first contributions deploying this approach compared disease-specific research funding by the National Institutes of Health, with measures of US disease burden (Gross et al., 1999). It found some diseases were relatively overfunded (e.g. AIDS, breast cancer, diabetes mellitus, and dementia) and others were relatively underfunded (e.g. chronic obstructive pulmonary disease, perinatal conditions and peptic ulcer). Notably though, the authors left it largely to the reader and commentators to decide whether their analyses constituted misalignments.

Extending the approach beyond the US, Røttingen et al. (2013) found 'only about 1% of all health R&D investments were allocated to neglected diseases' and a 'persistent imbalance between R&D investments and needs-based priorities'. The extreme disparity meant they could be explicit about misalignment. So, compared with Gross et al. (1999), they were more forthright about policy implications: 'The need to align investments in health research and development (R&D) with public health demands is one of the most pressing global public health challenges' (Røttingen et al., 2013).

A stream of further studies built on this work. One compares the production of global health knowledge (in the form of publications) to 'the global market for treatment' (based on multiplying DALYs by gross national income per capita) (Evans et al., 2014). Another adds a 'neglect factor', based on the ratio of disease burden to R&D expenditure (von Philipsborn et al., 2015). More recently, since the inception of the WHO's Global Observatory on Health R&D, studies have analysed funders, recipient countries, grant type and duration, product type and collaborations (Adam et al., 2019; Ralaidovy et al., 2020). All of these studies highlight conspicuous misalignments between biomedical research and global health needs in various ways, suggesting a degree of robustness to their overarching claims.

Probing what might be driving these kinds of misalignments, Yegros-Yegros et al. (2020) investigated the influence of geography, industry and publication incentives on health research efforts globally. They found that diseases that are more prevalent in high-income countries (HICs) 'generate ten-fold more research attention than those in low-income countries' and that researchers receive more citations when they work on HIC diseases. This is likely to be a reflection of research activity and funding being heavily concentrated in HICs, however it also suggests that academic publishing might incentivise researchers to focus on diseases of the rich, even researchers in low- and middle-income countries (LMICs), regardless of local LMIC priorities.

Despite the proliferation of research identifying misalignments, it can remain difficult to discern what 'correct' alignment would look like, and to what extent, if at all, the growth of targeted research will be able to address these societal needs. As such, all but the most extreme misalignments will remain highly contested. These questions should be included in a future research agenda in this area. An important strand for such an agenda is to recognise that analytical misalignments sometimes arise from the categories being used in the analysis. There is a need to appreciate *the nature of the categories* being targeted for research.

Diseases have come to occupy premier policy relevance in organising social resources towards addressing health problems. As a category, they have their own sets of causes and consequences. They bring together an array of symptoms, pathogens, treatments through a process of diagnosis (Rosenberg, 2002; Thagard, 1999). This means that there are multiple ways of grouping diseases into classes.

We highlight the prominence of neglected diseases as a category where 'classifications should be recognised as the significant site of political and ethical work that they are' (Bowker and Star, 2000). The category of neglected diseases is *doing work*, contributing to efforts to define a problem and attract more investment to address a moving target (Best, 2019; Blume,

Table 10.1   *Categories of disease and their performance*

Category of disease	A description of the category label and its social performance.
Preventable diseases	More than a quarter of the world's population does not have access to essential medicines (Chan, 2017). By highlighting that some diseases can be treated with basic drugs, this gives rise to the idea of preventable disease and premature deaths, or in Paul Farmer's terminology, 'stupid deaths' (Farmer, 2003).
Neglected diseases	These are distinguishable from preventable diseases because adequate treatments are not available yet. The focus is switched from access to existing medicine, to R&D for new or better medicine.
Rare and tropical diseases	Rare diseases have small market size because they affect few people. In contrast, tropical diseases have small market size because they affect a large number of poor people. So, the label serves to emphasise its geographical incidence rather than its relation to poverty or how deserving its patients might be.
Emerging diseases	This category serves to prompt urgent responses, marshal resources from security agendas that often have larger budgets, and encourage the strengthening of a global monitoring and detection apparatus.
Big three diseases	A sub-category that commands more than two-thirds of all global R&D funding for neglected diseases (Policy Cures Research, 2019) and highlights differing degrees of neglect within neglected diseases (von Philipsborn et al., 2015).

2003; Hacking, 1995; Mackenzie, 2006). Quantification of both disease burden and research investment allows classification into categories that facilitate commensurability. Both classification and quantification have been conceptualised as social processes, requiring social and intellectual effort to construct and maintain (Espeland and Stevens, 1998; Porter, 1995; Power, 1997).

For the purposes of targeting resources, focusing on diseases can make problems more comparable, and cast light on previously overlooked allocation choices. A variety of disease category labels have been deployed in a similar vein to the neglected diseases category to highlight the plight of those marginalised from health gains. Consider, for example, the variety of disease classes listed in Table 10.1 and the varying conceptualisations they invoke.

Despite attempts to define neglected diseases, in practice the grouping is nebulous and quickly decomposes into other, often overlapping, categories. The term 'neglected diseases' can be a shorthand reference to neglected tropical diseases (NTDs), which in turn are categorised differently across stakeholders (Hotez et al., 2020; Molyneux et al., 2021; WHO, 2021). Neglected diseases can also refer to a wider set of poverty-related and neglected diseases, where they include 'The Big Three': malaria, tuberculosis and HIV/AIDS (Cochrane et al., 2017). The Big Three are big in the sense that, together, they cause high mortality. Hotez (2013) argues that we should go further and talk about 'The Gang of Four' to include the morbidity of NTDs in terms of DALYs (as opposed to mortality). To complicate definitions further, some HIV/AIDS R&D funding is omitted because the disease is prevalent in HICs as well as in LMICs, and so some HIV/AIDS research funding cannot be attributed to being part of an effort to address neglected diseases (Moran et al., 2009).

This provides an illustration of *the ways in which we define the category of neglected diseases matters* – for example, if we exclude some investment in HIV/AIDS R&D, and if we emphasise morbidity (rather than only mortality), neglected diseases seem more neglected.

10.3   WHAT DO WE KNOW ABOUT UNINTENDED CONSEQUENCES OF FOCUSING RESEARCH FUNDING ON SPECIFIC SOCIAL OUTCOMES?

We identify six possible unintended consequences of targeting research funding to specific diseases. The discussion below suggests that many of these are likely to be relevant to research targeting more generally.

Firstly, the plethora of new actors and organisations targeted towards specific diseases or products has created coordination and prioritisation challenges. This has resulted in 'gaps in funding and distorted priorities' and has left LMICs 'in the position of having to accept the net result of multiple uncoordinated decisions rather than benefiting from careful planning and investment' (Hanson et al., 2012). If successful, continued increases in R&D funding for neglected diseases will lead to a need for large-scale clinical trials of new treatments and products and these will require even greater funding and coordination as well as local clinical trial capabilities (Moran et al., 2005). Thus, even if the main policy focus is on providing targeted R&D funding to solve a specific health problem, coordination and prioritisation challenges must be addressed.

Secondly, focusing research funding on addressing neglected diseases has increased the need to address social determinants of health, strengthen health research systems, and build research capacity. Addressing these needs may even achieve more, in terms overall health improvements, than efforts targeted at a particular disease (Chataway et al., 2019; Ncube and Chataway, 2019).

One possibility is that research funding targeting particular diseases has come in addition to these other priorities which have not seen similar increases in funding support. However, a more serious possibility is that targeted funding displaced these other priorities. It remains difficult to disentangle these two possibilities, but it is clear that targeting to particular diseases has become a general trend in global health.

Donors typically prefer 'vertical' disease-specific interventions, rather than 'horizontal' approaches, which would focus on strengthening entire health systems (Clinton and Sridhar, 2017). Vertical programmes are perceived as being easier to monitor and control, with results that are easier to measure. They are favoured by donors despite 'near universal consensus that optimal health systems are the key to improving health' (Clinton and Sridhar, 2017). With around 40 different global health PDPs, all implementing largely vertical strategies that collectively pull resources into particular disease areas, bottlenecks in health systems and research capacity are accentuated (Ncube and Chataway, 2019). One could see this as a natural consequence of the way neglect was constructed as an issue in need of addressing with R&D, as discussed in Section 10.2.

Thirdly, focusing research funding on neglected diseases helps sustain the false assumption that research capabilities can be accumulated automatically as a side effect of research targeting LMIC concerns – the mythology of 'learning by doing' (Bell and Pavitt, 1993; Scott-Kemmis and Bell, 2010). One reason the assumption does not hold is simply because remarkably little neglected disease research is in fact undertaken in LMIC countries. A recent analysis of the research funded by 10 major funders of health research revealed that 98.9% of biomedical research grants were allocated to researchers in HICs and only 0.2% to those in LICs (Ralaidovy et al., 2020).[4] Another reason is that not all forms of research activity will actually build capacity to the same extent or in the same ways. So, even if more research is localised in LMICs, it will not necessarily contribute to building capabilities without due consideration of the research system in which it is embedded (national or global). A more dedicated, and often broader effort that explicitly targets research capacity building is often needed.

Over recent years, more direct efforts at building research capacity building have been made (Cochrane et al., 2014; Ghaffar et al., 2008; Marjanovic et al., 2013). However, building research capacity is itself prone to overly narrow targeting. In practice, the challenge is often reduced to promoting knowledge transfer or technical training 'without parallel investments to develop and sustain the socioeconomic and political structures that facilitate knowledge creation' (Mormina, 2019).

One result of this focus is the salience of the 'brain drain' problem, whereby LMIC researchers emigrate to HICs (Ghaffar et al., 2008). An alternative would be to conceptualise knowledge production as a more collective process. This might instead emphasise weak local demand for trained researchers, and create an imperative to 'strengthen the different social, political and economic structures that make up a nation's innovation system' (Mormina, 2019). National system differences are important because research funding priorities can differ between HICs and LMICs. In HICs, funding rationales based on scientific excellence and national relevance can both be pursued, whereas in LMICs scarce resources may mean pursuing multiple rationales is not feasible (Chataway et al., 2019). Balancing capacity building imperatives and addressing national priorities may not align with current perceptions of scientific excellence (Chataway and Daniels, 2020). In response to this problem, some have called for a more pluralistic view of research excellence, one that includes research capacity building (Kraemer-Mbula et al., 2020).

Fourthly, researchers themselves may react to research targeting in unanticipated ways. Examples include: 'symbolic compliance'/window-dressing (modifying the language used to describe research without changing the content of the research); 'hoarding' (gathering more resources than needed to cope with funding cuts and the risk of failure; Gläser, 2019); 'bootlegging' (using resources that were meant for one purpose to fund another; Hackett, 1987); maintaining research portfolios (enabling researchers to drop unfundable lines, start fundable lines and change existing lines of research; Gläser et al., 2010); and constructing 'doable' problems linked to 'fundability' (Fujimura, 1987). Researchers may also engage in goal displacement (in which gaining a high score according to evaluation criteria becomes the goal, displacing other research goals); in task reduction (suppressing tasks which are not counted in the evaluation); or structural changes to publication activities and research capacity-building (de Rijcke et al., 2016). Laudel's chapter in this *Handbook* also analyses 'researchers' strategies for building and maintaining their funding portfolios' (Laudel, Chapter 16 in this *Handbook*).

Fifthly, targeting research may have contributed to the rise of project-funding. This has become an increasingly important mechanism for supporting research. This mechanism is not only likely to cause a narrowing of goals, as researchers feel pressured to respond to funder priorities, but also suffers from instability, which may discourage researchers from staying in underfunded research areas (Whitley et al., 2018). Even for those that might venture away from well-funded and stable research environments, project funding mechanisms tend to discourage researchers from moving into fields where they might not have a track record (Luukkonen, 2012). Of particular relevance to neglected diseases, LMIC researchers may be forced to adapt their research in more extreme ways owing to the scarcity of resources in their research environment and the 'high degree of authority over research agendas and methodologies' imposed by funders and research partners from the Global North (Laudel, Chapter 16 in this *Handbook*).

Lastly, the pathways for addressing a disease are not defined by mere dint of having targeted the disease category with research. The multiplicity of routes to the target, as well as the nature of the target itself can be contested, and they matter for both the effectiveness and legitimacy of the pathways. Non-local research funding allocations shape research targets and priorities in ways that may not be the most appropriate for local contexts in LMICs (Cochrane et al., 2017). For HIC funders, the 'choice of target area can reflect their own understandings rather than the needs and demands of low- and middle-income countries themselves' (Hanson et al., 2012). This is unlikely to produce long term solutions to the problems that matter to those living in LMICs (Cochrane et al., 2017) and it may result in the pursuit of technical options that seem strange and could subsequently lead one to misidentify the problem as a failure of research translation or 'implementation'.

A stark illustration can be found in podoconiosis, where exposure of bare feet to alkalic clay causes inflammation and progressive swelling (Deribe et al., 2020). Since there is some degree of genetic susceptibility, there is genetic research into podoconiosis. However, people would not contract podoconiosis if they had shoes to wear in areas of irritant soil, and 'footwear remains an unaffordable luxury for residents of most affected areas in the tropics' (Davey et al., 2007). For want of shoes, genetic research can seem a peculiar approach to pursue. This peculiarity is not well addressed by a framework that emphasises only a misalignment between research supply and societal needs. That framework would suggest more targeted research, whereas the issue in fact relates to the kinds of research (or non-research) approaches brought to bear upon the problem.

Targeting research towards specific diseases has not corrected an imbalance between laboratory science and social science that has been identified as a problem by many (Gilson et al., 2011; Ncube and Chataway, 2019). It may even have reinforced and exacerbated some imbalances, as the prominence of a particular line of research is more pro-actively enhanced and reinforced through disease-based framing.

For example, Chagas disease changed 'from a problem of precarious living conditions, to a problem of fumigation, and then a problem of basic research' (Kreimer and Zabala, 2007). Kreimer (2016) argued that by 'positioning the production of knowledge about the parasite's DNA center stage', researchers displaced 'other solutions to the Chagas problem, such as systematically fumigating rural houses'. He concluded that: 'In fact, less prestigious but more useful research could be conducted, such as the development of new kinds of insecticides. But such research would not allow the researchers to participate in international scientific networks' (Kreimer, 2016). The study illustrates the influence of the global science system, even on locally-oriented research topics.

To address these issues there is a need to build up local research capabilities, not only to absorb the knowledge being produced in HICs, but also to orient research in ways that better contribute to solving LMIC problems (Cochrane et al., 2017). In some ways, this is a re-iteration of the call made thirty years ago. The influential 10/90 report argued that 'Strengthening research capacity in developing countries is one of the most powerful, cost-effective, and sustainable means of advancing health and development' (CHRD, 1990).

10.4   (TARGETING CAN CREATE) A TRAGEDY OF THE EVALUATION COMMONS

Funding targeted to specific diseases often leads to evaluation based on metrics for specific disease-related outcomes. For example, funding for the provision of HIV/AIDs antiretroviral drugs can be evaluated by measuring reduction in HIV/AIDs disease burden. Moreover, focusing on specific diseases and the impact of R&D for those diseases can help maintain political support for research. Evaluations of this kind can offer a clear indication of return on investments.

In contrast, investments aimed at broader health system strengthening, research capacity building and overall health outcomes, are much more difficult to evaluate. The difference exacerbates a lack of evidence on the returns to health system strengthening and research capacity building efforts, relative to that of investments targeting specific diseases where the evaluation challenge is narrower. Part of the appeal of research targeting, then, is intimately tied to evaluation practice.

Evaluation difficulties stem from at least two sources that we discuss in turn: the involvement of a wider set of stakeholders; and data collection from LMICs with conceptual frameworks that highlight complementarities across systems.

Firstly, the tragedy of the evaluation commons is that, although complex evaluations of broad-remit programs can be of benefit to multiple stakeholders, their delivery is costly and labour-intensive. Moreover, it is harder to justify costs if benefits cannot be easily appropriated by those who pay for the evaluation.

One way to mitigate these problems is to share the costs (and benefits) of the evaluation between multiple stakeholders. However, multiple stakeholders may have goals that pull the evaluation in different directions, and make it difficult to provide clear evidence of returns on investment. Research evaluation can be have multiple purposes that include accountability, learning, advocacy and informing strategy; their design can be narrowly or broadly framed, deploying only a few or a wide array of indicators (Marjanovic et al., 2017). These different motives, framings and designs for evaluating can remain implicit, causing problems when deciding who should do the evaluating and how it should be done.

The allure of tightly framed evaluations providing clear evidence of returns on investment may inadvertently contribute to a narrowing of the research itself because activities that are not included in the evaluation might not get done. Broader goals such as health system strengthening and research capacity building may be displaced by the narrow goals that are measured more easily by evaluations taken on by fewer stakeholders. If these are not valued in evaluations, other more targeted investments may prevail, and the importance of health system strengthening and research capacity building may remain overlooked. The problem is pressing because the health of a population may not necessarily be improved by disease-specific success without complementary investments in systems and capacity.

Secondly, there is a lack of evidence that targeted research funding leads to better outcomes overall, and a lack of conceptual apparatus to facilitate the type of analysis that might support the necessary complementary investments. Rates of return on health research show high payback, but the evaluations are often framed around individual diseases (Guthrie et al., 2018). They do not establish a more comprehensive picture of the relationship between health research and returns to society. There remains considerable conceptual difficulty about how to measure these broader relationships. Importantly, studies of this kind have not included LMICs, and an absence of LMIC data makes that task difficult.

One study that examined the broad relationship between investment in poverty-related neglected diseases R&D, and health outcomes in LMICs, concluded that it was not possible to draw strong results about the benefits and issues on the basis of existing data. The data that would enable this kind of analysis would need to be very different and much more comprehensive than that which is currently collected (Cochrane et al., 2017).

An evaluation of the Swedish International Development Cooperation Agency component of the European Developing Country Clinical Trails Programme highlighted an additional problem, which stems from conceptual confusion about the intended outcomes of targeted funding mechanisms. It highlighted a lack of clarity on the extent to which the programme defined its mission in terms of R&D outputs and capacity building on the one hand, and broader health and societal outcomes on the other hand (Hanlin et al., 2020). A clearer distinction would have a profound impact on the type of evaluation that is required and raises questions about who should be responsible for collecting data and reporting. This kind of confusion arises from a widespread but often unevidenced *assumption* that health R&D will lead to positive health outcomes in LMICs (Cochrane et al., 2017).

In recent years, several research evaluation efforts have attempted to address this gap with broader evaluation frameworks. A Wellcome Trust report (2012) argued for integrating monitoring and evaluation into project plans from the start; involving stakeholders when deciding what to monitor and evaluate (including associated indicators and methods); and ensuring that monitoring and evaluation are properly resourced, practical, usable and proportionate.

RAND Europe developed a poverty-related neglected disease health research and innovation system framework to evaluate the impact of the EU's R&D funding for poverty-related neglected diseases in terms of how public research has been translated into new products and services. The framework highlights the 'different components of a health research and innovation system that need to "work together" to achieve desired impacts' (Cochrane et al., 2017). These include health research and innovation pathways; research and innovation system drivers; health system drivers; global health policy levers; and wider environmental drivers. This framework conceptualises the problem of addressing neglected diseases as inherently multifaceted, and public funding of targeted research as *one* response to *one* of the issues that have been identified as crucial parts of a wider health and innovation system.

The International Development Research Centre in Canada developed an evaluation framework called Research Quality Plus, which is 'a systems-informed approach to defining and evaluating the quality of research, and its positioning for use and impact' (IDRC, 2016). The framework emphasises multiple dimensions of quality assessment criteria that allow for varying contexts. This approach shows that research in the global south can be both rigorous and well-positioned for use; and that capacity strengthening and excellence can go hand in hand (Lebel and McLean, 2018).

Another response to these problems is to 'broaden out' the inputs to research evaluation and 'open up' the outputs (Ràfols and Stirling, 2021). The development of more plural and conditional indicators would make 'the perspectives or assumptions through which they are framed' more visible. Ràfols and Stirling note how the *methods used* in research evaluation and other types of social appraisal[5] influence the outputs, and so argue for the use of methods such as multicriteria mapping (MCM), which is a hybrid quantitative-qualitative method. MCM involves the appraisal of multiple options according to multiple perspectives and issues, and allows for consideration of uncertainties. The resultant mappings can be used to explore any salient grouping of the inputs, alongside qualitative reasons as to *why* some options perform better or worse under some conditions. There are many other methods which can help to broaden out and open up social appraisal.

10.5   CONCLUSION

In this chapter we examined an extreme case of efforts to target research towards addressing societal needs. We noted that R&D spending oriented to these needs has increased, and explained how this was facilitated by the emergence of a target category, namely that of neglected diseases.

We also argued however that there may be fundamental limits to a research-targeting approach. Perpetually increasing the funding for R&D may not unlock changes in health outcomes because of unintended consequences resulting from targeting funding towards specific diseases (see Bozeman's chapter in this *Handbook* for a discussion of other reasons for the 'research–health outcomes gap' in the US (Bozeman, Chapter 2 in this *Handbook*)). Research targeting may suffer from a lack of coordination; it can undermine efforts to strengthen local health systems; it leaves efforts to build research capacity unattended; it may result in unanticipated reactions by researchers in response to their funding environment; and it may favour some types of research over other approaches.

A better understanding of the relationship between scientific research and global health outcomes may help to avoid some of these unintended consequences and offer alternatives to research-targeting. This includes reconsidering the way funding mechanisms are designed predominantly around principles of research excellence, which means that increasing funding levels towards a specific target does not necessarily alter the balance and composition of research portfolios. Addressing problems in low- and middle-income countries may require not just more biomedical R&D, but also other kinds of research. Portfolio composition, as well as overall portfolio size, remains an important challenge. These problems are compounded by a tragedy of the evaluation commons, where more complex and challenging evaluation tasks are overlooked or underfunded.

We have also argued that some of these problems could be addressed by building up local research capabilities, not only to absorb the knowledge being produced in high-income countries, but also to orient research in ways that better contribute to solving low- and middle-income country problems. Cooperative forms of research with a wide range of stakeholders could also help to both orient and evaluate research. Broad methods of social appraisal and consultation (such as multicriteria mapping) could offer sense of when research is likely to be seen as a complement, or as a dominant input, for addressing a given target. This serves not only to set a direction for research but also lends greater legitimacy for pursuing research as a way of addressing social challenges.

Taken together, we see that the way a societal problem is framed and targeted by research interacts with research evaluation. Although we have focused on examining these issues in relation to the case of neglected diseases, research targeting to address societal problems is on the rise more generally. Thus, many of the issues highlighted here are relevant to the prevailing enthusiasm for targeting research towards society's 'Grand Challenges', in domains such as climate change, the Sustainable Development Goals and pandemics, and to how the burden of such challenges are distributed across high-income countries and other countries. We hope there is an appetite for developing a new research and policy agenda along these lines, for tackling the challenge of neglected diseases in particular, but also for addressing other urgent societal problems.

NOTES

1. The WHO launched its Special Programmes 'to develop or apply new technologies and strategies for the pressing health needs of people in developing countries' and the Program for Appropriate Technology in Health (PATH) in Seattle created product research and development programmes to begin to address health needs in developing countries (Mahoney and Morel, 2006).
2. Although there are some exceptions such as Drugs for Neglected Diseases initiative, whose remit spans a range of diseases, albeit within the same class of diseases (neglected diseases).
3. There was a growing recognition that better data infrastructure could support research funders who might want to invest in neglected diseases (Moran et al., 2009). Funded by the Gates Foundation and other global organisations, G-FINDER was founded, a publicly available tool that tracks product-related R&D funding flows for neglected diseases (Moran et al., 2009). Despite these improvements, there remains a lack of data from LMICs (Cochrane et al., 2017). The WHO has recently established a global observatory on health R&D.
4. This is not simply due to a low percentage of grants devoted to neglected diseases research (only 16% of grants were for infectious and parasitic diseases and only 1.1% for NTDs). Even *within* neglected diseases research, the vast majority was allocated to researchers in HICs.
5. Appraisal can be defined as 'the ensemble of processes through which knowledges are gathered and produced in order to inform decision-making and wider institutional commitments' (Leach et al., 2010).

REFERENCES

Adam, T., Ralaidovy, A. H., and Swaminathan, S. (2019). Biomedical research; What gets funded where? *Bulletin of the World Health Organization, 97*(8), 8–9.

Arrow, K. (1962). Economic welfare and the allocation of resources for invention. In R. Nelson (Ed.), *The rate and direction of inventive activity* (pp. 609–626). Princeton University Press.

Bell, M., and Pavitt, K. (1993). Technological accumulation and industrial growth: contrasts between developed and developing countries. *Industrial and Corporate Change, 2*(2), 157–210.

Best, R. K. (2019). *Common enemies: Disease campaigns in America.* Oxford University Press.

Block, F. (2008). Swimming against the current: The rise of a hidden developmental state in the United States. *Politics and Society, 36*(2), 169–206.

Blume, S. (2003). *Insight and industry: On the dynamics of technological change in medicine.* MIT Press.

Bowker, G., and Star, S. L. (2000). *Sorting things out: Classification and its consequences.* MIT Press.

Bush, V. (1945). *Science: The endless frontier.* United States Government Printing Office.

Chan, M. (2017). *Ten years in public health 2007–2017.* World Health Organization.

Chataway, J., and Daniels, C. (2020). The Republic of Science meets the Republics of Somewhere: Embedding scientific excellence in sub-Saharan Africa. In E. Kraemer-Mbula, R. Tijssen, M. Wallace, and R. McLean (Eds.), *Transforming research excellence* (pp. 39–58). African Minds.

Chataway, J., and Smith, J. (2006). The International AIDS Vaccine Initiative (IAVI): Is it getting new science and technology to the world's neglected majority? *World Development, 34*(1), 16–30.

Chataway, J., Brusoni, S., Cacciatori, E., Hanlin, R., and Orsenigo, L. (2007). The International AIDS Vaccine Initiative (IAVI) in a changing landscape of vaccine development: A public/private partnership as knowledge broker and integrator. *European Journal of Development Research, 19*(1), 100–117.

Chataway, J., Hanlin, R., Mugwagwa, J., and Muraguri, L. (2010). Global health social technologies: Reflections on evolving theories and landscapes. *Research Policy, 39*(10), 1277–1288.

Chataway, J., Dobson, C., Daniels, C., Byrne, R., Hanlin, R., and Tigabu, A. (2019). Science granting councils in Sub-Saharan Africa: Trends and tensions. *Science and Public Policy, 46*(4), 620–631.

Chen, A., Jacobsen, K., Deshmukh, A., and Cantor, S. (2015). The evolution of the disability-adjusted life year (DALY). *Socio-Economic Planning Sciences, 49*, 10–15.

CHRD. (1990). *Health research: Essential link to equity in development.* Oxford University Press.

Clinton, C., and Sridhar, D. (2017). *Governing global health: Who runs the world and why?* Oxford University Press.

Cochrane, G., Robin, E., Marjanovic, S., Diepeveen, S., Hanlin, R., Kryl, D., Muchova, L., Yaqub, O., and Chataway, J. (2014). *The African Institutions Initiative: Insights from the first four years.* RAND Europe and The Open University.

Cochrane, G., Morgan Jones, M., Marjanovic, S., MacLure, C., Varnai, P., Jongh, T. de, Rosemberg, C., Sadeski, F., Dani, S., Davé, A., Nooijen, A., Ghiga, I., Lepetit, L., Chataway, M., and Chataway, J. (2017). *Evaluation of the impact of the European Union's Research Funding for Poverty-related and Neglected Diseases.* European Commission.

Davey, G., Tekola, F., and Newport, M. (2007). Podoconiosis: Non-infectious geochemical elephantiasis. *Transactions of the Royal Society for Tropical Medicine and Hygiene, 101*(12), 1175–1180.

Deribe, K., Mackenzie, C., Newport, M., Argaw, D., Molyneux, D., and Davey, G. (2020). Podoconiosis: Key priorities for research and implementation. *Transactions of the Royal Society for Tropical Medicine and Hygiene, 114*, 889–895.

de Rijcke, S., Wouters, P., Rushforth, A., Franssen, T., and Hammarfelt, B. (2016). Evaluation practices and effects of indicator use – A literature review. *Research Evaluation, 25*(2), 161–169.

Espeland, W., and Stevens, M. (1998). Commensuration as a social process. *Annual Review of Sociology, 24*, 313–343.

Evans, J., Shim, J.-M., and Ioannidis, J. (2014). Attention to local health burden and the global disparity of health research. *PLoS ONE, 9*(4).

Farmer, P. (2003). *Pathologies of power: Health, human rights, and the new war on the poor.* University of California Press.

Foray, D., Mowery, D., and Nelson, R. (2012). Public R&D and social challenges: What lessons from mission R&D programs? *Research Policy, 41*(10), 1697–1702.

Fuchs, E. R. H. (2010). Rethinking the role of the state in technology development: DARPA and the case for embedded network governance. *Research Policy, 39*(9), 1133–1147.

Fujimura, J. H. (1987). Constructing 'do-able' problems in cancer research: Articulating alignment. *Social Studies of Science, 17*(2), 257–293.

GFHR (2000). *The 10/90 report on health research.* Global Forum for Health Research.

Ghaffar, A., Ijsselmuiden, C., and Zicker, F. (2008). *Changing mindsets: Research capacity strengthening in low- and middle-income countries.* CHRD, GFHR, UNICEF/UNDP/World Bank/WHO-TDR.

Gilson, L., Hanson, K., Sheikh, K., Agyepong, I., and Ssengooba, F. (2011). Building the field of health policy and systems research: Social science matters. *PLoS Medicine, 8*(8), 1–6.

Gläser, J. (2019). How can governance change research content? Linking science policy studies to the sociology of science. In S. Dagmar, S. Kuhlmann, and J. Stamm (Eds.), *Handbook on science and public policy* (pp. 419–447). Edward Elgar.

Gläser, J., Lange, S., Laudel, G., and Schimank, U. (2010). The limits of universality: How field-specific epistemic conditions affect authority relations and their consequences. In R. Whitley, J. Gläser, and L. Engwall (Eds.), *Reconfiguring knowledge production* (pp. 291–324). Oxford University Press.

Godin, B. (2005). *Measurement and statistics on science and technology: 1920 to the present.* Routledge.

Gross, C., Anderson, G., and Powe, N. (1999). The relation between funding by the National Institutes of Health and the burden of disease. *New England Journal of Medicine, 340*(24), 1881–1887.

Guthrie, S., D'Angelo, C., Ioppolo, B., Shenderovich, Y., and McInroy, G. (2018). *Evidence synthesis on measuring the distribution of benefits of research and innovation.* RAND Europe.

Hackett, E. (1987). Funding and academic research in the life sciences: Results of an exploratory study. *Science and Technology Studies, 5*(3/4), 134–147.

Hacking, I. (1995). *Rewriting the soul: Multiple personality and the sciences of memory.* Princeton University Press.

Hanlin, R., van't Hoog, A., Kruger, M., Mugwagwa, J., and Chataway, J. (2020). *Final report: An independent evaluation of Sida's support to projects in the scope of the EDCTP2 programme*. SIDA and EDCTP.

Hanson, K., Palafox, B., Anderson, S., Guzman, J., Moran, M., Shretta, R., and Wuliji, T. (2012). Pharmaceuticals. In M. Merson, R. Black, and A. Mills (Eds.), *Global health: Diseases, programs, systems and policies* (pp. 707–755). Jones & Bartlett Learning.

Hoogstraaten, M., Boon, W., and Frenken, K. (2020). How product development partnerships support hybrid collaborations dealing with global health challenges. *Global Transitions*, *2*, 190–201.

Hotez, P. J. (2013). *Forgotten people, forgotten diseases: The neglected tropical diseases and their impact on global health and development*. ASM Press.

Hotez, P. J., Aksoy, S., Brindley, P., and Kamhawi, S. (2020). What constitutes a neglected tropical disease? *PLoS Neglected Tropical Diseases*, *14*(1), e0008001.

IDRC. (2016). *Research quality plus: A holistic approach to evaluating Research*. International Development Research Center.

Keating, C. (2014). Ken Warren and the Rockefeller foundation's great neglected diseases network, 1978–1988: The transformation of tropical and global medicine. *Molecular Medicine*, *20*(December 1977), S24–S30.

Kraemer-Mbula, E., Tijssen, R., Wallace, M., McLean, R., Allen, L., Barrere, R., Chataway, J., Chavarro, D., Daniels, C., Lebel, J., Marincola, E., Mendizabal, E., Neylon, C., Ouattara, A., Raza, F., Sangaré, Y., Singh, S., Siregar, F., Ssembatya, V., and Sutz, J. (2020). Call to action: Transforming 'excellence' for the Global South and beyond. In E. Kraemer-Mbula, R. Tijssen, M. Wallace, and R. McLean (Eds.), *Transforming research excellence*. African Minds.

Kreimer, P. (2016). Co-producing social problems and scientific knowledge. Chagas disease and the dynamics of research fields in Latin America. In M. Merz and P. Sormani (Eds.), *The local configuration of new research fields* (pp. 173–190). Springer International.

Kreimer, P., and Zabala, J. P. (2007). Chagas disease in Argentina: Reciprocal construction of social and scientific problems. *Science, Technology and Society*, *12*(1), 49–72.

Kuhlmann, S., and Rip, A. (2019). Next generation science policy and Grand Challenges. In D. Simon, S. Kuhlmann, J. Stamm, and W. Canzler (Eds.), *Handbook on science and public policy* (pp. 12–25). Edward Elgar.

Leach, M., Scoones, I., and Stirling, A. (2010). Dynamic Sustainabilities: Technology, environment, social justice. In *Dynamic Sustainabilities: Technology, Environment, Social Justice*. Earthscan.

Lebel, J., and McLean, R. (2018). A better measure of research from the Global South. *Nature*, *559*, 23–26.

Lund Declaration (2009). *The Lund Declaration: Europe must focus on the Grand Challenges of our time* (July). Swedish EU Presidency.

Luukkonen, T. (2012). Conservatism and risk-taking in peer review: Emerging ERC practices. *Research Evaluation*, *21*(1), 48–60.

Mackenzie, D. (2006). *An engine, not a camera: How financial models shape markets*. The MIT Press.

Mahoney, R. T., and Morel, C. M. (2006). A Global Health Innovation System (GHIS). *Innovation Strategy Today*, *2*(1), 1–12.

Marjanovic, S., Hanlin, R., Diepeveen, S., and Chataway, J. (2013). Research capacity-building in Africa: Networks, institutions and local ownership. *Journal of International Development*, *25*, 936–946.

Marjanovic, S., Cochrane, G., Robin, E., Sewankambo, N., Ezeh, A., Nyirenda, M., Bonfoh, B., Rweyemamu, M., and Chataway, J. (2017). Evaluating a complex research capacity-building intervention: Reflections on an evaluation of the African Institutions Initiative. *Evaluation*, *23*(1), 80–101.

Mazzucato, M. (2018). *Mission-oriented research and innovation in the European Union: A problem-solving approach to fuel innovation-led growth*. European Commission.

Molyneux, D., Asamoa-Bah, A., Fenwick, A., Savioli, L., and Hotez, P. (2021). The history of the neglected tropical disease movement. *Transactions of the Royal Society for Tropical Medicine and Hygiene*, *115*(2), 169–175.

Moran, M., Ropars, A.-L., Guzman, J., Diaz, J., and Garrison, C. (2005). *The new landscape of neglected disease drug development*. Wellcome Trust.

Moran, M., Guzman, J., Ropars, A.-L., Mcdonald, A., Jameson, N., Omune, B., Ryan, S., and Wu, L. (2009). Neglected disease research and development: How much are we really spending? *PLoS Medicine, 6*(2), 137–146.

Mormina, M. (2019). Science, technology and innovation as social goods for development: Rethinking research capacity building from sen's capabilities approach. *Science and Engineering Ethics, 25*(3), 671–692.

MSF. (2001). *Fatal imbalance: The crisis in research and development for drugs for neglected diseases* (p. 32). Medecins Sans Frontiers and Drugs for Neglected Diseases initiative.

Ncube, V., and Chataway, J. (2019). Harnessing innovative HIV point-of-care testing for health systems strengthening: Early lessons from Zimbabwe. *Innovation and Development, 9*(2), 287–304.

Nelson, R. (1959). The simple economics of basic scientific research. *Journal of Political Economy, 67*(3), 297–306.

Policy Cures Research (2019). *G-FINDER 2019: Neglected disease research and development: Uneven progress* (p. 25). Policy Cures Research.

Policy Cures Research (2020). *G-FINDER 2020: Neglected disease research and development: Where to now?* Policy Cures Research.

Porter, T. (1995). *Trust in numbers: The pursuit of objectivity in science and public life.* Princeton University Press.

Power, M. (1997). *The audit society: Rituals of verification.* Oxford University Press.

Ràfols, I., and Stirling, A. (2021). Designing indicators for opening up evaluation. Insights from research assessment. In P. Dahler-Larsen (Ed.), *A research agenda for evaluation.* Edward Elgar.

Ralaidovy, A., Adam, T., and Boucher, P. (2020). Resource allocation for biomedical research: Analysis of investments by major funders. *Health Research Policy and Systems, 18*(1), 1–9.

Rosenberg, C. (2002). The tyranny of diagnosis: Specific entities and individual experience. *The Milbank Quarterly, 80*(2), 237–260.

Røttingen, J. A., Regmi, S., Eide, M., Young, A., Viergever, R., Ardal, C., Guzman, J., Edwards, D., Matlin, S., and Terry, R. (2013). Mapping of available health research and development data: What's there, what's missing, and what role is there for a global observatory? *The Lancet, 382,* 1286–1307.

Sampat, B. N. (2012). Mission-oriented biomedical research at the NIH. *Research Policy, 41*(10), 1729–1741.

Sarewitz, D. (1996). *Frontiers of illusion: Science, technology, and the politics of progress.* Temple University Press.

Schot, J., and Steinmueller, W. E. (2018). Three frames for innovation policy: R&D, systems of innovation and transformative change. *Research Policy, 47,* 1554–1567.

Scott-Kemmis, D., and Bell, M. (2010). The mythology of learning-by-doing in World War II airframe and ship production. *International Journal of Technological Learning, Innovation and Development, 3*(1), 1–35.

Stilgoe, J., Owen, R., and Macnaghten, P. (2013). Developing a framework for responsible innovation. *Research Policy, 42*(9), 1568–1580.

Stirling, A. (2009). *Direction, distribution and diversity! pluralising progress in innovation, sustainability and development.* STEPS Centre.

Thagard, P. (1999). *How scientists explain disease.* Princeton University Press.

Viergever, R. F. (2013). The mismatch between the health research and development (R&D) that is needed and the R&D that is undertaken: an overview of the problem, the causes, and solutions. *Global Health Action, 6*(22450).

von Philipsborn, P., Steinbeis, F., Bender, M. E., and Tinnemann, P. (2015). Poverty-related and neglected diseases – An economic and epidemiological analysis of poverty relatedness and neglect in research and development. *Global Health Action, 8,* 1–15.

Wellcome Trust. (2012). *Engaging with impact: How do we know if we have made a difference?* Wellcome Trust.

Whitley, R., Gläser, J., and Laudel, G. (2018). The impact of changing funding and authority relationships on scientific innovations. *Minerva, 56*(1), 109–134.

WHO (1996). *Investing in health research and development: Report of the Ad Hoc Committee on Health Research Relating to Future Invervention Options.* World Health Organization.

WHO (1999). *The world health report 1999: Making a difference.* World Health Organization.

WHO (2021). *Control of neglected tropical diseases.* WHO website. https://www.who.int/teams/control
-of-neglected-tropical-diseases.

World Bank (1993). *World development report 1993: Investing in health.* Oxford University Press.

Yegros-Yegros, A., van de Klippe, W., Abad-Garcia, M. F., and Ràfols, I. (2020). Exploring why global
health needs are unmet by research efforts: the potential influences of geography, industry and publication incentives. *Health Research Policy and Systems, 18*(47), 1–14.

11. The construction of competition in public research funding systems

Stefan Arora-Jonsson, Nils Brunsson and Peter Edlund

INTRODUCTION

During the twentieth century, the idea that scientists should compete for research funding became popular in public research systems across Europe (Lorenz, 2012). It is now often taken for granted that if scientists compete for funds, the funding will be allocated to the most deserving scholars, and that all scholars will exert themselves more. Some research supports this view, showing that competing for funds may expand the collaborations among, and boost the subsequent publications of, scientists (Aghion et al., 2010; Ayoubi et al., 2019). Yet studies also show that competition for funding can unleash rich-get-richer processes, and can incentivize researchers to go for 'safe bets' (Bloch et al., 2014; Bol et al., 2018). Despite these mixed outcomes, competition for research funding has become an almost obvious means to identify and support high-quality science in public systems (Sandström and van den Besselaar, 2018).

A commonly quoted reason for the increasingly hegemonic preference for competitive research funding suggests that competition is an inevitable outcome of a growing imbalance between increasing cohorts of researchers and a limited supply of research funds (Auranen and Nieminen, 2010; Münch and Baier, 2012). As we will demonstrate, a situation of scarcity does not, however, necessarily give rise to competition. Those who distribute research funding can organize it in ways that render the allocation of funds more or less likely to be interpreted as competition.

Funding systems are complex operations. There can be a variety of types of *potential competitors* – individual researchers, groups or universities, citizens of a certain nation state or scholars from other countries as well. What is *competed for* can be different across contexts. Money is common, but research funding can also come in the form of employment or a prize. Moreover, as Merton (1957) asserted, researchers often compete for status – which may or may not be linked to monetary resources. What participants *compete with* can also differ. Projects that describe future research is common, but scholars may also compete with past merits. Furthermore, the *timing* of competition can vary: competition can be continuous or episodic. All the types of funding decisions that we will describe are made at certain occasions, annually or less often. They therefore open up primarily for episodic competition, but they may lead to continuous competition as well (cf. Chadwick, 1859). There is also a wide variety of those who *organize* the allocation of funding – from wealthy individuals, to research councils or nation states or even international organizations – and who decide on the organization of the funding allocation such that it is more or less likely to be seen as competitive.

If we want to understand when and why the funding of research is competitive, it is crucial to find a way to sort through this complexity. In this chapter, we put forward a framework, based on the work of Arora-Jonsson et al. (2020, 2021), that allows an analysis of how funding may become competitive. Central to this framework is the conceptualization of competition as a socially constructed relationship, rather than a set of actions. It is necessary to specify who constructs competition; a specific instance of allocation of research money can be constructed differently (as competition or not) from different standpoints. An individual researcher may not construct the allocation of funds as competitive, even if the research council sees it as such, and vice versa.

We apply this framework to various forms of allocating research funds – through employment, prizes, block grants and project grants – to describe when each of these forms of allocating funds may be constructed as competitive. Although the framework allows for this analysis to be used from any vantage point (funder, researcher or outside observer), we consistently take the perspective of the applicant for funds – a researcher, a group of researchers or a university.

A FRAMEWORK FOR UNDERSTANDING COMPETITION

Broadly speaking, there is a clear idea of what constitutes a competitive situation. The common view is captured in Stigler's (1987: 531) definition of competition as a phenomenon that 'arises whenever two or more parties strive for something that all cannot obtain'. Although we agree with the broad characterization of what a competitive context is like, this definition does not allow us to ask how a context *came to be* competitive. In contrast, we follow earlier work to understand competition as consisting of four constituent elements (Arora-Jonsson et al., 2020).

The elements that comprise competition are:

- *actors* (i.e. individuals or organizations that see themselves, and are seen by others, as autonomous and distinctive entities capable of acting) involved in
- *relationships* (i.e. actors assessing their options for action by taking other actors' confirmed or presumed actions into account) revolving around material or symbolic goods, which are perceived as
- *scarce* (i.e. actors believe, and believe other actors also believe, the demand for particular goods exceeds their supply) and
- *desirable* (i.e. actors want to obtain, and sense other actors also want to obtain, a particular good).

A core assertion is that these elements are social constructions, i.e. contextual, and at times the result of directed construction efforts. The common definition of competition can thus be broken down to be read as the *concurrent construction* of parties (i.e. actors in relationships that strive for something desirable) that is perceived as scarce. When all these elements are constructed together, a situation is competitive. Two important implications for understanding when and why there is competition follow. First, if any of the elements are not successfully constructed (i.e. there is no conviction that there are actors, or that the actors have a relationship, or that actors desire something scarce), then there is no competition. Second, as the elements can be constructed differently from different vantage points (e.g. the applicant, the funder or an external observer), any analysis of a situation as competitive or not needs to be clear on its vantage point. A situation can be constructed as competitive from many different vantage points, but it does not have to be.

The remaining sections of the chapter are structured as follows. Next we deploy our theoretical framework to investigate block grants, employment and prizes as traditional ways of allocating funding. Then, we turn to the more novel way of allocating research funding through project grants. Across these sections, we discuss when allocations of funding are, or are not, constructed as competition and how this results from ways of organizing the allocation of research funds. We finish the chapter by offering policy implications and suggesting future inquiry avenues that centre on the construction and revocation of competition in public research systems.

EARLY FUNDING MODELS AND COMPETITION

Although the past three decades have witnessed a tremendous growth of research funding allocated through project grants to individual scientists or groups of scientists (Gläser and Laudel, 2016; Lepori et al., 2007; Skoie, 1996), such grants constitute only one way of allocating funding. Other ways of funding research include block grants to universities, employment and prizes.

Funding Directed at Organizations

Block grants comprise a traditional way of funding research where grants are allocated to universities and not directly to researchers. In public research systems, block grants have been, and still are, the largest source of funding for universities (Bégin-Caouette et al., Chapter 20 in this *Handbook*; Gläser and Laudel, 2016).

Governments have historically allocated block grants to universities in ways that have been difficult to construct as competition for research funding. One reason is that universities were, for a long time, not seen as actors with respect to attracting funding (Brunsson and Sahlin-Andersson, 2000). Instead, allocations were preceded by highly politicized procedures that, more often than not, involved extensive negotiations between government bureaucrats and university vice chancellors to determine the size and usage of block grants (Engwall, 2020; Gläser and Laudel, 2016). Universities thus stood relatively powerless with respect to their command of funding, and thereby were unlikely to perceive themselves and other universities as competitors for research funding.

Since the 1980s governments across Europe have increasingly begun to see universities as actors that should attract research funding independently. Efforts like these mainly derive from political pressures to create 'complete' (Brunsson and Sahlin-Andersson, 2000) public sector organizations, such as 'entrepreneurial universities' (Clark, 1998), that can mimic the (alleged) efficiency of private sector organizations. Governments have become organizers that, by encouraging universities to see themselves as actors, also encourage them to see themselves as competitors for block grants (Krücken, 2019; Musselin, 2018).

Constructing universities as competitors is not a straightforward matter, however. Historically, universities have been organized as heterogenous and highly decentralized entities (Cohen et al., 1972), perhaps primarily held together by their names and administrative units. The construction of actors has recently received assistance from various evaluations, including ratings, rankings, and other performance-based assessments, which have spread as prominent tools with which to scrutinize entire universities across Europe (Hicks, 2012). During such assessments, the quality of educational programmes, the number of doctoral degrees, and the impact of journal publications are aggregated and evaluated, along with the amount of funding that whole universities attract independently through their scientists. The construction of actors has been assisted by these performance-based evaluations because, in them, universities are repeatedly assessed as if they were single, bounded and coherent entities (Bomark, 2016). And the results of such assessments can create relationships among universities that are now able to constantly compare themselves with other universities.

Performance-based evaluations can, beside creating relationships, also generate very immediate material consequences for universities when governments connect assessment results to the allocation of block grants (Bégin-Caouette et al., Chapter 20 in this *Handbook*). This connection means that many universities nowadays compete for funding with their results in performance-based evaluations, and this compels them to routinely monitor the results of other universities (Krücken, 2019; Musselin, 2018). Such monitoring is typical of the comparative 'side-glances' (Geiger, 1941) that competitors engage in as they continuously seek to surpass one another. Routine monitoring among universities is thus likely to generate perceptions of continuous competition for research funding, although block grants are seldom allocated more than once a year. This is an example of how episodic competition can be turned into a continuous one.

Universities have not been the only entities subject to organizing efforts targeted at constructing actors that should attract research funding. Although entire universities constitute the primary targets of these efforts, governments across Europe have, since the early 2000s, also sought to construct various parts of universities, including milieus, programmes, and laboratories, as actors that are expected to attract funding (Musselin, 2013). Despite differences, Sweden's *Linnémiljöer*, France's *Grand Emprunt* and Germany's *Exzellenzinitiative* had in common that, as government packages to strengthen research, they all encouraged and accepted applications for funding from various parts of universities. The challenges associated with constructing parts of universities as actors, nonetheless, resemble some of the challenges associated with constructing whole universities as actors. Although certain organizational characteristics that facilitate the construction of actors can already be found in programmes and laboratories, extensive organizing efforts are required to demarcate boundaries around, concretize memberships in, and coordinate activities for milieus, as they typically feature loose constellations of scientists working under broad, umbrella-like research topics (Bomark, 2016).

Funding Contained in Employment

Another way to allocate research funding to scientists is through their employment positions (Musselin, 2009). Applying the framework to this form of allocating research funding suggests that it will be considered as competitive when the applicants for the job consider themselves as *actors* (able to influence the outcome of the employment process), involved in a *relationship* with other actors (at least being aware that there are other applicants for the position), *desiring* the funding that comes with the employment (and seeing the other applicants as also desiring this), and perceiving this kind of employment position as *scarce*.

Not everyone can be a competitor for the research funding that comes with academic employment. A standard limitation to being eligible is the requirement of a PhD in a relevant subject. This rules out some people from seeing this as a competition, but for the eligible ones the construction of actorhood is normally not a big challenge. Desire for the position and ensuing funds is affected by how the funds can be used. If the funder narrowly specifies what research the funding can be used for, desire is likely to be weak. On the other hand, the more research money is connected to the position, the more attractive it becomes. Traditionally professorships in the form of 'chairs' have been endowed with much more funding than other employment positions in Germanic, Anglo-Saxon, and Scandinavian public research systems (Clark, 1983; Muller-Carmen and Salzgeber, 2005). But chairs have been scarce, thus inviting competition. The competition is likely to be and remain episodic only, however, because chairs are normally offered only when an incumbent leaves.

Funding via Prizes

Prizes constitute another traditional way of allocating research funding to scientists in public systems (Zuckerman, 1992). As in the case of employment, allocating funding through prizes need not be intended to generate competition. Prize givers may only want to direct approval and acclaim towards certain scientists for their research accomplishments, perhaps hoping the scientific community will also start perceiving these accomplishments as approval- and acclaim-worthy (Best, 2008).

Yet prizes can also engender competition. Nomination procedures may help construct relationships between would-be contenders. Organizers often request nominations from various sources, including colleagues, department heads, university vice chancellors, and research council officers (Best, 2008). They want nominees with relatively equal merits, because such nominees are, in turn, expected to have relatively equal possibilities of winning (Allen and Parsons, 2006). However, scientists may be nominated without being asked for their previous consent (Merali, 2014) and the nominations do not have to be disclosed to the nominees. If scholars do not know that they are nominated their relationships are not affected; they may not be aware of the prize, and, if they are, they are up against vague masses of imagined competitors rather than specific ones (Werron, 2015). But sometimes funders publish lists of nominees in order to create drama and suspense (Goode, 1978) and increase attention for their prize. When scholars know that they and specific others are nominated, the likelihood of them constructing competition increases (Otner, 2018).

In some areas, prizes are abundant (Best, 2011). Many, if not most, prizes remain unknown to most scientists and prize givers have to make their prizes known. If they have enough money, they can create so-called mega prizes with which organizers – often US-based philanthropists, but also governments across Europe – allocate large monetary amounts to scientists (more than 1 million Euros each; Merali, 2014; Zuckerman, 1992). Such monetary amounts provide ample research possibilities that may contribute to the construction of desire for prizes.

Far from all prizes are associated with large monetary amounts, however. Some prizes mainly or only bestow status because, although they are devoid of money, competition for them is adjudicated by prominent peers. The status bestowed by prizes can, nonetheless, also engender desire. Merton (1957) argued that status per se tends to be regarded as the most desired reward among scientists and Weber (1968) argued that status may lead to further goods, including money. This suggests that prizes associated with status may generate much desire, and, by extension, construct a context seen as competitive among scientists who see themselves as potential recipients.

Desire for prizes can also be promoted by not limiting what can be done with the prize money (Franssen et al., 2018; Scholten et al., 2021). Givers of prizes without status can compensate by refraining from specifying what research recipients should conduct with their prize money (Franssen et al., 2018), or at least by refraining from monitoring its actual use. Funding allocated through prizes could thus provide support for explorations of unorthodox theories and lead to unexpected findings, and such funding conditions tend to be highly appreciated among scientists (Merton, 1973).

PROJECT GRANTS AND COMPETITION

With growing proportions of public funding allocated through project grants, governments have partly delegated their role as organizers to research councils. These councils construct competition through calls for applications, to which scientists respond by submitting project proposals. Once calls close, research councils utilize panellists as adjudicators to evaluate proposals and allocate project grants (Musselin, 2013). Adjudicators are central to the functioning of competition, much like the customer is in a market situation.

Project grants require much organisation to lead to competition. Scientists have not always perceived themselves and other scientists as competitors for grants. During long time periods, panellists were not seen as adjudicators in a competition, but instead as knowledgeable peers who helped scientists develop their project proposals through recurring dialogue and feedback. How can project grants be organized as competition? We structure our discussion around the activities intended to enhance actors, build relationships and stimulate a sense of scarcity and desirability of that which is to be competed for.

Enhancing Actors

The allocation of project grants will be constructed as competitive only if those that can be granted projects construct themselves and others as actors. Several grant schemes that encourage project proposals from scientists are simultaneously organized to restrict direct applications. This is particularly noticeable in early-career schemes that rely on nomination procedures. Here, the autonomy (and thus the actorhood) of early-career scientists as grant applicants is restricted to various degrees, because nominations from departments, universities, or research councils are required before any proposals can be submitted (Edlund, 2020). Early-career scientists are then, to a large extent, in the hands of other actors, including department heads, university vice chancellors, or research council officers. Project grant schemes relying on nominations have, at times, not even been perceived as a fair form of competition. Early-career scientists have argued that nominations are more based on the amity of grant applicants with vice chancellors or council officers (Lente, 2005; Watson et al., 2005).

Other grant schemes are organized not only to encourage, but also to accept, direct applications. The latter schemes construct early-career scientists as actors capable of applying for funding autonomously. Notable instances of such efforts include the project grants of the European Research Council (ERC) (Bohannon, 2006; Wolinsky, 2010). The proponents of these grants repeatedly asserted that the core idea was to allow direct applications that could provide many early-career scientists with long-awaited freedom to form their own research groups (Heldin, 2008). In disciplinary domains within which research groups constitute the main way of organizing scientific work, funding to individuals is nowadays understood as a 'Gordian knot that every early-stage scholar has to cut if she or he wishes to achieve an independent academic career' (Roumbanis, 2019b: 198).

Building New Relationships

Scientists who see themselves as actors with the capability of applying for research funding constitute a necessary, but not sufficient, condition for the construction of competition. Research councils may also need to assist in the establishment of new relationships.

Councils have tried to create new relationships that reach beyond national public funding systems (Thomas and Ramos-Vielba, Chapter 15 in this *Handbook*). Numerous governments in Europe, starting throughout the late 1990s, gradually opened national systems for panellists and grant applicants from abroad (Banchoff, 2002). One purpose was to avoid nepotistic relationships among national panellists and applicants that allegedly favour some scientists over others (Winnacker, 2008). Another purpose was to spur scientists not only to consider what familiar colleagues down the department corridor do, but also what unfamiliar colleagues on the other side of Europe may be doing (Serrano Velarde, 2018). This should be 'sobering', as many scientists had allegedly 'remained stuck in their immediate surroundings' (Winnacker, 2008: 126). Such an extension to more unfamiliar potential competitors can lead to vague, and perhaps anxiety-ridden and stress-inducing, perceptions among scientists because more competitors than before can apply for the same project grants (Werron, 2015).

On the other hand, research councils also curbed these perceptions somewhat, intentionally or not. The opening of national systems for foreign grant applicants has often been accompanied by restrictions, such as requirements that successful applicants must spend considerable time conducting research at host organizations located within those countries where funding is being provided (Gronbaek, 2003). Such requirements can be expected to reduce desire among foreign potential applicants, and therefore restrain the perceptions of local scientists of being in a relationship with those. After all, few potential, and eventually successful, grant applicants can be expected to relocate their offices, laboratories, and research groups in burdensome and time-consuming moves (Laudel, 2006). So, scientists may think that, in fact, they are not up against vague masses of international applicants, but that they are still competing against a smaller set of local scientists only.

Promoting Desire and Scarcity

Actors in relationships constitute two necessary elements, but they must also see these grants as scarce and desirable, and sense that they are seen as such by other scientists too.

The construction of project grants as scarce can be understood by considering that recent public sector reforms were partly launched to reduce expenditures associated with welfare states across Europe. Such reforms have contributed to a shortage of grants in public research systems, as the funding allocated by councils does not cover the funding required by scientists (Auranen and Nieminen, 2010; Münch and Baier, 2012). Desire is also salient, but, generally speaking, it can be regarded as inherent among scientists. They should, sooner or later, require funding to conduct any relatively continuous research (Thomas and Ramos-Vielba, Chapter 15 in this *Handbook*). But the way research councils organize their funding may affect the degree of desire among scientists.

At the European level, project grants were, up until the mid-2000s, mostly directed towards applied research endeavours conducted in multinational consortia composed of scientists, universities, and companies from several countries. Such grants did not generate much desire among scientists focusing on basic research endeavours. Those scientists often perceived

Europe-level funding as politically and bureaucratically controlled (Breithaupt, 2004; Reale et al., Chapter 7 in this *Handbook*). Many scientists refrained from applying (Schiermeier, 2002). Conversely, these experiences suggest that research councils may stimulate desire for their grants by reducing political and bureaucratic control (Cremonini et al., 2017). At the European level, ERC project grants were, from day one, portrayed as a-political and non-bureaucratic grants that enable the pursuit of unorthodox theories and unexpected findings (König, 2017). These portrayals made the ERC's project grants more desirable for basic scientists. The desirability was also assisted by generous grants and meticulous panellists, a combination that, early on, resulted in large resources being allocated to a few scientists. Such allocations show how the construction of project grants as scarce and desirable can intersect and overlap. Highly scarce grants become desirable because they give high status to the few who receive them (Edlund, 2020).

Adjudicating Ideas or Accomplishments

Funding can be differently organized also with respect to what the scientists are expected to compete *with*. In contrast to the allocation of funds through employment or prizes where the past merits of the applicants carry most weight, scientists compete for grants with project proposals containing future research ideas, That is, if nothing else, an image many councils across Europe cultivate as they launch calls expecting proposals to contain ground-breaking ideas (Heinze, 2008). Emphasizing the future-oriented features of project proposals, Braun (1998: 811) thus compared research councils to commercial banks: both are 'investing money into promising projects … based on the hope for future returns'.

However, 'it is difficult … to assess research that is not yet performed' (Langfeldt and Kyvik, 2011: 201). There are several indications that scientists do not solely, or not even mainly, compete for project grants on the basis of ideas contained in proposals. Like banks before issuing mortgages, to push that analogy, councils also conduct various background checks before allocating grants. These checks are deployed by research councils as part of organizing efforts seeking to alleviate the uncertainty that is inherently associated with future-oriented proposals. Councils often ask panellists not only to evaluate future research ideas, but also past research accomplishments, including patents and publications (van Arensbergen et al., 2014). Panellists, in addition, tend to take note of previously acquired funding, because 'getting a prestigious grant is already seen as a performance … and what one does with it seems less important' (Sandström and van den Besselaar, 2018: 380). The role of previously acquired research funding may fuel processes through which project grants are accumulated in patterns that resemble Merton's (1968) Matthew effect: the tendency that the rich get richer. After all, competition for funding from research grants may not be so different from competition for funding from prizes.

In further efforts to alleviate uncertainty, councils usually expect data, preliminary studies and other semi-completed research activities to be presented in proposals (Laudel, 2006). Such expectations could lead scientists to downplay the role of future research ideas in project proposals. There is, indeed, a growing perception that 'the system now favors those who can guarantee results rather than those with potentially path-breaking ideas that, by definition, cannot promise success' (Alberts et al., 2014: 5774). But how do scientists please panellists when research councils construct competition by, on the one hand, stressing the role of future ideas and, on the other hand, also emphasizing the role of past accomplishments? Whereas most scientists may need socialization into various application strategies (Roumbanis, 2019b), some scientists eventually learn to please adjudicators by crafting proposals that fuse the different, and, at times, contradictory, expectations of councils. Key to such fusions is that ground-breaking ideas are included in proposals, but positioned as non-essential for the completion of the projects (Franssen et al., 2018; Laudel, Chapter 16 in this *Handbook*).

IMPLICATIONS FOR POLICY AND RESEARCH

In this chapter, our aim has been to analyse when and why various ways of allocating funding, including employment, prizes, and block and project grants, are perceived as competition in public research systems. We employ a framework that suggests that such perceptions are cultivated through separate or collective efforts by organizers, potential competitors, and adjudicators to construct actors involved in relationships, which revolve around material or symbolic goods that are seen as scarce and desirable. More broadly, this framework suggests that competition is not a condition that simply 'arises' as is often imagined in economic theory (Arora-Jonsson et al., 2021), but most often is the result of decisions and organization, intended or not intended to enable the construction of competition. Below we draw out some implications of this way of thinking for research funding policy.

Easier and More Difficult Acts of Construction

Our chapter offers policy implications that merit consideration among governments and research councils seeking to deploy competition as their preferred means of allocating funding in public systems. We have argued that not all intentions to allocate funds in competition will be interpreted as such; efforts to construct competition can fail. There are easier and more difficult ways to construct competition.

Two dimensions merit particular consideration: whether funding is targeted at individuals or organizations, and whether it is directed towards basic or applied research. We suggest that it is easier to construct competition for research funding targeted at individuals than if it is targeted at organizations, because individual scholars are highly likely to perceive themselves, and are often perceived by others, as actors already. Organizations, on the other hand, often require extensive efforts to become seen as actors. We also suggest that it is easier to construct competition for funding of basic research endeavours than of applied research endeavours, because the former funding is typically infused with autonomy that is likely to increase desire, whereas the latter funding is often combined with control ambitions, which typically decreases desire.

Governments and research councils seeking to deploy competition as means of allocating research funding in public systems may also consider a third aspect: whether these allocations concern funding for shorter duration or longer duration. On the one hand, funding for shorter duration periods is likely to initiate competition among scholars more often, because constantly recurring allocations are needed, but such funding can also make competition less likely, because it allows less research time, which usually evokes less desire. Therefore, research funding for longer duration periods may make it easier to initiate competition.

Further Research Questions: Competition Among Funders and Revoking Competition

In addition to these policy implications, we believe our analysis opens avenues that can guide future inquiries on the construction of competition for public funding of research.

We used our theoretical framework to examine the construction of scientists and universities, and their milieus, programmes, and laboratories, as competitors for research funding. But, with a range of research councils operating across Europe (Thomas and Ramos-Vielba, Chapter 15 in this *Handbook*), they may also begin to see one another as competitors. Our framework could fruitfully be used for analysing the construction of councils as competitors. Such analyses would involve studies of how research councils are constructed as actors in relationships with other councils that similarly strive for scarce and desirable goods, including proposals from merited applicants, engagements from prominent panellists, and budgets from national governments or international organizations. What actors, if any, assist the construction of this competition by playing the roles as organizers? With what do research councils compete, and how do they portray themselves to become attractive? And how do the applicants, panellists, and governments or other organizations, now playing roles as adjudicators, select among councils to engage with?

Another suggestion for future inquiries would be to use our theoretical framework for understanding how competition is revoked. Such an inquiry is motivated by recent debates about alternatives to the use of competition in research funding, where it is argued that lotteries (Fang and Casadevall, 2016; Roumbanis, 2019a) or equipartitions (Bollen et al., 2014; Vaesen and Katzav, 2017) would generate improved conditions for high-quality science. But how can one revoke the sense of competition? Studies of multinational firms that have tried to revoke competition among their subsidiary units suggest that competition is a perception that may linger longer than expected – even when it is attempted to be organized away (Foureault, 2021). These findings are supported by recent experimental findings (Buser and Dreber, 2016; Johnson et al., 2006) showing that competition is generally simpler to construct than to revoke. We should investigate not only how competition can be stimulated by different ways of organizing, but also how it can be revoked by organization.

REFERENCES

Aghion, P., Dewatripont, M., Hoxby, C., Mas-Colell, A., and Sapir, A. (2010). The governance and performance of universities: Evidence from Europe and the US. *Economic Policy, 25*(61), 7–59.

Alberts, B., Kirschner, M. W., Tilghman, S., and Varmus, H. (2014). Rescuing US biomedical research from its systemic flaws. *Proceedings of the National Academy of Sciences, 111*(16), 5773–5777.

Allen, M. P., and Parsons, N. L. (2006). The institutionalization of fame: Achievement, recognition, and cultural consecration in baseball. *American Sociological Review, 71*(5), 808–825.

Arora-Jonsson, S., Brunsson, N., and Hasse, R. (2020). Where does competition come from? Organizational and institutional foundations. *Organization Theory, 1*(1), 1–24.

Arora-Jonsson, S., Brunsson, N., and Hasse, R. (2021). The origins of competition – institution and organization. In S. Arora-Jonsson, N. Brunsson, R. Hasse, and K. Lagerström (Eds.), *Competition. What it is and Why it Happens* (pp. 61–76). Oxford University Press.

Auranen, O., and Nieminen, M. (2010). University research funding and publication performance – An international comparison. *Research Policy, 39*(6), 822–834.

Ayoubi, C., Pezzoni, M., and Visentin, F. (2019). The important thing is not to win, it is to take part: What if scientists benefit from participating in research grant competitions? *Research Policy, 48*(1), 84–97.

Banchoff, T. (2002). Institutions, inertia and European Union research policy. *Journal of Common Market Studies*, *40*(1), 1–21.

Best, J. (2008). Prize proliferation. *Sociological Forum*, *23*(1), 1–27.

Best, J. (2011), *Everyone's a Winner. Life in Our Congratulatory Culture*. University of California Press.

Bloch, C., Krogh Graversen, E., and Skovgaard Pedersen, H. (2014). Competitive research grants and their impact on career performance. *Minerva*, *52*(1), 77–96.

Bohannon, J. (2006). *An Ambitious Effort to Plug Europe's 'Research Gap'*. Retrieved September 28 from https://www.sciencemag.org/careers/2006/10/ambitious-effort-plug-europes-research-gap.

Bol, T., de Vaan, M., and van de Rijt, A. (2018). The Matthew effect in science funding. *Proceedings of the National Academy of Sciences*, *115*(19), 4887–4890.

Bollen, J., Crandall, D., Junk, D., Ding, Y., and Börner, K. (2014). From funding agencies to scientific agency: Collective allocation of science funding as an alternative to peer review. *EMBO Reports*, *15*(2), 131–133.

Bomark, N. (2016). *Drawing Lines in the Sand: Organizational Responses to Evaluations in a Swedish University*. Department of Business Studies, Uppsala University.

Braun, D. (1998). The role of funding agencies in the cognitive development of science. *Research Policy*, *27*(8), 807–821.

Breithaupt, H. (2004). Push for innovation. *EMBO Reports*, *5*(4), 339–341.

Brunsson, N., and Sahlin-Andersson, K. (2000). Constructing organizations: The example of public sector reform. *Organization Studies*, *21*(4), 721–746. https://doi.org/10.1177/0170840600214003.

Buser, T., and Dreber, A. (2016). The flipside of comparative payment schemes. *Management Science*, *62*(9), 2626–2638.

Chadwick, E. (1859). Results of different principles of legislation and administration in Europe; Of competition for the field, as compared with competition within the field, of service. *Journal of the Statistical Society of London*, *22*(3), 381–420.

Clark, B. R. (1983). *The Higher Education System: Academic Organization in Crossnational Perspective*. University of California Press.

Clark, B. R. (1998). *Creating Entrepreneurial Universities: Organizational Pathways of Transformation*. Pergamon Press.

Cohen, M. D., March, J. G., and Olsen, J. P. (1972). A garbage can model of organizational choice. *Administrative Science Quarterly*, *17*(1), 1–25.

Cremonini, L., Horlings, E., and Hessels, L. K. (2017). Different recipes for the same dish: Comparing policies for scientific excellence across different countries. *Science and Public Policy*, *45*(2), 232–245.

Edlund, P. (2020). *Science Evaluation and Status Creation. Exploring the European Research Council's Authority*. Edward Elgar.

Engwall, L. (2020). The governance and missions of universities. In L. Engwall (Ed.), *Missions of Universities: Past, Present, Future* (pp. 1–19). Springer.

Fang, F. C., and Casadevall, A. (2016). Research funding: The case for a modified lottery. *mBio*, *7*(2), 1–7.

Foureault, F. (2021). Reversing competition – The case of corporate governance. In S. Arora-Jonsson, N. Brunsson, R. Hasse, and K. Lagerström (Eds.), *Competition. What it is and Why it Happens*. Oxford University Press.

Franssen, T. P., Scholten, W., Hessels, L. K., and de Rijcke, S. (2018). The drawbacks of project funding for epistemic innovation: Comparing institutional affordances and constraints of different types of research funding. *Minerva*, *56*(1), 11–33.

Geiger, T. J. (1941). *Konkurrence. En sociologisk analyse*. Universitetsforlaget.

Gläser, J., and Laudel, G. (2016). Governing science: How science policy shapes research content. *European Journal of Sociology*, *57*(1), 117–168.

Goode, W. J. (1978). *The Celebration of Heroes: Prestige as a Social Control System*. University of California Press.

Gronbaek, D. J. (2003). A European Research Council: An idea whose time has come? *Science and Public Policy*, *30*(6), 391–404.

Heinze, T. (2008). How to sponsor ground-breaking research: A comparison of funding schemes. *Science and Public Policy*, *35*(5), 302–318.

Heldin, C.-H. (2008). The European Research Council – A new opportunity for European science. *Nature Reviews Molecular Cell Biology*, *9*(5), 417–420.

Hicks, D. (2012). Performance-based university research funding systems. *Research Policy*, *41*(2), 251–261.

Johnson, M. D., Hollenbeck, J. R., Humphrey, S. E., Ilgen, D. R., Jundt, D., and Meyer, C. J. (2006). Cutthroat cooperation: Asymmetrical adaptation to changes in team reward structures. *Academy of Management Journal*, *49*(1), 103–119.

König, T. (2017). *The European Research Council*. Polity Press.

Krücken, G. (2019). Multiple competitions in higher education: A conceptual approach. *Innovation: Organization and Management*, *23*(6), 1–19.

Langfeldt, L., and Kyvik, S. (2011). Researchers as evaluators: Tasks, tensions and politics. *Higher Education*, *62*(2), 199–212.

Laudel, G. (2006). The art of getting funded: How scientists adapt to their funding conditions. *Science and Public Policy*, *33*(7), 489–504.

Lente, G. (2005). EURYI: Present procedure risks conflicts of interest. *Nature*, *437*(7056), 192.

Lepori, B., van den Besselaar, P., Dinges, M., Potì, B., Reale, E., Slipersæter, S., … van den Meulen, B. (2007). Comparing the evolution of national research policies: What patterns of change? *Science and Public Policy*, *34*(6), 372–388.

Lorenz, C. (2012). If you're so smart, why are you under surveillance? Universities, neoliberalism, and New Public Management. *Critical Inquiry*, *38*(3), 599–629.

Merali, Z. (2014). The new Nobels. *Nature*, *498*(7453), 152–154.

Merton, R. K. (1957). Priorities in scientific discovery: A chapter in the sociology of science. *American Sociological Review*, *22*(6), 635–659.

Merton, R. K. (1968). The Matthew effect in science. *Science*, *159*(3810), 56–63.

Merton, R. K. (1973). The normative structure of science. In N. W. Storer (Ed.), *The Sociology of Science. Theoretical and Empirical Investigations* (pp. 267–278). University of Chicago Press.

Muller-Carmen, M., and Salzgeber, S. (2005). Changes in academic work and the chair regime: The case of German business administration academics. *Organization Studies*, *26*(2), 271–290.

Münch, R., and Baier, C. (2012). Institutional struggles for recognition in the academic field: The case of university departments in German chemistry. *Minerva*, *50*(1), 97–126.

Musselin, C. (2009). *The Market for Academics*. Routledge.

Musselin, C. (2013). How peer review empowers the academic profession and university managers: Changes in relationships between the state, universities, and the professoriate. *Research Policy*, *42*(5), 1165–1173.

Musselin, C. (2018). New forms of competition in higher education. *Socio-Economic Review*, *16*(3), 657–683.

Otner, S. M. G. (2018). Near-winners in status competitions: Neglected sources of dynamism in the Matthew effect. *Journal of Management Inquiry*, *27*(4), 374–377.

Roumbanis, L. (2019a). Peer review or lottery? A critical analysis of two different forms of decision-making mechanisms for allocation of research grants. *Science, Technology, and Human Values*, *44*(6), 994–1019.

Roumbanis, L. (2019b). Symbolic violence in academic Life: A study on how junior scholars are educated in the art of getting funded. *Minerva*, *57*(6), 197–218.

Sandström, U., and van den Besselaar, P. (2018). Funding, evaluation, and the performance of national research systems. *Journal of Infometrics*, *12*(1), 365–384.

Schiermeier, Q. (2002). A window of opportunity. *Nature*, *419*(6903), 108–109.

Scholten, W., Franssen, T. P., van Drooge, L., de Rijcke, S., and Hessels, L. K. (2021). Funding for few, anticipation among all: Effects of excellence funding on academic research groups. *Science and Public Policy*, *48*(2), 265–275.

Serrano Velarde, K. (2018). The way we ask for money … The emergence and institutionalization of grant writing practices in academia. *Minerva*, *58*(1), 85–107.

Skoie, H. (1996). Basic research – A new funding climate? *Science and Public Policy*, *23*(2), 66–75.

Stigler, G. J. (1987). Competition. In J. L. Eatwell, M. Milgate, and P. K. Newman (Eds.), *The New Palgrave Dictionary of Economics* (pp. 531–536). Palgrave Macmillan.

Vaesen, K., and Katzav, J. (2017). How much would each researcher receive if competitive government research funding were distributed equally among researchers? *PLoS One*, *12*(9), 1–11.

van Arensbergen, P., van der Weijden, I. C. M., and van den Besselaar, P. (2014). Different views of scholarly talent: What are the talents we are looking for in science? *Research Evaluation*, *23*(4), 273–284.

Watson, D., Andersen, A. C., and Hjorth, J. (2005). Mysterious disappearance of female investigators. *Nature*, *436*(7048), 174.

Weber, M. (1968). Political communities. In G. Roth and C. Wittich (Eds.), *Economy and Society. An Outline of Interpretive Sociology* (pp. 901–940). University of California Press.

Werron, T. (2015). Why do we believe in competition? A historical–sociological view of competition as an institutionalized modern imaginary. *Distinktion: Journal of Social Theory*, *16*(2), 186–210.

Winnacker, E.-L. (2008). On excellence through competition. *European Educational Research Journal*, *7*(2), 124–130.

Wolinsky, H. (2010). Power to the scientists. *EMBO Reports*, *11*(10), 741–743.

Zuckerman, H. A. (1992). The proliferation of prizes: Nobel complements and Nobel surrogates in the reward system of science. *Theoretical Medicine*, *13*(2), 217–231.

PART III

INTERACTION OF FUNDING SYSTEMS WITH ORGANIZATIONAL STRUCTURES AND HIERARCHIES

12. Incentives, rationales, and expected impact: linking performance-based research funding to internal funding distributions of universities

Jussi Kivistö and Charles Mathies

INTRODUCTION

Despite the popularity and widespread attention of performance-based funding (PBF) across European higher education systems, we still know little about the impacts of PBF on behaviour and performance of universities (de Rijcke et al., 2015; Kivistö and Kohtamäki, 2016). Particularly, it is unclear to what extent the level of alignment of external and internal incentives influences the performance of universities. It is presumed that the internal incentive structures should be compatible and aligned with the incentives attached to external revenue streams of the university. This alignment is important because it expects to have a direct impact on the awareness and behaviour of organizational subunits and individuals leading to a higher level of productivity (Ziegele, 2008; Arnhold, Kivistö, Püttmann, Vossensteyn and Ziegele, 2018).

In this chapter, we aim to "open the black box" of universities aligning their internal funding distribution mechanism(s) with an external performance-based research funding system (PRFS) that includes external criteria and their associated incentives. More specifically, we focus on how system-level PRFSs affect universities' internal incentivization structures at the unit and individual levels and the expectations of how this behaviour may translate into changes in the research performance. We examine the rationales to align internal (organizational) funding mechanisms with external funding criteria, the expected outcomes, and the unintended effects. We focus on the tensions that may arise when a university adopts external criteria for its internal PRFS distribution. We conclude with our findings that internal PRFS are dependent on an intra-institutional causal chain of incentives and behavioural responses of individuals, both intended and unintended.

BACKGROUND

Many higher education systems, especially in Europe, have historically relied on the Humboldtian university tradition, with the autonomous professors playing a central role and collectively deciding on allocation of the institutional resources (Sörlin, 2007). In these systems, there was little oversight or external evaluation on how resources were spent and what was achieved with this spending. After World War II, many higher education systems experienced the financial consequences of massification and subsequently started introducing new managerial and funding paradigms (Herbst, 2007; Sörlin, 2007). The shift, in a majority of cases, was towards a performance-based regime with its roots in New Public Management

(NPM), introducing performance-based funding systems and business-oriented management practices (Checchi, Malgarini and Sarlo, 2019; Sörlin, 2007).

Jongbloed and Vossensteyn (2001) define PBF systems as funding mechanisms driven by the outputs of universities, which are represented by means of indicators within a funding formula or output criteria in budget negotiations. A primary defining feature of many PBF systems is the ex-post assessment of performance, although also ex-ante performance intentions (through performance agreements) can be qualified as PBF. Although PBF is used to promote transparency, accountability and legitimacy, the principal policy goal of it is to improve university performance by steering or aligning their activities towards the goals of the governance entity (Jongbloed, 2010; Kivistö and Kohtamäki, 2016).

By definition, PRFS can be considered as national systems of research output evaluation used to distribute research funding to universities (Hicks, 2009). Sivertsen (Chapter 6 in this *Handbook*) makes a useful distinction between three types of PRFSs: evaluation-based, indicator-based and performance-agreement driven systems. The focus of this chapter is solely on indicator-based PRFS.

Development of Research Performance-based Funding Schemes

Reinforced by growing global economic integration, the production, valorization, and application of knowledge as a key driver of global economic competitiveness (Jessop, 2017; Slaughter and Rhoades, 2004), one particular funding approach that has received more prominence over the last decades is PRFS. This is because universities and their research production processes are at the centre of and a key driver in the knowledge economy (e.g. Jessop, 2017; European Commission, 2020). This has helped reorient the relationship between higher education and governments towards stressing industrial and technological competitiveness, leading to increasing funding of research and development and efforts to support licensing and intellectual property stemming from publicly funded research (Jessop, 2017; Slaughter and Rhoades, 2004). At the same time, many nation states desire to increase the quality and effectiveness of their public research systems as they progressively invest money and see PRFS as a means to steer the research outputs resulting from this investment (Checchi et al., 2019; Zacharewicz, Lepori, Reale and Jonkers, 2019).

Countries adopt either a "formalized" or "non-formalized" evaluation process of their research performance. The formalized approach indicates the country has systemized the evaluation process through bibliometric data and formalized criteria (classifications of publishers and quality markers) to support the qualitative judgements by experts, while a non-formalized approach refers to a country not adopting a systemized evaluation process (Giménez-Toledo et al., 2019). Hicks (2012) provides five defining criteria of PRFS, including the following: research must be evaluated, the evaluation is ex-post, research outputs are evaluated, the distribution of government funding depends on the evaluation, and the system must be national. The final criterion emphasizes that PRFS are to be national systems and university "evaluations of their own research standing, even if used to inform internal funding distribution, are excluded" (Hicks, 2012, p. 252).

PRFS aim to encourage universities to improve their research production, in terms of quality and quantity, and steer them towards specific fields or areas of research (Geuna and Martin, 2003). There is also an expectation of "channelling" resources to the best performing universities, fuelling a competitive game based on outputs within higher education systems (Herbst,

2007). Most PRFS allocate funding at the institutional or departmental (aggregate) levels, but they often link to individual academics' behaviour (Aagaard, 2015). The prevailing thought is that incentives of PRFS "flow downwards", as their criteria are used to incentivize individual researchers' performance, particularly within the fields of social sciences and humanities (Aagaard, 2015; Bloch and Schneider, 2016; Haddow and Hammarfelt, 2019; Krog Lind, 2019).

The adoption of national PRFS criteria to allocate resources locally forms the central issue under examination in this chapter. We aim to understand how the external PRFS criteria can incentivize internal behaviour and research performance (for in-depth analysis of how PRFS impacts research performance, see chapter 6 by Sivertsen in this *Handbook*).

FROM EXTERNAL TO INTERNAL INCENTIVES: FOUR ASPECTS OF PRFS

System level PRFS rely on a rather simple behavioural assumption: financial incentives trigger productive behaviours *within universities*, which then translate to higher level of research performance *of universities*. Furthermore, there is evidence (see e.g. Jonkers and Zacharewicz, 2016; Mathies, Kivistö and Birnbaum, 2020) that the increasing competition for scarce resources among universities and other research organizations incentivizes the actors to maximize their revenues under the rules of a rigid allocation system that allocates a fixed budget. While there has been research on the effects of system level adoption of PRFS, there is limited work on the internal adoption, within a university or research organization, of PRFS for distributing research funding. Below, we describe, what are, in our opinion, four major aspects regarding the internal adoption of PRFS. These are (1) institutional autonomy, (2) the rationale for aligning external financial incentives with internal incentives, (3) expected outcomes, and (4) unintended effects.

Institutional Autonomy

The rationales for either supporting or opposing the use of PRFS at system level often relate to a university's chances of performing well in terms of the indicators and their weights in a system's funding formula. Presumably, research intensive universities are more in favour of PRFS indicators, such as the volume of external research funding or bibliometric indicators, than less research intensive universities. Furthermore, PRFS indicators can scale up and mutually reinforce each other. For instance, many European countries use research publications (scores in bibliometric evaluation or national publication classification systems), external research funding and awarded doctoral degrees as key performance indicators in allocating research funding (e.g. Jonkers and Zacharewicz, 2016; Claeys-Kulik and Estermann, 2015). The application of these three indicators in the funding formula simultaneously can create a knock-on effect, where being successful in one indicator increases the odds of being successful also in the other two: Research grants allow universities to recruit new doctoral students (who eventually complete a doctoral degree) and who publish co-authored publications with their supervisors, who are often the principal investigators of a research project. The same scaling up, however, is not often possible with those performance indicators that usually relate to education.

The introduction of system level PRFS often accompanies a greater level of institutional autonomy, which is often "traded" for increased accountability. With this line of thinking, institutional autonomy is valuable insofar as it allows universities to adopt adequate managerial tools to respond to PRFS incentives. Indeed, it is assumed that increased autonomy will stimulate intra-organizational engagement, creativity, and adaptability to local characteristics, which again will boost organizational efficiency and effectiveness (Aghion et al., 2010; Verhoest, Peters, Bouckaert and Verschuere, 2004). However, a frequently neglected insight is that with granting universities a greater level of autonomy, governments often pass the risk of failing research productivity to universities, via the PRFS, without compensating them for the risk-premium they must bear. This occurs particularly when the introduction of PRFS schemes is merely changing the mode of resource allocation without injecting any extra money into the system.

Increased institutional autonomy accompanied by PRFS, however, does not necessarily translate to a greater level of autonomy of university units. Since autonomy of universities is bound on a university being a legal person with legal responsibilities, this is likely to create more stringent internal accountability controls for units (who are not legal persons). Additionally, the treatment of unit-level financial surpluses is an important issue that is crossing the boundaries of university- and unit-level autonomy and interests. Standard alternatives for the treatment of unit surpluses are that units can either carry forward to the next budget year their entire surplus or a portion of their surplus, or "return" the surplus to the central administration. From the perspective of incentives, giving units freedom to pass on their surpluses and accumulate their wealth induces a risk that the higher unit level financial buffers reduce the expected efficacy of PRFS incentives, as they can be used as financial cushions allowing units to emphasize other objectives than those promoted by PRFS.

Lastly, organizational size may be important for the use of PRFS. Larger universities more often rely on standardized planning and control systems as means of coordination, whereas smaller universities can more easily coordinate by direct supervision or mutual adjustment. In smaller universities, the management is more able to have direct and continuous interaction with the units and their staff. This is more difficult in larger universities and, therefore, necessitates the use of more formal performance management tools, including PRFS formulae in allocating internal funds (Opstrup, 2017; Mintzberg, 1981; see also Massy, 2016).

Rationale for Aligning External Financial Incentives with Internal Incentives

Universities are regularly facing conflicting pressures from their external resource environment in how they manage themselves. Budgeting practices are one of the most important university internal governance tools to cope with these pressures (Lepori and Montauti, 2020). Making sure internal incentive structures are, if not compatible, at least non-conflicting with the ones generating the external revenue streams of the institution seems essential. From a logical perspective, having a misaligned incentive structure could increase the risks of misguided organizational behaviour vis-à-vis the logics of external revenue generation.

Compatibility essentially means ensuring the necessary level of alignment of external and internal financial incentives, but not necessarily copying the external incentives to internal ones, as the rationales and dynamics of internal allocations may differ from external ones. It is also not possible to tailor all organizational units (like faculties, schools, departments, institutes) of a university to equally match the external criteria. This means that some parts of a university will perform differently than others. For instance, faculties are composed of different disciplinary fields, which have differing chances of acquiring external research funding and publishing in high impact journals (e.g. STEM vs. humanities) and therefore differing behavioural logics as well.

There are only few empirical studies which have explored the similarities and differences between external and internal incentive structures in country contexts. These studies refer to Sweden (Hammarfelt, Nelhans and Eklund, 2016), Norway (Aagaard, 2015), Finland (Kivistö, Pekkola and Kujala, 2021) and Australia (Woelert and McKenzie, 2018). All these studies show similarities in terms of system level and university internal alignment in funding settings. For instance, in Finland only two universities out of 12 are applying an internal budgeting model where performance indicators are very different compared with the performance-based funding formula used by the Ministry of Education and Culture. Furthermore, most institutions follow closely the Ministry's weighting of particular indicators in their internal budgeting formula (see Kivistö et al., 2021). As also Aagaard (2015) has shown, this provides additional support to the assumption that PRFS "trickle down" to unit level, presumably for the same reasons they are applied in the system level.

The relative importance of academic core actives often differs between units. While research is a core activity within all academic units of universities, some departments offer more study programmes and service more students than others who perhaps focus more on research. As a result, teaching responsibilities take up more time in some units, thereby reducing the time available for research (Opstrup, 2017). University internal funding models are often compromises for allowing different types of performance profiles across units. For instance, when responding to state performance-based funding, universities often adjust some of the performance indicators in a way that best serves their own strategic goals, institutional culture or disciplines, or other specific organizational features (Arnhold et al., 2018).

It is important to note that applying system level PRFS incentives to academic sub-units via internal resource allocation is different from educational related performance incentives. Research activities are more individually focused with greater levels of academic autonomy than teaching activities, which are bound to a formal curriculum, shared among several teachers, and involve close interaction (co-production) with study services and administration. Of course, research is also a team product in some research fields more than in others (Checchi et al., 2019), but this makes performance management more challenging as the drivers of productivity are more individualized. Exactly because of this, compared with educational outputs, individual salary bonuses for high performing researchers are easier to attach to success in publishing or acquiring grants than, for instance, success in supervising students or educational degree completions.

Expected Outcomes

As PRFS policies become more and more common, so too should evidence on their efficacy, both at university and unit levels. To date, hard empirical evidence is still limited. However, some studies are available. For instance, in Finland, Mathies et al. (2020) found several changes in publication patterns, especially in social sciences and humanities (SSH), five years after the introduction of the weighted publication indicator in the national PBF model for universities. Himanen and Puuska (2022) found that introduction of the bibliometric indicator into the national funding model of Finnish universities has resulted in positive development in publication counts and that this is in line with the incentives set forth by this particular indicator. Similarly, Ossenblok, Engels and Sivertsen (2012) found publishing in English within SSH increased in Belgium (Flanders) and Norway after adopting a PRFS system. Earlier studies indicating that PRFS leads to changes in publication practices include Butler (2003), Jiménez-Contreras, de Moya Anegón and López-Cózar (2003), and Moed (2008). They refer to Australian, Spanish and UK contexts (see also Sīle and Vanderstraeten, 2019).

Strictly speaking, covariation (or absence of it) suggests that while there could be a positive or negative relationship between the use of PRFS and research performance, it does not guarantee it. Even though system level studies would be able to show publication patterns (or other outputs measured in PRFS systems) changing towards the goals stressed by the system's incentives, they have not been able to demonstrate why and how this actually occurs *within universities*. Studying the direct causation between changes in publication patterns and the internal use of PRFS would require the use of a well-designed quasi-experimental research setting with appropriate controls (see e.g. Tandberg and Hillman, 2013; Hillman, Tandberg and Gross, 2014).

The lack of empirical proof means that alternative causes of performance changes are still to a large extent unknown, even if we can observe and identify the PRFS as probably triggering these effects (Rabovsky, 2012). This means that the mechanisms that link PRFS and researchers' behaviour empirically, or at least present alternative causal factors which may have contributed to the observed changes in performance, are still to a large extent unknown (Sīle and Vanderstraeten, 2019; cf. Butler, 2003). Presumably, intra-institutional budgeting applying PRFS principles plays a big part in this, but there are several other potential factors influencing the outcomes – such as performance-based salary systems, academic career progression criteria (tenure track evaluations) and peer pressure.

Unintended Effects

PRFSs have the potential to induce several types of unintended effects if their incentives systematically change the behaviour of their target group in an unintended way (e.g. Frey and Osterloh, 2006; Kivistö, 2007). Despite the increased emphasis on the use of PRFS, we still have very little solid evidence also on unintended effects. Like with the expected outcomes, much of the discussion is based on anecdotal evidence, assumptions, or indirect evidence from some other PBF contexts.

PRFSs are subject to the same challenges as PBF systems in general. PRFSs rely on indicators that are observable and quantifiable, but as such are able to capture only limited aspects of total research performance. This opens up the possibility of dysfunctional behaviours, where "you only get what you pay for". Usual unintended effects are related to "gaming" the PRFS (Akerlof and Kranton, 2005). The gaming refers to behaviours where producing quantity becomes so important that the quality and ethical standards are systematically and purposefully neglected. Gaming is related to the so-called goal displacement phenomenon (Merton, 1968), where more meaningful but intangible goals are displaced by narrower but tangible goals. The unintended effects therefore relate to a "you get what you measure" type of behaviour, when neglecting the quality of the outputs by focusing on measurable quantity of outputs is possible. Concrete examples include "salami publishing" (unnecessarily dividing research results into the smallest publishable units), proposing relatively conservative but safe research projects (because mainstream research is more likely to receive funding than unorthodox, innovative research designs), and lowering the academic standards for PhD candidates (Weingart, 2005).

Empirical evidence for increased salami publishing seems mixed and discipline specific (see e.g. Frandsen, Eriksen, Hammer and Christensen, 2019) with its relation to PRFS seemingly largely unexplored. At the same time, splitting research into multiple publications might not necessarily be a questionable research practice, when, for instance, there is too much data for one paper, or interrelated papers may add or consolidate information. Further, there is considerable similarity and no clear demarcation between salami practices and duplicate publications. It can be difficult to determine whether a publication is a duplicate, as this is about dealing with different shades of grey (Norman and Grifths, 2008).

Another form of unintended effect is known as "cream skimming", where certain aspects of research output deemed valuable, but not actually rewarded in monetary terms, get ignored. For instance, research projects which would be academically more rewarding, but lack proper resources, may be ignored and replaced with projects for which it is easier to secure competitive funding but which have lesser academic value. Alternatively, domestic publications can be disregarded if international publications yield higher performance rewards. Sivertsen (Chapter 6 in this *Handbook*) has noted that, when indicators are connected to funding, they may narrow the focus of the organization only to those aspects which are financially attractive. Paradoxically, according to Sivertsen, to reach the aims of a PRFS more effectively, the consequences of funding should probably be minimalized.

Another presumably significant unintended effect is related to the so-called "crowding" effect (Frey, 1997; Frey and Jegen, 2001). It refers to the negative effect on employee motivation when a previously non-monetary relationship suddenly transforms into a monetary one (Tirole and Bénabou, 2006). The crowding effect means that the influence of external interventions, such as linking financial incentives to individual employee performance, depends on the individual's perception of these interventions, especially in situations where the employees have a high initial level of intrinsic motivation. Based on social–psychological insights, Frey (1997) argues that external rewards (creating extrinsic motivation) can "crowd out" intrinsic motivation and reduce employees' actual work efforts if they perceive the performance reward as a device to control their behaviour. Alternatively, Frey (1997) expects an external reward to "crowd in" intrinsic motivation if the affected individuals see the reward as a support to their own choices and values. In this case, the performance incentives serve as an acknowledgement of their work effort and increase morale and self-esteem while emphasizing self-determination (Frey, 1997; Frey and Jegen, 2001; Andersen and Pallesen, 2008). Given the basic characteristics of academic work and its emphasis on professional calling (deep alignment between their vocation and personal identity), most researchers and academics have presumably a high level of intrinsic motivation (Frey and Osterloh, 2006). For this reason, the "crowding" effect theory appears to be quite relevant for studying the effects of PRFS in universities and other research organizations.

Empirical evidence on the crowding in/out effect is, again, scarce. However, Andersen and Pallesen's (2008) study supports the conclusion that financial incentives can be important for academics. As suggested by crowding theory, the acceptance of the indicators by those who receive the budget is crucial for the effectiveness of the performance-related financial incentives. This suggests the more supportive (rather than controlling) researchers perceive the incentives to be, the more they motivate researchers to be more productive.

There are also other aspects which make PRFS use problematic. Sometimes units do not have (enough) control over the performance measures, implying the relation between effort and performance measures is less clear. For instance, units like departments may exhibit differing capacities to generate competitive research funding owing to their field or discipline, or they face human resource constraints beyond their own influence. It should be also noted that PRFS typically work poorly in cultures dominated by professional norms that denigrate speed and quantity of output relative to the quality, challenge, elegance, thoroughness, creativity or subtlety of the work done (cf. Baron and Kreps, 1999).

ANALYSIS AND DISCUSSION

Our analysis and discussion focus on examining the tension points that arise when a university adopts a PRFS for the internal distribution of research funding. A number of theoretical perspectives are helpful in understanding the behaviours of involved actors. However, we find that applying some of the traditional theoretical perspectives, such as a legitimacy-seeking approach and budgeting theories on research funding, are limited in understanding. This is mainly due to the incentives accompanying the "prestige" factor in academic publishing and the challenges in understanding the internalization of PRFS. We argue that agency theory can provide an alternative understanding of the incentives and motivations of the involved actors.

Legitimacy Seeking

Moll and Hoque (2011) suggest that university management can align its internal allocation system to external criteria as a way to seek legitimacy. The contention is that this allows university management to signal to its governance (oversight) entity (such as the board of trustees or ministry) that it is managing the university appropriately. This portrays "legitimacy as an unproblematic outcome of leaders choosing a strategy from a set of well-articulated responses" (Moll and Hoque, 2011, p. 99). This framework, while helpful in explaining the motivations of management, is limited in its explanation of the incentives of individual academics and units (faculties, departments) within an university. In many ways, this overstates how orderly the legitimization process is, as universities are not uniform actors and they differ in their responses (Moll and Hoque, 2011; Orton and Weick, 1990). Since the 1970s, one of the more common conceptions of universities is as a loosely coupled organization with limited direct links amongst organizational functions and units (Orton and Weick, 1990; Weick, 1976). Owing to this loose coupling, legitimacy seeking by management towards its oversight (governance) organization often fails owing to the subordinate units' ability to undermine the central management's directives. This avoidance behaviour is mainly due to differences in values and norms (Moll and Hoque, 2011). In other words, the structure and nature of universities lead to a diversity of motivations, incentives, and behaviours of their internal actors.

More specifically for research funding and PRFS, aligning internal allocation systems with external criteria to seek legitimacy is also problematic owing to the way prestige is associated with academic publishing. Within PRFS, funding ties directly with the number of and/or quality of publications. Individual scholars and units are interested in maximizing their prestige for a variety of reasons, from securing employment and evaluation of their performance to earning promotion and recognition within their field (Kwiek, 2021). While variation exists amongst fields, prestige typically comes in the form of highly recognized publications and funding (Kwiek, 2018; Melguizo and Strober, 2007; Mouritzen and Opstrup, 2020; Rosinger, Taylor, Coco and Slaughter, 2016). Prestige is field specific: what constitutes "high quality" or garners recognition in one field is not the same across all fields (Rosinger et al., 2016). Authors such as Bowen (1980), Garvin (1980), James (1990) and Massy (2016) emphasized that the motives and aspirations of universities are not associated with hard budget constraints, but with goals such as excellence, prestige, and influence. As the end result for legitimacy seeking behaviour being able to explain the incentivizing effect on individual academics and university units, there would need to be alignment between perceptions of multiple fields' prestige and excellence with the oversight criteria. As this is probably not the case for the vast majority of universities, the legitimacy seeking framework is limited for understanding the incentivizing effect of PRFS.

Budgeting Theory

Lepori and Montauti (2020) suggest universities are able to manage competing logics through "structured flexibility", i.e. a setting in which organizational structures frame and delimit local spaces of negotiation (see also Battilana, Sengul, Pache and Model, 2015). This allows universities to navigate complex and changing environmental conditions. Building on institutional logics, they suggest universities can find a balance between a *professional* logic and a *managerial* logic. The *professional* logic argues that managing universities should be driven by academic norms, with high levels of autonomy (i.e. funding and nomination decisions based on peer evaluation). The *managerial* logic argues universities to be managed like private companies, with central management being the core decision maker (i.e. funding decisions are made on concrete assessments and meeting strategic goals; Lepori and Montauti, 2020, p. 2). When organizations face a significant decision, they need a process to frame how the decision is made. On the one hand they need a flexible process to respond to changes in the environment and resource opportunities, but on the other hand they need established routines which promote rigidity (Chenhall, Hall and Smith, 2013; Gilbert, 2005; Lepori and Montauti, 2020). A "structured flexibility" permits the management of universities through competing logics, as the loose coupling (Orton and Weick, 1990; Weick, 1976) of universities provides opportunities where the boundaries of the competing logics are set within the university (Lepori and Montauti, 2020).

This framework is more accommodating than legitimacy seeking (Moll and Hoque, 2011) in explaining academics' behaviour, as it provides space for the *professional logic* of academics to influence university decision making. However, it has to deal with the similar issue of the different motivations and incentives influencing behaviours of individual actors in terms of prestige maximization (Kwiek, 2018, 2021; Mouritzen and Opstrup, 2020; Rosinger et al., 2016). This perhaps is most visible at field or disciplinary levels, that roughly translate to departmental units within a university. As prestige is field specific (Rosinger et al., 2016), operationalizing this in departments within universities suggests that departments, even if they had the jurisdiction (authority) to make decisions on resource allocation, would choose to follow or be incentivized by criteria based largely on what maximizes prestige within their field. Within a PRFS, where allocation criteria relate to specified forms of publications or publishers, there would need to be alignment between each department's (field) objectives for prestige and the university's allocation system and the PRFS criteria. As such, while the "structured flexibility" allows for the *professional* and *managerial* logics coexisting in operating a university, it is limited in understanding the incentivization of a PRFS owing to the disciplinary differences in terms of publishing for prestige maximization and the university's allocation system being at the institutional level (i.e. the funding criteria are the same for all departments/fields throughout the university).

Agency Theory

As a broader theoretical lens, we believe agency theory is a helpful framework for understanding the alignment and misalignment of interests and incentives between system level and institutional management, and between institutional management and subunits, and individual academics (e.g. Kivistö, 2007; Lane and Kivistö, 2008; Kivistö and Zalyevskaya, 2015). By virtue of its generic nature, agency theory is increasing in popularity as a conceptual tool for modelling the underlying dynamics of accountability and trust relationships in higher education settings (see e.g. Auld, 2010; Borgos, 2013; Enders, de Boer and Weyer, 2013; Kivistö and Zalyevskaya, 2015; Lane, Kinser and Knox, 2013; Kivistö, Pekkola and Lyytinen, 2017). It has, though, been less frequently applied in framing the budgeting and internal resource allocation decisions in universities.

Agency theory (Jensen and Meckling, 1976; Eisenhardt, 1989) analyses the relationship between two or more parties, in which one party (designated the principal) engages another party (designated the agent) to perform some task on its behalf. The theory assumes that principals often have problems controlling their agents. This is largely due to the self-interests of the agents (which trigger goal conflicts with their principal) and because agents often have better information about their own efforts than the principal (their actions are unobservable because of informational asymmetries). Together, the goal conflicts and informational asymmetries trigger conditions for the emergence of opportunistic, self-serving behaviour on the part of the agent (Kivistö and Zalyevska, 2015; Kivistö et al., 2017).

Agency theory proposes two alternative contractual strategies for principals to resolve the challenge posed by the agents' self-interests: one of increased monitoring (reducing informational asymmetries) and the other of outcome-based compensation (reducing goal conflicts). In intra-organization budgetary terms, the former is equivalent to input-based funding schemes, involving monitoring the unit-level use of funds, and the latter to performance-based funding, where the determination of budget allocations is related to unit-level performance. Both contractual options involve costs, benefits and risks, about which agency theory offers detailed insights.

The basic assumptions of agency theory are generic, to the extent that they are relevant regardless of the level of analysis. Agency theory is applicable to relationships (contractual or other) between individuals, units, and organizations (Kivistö, 2008). From this perspective, it suggests that, if a university does not align its internal funding criteria with the external funding mechanism, it will not perform well in meeting the external criteria, owing to potential or actual goal conflicts and informational asymmetries present in its internal organization.

A central question with regard to PRFS is how and to what extent the system-level incentives translate or incorporate into intra-institutional allocation practices. From the perspective of agency theory, principal–agent chains of relationships can replicate in a way where an agent of a higher-level relationship can also serve, simultaneously, as a principal in another relationship. This means that an institution's central management body can be acting simultaneously as both an agent (externally; the government agency is its principal) and a principal (internally, where subunits like departments or faculties are its agents). If we assume that system level incentives shape universities' behaviour, we need to also assume that the same incentives shape unit-level behaviour. This is because the university-level performance is an aggregated performance of the university's units. The logic of system-level PRFS indeed requires incentives trickle down (Aagaard, 2015) from the level of the public financing body to the level of units, and eventually, onto the level of research groups and individual researchers.

Tension Points

In order to highlight some of the most crucial tension points related to using PRFS in internal resource allocation models, we need to summarize the key assumptions on which PRFS is based. These assumptions are the following:

- That PRFS stimulates universities/units towards greater efficiency and quality, that is, better performance. By using PRFS, universities/units are encouraged to produce more and higher quality research outputs with the given resources, or the same amount and quality of outputs with a lower level of resources.
- That without PRFS, universities/units would not place enough emphasis on performance or would wilfully bypass their chances to improve their performance, unless there are clear incentives to do so. The former alternative refers to mismanagement while the latter to opportunistic, self-serving behaviour of the universities/units.

The validity of these two assumptions is based on two interconnected premises:

1. That universities/academic units are sensitive to financial incentives and that they find PRFS incentives valuable enough to change their behaviour (= *sufficient motivation*).
2. That universities/units have the necessary means to change their productive behaviour in line with the PRFS incentives if they want to do so (= *sufficient capability*).

If either of these two premises is not present, it is likely that PRFS will not produce its intended outcomes. We now turn to summarizing our analysis in the light of these assumptions and premises.

On Sufficient Motivation

Economic viability is a starting point for university- and unit-level operations. Therefore, when the basis of the amount of allocation is found in performance indicators, it is expected to undertake "rational" actions which are believed to result in higher levels of measured performance. However, it is unclear whether and to what point financial austerity increases the unit level's motivation for complying with financial stimuli. For instance, let us assume that the PRFS formula determines 30% of a unit's annual budget. Would those units, that are financially healthy, increase their effort at the same rate as those units who are in a financially difficult situation? Or would both these units aim to increase their efforts if the PRFS formula would determine 40% or even 70% of their budget? PRFS incentives are likely to have a greater impact under conditions where units experience financial austerity. Paradoxically this means that keeping units relatively poor without possibilities to accumulate financial buffers could actually improve the efficacy of PRFS approaches, given that units do not have alternative sources of revenue.

It is important to notice that the attention for financial incentives sometimes overeshadows the motivational factors affecting the behaviour of individual academics by highlighting the extrinsic motivation of academics. However, much of the academic motivation is related to intrinsic motivation: that is, academic curiosity, creating new knowledge and scientific discoveries is creating enjoyment and inherent satisfaction from academic work. In addition, other intrinsic, but more self-serving motivation comes also into play. Prestige, visibility, fame among peers and societal respect can also motivate academics (cf. Checchi et al., 2019). For instance, when studying the impact of performance-based incentives on Finnish academics, Kivistö et al. (2017) found that the motivation of senior level academics still related primarily to the acknowledgement and appreciation received from the academic community (academic prestige and respect among peers) and to the academic achievement itself, rather than to bureaucratic measurements and financial incentives (see also Frey and Osterloh, 2006). Even though this finding does not suggest that PRFS would not influence the behaviour of academics, it nevertheless implies that one should not overestimate the impact of PRFS, because of the intrinsic motivation of academics.

On Sufficient Capability

PRFS will only be effective if there is an initial misalignment in goals of the parties involved. If a university's management begins rewarding particular research outputs depending on the units' disciplinary nature and the individual academics' value system, the performance-oriented incentives may have no additional productive effect on the behaviour of the units or the academics. This means that the basis of PRFS's influence is always grounded on the assumption that there exist inefficiencies or "poor quality" which PRFS can fix. However, based on crowding hypotheses (see earlier in this chapter), PRFSs are prone to produce unintended effects in those cases where units already have reached their maximum efficiency level. If academics perceive the PRFS as a system of control and/or a sign of mistrust, rather than as a positive or encouragement mechanism, it is likely to create unintended impacts.

PRFS also assumes that next to an improvement potential there is a capability at the level of the unit to produce a higher level of performance, i.e. it suggests that there currently exists some degree of mismanagement that PRFS can fix. Mismanagement includes poor management or inadequate leadership, bad organizing, or ineffective governance structures (cf. Andrews, Boyne and Enticott, 2006). In cases where the management has no capabilities to improve performance because there is no clear production technology in place, or there are other intervening factors lying outside of the control of the management, improving performance can be difficult. Furthermore, university managers and individual academics are often in the middle of competing demands from various internal and external stakeholders (e.g. students, alumni, donors, industry, and multiple types of research financiers). The existence of numerous competing demands may in fact bring academics and university managers in situations where the task fulfilment for one resource provider may lead to a poorer performance vis-à-vis the performance metrics of other providers.

CONCLUSIONS

The logics behind PBFR models largely rely on similar assumptions to the ones underlying principal–agent relationships studied in agency theory. Governments (or other governance bodies, such as research councils) offering resources can be seen as principals, whereas universities and other research organizations act as agents. The classic principal–agent assumptions can help us understand the underlying logic of PRFS, its application in internal resource allocation and its potential to translate into changed behaviour of units and academics that leads to improvements in research performance. For this reason, internal funding schemes that fail to tie budgets to research outputs, such as publications or external funding, are more likely to result in inefficient outcomes from the principal's perspective. This is because these types of schemes have difficulties motivating the units and academics' behaviours.

The value of agency theory is that it provides a lens to understand the use of performance-based funding of research. It draws attention to information asymmetries (which explain the need to verify university/unit level performance) and goal conflicts (which explain the need to incentivize the university/unit). At the same time, it offers insights related to the difficulties of PRFS by addressing the challenges related to the measurability and controllability of research performance. Both of these are very relevant aspects for understanding the possibilities and limitations of research performance budgeting and its expected outcomes and unintended consequences.

Even though agency theory does not suggest that extrinsic motivation is the only source of motivation for human beings, the problem is that the theory fails to take into account other aspects of motivation. This takes us back to the somewhat simplistic, but crucial assumptions behind PRFS. Like agency theory, PRFS fails to take into account sources of intrinsic motivation and its unintended potential of crowding out this motivation.

Furthermore, agency theory assumes that the principal's goals and the PRFS are meaningful and legitimate, and that the agent receiving the resources should adopt these goals in return for these resources. Given the nature of research as an activity and universities being special organizations playing an important role in modern knowledge-driven societies, the system-level use of PRFS also creates a risk that universities copy and paste these PRFS models into their internal resource allocation schemes. For this reason, the selection of performance indicators and their weighting seems to be a crucial decision for the acceptance and efficacy of PRFS systems.

The knowledge about how and why universities internally respond to PRFS and what effects these responses create, remains still inconclusive. One major limitation is that empirical studies focusing on PRFSs require settings where systems have been in operation for a considerable time, and where systems allocate funding in a way and extent that creates strong enough incentives for universities to replicate system-level performance indicators internally. However, as this chapter has shown, some empirical findings indicate that the introduction of PRFS may have impacted publication behaviour among scholars, for instance by publishing more in those outlets that are rewarded through PRFS (Aagaard, 2015; Deutz, Drachen, Drongstrup, Opstrup and Wien, 2021; Mathies et al., 2020; Himanen and Puuska, 2022). Future empirical research should consider evaluating the effects of intra-institutional PRFS to better understand the design and the assumptions PRFSs are based on. In particular, future empirical research based on quasi experimental research designs which are able to provide proper counterfactuals would be particularly valuable.

REFERENCES

Aagaard, K. (2015). How incentives trickle down: Local use of a national bibliometric indicator system. *Science and Public Policy*, *42*, 725–737.

Aghion, P., Dewatripont, M., Hoxby, C., Mas-Colell, A., and Sapir, A. (2010). The governance and performance of universities: Evidence from Europe and the US. *Economic Policy*, *25*(61), 7–59.

Akerlof, G. A., and Kranton, R. E. (2005). Identity and the economics of organizations. *Journal of Economic Perspectives*, *19*(1), 9–32.

Andersen, L. B., and Pallesen, T. (2008). "Not just for the money?" How financial incentives affect the number of publications at Danish research institutions. International *Public Management Journal*, *11*, 28–47.

Andrews, R., Boyne, G. A., and Enticott, G. (2006). Performance failure in public sector. Misfortune or mismanagement? *Public Management Review*, *8*(2), 273–296.

Arnhold, N., Kivistö, J., Püttmann, V., Vossensteyn, H. and Ziegele, F. (2018). Bank reimbursable advisory service on higher education. Internal funding and governance in Latvia: Recommendations. In *World Bank Support to Higher Education in Latvia: Volume 2. Internal Funding and Governance*. Washington, DC: World Bank.

Auld, D. (2010). Strategic planning and the principal–agent issue in higher education leadership. *Academic Leadership*, *8*, 31–35.

Baron, J. N. and Kreps, D. N. (1999). *Strategic Human Resources: Frameworks for General Managers*. New York: John Wiley.

Battilana, J., Sengul, M., Pache, A., and Model, J. (2015). Harnessing productive tensions in hybrid organizations: The case of work integration social enterprises. *Academy of Management Journal*, *58*(6), 1658–1685.

Bloch, C. W., and Schneider, J. W. (2016). Performance-based funding models and researcher behavior: An analysis of the influence of the Norwegian Publication Indicator at the individual level. *Research Evaluation*, *25*(4), 371–382.

Borgos, J. (2013). Using principal–agent theory as a framework for analysis in evaluating the multiple stakeholders involved in the accreditation and quality assurance of international medical branch campuses. *Quality in Higher Education*, *19*, 173–190.

Bowen, H. (1980). *The Cost of Higher Education: How Much do Colleges and Universities Spend per Student and How Much Should they Spend?* San Francisco, CA: Jossey-Bass.

Butler, L. (2003). Modifying publication practices in response to funding formulas. *Research Evaluation*, *12*(1), 39–46.

Checchi, D., Malgarini, M., and Sarlo, S. (2019). Do performance-based research funding systems affect research production and impact? *Higher Education Quarterly*, *73*, 45–69.

Chenhall, R., Hall, M., and Smith, D. (2013). Performance measurement, modes of evaluation and the development of a compromising account. *Accounting, Organizations, and Society*, *38*, 268–287.

Claeys-Kulik, A-L., and Estermann, T. (2015). *Define Thematic Report: Performance-based Funding of Universities in Europe*. Brussels: European University Association.

de Rijcke, S., Wouters, P. F., Rushford, A. D., Franssen, T. P., and Franssen, B. (2015). Evaluation practices and effects of indicator use – A literature review. *Research Evaluation*, *25*(2), 161–169.

Deutz, D. B., Drachen, T. M., Drongstrup, D., Opstrup, N., and Wien, C. (2021). Quantitative quality: a study on how performance-based measures may change the publication patterns of Danish researchers. *Scientometrics*, *126*, 3303–3320.

Eisenhardt, K. (1989). Agency theory: An assessment and review. *Academy of Management Review*, *14*(1), 57–74.

Enders, J., de Boer, H., and Weyer, E. (2013). Regulatory autonomy and performance: The reform of higher education re-visited. *Higher Education*, *65*, 5–23.

European Commission. (2020). On achieving the European Education Area by 2025. Communication from the Commission to the European Parliament, the Council, the European Economic and Social Committee and the Committee of the Regions, COM(2020) 625 final. Brussels: European Commission.

Frandsen T., Eriksen M., Hammer D., and Christensen J. (2019). Fragmented publishing: A large-scale study of health science. *Scientometrics*, *119*, 1729–1743.

Frey, B. (1997). A constitution for knaves crowds out civic virtues. *Economic Journal, 107*(443), 1043–1053.

Frey, B., and Jegen, R. (2001). Motivation crowding theory. *Journal of Economic Surveys, 15*, 589–611.

Frey, B. and Osterloh, M. (2006). *Evaluations: Hidden Costs, Questionable Benefits, and Superior Alternatives*. Working Paper No. 302. Zurich: Institute for Empirical Research in Economics University of Zurich.

Garvin, D. A. (1980). *The Economics of University Behavior*. New York: Academic Press.

Geuna, A., and Martin, B. R. (2003). University research evaluation and funding: An international comparison. *Minerva, 41*, 277–304.

Gilbert, C. (2005). Unbundling the structure of inertia: Resource versus routine rigidity. *Academy of Management Journal, 48*, 741–763.

Giménez-Toledo, E., Mañana-Rodríguez, J., Engles, T., Guns, R., Kulczycki, E., Ochsner, M., Pölönen, J., Sivertsen, G., and Zuccala, A. (2019). Taking scholarly books into account, part II: A comparison of 19 European countries in evaluating and funding. *Scientometrics, 118*, 223–251.

Haddow, G., and Hammarfelt, B. (2019). Quality, impact, and quantification: Indicators and metrics use by social scientists. *Journal of the Association for Information Science and Technology, 70*(1), 16–26.

Hammarfelt B., Nelhans, G. and Eklund, P. (2016). The heterogeneous landscape of bibliometric indicators: Evaluating models for allocating resources at Swedish universities. *Research Evaluation, 25*(3), 292–305.

Herbst, M. (2007). *Financing Public Universities: The Case of Performance Funding*. Dordrecht: Springer.

Hicks, D. (2009). Evolving regimes of multi-university research evaluation. *Higher Education, 57*(4), 393–404.

Hicks, D. (2012). Performance-based university research funding systems. *Research Policy, 41*(2), 251–261.

Hillman, N. W., Tandberg, D. A., and Gross, J. P. (2014). Performance funding in higher education: Do financial incentives impact college completions? *The Journal of Higher Education, 85*(6), 826–857.

Himanen, L., and Puuska, H-M. (2022). Does monitoring performance act as an incentive for improving research performance? National and organizational level analysis of Finnish universities, Research Evaluation, *31*(2), 236–248.

James, E. (1990). Decision processes and priorities in higher education. In Hoenack, S. A. and Collins, E. L. (Eds.), *The Economics of American Universities. Management, Operations, and Fiscal Environment*. Albany, NY: State University of New York Press, 77–106.

Jensen, M. C., and Meckling, W. H. (1976). Theory of the firm: Managerial behavior, agency costs and ownership structure. *Journal of Financial Economics, 3*(4), 305–360.

Jessop, B. (2017). Varieties of academic capitalism and entrepreneurial universities. On past research and three thought experiments. *Higher Education, 73*, 853–870.

Jiménez-Contreras, E., de Moya Anegón, F., and López-Cózar, E. D. (2003). The evolution of research activity in Spain. *Research Policy, 32*(1), 123–142.

Jongbloed, B. (2010). *Funding Higher Education: A View Across Europe*. Brussels: European Centre for Strategic Management of Universities.

Jongbloed, B., and Vossensteyn, H. (2001). Keeping up performances: An international survey of performance-based funding in higher education. *Journal of Higher Education Policy and Management, 23*(2), 127–145.

Jonkers, K., and Zacharewicz, T. (2016). *Research Performance Based Funding Systems: A Comparative Assessment*. JRC Working Papers. Luxembourg: Publications Office of the European Union.

Kivistö, J. (2007). *Agency Theory as a Framework for the Government–University Relationship*. Doctoral dissertation. Higher Education Finance and Management Series. Tampere: Tampere University Press.

Kivistö, J. (2008). Agency theory as a framework for government–university relationship: Assessment of the theory. *Journal of Higher Education Policy and Management, 30*(4), 339–350.

Kivistö, J., and Kohtamäki, V. (2016). Does performance-based funding work? Reviewing the impacts of performance-based funding on higher education institutions. In Pritchard, R., Pausits, A., and Williams, J. (Eds.) *Positioning Higher Education Institutions: From Here to There*. Rotterdam: Sense, pp. 215–226.

Kivistö, J., and Zalyevska, I. (2015). Agency theory as a framework for higher education governance. In Huisman, J., de Boer, H., Dill, D., and Souto-Otero, M. (Eds.) *The Palgrave International Handbook of Higher Education Policy and Governance*. Basingstoke: Palgrave Macmillan, pp. 132–151.

Kivistö, J., Pekkola, E., and Lyytinen, A. (2017). The influence of performance-based management on teaching and research performance of Finnish senior academics. *Tertiary Education and Management*, *23*(3), 260–275.

Kivistö, J., Pekkola, E., and Kujala, E. (2021a). *Selvitys yliopistojen sisäisistä rahoitusmalleista. Osa 1: Yliopistojen sisäiset rahoitusmallit*. Helsinki: Professoriliitto ry.

Krog Lind, J. (2019). The missing link: How university managers mediate the impact of a performance-based research funding system. *Research Evaluation*, *28*(1), 84–93.

Kwiek, M. (2018). High research productivity in vertically undifferentiated higher education systems: Who are the top performers? *Scientometrics*, *115*, 415–462.

Kwiek, M. (2021). The prestige economy of higher education journals: A quantitative approach. *Higher Education*, *81*, 493–519.

Lane, J. E., and Kivistö, J. (2008). Interests, information, and incentives in higher education: Principal agent theory and its potential applications to the study of higher education governance. In Smart, J. C. (Ed.) *Higher Education: Handbook of Theory and Research. Volume XXIII*. Berlin: Springer, pp. 141–179.

Lane, J. E., Kinser, K., and Knox, D. (2013). Regulating cross-border higher education: A case study of the United States. *Higher Education Policy*, *26*, 147–172.

Lepori, B., and Montauti, M. (2020). Bringing the organization back in: Flexing structural responses to competing logics in budgeting. *Accounting, Organizations and Society*, *80*, 1729–1743.

Massy, W. F. (2016). *Re-engineering the University*. Baltimore, MD: Johns Hopkins University Press.

Mathies, C., Kivistö, J., and Birnbaum, M. (2020). Following the money? Performance-based funding and the changing publication patterns of Finnish academics. *Higher Education*, *79*, 21–37.

Melguizo, T., and Strober, M. (2007). Faculty salaries and the maximization of prestige. *Research in Higher Education*, *48*(6), 633–668.

Merton, R. K. (1968). *Social Theory and Social Structure* (enlarged ed.). New York: The Free Press.

Mintzberg, H. (1981). Organizational design: Fashion or fit? *Harvard Business Review*, (January–February), 103–116.

Moed, H. F. (2008). UK research assessment exercises: Informed judgments on research quality or quantity? *Scientometrics*, *74*(1), 153–161.

Moll, J., and Hoque, Z. (2011). Budgeting for legitimacy: The case of an Australian university. *Accounting, Organizations, and Society*, *36*, 86–101.

Mouritzen, P. E., and Opstrup, N. (2020). *Performance Management at Universities: The Danish Bibliometric Research Indicator at Work*. Basingstoke: Palgrave Macmillan.

Norman, I., and Grifths, P. (2008). Duplicate publication and "salami slicing": Ethical issues and practical solutions. *International Journal of Nursing Studies*, *45*(9), 1257–1260.

Opstrup, N. (2017). When and why do university managers use publication incentive payments? *Journal of Higher Education Policy and Management*, *39*(5), 1–16.

Orton, J. D., and Weick, K. (1990). Loosely coupled systems: A reconceptualization. *The Academy of Management Review*, *15*(2), 203–223.

Ossenblok, T. L. B., Engels, T. C. E., and Sivertsen, G. (2012). The representation of the social sciences and humanities in the Web of Science – a comparison of publication patterns and incentive structures in Flanders and Norway (2005–9), *Research Evaluation*, *21*(4), 280–290.

Rabovsky, T. M. (2012). Accountability in higher education: Exploring impacts on state budgets and institutional spending patterns. *Journal of Public Administration Research and Theory*, *22*(4), 675–700.

Rosinger, K., Taylor, B., Coco, L., and Slaughter, S. (2016). Organizational segmentation and the prestige economy: Deprofessionalization in high- and low-resource departments. *Journal of Higher Education*, *87*(1), 27–54.

Slaughter, S., and Rhoades, G. (2004). *Academic Capitalism and the New Economy: Markets, State, and Higher Education*. Baltimore, MD: Johns Hopkins University Press.

Sīle, L., and Vanderstraeten, R. (2019). Measuring changes in publication patterns in a context of performance-based research funding systems: The case of educational research in the University of Gothenburg (2005–2014). *Scientometrics*, *118*, 71–91.

Sörlin, S. (2007). Funding diversity: Performance-based funding regimes as drivers of differentiation in higher education systems. *Higher Education Policy*, *20*, 413–440.

Tandberg, D., and Hillman, N. (2013). *State Performance Funding for Higher Education: Silver Bullet or Red Herring*. WISCAPE Policy Brief, 18. Madison, WI: University of Wisconsin – Madison, Wisconsin Center for the Advancement of Postsecondary Education.

Tirole, R., and Bénabou, R. (2006). Incentives and pro-social behaviour. *American Economic Review*, *96*(5), 1652–1678.

Verhoest, K., Peters, G. B., Bouckaert, G., and Verschuere, B. (2004). The study of organisational autonomy: A conceptual review. *Public Administration and Development*, *24*, 101–118.

Weick, K. (1976). Educational organizations as loosely coupled systems. *Administrative Science Quarterly*, *21*(1), 1–19.

Weingart, P. (2005). Impact of bibliometrics upon the science system: Inadvertent consequences? *Scientometrics*, *62*, 117–131.

Woelert, P., and Mckenzie, L. (2018). Follow the money? How Australian universities replicate national performance-based funding mechanisms. *Research Evaluation*, *27*, 184–195.

Zacharewicz, T., Lepori, B., Reale, E., and Jonkers, K. (2019) Performance-based funding in EU-member states: A comparative assessment. *Science and Public Policy*, *46*(1), 105–115.

Ziegele, F. (2008). *Management of Financial Resources. Intensive Blended Learning University Leadership and Management Training Programme (UNILEAD)*. Oldenburg: Carl von Ossietzky University of Oldenburg.

13. Research funding in the context of high institutional stratification: policy scenarios for Europe based on insights from the United States[1]

Arlette Jappe and Thomas Heinze

13.1 INTRODUCTION

Top research universities in the United States are much admired by the rest of the world for their superior research performance and their formidable wealth. Many countries in Europe strive to emulate their success and seek to concentrate governmental funding in their best performing universities in turn. But it has also long been recognized that the organizational field of doctoral universities in the United States is characterized by pronounced stratification and fierce competition for educational prestige. Social closure effectively limits the upward social mobility of universities, faculty scientists, and students.

This chapter argues that research funding policies should not be conceived in isolation from knowledge about institutional structures of university systems. Instead, investigating the interaction between research funding and university system stratification is necessary to learn more about long-term structural effects of different funding policies. As a review, this chapter combines previously disjoint literatures that shed light on university system stratification in the United States. We consider basic findings concerning the comparability of the situation in Europe with that in the United States and discuss two scenarios for research funding policies in Europe.

The chapter is structured as follows. Section 13.2 introduces a theoretical account of the relationship between organizational status and scientific quality. Throughout this chapter, we use "status" as the general term that applies to organizations as well as individuals. In the case of universities, status is referred to more specifically as organizational "prestige", whereas "reputation" denotes the status of individual scientists. Reputation means recognition for relevant scientific contributions by fellow scientists. Reputation is to be distinguished from occupational status of individuals within organizations such as "full professor" or "head of laboratory". The first section describes how scientific competition is linked to organizational competition via inter-individual differences in scientific productivity.

As part of a handbook on research funding, this chapter is focused on research universities. Doctoral research universities are defined by the Carnegie classification as institutions that annually have awarded at least 20 research/scholarship doctoral degrees and had at least $5 million in total research expenditures.[2] Research universities are but one of six categories of colleges that scholars distinguish in the United States: baccalaureate colleges (liberal arts colleges), comprehensive colleges (baccalaureate and advanced degrees), research universities (focused on more advanced degrees and knowledge creation), associate degree colleges (community colleges), special-focus institutions (theology, medicine, law, art), and for-profit entities (special focus, baccalaureate, associate, and advanced degrees) (Scott and Biag, 2016: 28). In its most recent report, the population of 418 doctoral universities was further subdivided by Carnegie into "very high research" (131 higher education institutions, HEIs), "high research" (135), and "doctoral/professional universities" (152) (IUCPR, 2018).

Sections 13.3–13.5 characterize stratification within the segment of research universities in the United States from different angles. Section 13.3 treats characteristics of positional competitions for university prestige. Section 13.4 summarizes findings on the concentration versus dispersion of research expenditures. Section 13.5 reviews findings on the measurement of university prestige based on faculty exchange networks. Section 13.6 refers to the European Tertiary Education Register (ETER) to consider the broad comparability between research universities in Europe and the United States. Based on the results of Sections 13.3–13.6, we sketch two scenarios for the future of European research universities, with conclusions for research funding policy (Section 13.7).

This overview of interdisciplinary findings demonstrates that stratification of research universities in the United States is accompanied by social closure and reduced social mobility on several levels, from students to individual scientists to research organizations. We conclude from this body of research that university system stratification and social closure are part of the long-term societal impacts of research funding. The more an organizational prestige hierarchy solidifies, the more the discretionary influence of public policy on eventual funding distributions can be expected to diminish (Bozeman, Chapter 2 in this *Handbook*). Therefore, the design details of competitive funding instruments appear less decisive for long-term distributive outcomes than governments' overall strategic direction on the question of vertical differentiation versus system expansion.

13.2   ORGANIZATIONAL PRESTIGE AND SCIENTIFIC QUALITY

In general terms, scientific progress is characterized by a fundamental tension between originality or novel contributions on one side and disciplinary traditions or more established knowledge on the other (Heinze and Münch, 2016; Polanyi, 1969). Scientific competition takes place between individual scientists and their research groups in intellectual fields (Whitley, 2000), as well as between competing research programs (Lakatos, 1970). While organizations do not literally engage in intellectual competition, they support individual competitors so that organizational capabilities and resources have an influence on intellectual developments. Viewed from this analytical angle, universities primarily fulfill various administrative and professional functions, such as acting as employers, providing basic funding, managing external research grants, being a platform for collaboration, connecting research and teaching, and training young scientists. Furthermore, as institutions in democratic societies, universities act as fiduciaries for intellectual freedom and scientific renewal (Parsons and Platt, 1974).

Organizational competition can be linked to intellectual competition on the basis of inter-individual differences in scientific productivity. Bibliometric studies have consistently shown that the inter-individual distribution of scientific performance is extremely skewed. A small subset of the population of scientists produces the bulk of publications and accumulates an even larger proportion of all citations, a pattern that persists across disciplines (Ioannidis, Boyack, and Klavans, 2014; Nielsen and Andersen, 2021; Ruiz-Castillo and Costas, 2014; Seglen, 1992). In a stratified organizational field, universities compete primarily for individual scientific talent and reputation. In the fourth section, we show that university prestige can be measured in terms of faculty hiring as status-deferent behaviour. In reality, inter-university competition is more multidimensional, as it is also about attracting student talent. But the relevant dimensions are not independent. Other dimensions of organizational competition, such as competition for research money, follow suit.

How does organizational competition influence scientific competition? On a general level, two different accounts are available in the literature. Authors more concerned with scientific competition have argued that a concentration of talent can be beneficial because it supports and enhances scientists' individual and collective productivity (Allison and Long, 1990). In this view, an important function of elite universities is to create an environment that supports highly creative research (Heinze, Shapira, Rogers, and Senker, 2009; Hollingsworth, 2004). Furthermore, rich elite institutions are able to attract from across the world individuals with scientific talent who cannot find comparable working conditions elsewhere (Stephan and Levin, 2007). A related idea in research funding policy is that excellent research requires "critical mass". While this concept defies a precise numerical definition, it suggests that scientific capabilities and/or resources must be concentrated beyond a certain threshold to enable a self-reinforcing productive process (Aksnes, Benner, Borlaug, and Hansen, 2012; OECD, 2014). A recent review concerning funding concentration at the individual and group levels is provided by Aagaard, Kladakis, and Nielsen (2020).

Authors more interested in organizational competition have argued that stratification provides informational advantages, as it structures the competitive arena in such a way that a complex and dynamic situation (intellectual competition) is transformed into a stable and obvious situation (organizational hierarchies), enabling stable expectations on the part of different market agents. A diverse literature on organizational status in markets treats status as a "quality signal" in the face of information uncertainty (Piazza and Castelluci, 2014; Podolny, 1993; Sauder, Lynn, and Podolny, 2012). This notion of signaling is also applicable in the context of research organizations. Here, widespread uncertainty about "true" quality is primarily a result of scientific specialization.

Signaling has practical importance for research funding, because the "true" scientific quality of an individual contribution, a project proposal, or a researcher's performance can be judged independently and proficiently only by experts or peers from the same field (Whitley, 2000). All others have to rely on expert evaluation and cannot claim an independent judgment of their own. Making matters worse, experts often do not agree in their assessment, and less so for more creative and more risky contributions. As a consequence, organizational processes such as hiring or resource allocations often lead to situations where non-experts are required to take decisions on the relative merit of scientific competitors (Heinze and Jappe, 2020).

The literature on organizational status in markets maintains that stable stratification can structure the competitive arena in a way that mutual observation of status-deferent behavior could reasonably precede or even replace expert judgments of quality. To the extent that there is a commonly recognized gradient of prestige, high-status universities have an advantage in recruiting those individuals with the strongest scientific performance. The more an organizational prestige hierarchy mirrors a true differentiation of departments according to scientific performance, or correlates with the latter, the more organizational status becomes meaningful as a signal of quality (Sauder et al., 2012).

A further implication of the status-in-markets perspective is that markets tend to split up into status segments, effectively reducing the number of direct competitors. In the case of universities, status segments seem particularly relevant for the selection of collabora-tors. Jones, Wuchty, and Uzzi (2008) found that teamwork in science increasingly spans inter-organizational boundaries and that elite US universities play a dominant role in national co-authorships. The top-tier universities held places in 60 percent of multi-university collabo-rations in Science and Engineering and 56 percent in Social Sciences in the period 2001–2005 (Web of Science).

Between-university collaborations are frequent not only in publications but also in funding proposals. Therefore, a similar extent of segmentation and functional dominance of elite schools can be expected in national "quasi-markets" for research funding, despite the fact that competitions are construed in different ways for different funding instruments (Arora-Jonsson, Brunsson, and Edlund, Chapter 11 in this *Handbook*). Market segmentation means that an organizational prestige hierarchy becomes well defined and solid in the perception of market agents and that segments permanently offer different opportunity structures for individual scientists (Section 13.5). In this way, a prestige hierarchy can become a self-reinforcing mech-anism of funding concentration.

While the status-in-markets perspective underscores functional advantages in that status hierarchies reduce situational complexity, other studies also point to disadvantages of organ-izational stratification for scientific competition. A central problem is that the observation of scientific performance does not remain unaffected by status positions, for either individuals or organizations. Since scientific performance (or productivity) is often measured on the basis of publications and citations, bibliometrics can illustrate this point.

Bibliometric methods have inherent limitations when it comes to the distinction between quality and status. These limitations are directly related to the act of reference selection in scientific writing (for an overview, see Aksnes, Langfeldt, and Wouters, 2019). In most cases, authors select references for specific aspects of scientific content or quality, while in other cases, they also select references out of deference to the reputation of particular colleague-competitors within their respective intellectual field. The act of citing colleagues with a strong reputation can enhance the credibility and legitimacy of particular propositions and can also refer to shared scientific beliefs, so that status deference in scientific work should not per se be deemed problematic. Yet, the extent to which the selection of references is based on independent assessments of quality or rather reflects the mutual observation of status-deferent behavior in research communities cannot be decided on the basis of citation data alone.

While the relation of content quality and author status in citations cannot be disentangled for individual publications, bibliometric studies show that reputation produces network effects in citation data ("preferential attachment"). On the individual level, these effects have been referred to as "cumulative advantage" (Barabási et al., 2002; DiPrete and Eirich, 2006). Cumulative effects have also been observed at the level of universities. Several studies have reported super-linear scaling of citations with university size (as measured in publications or in research expenditures), which means that citation numbers increase disproportionately with organizational size (Lepori, Geuna, and Mira, 2019; van Raan, 2013).

So far, it has not been determined whether these organizational effects can be explained by the aggregated reputation of affiliated scientists or whether there are independent organ-izational effects that would indicate productivity advantages connected to university size or university prestige. In any event, the measurement of scientific quality and status appears to be closely associated in citation data on multiple levels. Consequently, while citation data can reduce uncertainty concerning the quality of scientific work, they cannot determine quality independently of status positions within the science system.

A related problem is that status hierarchies can filter ideas and might reduce intellectual renewal. Certainly, the logic of a status-deferent social exchange and resulting status hierarchies stand in fundamental tension with the epistemic norms of a rational exchange of arguments. Network science offers an analytical perspective to connect the two. It maintains that hubs in a network have higher diffusion power compared with that of nodes that are less well connected. It follows that ideas from the periphery need to be more persuasive – that is, have stronger arguments, higher originality and relevance, and stronger rhetorical qualities – to successfully spread in a network, compared with ideas originating from a tightly interconnected "rich core" structure (Morgan, Economou, Way, and Clauset, 2018).

High-status actors, such as disciplinary elites, will at times effectively delay or suppress the adoption and growth of new ideas in their particular domain of competence (Heinze and Münch, 2016; Whitley, Gläser, and Laudel, 2018). If research funding aims to support invention and intellectual renewal, it appears recommendable not to follow the signals of reputation and prestige alone, mechanically enforcing the hierarchical re-organization and centralization of universities, but to carefully observe unfolding tensions between established disciplinary hierarchies and efforts to establish more innovative and interdisciplinary research areas, and more generally to support intellectual diversity (Heinze and Münch, 2016; Münch, 2014).

13.3   POSITIONAL COMPETITION FOR UNIVERSITY PRESTIGE

While some insights from the market-oriented literature on organizational status also apply to universities, universities are not just any market when it comes to the phenomenon of social status. This section refers to the situation in the United States, where the competition for prestige between top universities appears to be so entrenched that it has been characterized by economists as an instance of "positional competition", the characteristics of which are analytically defined in contrast to more classical market situations (Frank and Cook, 2010/1995; Podolny, 1993; Winston, 1999). This applies to universities on two different levels. On the one hand, universities, through graduation, confer the certificates needed for entry to professional careers and thus for access to high occupational and income status at later stages. On the other hand, universities as organizations compete for talent on all steps of the academic career ladder, from high school seniors to Nobel Prize winners.

Frank and Cook (2010/1995) argue that digitalized economies are increasingly characterized by "winner-take-all markets" and that this phenomenon is important for the explanation of increasing income inequality in the United States and other modern economies. Those careers that lead to the highest incomes in US society, including finance, corporate-oriented law firms, or corporate management, can be conceived of as a "series of elimination tournaments". This expression both highlights the intensity of the competition and, through the notion of a "tournament", implies that the competition is primarily about the winner gaining higher status than the losers. The final winners, that is, those who persevere and reach the top of the hierarchy, eventually receive disproportionate rewards to a degree comparable only to the elevation of stars in sports or music or similar "winner-take-all markets" (Frank and Cook, 2010/1995).

Graduation from elite universities has long been a prerequisite for access to careers in high-status firms (Frank and Cook, 2010/1995), but also within academia (Section 13.5). As a result, high school seniors with the highest test scores compete for a limited set of study places and increasingly concentrate at the most prestigious universities (Winston, 1999). This competition among prospective students is about access to occupational status at a later stage, when university prestige is evaluated as a status attribute of individuals. Elite universities therefore function as gatekeepers for those careers that lead to the highest ranks in society.

The competition between universities for the best students differs from a more typical market situation in that top universities do not expand their enrolments in response to rising demand. Crow and Dabars (2015) criticized US elite universities for keeping the number of study places artificially restricted in order to maintain or even increase the distinctive value of the positional good which they offer. According to these authors, selectivity of study access is unwarrantedly interpreted as a signal of educational quality. Rather, they argued that a large and demographically diverse pool of talent in the United States remains untapped as a result of this policy. In any case, strong selectivity leads to a situation where relative advantages in performance become more important than absolute performance, which is a defining characteristic of positional competitions. Small differences in performance can thus lead to enormous differences in outcome (Frank and Cook, 2010/1995).

The perception of a scarcity of top positions among universities is also enforced by public rankings. University rankings can produce reactive effects in the sense that differences in performance between study programs that were once small and difficult to measure later become real and solidified as an effect of the repeated communication of initial differences in departmental prestige (Espeland and Sauder, 2007). Clauset, Arbesman, and Larremore (2015: SM) also investigated to what extent prestige rankings based on faculty placement data are associated with rank uncertainties and found large uncertainties for intermediate ranks but relatively low uncertainty for very high- or very low-prestige universities.

From the perspective of research funding, it is important to recognize that assumptions of classical economic theory regarding an efficient allocation of resources through markets do not necessarily apply to situations of positional competition among elite US universities. On the contrary, competitors are here compelled to make every investment that could lead to a positional advantage. Since the number of top positions is limited from the outset, these competing investments can be mutually offsetting and may eventually fail to achieve any positional gains. This type of competitive game has therefore been called a "positional arms race" (Frank and Cook, 2010/1995; Winston, 2000). Positional arms races can encourage investments that are wasteful from the perspective of society at large (Winston, 2004).

Likewise, research funding policy should consider that the positional arms race in inter-university competition is inherently linked to a global race in science and technology. The competitive structure of the US higher education system can perhaps best be interpreted to the effect that research universities become aligned to an arms race that ultimately is not about national but about global leadership (Heinze, Pithan, and Jappe, 2019; Leydesdorff and Wagner, 2009). From the perspective of a global race in science and technology, questions regarding the efficient allocation of societal resources appear almost subordinate. At the least, it could be argued that the economic gains through technology leadership in the past have more than compensated any potential efficiency losses for the United States, as the histories of big tech firms in Silicon Valley or the biotech industry illustrate (Jasanoff, 2006; Saxenian, 1994).

13.4 CONCENTRATION OF RESEARCH FUNDING AND SOCIAL CLOSURE AT THE LEVEL OF UNIVERSITIES

The concentration of research resources is an important indicator for the measurement of stratification within a university system, and one that directly relates to research funding. This section reviews empirical findings on the concentration of research expenditures in US universities. Proponents of university system stratification hold that the concentration of resources should follow the concentration of performance. In the hands of the most capable individuals, research money is expected to generate the most benefits. The analytical question of whether this constitutes an efficient allocation of resources through market mechanisms or whether the situation could be more adequately analyzed as a positional arms race cannot be decided on the basis of these descriptive findings.

After a period of strong expansion of research universities from the 1960s until the 1980s, a political consensus against further dispersion emerged in the early 1990s, according to Geiger and Feller (1995). Proponents argued that as a result of the expansion of research capacities, federal research funding would be spread out too thinly to continue to support excellence. In a similar vein, Hicks and Katz (2011: 142) state that "cumulative advantage in scientific performance establishes a conflict between efficiency and equity considerations in public funding of research", and argued that decision makers will probably not dare to concentrate funding as much as would be justified by differences in merit. They make the criticism that a concentration of funding equivalent to the concentration in performance is difficult to assert politically because of a widespread attitude of "inequality aversion" (Hicks and Katz, 2011: 149).

The development of research funding concentration in US HEI is less well studied empirically than one might assume in light of this important political debate. Davies and Zarifa (2012) investigated the development of university income and expenditure concentration in the period 1971–2006, comparing the United States and Canada. This study documented a very unequal distribution of resources among universities and four-year colleges. Research-related income is the most highly concentrated of all income streams: in 2006, "federal grants per student" (FTE) had the highest concentration (private sector Gini: 0.86; public sector Gini: 0.71), followed by "provincial/state grants per student" (private sector Gini: 0.78; public sector Gini: 0.75). By comparison, "course/tuition fees" showed less concentration across HEIs (private sector Gini: 0.30; public sector Gini: 0.29), while the "revenues and investment returns" ranged in between (private sector Gini, 0.51; public sector Gini, 0.58).

As regards the long-term development over 35 years, the study documented an increasing separation between the "masses" of HEIs and a small number of extremely wealthy institutions. Upper outliers in terms of total income and expenditures per student already existed in the 1970s, but increasingly they "have pulled away from the pack". On the basis of boxplot distributions, Davies and Zarifa (2012: 150) characterized US HEI as "a hierarchical system dominated by a small number of super-resourced, elite institutions that are highly distinct from the masses". The Gini index of federal research funding inequality was similar in 2006 to that in 1971, after having temporarily decreased in the decades between (mid-1970s to mid-1990s).

Brint and Carr (2017) investigated concentration of input and output indicators and mobility among US research universities over the period 1980–2010, building on Geiger and Feller (1995). Their sample includes 188 top research universities in terms of R&D expenditures, and is thus a more selective sample than that studied by Davies and Zarifa (2012). As measures of research output, Brint and Carr used Web of Science publications (whole counts) and cumulative citations. The study produced two main findings. First, the period of 1980–2010 was marked by steady and impressive growth in input and output indicators on both the system and campus levels. The strongest growth was in R&D expenditures (a 964% increase in 2010 prizes), followed by publications (190%) and citations (146%). At the same time, inequality remained virtually unchanged. While the first quartile of institutions lost slightly in its proportion of R&D spending, from more than 60 to closer to 50 percent, its proportion of publications remained constant at about 55 percent with citations at 60 percent. Gini coefficients for the entire sample (1980 versus 2010) declined slightly for R&D spending (0.52 versus 0.48) and citations (0.59 versus 0.56) and remained constant for publications (0.48).

Second, the study investigated the inter-decile mobility of institutions on the same indicators. Only a small number of institutions rose or fell by more than one decile over the 30 year period. In R&D expenditures, slightly more than 20 percent of the sample moved up or down more than one decile, in publications 14 percent and in citations 12 percent. Only 7–8 percent of institutions experienced long-term upward mobility. Some did enter or exit the set of top universities, but Brint and Carr argue that most of these movements happened at the bottom of the list. The authors conclude that "long-range upward mobility was not a prominent feature of the system of scientific production in US research universities during the study period" (Brint and Carr, 2017: 450).

Taken together, available studies document strong inequality among US HEIs generally and research universities in particular in terms of research funding and performance. Brint and Carr argue that the process of resource dispersion that was found by Geiger and Feller for the 1980s did not continue through the following two decades despite strong growth in R&D expenditures. They describe a stable concentration of resources accompanied by increasing R&D expenditures per unit of research output (publications and citations). Although these results do not contradict the proposition that a strong concentration of resources is beneficial for performance at the top of a university system, they also document social closure on the level of universities as organizations. Over a period of decades, the authors found that there were very few newcomers to the high-performing core of the system.

13.5   CONCENTRATION OF FACULTY PLACEMENTS AND SOCIAL CLOSURE AT THE LEVEL OF SCIENTISTS

This section reviews results from faculty placement studies, which provide more detailed insights into the social structure of US HEIs. Recruitment networks can serve as the basis for determining prestige hierarchies among university departments. Prestige is thus conceived not as an attribute attached to an individual department, but derives empirically from the respective departments' positions in a social exchange network (Burris, 2004: 240). The measurement of organizational status based on hiring therefore constitutes an instance of an "objective" or structural definition of status, in contrast to an understanding of status as "subjective" evaluation, which might for instance be operationalized through expert opinions (D'Aveni, 1996; Piazza and Castelluci, 2014).

Faculty placement studies investigate networks of "PhD exchange" among university departments (Burris, 2004), based on "who hires whose graduates as faculty" (Clauset, Arbesman, and Larremore, 2015: 1). They have been conducted for a range of mostly social science disciplines in the United States, including sociology (Shichor, 1970); economics

(Pieper and Willis, 1999); sociology, history and political science (Burris, 2004); political science (Fowler, Grofman, and Masuoka, 2007); mathematics (Myers, Mucha, and Porter, 2011); law (Katz, Gubler, Zelner, and Bommarito, 2011); communication (Barnett, Danowski, Feeley, and Stalker, 2010; Mai, Liu, and González-Bailón, 2015); and anthropology (Kawa, Michelangeli, Clark, Ginsberg, and McCarty, 2019). Clauset et al. (2015) use the most advanced methods, covering computer science, business, and history.

All available studies show that US faculty (tenure track, tenure) production is skewed so that the most prestigious departments fill a disproportionate share of faculty positions. Clauset et al. (2015) find that 25 percent of research universities produced 71 to 86 percent of all tenure-track faculty in the disciplines of computer science, business, and history during 2011–2013. Fifty percent of all faculty graduated from only 18, 16, and 8 departments in computer science, business, and history, respectively. Pieper and Willis (1999) found that 66 percent of economics faculty had graduated from the top 20 placing programs in 1992. Burris (2004) found 77 percent of history, 74 percent of political science, and 69 percent of sociology faculty were recruited from the respective top 20 placing programs in 1995. In communication, the top 20 placing programs filled 58 percent of faculty positions in 2007 (Barnett et al., 2010). Thus, top placing departments in each discipline compete for a limited set of faculty positions as a central resource of future academic research.

Since recruitment networks consist of behavioural data that are based on collective assessments by disciplinary peers, their conceptual and empirical validity appears superior to reputational survey data as used in popular news rankings. Several studies report moderate to strong correlations with rankings by US News and World Report (Clauset et al., 2015; Fowler et al., 2007) and National Research Council's rankings (Barnett et al., 2010; Burris, 2004; Clauset et al., 2015). An important limitation of the available research is its focus on the social sciences. With the exception of a study of computer science and one of mathematics, to date we do not know if these above-mentioned findings can be extended to the natural sciences, engineering, and medicine, where academic job markets are generally larger (Rosvall and Bergstrom, 2011: figure 3), comprising more institutions with larger average department sizes.

Steep faculty placement hierarchies imply that, in most cases, faculty will hold positions at departments with less prestige than their respective PhD faculties. Clauset et al. determined that downward movement occurred in 86 (business) to 91 percent (history) of placements. Thus, prestige hierarchies also imply that upward social mobility of scientists is rare compared with downward mobility, even if seen over a sample of faculty of all stages of seniority (Clauset et al., 2015: S4). Women from top institutions were found to move somewhat further down the hierarchy than men in the disciplines of computer science and business, but not in history (Clauset et al., 2015: S5).

In addition, faculty placement studies show "rich-club ordering" in inter-departmental recruitment networks, defined as "the tendency of nodes with a high degree to be more interconnected than expected" (Cinelli, 2019: 1). "The notion of a rich-club describes nodes which are essentially the hub of a network, as they play a dominating role in structural and functional properties" (Ma, Mondragon, and Latora, 2015: 1). Rich-club organization has implications in terms of status in that a high-status group constitutes a segment separated from the rest. But the functional dominance goes further than mere status differentiation. Nodes that belong to the(se) hub(s) have higher diffusion power across the network, so that network structures influence intellectual competition, a case of functional domination.

Viewing scientists as carriers of ideas, faculty hiring becomes a process of transmission of ideas. As each applicant is knowledgeable of an individual set of research topics, intellectual traditions, and associated skills, recruiting can be conceived as an organizational process of selecting and adapting particular (new) ideas and capabilities. This cognitive diffusion was investigated in a modelling study by Morgan et al. (2018), who studied how faculty-hiring networks could influence the spread of ideas in computer science. Their model shows that ideas from prestigious universities tend to spread farther than those originating from less prestigious universities, for ideas of similar quality. The effect of prestige is stronger for ideas of lower transmissibility (lower quality) and weaker for ideas of higher transmissibility (higher quality).

In sum, faculty placement studies document, first, competition among US research universities for faculty positions as the most central resource for academic research. This competition is organized within disciplines and is dominated by a handful of elite departments. Across studies, the top 20 departments fill between two-thirds and four-fifths of research positions of the investigated disciplines. Second, available studies strongly suggest that prestige translates into intellectual domination through a shared preference for education from elite departments and the associated reproduction of selected intellectual traditions. Third, these studies reveal that faculty regularly move down the prestige hierarchy from PhD to academic employment, with very few cases of upward mobility. In other words, social closure of academic career paths in the investigated fields had regularly already occurred at the stage of graduate admission. This early timing of social closure aggravates the danger of a predominance of cultural status norms and intellectual tastes within fields over careful (status-independent) assessment of scientific talent.

13.6   COMPARABILITY OF UNIVERSITY SYSTEMS IN THE UNITED STATES AND EUROPE

At present, the European situation differs from that in the United States in important respects. The European university system is more heterogeneous and less integrated by a coherent and stratified network structure. Capabilities for excellent research are more distributed (Bonaccorsi, Cicero, Haddawy, and Hassan, 2017). The European institutional landscape as a whole is also endowed with substantially less resources. From the vantage point of positional competitions for university prestige and global tech races, these are important disadvantages. Yet from the perspective of education and social mobility in democratic knowledge societies, we argue that the current dispersal of HEI capabilities could be turned into an advantage through ambitious policies of system expansion.

To what extent can Europe be regarded as a single university system? The European Higher Education Area, the Bologna Process, and the European Framework Programs are all important political instruments towards integration of European HEI. Yet, by comparison with the prominence of national university systems, it is still not very common in the HEI literature to study universities in Europe as one region. ETER has made important progress in data provision to describe the European landscape of HEI. For the academic year 2016/2017, ETER contained organizational information on HEIs from more than 30 countries, including the EU, EFTA, non-EU Balkan States, and Turkey.

Table 13.1   *Comparison of European and US HEI systems, number (percentage)*

2013	Europe			United States		
	HEIs	Enrolments	Staff	HEIs	Enrolments	Staff
Doctoral universities[a]	564	11,200,000	671,044	366	6,291,367	469,233
	(25)	(66)	(70)	(11)	(46)	(56)
Masters' colleges and	545	3,759,457	184,660	815	4,550,288	212,263
universities[b]	(24)	(22)	(19)	(25)	(33)	(25)
Other HEIs[c]	1,134	2,098,621	106,646	2,106	2,827,541	161,234
	(51)	(12)	(11)	(64)	(21)	(19)
Total	2,243	17,058,078	962,350	3,287	13,669,196	842,730
	(100)	(100)	(100)	(100)	(100)	(100)

Notes:
[a] HEIs with at least 20 ISCED 8 degrees in the year.
[b] HEIs with fewer than 20 ISCED 8 degrees and at least 50 ISCED 8 degrees.
[c] Baccalaureate colleges, baccalaureate/associate colleges, focused institutions, and unclassified.
Source: Lepori et al. (2019: S3).

Based on ETER and IPEDS data, the European HEI system appears roughly comparable with the US HEI system in terms of number of institutions and number of students. According to Lepori et al. (2019), who applied the Carnegie Classification to European HEIs, 88 percent of 17 million FTE students were enrolled in the two largest categories of "doctoral universities" and "master's colleges and universities" in Europe in 2013, compared with 79 percent of 14 million FTE students in the United States (Table 13.1). According to Lepori et al. (2019), the major difference between the systems is in resource provision. Not only is the total amount of revenue in the US HEI system much larger than it is in Europe, it is also more concentrated at the top. In Europe, the distribution of revenues tends to mirror the distribution of academic staff (FTE), whereas in the United States, revenues are more concentrated than academic staff (Lepori et al., 2019: figure 6). In 2013, only three European universities (Cambridge, Oxford, University College London) had budgets of more than 1 billion Euros, compared with 50 universities in the United States, including 16 top universities with budgets of more than 2 billion Euros. The authors conclude that the "gap in research excellence" between Europe and the United States is essentially a gap in resources.

The composition of funding streams accentuates these differences. For most European HEIs, basic government allocation still represents the largest share of funds, while other sources are only complementary, with the exceptions of private for-profit HEIs and publicly funded UK universities that are mostly funded through student fees. In contrast, in the United States, student fees are the most important source of funding for medium-sized HEIs with annual budgets of up to 500 million Euros; while for large HEIs (500–999 million and 1.000–1.999 million Euros annually), the funding streams of student fees, third-party funding, and private donations are of similar average magnitudes. In the group of the richest 16 universities with revenues above 2 billion euros in 2013, private donations are the dominant funding stream, constituting 49 percent of annual revenues (Lepori et al., 2019: 12). The distinction between public and private HEIs is complicated by the fact that governmental research funding is concentrated at the same segment of top universities as private donations (Bozeman, 2013).

In contrast to the United States, Europe does not function as one single academic job market but is structured by national university systems that have become increasingly interconnected through research collaborations and scientific mobility (Cañibano, D'Este, Otamendi, and

Woolley, 2020; Musselin, 2004). As a consequence, the methodical approach of faculty placement studies cannot be directly transferred to the European scale. Researchers with a strong reputation are more widely distributed in Europe compared with the United States, where the same set of elite universities excel across a wide range of fields (Bonaccorsi et al., 2017). From the perspective of the hierarchical interdependencies between academic departments in the United States, European HEIs are often perceived as peripheral.

National university systems in Europe differ regarding the extent to which they concentrate excellent researchers at prestigious universities. On one side, there is the UK with an entrenched prestige hierarchy. The five richest European HEIs in terms of annual budget are all located in England: Cambridge, Oxford, University College London, Manchester, and Imperial College London (ETER, 2019b: 18, 20). The UK has a policy of concentrating public research funding at the top, through the Research Excellence Framework (Geuna and Piolatto, 2016), as well as through competitive project funding (Ma et al., 2015). On the other side, the Netherlands exemplifies a more equitable policy, seeking to advance all their 13 research universities to the top segment in Europe. Both countries are very successful through the lens of bibliometric performance metrics (Bonaccorsi et al., 2017).

On the European level, the Framework Programs (FPs) act as a mechanism of resource concentration. Lepori, Veglio, Heller-Schuh, Scherngell, and Barber (2015) found that FP participation is concentrated among a small subset of large and visible HEIs and turns out to be more concentrated than academic staff, PhD students, or publication output. A group of 157 HEIs with more than 50 participations each accounted for 72 percent of all HEI participations in 2011. Among these 157 HEIs, 148 were also included in the Leiden Ranking based on their output of publications and citation impact. This group represents 15 percent of PhD-awarding universities in Europe. Other studies have investigated collaboration networks and found that participation remains highly stable over time (Enger, 2018). These findings indicate that FPs might develop into a powerful mechanism of system stratification and funding market segmentation. The average annual budget of Horizon Europe (2021–2027)[3] is approximately four times that of FP 5 (1999–2002) in current prizes (Reillon, 2017).

13.7   CONCLUSIONS: TWO RESEARCH POLICY SCENARIOS

Thus far, this chapter has reviewed findings on university system stratification in the United States from an interdisciplinary perspective. What lessons can be drawn for research policy in Europe? In this section, we delineate two scenarios for the future of the European university landscape concerning the long-term impact of research funding. These scenarios are distinguished by the extent to which policies of funding concentration are counterbalanced by strategies to expand the landscape of European research universities.

Since the 1990s, many European countries have implemented policies that have either the explicit objective or the unintended consequence of resource concentration (Reale, 2017). A common rationale for such policies is that universities should compete for research funding as an incentive to increase performance (Sivertsen, Chapter 6 in this *Handbook*). Performance-based funding is the category of instruments with the broadest scope (Zacharewicz, Lepori, Reale, and Jonkers, 2019), such as the Research Excellence Framework in the UK and the Italian Valutazione della Qualità della Ricerca (Geuna and Piolatto, 2016). The scope of research excellence schemes is more restricted, aiming to concentrate investment at selected centres and thus create a critical mass of internationally visible research (Aksnes et al., 2012; OECD, 2014). Even without instruments that specifically target the organizational level (universities, research centres), project funding can have resounding effects of institutional resource concentration (Ma et al., 2015).

Based on the American experience, one might expect that policies of vertical differentiation and resource concentration could eventually lead to a point at which HEI system stratification would become a self-reinforcing and irreversible dynamic. Current funding policies suggest that this tipping point has not yet been reached on a European scale, as many European countries are still struggling with schemes to increase the organizational capabilities and performance orientation of their research universities. An exception is the UK, where the Research Excellence Scheme converges with project funding to amplify resource concentration. As a result, a few UK-based elite universities have the largest budgets in Europe and also occupy leading positions in global prestige rankings.

At the same time, Europe as a region is undergoing a historical phase of HEI system expansion. During the 70 years from 1945 to 2015, the number of universities more than tripled, from fewer than 400 to almost 1,300 institutions (ETER, 2019a: 22). This expansion can be broken down into different waves across sub-regions and time periods (ETER, 2019a). From the macro perspective of European societies, the long-term expansion of HEIs is about the changing qualifications required by modern economies. From the micro perspective of individual citizens, the expansion of HEIs is about individual chances for social mobility and access to higher-income and higher-status occupations, often achieved only over the course of successive generations. From either view, HEI expansion is essential for future participation in a European knowledge society.

Based on these trends, two scenarios can be distinguished. Both assume that national and European policies of funding concentration enforce a vertical differentiation of the HEI landscape. We further assume that a commonly recognized university prestige hierarchy would develop into a self-reinforcing mechanism of resource concentration. Given that, across scientific disciplines, the most capable scientists would come to work at the same top European institutions, this would also imply a stronger European integration of academic labour markets.

First, in the "elitist scenario", the self-reinforcing prestige hierarchy will reach a tipping point where markets for research funding and collaboration split up into different segments. The collaborative linkages between organizations in the top segment will intensify to the extent that the whole network becomes functionally dominated by a "rich club" of tightly connected HEIs. Compared with the current situation, there will be a bigger number of large and internationally visible European HEIs that successfully compete with top universities from the United States and other world regions (Lepori et al., 2019). This group of highly prestigious HEIs will orchestrate the broader organizational network in terms of access to European and national funding sources (Ma et al., 2015). The number of Nobel Prizes and high tech firms in Europe will rise, to an extent that will depend also on the wealth and deregulation of European HEIs.

The downside of this concentrated effort is that most European regions will remain lastingly peripheral to the global science system and to the European knowledge society more generally. Policies of vertical differentiation, such as the Italian Valutazione della Qualità della Ricerca, will have desiccated research capabilities in economically weaker and more peripheral regions by promoting a more centralized organization. Positional competition will also lead to surging costs of research in Europe's centres of excellence. As a corollary of social closure, the number of prestigious universities and the size of their educational offerings will expand, yet not in proportion to a growing demand for high-quality education. Access to these prestigious universities will become super-exclusive. As a consequence, migration of young people from Southern, Eastern, and Central Europe to the established hubs of the knowledge society will continue and accelerate (Pruvot, Estermann, and Lisi, 2018). In sharp contrast to the urban lifestyle, cultural diversity, and progressive values cultivated in those hubs, adverse anti-EU, anti-elite, and anti-science attitudes will take root in the periphery (Dijkstra, Poelman, and Rodríguez-Pose, 2020).

Second, in the "expansive scenario", the knowledge society will be geographically expanded to develop a larger number of nodes with higher connectivity (Rodríguez-Pose and Griffiths, 2021; van Raan, 2022). There will still be policies of vertical differentiation in order to enhance the performance level of the strongest research universities, and there will still be research funding concentration at national top institutions. But these policies will be combined with and counterbalanced by political strategies to systematically expand the top segment of European research universities.

In the "expansive scenario", European research policy will be connected to European cohesion policies with the aim of successfully developing new research universities, either from scratch or as upgrades (or mergers) of existing institutions. New research universities or universities with new research capabilities will be established one by one in Southern, Eastern, and Central Europe, and the wealthier scientific nations in Northern and Western Europe will strive to compete and amplify European efforts at HEI building. A major advantage of this scenario is that new and interdisciplinary research areas will be established more swiftly and with higher frequency, generating a dynamism of innovation and strong societal impact. In this way, two well-known institutional deficiencies of European universities are addressed: first, the deferred and mostly hesitant uptake of new scientific fields (Ben-David, 1971), and second, the widespread fragmentation of scientific capabilities (Bonaccorsi et al., 2017).

In the "expansive scenario", European policy ensures that there will be successive waves of new entrants to a growing field of leading research universities. Instead of social closure on all levels, European policy will act to expand the opportunities for students and scientists with strong talent, increasing participation from different social and cultural backgrounds and the proportion of women and minorities among faculty. European research policy supports the integration of newcomer organizations into international networks of research collaboration. As the organizational field of the European research university will continue to grow, positional competition will become less dominant overall, compared with its role in the "elitist" scenario.

The downside of the "expansive scenario" is that it is expensive and would have to be followed through for quite some time in order to bear fruit. Clearly, not every new research organization or institutional upgrade will become a success. Much learning and entrepreneurial dynamism will be required, as exemplified by the organizational transformation of Arizona State University (Crow and Dabars, 2015). There is a serious risk that European research funding would become diluted away from its most capable centres of excellence and that dispersion would threaten critical mass and weaken international competitiveness. So overall, the amount of investment necessary to achieve the aims of the "expansive scenario" will be of an even larger scale than that required in the "elitist scenario".

Given the large scale of investment that a strategic expansion of European research universities would require, the funding would have to come (in part) from a rededication of

European regional and cohesion funds, thus combining objectives of research and innovation policy, higher education, regional development, and cohesion. Clearly, one of the main political challenges in this regard will be to define policy instruments that would go beyond the current European Framework Programmes (Lepori et al., 2015; Reillon, 2017) or the European Research Council (Beerkens, 2019; Luukkonen, 2014). Such new instruments would have to enable the EU to subsidize a permanent supply of faculty positions at European research universities in collaboration with member states, and to create selection procedures for European cities to qualify as locations for such an institutional boost to their scientific and innovative capabilities (Rodríguez-Pose and Griffiths, 2021; van Raan, 2022).

If pursued with long-term consistency and ambition, the investment in an expansive university policy would probably enhance the performance and stability of the European knowledge society as a whole. More talent would be tapped and less cultural cleavage and political disruption would occur, compared with the "elitist scenario". Europe as a world region could develop a strong economic dynamism alongside with ecological sustainability, and become a more educated and more equitable place to live, in comparison with the outcomes of current development paths followed by the United States.

NOTES

1. This work was funded by the Novo Nordisk Foundation as part of the project 'Promoting the socio-economic impact of research – The role of funding practices (PROSECON)', grant number NNF18OC0034422.
2. https://carnegieclassifications.iu.edu/classification_descriptions/basic.php, last accessed 25 January 2022.
3. https://ec.europa.eu/info/horizon-europe_en, last accessed 25 January 2022.

REFERENCES

Aagaard, K., Kladakis, A., and Nielsen, M. W. (2020). Concentration or dispersal of research funding? *Quantitative Science Studies*, *1*(1), 117–149.

Aksnes, D. W., Benner, M., Borlaug, S. B., and Hansen, H. F. (2012) Centres of Excellence in the Nordic countries. A comparative study of research excellence policy and excellence centre schemes in Denmark, Finland, Norway and Sweden. Working Paper 4/2012. Oslo: NIFU.

Aksnes, D. W., Langfeldt, L., and Wouters, P. (2019). Citations, citation indicators, and research quality: An overview of basic concepts and theories. *Sage Open*, *9*(1), 1–17.

Allison, D. P., and Long, J. S. (1990). Departmental effects on scientific productivity. *American Sociological Review*, *55*(4), 469–478.

Barabási, A. L., Jeong, H., Néda, Z., Ravasz, E., Schubert, A., and Vicsek, T. (2002). Evolution of the social network of scientific collaborations. *Physica A: Statistical Mechanics and its Applications*, *311*(3–4), 590–614.

Barnett, G. A., Danowski, J. A., Feeley, T. H., and Stalker, J. (2010). Measuring quality in communication doctoral education using network analysis of faculty-hiring patterns. *Journal of Communication*, *60*(2), 388–411.

Beerkens, M. (2019). The European Research Council and the academic profession: Insights from studying starting grant holders. *European Political Science*, *18*(2), 267–274.

Ben-David, J. (1971). *The Scientist's Role in Society. A Comparative Study*. Englewood Cliffs, NJ: Prentice-Hall.

Bonaccorsi, A., Cicero, T., Haddawy, P., and Hassan, S.-U. (2017). Explaining the transatlantic gap in research excellence. *Scientometrics*, *110*, 217–241.

Bozeman, B. (2013). What organization theorists and public policy researchers can learn from one another: Publicness theory as a case-in-point. *Organization Studies, 34*(2), 169–188.

Brint, S., and Carr, C. E. (2017). The scientific research output of US research universities, 1980–2010: Continuing dispersion, increasing concentration, or stable inequality? *Minerva, 55*(4), 435–457.

Burris, V. (2004). The academic caste system: Prestige hierarchies in PhD exchange networks. *American Sociological Review, 69*, 239–264.

Cañibano, C., D'Este, P., Otamendi, F. J., and Woolley, R. (2020). Scientific careers and the mobility of European researchers: an analysis of international mobility by career stage. *Higher Education, 80*(6), 1175–1193.

Cinelli, M. (2019). Generalized rich-club ordering in networks. *Journal of Complex Networks, 7*(5), 702–719.

Clauset, A., Arbesman, S., and Larremore, D. B. (2015). Systematic inequality and hierarchy in faculty hiring networks. *Science Advances, 1*, e1400005.

Crow, M. M., and Dabars, W. B. (2015). *Designing the New American University.* Baltimore, MD: Johns Hopkins University Press.

D'Aveni, R. (1996). A multiple-constituency, status-based approach to interorganizational mobility of faculty and input–output competition among top business schools. *Organization Science, 7*(2), 166–189.

Davies, S., and Zarifa, D. (2012). The stratification of universities: Structural inequality in Canada and the United States. *Research in Social Stratification and Mobility, 30*(2), 143–158.

Dijkstra, L., Poelman, H., and Rodríguez-Pose, A. (2020). The geography of EU discontent. *Regional Studies, 54*(6), 737–753.

DiPrete, T. A., and Eirich, G. M. (2006). Cumulative advantage as a mechanism for inequality: A review of theoretical and empirical developments. *Annual Reviews in Sociology, 32*, 271–297.

Enger, S. G. (2018). Closed clubs: Network centrality and participation in Horizon 2020. *Science and Public Policy, 45*(6), 884–896.

Espeland, W. N., and Sauder, M. (2007). Rankings and reactivity: How public measures recreate social worlds. *American Journal of Sociology, 113*, 1–40.

ETER (2019a). Dual vs. unitary systems in higher education. European Tertiary Education Register. Analytical Report 2019-3.

ETER (2019b). How are European Higher Education Institutions funded? New evidence from ETER microdata. European Tertiary Education Register. Analytical Report 2019-2.

Fowler, J. H., Grofman, B., and Masuoka, N. (2007). Social networks in political science: Hiring and placement of PhDs, 1960–2002. *PS: Political Science and Politics, 40*(4), 729–739.

Frank, R. H., and Cook, P. J. (2010/1995). *The Winner-Take-All Society. Why the Few at the Top Get so Much More Than the Rest of Us.* New York: Virgin Books.

Geiger, R. L., and Feller, I. (1995). The dispersion of academic research in the 1980s. *Journal of Higher Education, 66*, 336–360.

Geuna, A., and Piolatto, M. (2016). Research assessment in the UK and Italy: Costly and difficult,but probably worth it (at least for a while). *Research Policy, 45*, 260–271.

Heinze, T., and Jappe, A. (2020). Jurisdiction of bibliometrics. In R. Ball (Ed.), *Handbook Bibliometrics* (pp. 91–98). Berlin: DeGruyter.

Heinze, T., and Münch, R. (2016). Editor's introduction: Institutional conditions for progress and renewal in science. In T. Heinze and R. Münch (Eds.), *Innovation in Science and Organizational Renewal. Sociological and Historical Perspectives* (pp. 1–20). New York: Palgrave Macmillan.

Heinze, T., Shapira, P., Rogers, J., and Senker, J. (2009). Organizational and institutional influences on creativity in scientific research. *Research Policy, 38*(4), 610–623.

Heinze, T., Pithan, D., and Jappe, A. (2019). From North American hegemony to global competition for scientific leadership. Insights from the Nobel population. *PLoS ONE, 14*(4), e0213916.

Hicks, D. M., and Katz, S. (2011). Equity and excellence in research funding. *Minerva, 49*(2), 137–151.

Hollingsworth, J. R. (2004). Institutionalizing excellence in biomedical research: The case of the Rockefeller University. In D. H. Stapleton (Ed.), *Creating a Tradition of Biomedical Research. Contributions to the History of the Rockefeller University* (pp. 17–63). New York: Rockefeller University Press.

Ioannidis, J. P. A., Boyack, K. W., and Klavans, R. (2014). Estimates of the continuously publishing core in the scientific workforce. *PLoS ONE*, *9*(7), e101698.

IUCPR. (2018) *The Carnegie Classification of Institutions of Higher Education, 2018 edition*. Bloomington, IN: Indiana University Center for Postsecondary Research.

Jasanoff, S. (2006). Biotechnology and empire. The global power of seeds and science. *Osiris*, *21*(1), 273–292.

Jones, B. F., Wuchty, S., and Uzzi, B. (2008). Multi-university research teams: Shifting impact, geography, and stratification in science. *Science*, *322*, 1259–1262.

Katz, D. M., Gubler, J. R., Zelner, J., and Bommarito, M. J. (2011). Reproduction of hierarchy – A social network analysis of the American law professoriate. *Journal of Legal Education*, *61*, 76.

Kawa, N. C., Michelangeli, J. A. C., Clark, J. L., Ginsberg, D., and McCarty, C. (2019). The social network of US academic anthropology and its inequalities. *American Anthropologist*, *121*(1), 14–29.

Lakatos, I. (1970). Falsification and the methodology of scientific research programmes. In I. Lakatos and A. Musgrave (Eds.), *Criticism and the Growth of Knowledge* (pp. 91–196). Cambridge: Cambridge University Press.

Lepori, B., Veglio, V., Heller-Schuh, B., Scherngell, T., and Barber, M. (2015). Participations to European Framework Programs of higher education institutions and their association with organizational characteristics. *Scientometrics*, *105*, 2149–2178.

Lepori, B., Geuna, A., and Mira, A. (2019). Scientific output scales with resources. A comparison of US and European universities. *PLoS ONE*, *14*(10), e0223415.

Leydesdorff, L., and Wagner, C. S. (2009). Is the United States losing ground in science? A global perspective on the world science system. *Scientometrics*, *78*, 23–36.

Luukkonen, T. (2014). The European Research Council and the European research funding landscape. *Science and Public Policy*, *41*(1), 29–43.

Ma, A., Mondragon, R. J., and Latora, V. (2015). Anatomy of funded research in science. *Proceedings of the National Academy of Sciences of the United States of America*, *112*(48), 14760–14765.

Mai, B., Liu, J., and González-Bailón, S. (2015). Network effects in the academic market: Mechanisms for hiring and placing PhDs in communication (2007–2014). *Journal of Communication*, *65*(3), 558–583.

Morgan, A. C., Economou, D. J., Way, S. F., and Clauset, A. (2018). Prestige drives epistemic inequality in the diffusion of scientific ideas. *Epj Data Science*, *7*. https://doi.org/10.1140/epjds/s13688-018-0166-4.

Münch, R. (2014). *Academic Capitalism. Universities in the Global Struggle for Excellence*. New York: Routledge.

Musselin, C. (2004). Towards a European academic labour market? Some lessons drawn from empirical studies on academic mobility. *Higher Education*, *48*(1), 55–78.

Myers, S. A., Mucha, P. J., and Porter, M. A. (2011). Mathematical genealogy and department prestige. *Chaos: An Interdisciplinary Journal of Nonlinear Science*, *21*(4), 041104.

Nielsen, M. W., and Andersen, J. P. (2021). Global citation inequality is on the rise. *PNAS*, *118*(7), e2012208118.

OECD (2014) *Promoting Research Excellence: New Approaches to Funding*. Paris: OECD.

Parsons, T., and Platt, G. M. (1974). *The American University*. Cambridge, MA: Harvard University Press.

Piazza, A., and Castelluci, F. (2014). Status in organization and management theory. *Journal of Management*, *40*(1), 287–315.

Pieper, P. J., and Willis, R. A. (1999). The doctoral origins of economics faculty and the education of new economics doctorates. *The Journal of Economic Education*, *30*(1), 80–88.

Podolny, J. M. (1993). A status-based model of market competition. *American Journal of Sociology*, *98*, 829–872.

Polanyi, M. (1969). *Knowing and Being. With an Introduction by Marjorie Grene*. Chicago, IL: Chicago University Press.

Pruvot, E. B., Estermann, T., and Lisi, V. (2018) Public Funding Observatory Report 2018. European University Association. www.eua.eu/publicfundingobservatory.

Reale, E. (2017). *Analysis of National Public Research Funding (PREF) Final Report*. Luxembourg.

Reillon, V. (2017) EU framework programmes for research and innovation. Evolution and key data from FP1 to Horizon 2020 in view of FP9. European Parliamentary Research Service EPRS.

Rodríguez-Pose, A., and Griffiths, J. (2021). Developing intermediate cities. *Regional Science Policy and Practice*, *13*, 441–456.

Rosvall, M., and Bergstrom, C. T. (2011). Multilevel compression of random walks on networks reveals hierarchical organization in large integrated systems. *Plos ONE*, *6*(4), e18209.

Ruiz-Castillo, J., and Costas, R. (2014). The skewness of scientific productivity. *Journal of Informetrics* (8), 917–934.

Sauder, M., Lynn, F., and Podolny, J. M. (2012). Status: Insights from organizational sociology. *Annual Review of Sociology*, *38*, 267–283.

Saxenian, A. (1994). *Regional Advantage. Culture and Competition in Silicon Valley and Route 128*. London: Harvard University Press.

Scott, W. R., and Biag, M. (2016). The changing ecology of US higher education: An organization field perspective. In *The University Under Pressure*. Research in the Sociology of Organizations, 46 (pp. 25–51). Bingley: Emerald.

Seglen, P. O. (1992). The skewness of science. *American Society for Information Science Journal*, *43*, 628–638.

Shichor, D. (1970). Prestige of sociology departments and the placing of new PhDs. *The American Sociologist*, 157–160.

Stephan, P. E., and Levin, S. G. (2007). Foreign scholars in U.S. science: Contributions and costs. In P. E. Stephan and R. G. Ehrenberg (Eds.), *Science and the University* (pp. 150–173). Madison, WI: University of Wisconsin Press.

van Raan, A. F. (2013). Universities scale like cities. *PLoS ONE*, *8*(3), e59384.

van Raan, A. F. (2022). German cities with universities: Socioeconomic position and university performance. *Quantitative Science Studies*, *3*(1), 265–288.

Whitley, R. (2000). *The Intellectual and Social Organization of the Sciences. 2nd Edition*. Oxford: Oxford University Press.

Whitley, R., Gläser, J., and Laudel, G. (2018). The impact of changing funding and authority relationships on scientific innovations. *Minerva*, *56*(1), 109–134.

Winston, G. C. (1999). Subsidies, hierarchy and peers: The awkward economics of higher education. *Journal of Economic Perspectives*, *13*(1), 13–36.

Winston, G. C. (2000) The positional arms race in higher education. WPEHE Discussion Paper, No. 54. Williamstown, MA: Williams College, Williams Project on the Economics of Higher Education.

Winston, G. C. (2004). Differentiation among US colleges and universities. *Review of Industrial Organization*, *24*(4), 331–354.

Zacharewicz, T., Lepori, B., Reale, E., and Jonkers, K. (2019). Performance-based research funding in EU Member States – A comparative assessment. *Science and Public Policy*, *46*(1), 105–115.

14. Public research organisations and public research funding[1]

Laura Cruz-Castro and Luis Sanz-Menéndez

INTRODUCTION

In 2019, the world research and development (R&D) expenditure was more than 2.2 trillion US dollars – according to UNESCO almost 1.8% of the world gross product. Although the business enterprise sector has taken the global lead in financing and executing research, governments' total R&D financing is still very significant, representing 0.61% of the GDP in the Organisation for Economic Co-operation and Development (OECD) economies.

From the point of view of the government, the funding of R&D may operate directly and indirectly – the balance between the direct performance of R&D activities by institutions that belong to the government sector and indirect support from government to R&D actors through various types of funding has changed; the modalities of government funding have also evolved over time in many countries (Larrue et al. 2018).

Governments and the public sector in general also continue to play an important role performing R&D. In general, the share of governments in the performance of R&D (that is, in institutions controlled by them), seems to have decreased (measured as a percentage of the total gross expenditure in R&D, GERD) in the OECD countries or, at least, in an important group of them. Despite a general reduction of governmental role (Poti and Reale 2000), the degree of governments' involvement in the performance of R&D is very heterogeneous. The reasons are partly historical and country specific, for instance, the persistence of some missions around the public production of knowledge (Mazzucato 2018), public sector reforms (e.g. Boden et al. 2004 for UK) and the integration of government research institutes in universities (e.g. Aagaard et al. 2016 for Denmark) have affected countries in different ways.

The aim of this chapter is to address the relationship between public R&D organisations and R&D public funding. The chapter focuses on the analysis of a diverse set of organisations that carry out R&D, which do not depend on companies or universities, and on which the government exerts influence or control through various channels.

The research organisations under public or government control have traditionally been called the government sector (Marcson 1972), but the empirical reality, the concept and the categories to describe the 'influence' of government in R&D activities have changed over time; for instance, government research laboratories (OECD 1989) or public research institutions (OECD 2011) are labels that comprise various types of entities such as research institutes, councils or academies of sciences, or governments' R&D centres with specific missions.

The focus on which dimension of government influence is relevant for categorising them as public research organisations (PROs) (Sanz-Menéndez et al. 2011) has been changing from administrative dependence or legal status to their effective control, funding or the performing of 'public missions'. Behind the new names or uses of the traditional concepts, new dynamics are identifiable, especially the increasing diversity of sources of funding, the execution of public missions or the provision of public goods. This concept (PROs) allows for classification and is useful for interpretative purposes, as well as for addressing some of the processes of change, evolution and the emergence of new organisational types under government influence. Although sometimes universities, as a result of local circumstances, are also included under the PRO category, here we use the term PRO to refer exclusively to organisations that do not have teaching as one of their main missions.

The chapter addresses three broad topics that can be organised around the following questions in different levels: conceptual, descriptive and causal. The first relates to the characterisation of public research organisations: what is the public or government R&D sector? How to characterise the variety of organisations within the public research sector? How has it changed? The second refers to the variation of sources of funding (volume and composition) of PROs. The issue is important because the emergence of new types of PRO and their corresponding missions is related to different forms of government funding and other types of influence. The third relates to the consequences of different types of funding on some of the internal dynamics of PROs: what are the expected effects of funding modalities on managerial strategic capacity and researchers' autonomy? Does this change depend on structural characteristics?

These are relevant academic and policy questions. The literature still suffers from a lack of consideration and understanding of the internal diversity of PROs. Additionally, government R&D funding and the promotion of research organisations are decisive instruments of science and innovation policies (Joengbloed and Lepori 2015; OECD 2018); funding portfolios are expected to differ by PRO type but the empirical evidence is scant. Finally, research funding is a key management tool in research organisations (Borsi 2021) and organisational theory is underdeveloped regarding the effects of funding modes on the knowledge production (Gläser and Laudel 2016) and other internal dynamics.

In the view of the size and the role that government R&D laboratories continue to play in many countries, it is surprising that PROs have received so little systematic attention among research policy scholars and analysts.

The rest of the chapter is organised as follows: in the next section, we delimitate the public sector research sector (PSR) domain presenting some positioning data in different countries. The chapter follows with a review of the classifications of PROs and the role of funding in the typologies; we analyse the issue from two different approaches, which correspond to ideal types and taxonomies respectively. In the following section, we highlight the importance of the missions in accounting for the increasing diversity of PROs and explore the variation of funding sources across some examples of different types of PRO. Next we turn to the PROs as strategic actors and present some plausible connections between different types of research funding and authority relations. The chapter ends with some concluding remarks and some methodological considerations.

THE FUNDING OF PUBLIC RESEARCH ORGANISATIONS: MAPPING THE DIFFERENCES

The existing literature, classification and measurement of the public sector research rely strongly on classificatory standards and an official dataset: the OECD Frascati Manual (OECD 2015), also adopted by UNESCO and EUROSTAT. We use the concept of PSR to include both public higher education institutions (HEIs) and government sector organisations (Senker

2006; Larédo and Mustar 2004), an aggregation of two different 'Frascati sectors'. For our purposes, we keep the concept of PROs to refer to organisations mainly dedicated to research without any teaching under the control, or influence of government, developing public missions or providing public goods (Cruz-Castro et al. 2020).

The official R&D statistics provide some proxies for the role of governments in R&D and trends. The problem is that they make it difficult to understand relevant changes in the PROs related to policy and funding. Currently, the analyses merely highlight formal changes, present differences because countries use various implementation criteria (e.g. in France and Spain similar entities (CNRS and CSIC) are classified in different sectors) and hide the role of governments in funding other organisations that perform public missions (e.g. some not for profit institutions).

We are interested in the membership of a group of organisations that we conceptualise as PROs, but most of the standard data reports the government sector. As mentioned, governments' total R&D financing is very significant (equivalent to 0.61% of the GDPs in the OECD economies and 0.63% in EU-27 countries for 2019), but with big variance across countries; while in some research-intensive countries (e.g. Korea or Norway), it accounts for almost 1% of GDP, in other countries, it is only one quarter as much.

Despite the fact that the government sector's contribution (percentage) to GERD has diminished by almost 50% since the beginning of the 1980s, the government sector still represents 9.7% of GERD in the OECD countries and 11.4% in the EU-27. However, there are relevant differences between countries regarding the role of governments in the direct performance of R&D, and most of them are related to the relative salience of their Higher Education sector.

The changes in the different countries can be observed in Figure 14.1, where the share of the government sector (as a percentage of the PSR) is presented in 1995 and in 2019. The figure portrays considerable diversity. There is a group of countries, which appear below the diagonal, that have reduced the government sector to a minimum and have concentrated public support on the HE sector (countries also known for having implemented major reforms). In others, the distribution has not been greatly altered, but there are also cases, located in the figure up to the diagonal, in which the weight of the government sector has slightly increased (e.g. Belgium, Turkey, Argentina, Slovenia, Greece, etc.).

Figure 14.2 shows, for 2019, the relationship between higher education and government R&D expenditures as a percentage of the GDP (horizontal axis) and the share of the government sector in the PSR. The situation of the countries is again very heterogeneous. However, in those in which the weight of the public sector is large in terms of GDP, there are some that clearly maintain the relevance of the government sector (Germany, Korea, United States, etc.), and others in which the government is very small. Interestingly, the trend line shows a general pattern of reduction of the share of the government sector as the size of the PSR increases over the GDP. In sum, there is weak relationship between the weight of the PSR in the GDP and the share of the government sector in the PSR; it looks like that there are country path-dependencies.

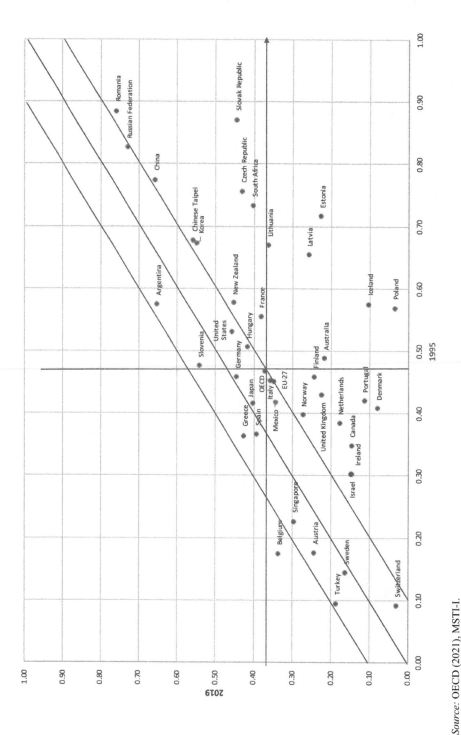

Source: OECD (2021), MSTI-I.

Figure 14.1   *Government sector share on public sector research, 1995 and 2019*

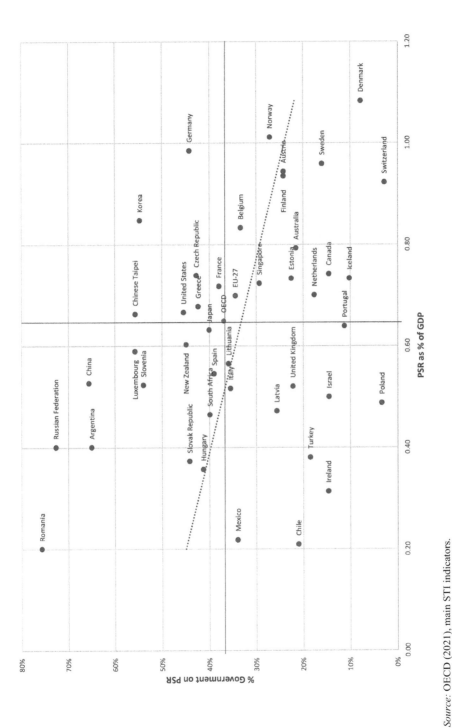

Source: OECD (2021), main STI indicators.

Figure 14.2   *Share of government and public sector research R&D expenditure (as a percentage of GDP), 2017*

GOVERNMENT INFLUENCE AND PUBLIC RESEARCH ORGANISATIONS: A REVISION OF EXISTING CLASSIFICATIONS

Our interest in conceptual precision and the reduction of conceptual stretching and travelling is related to the problems that traditional sectoral classifications entail for the analysis of changes and dynamics, and the understanding of internal diversity.

Firstly, they make the categorisation of some organisations difficult, given the increased blurred boundaries between different actors. Second, they are ill-suited to reveal some new forms of government intervention and, more importantly, the transformation of research performing organisations, because they do not allow for comparing the commonalities of organisations assigned to different institutional sectors.[2] Finally, sectoral classifications fall short of capturing the emergence of some new types of research organisations, usually with a not for profit legal status, promoted by governments on the boundaries of HEIs, or centres to stimulate technology transfer to industry.

Organisational funding is entangled with organisational types and this is why categorisation is an essential issue. In this section we review some of the literature that has addressed the classification of PRO with more or less emphasis in the funding dimension, highlighting the heterogeneity of the sector. This literature is very diverse in approaches and goals.

First, we find studies with a descriptive and measurement focus that have in general followed the guidelines defined by the formal *ex ante* classifications of the sectors; this approach is rather static and makes it difficult to identify processes of evolution and change, and the blurring of boundaries between sectors that requires more granularity.

Second, research with an analytical and empirical approach addressing dynamics of change of the influence of government has considered, either implicitly or explicitly, the idea of publicness associated with a continuum that moves between the government and the market.

Third, there is also some literature, linked to normative approaches, with proposals about how R&D and innovation policies should operate or how the organisations should be managed; these approaches usually highlight the relationship between the various sectors, especially science–industry, and its benefits; the focus is on improving performance and efficient management.

Yet categorisation processes are also defined by the different dimensions they use, the purpose they serve and the methodology they apply.

Firstly, the different classifications use a diversity of organisational attributes or dimensions. Categorisation entails the selection of one or more dimensions of the object in a vector space and the application of a procedure known as reduction. The legal status or legal nature, the control of decisions, the public missions (objectives) assumed by organisations, and the sources of funding are the dimensions that have been used most frequently.

Secondly, classifications may have several purposes. To classify is to reduce the complexity and select parts of the reality. Classification is often part of the description, but it is also used to analyse heterogeneity, monitor changes or construct plausible hypotheses about the behaviour of organisations.

Thirdly, in what is referred to methodological considerations, research in this area is characterised by a predominance of case-based analyses of organisations, which usually refer to individual countries. In terms of classificatory strategies, two main approaches have been followed: 'Ideal types' and empirical 'Taxonomies' based on the selection of attributes, with two corresponding strategies – classifying according to *ex ante* definitions or classifying based on *ex post* emergent properties of the organisational attributes.

Categorisation Criteria Associated with the Concept of a PRO

Regarding dimensions, three are worth highlighting in the literature: organisational settings, missions and funding sources. Cole (1979) analysed the different environments of research units, in academia and other institutional arrangements. He proposed a two-way cross-classification of research units based on two dimensions, namely, scientific field and type of organisation (university, academies of science, government and industry). In his view, the resulting categories would show differences in three related areas: research orientation, research output and research settings, the latter referring mainly to patterns of influence regarding research priorities. The primary distinction in the resulting typology was the organisational setting, although the additional dimension of the 'nature of research outputs' was often included.

This approach has been used in historical accounts. Van Roij (2011) developed an empirical taxonomy of research organisations (laboratories), based on three different types of knowledge production. He combined three dimensions: the type of knowledge production, its orientation, and its ownership; these three dimensions constitute the profile of a specific laboratory, but can also be used to build a set of laboratory types; in addition to the archetypal laboratory types – university and R&D labs – six additional types were identified (three of them associated with industry).

Over the last 20 years, the idea of organisational missions or objectives has gained salience as the principal dimension of PRO diversity, beyond traditional ones like ownership and control. This is the approach taken by Arnold, Barker and Slipersæter (2010), who classified 'research institutes' into three main categories: government laboratories, academic institutes, and research and technology organisations (RTOs). Their classification is based on one dimension and refers to the 'principal mission' as the key criterion: mission-oriented research, basic science, and oriented and applied research (to service industry and innovation). The OECD (2011) has also adopted this approach. The rationale behind this classification is mainly related to the importance of empirical groups and self-identification, and combines elements of history, evolution and current features.

Philipps (2013) examined the variations in the descriptions of German extra-university research institutes. He studied the mission statements and self-descriptions from Max Planck institutes, Fraunhofer institutes and government research agencies in the material sciences field, in order to discuss differences and to understand how they coped with external expectations. More recently, de la Torre et al. (2021) have classified UK PROs according to their knowledge transfer profiles that appear related to the knowledge field specialisation.

Finally, funding sources have also been used to show PRO diversity. Wilts (2001) advancing an underlying theory about what determines the nature of organisations, developed a typology of research organisations based on their responsiveness to external goal settings, channelled through funding. He empirically illustrated the types with cases of organisations performing economic research in Germany, in the university and non-university sectors.

Also paying attention to funding, Sanz-Menéndez and Cruz-Castro (2003) analysed the PROs – government-owned research councils and mission-oriented institutes – and their organisational responses to changes in the funding environment in the context of crisis. In further work,

Cruz-Castro et al. (2012) analysed two groups of research institutes (based on differentiated ownership) and checked their funding portfolios (sources and size) to assess the influence of external actors. The result was a taxonomy in which the institutes were located empirically, and the positions of some research organisations in the groups did not correspond with the expectations emerging from classical sectoral divisions, based on ownership and control. The positioning of the centres in terms of funding portfolios revealed a much more complex characterisation, one that was also related to the mission and type of research activities developed by the PRO.

Typologies and Taxonomies

Regarding methodological strategies, Michael Crow and Barry Bozeman (Crow and Bozeman 1987a, b, 1998; Bozeman and Crow 1990) attempted to distance themselves from the traditional focus on ownership or legal status of research organisations. They first developed a typology using two principal dimensions: government influence (mainly in terms of funding) and market influence (the type of technology or specialisation that shapes the degree of private appropriability of the technology).

Further, Crow and Bozeman developed the idea of 'environmental taxonomy' to capture the diversity of research organisations and to overcome some of the limitations of the sector-based framework. The taxonomy was a nine-cell which analysed empirically what they called laboratories according to their levels of government and market influence, with public science displaying high government and low market influence, and private technology showing low government and high market influence.

More recently, Sanz-Menéndez et al. (2011), later reproduced in Cruz-Castro et al. (2015), developed a typology of PROs, combining two basic criteria or dimensions to define ideal types. They identified two principal attributes of research organisations likely to condition R&D activities and funding strategies: (1) the degree of external autonomy and resource dependence of the organisation – for instance in terms of funding, human resources and access to external knowledge – and the extent of managerial independence and discretion over resources; and (2) the type of internal authority structure which characterises the functioning of the organisation, and more precisely the relationship between research professionals and the management of their organisation. The two dimensions reflected, on the one hand, the organisational dependence on the environment and, on the other hand, the relative authority of the managers versus the researchers/employees (Table 14.1).

Four ideal types of PRO were identified according to their position in the two dimensions: mission-oriented centres (MOCs), public research centres and councils (PRCs), research and

Table 14.1   Classification of (ideal type) PROs according to external autonomy and internal authority

PRO management		Degree of internal authority (command and control/hierarchy)	
		+	−
Degree of external organisational autonomy from governments	+	RTO	IRI
	−	MOC	PRC

Note: RTO, Research and technology organisations; MOC, mission-oriented centres; IRI, independent research institutes; PRC, public research centres and councils.
Source: Own elaboration based on Sanz-Menéndez et al. (2011).

technology organisations (RTOs) and independent research institutes (IRIs). The connection of the different types with roles and specific functions regarding knowledge production is interesting; for example, MOCs with the role of providing knowledge and technological capabilities to support policymaking; PRCs performing basic and applied research in several fields; IRIs as publicly supported institutes performing both basic and applied research focused on issues or problems rather than fields; and RTOs pursuing research of interest for industry (Sanz-Menéndez et al. 2011).

This typology highlights the main features to understand behaviour but sometimes, when applying ex-ante classifications, empirical cases do not fit with expectations correctly, owing to the complexity of transforming concepts into indicators. While ideal types may help to improve conceptualisation, they may encounter difficulties of measurement when confronted with existing data.

In a recent work, Cruz-Castro et al. (2020) complemented the approach with a taxonomy of almost 200 empirical cases of PROs, from eight different countries, and they constructed an *ex post* classification based on clustering some PRO attributes. Their findings highlighted the salience of the organisational mission in the correct classification of cases (see Table 14.2).

To provide the reader with some examples of existing organisations that could fit in the PRC category, we could mention the national academies of science or national research councils, like traditionally CONICET in Argentina, CNR in Italy, CSIC in Spain, etc. They largely represent the classical model of academic science organisation. MOCs are usually embedded in the structures of the public administration in the areas of health, energy and environment, agriculture, defence, etc.: in agriculture (INRAE – France, INTA – Argentina), defence and aerospace (NASA – United States), energy and the environment (CERI – Canada, CIEMAT – Spain) and health (INSERM – France, INSA – Portugal). Examples of IRI are new research institutes (like CNIO or CRG in Spain or INMEGEN in Mexico), some of them hybrids (Guldbransen 2011) by nature, that combine fundamental research in some scientific domains with a strong mandate of addressing social or economic problems. RTOs are centres with the general mission of promoting industrial competitiveness such as TNO in the Netherlands, Tecnalia in Spain, SINTEF in Norway and FhG in Germany to name a few.

In the rest of the chapter, we use the classification of Tables 14.1 and 14.2; in the following section we complement the taxonomy with examples of the type, volume and share of diverse

Table 14.2   *Emerging types of PRO: taxonomy results of four dimensions and dominant characterisation of each dimension*

	IRI	PRC	RTO	MOC
Principal mission	Develop knowledge	Develop knowledge	Generate economic value	Contribute to solve public policy issues
Legal status	Not for profit institution	Public	Not for profit institution or private	Public
Orientation of R&D activity	Basic/applied research	Basic/applied research	Experimental development	Applied research
Country examples	CRG (Es), INMEGEN (Mx)	MPG (De), CSIC (Es), CONICET (Ar), CNR (It)	TNO (Nl), SINTEF (No), FhG (De)	INRAE (Fr), CERI (Ca), NASA (Us), INSA (Pt)

Source: Adapted from Cruz-Castro et al. (2020).

funding sources in some empirical cases of PROs. Then we add to the typology by addressing the management structure dimension.

VARIATION OF FUNDING ACROSS PROS AND THE RELEVANCE OF MISSIONS

In general, PRCs and MOCs, that usually receive more direct public funding, have longer institutional histories compared with IRIs and RTOs, but interestingly, the latter have attracted more recent scholarly attention; this attention could be related to the dynamics in the public funding environment since the end of the 1990s.

Two general dynamics are important as contextual factors that are likely to have affected the emergence of new types of PRO, the transformation of old ones into new classes, as well as the variation in the sources and types of research funding across them: on the one hand, the increasing importance of the role of 'intermediation' between other (more consolidated) sectors (academy and industry) assigned to some PROs (Azagra-Caro 2011) and, on the other hand, the promotion of public institutes around the idea of excellent science with social relevance. Correspondingly, from the perspective of policy intervention, two main institutional logics (Cruz-Castro and Sanz-Menéndez 2007) have emerged, with consequences in terms of funding: on the one hand, organisations fulfilling the mission of 'intermediation' and servicing to the industry and innovation and, on the other hand, organisations pushing science in the knowledge frontier and 'excellence' and the so called 'Pasteur's quadrant' research (Stokes 1997). The first has been related to a greater relevance of contract research funding, and the second to the increasing role of programmatic funding.[3]

Whereas government laboratories have seldom been the subject of descriptive or comparative international studies, PROs linked to the mission of 'technology transfer' and 'science–industry' relationships have attracted more attention. These themes were already present in the first works of Bozeman, Crow and collaborators, but along with the emphasis on instruments of technology and innovation policy, we have witnessed the 'emergence' or, perhaps, greater visibility of a type of applied R&D entity supported by governments, to provide knowledge to industry, first named research and technology institutes (Arnold et al. 1998) and, later on, RTOs (Preissl 2006; Leijten 2007; Sharif and Baark 2011; Albors-Garrigós et al. 2014). They are now popular in many countries along with the specific action of interest groups (EARTO in Europe).

Therefore, the RTO is not a new phenomenon. Applied research organisations (contract research organisations) have for a long time existed in some countries, sharing the ecosystem with other types of governmental laboratories. Early in the aftermath of the Second World War, and clearly since the 1960s, in some European countries institutions were promoted by governments with the main mission of providing technological knowledge and innovation services to industry (e.g. FhG in Germany); in some others, PROs traditionally under the government sector reinforced their orientation to support industry (e.g. TNO in The Netherlands) working as contract research organisations, but with significant government support. In other cases, support was provided to 'research associations', 'technology institutes', 'technology centers' (Barge-Gil and Modrego-Rico 2008; Mas-Verdú 2007) or 'cooperative centres' (Boardman and Gray 2010).

Governments have also promoted and funded, especially in good budgetary times, new organisations pushing science in the knowledge frontier and 'excellence'. Programmes of excellence (OECD 2014; Hellström 2018) have been launched in various countries and, in many cases, their role has been the creation and funding of new PROs. Associated with the so-called Pasteur quadrant (Stokes 1997) and the 'transformative organisations' (Hollingsworth 2006), governments have increasingly promoted a group of PROs around the mission of producing scientifically excellent and socially relevant research (Martínez et al. 2013). Programmatic and public competitive funding are typically associated with this type of PRO, that we have called IRI. Related, some types of PRO may be an important tool to achieve mission-oriented policy goals, and increase their salience in relation to universities; precisely, Bührer, Seus and Walz in Chapter 9 in this *Handbook*, referring to Germany, discuss the limitations of targeting through research programmes in an environment where universities receive funding mostly based on scientific performance.

Funding sources and modalities are likely to differ by PRO type, but there is a lack of empirical studies on the topic and the scant literature is case based. Cruz-Castro et al. (2012) analysed the correlation between third party funding sources (competitive public and industrial contract research) and the legal nature of two different types of PRO: PRCs and RTOs. The results found empirical patterns, but a low correlation between the legal nature and the funding portfolio. In fact, among the empirical types, there were all kinds of particular cases that needed additional variables, such as the mission, the relationship of the technology (the type knowledge produced) with the market and the incentive systems in place, to make sense. In sum, publicness was not determined solely either by the legal status or by the predominance of a source of funding in a particular PRO.

In our view, the effects of funding sources portfolios are mediated by the PRO mission. Only if the mission is legitimated as a public objective (e.g. providing knowledge services to industry or advancing the research frontier and excellence) and recognised as a public mission will public funding affect the organisational nature. This applies regardless of the amount of finance that the direct public funds represent, and even if such an amount of resources is limited (as it is the case, for instance, in some FhG institutes, where the direct public funding is kept around 30%).

There is no systematic cross-country and valid data collection on the different sources of funding for the types of PRO. In fact, the PRO funding portfolios are national and context dependent (Thèves et al. 2007), and they are very much affected by the public budget cycle (Cruz-Castro and Sanz-Menéndez 2016). In Table 14.3, we compare PROs from the same type, that in different countries have very different portfolios of funding, and different types of PRO with similar funding portfolios. Albeit this handbook is concerned mainly with public funding, it is important to pay attention to the broader funding portfolio of these organisations, especially after we have shown that funding modalities do not become generally part of the concept.

It seems that there is a pattern of PRO government funding by country, that could be either intentional or the result of budgetary pressures, in which there are general smaller shares of direct funding to RTO and IRI than to PRC and MOC. A reduction of the share of core public funding (block grant) could be used by governments to steer the direction of research according to the missions. To respond to such steering, organisations need autonomy, and competitive public funding and private research funding need to be available too. Public competitive funding (especially EU) appears to be a source of funding increasingly used by RTO and IRI,

Table 14.3   *Types, volumes and shares of funding in different PROs*

	MPG (DE)	CSIC (ES)	CNR (IT)	FhG (DE)	Tecnalia (ES)	INRAE (FR)	CRG (ES)
PRO type	PRC	PRC	PRC	RTO	RTO	MOC	IRI
Total budget (2020 or nearest year (million €))	2400	763	900	2800	114	999	43
A. Government direct funding (percentage of total)	85%	62%	60%	30%	20%	80%	50%
B. Total third party funding (percentage of total)	13%	36%	40%	65%	78%	20%	50%
B1. Public competitive funding (regional, national) (percentage of total)		20%		30%	10%		20%
B1.2. Competitive funding from EU (percentage of total)	4%	12%	5%	5%	18%	3%	25%
B2. Commissioned 'contract research' (percentage of total)		3%		30%	50%		5%
C. Other sources of funding (percentage of total)	2%	2%		5%	2%		

Note: Share estimates based on average bi-annual data, when available, and EU Cordis.
Sources: Annual Reports, financial statements and PRO web pages.

to enlarge their capabilities, but systematic evidence is limited. As expected, contract research funding is very relevant in RTO.

The consequences of the different funding modalities and portfolios have been addressed empirically regarding the so-called 'protected space' for scientific innovations (Whitley 2014) and, analytically, in relation the balance of the authority sharing within organisations (Cruz-Castro and Sanz-Menéndez 2018; Whitley 2019), an issue that will be examined in the next section.

TYPES OF FUNDING AND THE BALANCE BETWEEN AUTHORITY AND AUTONOMY WITHIN DIFFERENT PROS

In this section we address how different types of funding may affect the authority sharing and autonomy of researchers and managers in different organisational settings. Our argument, which we elaborate below, is that the effects of funding modalities on the strategic capability of PROs, or on their authority sharing[4] depend on the structural features of the PRO.

Research policy discourse has emphasised the desirability of PROs strengthening their strategic capacities or their 'organisational actorhood' (Krücken and Meier 2006; Whitley 2011). For that they need resources and autonomy. Organisational autonomy does not only derive from legal status and the political structure. Resource dependency theorists have shown that the power of organisational actors is contingent on their control of critical resources. Some previous literature related to the impact of funding on organisations has considered the relationship between funders and researchers (Braun 1993) as if the researcher was not part of an organisation. Recent research has advanced propositions that include additional intervening variables (Cruz-Castro and Sanz-Menendez 2018), among which the funding modalities are especially relevant.[5]

We cannot forget that PROs as professional organisations have traditionally been depicted as loosely coupled. In contrast, policy reforms have emphasised the role of governments in steering research. For organisations to steer and act strategically, they need internal authority, which may come from different sources.

The overall level of recurrent research funding of a PRO (block grants) determines its resource dependence and interacts with its structural attributes, affecting and in some cases modifying internal authority structures. The key difference is whether funding instruments target the organisation or the researcher. Funding instruments targeted on the organisation (programme funding, organisational excellence programmes, etc.) may provide the managers of research organisations with important resources for strategic behaviour. However, it is also important to consider the strings with which funding reaches the organisation.

Considering only funding proceeding directly from government (block grants), there can be, to simplify, two types of organisational funding: earmarked and discretionary. In some PROs, the bulk of earmarked funding is for basic operational costs and the biggest share is usually reserved to pay the salaries of permanent researchers (Coccia 2019); for example, the total labour cost of the Spanish largest PRC, the CSIC, amounted to almost 60% of the total expenditures, and that comes mainly from government transfers. By definition, earmarked funds, owing to their reserved nature, allow little room for manoeuvre regarding their use; managers of PROs receiving predominantly this type of funding are likely to have less influence over the strategic research agenda than managers receiving greater shares of discretionary research funds.

In contrast, in general, direct organisational funding which reaches a PRO without strings might be a powerful mechanism in the hands of the managerial level to influence the direction of research programmes and agendas. Discretion in the use of such funds affords managers more authority, but at the same time they become more accountable to funders. Some funding instruments could make the PRO compete for this type of funding (e.g. performance-based schemes used in some university systems but not developed for PROs), while others will involve organisations being held accountable for the accomplishment of science and development objectives (e.g. programme funding[6]). The growing importance of this kind of policy instrument in many research systems is in line with the policy rationales of granting PROs more autonomy in their operations and, occasionally, providing managers with more leverage; for example, in Spain the Excellence Programme Severo Ochoa was designed to empower scientific directorships with organisational funding resources.

PROs may also be funded by industry in the form of contracts or donations; this is an important source especially in RTOs. This type of funding is usually linked to specific projects, activities or services, and the room for manoeuvre of the PRO leadership concerning those resources will depend on the existing control structure of the organisation. Some RTOs get almost half of their income from contract research and services to industry, while in PRCs the share of industry funding is small. For example, comparing within the same national context, in a typical PRC (the Spanish CSIC) industry funding represents less than 5% of the total, while in the largest RTO (Tecnalia) 46% of income comes from the business sector.

Turning to individual funding, it can be said that in general terms individual funding reinforces the internal authority of researchers versus managers and therefore the autonomy of the former.

Third party funding coming from competitive public sources (domestic or European) could be higher in PROs like IRIs, with high levels of autonomy of individual researchers and limited

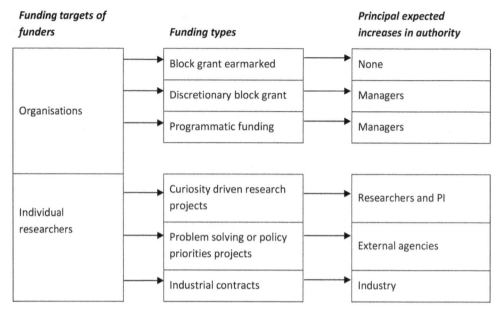

Source: Adapted from Cruz-Castro and Sanz-Menéndez (2018).

Figure 14.3   Expected effect of funding types on different funding targets

institutional block grant funding, probably driven by reputational effects. There are cases of PROs, especially among the IRIs, in which the ability to get competitive project funding by principal investigators (PIs) and researchers is almost a condition for recruitment and employment. In these cases, PI and researchers become 'entrepreneurs' that gain autonomy and authority. For example, some IRIs are designed to work in the competitive funding mode (e.g. in the Spanish Centre for Genomic Regulation (CRG), almost a quarter of expenditures are obtained from EU competitive funding sources, specially the ERC and H2020); on the opposite side of the spectrum, the German MPG, owing to its high level of internal resources, becomes involved in the competition for funding only for the most prestigious and generous schemes. For the moment, it seems that MOCs are less involved in getting public competitive funding, unless there are specific dedicated programmes, such as EURATOM nuclear energy.

These general propositions about the expected effects of different types of funding are mediated by the structural attributes of the different types of PRO, among them, the managerial structures. In Table 14.4, we take into account the diversity of management structures dominant in different types and consider the funding of organisations and researchers as exogenous variables.

In the case of PRCs, resembling the typical case of public academic science organisations, increases in earmarked block grant funding are not likely to affect the dominance of researchers' authority typical of this configuration. Although the management may be formally hierarchical, the seniority and tenure-based structure in many of this type of PRO makes managerial discretion over earmarked funding rather limited. However, larger shares of discretionary block funding are likely to improve the leverage position of managers to employ such resources to promote the strategic aims of the organisation.

Table 14.4   *Differences in management structures according to types of PRO*

Management structures	Typology of PROs		
	PRCs	MOC/RTOs	IRIs
Management type	Hierarchical but weak, penetrated by researchers	Hierarchical, strong managerial	Hierarchical, dual, mixing administrators and researchers
Managerial discretion over collective resources (block grant or programmatic funding)	Limited	High	High
Researchers' discretion over individual project and contract funding	High	Low	High to medium for project leaders and PI

Source: Cruz-Castro and Sanz-Menéndez (2018).

Perhaps one of the most important differences between PRC on the one hand, and the way of organising research characteristic of MOCs and RTOs on the other hand, relates to managerial discretion over collective resources (scientific and technical infrastructures and facilities, among others). In MOCs, the dominance of managerial authority is unlikely to be affected by increases in earmarked block grant funding; the case of discretionary research block funding is different, especially when it is instrumented through programme funding, which is likely not only to further reinforce managerial authority with respect to researchers, but also to increase managerial accountability and therefore the influence of external sponsors over this type of PRO oriented to specific goals.

Independent research institutes have a more hybrid nature regarding management, and often a dual hierarchical model, in which leadership is strong, but there is a partial delegation of strategic decisions to principal investigators. In this type of PRO, increases in discretionary block grant funding, especially if they are instrumented through 'programmatic funding', will reinforce the standing of the managerial leadership. In the context of the strongly performance-based management typical of this structural configuration, these augmented discretionary resources could be used by managers to attract researchers to the strategic visions adopted by the organisation, by allocating incentives or simply by giving greater internal resources to specific lines of research.

CONCLUSION

In this chapter, we have argued that the standard statistical classifications of the public sector research organisations fall short of capturing the growing variety in the field given the blurred boundaries between different actors, and the emergence of new organisational types. Therefore, more nuanced analyses are needed. Although academic and policy research have increasingly paid attention to PROs in the context of the debates about research governance and funding, the literature is still limited in comparison with higher education institutions studies.

Funding trends have changed over time, but the degree and type of change depend very much on the countries. Within this heterogeneity, the few available evidence suggests that, as for PROs, rather than funding modalities, what has changed in several countries is the balance between the direct transfer of resources they get and the third party funding (including government competitive funding) of research activities. This is in contrast with university funding in some countries, where much of the change has been in modalities.

Although the PRO sector exhibits high internal diversity, it is still quite distinct compared with higher education institutions. Much of the discussion about the changing funding environment of universities cannot be applied to PROs; specifically, concerning performance-based research funding in countries where governments have introduced this type of funding, they have generally introduced a competition mechanism. This hardly applies to the PRO sector (regardless organisational type). In this sense, it is important to distinguish performance-based research funding systems from performance-based internal incentives, as Kivistö and Matthies do in Chapter 12 in this *Handbook*; we do not include here 'excellence funding schemes' (Hellström 2018) as part of the performance-based research funding systems. Whereas the first pertain to the organisational funding level and it is unlikely to be found in the PRO sector, the latter (which may be used by universities and some PROs alike) apply to subunits (departments, groups or individuals).

We have focused on analytical issues rather than on empirical developments. We have highlighted the need for conceptual precision regarding the categories that refer to the set of organisations executing R&D activities, which are controlled or influenced by the government in various ways. In this sense, there is still significant ambiguity as to what is considered public, and whether the main criteria should be the legal ownership, the sources of funding, the decision-making or control procedures, or the organisational missions. It is fair to say that, over the last 20 years, organisational missions or objectives have gained salience as the principal dimension of PRO classifications, beyond traditional ones like ownership and control.

The evolution of the concepts has gone in parallel with the emergence of new realities and new labels. Under a diversity of labels, two main institutional logics have emerged in the PRO field: one linked to the mission of intermediation and servicing to the industry and innovation, and another pushing science in the knowledge frontier and promote excellence. These emerging institutional logics have had their funding correlates in the prevalence of private funding in RTO, and in the creation of publicly promoted science-oriented new institutes where programmatic funding is relevant.

On the methodological side, we have found in the literature a combination of typological and taxonomical approaches. Each has advantages and disadvantages for addressing diversity. Although classifications based on ideal types allow for identifying the analytical features or the necessary variables to understand organisational heterogeneity, when the *ex ante* classification is applied to the empirical cases, some may not fit with expectations correctly; we need to acknowledge that transforming concepts into indicators for measuring attributes is complex. While ideal types may help to improve conceptualisation, researchers may encounter measurement problems when trying to apply the typology existing data. In this case, taxonomies may allow for a better classification based on *ex post* emergent properties of the organisational attributes.

Funding sources and modalities are likely to differ by PRO type. There is a lack of empirical studies on the topic, especially from a comparative perspective, that is related to the fact that the funding portfolios of PROs are highly national and context dependent. Acknowledging this, we have documented the variation with some examples of large PROs in different countries. As expected, and in close relation with the organisational missions, the weight of governments' block grants in the total income of PRCs and MOCs is bigger than in RTOs and IRIs, where third-party funding, including governmental competitive funding, is more relevant.

We have argued, in accordance with recent research, that funding modalities (either public of private) affect the 'nature' of the organisations regardless their legal status and the level of public funding, and that the key intermediary variable is the organisational mission. Indeed, funding modalities matter, and they have consequences for the authority structures of PROs, the relative autonomy of researchers, and therefore for the strategic capabilities of the organisation. In general, individual funding reinforces the autonomy of researchers and discretionary block funding (especially programme based) reinforces managerial authority, but it is important to acknowledge that these effects are mediated by structural factors embedded in the typology of PROs itself. Although we acknowledge that the funding composition is likely to strongly differ by type, under specific national conditions, we believe that the general propositions advanced in the chapter may serve as the basis for empirical testing. Finally, what clearly emerges is that the governments, independent of the direct ownership and control of PROs, continue to influence the various types of PRO by different mechanisms.

On the methodological challenges ahead, we have identified a need to develop empirical research, and to move from local case studies to a more systematic comparative analysis. Recent initiatives of international datasets could provide better opportunities to analyse and construct better theories and understanding; among the initiatives we can mention OrgReg (Lepori 2020) and the Research Organisation Registry (ROR) (https://ror.org).

NOTES

1. We thank the editors, Inga Ulnicane and the participants in the EU-SPRI 2021 session for comments and suggestions to an earlier version. We also acknowledge funding from the Spanish Funding Agency (AEI) grant (CSO2016-79045-C2-1-R).
2. There is a new specific and revised version, in the Frascati Manual, of the recommendations about how to classify difficult cases in the boundaries of the different sectors.
3. In contrast with development in HEIs (see Chapter 12 by Kivistö and Matthies, and Chapter 6 by Sivertsen in this *Handbook*) there is no evidence that performance-based funding has affected PRO in a significant way.
4. We adopt the idea of authority sharing (Whitley 2019).
5. In the remainder of the section we draw upon that previous work.
6. See Reale, Gulbrandsen and Scherngell, Chapter 7 in this *Handbook*, for an analysis of research programmes as funding instruments.

REFERENCES

Aagaard, K., Hansen, H. F., and Rasmussen, J. G. (2016). Mergers between governmental research institutes and Universities in the Danish HE sector. *European Journal of Higher Education*, 6(1), 41–55.
Albors-Garrigós, J., Rincon-Diaz, C. A., and Igartua-Lopez, J. I. (2014). Research technology organisations as leaders of R&D collaboration with SMEs: Role, barriers and facilitators. *Technology Analysis and Strategic Management*, 26(1), 37–53.
Arnold, E., Rush, H., Bessant, J., and Hobday, M. (1998). Strategic planning in research and technology institutes. *R&D Management*, 28(2), 89–100.
Arnold, E., Barker, K., and Slipersæter, S. (2010). *Research Institutes in the ERA*. Brussels: EC. https://www.escholar.manchester.ac.uk/uk-ac-man-scw:99014. Accessed 10 Apr 2022.

Azagra-Caro, J. M. (2011). Do public research organisations own most patents invented by their staff? *Science and Public Policy, 38*(3), 237–250.

Barge-Gil, A., and Modrego-Rico, A. (2008). Are technology institutes a satisfactory tool for public intervention in the area of technology? A neoclassical and evolutionary evaluation. *Environment and Planning C: Government and Policy, 26*(4), 808–823.

Boardman, C., and Gray, D. (2010). The new science and engineering management: cooperative research centers as government policies, industry strategies, and organisations. *Journal of Technology Transfer, 35*(5), 445–459.

Boden, R., Cox, D., Nedeva, M., and Barker. K. (2004). *Scrutinising Science: The Changing UK Government of Science*. Basingstoke: Palgrave. Macmillan.

Borsi, B. (2021). The balanced state of application-oriented public research and technology organisations. *Science and Public Policy, 48*(5), 612–629.

Bozeman, B., and Crow, M. (1990). The environments of U.S. R&D laboratories: Political and market influences. *Policy Sciences, 23*(1), 25–56.

Braun, D. (1993). Who governs intermediary agencies? Principal–agent relations in research policy-making. *Journal of Public Policy, 13*(2), 135–162.

Coccia, M. (2019). Metabolism of public research organisations: How do laboratories consume state subsidies? *Public Organisation Review, 19*(4), 473–491.

Cole, G. A. (1979). Classifying research units by patterns of performance and influence: A typology of the round 1 data. In: F. M. Andrews (Ed.) *Scientific Productivity: The Effectiveness of Research Groups in Six Countries*, pp. 353–404. Cambridge: Cambridge University Press/Unesco.

Crow, M., and Bozeman, B. (1987a). R&D laboratory classification and public policy: The effects of environmental context on laboratory behavior. *Research Policy, 16*(5), 229–258.

Crow, M. M., and Bozeman, B. L. (1987b). A new typology for R&D laboratories: Implications for policy analysts. *Journal of Policy Analysis and Management, 6*(3), 328–341.

Crow, M., and Bozeman, B. (1998). *Limited by Design. R&D Laboratories in the U.S. National Innovation System*. New York: Columbia University Press.

Cruz-Castro, L., and Sanz-Menéndez, L. (2007). New legitimation models and the transformation of the public research organisational field. *International Studies of Management and Organisation, 37*(1), 27–52.

Cruz-Castro, L., and Sanz-Menéndez, L. (2016). The effects of the economic crisis on public research: Spanish budgetary policies and research organizations. *Technological Forecasting and Social Change, 113*, 157–167.

Cruz-Castro, L., and Sanz-Menéndez, L. (2018). Autonomy and authority in public research organisations: Structure and funding factors, *Minerva, 56*(2), 135–160.

Cruz-Castro, L., Sanz-Menéndez, L., and Martínez, C. (2012). Research centers in transition: Patterns of convergence and diversity. *The Journal of Technology Transfer, 37*(1), 18–42.

Cruz-Castro, L., Jonkers, K., and Sanz-Menéndez, L. (2015). The internationalization of Research Institutes. In L. Weidlin and M. Nedeva (Eds.) *Towards European Science. Dynamics and Policy of an Evolving European Research Space*, pp. 175–198. Cheltenham: Edward Elgar.

Cruz-Castro, L., Martínez, C., Peñasco, C., and Sanz-Menéndez, L. (2020). The classification of public research organisations: Taxonomical explorations. *Research Evaluation, 29*(4), 377–391.

de la Torre, E. M., Ghorbankhani, M., Rossi, F., and Sagarra, M. (2021). Knowledge transfer profiles of public research organisations: The role of fields of knowledge specialisation. *Science and Public Policy, 48*(6), 860–876.

Gläser, J. and Laudel, G. (2016). Governing science. *European Journal of Sociology, 57*(1), 117–168.

Gulbrandsen, M. (2011). Research institutes as hybrid organisations: Central challenges to their legitimacy. *Policy Sciences, 44*(3), 215–230.

Hellström, T. (2018). Centres of excellence and capacity building: From strategy to impact. *Science and Public Policy, 45*(4), 543–552.

Hollingsworth, J. R. (2006). A path-dependence perspective on institutional and organisational factors shaping major scientific discoveries. In J. Hage and M. Meeus (Eds.) *Innovation, Science, and Institutional Change: A Research Handbook*, pp. 423–442. Oxford: OUP.

Jongbloed, B., and Lepori, B. (2015). The funding of research in higher education: Mixed models and mixed results. In J. Huisman, H. de Boer, D. D. Dill, and M. Souto-Otero (Eds., *The Palgrave*

International Handbook of Higher Education Policy and Governance, pp. 439–462. Basingstoke: Palgrave Macmillan.

Krücken, G. and Meier, F. (2006). Turning the university into an organisational actor. In S. D. Gili, J. W. Meyer, and H. Hwang (Eds.) *Globalization and Organisation. World Society and Organisational Change*, pp. 241–257. Oxford: Oxford University Press.

Larédo, P., and Mustar, P. (2004). Public sector research: A growing role in innovation systems. *Minerva*, *42*(1), 11–27.

Larrue, P., Guellec, D., and Sgard, F. (2018). New trends in public research funding. In *OECD Science, Technology and Innovation Outlook 2018*, pp. 185–204. Paris: OECD Publishing.

Leijten, J. (2007). The future of RTOs: A few likely scenarios. In: M. Akrich and R. Miller (Eds.) *The Future of Key Research Actors in the European Research Area*, pp. 119–138. Luxembourg: European Commission.

Lepori, B. (2020). A register of public-sector research organisations as a tool for research policy studies and evaluation. *Research Evaluation*, *29*(4), 355–365.

Marcson, S. (1972). Research Settings. In: S. Z. Nagi and R. G. Corwin (Eds.) *The Social Context of Research*, pp. 161–191. London: Wiley-Interscience.

Martínez, C., Azagra-Caro, J. M., and Maraut, S. (2013). Academic inventors, scientific impact and the institutionalisation of Pasteur's quadrant in Spain. *Industry and Innovation*, *20*(5), 438–455.

Mas-Verdú, F. (2007). Services and innovation systems: European models of Technology Centres. *Service Business*, *1*(1), 7–23.

Mazzucato, M. (2018). Mission-oriented innovation policies: Challenges and opportunities. *Industrial and Corporate Change*, *27*(5), 803–815.

OECD (1989). *The Changing Role of Government Research Laboratories*. Paris: OECD.

OECD (2011). *Public Research Institutions. Mapping Sector Trends*. Paris: OECD.

OECD (2014). *Promoting Research Excellence: New Approaches to Funding*. Paris: OECD.

OECD (2015). *Frascati Manual 2015. Guidelines for Collecting and Reporting Data on Research and Experimental Development*. Paris: OECD.

OECD (2018). *Science, Technology and Innovation Outlook 2018: Adapting to Technological and Societal Disruption*. Paris: OECD Publishing.

OECD (2021). Main Science and Technology Indicators (MSTI), 1. OECD. https://www.oecd.org/sti/msti.htm.

Philipps, A. (2013). Mission statements and self-descriptions of German extra-university research institutes: A qualitative content analysis. *Science and Public Policy*, *40*(5), 686–697.

Potì, B., and Reale, E. (2000). Convergence and differentiation in institutional change among European public research systems: The decreasing role of public research institutes. *Science and Public Policy*, *27*(6), 421–431.

Preissl, B. (2006). Research and technology organisations in the service economy. *Innovation: The European Journal of Social Science Research*, *19*(1), 131–146.

Sanz-Menéndez, L., and Cruz-Castro, L. (2003). Coping with environmental pressures: Public research organisations' responses to funding crises. *Research Policy*, *32*(8), 1293–1308.

Sanz-Menéndez, L., Cruz-Castro, L., Jonkers, K., Derrick, G. E., Bleda, M., and Martínez, C. (2011). *Public Research Organisations*. Paris: OECD-IPP Policy Briefs. https://www.researchgate.net/publication/287595871_Policy_Brief_-_public_research_organisations. Accessed 10 Apr 2022.

Senker, J. (2006). Reflections on the transformation of European public-sector research. *Innovation: The European Journal of Social Science Research*, *19*(1), 67–77.

Sharif, N., and Baark, E. (2011). The transformation of research technology organisations (RTOs) in Asia and Europe. *Science, Technology and Society*, *16*(1), 1–10.

Stokes, D. E. (1997). *Pasteur's Quadrant. Basic Science and Technological Innovation*. Washington, DC: The Brookings Institution.

Thèves, J., Lepori, B., and Larédo, P. (2007). Changing patterns of public research funding in France. *Science and Public Policy*, *34*(6), 389–399.

Van Rooij, A. (2011). Knowledge, money and data: An integrated account of the evolution of eight types of laboratory. *The British Journal for the History of Science*, *44*(3), 427–448.

Whitley, R. (2011). Changing governance and authority relations in the public sciences. *Minerva*, *49*(4), 359–385.

Whitley, R. (2014). How do institutional changes affect scientific innovations? The effects of shifts in authority relationships, protected space, and flexibility, *Research in the Sociology of Organizations*, *42*, 367–406.

Whitley, R. (2019). Changing science policies, authority relationships and innovations in public science systems. In S. Dagmar, S. Kuhlmann, J. Stamm, and W. Canzler (Eds.) *Handbook on Science and Public Policy*, pp. 204–226. Cheltenham: Edward Elgar.

Wilts, A. 2000. Forms of research organisation and their responsiveness to external goal setting. *Research Policy*, *29*(6), 767–781.

PART IV

RESEARCHERS' INTERACTION WITH THE FUNDING ENVIRONMENT

15. Reframing study of research(er) funding towards configurations and trails[1]

Duncan A. Thomas and Irene Ramos-Vielba

INTRODUCTION

Research funding has become a complicated issue across many fields of contemporary science (Wagner, 2019). Public research funding particularly has undergone major changes, primarily in Europe, but also beyond (Paradeise and Thoenig, 2015; Cocos and Lepori, 2020). New directions are pursued in research governance and funding policies, and in the way public ministries and funding agencies handle policy instrument design and resource allocation. Also, evaluation, monitoring and accountability practices have changed (Lepori and Reale, 2019). There is also increasing diversification and hybridity in how scientific and societal objectives are pursued through public research funding programmes at national and supranational levels (Aagaard et al., 2021a).

For individual researchers, these multi-layered changes percolate through, to make their funding situations also more complicated. Researchers may have to engage with more varied funders, funders' aims and funding forms. Any public funding source a researcher now accesses no longer resembles its previously stable, *laissez faire* nature (Lepori and Reale, 2019; Cocos and Lepori, 2020). Public funding has traditionally been almost automatically internally granted to researchers, with few strings attached, after state allocation of block grants to research organisations. Nowadays, researchers may have no institutionally funded time for research. They instead apply – often externally, individually, in competition with peers – to periodic calls from funding agencies. These may feature socio-economic priorities, set by national ministries and intergovernmental bodies (Reale et al., Chapter 7 in this *Handbook*). Such funding can be short-term, project-based and targeted towards prespecified problems and audiences. This potentially reduces researchers' freedom to self-determine directions they wish to follow, which research questions they would like answered, methods and equipment they prefer to use, and their collaboration choices (Franssen et al., 2018; Gläser et al., 2022; Laudel, Chapter 16 in this *Handbook*).

This changed funding reality is understudied (Hallonsten, 2014; Gläser and Serrano Velarde, 2018; Aagaard et al., 2021a). Researchers themselves are aware of changing resource dependencies. They react to, and potentially shape, their funding environment, its contingencies and unpredictability, and can be strategic in acquiring funding (Hallonsten, 2014; Laudel, Chapter 16 in this *Handbook*). To support their goals, researchers may apply not only for one funding source, or simply to their traditional, domestic-national public funders. They may also apply to a diverse range of public, private, not-for-profit, foreign-national, and supranational funders (Gläser and Serrano Velarde, 2018; Aagaard et al., 2021a). A consequence is that how individual research(er) funding is *studied* needs to change in order to accommodate such complicated situations. Previously, it may have sufficed, or satisfied funders' accountability needs, to study funding by assuming each researcher has one primary source influencing their research. Today, we should at least accept that researchers may hold variegated funding, possibly involving many overlapping characteristics, and having multiple potential influences upon their research.

In this chapter, we present two new frames to attempt a reframing of the study of research(er) funding. We define a researcher's 'funding configuration' and 'funding trail'. These concepts capture that a researcher may concurrently, and over time, combine various public and other funding sources, all of which may somehow influence them. Without this reframing, we argue our analytical ability is limited to address the effectiveness of research funding policies, programmes, and practices in contemporary research contexts. To position our frames, we first revisit funding changes. We then define configurations and trails, discuss what they afford analytically, and conclude with some further study considerations and policy implications.

Why Reframe the Study of Research(er) Funding?

Four interconnected trends for research funders and funding necessitate a reframing. First, funding landscapes are less geographically confined. They operate as multi-level, geographic border-crossing realities, spanning thematic and disciplinary boundaries. A researcher's funding opportunities are not confined to major, national, public funders. Multiple funders across different countries can support the same research(ers), overlapping topics and missions (Lepori, 2011). Second, there is a greater variety of funders. This extends to a researcher's diverse funding opportunities and characteristics, linked to differing research and funding policy rationales and priorities, and the emergence of new funders (Boon and Edler, 2018; Kuhlmann and Rip, 2018; Lepori and Reale, 2019; Wagner, 2019; Reale et al., Chapter 7 in this *Handbook*). This enables researchers to bid for, win, and then configure heterogenous individual funding situations, mobilising funding from diverse funders across geographic areas, and directed towards possibly varying objectives (Aagaard et al., 2021a).

Third, funding can be increasingly hybrid. Funding programmes, often designed by policymakers and managed by funding agencies, can pursue not one but multiple simultaneous objectives (Sörlin, 2007; Gläser and Serrano Velarde, 2018; Lepori and Reale, 2019; Thomas et al., 2020; Reale et al., Chapter 7 in this *Handbook*). Traditional labels may still be used to describe research funding instruments within programmes, like 'excellence', 'academic', 'innovation', 'strategic', and 'mission' (Cremonini et al., 2017; Reale, 2017; Aagaard et al., 2021a). Traditional instrument types remain in use, like 'institutional funding', 'project funding', 'personal grants', 'centres of excellence', and 'network' funding (Cocos and Lepori, 2020). However, once programmes are translated into specific funding calls, and after resources are negotiated and awarded to fund research proposals, each researcher's 'funding instrument grant' – as we will refer to it – bears, we would argue, *observable* traces of whatever bespoke *multi-level funding context* spawned it.

For this chapter, these first three trends all direct our focus towards a study of funding at the *individual researcher's* level. This level of 'individual organising' (Hallonsten, 2014) is where traces of policy and funding instrument characteristics accumulate, driving various use dynamics and outcomes. Researchers act and strategize about (co-)use of features their funding grants afford (Hellström and Jacob, 2017). They use their specialist knowledge to leverage funding to advance their cognitive career ambitions, to contribute to growth of their knowledge communities, and to satisfy research organisations, funders and evaluators (Gläser, 2019; Thomas et al., 2020; Ramos-Vielba et al., 2022).

The fourth trend concerns the research fields around researchers. Certain fields are already inherently multi-funder or 'co-funding network' environments, where researchers co-using funding (through matching or co-funding) is practically taken for granted (Shapira and Wang, 2010; Hellström and Jacob, 2017; Aagaard et al., 2021a; Vasan and West, 2021). These researchers have to use multiple grants to address larger scale research activities, research topics, objects and experimental scope than is possible with project-based, isolated grants alone (Luukkonen and Thomas, 2016; Laudel, Chapter 16 in this *Handbook*). This field level, however, also connects to individual researchers. Fields are intertwined with changing political accountability for public resources, and new ways of governing and evaluating research(er) performance. Funding use may be steered by science policies that are increasingly being perceived as belonging to a neoliberal, capitalist, New Public Management, nationally and internationally competitive, benchmarked, concentrated and highly selective arena (Bourdieu, 1991; Slaughter and Rhoades, 2004; Whitley et al., 2010; Lorenz, 2012; Bloch and Sørensen, 2015; Aagaard, 2017; Young et al., 2017). Use of formal and informal, summative and formative, national and local performance-based evaluation arrangements is spreading (Sivertsen, 2020; Hallonsten, 2021). Individual researchers' academic careers have become predicated on how such arrangements measure 'success'. This can include funding success, for instance, whether a researcher acquires prestigious grants, and how many publications in high esteem journals were published using their funding (Franssen and de Rijcke, 2019; Hammarfelt et al., 2020). Funding acquisition and use are increasingly phenomena about which researchers are held accountable *individually*, regardless of whether it is reasonable to consider they can control the largely *systemic* dynamics of contemporary global funding environments.

Despite these trends, framing the study of individual researchers to account for such complicated funding situations is not a dominant tradition. Instead, it is more popular to explore single funding grants in isolation, like assessing only the most prestigious or largest grant a researcher holds (Thomas and Nedeva, 2012; Laudel and Gläser, 2014). This might originate in how studies have been funded, and because of intractable methodological challenges. Funders often commission linear, audit-like policy evaluations to satisfy political accountability to the state and stakeholders. Funders expect to see their funding audited separately from other resources, to emphasise a distinctive value added (Thomas et al., 2020). Methodologically, assessing how funding causally influences research *even just for one grant* is daunting, requiring cautious study of *single* not *multiple* funding grants. A key difficulty is accounting for many mediating factors apart from funding that can influence research. These can include the researchers' intrinsic and extrinsic motivations, scientific and societal expressions of knowledge production, their research organisation and research field conditions, and country or academic career specificities (Thomas and Nedeva, 2012; Cunningham et al., 2014; D'Este et al., 2018; Gläser, 2019; Smit and Hessels, 2021).

An unintended consequence of single grant studies is they omit real-world complexity and overlook trends towards more complicated researcher funding situations. Such studies have helped build understanding of why such situations are increasingly occurring. They highlight international and interdisciplinary collaboration is growing, and that more 'team science' and massively-collaborative research is now being done, as evidenced by a rising hyper-authorship of papers in selected fields. Studies have observed funders increasingly prioritising cross-sectoral, trans-disciplinary working to tackle societal challenges, thus making research more complex (Shapira and Wang, 2010; Ioannidis et al., 2018; Adams et al., 2019; Schneider et al., 2019; Wu et al., 2019; Wang and Barabási, 2021; Ramos-Vielba et al.,

2022). Such work, however, does not help us determine whether most researchers now face complicated funding situations. We can see they may, if they work in highly applied *fields*, are *group leaders* or *elite* scientists (Luukkonen and Thomas, 2016; Aagaard et al., 2021a). We might speculate that complicated, individual researcher funding situations are – or soon may become – a 'new normal' across science, given the trends we have mentioned. Regardless of this phenomenon's current scope, however, it at least seems timely to develop new study frames to be able to explore them.

DEFINING THE FRAMES

To introduce our two study frames, we first define funding instrument grants and the funder–researcher relationship within which they are located. We next define researcher funding configurations and trails, then introduce descriptors to explore them.

Funding Instrument Grants and Funder–Researcher Relationships

A multi-level understanding of funding policy, programmes and instruments informs our frames. We begin from any funder's most basic unit of resource provision that engages an individual researcher – a 'funding instrument grant'. This unit is shaped by a specific funding instrument format, but it is neither just a 'grant' nor strictly an 'instrument'. It can be said to *embody* specific instrument characteristics, and traces of the policy and programme levels that moulded that class of instrument. Yet, this is all expressed in a *discrete* grant awarded to a *particular* researcher. Such funding instrument grants can thus be of many kinds, individual or team-based. They could be an externally funded project, an individual fellowship, a fixed-duration funding of a centre of excellence, or a project-like internal funding allocation for a special purpose (Luukkonen and Thomas, 2016).

The grant additionally has a funding *contract* bounding the agreed award. It delineates how adherence of the performed research to the agreed research may be enforced by the funder. For public and private external funders, this contract is often material. Such enforcement may be codified and legally binding, typically between the researcher's organisation and the funder (Steele et al., 2019). For internal funding, enforcement may be tacit, codified as specified 'free research' time in a researcher's employment contract, or some formal commitment of in-kind funding to match an external grant, for example.

We assume a two-way funder–researcher relationship exists for every funding instrument grant a researcher holds (Guston and Keniston, 1994; Braun, 1998, 2003; Hessels et al., 2019). Each relationship has context-specific strategy and response dynamics (see Figure 15.1). Funders express their strategies through programmes, informed by political and policy expressions of societal needs and scientific expectations, and their own priorities and practices. Funding programmes are deployed via various funding instruments. These are offered to researchers through periodic or one-off calls for proposals, communicated via documents, web portals, and information events. Funders respond to submitted proposals – and accompanying material such as CVs and track records – with review processes and award negotiation, and by monitoring how a researcher's performed research adheres to what was originally agreed. Researchers will be strategic in deciding whether a call warrants a response to write and submit a proposal to acquire the grant (Laudel, Chapter 16 in this *Handbook*). A minority of

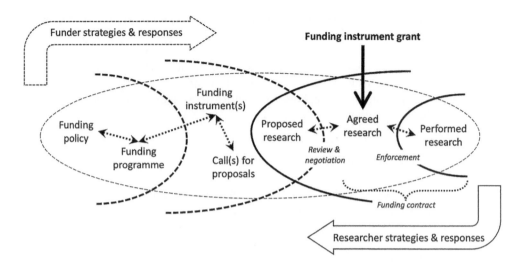

Figure 15.1   *The funder–researcher relationship for each funding instrument grant*

(elite) researchers may also influence funding policy and programme designs in their field, by being individual members of funder advisory and executive structures (Braun, 1998, 2003).

Within this relationship scheme, funding call documents will codify certain specifications and requirements. These are contextualised by a researcher's subjective understanding of tacit funder expectations, based on their previous experience or 'anticipation' of funder evaluative behaviours (Hammarfelt et al., 2020). This also may be informed by any impressions a researcher gleans from funder information events. Each grant a researcher ends up holding thus bears certain objective traces of these multi-level funding policy, programme and instrument design features, as well as of the researcher's subjective understanding of that funder's context and history.

Such funding instrument grants can be studied by examining their original call requirements, instrument, programme and policy documents, and by exploring researcher expectations regarding these materials. For this chapter, we focus only on objective, *ex ante* grant descriptors and not on researcher-subjective expectations. We include enforcement as a descriptor for how the contract might unfold, but only to register how such matters are specified beforehand. This operationalises the 'funding instrument grant' as a relatively standardised unit for study. Table 15.1 lists descriptors that we expect are both registerable to characterise, and meaningful for any later study of potential influences for research(ers) – i.e. those arising from *use* of such funding instrument grants (Aagaard et al., 2021a, b; Ramos-Vielba et al., 2022).

The data for the descriptor's size, duration and expenditures coverage is often codified in funding documents. These values are typically static, except for changes to consortia composition or revisions like funded or unfunded extensions. This first set of descriptors aims to capture variations in resource intensity, which could later be analysed, and is known to have the potential to affect research (Laudel, Chapter 16 in this *Handbook*). The different roles of the funded researchers are also probably important to register. A researcher's funding centrality, in being principal investigator, co-investigator or team member, hypothetically may enable certain degrees of control over how funding is used, co-used with other funding, and regarding what research is ultimately done and with whom. This descriptor provides an objective

Table 15.1   *Funding instrument grant descriptors, details and purposes*

Descriptor	Detail	Descriptive and analytical purpose
Size	Absolute size (local currency amount researcher receives) Relative size (small, medium, large versus what is average for the field and/or country context)	Potential strength of influence of funding contract and its characteristics over research directions; can be compared with other funding contracts researcher has previously held, or ones they concurrently hold
Duration	Absolute length (funded years) Relative length (short, moderate, long versus average for field and country)	
Coverage	Operational expenditures funded Capital expenditures funded	Influences research directions via which personnel, equipment, experimental materials, data and infrastructures are funded
Role	Principal investigator (PI) Co-investigator (Co-I) Team member	Potential influence over directions of funded research and how the researcher's career may be affected by the funded research
Practices	Problem specifications Output specifications	Number and varieties of research problems and outputs that are being funded
Networks	Collaborator specifications (academic, non-academic)	Number and varieties of academics (and from which disciplines) and non-academics (and from which sectors) that are being funded
Type	Non-profit, public, private, public–private mix, internal	Proxies for funders' potentially differing policy, programme, instrument rationales and designs; enables tracing back effects to funders, and reflecting on instruments designs associated with particular funder types, origins
Origin	Domestic-national, foreign-national, supranational	
Enforcement	Administrative Epistemic (process, event series, one-off)	How adherence of performed to agreed research is enforced; how this may influence research and researcher's future funding prospects

measure, but nevertheless only a proxy for later enacted authority (Whitley et al., 2010). There may be divergence between the *ex ante*, notional label and measure of control, and the *ex post* authority a researcher later *exerts* (and which would require detailed study).

Descriptors indicating which research practices and networks are funded are also proxies. They allow some consideration of which scientific and socio-economic needs and possibilities, political, administrative and societal stakeholders are associated with the funded research (cf. Ramos-Vielba et al., 2022). They will enable a separate analytical focus on which *specific actors* were targeted to do and to (later) use the funded research, contrasted with what then actually happened. *Practices* enable later analytical focus concerning how the funded research topic was funder prespecified, similarly for funded research outputs, their forms, and orientations. Were funded outputs required to reach beyond academic audiences and did they? Was patenting activity, product or service development expected, and did it occur? *Ex post* analysis could then analyse whether these funding conditions can be associated with particular kinds of research activities and behaviours. *Networks* similarly enable a focus on the number and variety of academics to be involved being funder prespecified. Did the funding requirements require funded academics to come from similar or differing disciplines and did this happen? Were non-academics required to be involved, and from which commercial, non-profit, civic or other sectors? What happened in reality and how did this influence the funded research?

Registering variations in these funding descriptors systematically then aims to enable a separate, later analysis of influences related to collaboration compositions and intensities, as these are known to affect how research is done (Laudel, Chapter 16 in this *Handbook*). This can be in how certain actors distinctly co-produce knowledge, co-design research problems, supply key data and materials and more (Ramos-Vielba et al., 2022; see also Gläser et al., 2022, for a discussion of influences due to actors from civil society, funding agencies, industry, the military, states, and universities). Funder type and origin register which kinds of funders are involved. Was it a non-profit, public, private, mixed, internal, domestic, foreign or supranational funder? Each funder type and origin may be a proxy for distinct classes of funding designs, sizes, durations and orientations. These are again objective descriptors, serving as proxies to study whether certain funding types and origins are associated with particular forms of observed research changes.

We lastly include a descriptor of whether adherence between the performed and agreed research is enforced. This should be registered from the codified, *ex ante* flexibility the funder indicates will be contractually afforded to the researcher, for them later to adjust scientific, technical and collaboration parameters after the funded research begins (see also 'flexibility of use' in Laudel and Gläser, 2014). This provides another descriptor to use in later estimating apparent funder influence over research. How enforcement is pre-specified, then later enacted, may vary. However, it probably cannot overreach the contract legal terms. Such 'enforcement' is understudied (Langfeldt and Scordato, 2015; Roumbanis, 2019; Steele et al., 2019; Aagaard et al., 2021b). However, we might suggest enforcement *timing* can vary for this descriptor. It may be processual, where funder-mandated stakeholders, scientific officers or industry advisors participate throughout the funded research. It may be a series of events, with multiple stage-gates such as mid-term review plus final reporting. It may require external stakeholders attend only selected, key project meetings. It could be very light touch, stipulating only one-off final reporting of the research.

We can also imagine varying enforcement *intensity*. There could be simple *administrative* accountability for resource use, but no contractual funder mandate to request changes to the performed research, even if it deviates from what was originally agreed. Alternatively, *epistemic* enforcement may occur, where the funder has authority to ensure strict adherence (Steele et al., 2019). Some industry funders enforce contracts this way, by suppressing publication of undesired research results, steering research to avoid negative findings, mandating data deletion, terminating funding prematurely, or denying any future grants to a researcher (Steele et al., 2019; McCrabb et al., 2021).

Defining Individual Researcher Funding Configurations

To capture funding instrument grants for researchers, we assume they may hold one or more grants at once – originating from the same or from multiple funders. A researcher can be involved in multiple funder–researcher relationships, simultaneously superimposed. Our first study frame captures these instances as an 'individual researcher funding configuration'. This is defined as:

> An inventory, covering a specified time window, of all an individual researcher's concurrent funding instrument grants from any funder, with potential for co-use, and embedded in funder–researcher relationships.

The configuration collects all a researcher's concurrent, potentially overlapping funding instrument grants within a specified time window, thus extending the study beyond single, isolated grants. The time window can be specified to match the start and end of a funding instrument grant that is of analytical interest (Figure 15.2). What constitutes 'analytical interest' should be driven by a research question. For example, a prestigious personal funding grant, claiming to support ambitious research, could be explored to assess whether outcomes seemingly associated with it were attributable to it being used alone or are the result of the use of all or part of a broader configuration of the researcher's grants. Separately, outcomes of a societally targeted team project funding grant could be explored to assess whether they were shaped by any other funding present during the respective start and date ends. At a larger scale, a configuration lens could be applied to a long-term, capacity-building international centre of excellence. This might uncover additional dynamics of influence from concurrent funding during that centre's specific time window (Luukkonen and Thomas, 2016; Borlaug and Langfeldt, 2020; Reale et al., Chapter 7 in this *Handbook*).

Additional analytical interests could be imagined. Researchers with very homogenous or heterogenous configurations could be compared. Does the variety make a difference, and in which research field and country settings? A configuration approach could enable other questions. For example, in a given context, do certain researchers (not) seek a specific grant because it is highly (in)compatible with other concurrent funding in their configuration? Separately, do otherwise seemingly similar researchers use an identical grant differently because their configurations differ and affect the observed outcomes? Clearly, despite taking a multiple funding perspective, a configuration approach can still be used to focus on single key grants that policymakers and funders consider noteworthy. The distinction is they then frame them as only one part of a potentially broader aggregate unit that may also influence outcomes. This also orients the study towards grants as aggregate units, which researchers may strategize around, and may co-use by 'bundling' or 'hoarding' them together in novel or unexpected ways (Hellström and Jacob, 2017; Laudel, Chapter 16 in this *Handbook*).

Whatever the analytical interest, the configuration time window needs bounding. It is likely that certain other grants do not fit entirely within the start or end dates of the particular grant (see Figure 15.2). Fuzziness in bounding the period may be needed. Is there overlap with prior research lines and research collaborators? Similarly, acquisition of new grants after the start but before the end date may be included, for example to analyse path dependency dynamics.

Even if they share an aggregate focus, we also consider configurations as distinct from research 'funding portfolios'. Funding portfolios have been considered a *funder* level phenomenon (Molnar et al., 2015; Rahkovsky et al., 2021) and a *research field* level one (Shapira and Wang, 2010; Wang and Shapira, 2011; Luukkonen and Thomas, 2016; Degn et al., 2019). Internal funding mixes in public research organisations have been called portfolios (Balaji et al., 2007; Lepori et al., 2016). Other studies have included both internal and external funding to be organisations' funding portfolios (Scholten et al., 2021). Our closest match is with work on 'researcher funding portfolios' by Laudel (Chapter 16 in this *Handbook*) and the spirit of calls for more attention to researchers' 'funding arrangements' (Gläser and Serrano Velarde, 2018). We consider 'portfolios' as somewhat static and passive, and see 'configuring' as dynamic and active, involving both funding acquisition (Laudel, Chapter 16 in this *Handbook*) and conditions or practices of use (Laudel, 2006a; Grimpe, 2012; Luukkonen and Thomas, 2016).

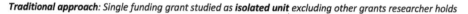

Traditional approach: *Single funding grant studied as* **isolated unit** *excluding other grants researcher holds*

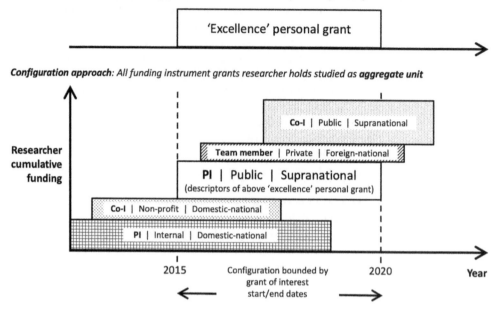

Figure 15.2   *Studying a single grant in isolation versus the aggregate researcher funding configuration*

The particular case of researchers' funding co-use, we believe, warrants particular foregrounding as a configuration-related dimension. Co-use dynamics have been misclassified, in our view, as borderline questionable practice. Situations where researchers acquire multiple grants to perform similar research have been implied to be cases of 'double-dipping' or researchers being 'over-funded' (see Wang and Shapira, 2011; Rigby and Julian, 2014). Such phrasings doubtless sound alarm bells for funders. The configuration frame instead views these situations as neither inherently positive nor negative, but invites further analysis. For instance, such configurational dynamics may be commonplace or even indispensable in certain fields and contexts. They may be an unavoidable 'new normal' in some parts of contemporary science.

However, these researcher level co-funding behaviours are also understudied. Promising avenues to explore them include focusing on the researchers' funding acquisition and use strategies in particular funding environments, and how this relates to researchers' adaptation of research content (Laudel, Chapter 16 in this *Handbook*). Beyond this, we can only tentatively sketch some co-use aspects for future study. A focus could be placed upon individual researcher level bricolage, serendipity and 'making do', whenever certain resources in a configuration are not ideally suited for whatever purposes a researcher intends to use them for. We may survey if certain researchers create new opportunities by configuring funding, transcending what is possible using separate single grants alone (Merton and Barber, 2004; Baker, 2007; Halme et al., 2012; Scholten et al., 2021). We might explore which researchers see or enact co-use opportunities, then know how to 'bundle' multiple funding affordances together across separate grants (Cunha et al., 2014; Hellström and Jacob, 2017). It could also be studied if researchers co-use grants in ways that exceed funders' original intentions, thus triggering appreciation or, potentially, enforcement. Similarly, it could be explored how a researcher's configuring is influenced by the research field(s) they are active in, the researcher's reputation, and which funders the researcher can access. We might also explore whether elite scientists, already known to have greater access to funding in most fields, enjoy or enact higher degrees of freedom to configure funding co-use than others (cf. Bourdieu, 1991; Laudel, 2006b; Ioannidis et al., 2018; Aagaard et al., 2020).

Configuration Characteristics

We also propose configurations as having identifiable overall characteristics. This could be simply whether they are 'homogenous' or 'heterogenous', once characterised via selected descriptors as shown in Table 15.1. What homogeneity and heterogeneity mean for influencing research(ers) is likely heavily context specific, however. For instance, some researchers may 'benefit from the mess' of a heterogenous grant mix, while others may not (Hallonsten, 2014). Configuration 'success' may thus depend not only on particular mixes of funding features but also on researcher capacity to (co-)use grants, and tolerance for any frictions this may generate for them over time (Hellström and Jacob, 2017).

Another stylised configuration characteristic could be whether grants in a configuration can be considered as supporting complementary research problems and collaborations. This complementarity characteristic could then be contrasted with notional control over grants, as suggested earlier, in terms of the apparent majority role of principal investigator (PI), co-investigator (Co-I, a key participant but without the overall authority of the PI) or team member of the researcher in question, across their configuration of grants. To determine majority, one could weigh roles by grant size and duration. Figure 15.3 illustrates such a hypothetical combination of two characteristics, from combining 'complementarity' and 'control' dimensions. It also speculates how one might imagine connecting certain degrees of these dimensions to potential influence for the research(er). Future analysis of these, or potentially other aspects, would of course need more robust operationalisation of the dimensions and degrees involved than illustrative examples, and require empirical study of particular cases.

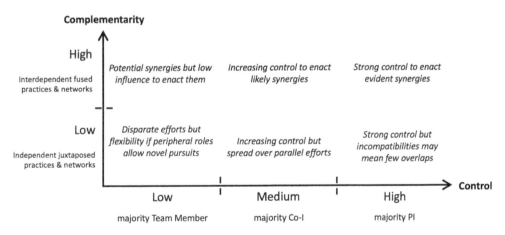

Figure 15.3   Example configuration characteristics based on complementarity and control dimensions

The aim here is simply to flag the idea that determining how and which configuration characteristics are distributed across a particular research area could inform better funding policy and instrument designs. Exploring configuration characteristics might help funders design better instruments, by taking into account their potential complementarity for co-use, and generally considering whether and how their own instruments fit with instruments provided by other funders active in the same funding environment.

Funding Trails of Individual Researchers

Our second study frame is the 'individual researcher funding trail'. This extends the configuration to cover the researcher's scientific lifetime, not just the start and end dates of a grant of interest. It aims to enable the study of long-term dynamics, like recurrent funding acquisition and co-use. Trails could help explore long-term effects of researcher funding acquisition strategies, for instance (see Laudel, Chapter 16 in this *Handbook*). This may reveal timing and sequencing effects in *when* a researcher acquires or co-uses grants. It could also help to investigate path dependency and funding concentration, through analysis of how researchers' past funding situations associate with future ones.

Studying which funding trails exist in a research area might also later be used to explore which researchers are repeatedly (un)successful in acquiring certain grants. This could help reveal funding situations associated with gender-based and other intersectional inequalities and funding concentrations (Cruz-Castro and Sanz-Menéndez, 2019; Aagaard et al., 2020; Kozlowski et al., 2022). Future questions could include, are all types of researchers constantly financed, or do some experience funding discontinuities? Which grants cause funding discontinuities, and how do researchers cope with them? Do researchers use internal, institutional funding to bridge gaps, and does any grant co-use yield long-term advantages? These questions are outside the scope of this current chapter. However, they could be addressed in the future, using suitable, trail-based approaches. These might also focus on any ongoing roles for *internal* funding, as this might otherwise be overlooked, given that changing *external* funding dynamics are receiving much of the scholarly attention.

Studying trails could also help to analyse instances of difficulties or successful synergies researchers encounter when co-using certain grants. This could, for example, highlight which capacities researchers need to navigate increasingly complicated funding situations. For policymakers and funders, knowing what funding trails exist, and what capacities researchers possess, might help them understand instances where certain researchers successfully achieve intended outcomes from funding, but others do not. Is this related to deficient funding design, or a signal that improved funder-to-funder coordination is needed? With data and analysis from trail-based studies, funders may then be able to adjust their funding approaches accordingly.

Like configurations, trails might be considered to have overall characteristics. Figure 15.4 suggests an example, illustrating a researcher seemingly experiencing decreasing funding complementarity and control, as one key characteristic of their trail. Analysis of such a trail could explore why this researcher is developing this way. A trail lens could help illustrate this kind of funding situation, through highlighting apparent patterns of increasing or decreasing control, inferred from a researcher's sequence of PI and Co-I grants, over time.

Here the figure's upper part separately stylises apparent complementarity of this researcher's research. Using appropriate descriptors, this could be explored in future studies to examine the consequences of cases such as the one illustrated. What are the effects of a researcher

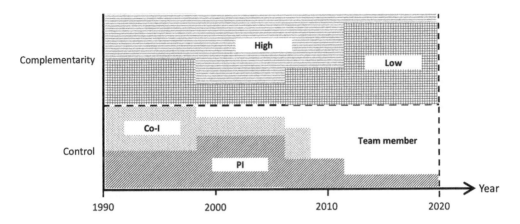

Figure 15.4   *Example funding trail with decreasing control and complementarity over time*

perhaps having fewer interdependent funded research questions, methods, equipment, and collaborators over time, such as the case illustrated in this trail shows? Analysis of these kinds of funding dynamics might then help to inform policymakers and funders to make decisions and to design instruments.

DISCUSSION

We now discuss challenges to use the frames we have proposed. The challenges refer to the limited data available on researcher funding, and the influence of changing funding configurations and trails on changing research. We also discuss how in the future we might expand the current individual level focus of the frames.

Funding Data Availability

Registering configurations or trails requires tracing researcher funding instrument grants. Most researchers do not prioritise public sharing of complete, accurate records of their funding, although some do publicise their external grants. Institutional funding often remains invisible, even though some researchers are likely to use internal funding.

Tracing suitable funding data is a challenge, even though public research funding information systems exist. Online, free access, national and supranational funder/funding databases contain data, but often with partial coverage. Examples include CRIStin Norway's Current Research Information System, which has data only from 2004 onwards. There is also RePORTER, the USA National Institutes of Health Research Portfolio Online Reporting Tools Expenditures and Results, with data from 1985. CORDIS, the European Commission Community Research and Development Information Service, has data from 1990, but at research organisation and not researcher level. Paywalled databases like Digital Science's Dimensions (Herzog et al., 2020) can claim a high coverage of funding information, and aggregate across public and private sources. Yet, these still may have only partial records and exhibit limitations tracing back to the original datasets. Similarly, websites of research organisations may publish researchers' work and CVs, but they provide uneven funding data. Academic network websites, like ORCID and ResearchGate, and personal academic blogs, often show the researchers' career positions, publications, and project descriptions, but often do not provide funding data.

Research organisations and funders internally hold researcher funding data. Access to this data needs to be negotiated across multiple research performers and funders, with each possibly using differing data protection and disclosure practices. Publication acknowledgements can provide funding data, but often without funding-researcher attribution, implying it may not be known which author had which funding. Funding size or duration are also rarely acknowledged in publications (Aagaard et al., 2021a). Studying acknowledgements also requires access to paywalled databases, and runs into limited systematic coverage of funding-related paratexts (Clarivate's Web of Science has this from late-2008 only). For now, the approach we recommend is some context-specific combination of desk-based research, funding acknowledgements study, surveying and interviewing researchers, and mixed method case studies addressing not only funded academics but also any funded non-academics (Bone et al., 2019; Aagaard et al., 2021a). This still has certain limitations, but we have found it can yield sufficient data to reconstruct researcher funding configurations and trails.

Funding Influencing Research

Another challenge is connecting changing configurations and trails to changing research. Funding is not the only influence to consider. Research can be shaped by multiple, interconnected factors. This makes designing causal funding studies onerous (Laudel and Gläser, 2014; Gläser and Serrano Velarde, 2018; Gläser, 2019). Previous literature has highlighted areas of funding effects to consider. These are somewhat fragmented, but indicate: funding can change whether novel topics and long-term intellectual innovations are researched; short-term project-based, and narrowly prioritised funding can reduce the resilience of research(ers) to respond to societal shocks; explicit funder requirements for specified topics to be tackled, by particular funded consortia compositions, can lead to more users- and use-based perspectives being included in funded research than would occur without such intervention; and, funding requirements for openness can affect researcher choices about whether to keep their materials, methods and findings secret or not (Bourke and Butler, 1999; Geuna, 2001; Laudel, 2006a; Lepori et al., 2007; Hong and Walsh, 2009; Evans, 2010; Hallonsten, 2014; Czarnitzki et al., 2015; Franssen et al., 2018; Franssen and de Rijcke, 2019; Perkmann et al., 2021; Ryan, 2021; Gläser et al., 2022).

Despite knowing these effect areas exist, we have limited robust methods to connect changing funding with them. Arguably the most developed approach has been to study research change by analysing changing publication content, then to study how this translates into changed pursuit of research topics, problems, methods, experiments and research outputs. Here, researcher 'research trails' need to be reconstructed and then connected to funding situations. Whether a researcher is pursuing one or multiple research 'lines' is first inferred from sequences of papers they have (co-)authored. Overlapping cited references – strictly, the degree of bibliographic coupling between them – is visualised in a plot of apparent research lines. These are discussed in detail, via a 'scientifically informed' interview with a researcher (Laudel and Gläser, 2007; Gläser and Laudel, 2015a). This can then be used to attempt to associate changing funding with changing 'epistemic properties' of research. This can address any changes in theories and methods that are used, research objects and timescales, topic ambition and novelty, and which experiments are being planned and conducted (Gläser and Laudel, 2015b; Laudel, Chapter 16 in this *Handbook*). Configurations and trails are amenable to this same approach. Changing research trails could, in future studies, be associated with underlying dynamics of funding configurations and trails.

Configurations and trails could also be used to study other aspects, in particular, funding co-use. For instance, is this shaped by – or does it shape – research trails? Additional study questions could include:

- Why are some concurrent grants used together or separately, and how does this influence the research(er)?
- What tangible materials and intangible knowledge overlap across concurrent funding, including via any academic and non-academic collaborators?
- When are concurrent grants co-used to purchase, develop, use or maintain equipment, materials and data, and how does this affect the research(er)?
- How does co-use affect project management and administration of the research(er)?

Framing Funding of Collaborating Researchers

Our frames address *individual* researchers. Yet we know much science is now done by organisation-based groups, pan-organisation teams, inter- or transdisciplinary collaborations, and across global knowledge networks (Hallonsten, 2014; Ioannidis et al., 2018; Adams et al., 2019; Aagaard et al., 2021a; Ramos-Vielba et al., 2022). Funding changes for *collaborating* researchers are therefore also important to consider. Our frames do already somewhat position researchers as individuals collaborating with other researchers. This can invite attention to interconnections within configurations, such as with funding of Co-Is and other team members.

To capture collaborative funding dynamics more comprehensively, we might later consider other levels of analysis, for instance at field or organisation level. Alternatively, we could explore 'funding amalgamations' (Aagaard et al., 2021a). These frame a larger unit of all the funding of all participants working on a specified collaborative research activity, like a multi-authored paper or team research project. Bounding amalgamations would be challenging, and requires a difficult tracing of funding data for a larger number of researchers. Nevertheless, they could be explored in future research.

CONCLUSIONS

In this chapter we argued that multi-level research funding changes necessitate the development of new frames for the study of funding. We positioned and defined two frames, addressing funding at the individual researcher level. Our aim was to reframe the study of individual research(er) funding to enable exploration of funding interdependencies seemingly now growing across contemporary science. The frames also focus on whether such complicated funding contexts render invalid the continuing attempts to study single funding grants in isolation. The frames also imply certain changes to the design and use of research funding policies, programmes and instruments:

- *Instrument design* and *allocation* could consider how many grants and complementary research practices and networks exist in a given research area, and whether synergies or frictions are being caused, once researchers configure and co-use funding in context.
- *Coordination* with other funders might increase across policies, programmes, instruments, calls and enforcement, by recognising and enabling co-use in certain contexts.
- *Concentration* may be a larger concern than already suspected (Aagaard et al., 2020) after reframing funding landscapes through the lenses of configurations and trails. Instruments and their allocation may need to be revisited to safeguard equity, diversity and related resilience in science.
- *Influence* levels we might expect funders to exert, even prestigious ones like the European Research Council (Thomas and Nedeva, 2012), may need to be revisited, after we take into account configuration and co-use dynamics in selected contexts.

To close, we hope our proposed frames inspire scholars, policymakers and funders to analyse critically funding designs and allocations. We also hope the frames may help build greater understanding of why and how researchers use funding in particular ways, so researchers can continue to pursue their diverse scientific and societal goals, not unnecessarily impeded by problematic funding features and perspectives.

NOTE

1.   A Novo Nordisk Foundation grant NNF18OC0034422 (PROSECON) supported this research.

REFERENCES

Aagaard, K. (2017). The evolution of a national research funding system: Transformative change through layering and displacement. *Minerva*, 55, 279–297.

Aagaard, K., Kladakis, A., and Nielsen, M.W. (2020). Concentration or dispersal of research funding? *Quantitative Science Studies*, 1(1), 117–149.

Aagaard, K., Mongeon, P., Ramos-Vielba, I., and Thomas, D.A. (2021a). Getting to the bottom of research funding: Acknowledging the complexity of funding dynamics. *PLOS ONE*, 16(5), e0251488. https://doi.org/10.1371/journal.pone.0251488.

Aagaard, K., Ramos-Vielba, I., and Thomas, D.A. (2021b, 11 February). Funders use of 'targeting' and 'enforcement' to shape research for societal impact [paper presentation]. (How) does governance matter? Berlin, Germany. https://www.ucviden.dk/en/publications/funders-use-of-targeting-and-enforcement-to-shape-research-for-so.

Adams, J., Pendlebury, D., Potter, R., and Szomszor, M. (2019). *Global Research Report: Multi-Authorship and Research Analytics*. Beijing, China: Clarivate Analytics Institute for Scientific Information Web of Science Group.

Baker, T. (2007). Resources in play: Bricolage in the Toy Store(y). *Journal of Business Venturing*, 22(5), 694–711. https://doi.org/10.1016/j.jbusvent.2006.10.008.

Balaji, R.V., Knisely, C., and Blazyk, J. (2007). Internal grant competitions: A new opportunity for research officers to build institutional funding portfolios. *Journal of Research Administration*, 38(2), 44–50.

Bloch, C., and Sorensen, M.P. (2015). The size of research funding: Trends and implications. *Science and Public Policy*, 42(1), 30–43.

Bone, F., Hopkins, M.M., Ràfols, I., Molas-Gallart, J., Tang, P., Davey, G., and Carr, A.M. (2019). DARE to be different? Applying diversity heuristics to the analysis of collaborative research. SPRU Working Paper Series (SWPS), 2019-09, 1–31. Retrieved 28 March 2022, from http://sro.sussex.ac .uk/id/eprint/86414/.

Boon, W., and Edler, J. (2018). Demand, challenges, and innovation. Making sense of new trends in innovation policy. *Science and Public Policy*, 45(4), 435–447.

Borlaug, S.B., and Langfeldt, L. (2020). One model fits all? How centres of excellence affect research organisation and practices in the humanities. *Studies in Higher Education*, 45(8), 1746–1757.

Bourdieu, P. (1991). The peculiar history of scientific reason. *Sociological Forum*, 6(1), 3–26. https:// doi.org/10.1007/BF01112725.

Bourke, P., and Butler, L. (1999). The efficacy of different modes of funding research: Perspectives from Australian data on the biological sciences. *Research Policy*, 28(5), 489–499.

Braun, D. (1998). The role of funding agencies in the cognitive development of science. *Research Policy*, 27(8), 807–821. https://doi.org/10.1016/s0048-7333(98)00092-4.

Braun, D. (2003). Lasting tensions in research policy-making – A delegation problem. *Science and Public Policy*, 30(5), 309–321.

Cocos, M., and Lepori, B. (2020). What we know about research policy mix. *Science and Public Policy*, 47(2), 235–245. https://doi.org/10.1093/scipol/scz061.

Cremonini, L., Horlings, E., and Hessels, L.K. (2017) Different recipes for the same dish: Comparing policies for scientific excellence across different countries. *Science and Public Policy*, 45(2), 232–245.

Cruz-Castro, L., and Sanz-Menéndez, L. (2019). Grant allocation disparities from a gender perspective: Literature review. Synthesis Report. GRANteD Project D.1.1. http://dx.doi.org/10.20350/ digitalCSIC/10548.

Cunha, M.P.E., Rego, A., Oliveira, P., Rosado, P., and Habib, N. (2014). Product innovation in resource-poor environments. *Journal of Product Innovation Management*, 31, 202–210. https://doi .org/10.1111/jpim.12090.

Cunningham, J., O'Reilly, P., O'Kane, C., and Mangematin, V. (2014). The inhibiting factors that principal investigators experience in leading publicly funded research. *The Journal of Technology Transfer*, 39, 93–110, https://doi.org/10.1007/s10961-012-9269-4.

Czarnitzki, D., Grimpe, C., and Pellens, M. (2015). Access to research inputs: Open science versus the entrepreneurial university. *The Journal of Technology Transfer*, 40(6), 1050–1063.

Degn, L., Mejlgaard, N., and Schneider, J.W. (2019). Using mixed methods to map vaguely defined research areas. *Research Evaluation*, 28(4), 394–404. https://doi.org/10.1093/reseval/rvz025.

D'Este, P., Ramos-Vielba, I., Woolley, R., and Amara, N. (2018). How do researchers generate scientific and societal impacts? Toward an analytical and operational framework. *Science and Public Policy*, 45(6), 752–763.

Evans, J.A. (2010). Industry collaboration, scientific sharing, and the dissemination of knowledge. *Social Studies of Science*, 40(5), 757–791.

Franssen, T., and de Rijcke, S. (2019). The rise of project funding and its effects on the social structure of academia. In F. Cannizzo and N. Osbaldiston (Eds.), *The Social Structures of Global Academia* (pp. 144–161). Abingdon: Routledge Advances in Sociology.

Franssen T., Scholten W., Hessels L.K., and de Rijcke S. (2018). The drawbacks of project funding for epistemic innovation: Comparing institutional affordances and constraints of different types of research funding. *Minerva*, 56(1), 11–33. https://doi.org/10.1007/s11024-017-9338-9.

Geuna, A. (2001). The changing rationale for European university research funding: Are there negative unintended consequences? *Journal of Economic Issues*, 35(3), 607–632, https://doi.org/10.1080/ 00213624.2001.11506393.

Gläser, J. (2019). How can governance change research content? Linking science policy studies to the sociology of science. In D. Simon, S. Kuhlmann, J. Stamm, and W. Canzler (Eds.), *Handbook on Science and Public Policy* (pp. 419–447). Cheltenham: Edward Elgar.

Gläser, J., and Laudel, G. (2015a). A bibliometric reconstruction of research trails for qualitative investigations of scientific innovations. *Historical Social Research – Historische Sozialforschung*, 40, 299–330.

Gläser, J., and Laudel, G. (2015b). Cold atom gases, hedgehogs, and snakes: The methodological challenges of comparing scientific things. *Nature and Culture*, 10(3), 303–332. http://www.jstor.org/stable/26206097.

Gläser, J., and Serrano Velarde, K. (2018). Changing funding arrangements and the production of scientific knowledge: Introduction to the Special Issue. *Minerva*, 56(1), 1–10.

Gläser, J., Ash, M., Bünstorf, G., Hopf, D., Hubenschmid, L., Janßen, M., Laudel, G., Schimank, U., Stoll, M., Wilholt, T., Zechlin, L., and Lieb, K. (2022). The independence of research – A review of disciplinary perspectives and outline of interdisciplinary prospects. *Minerva*, 60, 105–138. https://doi.org/10.1007/s11024-021-09451-8.

Grimpe, C., (2012). Extramural research grants and scientists' funding strategies: Beggars cannot be choosers? *Research Policy*, 41, 1448–1460.

Guston, D.H., and Keniston, K. (Eds.) (1994). *The Fragile Contract: University Science and the Federal Government*. Cambridge, MA: MIT Press.

Hallonsten, O. (2021). Stop evaluating science: A historical–sociological argument. *Social Science Information*, 60(1), 7–26. https://doi.org/10.1177/0539018421992204.

Hallonsten, O. (2014). How scientists may 'benefit from the mess': A resource dependence perspective on individual organizing in contemporary science. *Social Science Information*, 53(3), 341–362. https://doi.org/10.1177/0539018414524037.

Halme, M., Lindeman, S., and Linna, P. (2012). Innovation for inclusive business: Intrapreneurial bricolage in multinational corporations. *Journal of Management Studies*, 49(4), 743–784.

Hammarfelt, B., Rushforth, A.D., and de Rijcke, S. (2020). Temporality in academic evaluation: 'Trajectoral thinking' in the assessment of biomedical researchers. *Valuation Studies*, 7(1), 33. https://doi.org/10.3384/VS.2001-5992.2020.7.1.33.

Hellström, T., and Jacob, M. (2017). Policy instrument affordances: A framework for analysis. *Policy Studies*, 38(6), 604–621.

Herzog, C., Hook, D., and Konkiel, S. (2020). Dimensions: Bringing down barriers between scientometricians and data. *Quantitative Science Studies*, 1(1), 387–395. https://doi.org/10.1162/qss_a_00020.

Hessels, L.K., Franssen, T., Scholten, W., and De Rijcke, S. (2019). Variation in valuation: How research groups accumulate credibility in four epistemic cultures. *Minerva*, 57(2), 127–149.

Hong, W., and Walsh, J.P. (2009). For money or glory? Commercialization, competition, and secrecy in the entrepreneurial university. *The Sociological Quarterly*, 50(1), 145–171.

Ioannidis, J., Klavans, R., and Boyack, K. (2018). Thousands of scientists publish a paper every five days. *Nature*, 561, 167–169. https://doi.org/10.1038/d41586-018-06185-8.

Kozlowksi, D., Larivière, V., Sugimoto, C.R., and Monroe-White, T. (2022). Intersectional inequalities in science. *PNAS*, 119(2), e2113067119, 4 January. https://doi.org/10.1073/pnas.2113067119.

Kuhlmann, S., and Rip, A. (2018). Next-generation innovation policy and grand challenges. *Science and Public Policy*, 45(4), 448–454.

Langfeldt, L., and Scordato, L. (2015). Assessing the broader impacts of research: A review of methods and practices. NIFU Working Paper 8/2015. Oslo: NIFU.

Laudel, G. (2006a). The art of getting funded: How scientists adapt to their funding conditions. *Science and Public Policy*, 33(7), 489–504.

Laudel, G. (2006b). The 'quality myth': Promoting and hindering conditions for acquiring research funds. *Higher Education*, 52, 375–403. https://doi.org/10.1007/s10734-004-6414-5.

Laudel, G., and Gläser, J. (2007). Interviewing scientists. *Science, Technology and Innovation Studies*, 3(2), 91–111. http://dx.doi.org/10.17877/DE290R-983.

Laudel, G., and Gläser, J. (2014). Beyond breakthrough research: Epistemic properties of research and their consequences for research funding. *Research Policy*, 43, 1204–1216.

Lepori, B. (2011). Coordination modes in public funding systems. *Research Policy*, 40, 355–367.

Lepori, B., and Reale, E. (2019). The changing governance of research systems. Agencification and organizational differentiation in research funding organizations. In D. Simon, S. Kuhlmann, J. Stamm and W. Canzler (Eds.), *Handbook on Science and Public Policy* (pp. 448–463). Cheltenham: Edward Elgar.

Lepori, B., van den Besselaar, P., Dinges, M., van der Meulen, B., Potì, B., Reale, E., Slipersaeter, S., and Theves, J. (2007). Indicators for comparative analysis of public project funding: Concepts, implementation and evaluation. *Research Evaluation*, 16(4), 243–255. https://doi.org/10.3152/0958 20207x260252.

Lepori, B., Wise, M., Ingenhoff, D., and Buhmann, A. (2016). The dynamics of university units as a multi-level process. Credibility cycles and resource dependencies. *Scientometrics*, 109(3), 2279–2301.

Lorenz, C. (2012). If you're so smart, why are you under surveillance? Universities, neoliberalism, and New Public Management. *Critical inquiry*, 38(3), 599–629.

Luukkonen, T., and Thomas, D.A. (2016). The 'negotiated space' of university researchers' pursuit of a research agenda. *Minerva*, 54(1), 99–127. https://doi.org/10.1007/s11024-016-9291-z.

McCrabb, S., Mooney, K., Wolfenden, L., Gonzalez, S., Ditton, E., Yoong, S., and Kypri, K. (2021) 'He who pays the piper calls the tune': Researcher experiences of funder suppression of health behaviour intervention trial findings. *PLoS ONE*, 16(8), e0255704. https://doi.org/10.1371/journal.pone .0255704.

Merton, R.K., and Barber, E. (2004). *The Travels and Adventures of Serendipity. A Study in Sociological Semantics and the Sociology of Science*. Princeton, USA: Princeton University Press.

Molnar, A., McKenna, A.F., Liu, Q., Vorvoreanu, M., and Madhavan, K. (2015). Using visualization to derive insights from research funding portfolios. *IEEE Computer Graphics and Applications*, 35(3), 91–c3.

Paradeise, C., and Thoenig, J.C. (2015). *In Search of Academic Quality*. London: Macmillan.

Perkmann, M., Salandra, R., Tartari, V., McKelvey, M., and Hughes, A. (2021). Academic engagement: A review of the literature 2011–2019. *Research Policy*, 50(1), 104114. https://doi.org/10.1016/j .respol.2020.104114.

Rahkovsky, I., Toney, A., Boyack, K.W., Klavans, R., and Murdick, D.A. (2021). AI research funding portfolios and extreme growth. *Frontiers in Research Metrics and Analytics*, 6, 11.

Ramos-Vielba, I., Thomas, D.A., and Aagaard, K. (2022). Societal targeting in researcher funding: An exploratory approach. *Research Evaluation*, rvab044. https://doi.org/10.1093/reseval/rvab044.

Reale, E. (2017). Analysis of national public research funding (PREF). Final report. https://doi.org/10 .2760/19140.

Rigby, J., and Julian, K. (2014). On the horns of a dilemma: Does more funding for research lead to more research or a waste of resources that calls for optimization of researcher portfolios? An analysis using funding acknowledgement data. *Scientometrics*, 101(2), 1067–1075.

Roumbanis, L. (2019) Symbolic violence in academic life: A study on how junior scholars are educated in the art of getting funded. *Minerva*, 57, 197–218. https://doi.org/10.1007/s11024-018-9364-2.

Ryan, T.R. (2021). The production and public dissemination of scientific knowledge in university–industry projects. PhD Dissertation, Aarhus University, Denmark: Forlaget Politica.

Schneider, F., Buser, T., Keller, R., Tribaldos, T., and Rist, S. (2019). Research funding programmes aiming for societal transformations: Ten key stages. *Science and Public Policy*, 46(3), 463–478.

Scholten, W., Franssen, T.P., van Drooge, L., de Rijcke, S., and Hessels, L.K. (2021). Funding for few, anticipation among all: Effects of excellence funding on academic research groups. *Science and Public Policy*, 48(2), 265–275. https://doi.org/10.1093/scipol/scab018.

Shapira P., and Wang J. (2010). Follow the money. *Nature*, 468(7324), 627–628. https://doi.org/10.1038/ 468627a.

Sivertsen, G. (2020). Problems and considerations in the design of bibliometric indicators for national performance-based research funding systems. *Przegląd Prawa Konstytucyjnego*, 55(3), 109–118. https://doi.org/10.15804/ppk.2020.03.06.

Slaughter, S., and Rhoades, G. (2004). *Academic Capitalism and the New Economy: Markets, State, and Higher Education*. Baltimore, MD: Johns Hopkins University Press.

Smit, J.P., and Hessels, L.K. (2021). The production of scientific and societal value in research evaluation: A review of societal impact assessment methods. *Research Evaluation*, 30(3), 323–335. https:// doi.org/10.1093/reseval/rvab002.

Sörlin, S. (2007). Funding diversity: Performance-based funding regimes as drivers of differentiation in higher education systems. *Higher Education Policy*, 20(4), 413–440.

Steele, S., Ruskin, G., McKee, M., and Stuckler, D. (2019). 'Always read the small print': A case study of commercial research funding, disclosure and agreements with Coca-Cola. *Journal of Public Health Policy*, 40, 273–285. https://doi.org/10.1057/s41271-019-00170-9.

Thomas, D., and Nedeva, M. (2012). Characterizing researchers to study research funding agency impacts: The case of the European Research Council's Starting Grants. *Research Evaluation*, 21(4), 257–269. https://doi.org/10.1093/reseval/rvs020.

Thomas, D.A., Nevada, M., Tirado, M.M., and Jacob, M. (2020). Changing research on research evaluation: A critical literature review to revisit the agenda. *Research Evaluation*, 29(3), 275–288. https://doi.org/10.1093/reseval/rvaa008.

Vasan K., and West J.D. (2021). The hidden influence of communities in collaborative funding of clinical science. *Royal Society Open Science*, 8(210072), 1–18. https://doi.org/10.1098/rsos.210072.

Wagner, C.S. (2019). Global science for global challenges. In D. Simon, S. Kuhlmann, J. Stamm, and W. Canzler (Eds.), *Handbook on Science and Public Policy* (pp. 92–103). Cheltenham: Edward Elgar.

Wang, D., and Barabási, A. (2021). *The Science of Science*. Cambridge: Cambridge University Press. https://doi.org/10.1017/9781108610834.

Wang J., and Shapira, P. (2011). Funding acknowledgement analysis: An enhanced tool to investigate research sponsorship impacts: The case of nanotechnology. *Scientometrics*, 87(3), 563–586.

Whitley, R., Gläser, J., and Engwall, L. (2010). *Reconfiguring Knowledge Production: Changing Authority Relationships in the Sciences and their Consequences for Intellectual Innovation*. Oxford: Oxford University Press.

Wu, L., Wang, D., and Evans, J.A. (2019). Large teams develop and small teams disrupt science and technology. *Nature*, 566, 378–382. https://doi.org/10.1038/s41586-019-0941-9.

Young, M., Sørensen, M.P., Bloch, C., and Degn, L. (2017). Systemic rejection: Political pressures seen from the science system. *Higher Education*, 74(3), 491–505.

16. Researchers' responses to their funding situation

Grit Laudel

INTRODUCTION

Over the last decades, the funding of research has changed drastically in many OECD countries. The basic structure of funding has shifted from recurrent funding to a split funding mode with recurrent and competitive grant funding. Several chapters in this *Handbook* illustrate that competition for project grants has increased, and success rates have decreased, ever since. In addition, funding instruments are increasingly used to encourage contributions to commercial and public policy goals. Finally, higher education reforms made university funding contingent on performance (Whitley, 2010). As a result of these changes, many researchers face an increasingly turbulent resource environment, in which securing funding becomes a more and more challenging task.

Researchers have responded to their perceptions of changing resource environments by developing a variety of strategies for securing funding that sustains their research. These strategies inform and shape researchers' interactions with their resource environment, affect the amount and kinds of resources available to them, and influence the conduct and content of their research. How researchers respond to their funding situation has consequences for the direction and quality of their research. Strategies for securing funding must therefore be included in the explanation of processes of funding and their effects, and should be taken into account when funding instruments are designed.

Given their pivotal role, the strategies of researchers concerning their funding and the effects of researchers' strategic behaviour have received surprisingly little attention in science studies. Almost 20 years ago, Morris (2003, p. 359) observed that the agency of researchers has been neglected in studies of the impact of funding policies. This situation remains more or less unchanged. While researchers' actions of securing funding are noted in passing in many case studies, only very few scholars have made attempts to systematically study these actions, the strategies underlying them and their impact on research, such as Morris (2000, 2003), Laudel (2006), Leišytė (2007).

The aim of this chapter is to develop a systematic account of what is known about researchers' strategies to secure funding, to highlight the conditions under which particular strategies are utilized, and to outline necessary steps towards a middle-range theory of relationships between funding conditions and the conduct and content of research. I begin by presenting a sociological perspective on the strategic actors – individual researchers – and their research situations. In the main part of the chapter, I use the literature to build a typology of strategies available to researchers. While little is known about conditions triggering particular strategies, a strong argument can be built that the utility and applicability of strategies is field specific, i.e. it depends on the epistemic properties of research. Some consequences of the application of funding strategies for the content of research are examined before, finally, conclusions are drawn.[1]

RESEARCHERS AND THEIR SITUATIONS

Our starting point is the consideration of the researcher as an actor capable of formulating and implementing strategies for action. While this observation appears trivial at first glance, it is important for three reasons. First, discussing researchers as strategic actors ascribes them a minimum level of autonomy, i.e. they must have a certain degree of control over the formation of goals and the choice of approaches (Gläser et al., 2022), and they must have the authority to acquire and use resources for sustaining their research (Morris, 2003, p. 365). This requisite autonomy and authority are provided to researchers on most positions in public research organizations when they execute the role of a "colleague" in their scientific community (Laudel and Gläser, 2008).

Understanding strategies to secure research funding requires linking them to the researcher's interests. This chapter builds on the premise that researchers' primary motive is to sustain their research, because continuously doing research is an important aspect of their identity (Gläser, 2019, p. 431). This is why, secondly, a researcher's goals and approaches must be the starting point of any analysis. Researchers balance their own interests with others' expectations when developing and applying funding strategies: "In order to continuously conduct research, researchers need to select problems and approaches that create a sufficient agreement between their own interests, the community's expectations concerning relevant and reliable contributions, and expectations by external actors" (ibid., pp. 436–437). The balancing may have different outcomes, which include a perfect alignment of interests and various forms of compromises between researchers' interests and interests inscribed in funding instruments (Thomas and Ramos-Vielba, Chapter 15 in this *Handbook*).

Thirdly, the extent to which actions are consciously directed towards achieving goals varies, with strategic actions at one end of the spectrum and routine actions at the other. This variance has first been noted by Weber (1922 [2019], p. 98). It also applies to an actor's strategies, which I understand here as planned patterns of actions whose purpose is to achieve a specific type of situational change. Such strategies will be analysed here as ideal types of consciously selected sets of actions, which, however, may also be applied by researchers who are not fully aware of the underlying strategy. How much researchers are aware of the fact that they implement a particular strategy is an empirical question.

Balancing one's research interests with external interests inscribed in funding instruments or with the interests of other actors involved in the process of funding research may be conceptualized as balancing research portfolios and funding portfolios. In the course of their careers, researchers develop a sequence of thematically interconnected research processes in which findings from earlier research projects serve as input in later projects (Laudel and Gläser, 2008). These research processes constitute one or several distinct "research trails" (Chubin and Connolly, 1982, p. 295). If we now regard a researcher's situation at a specific point in time, we see them managing a "research portfolio", which consists of one or multiple research trails (Gläser et al., 2010, p. 305; Gläser, 2019, p. 439; for similar definitions see Lukkonen and Thomas, 2016, p.102; Wallace and Rafols, 2015, p. 93; Rushford et al., 2019, p. 213). This portfolio includes projects a researcher currently works on, as well as potential projects and research trails, i.e. those they intend to start, would like to start or at least consider possible. Maintaining an identity as a researcher requires sustaining a research portfolio of at least one research trail. For this purpose, a researcher must acquire and manage resources, i.e. manage a funding portfolio (Barrier, 2011, pp. 525–528).[2] A funding portfolio consists of existing resources and latent funding opportunities. "Co-funding behaviour" is common, i.e. seeking funding for a research trail from multiple sources (Thomas and Ramos-Vielba, Chapter 15 in this *Handbook*).

The extent to which a researcher's research and funding portfolios correspond to each other is crucial for the opportunities researchers have to achieve their goals. This correspondence is therefore likely to be one of the most important conditions that shape researchers' strategic actions. Funding strategies can thus be defined as planned patterns of actions whose purpose is to achieve a match between *funding* and *planned research*. This definition implies that researchers' funding strategies may change the funding, the research, or both.

The utilization of funding strategies and their success depend on a variety of conditions which can be pointed out here but cannot be elaborated within the confines of this chapter (or indeed without further research). It is important to note that when acquiring and managing resources, researchers do not respond to funding opportunities or constraints alone. Researchers always respond to the totality of their situation, of which the funding conditions and opportunities are only a part. Other conditions include, among others, the nature of competition in a researcher's community, the researcher's career situation (Melkers et al., Chapter 18 in this *Handbook*), organizational evaluation cycles and general infrastructural conditions.

For example, the range of strategies available to a researcher depends on their status in the community. Elite researchers may select other strategies than non-elite members. This status is related to, but does not always coincide with, community perceptions of the quality of a researcher's work. Institutional conditions of actions that shape opportunities to apply particular strategies include rules set by funders of research (particularly eligibility rules), other rules governing the conduct of research, the exercise of authority by other actors like the research organization and expectations of the scientific community. The applicability and presence of particular strategies also depend on field-specific epistemic properties of research, which will be briefly discussed later.

RESEARCHERS' STRATEGIES FOR BUILDING AND MAINTAINING THEIR FUNDING PORTFOLIOS

Categorizing Strategies – A Mission Impossible?

Providing a systematic overview of researchers' strategies of building and maintaining their funding portfolios is not an easy task. In most empirical studies of research funding, strategies are identified inductively from the empirically observed patterns of actions with little reference to prior research. As a consequence, similar responses have been labelled differently in various studies. A second problem is that researchers respond to their situations, which consist of other opportunities and pressures beside their funding situation. These factors are often difficult to disentangle owing to a lack of detail in empirical descriptions in the literature.

Studies that try to theoretically ground their discovery of strategies usually resort to organizational sociology and its work on strategic responses by organizations to their environments.

This approach can be justified by an analogy between organizations and researchers, namely that both can be considered to maintain a specific "core technology" in more or less turbulent environments. This observation led to the consideration of research groups as "quasi-firms", because they "have firm-like qualities, especially under conditions in which research funding is awarded on a competitive basis" (Etzkowitz, 2003, p. 109). Although this thought has been frequently reiterated, it has not led to a fully fledged theoretical account that could guide empirical investigations of researchers' funding strategies or to a systematization of empirically observed strategies.

Although no systematic account of researchers' strategies has been developed (the conceptual attempt by Hallonsten (2014) is neither specific enough nor exhaustive), theoretical approaches from organizational theory have been used as heuristics to categorize inductively reconstructed strategies of researchers (e.g. Leišytė, 2007, pp. 23–41; Gläser, 2019, p. 438). Among these are Thompson's account of organizations' strategies to maintain their core technologies in the face of changing environments (Thompson, 1967), resource dependency theory, which addresses the strategies adopted by organizations for securing resources (Pfeffer and Salancik, 2003 [1978]), and Oliver's (1991) account of organizational responses to institutional pressures. All three approaches have in common that they capture strategies of organizations as responses to environmental changes. Unfortunately, these contributions to organizational theory did not result in a consistent conceptual framework that could be used for categorizing the empirically derived strategies of researchers. For this reason, I use in this chapter ideas from organizational theory as heuristic tools where I see fit.

My point of departure is a distinction of four possible targets of researchers' strategies, namely their resource environment, the resource acquisition process, the resources available to them, and the research content itself (Figure 16.1). The distinction between the four targets is analytical in that targeting one of the elements often will have consequences for another. In the next section I discuss these strategies in detail.

Changing the Resource Environment

Modifying the resource environment

Researchers can attempt to improve their chances of acquiring funding by proactively shaping expectations and the behaviour of actors that provide resources. This strategy has first been discussed in the context of the debate on "planned research" in the 1970s. Researchers who studied the genesis of major state funding programmes (e.g. those implemented in the US "war on cancer") found that these programmes were developed with active participation of elite researchers, and could not in fact have been developed without them. Funding programmes were developed in so-called "hybrid communities" (Van den Daele et al., 1977, p. 228), which consist of researchers, science policy makers and other societal actors. Researchers who are members of these hybrid communities attempt to shape funding programmes according to their research interests. A similar observation has been made with regard to funding councils. Braun (1998) argued that that the translation of policy interests into expectations concerning the directions of research is only possible with the help of researchers.

At the national level, members of the elite are more often involved in the shaping of funding programmes than other researchers. They play also an active role in the emergence of new research and technology fields (e.g. Barrier, 2011, p. 522; van Lente and Rip, 1998; Reinecke, 2021). At the organizational level, researchers also compete for the resources of their univer-

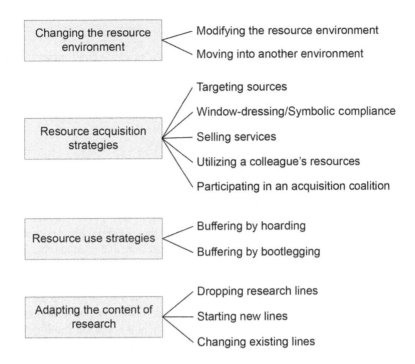

Figure 16.1   Researchers' strategic responses to their funding situations

sities, and can attempt to influence their university's internal funding schemes. In particular, the "profile building" of universities is supported by a concentration of resources, which motivates researchers to make the profile include their research topics (Meier and Schimank, 2010; Weyer, 2018). The same strategy has been applied to make certain topics part of the departmental research agenda (Leišytė, 2007, p. 226).

Moving into another environment
Researchers can change their resource environment by moving into another environment. When researchers commercialize their research results through academic spin offs, this is sometimes done with the aim to earn money that supports one's research (Laudel, 2006, p. 495; Nilsson et al., 2010; Lam, 2010; Lam and de Campos, 2015).[3] Commercialization positions the researcher in an additional environment, which in most cases is an industry. It usually requires long-term endurance, and the hoped-for financial revenues may not occur (Zomer et al., 2010, pp. 344–345; Lam, 2010, p. 323). A whole range of legal, economic, cultural conditions must be fulfilled to support entrepreneurial activities, as numerous studies on academic entrepreneurship have shown. If successful, this strategy may lead to the acquisition of substantial additional resources. It can of course be used only by those whose work produces applications that can be commercialized.

Resource Acquisition Strategies

We now consider a set of strategies related to an existing research environment, namely targeting particular sources, symbolic compliance, selling services and enrolling collaborators, as well as joining an acquisition coalition. At least some of these strategies have been frequently observed and they are likely to be applied by researchers from different career stages and research fields.

Targeting particular sources

Researchers have been observed to target any source, an "easy" source, or an appropriate source of funding (Laudel, 2006, p. 495; cf. also O'Kane, 2015, pp. 207–208). For maintaining and extending their research portfolios, researchers may target *any funding source* for which they are eligible – both those that are highly appropriate and some that may be less appropriate (see also Morris, 2003, p. 366). These sources could include internal university schemes, all funding agencies and their various programmes, private donors and foundations, and industry funding. Given the worldwide trend of shrinking success rates of grants, this strategy is likely to become more and more common.

The range of funding sources which this strategy includes depends on the diversity of a research system's funding sources and on the researcher's research portfolio. Researchers in the Global South often find themselves in a situation where no national funding for research is available, so that donors from a Western country are the only source they can target (Ishengoma, 2017; Bradley, 2017, p. 57). This "donor-driven research" usually makes North–South collaborations a prerequisite for funding, adds an extra layer of agenda negotiations and "creates a problematic starting point for articulating common research goals" (Bradley, 2017, p. 47).

A major disadvantage of targeting any funding source is that the application of this strategy multiplies the time necessary for preparing grant proposals when there are many possible sources. Therefore, some researchers have been observed to only target an *"easy" source*. Researchers weigh up the estimated effort for grant writing and administration against the perceived likelihood of success and the size of the grants, and target only sources that promise "easy" money.

The strategy of targeting an *"appropriate" source* describes the attempt to find a close match between research content and funding sources by looking for a funding programme that fits the designed content. This strategy has been exemplified in studies of funding programmes with the purpose to promote unconventional research ("breakthrough research" or scientific innovation) that is important for the progress of a whole research field. These funding schemes differ from conventional schemes, as they are characterized by large and flexible budgets, long time horizons and risk-tolerant selection processes (Heinze, 2008; Laudel and Gläser, 2014). The most prominent example in that respect is the European Research Council's grant scheme. Similar schemes exist in many national research systems.[4]

Research aiming at scientific innovations is characterized by specific epistemic properties, such as a long duration of research processes (long *Eigentime*), high technical and strategic uncertainty, deviation from standards for the choice of problems, or methods (Laudel and Gläser, 2014). Researchers who plan to conduct this kind of research are likely to select "targeting an appropriate source" as a funding strategy, simply because this is often the only way they can get their research funded.

As this strategy is characterized by creating as much as possible a fit between research content and institutional form, it is less likely that researchers need to adapt their research than in the case of targeting easy sources or targeting all sources. However, researchers must be in a situation where they can afford this highly selective strategy.

Window dressing or symbolic compliance

Window dressing (Oliver, 1991, p. 154) or symbolic compliance (Leišytė, 2007) is a strategy which presents research as meeting a funding agency's expectations even if it does not (Barrier, 2014; Chubin and Hackett, 1990; Leišytė, 2007; Morris, 2003). For example, evolutionary biologists put their research into "a climate coat" or gave it a "clinical touch" (Morris, 2000, p. 433). This strategy largely depends on a funder's unwillingness or inability to conduct in-depth checks of actual compliance. This strategy is usually understood as a mere change of the representation of research that leaves the content of research completely unchanged. Still, it cannot be ruled out that subtle changes in the research occur.

Selling services

Some researchers were observed to secure funding by splitting their time and capacity to use some of it to sell services to external clients. They performed routine tasks for clients (industry, or other sponsors) and the money they received could be used to fund their research (Laudel, 2006, p. 495; Gläser et al., 2010, p. 307; Hessels et al., 2011, p. 562). Computer scientists in East Africa also depended on consultancy work for creating time and money to conduct research as well as to support their salaries (Harsh et al., 2018).

Utilizing a colleague's resources

If resources are not sufficient to fund all tasks of a research project, researchers may acquire the support of collaborators. Necessary contributions to a project for which no funding can be obtained are acquired from colleagues, and are usually "paid for" with co-authorships (or with a contribution to their project). This way, a research group can add a colleague's resources to its funding portfolio. For example, Australian researchers spent several months a year using better equipped laboratories overseas (Laudel, 2006, p. 495). Biologists in the UK used collaborations for "circumventing the problem of funding in-house expertise" (Morris, 2000, p. 441). Researchers in the nanosciences realize their research programmes as long-term collaborative endeavours in which they combine the capabilities to synthesize materials of one group with the measurement infrastructure (and skills) of one or more other groups (Ulnicane, 2014; see also Barrier, 2011, p. 523). This kind of "extended laboratory" seems to be very common in material science. Also, researchers in developing countries often rely on facilities of better equipped collaborators (Beaudry et al., 2018, pp. 79–80).

Participating in an acquisition coalition

The last resource acquisition strategy describes the collective action of researchers with the main aim of jointly acquiring funding. This strategy is a response to the increasing popularity of large inter- or transdisciplinary research networks, including "centres of excellence". In order to be eligible for these funding programmes, applicants must meet several formal criteria, which may include a minimum size, the participation of a minimum number of disciplines, or the participation of non-researchers. Examples include many EU funding programmes (e.g. the EU Flagship Programme) and national programmes for long-term funding like the German

DFG's funding programme for Collaborative Research Centres (*Sonderforschungsbereiche*) and the numerous collaborative funding schemes for "excellence" (Hellström et al., 2018; Borlaug and Langfeldt, 2020).

While grant-funded networks are often a necessary structure for collaborative, interdisciplinary or transdisciplinary research, they can also be targeted by coalitions of researchers who collectively apply window dressing, by exaggerating their collaboration and its benefits in order to access large amounts of long-term funding (Hessels and Kingstone, 2019).

Strategies of Resource Use

In the literature of organizational responses to their environment, *buffering* is described as a strategy to create reserves that can be used when resource supplies worsen. Buffering is a response to three processes. First, the increasing competition for funding reduces chances of success and increases the likelihood of periods of scarcity. Secondly, the shift from recurrent funding to competitive project funding comes with a loss of flexibility, because resources are provided only for specific projects. There is no slack funding (Hackett, 1987, p. 144). Thirdly, competitive funding usually requires researchers "to bring novel work to a fundable stage" without funding (Morris, 2000, p. 446), i.e. preliminary work is usually needed for grants to be successful.

Two forms of buffering can be distinguished (Gläser, 2019, p. 438). First, researchers *"hoard"*. Given the overall declining success rates of grant applications, a widespread practice seems to be to acquire as much money as possible for each project, sometimes by applying for several grants for the same project. This way researchers cope with cuts and the risk of failure.

A second practice is *"bootlegging"* (Hackett, 1987, p. 143), where researchers use resources for another purpose than they were originally dedicated for. Researchers' "bootlegging" has been frequently observed, e.g. for German and Australian physicists (Laudel, 2006, p. 496; Gläser et al., 2016), British bioscientists (Morris, 2003, p. 365), computer scientists in several African countries (Harsh et al., 2019, pp. 64–66) and US space scientists (Reinecke, 2021, pp. 18, 21).

Adapting the Content of Research

The strategies described so far have not directly touched a researcher's research portfolio but were aimed at acquiring and using resources for research that is left unchanged in terms of content. Researchers will usually try to use these strategies. However, if they are not successful, they "need to adapt their research content to anticipated or actual external expectations", in this case: expectations of funders (Gläser, 2019, p. 439). The adaptation of a research portfolio to the funding situation includes four strategic responses (Gläser et al., 2010, pp. 305–306):

- to drop "unfundable" research trails;
- to start "fundable" research trails;
- to avoid (and not start) research trails; or
- to change the direction of existing research trails to adapt them to funding opportunities.

These strategies were observed in Australian universities, where biologists avoided research projects which they considered "unfundable" in the national funding environment. Australian researchers in several fields moved towards more applied research and to the mainstream by dropping "unfundable" (basic) research trails and starting "fundable" research trails that were closer to applications or to the mainstream of their community (ibid., p. 307). Similarly, US biologists moved towards research with biomedical applications, as they could not acquire funding for their basic research (Hackett, 1987, p. 142).

If researchers have only one research trail, and if this research trail does not match the expectations of external funders, they may feel forced to change its content to achieve a match. This strategy is dangerous insofar as researchers might need to give up their own interests or start working on topics that are not relevant to their scientific communities (Gläser, 2019, p. 439). It is therefore more likely that researchers attempt to cope with the consequences of not receiving funding or not receiving the amount they need (Hackett, 1987, pp. 142–143). Such consequences include scarcity of resources and scarcity of time.

Indeed, this strategy has been frequently observed under conditions of scarcity (Gläser et al., 2010). It has been applied to both current research and to funding proposals. Researchers reduced their current research to the projects of graduate students they supervised because funding for these projects was guaranteed by the university. They stretched or "retarded" their research, either by temporarily abandoning it when there was no time or no funding, or by slowing it (Lange, 2007, pp. 166–167; Gläser et al., 2010, p. 307). Further, researchers reduced the empirical basis of their research by investigating fewer objects, conducting fewer experiments and applying fewer methods (e.g. biologists). Geologists selected cheaper and fewer sites for fieldwork, political scientists investigated fewer cases and conducted fewer interviews, historians visited fewer archives and spent less time there (Gläser et al., 2010, p. 309). Some of these adaptations are likely to have affected the quality of the research.

The prospective adaptation of research content to the perceived opportunities of funding them has also been observed. Researchers perceived peer review being biased towards mainstream and low-risk research, and responded accordingly by adapting their research proposals, e.g. by applying for low-risk research only (Hackett, 1987; Morris, 2000, pp. 445–446; Laudel, 2006, p. 497; Leišytė, 2007). Likewise, archaeologists in Finland adjusted their grant proposal by avoiding resource-intensive fieldwork-oriented research (Luukkonen and Thomas, 2016, p. 119).

Extreme forms of adaptations have been frequently observed for researchers in the Global South, where funders and research partners from the Global North often have a high degree of authority over research agendas and methodologies, up to the point where the researchers from the Global South end up doing merely consultancy work (Ishengoma, 2017; Bradley, 2017, p. 60). African biomedical researchers' task was reduced to supporting data collection (Connell et al., 2018, p. 48; Moyi Okwaro and Geissler, 2015). Drastic forms of changing research content were observed among donor-funded social scientists, who were asked to apply quantitative methods or move from studying gender into studying religious radicalization (Sabzalieva, 2020, p. 104).

IMPACT OF EPISTEMIC PROPERTIES OF FIELDS ON THE LIKELIHOOD OF FUNDING STRATEGIES

As stated before, researchers' responses to their funding situation depend on a whole range of factors. A condition that is often overlooked in empirical studies is the epistemic properties of the research for which funding is sought. These epistemic properties influence the repertoire

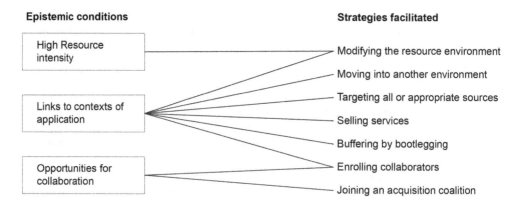

Epistemic conditions

- High Resource intensity
- Links to contexts of application
- Opportunities for collaboration

Strategies facilitated

- Modifying the resource environment
- Moving into another environment
- Targeting all or appropriate sources
- Selling services
- Buffering by bootlegging
- Enrolling collaborators
- Joining an acquisition coalition

Figure 16.2   Examples of epistemic conditions of research facilitating strategies for building funding portfolios

of responses available to a researcher (Gläser et al., 2010; Gläser, 2019, pp. 439–441). Given our meagre knowledge about researchers' responses to their funding situation, it is not surprising that we know even less about how these responses are modified by epistemic properties of research. Such influences can be elucidated by discussing three examples of epistemic conditions and their connection to funding strategies, about which at least some empirical knowledge exists (Figure 16.2).

There is no doubt that research processes differ with respect to their resource intensity, their links to application contexts and their collaboration intensity. Turning to resource intensity first, we can observe a spectrum from very low resource intensity of research that requires little more than the researcher's salary and library access, all the way through to the extremely high resource intensity of research that depends on investments in the hundreds of million euros. If the resource intensity of a research portfolio is low, it may be possible to sustain it without any external research funding. This has for example been observed for pure mathematics (Gläser and Laudel, 2007). In contrast, a high resource intensity of research forces researchers to acquire resources if they want to conduct this research. "Big science" research depends on the success of the scientific elite in influencing science policy, which in turn may depend on convincing the scientific community first. For example, the funding for the world's first X-ray free electron laser could be secured when several US physicists convinced their scientific communities of its usefulness, and science policy – the Department of Energy – to invest in it (Heinze and Hallonsten, 2017, p. 311). In a similar situation, gravitational wave researchers got very concerned about a claim by one of them to have discovered gravitational waves, because this claim endangered a campaign for funding for a large detection array for gravitational waves (Collins, 1999).

If research can be linked to contexts of application, modifying the resource environment by initiating new funding programmes is easier than in the case of basic research, because science policy is more likely to fund research that promises economic benefits (Hedgecoe, 2003; Ulnicane, Chapter 4 in this *Handbook*, on the EU policy's dominant frame of economic competitiveness which informs their funding policy). Researchers conducting applied research can move more easily into another environment through commercial activities and they can sell services and enrol collaborators, e.g. from industry. With an increasing interest of science policy in many countries in the funding of economically useful research, those who conduct this kind of research are able to target many more sources and have more chances of finding funding sources that match their research portfolio. Being able to tap into more funding sources as well as into sources with few or even no restrictions on use facilitates buffering by bootlegging.

Finally, in research fields with high collaboration intensity there are better chances of enrolling collaborators to compensate for missing funding. These fields also offer better chances for building an acquisition coalition.

CONSEQUENCES OF THE APPLICATION OF FUNDING STRATEGIES FOR THE CONTENT OF RESEARCH

The application of all funding strategies may alter the content of research. This is most obvious for strategies aimed at adapting the content of research to the available funding. However, the use of other strategies might also be accompanied by changes to the content of research. The strategy of modifying the resource environment by lobbying for the creation of funding programmes that match one's own research may not be completely successful, which means that research needs to be adapted to cope with the mismatch. Similarly, window dressing is intended to remain at the level of framing, but the different framing of research may have consequences for its content. Selling services takes time away from research, enrolling collaborators requires a consideration of their interests, and bootlegging may take resources away from other research projects. In all these cases, some adaptation of the content of research may occur.

The causal attribution of changes in research to the application of funding strategies is exceedingly difficult. As I already indicated, funding is an important but not the only condition of research. The effects of choosing funding strategies and of their success are overlaid by other factors that contribute to the situation of researchers. Causally attributing changes in research content to funding conditions requires consideration of these conditions of research.

Consequences for Research in General

Although we have far too little information about the consequences of the application of funding strategies for the conduct and content of research, three broad trends can be derived from empirical studies. First, most researchers see their research becoming increasingly precarious, because the competition for funding increases. Second, many researchers appear to be able to maintain their research by successfully applying the strategies described in the previous section. For example, little change of research agendas was found when researchers moved into an industrial environment by creating academic spin-offs (Shinn and Lamy, 2006; Zomer et al., 2010; Perkmann et al., 2013, pp. 428–429). However, indirect effects cannot be ruled out. For example, a scientist's research portfolio may change, because their greater awareness of practical problems makes them include more applied research. Other researchers also used funding opportunities to develop their research portfolios according to their own interests (Morris, 2000, p. 434).

Third, researchers are increasingly forced to respond to the growing competition for funding by turning to strategies that require changes in the conduct and content of research. The epistemic consequences of these strategies include a loss of epistemic diversity, risk avoidance and moves toward mainstream research or applied research. The "downgrading" also made research less valid and reliable (Morris, 2000; Gläser et al., 2010). Australian researchers who worked under conditions of considerable scarcity of funds were found to decelerate otherwise unchanged research, to gradually narrow their research portfolios and to limit data collection, thereby reducing the validity and reliability of research (Gläser et al., 2010, pp. 309–310). These effects are field-specific, i.e. they depend on the resource intensity and epistemic practices of fields in relation to properties of the resource environments (their diversity, richness and tolerance for certain topics) and strategies applied by researchers. Funding landscapes which favoured research that is relevant for the solution of societal problems made researchers move to more applied research, as they chose respective research problems or objects (Gläser et al., 2010, pp. 309–310; Blumenthal et al., 1996; Lam, 2010; Luukkonen and Thomas, 2016, p.120). Agricultural cell biologists, working in a scarce funding landscape, changed their topics towards human medical research (Hessels et al., 2011, p. 562).

Finally, many researchers in the Global South had to negotiate research agendas with multiple actors (Bradley, 2017) and often seem to have very limited authority over research goals and approaches (see Chapter 10 by Coburn et al. in this *Handbook*). Particularly in the biomedical sciences this led to the conduct of dependent research (Moyi Okwaro and Geissler, 2015).

Consequences for Scientific Innovations

An epistemic consequence that is rarely mentioned in the literature on research funding is the impact of changing funding conditions and researchers' strategies on opportunities to create and develop scientific innovations. To the extent to which such research requires stable funding, the uncertainties of grant funding tend to make scientific innovations less likely. Indeed, core institutional funding that could be flexibly used was found pivotal in developing innovations in nanotechnology and human genetics (Heinze et al., 2009, p. 618).

Funding agencies responded to the danger of crowding out innovations by creating specific schemes to promote "breakthrough research". These "excellence" schemes appear to be successful in that unconventional research ideas have actually been selected through peer review (Grant and Allen, 1999; Heinze, 2008; Lal et al., 2011; Luukkonen, 2012; Laudel and Gläser, 2014). They create new "appropriate sources" for researchers with unconventional ideas that require unconventional funding, and targeting these sources likely led to successful scientific innovations. However, a systematic study of the effects of such grants on the content of research is still lacking.

While appropriate for some kinds of scientific innovations, grants for "breakthrough research" still pose restrictions on the ways in which the money can be used, and may therefore not be appropriate for all research problems. In a study of Dutch elite researchers, Franssen et al. (2018) compared projects funded by grants for scientific innovations (grants of the European Research Council and other grants) to projects funded by an even less constraining source of funding, namely prizes. They found that researchers used the project grants for research that included high-risk elements but also tended to exploit discoveries previously made. In contrast, the prize funding allowed to deviate from epistemic and organizational standards: "The Spinoza prize in the humanities is used to create a network of scholars across Europe, as well as a digital infrastructure and a small local organization of mostly student-assistants to organize the network as well as the digital infrastructure. In the geosciences group a new tenure track researcher is hired who can enrich the research agenda of the group through her knowledge of genetics. In the mathematics group a new professor is hired who is able to create a more lively and vibrant academic community" (Franssen et al., 2018, p. 31).

Despite the rise of funding schemes for exceptional research and the availability of prizes (even if they are few), at least some scientific innovations are still developed with conventional three-year grants. This was studied in a large comparative project on national conditions for the development of scientific innovations. The three innovations studied included the experimental realization of Bose–Einstein–Condensation in physics, evolutionary-developmental biology (evo-devo) and international comparative large-scale assessment of student performance (ILSA) in educational science (Whitley et al., 2018). It turned out that the expected success of funding strategies played a major role in the researchers' decisions to develop an innovation. Innovations that required exceptional resources and a long time horizon were only taken up by those who believed they would be able to build this necessary protected space. Several physicists delayed their work on Bose–Einstein–Condensation because they lacked access to the necessary infrastructure or because they felt unable to compete with other groups because of insufficient access to resources. The physicists used funding by bootlegging money from other grants and they applied for new grants, usually from conventional grant schemes (see also Heinze et al., 2009, p. 618). The problem of short grant cycles could be overcome by applying for consecutive grants without being able to present substantial results. This practice needed to be tolerated by funding agencies, which some of them did even though the majority of the scientific community did not believe in the success of this research. Above-average governmental investments for evo-devo and for ILSA occurred in exceptional cases at non-university institutes in Germany and at universities in Switzerland. The support of basic research by research organizations and funding organizations has been crucial for two of the innovations, whereas the lack of it led to a nearly complete crowding out of evo-devo research in the Netherlands (Laudel and Weyer, 2014).

Again, it should be emphasized that the successful development of innovations was not an effect of national funding conditions only, but also depended on a variety of other conditions, including epistemic traditions in scientific communities, the structure of national career paths and practices of evaluations in universities.

CONCLUSIONS

The transition from exclusive block funding of universities and research organizations to a split funding mode of block funding and competitive grant funding forces most researchers to actively construct a match between resources – their funding portfolio – and their research portfolio. To do this, they employ strategies for changing their funding environment, acquiring resources, using resources, and adapting their research portfolios. While these strategies have been constructed as patterns of highly rational actions, this does not mean that the strategies are always applied consciously and based on rational considerations. On the contrary, the patterns identified in this chapter are likely to be habitually applied. Researchers might even be pressured by managers to apply particular strategies. In both cases, strategies may not match the situation researchers perceive.

The attempt to systematize funding strategies shows that we are still far away from a middle-range theory that links the macro-level of funding landscapes and policies to micro-level responses and their effects. Owing to the mostly descriptive nature of many studies, the causal mechanisms operating between the macro-level of funding, the researcher's strategic responses to them and changes in the content of research have not yet been identified. Building such a theory requires first and foremost systematic comparative research, i.e. research that is internationally comparative (in order to assess the impact of different funding and wider institutional environments), field-comparative (in order to assess the impact of different epistemic properties) and comparative in its approach to researchers' responses to their funding situation. These comparative studies should not be limited to the Global North, but should systematically include the extreme funding situations in the Global South.

Studies on academic entrepreneurship could make important contributions. So far, they usually neglect the overall research portfolio and situation of a researcher. If they would position a university researcher's entrepreneurial activities and the funding resulting from it into his or her overall research situation (including individual research and funding portfolios), then this could be another important source for empirical findings about the researchers' strategic responses.

The empirical search for these strategies requires adequate support by theoretical frameworks that capture researchers' specific situations and actions, and can be operationalized for empirical investigations. Concepts from organizational theory seem to be a good starting point, but need to be adapted to the specific nature of research. Ideally, research-specific theoretical concepts must guide empirical investigations instead of serving *ex post* as labels of inductively derived strategies. A concept that has proven useful in integrating these influences is that of "protected space". Protected space is the time horizon for which scientists can autonomously use a specific research capacity (human and material resources), including their own time, without hierarchical intervention and without reputational consequences that would endanger their future research (Whitley and Gläser, 2014, p. 8). Dimensions of protected space include discretion over resources, the time horizon of the protection and the thematic breadth that is protected. Researchers actively construct protected space by, among other things, applying the funding strategies discussed in this chapter.

Finally, the effects of researchers' responses to their funding situation can only be understood if funding is considered as just one condition among others that make up a researcher's overall situation. Analyses of funding strategies need to be theoretically and empirically embedded in the analysis of researchers' attempts to sustain their research under changing economic, institutional and epistemic conditions of research.

NOTES

1. I thank Jochen Gläser, Stefan Skupin, Duncan Thomas and the editors (particularly Ben Jongbloed) for their critical reading and insightful comments.
2. The funding configurations introduced by Thomas and Ramos-Vielba (Chapter 15 in this *Handbook*) don't appear to take potential funding sources (which are the target of funding strategies) into account.
3. Patenting would be another way of moving to an industrial resource environment to earn money for research. However, researchers have very little control over the distribution of revenues, and most patents do not lead to commercial success (Sampat, 2006; Mowery et al., 2001).
4. For example, in Germany (the Reinhart-Kosseleck grant), the US (the NIH Director's Pioneer Award), the Netherlands (the Vidi and Vici grants) and Austria (the START grant).

REFERENCES

Barrier, J. (2011). La science en projets: Financements sur projet, autonomie professionnelle et transformations du travail des chercheurs académiques. *Sociologie du travail, 53*(4), 515–536.

Barrier, J. (2014). Merger mania in science: Organizational restructuring and patterns of cooperation in an academic research centre. In R. Whitley, and J. Gläser (Eds.), *Organizational Transformation and Scientific Change: The Impact of Institutional Restructuring on Universities and Intellectual Innovation* (Vol. 42, pp. 141–172). Bingley: Emerald Group.

Beaudry, C., Mouton, J., and Prozesky, H. (2018). *The Next Generation of Scientists in Africa*. Cape Town: African Minds.

Blumenthal, D., Campbell, E. G., Causino, N., and Seashore, K. L. (1996). Participation of life-science faculty in research relationships with industry. *The New England Journal of Medicine, 335*(23), 1734–1739.

Borlaug, S. B., and Langfeldt, L. (2020). One model fits all? How centres of excellence affect research organisation and practices in the humanities. *Studies in Higher Education, 45*(8), 1746–1757.

Bradley, M. (2017). Whose agenda? Power, policies, and priorities in North–South research partnerships. In L. J. A. Mougeot (Ed.), *Putting Knowledge to Work: Collaborating, influencing and learning for international development* (pp. 37–69). Ottawa: Practical Action.

Braun, D. (1998). The role of funding agencies in the cognitive development of science. *Research Policy, 27*(8), 807–821.

Chubin, D. E., and Connolly, T. (1982). Research trails and science policies. In N. Elias, H. Martins, and R. Whitley (Eds.), *Scientific Establishments and Hierarchies* (pp. 293–311). Dordrecht: Reidel.

Chubin, D. E., and Hackett, E. J. (1990). *Peerless Science: Peer Review and U.S. Science Policy*. Albany, NY: State University of New York Press.

Collins, H. M. (1999). Tantalus and the aliens: Publications, audiences and the search for gravitational waves. *Social Studies of Science, 29*(2), 163–197.

Connell, R., Pearse, R., Collyer, F., Maia, J. M., and Morrell, R. (2018). Negotiating with the North: How Southern-tier intellectual workers deal with the global economy of knowledge. *The Sociological Review, 66*(1), 41–57.

Etzkowitz, H. (2003). Research groups as "quasi-firms": The invention of the entrepreneurial university. *Research Policy, 32*(1), 109–121.

Franssen, T., Scholten, W., Hessels, L. K., and de Rijcke, S. (2018). The drawbacks of project funding for epistemic innovation: Comparing institutional affordances and constraints of different types of research funding. *Minerva, 56*(1), 11–33.

Gläser, J. (2019). How can governance change research content? Linking science policy studies to the sociology of science. In D. Simon, S. Kuhlmann, J. Stamm, and W. Canzler (Eds.), *Handbook on Science and Public Policy* (pp. 419–447). Cheltenham: Edward Elgar.

Gläser, J., and Laudel, G. (2007). Evaluation without Evaluators: The impact of funding formulae on Australian University Research. In R. Whitley, and J. Gläser (Eds.), *The Changing Governance of the Sciences: The Advent of Research Evaluation Systems* (pp. 127–151). Dordrecht: Springer.

Gläser, J., Lange, S., Laudel, G., and Schimank, U. (2010). The limits of universality: How field-specific epistemic conditions affect authority relations and their consequences. In R. Whitley, J. Gläser, and L. Engwall (Eds.), *Reconfiguring Knowledge Production: Changing authority relationships in the sciences and their consequences for intellectual innovation* (pp. 291–324). Oxford: Oxford University Press.

Gläser, J., Laudel, G., and Lettkemann, E. (2016). Hidden in plain sight: The impact of generic governance on the emergence of research fields. In M. Merz and P. Sormani (Eds.), *The Local Configuration of New Research Fields* (Vol. 29, pp. 25–43). Heidelberg: Springer.

Gläser, J., Ash, M., Buenstorf, G., Hopf, D., Hubenschmid, L., Janßen, M., Laudel, G., Schimank, U., Stoll, M., Wilholt, T., Zechlin, L., and Lieb, K. (2022). The independence of research – a review of disciplinary perspectives and outline of interdisciplinary prospects. *Minerva, 60*(1), 105–138.

Grant, J., and Allen, L. (1999). Evaluating high risk research: an assessment of the Wellcome Trust's Sir Henry Wellcome Commemorative Awards for innovative research. *Research Evaluation, 8*(3), 201–204.

Hackett, E. J. (1987). Funding and academic research in the life sciences: Results of an exploratory study. *Science and Technology Studies*, 5(3/4), 134–147.

Hallonsten, O. (2014). How scientists may "benefit from the mess": A resource dependence perspective on individual organizing in contemporary science. *Social Science Information*, 53(3), 341–362.

Harsh, M., Bal, R., Wetmore, J., Zachary, G. P., and Holden, K. (2018). The rise of computing research in East Africa: The relationship between funding, capacity and research community in a nascent field. *Minerva*, 56(1), 35–58.

Harsh, M., Holden, K., Wetmore, J., Zachary, G. P., and Bal, R. (2019). Situating science in Africa: The dynamics of computing research in Nairobi and Kampala. *Social Studies of Science*, 49(1), 52–76.

Hedgecoe, A. M. (2003). Terminology and the construction of scientific disciplines: The case of pharmacogenomics. *Science, Technology and Human Values*, 28(4), 513–537.

Heinze, T. (2008). How to sponsor ground-breaking research: A comparison of funding schemes. *Science and Public Policy*, 35(5), 802–818.

Heinze, T., and Hallonsten, O. (2017). The reinvention of the SLACNational Accelerator Laboratory, 1992–2012. *History and Technology*, 33(3), 300–332.

Heinze, T., Shapira, P., Rogers, J. D., and Senker, J. M. (2009). Organizational and institutional influences on creativity in scientific research. *Research Policy*, 38, 610–623.

Hellström, T., Jabrane, L., and Brattström, E. (2018). Center of excellence funding: Connecting organizational capacities and epistemic effects. *Research Evaluation*, 27(2): 73–78.

Hessels, R. S., and Kingstone, A. (2019). Fake collaborations: Interdisciplinary science can undermine research integrity. Preprint. PsyArXiv. June 29. doi:10.31234/osf.io/rqwea

Hessels, L. K., Grin, J., and Smits, R. E. H. M. (2011). The effects of a changing institutional environment on academic research practices: Three cases from agricultural science. *Science and Public Policy*, 38(7), 555–568.

Ishengoma, J. M. (2017). North–South research collaborations and their impact on capacity building: A Southern perspective. In T. Halvorsen and J. Nossum (Eds.), *North–South Knowledge Networks: Towards Equitable Collaboration Between: Academics, Donors, and Universities* (pp. 149–186). Cape Town: African Minds.

Lal, B., Hughes, M. E., Shipp, S., Lee, E., C., Marshall Richards, A., and Zhu, A. (2011). *Outcome Evaluation of the National Institutes of Health (NIH) Director's Pioneer Award (NDPA), FY 2004–2005*. Retrieved from Washington: https://commonfund.nih.gov/sites/default/files/HRHR PA FY 2004–2005 Outcome Evaluation.pdf.

Lam, A. (2010). From "Ivory Tower Traditionalists" to "Entrepreneurial Scientists"? *Social Studies of Science*, 40(2), 307–340.

Lam, A., and de Campos, A. (2015). "Content to be sad" or "runaway apprentice"? The psychological contract and career agency of young scientists in the entrepreneurial university. *Human Relations*, 68(5), 811–841.

Lange, S. (2007). The basic state of research in Germany: Conditions of knowledge production pre-evaluation. In R. Whitley and J. Gläser (Eds.), *The Changing Governance of the Sciences* (Vol. 26, pp. 153–170). Dordrecht: Springer.

Laudel, G. (2006). The art of getting funded: How scientists adapt to their funding conditions. *Science and Public Policy*, 33(7), 489–504.

Laudel, G. and J. Gläser (2008). From apprentice to colleague: The metamorphosis of early career researchers. *Higher Education*, 55, 387–406.

Laudel, G., and Gläser, J. (2014). Beyond breakthrough research: Epistemic properties of research and their consequences for research funding. *Research Policy*, 43(7), 1204–1216.

Laudel, G., and Weyer, E. (2014). Where have all the scientists gone? Building research profiles at Dutch universities and its consequences for research. In R. Whitley and J. Gläser (Eds.), *Organizational Transformation and Scientific Change: The Impact of Institutional Restructuring on Universities and Intellectual Innovation* (Vol. 42, pp. 111–140). Bingley: Emerald Group.

Leišytė, L. (2007). *University Governance and Academic Research: Case Studies of Research Units in Dutch and English Universities*. Enschede: CHEPS, University of Twente.

Luukkonen, T. (2012). Conservatism and risk-taking in peer review: Emerging ERC practices. *Research Evaluation*, 21(1), 48–60.

Luukkonen, T., and Thomas, D. A. (2016). The "negotiated space" of university researchers' pursuit of a research agenda. *Minerva*, *54*(1), 99–127.

Meier, F., and Schimank, U. (2010). Mission now possible: Profile building and leadership in German universities. In R. Whitley, J. Gläser, and L. Engwall (Eds.), *Reconfiguring Knowledge Production: Changing Authority Relationships in the Sciences and their Consequences for Intellectual Innovation* (pp. 211–236). Oxford: Oxford University Press.

Morris, N. (2000). Science policy in action: Policy and the researcher. *Minerva*, *38*(4), 425–451.

Morris, N. (2003). Academic researchers as "agents" of science policy. *Science and Public Policy*, *30*(5), 359–370.

Mowery, D. C., Nelson, R. R., Sampat, B. N., and Ziedonis, A. A. (2001). The growth of patenting and licensing by U.S. universities: an asssessment of the effects of the Bayh–Dole Act of 1980. *Research Policy*, *30*, 99–119.

Moyi Okwaro, F., and Geissler, P. W. (2015). In/dependent collaborations: Perceptions and experiences of African scientists in transnational HIV research. *Medical Anthropology Quarterly*, *29*(4), 492–511.

Nilsson, A. S., Rickne, A., and Bengtsson, L. (2010). Transfer of academic research: Uncovering the grey zone. *The Journal of Technology Transfer*, *35*(6), 617–636.

O'Kane, C., Cunningham, J., Mangematin V., and O'Reilly, P. (2015). Underpinning strategic behaviours and posture of principal investigators in transition/uncertain environments. *Long Range Planning*, *48*(3), 200–214.

Oliver, C. (1991). Strategic responses to institutional processes. *Academy of Management Review*, *16*(1), 145–179.

Perkmann, M., Tartari, V., McKelvey, M., Autio, E., Broström, A., D'Este, P., Sobrero, M. (2013). Academic engagement and commercialisation: A review of the literature on university–industry relations. *Research Policy*, *42*(2), 423–442.

Pfeffer, J., and Salancik, G. R. (2003 [1978]). *The External Control of Organizations: A Resource Dependence Perspective*. Stanford, CA: Stanford University Press.

Reinecke, D. (2021). When funding fails: Planetary exploration at NASA in an era of austerity, 1967–1976. *Social Studies of Science*, *51*(5), 750–799. https://doi.org/10.1177/03063127211021913.

Rushforth, A., Franssen, T., and de Rijcke, S. (2019). Portfolios of worth: Capitalizing on basic and clinical problems in biomedical research groups. *Science, Technology, and Human Values*, *44*(2), 209–236.

Sabzalieva, E. (2020). Negotiating international research collaborations in Tajikistan. *Journal of Studies in International Education*, *24*(1), 97–112.

Sampat, B. N. (2006). Patenting and US academic research in the 20th century: The world before and after Bayh–Dole. *Research Policy*, *35*: 772–789.

Shinn, T., and Lamy, E. (2006). Paths of commercial knowledge: Forms and consequences of university–enterprise synergy in scientist-sponsored firms. *Research Policy*, *35*(10), 1465–1476.

Thompson, J. D. (1967). *Organizations in Action*. New York: McGraw Hill.

Ulnicane, I. (2014). Why do international research collaborations last? Virtuous circle of feedback loops, continuity and renewal. *Science and Public Policy*, *42*(4), 433–447.

Van den Daele, W., Krohn, W., and Weingart, P. (1977). The political direction of scientific development. In E. Mendelsohn, P. Weingart, and R. D. Whitley (Eds.), *The Social Production of Scientific Knowledge* (pp. 219–242). Dordrecht: Reidel.

van Lente, H., and Rip, A. (1998). The rise of membrane technology: From rhetorics to social reality. *Social Studies of Science*, *28*(2), 221–254.

Wallace, M. L., and Rafols, I. (2015). Research portfolio analysis in science policy: Moving from financial returns to societal benefits. *Minerva*, *53*(2), 89–115.

Weber, M. (1922 [2019]). *Economy and Society. I: A New Translation/Max Weber*, edited and translated by Keith Tribe. Cambridge, MA: Harvard University Press.

Weyer, E. (2018). *From Loose to Tight Management. Seeking Evidence of Archetype Change in Dutch and English Higher Education*. Wiesbaden: Springer.

Whitley, R. (2010). Reconfiguring the public sciences: The impact of governance changes on authority and innovation in public science systems. In R. Whitley, J. Gläser, and L. Engwall (Eds.), *Reconfiguring Knowledge Production: Changing Authority Relationships in the Sciences and their Consequences for Intellectual Innovation* (pp. 3–47). Oxford: Oxford University Press.

Whitley, R., and Gläser, J. (2014). Editor's introduction. In R. Whitley and J. Gläser (Eds.), *Organizational Transformation and Scientific Change: The Impact of Institutional Restructuring on Universities and Intellectual Innovation* (Vol. 42, pp. 1–15). Bingley: Emerald Group.

Whitley, R., Gläser, J., and Laudel, G. (2018). The impact of changing funding and authority relationships on scientific innovations. *Minerva, 56*(1), 109–134.

Zomer, A. H., Jongbloed, B. W. A., and Enders, J. (2010). Do spin-offs make the academics' heads spin? *Minerva, 48*(3), 331–353.

17. Gender and underrepresented minorities differences in research funding[1]

Laura Cruz-Castro, Donna K. Ginther and Luis Sanz-Menéndez

INTRODUCTION

This review is about the relationship between research funding allocation, gender and underrepresented minorities (URM). Research on gender and URM disparities in research funding is relevant as it speaks directly to the unexplained gaps in career advancement by illuminating potential effects of gender, race and ethnicity characteristics on productivity, reputation and compensation, offering potential explanations for the distribution of other types of organizational resources and career opportunities.

The allocation of research funding is generally performed by the funding bodies, and it has been traditionally expected to operate under some values and principles shared by the science community such as merit-based allocations and equity and not be based on any ascriptive feature of the individuals, like gender, race or ethnicity. Additionally, social and policy pressures for the adoption of other social values exist, such as gender and race equality, or more generally, the observation of non-discriminatory practices. Despite the abundant literature on gender inequality in academia (see Ceci et al. 2014 for a review) and much less regarding URM (National Center for Science and Engineering Statistics 2021; Bernard and Cooperdock 2018), research remains largely inconclusive as to whether disparities are mainly the result of structural differences, self-selection or the effect of different types or discrimination or bias during the review and allocation processes. We will argue that there are analytical gaps as well as methodological challenges that should be addressed in order to increase the robustness of research on this topic.

The scope of this review refers to the recent situation of research funding in various countries and agencies with a focus on gender and URM disparities. It also tries to assess the changing trends. We consider research funding allocation as a process and at each phase there are factors that lead to disparities in funding outcomes across groups. Adopting this type of dynamic perspective means that cumulative effects play a relevant role. We focus on grant funding and not on baseline funding allocated through, for instance, hiring. We do not cover issues related to how research funding supports careers since this is addressed in Melkers, Woolley and Kreth (Chapter 18 in this *Handbook*). Furthermore, given the complexity and specificity of research funding allocation practices across agencies and countries, their variations and their context dependent effects, we do not discuss funding agency policies designed to provide a more equitable allocation of funding.

GENDER AND RACE DIFFERENCES IN FUNDING

The allocation of research funding is a multistep and multi-actor process involving application, evaluation, allocation and funding outcomes. This chapter is organized to examine gender and URM differences at each stage of the funding process:

1. Do women or URM have a lower probability of applying for research grants from a competitive funding source? If so:
2. What are the factors that could account for a lower involvement in applications for funding?
3. Do women or URM have a lower probability of receiving a grant (or receiving less funding) from competitive funding sources? If so:
4. Are differences in outcomes mainly explained by merit or past performance differences between groups? Or could be they (partially) the effect of some implicit or explicit bias? If the latter is the case:
5. Does the peer review process account for the observed differences in outcomes?

Some research has shown that women and URM receive fewer research grants and less funding (see Bloch, Kladakis and Sørensen, Chapter 8 in this *Handbook* for an analysis of the equality implications of increased funding sizes), in comparison with the other groups, in individual funding agencies in specific fields and under different evaluation criteria (Sato et al. 2021 list a few for gender; Ginther et al. 2011; Hoppe et al. 2019; Erosheva et al. 2020). These disparities, if unrelated to past performance, may suggest the existence of bias.

Figure 17.1 uses data on research success rates by gender and country in Europe and the US in 2017. In only eight of the 26 comparisons do women have equal or higher success rates than men (shown with asterisks in the figure). Notably at the National Institutes of Health (NIH) in the US, women have success rates that are equal to men's and at the US National Science Foundation, women's success rates are higher. Women's success rates are also notably higher in smaller countries such as Bulgaria and Iceland. We cannot do this same kind of analysis by race because in many countries that data is not collected.

The main problem for the analysis of disparities is the identification of the causal mechanisms involved (Reskin 2003). Establishing that funding disparities are related to or are the result of previous differences, self-selection, segregated structures, discrimination practices or biased evaluations requires addressing the underlying mechanisms and moving into the sphere of available theories.

On the methodological side, most of the evidence in this domain is observational, and very few experimental or controlled field studies have been conducted. As we review the literature, we discuss the wide variety of methodologies used to analyse and explain gender, race, and ethnicity differences in research funding. Additionally, the majority of studies have important limitations regarding representativeness, generalizability or external validity as they generally analyse funding processes in a specific context or academic field. Since the funding contexts are very diverse, variation is inevitable but the lack of systematic reporting of the context makes the evidence partial and inconclusive even across studies addressing similar research questions.

In sum, most of the existing literature could be regarded as a series of informative independent studies where many of the potential explanations are related to the specific context of the observations.

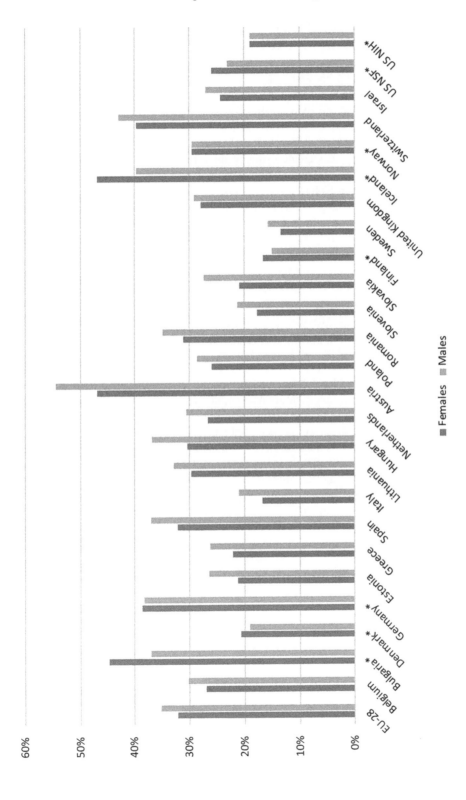

Figure 17.1   Success rates by gender in Europe and the US, 2017

THE EFFECTS OF PREVIOUS DIFFERENCES IN THE STRUCTURE OF OPPORTUNITIES FOR RESEARCH FUNDING

One implication of studying processes is that achievements such as research funding are not independent from other science outputs such as publications and work cumulatively. Merton acknowledged the Matthew effect (Merton 1968) where resources are more likely to flow to established scientists. Cumulative advantage (DiPrete and Eirich 2006) will also play a role in research funding.

Previously existing differences create different opportunity structures for various groups that affect the probabilities of grant application or success. The literature, especially regarding female underrepresentation in STEM careers, is abundant. In the study of gender and URM inequalities, the list of potential previous factors, structures and events that influence disparities in application and funding is long. Previous reviews have summarized some of the facts and theories regarding gender (e.g. Ceci and Williams 2011; Ceci et al. 2014; Williams and Ceci 2015; Kahn and Ginther 2018; Cruz-Castro and Sanz-Menéndez 2020).

Any serious analysis of funding disparities among social groups needs to take account of previous differences in merit or past performance including publications, citations and journal impact factors. The traditional empirical claim has been that men on average publish more papers and receive more citations than female scientists (Cole and Zuckerman 1984; Xie and Shauman 1998; van den Besselaar and Sandström 2016 among others). A trend towards closing the gap in citation and journal impact factor of publications has also been reported in the literature by Xie and Shauman (1998) and Bello and Galindo-Rueda (2020) as well as the finding that the productivity of both men and women increases with scientific rank. Ginther et al. (2018) found that Black investigators who applied for funding from the NIH published fewer papers in lower-impact journals than white investigators. Additional research finds that men typically get more credit for co-authored papers in tenure decisions (Sarsons 2017; Sarsons et al. 2021) and that women are held to higher standards when trying to publish in top journals (Hengel and Moon 2020; Card et al. 2020). Research also reports that in highly selective research institutions the relationship between gender and publications is relatively small for PhD students compared with faculty supervisors (Pezzoni et al. 2016).

Additionally, the gender gap in citations remains important, as well as the gaps in the elite ranges of performance (Aguinis et al. 2018). Recent research confirms that women authors have been persistently underrepresented in high-profile journals (Shen et al. 2018). According to Larivière and Sugimoto (2017) using Elsevier data, the average impact factors of journals for men and women are much closer to parity than citations and the gap in citations is much greater than the gap in impact factors that always favours men. Nevertheless, the Ceci et al. (2014) review of the research shows that women's average citations per publication are not different from men's.

The issue is then how much of the funding gap is explained by the publication and citation gaps. Some studies have shown that Black researchers publish less than white researchers, and this explains about half of the Black/white funding gap (Ginther et al. 2018).

Several explanations of the gender productivity gap have been proposed: cumulative disadvantage (Zuckerman 2001), career attrition (Huang et al. 2020), family formation (Long 1992; Symonds et al. 2006; Hunter and Leahey 2010), life choices and social pressures (Ceci and Williams 2011), lower specialization (Leahey 2006; Conti et al. 2014), access to resources

(Xie and Shauman 1998), and weaker collaboration and co-authoring networks (Mcdowell et al. 2006; Lee and Bozeman 2005; Ductor 2015; Elsevier 2018; Ginther et al. 2018).

We also need to pay attention to differences by URM and gender in factors that may represent more reputation than merit but that are used in practice in the funding evaluation: earlier grants, quality of networks, PhD granting institution, postdoctoral training, current academic status and employing institution. At the same time, many funding instruments have formal eligibility criteria or evaluation practices that have associations with academic status, because they are designed and targeted at researchers at specific career stages (Melkers, Woolley and Kreth, Chapter 18 in this *Handbook* review this type of career-oriented grants).

The distribution of groups across academic organizations by research intensity, reputation and resources is segregated. Women tend to work at universities with lower reputation, have more part-time jobs and focus more on teaching (Elsevier 2017; Gibney 2016) and service (Guarino and Borden 2017; Babcock et al. 2017). The US National Science Foundation (NSF) reports that, as of 2017, 37.8% of the academic doctoral workforce were female and 8.9% were URM. The share of tenured faculty at four-year universities is lower with 31.2% of tenured faculty being female and only 4% of tenured faculty being URM (National Science Foundation, National Center for Science and Engineering Statistics 2019).

Although the literature is dominated by case studies of the US, there is some research in European universities with results along the same lines. For instance, Conti and Visentin (2015) found that female PhDs are less likely than men to be employed in highly ranked universities in science and engineering in Sweden and Switzerland even after controlling for their research output. According to European Commission data, on average, only 7.4% of female academics in Europe hold the highest research position, compared with 16.7% for men (European Commission 2019). However, most of the measurements concerning the scarcity of women at the top of the academic and scientific hierarchy are cross-sectional and not longitudinal.

These systemic or structural differences accumulate and may result in lower productivity and impact and lower access to institutional resources (Holliday et al. 2015). The much-cited work of Xie and Shauman (1998) already highlighted that the primary factor affecting women scientists' research productivity was their overall structural position, such as institutional affiliation and rank; when type of institution, teaching load, funding level and research assistance were controlled for, the productivity gender gap disappeared. More recent evidence (Rørstad and Aksnes 2015) also stresses the importance of the academic position and availability of research funds. An important methodological consideration is that interaction effects with gender and URM are worth further examination. In the US, intersectionality is the interaction of racial and gender disadvantage, often referred to as the "double-bind". Ginther and Kahn (2013) found that women of colour do obtain tenure-track jobs, but they are more likely to be employed at minority-serving institutions.

APPLICATION BEHAVIOUR: DO WOMEN AND UNDERREPRESENTED MINORITIES APPLY LESS FOR FUNDING? IF SO, WHY?

Application behaviour is difficult to study.[2] Unfortunately, research funding agencies do not typically grant researchers access to individual-level application data. In the US, funding agencies provide aggregate data on applications in the form of "success rates" for women (e.g. the probability of receiving an award conditional on making an application). The NIH does not yet publish data on success rate by race/ethnicity.[3]

Any measure of the decision to apply depends on the number of women or URM researchers in a scientific field, whether the work requires funding, and the unobserved incentives (or lack thereof) to submit applications. A simple count of the number of women and URM employed in academia would over-estimate the applicant pool, making it difficult to evaluate whether there are gender and race/ethnicity differences in the propensity to apply.

Differences – at least the gender ones – are becoming smaller over time, but they are persistent (Ceci et al. 2014; Ceci and Williams 2011; Kahn and Ginther 2018). Regarding the causes, as noted by Stephan and El Ganainy (2007), there are structural factors that may result in women or URM being employed in non-research institutions (demand factors), as well as unobserved factors affecting supply (including attitudes towards competition, preferences about work–life balance, family variables).[4]

While many factors affect both men and women, some disproportionately stop women from making applications, especially if they are formalized in the eligibility criteria of the calls for proposals. For instance, rank or employment criteria established by research funders to define who can apply for research funding can produce a gender and URM disadvantage at the application stage because more women and URM are employed on fixed-term contracts, part-time posts and at lower academic ranks. British higher education survey data (Blake and La Valle 2000) showed that women were less likely than men to be eligible for the grants owing to their type of employment. They also found that men were more likely to apply as principal investigator than women, a result that could be explained by differences in seniority. Interestingly, women were more likely than men to have applied for their salary to be paid by the grant, which suggests a higher representation of women in non-permanent posts. In sum, many of the gender differences in application behaviour identified in the survey were rooted in higher education institutions' employment practices. Another example is the geographical mobility requirement of some European early and mid-career grants which may disadvantage women given their lower propensity to international mobility (Guthrie et al. 2017; Shauman and Xie 1996).

Unobserved self-selection also plays a role. Self-selection means that not everyone in the population of researchers who is eligible to apply for funding does so. In the case of women, mechanisms identified in the literature include: "shying away from competition" (Niederle and Vesterlund 2007), being more responsive to negative feedback (Kugler et al. 2017), being more shaped by "previous rejection experiences" (Brands and Fernandez-Mateo 2017; Ginther, Kahn and Schaffer 2016), and being more affected by "unprofessional reviews" (Silbiger and Stubler 2019 also for URM). However, Ley and Hamilton (2008) data suggest that a large fraction of female biomedical scientists choose to leave US NIH-funded career pipeline at the transition to independence from late postdoctoral to faculty position or early faculty years. Since men and women have near-equal NIH funding success at all stages of their careers, it is very unlikely that female attrition is due to negative selection from NIH grant-funding decisions. Hosek et al. (2005) and Pohlhaus et al. (2011) also found a gender gap in subsequent application rates, especially for NIH Type 2 awards.

We must acknowledge that the literature reports contradictory findings and is rather inconclusive about the causes of differences in application. One reason for this lack of robustness is that studies seldom take feedback dynamics into account. An exception is the study of Bol et al. (2018) in which they analyse recent PhD grant proposal submissions and find that early funding introduces a growing funding gap in favour of winners over the following eight years. They conclude that the emergent funding gap is partly created by applicants, who after failing to get one grant, apply for another less often. Application behaviour could also be conditional on the information about the level of competition in previous rounds, and the pressures that researchers face in their own institutions to get funding.

Funding Disparities: Diverse Approaches, Divergent Findings

The empirical literature addressing funding disparities is mostly focused on research funding of individual grants; this is partly explained because it is easier in econometric models to test the explanatory power of individual variables such as race, gender and age to determine whether these factors "explain" the funding outcome. Team science (instrumented by other type of grants) makes the study of inequality much more complex.

Data on the distribution of federal research funding in the US and EU

Existing research could be organized according to the methodology used. First, there is some descriptive evidence of the differences by gender and race in funding outcomes and more recently success rates (see for example, NIH Reporter). This approach has been used by the funding agencies but also in some academic literature. This type of study does not generally account for differences in individual productivity, institutional affiliation or previous funding.

We add to this literature in two ways. First, we use data from the European Research Council (ERC), the NSF and the NIH to show applications and awards by gender and a broad field including life (biomedical) science, physical sciences and engineering, and social, behavioural and economic sciences and humanities. Figure 17.2 shows trends in the number of applications and awards to the ERC from 2014 to 2019 by broad field. In both life science and social science and humanities the share of female applicants increased each year. In contrast, applications from women in physical sciences and engineering were flat in the past few years, but the share of awards for female applicants was higher especially by 2019. The share of awards was lower in the life sciences than the share of applications, but higher for the years of 2017 and 2018 in social sciences and humanities.

We performed the same analysis using data from the US NIH and NSF. Life sciences are proxied by NIH funding to biomedical researchers. Our measure of physical sciences and engineering in the US is the sum of total applications and awards (and those by gender) across the NSF's Computer and Information Sciences and Engineering, Engineering, Geoscience, and Mathematics and Physical Science Directorates. The measure of social sciences comes from the Social, Behavioural and Economic Sciences Directorate at NSF. Figure 17.3 shows trends in applications and awards in the US. These data show relative parity or a female advantage in research funding at the NIH and NSF. Women make up larger shares of applicants and awards at NIH, and as of 2019 receive the same share of awards as applications (34%). Applications by females in physical science and engineering at the NSF have been flat at between 18 and 19%; however the share of females receiving awards has exceeded the share of applicants for every year. Females as a share of applicants in social and behavioural science at NSF have trended downward from a peak of 35% in 2016. However, the share of female grantees exceeded the share of applicants for every year except one.

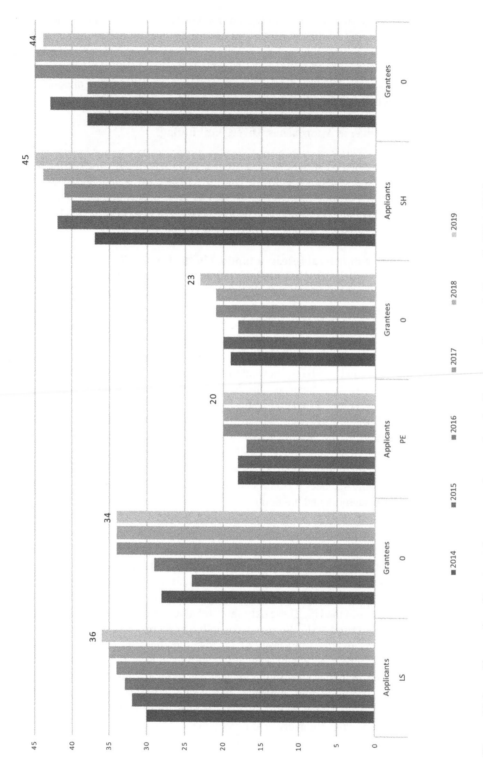

Figure 17.2   Share of applicants and grantees who are female, European Research Council, 2014–2019

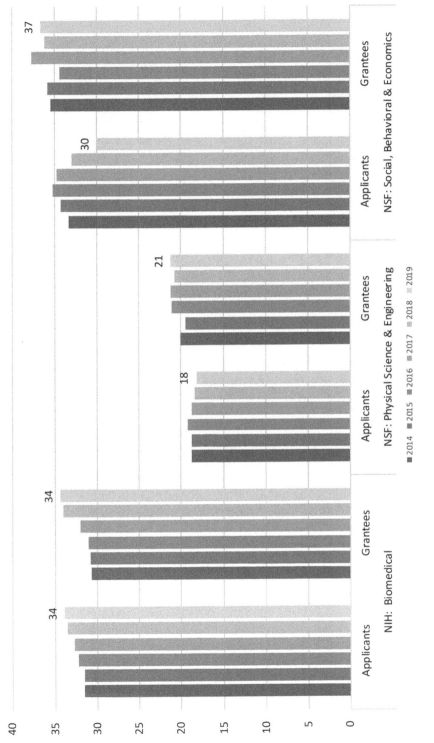

Figure 17.3   Share of applicants and grantees who are female by broad field, National Institutes of Health and National Science Foundation 2014–2019

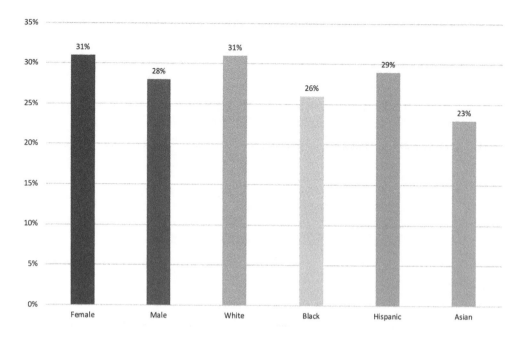

Figure 17.4   NSF funding rates by demographic group, fiscal year (FY) 2019

Finally, Figure 17.4 compares funding rates by gender and race/ethnicity. It shows that women are 3 percentage points more likely to receive NSF funding than men. White and Hispanic researchers have higher funding rates (31 and 29% respectively) than Black (26%) and Asian (23%) researchers.

Why do the numbers from the ERC, NIH and NSF differ so much from the data by country that we showed in Figure 17.1? First, it could be that the various funding mechanisms within each country differ significantly, thus creating disadvantages for women. For example, the success rates vary dramatically across countries with places like Austria, Iceland and Switzerland funding over 40% of proposals. The correlation between the average success rate in the country and the difference in the female–male success rate is 0.29, indicating that as success rates increase the female–male gap falls. Second, the ERC, NIH and NSF are highly competitive research funders. As a result, the women who apply to these funders may be positively selected, especially in fields where women are relatively underrepresented such as physical sciences and engineering. Third, the trends at ERC, NIH and NSF suggest that women's funding success has improved over time. Thus, data from 2017 across these countries may not reflect the progress that women have continued to make.

From data to explanation gender
There is a second type of observational evidence that includes some correlational and causality approaches. This is the type of evidence that is dominant in the academic literature. Most empirical studies of this type include some characteristics of the applicants that in the best cases also incorporate some indicators of merit or performance; however, this research is rather fragmented and with findings in opposite directions. Some studies have reported lower evaluation scores for female applicants even when accounting for relevant factors

related to productivity, seniority or discipline. The seminal papers of Wennerås and Wold (1997), Tamblyn et al. (2018) and Bornmann et al. (2007) can be cited. On the contrary, other research has argued for the absence of a gender effect in the review (Warner et al. 2016; Marsh et al. 2009; Ginther et al. 2016). Replicating the Wennerås and Wold study a decade later, Sandström and Hallsten (2008) found nepotism but not gender bias.

In a meta-analysis of 21 studies of funding success rates, Bornmann et al. (2007) found that although the estimates of the gender effect varied substantially from study to study, among grant applicants, men had statistically significant greater odds of receiving grants than women by about 7%. Van der Lee and Ellemers (2015a,b) found that gender disparities were most prevalent in scientific disciplines with the highest number of applications and with equal gender distribution among the applicants (i.e. life sciences and social sciences), but when this was controlled for, the data no longer supported the gender gap (Volker and Steenbeek 2015). Methodologically, this is an example of how disregarding an exogenous variable can produce a statistical artefact. Stratifying datasets according to key variables like application rate, academic rank or scientific field (Sato et al. 2021) may yield more robust results.

In the US, Hosek et al. (2005) using data from three federal agencies (NSF, NIH and US Department of Agriculture) found no gender differences in federal grant funding outcomes when they adjusted for other characteristics of applicants, including the researcher's discipline, institution, experience, and past research output. They found, however, a gender gap in the average amount of funding that females received relative to their male counterparts; they also reported a gender gap in subsequent application rates. The most recent evidence of the NIH shows that gender differences in the size of grants awarded to comparable first-time female and male principal investigators exist, also if one looks at top research institutions only. In most grant types, men get more than women, but for R01 grants (the most frequent award), women receive larger grants (Oliveira et al. 2019). Other research showed that success chances were not significantly different after controlling for productivity (Boyle et al. 2015). Part of the inconclusiveness of the literature relates to how applicants' productivity is measured in empirical research, the variety of bibliometric measures used and how to account for differences in application behaviour.

From data to explanation URM
There is limited but growing research on race/ethnicity differences in research funding. The paucity of this research can be linked to lack of access to administrative data on grant applications that identify the race/ethnicity of applicants. Race and ethnicity are not measured as part of the application process outside of the US. As a result, all of this research has been conducted in collaboration with staff at the NIH. Ginther et al. (2011) found that Black researchers were one-third as likely to receive NIH funding as white applicants after controlling for employer characteristics, previous research funding and publications. Ginther et al. (2012) found that Black MDs at medical schools were not disadvantaged in NIH funding after controlling for whether the applications included human subjects. There is only one paper on potential intersectional disadvantages in research funding. Ginther et al. (2016) found that women of colour did not experience a double bind, and that white women were somewhat more likely to receive NIH funding that white men. Ginther et al. (2018) used improved measures of publications and bibliometrics to show that half of the Black–white NIH funding gap could be explained by lower publication rates by Black researchers. This work was revisited using a new sample of NIH data. Hoppe et al. (2019) found that topic choice alone accounted for over 20% of the

funding gap between African American/Black (AA/B) scientists relative to white scientists in NIH R01 after controlling for multiple variables, including the applicant's prior achievements. However, after controlling for funding rates at NIH institutes or centres, topic choice no longer explains the funding gap between AA/B scientists (Lauer et al. 2021).

Finally, there is a third type of evidence emerging from experimental, quasi-experimental, field or controlled experiments usually linked to test causality approaches in evaluation contexts. However, most of this literature is not about research funding, but about hiring or more generally research evaluation. An exception is the recent study of Forscher et al. (2019) where the applicant's gender and race were manipulated in a simulation of an actual grant evaluation process and found no effect of gender or race in the review.

The Role of the Evaluation Processes

In an interesting review, Heilman (2001) identified a number of organizational conditions that may contribute to the undervaluation of women and URM performance: first, ambiguity in evaluation criteria that may introduce bias to fit preconceived ideas about capacity and performance; second, the lack of structure in evaluation and decision-making processes; third, ambiguity about the source of successful performance – for example, when science is produced by teams it may distort the contributions of individual scientists (de Fontenay et al. 2018); and fourth, ambiguity about the reasons for past success where diversity programmes may have unintended consequences in terms of perception of preferential treatment along the career.

Peer review as a context-specific process

In addition to the methodological differences in previous research, there are "contextual" factors that should be reported to have a better assessment of findings and claims of research about the uses of peer review for funding allocation; in exploring causality, similar factors, in different contexts, could produce diverse outcomes.

Peer review in funding agencies is not homogenous and it does not have standardized criteria and processes all over the world (Langfeldt et al. 2020), despite the existence of "manuals" or handbooks (Moghissi et al. 2013). Therefore, most analyses could be treated as case studies that provide some evidence but may not have external validity.

At the same time, reviewers report different preferences about the merit criteria in evaluations (Cruz-Castro and Sanz-Menéndez 2021), and they may have different or inconsistent views regarding what constitutes individual "merit" or "research quality" (Pier et al. 2018), or how to address the matching between the definition of "worth" of the specific calls of the funding agencies and their own criteria. Moreover, funding agencies sometimes include policy goals that may interfere with the objective of funding solely on the basis of merit and scientific quality potentially introducing biases in the review process (Costello 2010).

The amount of time for decision making and the available information are relevant contextual factors. It is known that reviewers, who operate under time limitations, use cognitive shortcuts (bibliometrics, "reputation" signals like the PhD-granting or employing university, quality of networks and previous grants, for example).

The evaluation design (individual reviews, panels, commissions) may involve problems of aggregation. If the review is made based on single evaluators, and there is only a pair who deal independently with each proposal, there is more room for potential bias in the outcome, resulting from a kind of series of measurement errors. The role of peer review and administrative discretion in the funding agencies (Ginther and Heggeness 2020; Goldstein and Kearney 2016) and whether different phases of the evaluation involve different or the same reviewers are also relevant.

In sum, each peer review occurs somehow on a case-by-case basis where each aspect will produce various degrees of influence within every funding context. When addressing the possible factors involved in evaluation bias, the literature has addressed various relevant factors: some are related to panel composition (social dynamics); others to evaluation tools, procedures, and criteria (evaluation methods); and a third type of factors refers to cognitive mechanisms, mainly stereotypes.

The effects of panel composition: who evaluates and who decides

Most empirical evidence about the impact of reviewers' gender on differential evaluation by gender has found no significant effect (Bornmann et al. 2007; Marsh et al. 2009, 2011). For instance, Mutz et al. (2012) evaluated the grant peer review process at the Austrian Science Fund with respect to gender over 10 years (8,496 research proposals across all disciplines, rated by more than 18,000 reviewers in almost 24,000 reviews) and found no effect of the gender of applicants and reviewers.

Likewise, based on 10,023 reviews by 6,233 external assessors of 2,331 proposals from social science, humanities and science disciplines, Marsh et al. (2011) found, moreover, that these non-effects of gender generalized over reviewer's gender (contrary to a matching hypothesis), discipline, reviewers chosen by the researchers themselves compared with those chosen by the funding agency, and country of the reviewers. From the side of the funding agencies, statistics collected by the ERC found no correlation between the percentage of women on its evaluation panels and female success rates (Vernos 2013).

Years ago, based on reviews of around 15,000 grant proposals to the economics programme of the National Science Foundation, Broder (1993) presented evidence of significant differences in the reviewing of female and male authors by male and female referees but in the opposite direction. Even when author quality was controlled for by comparing ratings on the same proposal, female reviewers rated female-authored proposals lower than did their male colleagues while no gender differences in the review of male proposals was observed.

Social connections have also been shown to play a role. A study recently reported in *Nature* news (Singh Chawla 2019) examined more than 38,000 reviews from nearly 13,000 Swiss National Science Foundation proposals by about 27,000 peer reviewers from all disciplines between 2006 and 2016. The findings were that reviewers nominated by applicants were more likely to give these applicants higher evaluation scores than referees chosen by the Swiss National Science Foundation (Severin et al. 2020). However, not all agencies allow for suggesting or vetoing application reviewers.

Peer review evaluation methods

In peer review panels, bibliometrics and impact factors are often used as a proxy for excellence, quality, and ability. For some, these metrics are gender-blind but some case studies have argued that the use of this type of indicators widen the gender gap in research performance (Nielsen 2017, 2018). Furthermore, Eyre-Walker and Stoletzki (2013) consider the IF a poor measure of merit.

The degree to which the evaluation focuses on candidates or proposals (or both) and in what order have additional explanatory power. An experiment-based paper found that gender gaps in grant funding were attributable to less favourable assessments of women as principal investigators, not of the quality of their proposed research (Witteman et al. 2019 in their study of the Canadian Institutes of Health Research). Van der Lee and Ellemers (2015a) found similar results in their study of research funding in the Netherlands. However, an analysis of the peer review reports of the ERC starting grants showed that when both the CV and the proposal are assessed without blinding, a high level of correlation between both marks was found (Van den Besselaar and Moom 2020).

The literature also shows that the transparency, clarity and wording of the reviews may have a negative impact on gender differences in the award rates (Magua et al. 2017; Kaatz et al. 2015). Even the type of scales can produce a gendered impact as some numbers may convey symbolic value, with females getting lower scores in 10-point scales than in six-point scales (Rivera and Tilcsik 2019).

The evidence has found little evidence of the impact of blinded peer review on grant application funding (Tricco et al. 2017). However, Kolev et al. (2019) found that women were disadvantaged in anonymized reviews. In response to the race/ethnicity differences in NIH funding, the Centre for Scientific Review conducted an anonymization study. Nakamura et al. (2021) found that anonymization did not affect scores received by Black applicants but slightly worsened the scores for white applicants. Furthermore, anonymization did not prevent reviewers from identifying 20% of the investigators.

The amount of information available to the panels, the formalization of evaluation criteria and timeframe in funding organizations may leave more (or less) room for the activation preconceived stereotypes about differences in performance and quality.

Cognitive factors and stereotyping

One of the sources of bias in judgements is stereotyping. Stereotyping is a cognitive shortcut. When processing information, individuals tend to consider observations that match their stereotypical expectations as more reliable and informative than counter-stereotypical observations (Ellemers 2018).

Most of the evidence on the topic of stereotyping is experimental and although we have not found much specific research related to funding evaluations, findings in related areas provide some useful insights. Heilman (2012) acknowledges that in the vast majority of studies on gender stereotypes no differences have been found in the reactions between female and male respondents; a possible explanation is that stereotypes are widespread in society and affect both men and women alike.

Using an experimental design, Carli et al. (2016) found that the higher the proportion of women in a scientific field, the more similar the stereotypes in that field were to stereotypes about women. Their results were congruent with theories that report incompatibility of female gender stereotypes with stereotypes about high-status occupational roles, since women were perceived to lack the qualities needed to be successful scientists. These qualities include a number of agentic traits related to assertiveness, independence, competency and leadership. Organizational interventions to prevent gender and URM bias arising from stereotypes are mostly centred on raising awareness, and also on the provision of information to forestall the use of expectations to "fill in the blanks", but generally no impact analyses have been conducted or published.

CONCLUSION

Our analysis of recent data from the US and Europe shows a different picture than the one painted by the literature. Women have made progress in terms of applications and awards on both sides of the Atlantic, especially at the most competitive funding agencies: the ERC, NIH and NSF. Women have greater funding success at the US NSF than men using the most recent year of data available. Our data also show that there is a race/ethnicity gap in research funding. Even an impressionistic comparison of the amount of literature that claims that gender bias exists and persists with the literature that claims that it is diminishing or disappearing makes clear the division. However, it is important is to pay attention to rival explanations of gender gaps and be careful with inferring processes from outcomes. Ceci et al. (2014) published an overview of the empirical evidence up to then about gender bias in science. In their view the unequal position of women in science would be based on quality differences which are partly the product of women's own career choices and partly the product of discriminatory arrangements not in science but in society at large. The data we have presented in this chapter support that view.

Although the argument that gender gaps in career advancement are mainly explained by differential performance and previous career choices may be analytically appealing, there is also evidence that the higher we go in the academic hierarchy, the more difficult is to disentangle performance and career differences from other factors that impede women's entry into the most elite ranks. In an recent paper, Treviño et al. (2018) analyse differential appointments by gender to the rank of named professorships in a sample of over 500 management professors at tier 1 American research universities, and found adverse gender effects after controlling for performance.

The literature has yielded heterogeneous results and whereas some show clear effects of the various potential sources of bias, others find only moderate or weak effects. The lack of common definitions, samples and methods is the most likely explanation of such heterogeneity. In order to test causality of gender or institutional bias, the literature has increasingly introduced measures of performance into the analyses, and it is slowly adopting experimental approaches based on randomized control trials. In terms of methodology, we have identified a need for more conceptual precision, the introduction of funding agency contextual factors, the stratification of samples, common measures of individual productivity, longitudinal analysis and feedback dynamics.

Underscoring all of this contradictory evidence is a lack of clear data on the potential applicant pool, applications and awards by gender and race/ethnicity. Science funding agencies allocate public money to create the public good of scientific discovery. In this era of heightened awareness of gender and race/ethnicity disparities in socioeconomic outcomes, reporting research funding allocations by demographic characteristics is essential.

Research universities collect data on research funding at the individual level; making this data available for research purposes would be an important advance in data availability. The Institute for Research on Innovation and Science (IRIS) at the University of Michigan curates the UMETRICS data. IRIS is a consortium of over 30 research universities in the US that share administrative data on research awards and expenditures. The UMETRICS data has been used to track the impact of expenditures on research, publications, patents, and careers. However, it is missing information on the application process. The ERC does not allow access to its administrative funding data, and there are higher barriers to accessing personal data across the

European Union. In the US, the NIH has allowed selective access to its administrative data for research purposes (e.g. Ginther et al. 2011). In contrast, the NSF has not made its administrative data available to researchers. Placing NIH and NSF data in the Federal Research Data Center network would jump-start fundamental research on gender, race and ethnicity differences in research funding. Access to high-quality administrative data would allow for improved methodological approaches to understanding these differences in research funding.

There is an ongoing debate in science policy about inequality in the distribution of resources that links with a broader discussion on the relationship between excellence, merit, equity and equality (Hicks and Katz 2011). Equality is a public value, that is far from being a universally consensual one (see Bozeman, Chapter 2 in this *Handbook* for an analysis of the relationship between public funding and public values). Equality is not a predominant norm in the distribution of rewards within the science system. The political and policy systems often introduce the equity dimension in the distribution of resources.

Different research funding organizations may have different values, depending on their mission, and national research councils, private foundations or state agencies may have their own policy objectives which may be more or less aligned with the scientific communities' norms and practices. Funders have latitude in how they allocate resources. A main policy implication is that a variety of funding agencies may be better equipped to address some of the pending challenges highlighted in the chapters of this volume dealing with the individual level. When resources are concentrated in a single source, that funder may have less flexibility in allocating resources more broadly.

We began this review by noting that much of the literature was a series of informative independent studies where many of the potential explanations depend upon the context. Future research should attempt to move beyond description towards explanation. Doing so will require access to information on grant applications as well as awards. Furthermore, researchers are only scratching the surface about the role of peer review in research funding allocations. To the extent that we continue to observe gender and race/ethnicity differences in research funding, a deeper understanding of peer review is warranted.

NOTES

1.   This research was funded by EU H2020 GA-824574 awarded to Cruz-Castro and Sanz-Menéndez. It was also funded by NSF grant SES-1538797 to Ginther. We thank the editors, Julia Melkers and the participants in the EU-SPRI 2021 session for comments and suggestions to an earlier version.
2.   Laudel, Chapter 16 in this *Handbook* contributes with an analytical exercise on the classification of the researchers' strategies to acquire research funding resources.
3.   The NIH Advisory Committee to the Director Working Group on Diversity in 2021 recommended that the NIH report NIH funding success rates by race/ethnicity. https://acd.od.nih.gov/documents/presentations/02262021Diversity.pdf. The National Science Foundation is required by law to report on women, minorities, and persons with disabilities in science https://ncses.nsf.gov/pubs/nsf21321/.
4.   In 2010, the European Research Council increased the window of grant eligibility for applicants with children; the number of female applicants increased, as did the number of male applicants, so the gap did not narrow, a finding which suggests that gender-neutral policies may have unintended effects.

REFERENCES

Aguinis, H., Ji, Y. H., and Joo, H. (2018). Gender productivity gap among star performers in STEM and other scientific fields. *Journal of Applied Psychology*, July 19, 1–24. https://doi.org/10.1037/apl0000331.

Babcock, L., Recalde, M. P., Vesterlund, L., and Weingart, L. (2017). Gender differences in accepting and receiving requests for tasks with low promotability. *American Economic Review*, *107*(3), 714–747. https://doi.org/10.1257/aer.20141734.

Bello, M., and Galindo-Rueda, F. (2020). *The 2018 OECD International Survey of Scientific Authors*. OECD Science, Technology and Industry Working Papers 4/2020 https://doi.org/10.1787/18d3bf19 -en.

Bernard, R. E., and Cooperdock, E. H. G. (2018). No progress on diversity in 40 years. *Nature Geoscience*, *11*(5), 292–295. https://doi.org/10.1038/s41561-018-0116-6.

Blake, M., and La Valle, I. (2000). *Who Applies for Research Funding?* Wellcome Trust. https://wellcomecollection.org/works/qctj6ypv.

Bol, T., Vaan, M. de, and Rijt, A. van de. (2018). The Matthew effect in science funding. *Proceedings of the National Academy of Sciences*, *115*(19), 4887–4890. https://doi.org/10.1073/pnas.1719557115.

Bornmann, L., Mutz, R., and Daniel, H. (2007). Gender differences in grant peer review: A meta-analysis. *Journal of Informetrics*, *1*(3), 226–238. https://doi.org/10.1016/j.joi.2007.03.001.

Boyle, P., Smith, L., Cooper, N., Williams, K., and O'Connor, H. (2015). Women are funded more fairly in social science. *Nature*, *525*. https://doi.org/10.1038/525181a.

Brands, R. A., and Fernandez-Mateo, I. (2017). Leaning out: How negative recruitment experiences shape women's decisions to compete for executive roles. *Administrative Science Quarterly*, *62*(3), 405–442. https://doi.org/10.1177/0001839216682728.

Broder, I. E. (1993). Review of NSF economics proposals: Gender and institutional patterns. *The American Economic Review*, *83*(4), 964–970.

Card, D., DellaVigna, S., Funk, P., and Iriberri, N. (2020). Are referees and editors in economics gender neutral? *The Quarterly Journal of Economics*, *135*(1), 269–327. https://doi.org/10.1093/qje/qjz035.

Carli, L. L., Alawa, L., Lee, Y., Zhao, B., and Kim, E. (2016). Stereotypes about gender and science: Women ≠ scientists. *Psychology of Women Quarterly*, *40*(2), 244–260. https://doi.org/10.1177/0361684315622645.

Ceci, S. J., and Williams, W. M. (2011). Understanding current causes of women's underrepresentation in science. *Proceedings of the National Academy of Sciences*, *108*(8), 3157–3162. https://doi.org/10.1073/pnas.1014871108.

Ceci, S. J., Ginther, D. K., Kahn, S., and Williams, W. M. (2014). Women in academic science: A changing landscape. *Psychological Science in the Public Interest*. https://doi.org/10.1177/1529100614541236.

Cole, J., and Zuckerman, H. (1984). The productivity puzzle: Persistence and change in patterns of publication of men and women scientists. *Advances in Motivation and Achievement*, *2*, 217–258.

Conti, A., and Visentin, F. (2015). Science and engineering Ph.D. students' career outcomes, by gender. *PLoS One*, *10*(8), e0133177. https://doi.org/10.1371/journal.pone.0133177.

Conti, A., Denas, O., and Visentin, F. (2014). Knowledge Specialization in Ph.D. Student Groups. *IEEE Transactions on Engineering Management*, *61*(1), 52–67. https://doi.org/10.1109/TEM.2013 .2283039.

Costello, L. C. (2010). Perspective: Is NIH funding the "best science by the best scientists"? A critique of the NIH R01 research grant review policies. *Academic Medicine*, *85*(5), 775–779. https://doi.org/10.1097/ACM.0b013e3181d74256.

Cruz-Castro, L., and Sanz-Menéndez, L. (2020). *Grant Allocation Disparities from a Gender Perspective: Literature Review. Synthesis Report*. https://doi.org/10.20350/digitalCSIC/10548.

Cruz-Castro, L., and Sanz-Menéndez, L. (2021). What should be rewarded? Gender and evaluation criteria for tenure and promotion. *Journal of Informetrics*, *15*(3), 101196. https://doi.org/10.1016/j.joi .2021.101196.

de Fontenay, C., Lim, K., Snashall-Woodhams, N., and Basov, S. (2018). *Team Size, Noisy Signals, and the Career Prospects of Academic Scientists* (SSRN Scholarly Paper ID 3098510). Social Science Research Network. https://doi.org/10.2139/ssrn.3098510.

DiPrete, T. A., and Eirich, G. M. (2006). Cumulative advantage as a mechanism for inequality: A review of theoretical and empirical developments. *Annual Review of Sociology*, *32*, 271–297. JSTOR.

Ductor, L. (2015). Does co-authorship lead to higher academic productivity? *Oxford Bulletin of Economics and Statistics*, *77*(3), 385–407. https://doi.org/10.1111/obes.12070.

Ellemers, N. (2018). Gender stereotypes. *Annual Review of Psychology*, *69*(1), 275–298. https://doi.org/10.1146/annurev-psych-122216-011719.

Elsevier (2017). *Gender in the Global Research Landscape Report*. https://www.elsevier.com/research-intelligence/resource-library/gender-report.

Elsevier (2018). *Gender in the Global Research Landscape*. *Research Intelligence*. https://www.elsevier.com/research-intelligence/campaigns/gender-17.

Erosheva, E. A., Grant, S., Chen, M.-C., Lindner, M. D., Nakamura, R. K., and Lee, C. J. (2020). NIH peer review: Criterion scores completely account for racial disparities in overall impact scores. *Science Advances*, *6*(23), eaaz4868. https://doi.org/10.1126/sciadv.aaz4868.

European Commission (2019). *She Figures 2018*. https://doi.org/10.2777/936.

Eyre-Walker, A., and Stoletzki, N. (2013). The assessment of science: The relative merits of post-publication review, the impact factor, and the number of citations. *PLoS Biology*, *11*(10), e1001675. https://doi.org/10.1371/journal.pbio.1001675.

Forscher, P. S., Cox, W. T. L., Brauer, M., and Devine, P. G. (2019). Little race or gender bias in an experiment of initial review of NIH R01 grant proposals. *Nature Human Behaviour*, *3*(3), 257–264. https://doi.org/10.1038/s41562-018-0517-y.

Gibney, E. (2016). Women under-represented in world's science academies. *Nature*, 3–5. https://doi.org/10.1038/nature.2016.19465.

Ginther, D. K., and Heggeness, M. L. (2020). Administrative discretion in scientific funding: Evidence from a prestigious postdoctoral training program. *Research Policy*, *49*(4), 103953. https://doi.org/10.1016/j.respol.2020.103953.

Ginther, D. K., and Kahn, S. (2013). Seeking solutions: Maximizing American talent by advancing women of color in academia: Summary of a conference. In National Research Council (Ed.), *Seeking Solutions: Maximizing American Talent by Advancing Women of Color in Academia: Summary of a Conference* (pp. 71–93). The National Academies Press. https://doi.org/10.17226/18556.

Ginther, D. K., Schaffer, W. T., Schnell, J., Masimore, B., Liu, F., Haak, L. L., and Kington, R. (2011). Race, ethnicity, and NIH research awards. *Science*, *333*(6045), 1015–1019. https://doi.org/10.1126/science.1196783.

Ginther, D. K., Haak, L. L., Schaffer, W. T., and Kington, R. (2012). Are race, ethnicity, and medical school affiliation associated with NIH R01 Type 1 award probability for physician investigators? *Academic Medicine*, *87*(11), 1516–1524. https://doi.org/10.1097/ACM.0b013e31826d726b.

Ginther, D. K., Kahn, S., and Schaffer, W. T. (2016). Gender, race/ethnicity, and National Institutes of Health R01 research awards: Is there evidence of a double bind for women of color? *Academic Medicine*, *91*(8), 1098–1107. https://doi.org/10.1097/ACM.0000000000001278.

Ginther, D. K., Basner, J., Jensen, U., Schnell, J., Kington, R., and Schaffer, W. T. (2018). Publications as predictors of racial and ethnic differences in NIH research awards. *PLoS One*, *13*(11), e0205929. https://doi.org/10.1371/journal.pone.0205929.

Goldstein, A., and Kearney, M. (2017). Uncertainty and individual discretion in allocating research funds. *SSRN Electronic Journal*. https://doi.org/10.2139/ssrn.3012169.

Guarino, C. M., and Borden, V. M. H. (2017). Faculty service loads and gender: Are women taking care of the academic family? *Research in Higher Education*, *58*(6), 672–694. https://doi.org/10.1007/s11162-017-9454-2.

Guthrie, S., Lichten, C. A., Corbett, J., and Wooding, S. (2017). *International Mobility of Researchers: A Review of the Literature*. RAND Corporation. https://www.rand.org/pubs/research_reports/RR1991.html.

Heilman, M. E. (2001). Description and prescription: How gender stereotypes prevent women's ascent up the organizational ladder. *Journal of Social Issues*, *57*(4), 657–674. https://doi.org/10.1111/0022-4537.00234.

Heilman, M. E. (2012). Gender stereotypes and workplace bias. *Research in Organizational Behavior*, *32*, 113–135. https://doi.org/10.1016/j.riob.2012.11.003.

Hengel, E., and Moon, E. (2020). *Gender and Quality at Top Economics Journals* (Working Paper No. 202001). University of Liverpool, Department of Economics. https://econpapers.repec.org/paper/livlivedp/202001.htm.

Hicks, D., and Katz, J. S. (2011). Equity and excellence in research funding. *Minerva*, *49*(2), 137–151. https://doi.org/10.1007/s11024-011-9170-6.

Holliday, E., Griffith, K. A., De Castro, R., Stewart, A., Ubel, P., and Jagsi, R. (2015). Gender differences in resources and negotiation among highly motivated physician-scientists. *Journal of General Internal Medicine*, *30*(4), 401–407. https://doi.org/10.1007/s11606-014-2988-5.

Hoppe, T. A., Litovitz, A., Willis, K. A., Meseroll, R. A., Perkins, M. J., Hutchins, B. I., Davis, A. F., Lauer, M. S., Valantine, H. A., Anderson, J. M., and Santangelo, G. M. (2019). Topic choice contributes to the lower rate of NIH awards to African-American/black scientists. *Science Advances*, *5*(10), eaaw7238. https://doi.org/10.1126/sciadv.aaw7238.

Hosek, S. D., Cox, A. G., Ghosh-Dastidar, B., Kofner, A., Ramphal, N. R., Scott, J., and Berry, S. H. (2005). *Gender Differences in Major Federal External Grant Programs*. https://www.rand.org/pubs/technical_reports/TR307.html.

Huang, J., Gates, A. J., Sinatra, R., and Barabási, A.-L. (2020). Historical comparison of gender inequality in scientific careers across countries and disciplines. *Proceedings of the National Academy of Sciences*, *117*(9), 4609–4616. https://doi.org/10.1073/pnas.1914221117.

Hunter, L. A., and Leahey, E. (2010). Parenting and research productivity: New evidence and methods. *Social Studies of Science*, *40*(3), 433–451. https://doi.org/10.1177/0306312709358472.

Kaatz, A., Magua, W., Zimmerman, D. R., and Carnes, M. (2015). A quantitative linguistic analysis of National Institutes of Health R01 application critiques from investigators at one institution. *Academic Medicine*, *90*(1), 69–75. https://doi.org/10.1097/ACM.0000000000000442.

Kahn, S., and Ginther, D. (2018). Women and science, technology, engineering, and mathematics (STEM): Are differences in education and careers due to stereotypes, interests, or family? In S. L. Averett and L. M. Argys (Eds.), *The Oxford Handbook of Women and the Economy*. New York: Oxford University Press. https://doi.org/10.1093/oxfordhb/9780190628963.001.0001.

Kolev, J., Fuentes-Medel, Y., and Murray, F. (2019). *Is Blinded Review Enough? How Gendered Outcomes Arise Even Under Anonymous Evaluation* (Working Paper No. 25759). National Bureau of Economic Research. https://doi.org/10.3386/w25759.

Kugler, A. D., Tinsley, C. H., and Ukhaneva, O. (2017). *Choice of Majors: Are Women Really Different from Men?* (Working Paper No. 23735). National Bureau of Economic Research. https://doi.org/10.3386/w23735.

Langfeldt, L., Reymert, I., and Aksnes, D. W. (2020). The role of metrics in peer assessments. *Research Evaluation*, *30*(1), 112–126. https://doi.org/10.1093/reseval/rvaa032.

Lauer, M. S., Doyle, J., Wang, J., and Roychowdhury, D. (2021). Associations of topic-specific peer review outcomes and institute and center award rates with funding disparities at the National Institutes of Health. *ELife*, *10*, e67173. https://doi.org/10.7554/eLife.67173.

Larivière, V., and Sugimoto, C. R. (2017). The end of gender disparities in science? If only it were true … . *CWTS*. https://www.cwts.nl:443/blog?article=n-q2z294.

Leahey, E. (2006). Gender differences in productivity: Research specialization as a missing link. *Gender and Society*, *20*(6), 754–780. https://doi.org/10.1177/0891243206293030.

Lee, S., and Bozeman, B. (2005). The impact of research collaboration on scientific productivity. *Social Studies of Science*, *35*(5), 673–702. https://doi.org/10.1177/0306312705052359.

Ley, T. J., and Hamilton, B. H. (2008). The gender gap in NIH grant applications. *Science*, *322*(5907), 1472–1474. https://doi.org/10.1126/science.1165878.

Long, J. S. (1992). Measures of sex differences in scientific productivity. *Social Forces*, *71*(1), 159–178. JSTOR. https://doi.org/10.2307/2579971.

Magua, W., Zhu, X., Bhattacharya, A., Filut, A., Potvien, A., Leatherberry, R., Lee, Y.-G., Jens, M., Malikireddy, D., Carnes, M., and Kaatz, A. (2017). Are female applicants disadvantaged in National Institutes of Health peer review? Combining algorithmic text mining and qualitative methods to detect evaluative differences in R01 reviewers' critiques. *Journal of Women's Health*, *26*(5), 560–570. https://doi.org/10.1089/jwh.2016.6021.

Marsh, H. W., Bornmann, L., Mutz, R., Daniel, H.-D., and O'Mara, A. (2009). Gender effects in the peer reviews of grant proposals: A comprehensive meta-analysis comparing traditional and multilevel approaches. *Review of Educational Research*, *79*(3), 1290–1326. https://doi.org/10.3102/0034654309334143.

Marsh, H. W., Jayasinghe, U. W., and Bond, N. W. (2011). Gender differences in peer reviews of grant applications: A substantive-methodological synergy in support of the null hypothesis model. *Journal of Informetrics*, *5*(1), 167–180. https://doi.org/10.1016/j.joi.2010.10.004.

Mcdowell, J. M., Singell Jr, L. D., and Stater, M. (2006). Two to tango? Gender differences in the decisions to publish and coauthor. *Economic Inquiry*, *44*(1), 153–168. https://doi.org/10.1093/ei/cbi065.

Merton, R. K. (1968). The Matthew effect in science: The reward and communication systems of science are considered. *Science*, *159*(3810), 56–63. https://doi.org/10.1126/science.159.3810.56.

Moghissi, A. A., Love, B. R., and Straja, S. R. (2013). *Peer Review and Scientific Assessment: A Handbook for Funding Organizations, Regulatory Agencies, and Editors*. Institute for Regulatory Science.

Mutz, R., Bornmann, L., and Daniel, H.-D. (2012). Does gender matter in grant peer review? An empirical investigation using the example of the Austrian science fund. *Zeitschrift für Psychologie/Journal of Psychology*, *220*(2), 121–129. http://dx.doi.org.ezproxy1.lib.asu.edu/10.1027/2151-2604/a000103.

Nakamura, R., Mann, L. S., Lindner, M. D., Braithwaite, J., Chen, M. C., Vancea, A., Byrnes, N., Durrant, V., and Reed, B. (2021). An experimental test of the effects of redacting grant applicant identifiers on peer review outcomes. *bioRxiv*. https://doi.org/10.1101/2021.06.25.449872.

National Center for Science and Engineering Statistics (2021). *Women, Minorities, and Persons with Disabilities in Science and Engineering: 2021*. Special Report NSF 21-321. Alexandria, VA: National Science Foundation. https://ncses.nsf.gov/wmpd.

National Science Foundation, National Center for Science and Engineering Statistics (2019). *Women, Minorities, and Persons with Disabilities in Science and Engineering: 2019*. Special Report NSF 19-304. Alexandria, VA. https://www.nsf.gov/statistics/wmpd.

Niederle, M., and Vesterlund, L. (2007). Do women shy away from competition? Do men compete too much? *The Quarterly Journal of Economics*, *122*(3), 1067–1101. https://doi.org/10.1162/qjec.122.3.1067.

Nielsen, M W. (2017). Gender and citation impact in management research. *Journal of Informetrics*, *11*(4), 1213–1228. https://doi.org/10.1016/j.joi.2017.09.005.

Nielsen, M. W. (2018). Scientific performance assessments through a gender lens. *Science and Technology Studies*, *31*(1), 2–30. https://doi.org/10.23987/sts.60610.

Oliveira, D. F. M., Ma, Y., Woodruff, T. K., and Uzzi, B. (2019). Comparison of National Institutes of Health grant amounts to first-time male and female principal investigators. *JAMA*, *321*(9), 898–900. https://doi.org/10.1001/jama.2018.21944.

Pezzoni, M., Mairesse, J., Stephan, P., and Lane, J. (2016). Gender and the publication output of graduate students: A case study. *PLoS One*, *11*(1), e0145146. https://doi.org/10.1371/journal.pone.0145146.

Pier, E. L., Brauer, M., Filut, A., Kaatz, A., Raclaw, J., Nathan, M. J., Ford, C. E., and Carnes, M. (2018). Low agreement among reviewers evaluating the same NIH grant applications. *Proceedings of the National Academy of Sciences*, *115*(12), 2952–2957. https://doi.org/10.1073/pnas.1714379115.

Pohlhaus, J. R., Jiang, H., Wagner, R. M., Schaffer, W. T., and Pinn, V. W. (2011). Sex differences in application, success, and funding rates for NIH extramural programs. *Academic Medicine*, *86*(6), 759–767. https://doi.org/10.1097/ACM.0b013e31821836ff.

Reskin, B. F. (2003). Including mechanisms in our models of ascriptive inequality: 2002 presidential address. *American Sociological Review*, *68*(1), 1–21. JSTOR. https://doi.org/10.2307/3088900.

Rivera, L. A., and Tilcsik, A. (2019). Scaling down inequality: Rating scales, gender bias, and the architecture of evaluation. *American Sociological Review*, *84*(2), 248–274. https://doi.org/10.1177/0003122419833601.

Rørstad, K., and Aksnes, D. W. (2015). Publication rate expressed by age, gender and academic position – A large-scale analysis of Norwegian academic staff. *Journal of Informetrics*, *9*(2), 317–333. https://doi.org/10.1016/j.joi.2015.02.003.

Sandström, U., and Hällsten, M. (2008). Persistent nepotism in peer-review. *Scientometrics*, *74*(2), 175–189. https://doi.org/10.1007/s11192-008-0211-3.

Sarsons, H. (2017). Recognition for group work: Gender differences in academia. *American Economic Review*, *107*(5), 141–145. https://doi.org/10.1257/aer.p20171126.

Sarsons, H., Gërxhani, K., Reuben, E., and Schram, A. (2021). Gender differences in recognition for group work. *Journal of Political Economy*, *129*(1), 101–147. https://doi.org/10.1086/711401.

Sato, S., Gygax, P. M., Randall, J., and Schmid Mast, M. (2021). The leaky pipeline in research grant peer review and funding decisions: Challenges and future directions. *Higher Education*, *82*(1) 145–162. https://doi.org/10.1007/s10734-020-00626-y.

Shauman, K. A., and Xie, Y. (1996). Geographic mobility of scientists: Sex differences and family constraints. *Demography*, *33*(4), 455–468. https://doi.org/10.2307/2061780.

Severin, A., Martins, J., Heyard, R., Delavy, F., Jorstad, A., and Egger, M. (2020). Gender and other potential biases in peer review: Cross-sectional analysis of 38 250 external peer review reports. *BMJ Open*, *10*(8), e035058. https://doi.org/10.1136/bmjopen-2019-035058.

Shen, Y. A., Webster, J. M., Shoda, Y., and Fine, I. (2018). Persistent underrepresentation of women's science in high profile journals. *BioRxiv*, 275362. https://doi.org/10.1101/275362.

Silbiger, N. J., and Stubler, A. D. (2019). Unprofessional peer reviews disproportionately harm underrepresented groups in STEM. *PeerJ*, *7*, e8247. https://doi.org/10.7717/peerj.8247.

Singh Chawla, D. (2019). "Friendly" reviewers rate grant applications more highly. *Nature*, 17 April, news. https://doi.org/10.1038/d41586-019-01198-3.

Stephan, P. E., and El-Ganainy, A. (2007). The entrepreneurial puzzle: Explaining the gender gap. *The Journal of Technology Transfer*, *32*(5), 475–487. https://doi.org/10.1007/s10961-007-9033-3.

Symonds, M. R. E., Gemmell, N. J., Braisher, T. L., Gorringe, K. L., and Elgar, M. A. (2006). Gender differences in publication output: Towards an unbiased metric of research performance. *PLoS One*, *1*(1), e127. https://doi.org/10.1371/journal.pone.0000127.

Tamblyn, R., Girard, N., Qian, C. J., and Hanley, J. (2018). Assessment of potential bias in research grant peer review in Canada. *CMAJ: Canadian Medical Association Journal*, *190*(16), E489–E499. https://doi.org/10.1503/cmaj.170901.

Treviño, L. J., Gomez-Mejia, L. R., Balkin, D. B., and Mixon, F. G. (2018). Meritocracies or masculinities? The differential allocation of named professorships by gender in the academy. *Journal of Management*, *44*(3), 972–1000. https://doi.org/10.1177/0149206315599216.

Tricco, A. C., Thomas, S. M., Antony, J., Rios, P., Robson, R., Pattani, R., Ghassemi, M., Sullivan, S., Selvaratnam, I., Tannenbaum, C., and Straus, S. E. (2017). Strategies to prevent or reduce gender bias in peer review of research grants: A Rapid scoping review. *PLoS One*, *12*(1), 1–12. https://doi.org/10.1371/journal.pone.0169718.

van den Besselaar, P., and Moom, Ch. (2020). Gender differences in research grant allocation – A mixed picture. Preprint. https://www.researchgate.net/publication/344461914_Gender_bias_and_grant_allocation_-_a_mixed_picture.

van den Besselaar, P., and Sandström, U. (2016). Gender differences in research performance and its impact on careers: A longitudinal case study. *Scientometrics*, *106*(1), 143–162. https://doi.org/10.1007/s11192-015-1775-3.

van der Lee, R., and Ellemers, N. (2015a). Gender contributes to personal research funding success in The Netherlands. *Proceedings of the National Academy of Sciences*, *112*(40), 12349–12353. https://doi.org/10.1073/pnas.1510159112

van der Lee, R., and Ellemers, N. (2015b). Reply to Volker and Steenbeek: Multiple indicators point toward gender disparities in grant funding success in The Netherlands. *Proceedings of the National Academy of Sciences*, *112*(51), E7038–E7038. https://doi.org/10.1073/pnas.1521331112.

Vernos, I. (2013). Quotas are questionable. *Nature*, *495*, 39.

Volker, B., and Steenbeek, W. (2015). No evidence that gender contributes to personal research funding success in The Netherlands: A reaction to van der Lee and Ellemers. *Proceedings of the National Academy of Sciences*, *112*(51), E7036–E7037. https://doi.org/10.1073/pnas.1519046112.

Warner, E. T., Carapinha, R., Weber, G. M., Hill, E. V., and Reede, J. Y. (2016). Faculty promotion and attrition: The importance of coauthor network reach at an academic medical center. *Journal of General Internal Medicine*, *31*(1), 60–67. https://doi.org/10.1007/s11606-015-3463-7.

Wennerås, C., and Wold, A. (1997). Nepotism and sexism in peer-review. *Nature*, *387*, 341–343. https://doi.org/10.1038/387341a0.

Williams, W. M., and Ceci, S. J. (2015). National hiring experiments reveal 2:1 faculty preference for women on STEM tenure track. *Proceedings of the National Academy of Sciences*, *112*(17), 5360–5365. https://doi.org/10.1073/pnas.1418878112.

Witteman, H. O., Hendricks, M., Straus, S., and Tannenbaum, C. (2019). Are gender gaps due to evaluations of the applicant or the science? A natural experiment at a national funding agency. *The Lancet*, *393*(10171), 531–540. https://doi.org/10.1016/S0140-6736(18)32611-4.

Xie, Y., and Shauman, K. A. (1998). Sex differences in research productivity: New evidence about an old puzzle. *American Sociological Review*, *63*(6), 847–870. https://doi.org/10.2307/2657505.

Zuckerman, H. (2001). The careers of men and women scientists: Gender differences in career attainment. In M. Wyer, M. Barbercheck, D. Cookmeyer, H. Ozturk, and M. Wayne (Eds.), *Women, Science, and Technology: A Reader in Feminist Science Studies* (pp. 69–78). New York: Routledge. https://doi.org/10.4324/9780203427415.

18. Research funding and scientific careers

Julia Melkers, Richard Woolley and Quintin Kreth

INTRODUCTION

Research grants, by their very nature, provide critical career-relevant resources and opportunities, often a determining factor in a researcher's career advancement, mobility, and overall trajectory. While funding opportunities themselves are increasing in size (Bloch, Kladakis and Sørensen, Chapter 8 in this *Handbook*), expectations and competition for those awards is intensifying. Within this funding ecosystem, researchers demonstrate varied motivations to pursue competitive funding (Lam, 2011), adapting their behaviours to available funding opportunities (Serrano Velarde, 2018). For those who are successful, rewards in the form of opportunities and recognition can shape research foci and offer potentially career-changing outcomes. In recognition of the crucial importance of timely funding awards and impacts, many national funding systems specifically target researchers at different career stages, both for purposes of broader inclusion and to satisfy distinct career-building objectives (Millsap et al., 2001).

At the most fundamental level, research funding is instrumental, providing direct support for a researchers' salary and/or for the resources that enable scientific inquiry: access to data, equipment and materials; freeing up time from other obligations; incorporation of additional research personnel; and other assets. The resulting generation of new knowledge further enables the researcher to produce, communicate, and disseminate these discoveries, typically in products that cumulatively further one's career, including publications and patents that then attract subsequent grant funding. In the most general terms, success in grant-getting is thus crucial for the development of the professional careers of those who lead or participate in funded research. As scholars have noted, the distribution of funding is not normal in any way (Hicks and Katz, 2011), and multiple factors may influence the propensity to seek funding. For example, the precise effects of research funding on research careers will also differ depending on the academic career stage of those who benefit (Laudel and Gläser, 2008). The strategies that researchers adopt to secure funding for research will thus vary according to multiple factors, including their career stage and the specific resource demands of their field or discipline.

Our aim in this chapter is to develop an account of what we know about how research funding matters to academic career progress and transitions. We explore the catalytic human capital outcomes of grant funding, relevant to a career-stage model of research careers. Complementing Laudel's chapter (Chapter 16 in this *Handbook*) on researchers' funding acquisition strategies, we provide an overview of the state of knowledge on the relationship between funding and research careers. To illustrate, we identify several important trends in research funding and their consequences for the support of research careers, using examples of career-specific funding mechanism in several national systems. We organize our discussion around career stages to highlight the early, mid and later career factors relevant to the design of funding instruments and how career scripts are reflected in, and potentially shaped by, these career-stage-specific instruments. Finally, we address current knowledge gaps relevant to improving our understanding of the relationships between research funding and academic careers, accompanied by suggestions for a future research agenda.

Furthermore, we focus on the competitive funding of research and how these mechanisms support and affect academic careers, through both direct and indirect mechanisms. This complement's Horta and Li's chapter (Chapter 19 in this *Handbook*) on the impacts of research funding on scholarly activities. Funding for research that supports research careers *directly* tends to take the form of individual fellowships and grants designed and targeted at researchers at specific career stages. These awards explicitly aim to support transition through different career stages. Research funding that supports research careers *indirectly* takes the main form of research project grants, which typically cover the costs of the research and equipment as well as technical personnel required to carry out the proposed research. For permanent faculty, these awards provide technical and human capital resources, while also freeing up time from other obligations, such as teaching. For 'soft money' positions, these awards are especially crucial in the perpetuation of careers for those researchers, who lack either a permanent organizational position or a personal fellowship. Understanding this competitive context within the expected norms and scripts of a research career helps us to move beyond a simple 'money matters' perspective and attend to the roles of research funding at critical career stages.

In the main section of this chapter, we focus on how funding supports research careers at successive career stages. In so doing, we compare the effects of direct and indirect support for research careers provided by competitive funding mechanisms, highlighting the relative importance of these approaches in different science systems. However, prior to this we need to provide at least a minimal overview of what we understand by an 'academic research career'.

ACADEMIC RESEARCH CAREERS

An academic research career is a professional work life lived through the production of scientific knowledge (Cañibano et al. 2019). Definitions of research careers emphasize the continuous learning and accumulation of competences and connections (Bozeman et al., 2001), integrated in evolving role sets (Laudel and Gläser, 2008). The term 'research career' is also a conceptual and analytical category that mediates between individual work lives and the institutional processes and conditions that are necessary for the conduct of scientific research.

The only comprehensive theoretical framework for analysing academic research careers is the 'three careers' model (Gläser and Laudel, 2015). In this model, researchers have three overlapping institutional career contexts: a cognitive career of 'thematically connected problem solving processes in which findings from earlier projects serve as input in later projects'; a community career or 'series of status positions in the scientific community that are defined by the reputation a researcher has accrued and corresponding role expectations'; and an organizational career, 'a sequence of organisational positions which, through organisational role expectations, are linked to expectations concerning the conduct and content of research and opportunities to conduct research (access to salary, infrastructure, and other resources)' (Laudel and Bielick, 2019: 3–4). Research careers are produced by the three overlapping institutional processes, with researchers passing through a succession of career stages – apprentice, colleague, master, elite – regulated by their research achievements and the acceptance and recognition of those within their peer community, which is the gatekeeper for obtaining stable organizational positions and further research funds (Gläser and Laudel, 2015).

The question of how individual career decisions and these complex institutional contexts interact to produce 'typical' or 'ideal-type' patterns of research careers enters into the structure–agency problem in social theory. Pierre Bourdieu (1975, 2004) applied his general sociological theory in his writings on the scientific field. Bourdieu understood the scientific career trajectory as series of competitive 'position-takings' within the scientific field, that are largely determined by an individual's embodied set of pre-reflexive dispositions or *habitus*, resolving the structure–agency problem at the level of practice. Bourdieu's approach captures well the (elite) 'vocational' component of 'being' a scientist, based on forces of social reproduction, ascribed social capitals and embodied comportment in the social spaces governing scientific work. However, it is perhaps more limited in how it accounts for individual agency, particularly in reflexively objectifying (and quantifying) research performance and strategizing a sequence of future 'career moves' in current decision-making processes.

In contrast, Laudel and colleagues (2019) develop the analytical category of career 'script' as mediating between individual agency and institutional conditions and processes. Building on the work of Barley (1989) they define career scripts as 'collectively shared interpretive schemes' that describe successful career trajectories. Individuals research career perceptions and decisions will tend to conform to the available scripts shared and enacted within their disciplinary community. The script concept attempts to resolve the structure–agency problem through a dialogic process of interaction between agents and the structural conditions of research. Scripts provide more room for conscious individual decision-making processes than Bourdieu's practice theory approach. Laudel and colleagues (2019) endeavour to strike a balanced position on the degree that scripts are determined by institutions and organizations or emerge from individual actions and patterns of behaviour. Yet how these shared career scripts emerge, circulate and evolve remains an ongoing challenge for this type of theoretical approach.

The concept of career scripts is useful for our examination of the effect of research funding on research careers. Funders determine much of organizational context of research careers and funding instruments by establishing formal funding criteria (rules) that have direct and indirect effects on research career outcomes. Thus, we can conceive of the funding criteria used in instruments designed to support research careers as contributing to the discursive production of career scripts. Where a research funding organization is closely aligned with the scientific community, as is the case with many traditional research councils (Braun, 1998), these criteria may reflect community norms and expectations. However, other types of funders, such as those aligned more closely with state authorities or private foundations, may set funding criteria that reflect other policy agendas such as national research priorities or societal missions. If we understand research funding criteria as contributing to the active 'scripting' of research careers, then we might also interpret trends in such programmes and criteria as evidence of evolving expectations about academic research careers. Whether changes in research career expectations are driven by scientific communities or institutional stakeholders, or reflect a settlement between these different interests, remains an empirical question. We will keep these theoretical considerations in mind and refer to them where appropriate in our review of competitive funding support for research careers.

RESEARCH FUNDING AND ACADEMIC RESEARCH CAREERS

This section links competitive research funding mechanisms to the development of academic careers across time. It is organized around career stages to highlight the early, mid and later career factors relevant to the design of funding instruments and how career scripts are reflected in, and potentially shaped by, these instruments. We refer to the 'three career' model (Gläser and Laudel, 2015) to illustrate how funding supports different career processes. We use US and European examples (Table 18.1) to illustrate and highlight different funding approaches, instruments, and priorities, that together configure grant-getting opportunities for researchers at successive career stages.

In considering the impact of funding on research careers, it is also important to note country differences in the opportunities and structures of these careers. Each country has its own historically and culturally shaped set of authority relations in which higher education institutions are embedded (Whitley et al., 2010). Covering the diversity of national systems in the EU is beyond the scope of this chapter; however, it is important to note that academic staff structures in Europe also vary between systems based on a chair model (e.g. France, Germany) or a department model (e.g. UK, similar to the US). The chair model creates high-level competition for well-funded professorial positions, which are difficult to obtain and come with considerable administrative responsibility and political influence (Neave and Rhoades, 1987), but also with recurring research budgets that provide additional discretionary resources. The department model is less hierarchical and collegial responsibilities more distributed across members at different career levels, with promotion and career development within an organization being more common (Neave and Rhoades, 1987). These variations may result in different needs and reward structures, as well as career implications, for funding acquisition by researchers at different career stages.

Research Funding for Doctoral Researchers (Apprentice Career Stage)

The doctoral phase establishes the initial base for building a research career. Training in problem identification and specification and technical capabilities shapes the cognitive and the peer community context. Very rarely does doctoral funding promise any type of continuity or permanence in terms of secure organizational positions.

Research funding at the doctoral stage initiates one's career. It can provide immediate benefits to doctoral students, allowing them to concentrate full-time on producing the outputs that can shape early career opportunities and trajectory. Given the relative prestige of these awards, they also provide longer-term reputational effects, which may facilitate career mobility and advancement. There are different models for providing doctoral stage scholarships or awards. We can distinguish between *early pursuit* of direct competitive funding and the more common *opportunistic* research funding provided to doctoral students at this same career stage.

Least common and highly competitive are doctoral student fellowships or dissertation awards that are parallel to later career awards. Longstanding mechanisms such as the graduate research fellowship (offered by the US National Science Foundation for well over half a century) provide very early career trainees with an element of research independence, suggesting the ability to accelerate that career transition at the pre-doctoral stage. Horta and colleagues (2018) found stronger positive effects on post-graduation research productivity and capacity among doctoral trainees who received competitive individual research grants

Table 18.1 Prestigious competitive individual research career awards, US and EU

Agency	Career stage	Mechanism	Origin	Length	Funding limits	Focus
US NSF	Doctoral	Graduate Research Fellowship	1952	5 years	$140k	NSF Fellows are anticipated to become knowledge experts who can contribute significantly to research, teaching, and innovations in science and engineering.
	Postdoc	Postdoctoral Research Fellowship	–	1–3 years	$200k	The programme is intended to recognize beginning investigators of significant potential and provide them with experience in research that will broaden perspectives, facilitate interdisciplinary interactions and help establish them in leadership positions.
	Early Career	NSF CAREER	1994	3–5 years	$2,100k	This programme enhances and emphasizes the importance the Foundation places on the development of full, balanced academic careers which include both research and education.
	Mid career	Mid-Career Advancement	2020	3 years	$2,000k	The Mid-Career programme helps ensure the health and vitality of science at a sensitive career stage. It also aims to lift some of these constraints to support your scientific research career and help build and retain a more diverse science and engineering workforce.
EU/ERC	Doctoral and postdoc	Marie Skłodowska-Curie Individual Fellowships	1996	2–3 years	$170k	Support for excellent principal investigators at the career stage at which they are starting their own independent research team or programme.
	Early career	ERC Starting Grants	2007	5 years	$3,000k	An ERC grant can cover up to 100% of the total eligible direct costs of the research plus a contribution of 25% of the total eligible costs towards indirect costs.
	Mid career	ERC Consolidator Grants	2007	5 years	$3,650k	Support for excellent principal investigators at the career stage at which they may still be consolidating their own independent research team or programme. Principal investigators must demonstrate the ground-breaking nature, ambition and feasibility of their scientific proposal.
	Senior career	ERC Advanced Grants	2007	5 years	$4,250k	Support for excellent principal investigators at the career stage at which they are already established research leaders with an organized track record of research achievements. Principal investigators must demonstrate the ground-breaking nature, ambition and feasibility of their scientific proposal.

compared to individuals who held research assistantships, which we discuss below. Given the increasingly competitive academic job market worldwide, access to (or exclusion from) early-career funding through opportunities or competitive acquisition of prestigious awards can have long-lasting career effects.

Most often in the US, research funding at the trainee stage takes the form of opportunities for research assistantships. These are the most common form of doctoral student funding supported by the US National Science Foundation, accounting for the vast majority (82%) of their total doctoral student support (Muller-Parker et al., 2020; National Science Foundation, 2019). For doctoral students, the opportunity to procure a research assistantship or fellowship, particularly if accompanied by a tuition waiver, makes the pursuit of a doctoral degree more viable and affordable, especially relevant in the US, where tuition for graduate education can be several times the cost of room and board (Knight et al., 2018; National Center for Science and Engineering Statistics, 2019). Alternative support may come from teaching assistantships, but at a cost. Studies of early-career funding mechanisms show that funded doctoral students are more likely to finish their PhD (Chapman and McCauley, 1993) and are more likely to remain in academic research following their PhD (Graddy-Reed et al., 2021). Further, teaching assistantships have weaker effects on degree completion than research assistantships and fellowships (Denton et al., 2020), suggesting that other aspects of the research assistantship experience matters for early career success.

Perhaps most impactful for career development, research assistantships provide the opportunity for doctoral students to actively engage in hands-on research at an early stage. This enables research and team-related skill development, navigating the realities, and failures of the research process, while providing access to materials, equipment and other opportunities that may accelerate and enrich the doctoral experience (Denton et al., 2020; Grote et al., 2021). These gains in experience and research skills, as well as establishing an early publication record, can in turn enhance career advancement, easing the transition from trainee to active researcher (Pinheiro et al., 2014; Horta and Santos, 2016). Yet these resources can also be unstable, forcing students to join new projects when existing funding becomes depleted, which can be disruptive and result in slower progress to degree (Horta et al., 2018).

In Europe, funding of doctoral students varies considerably between national systems. In chair model systems (e.g. France and Germany), well-funded professorial positions enable supporting doctoral students as part of a professor's recurrent research budget. Under the department model, processes for hiring and promotion can become relatively bespoke and reflective of incumbent staff preferences, with only minimal administrative influence. Universities in Europe thus have varying degrees of autonomy over financial, organizational, academic and hiring matters (Estermann et al., 2011), including over arrangements for doctoral education. In the Netherlands, for example, most doctoral students are directly employed by the university of their supervisor once their PhD proposal has been accepted, while a range of awards are available from different types of supporting organizations, most commonly to support international students. In the UK, doctoral students are typically supported by graduate teaching assistantships

Research Funding for Postdoctoral/Early Faculty Career (Apprentice to Colleague Stage)

There is considerable variation among funding agencies in the definitions of scientific career stages, particularly 'early career' (Bazeley, 2003; Bosanquet et al., 2017; Nicholas et al., 2017). Indicators typically include, for example, years elapsed since earning one's doctorate, number of tenure-track positions held, tenure status, job title and (controversially) sometimes age. Some agencies take a more achievement-based approach. For instance, the US NIH defines 'early-stage investigators' as researchers who are less than 10 years post-PhD and/ or medical residency *and* have not served as a principal investigator (PI) on a 'substantial independent research award'. There is also considerable variation in the extent to which these agency definitions have built-in flexibility for nontraditional academic careers and hardship. Overall, while specific definitions of 'early career' vary, they consistently reflect the theoretical idea of the developing scholar (or 'apprentice'; Laudel and Gläser, 2008) – a scholar engaged in the development of an independent research programme.

The acquisition of a competitive research award as PI at the postdoctoral and/or early career stage is a critical step in establishing one's self as an independent researcher and 'colleague' (Laudel and Gläser, 2008). For academic careers, acquisition of funding demonstrates researcher capacity and quality, marks the ability of an individual to function as an independent researcher (Heggeness et al., 2018; Laudel and Gläser, 2008), and matters in most disciplines for tenure, career advancement, and mobility. Taking the long view, receipt of direct funding that supports early-career continuity and the capacity to conduct high quality research can have long-lasting beneficial effects. Funding for early-career researchers can both increase research production and accelerate career advancement and mobility (Graddy-Reed et al., 2021). In fact, mobility at the postdoctoral stage has become increasingly ingrained as a 'rite of passage' in the scripts of academic research careers (Ackers, 2008), albeit this mobility may fulfil different functions in different disciplines (Laudel and Bielick, 2019, table 5). The uncertainty over future employment, and hence the viability of the research career, along with an explicit or implicit requirement to move between organizations and/or countries, is why the postdoctoral stage is where most direct funding support for academic research careers is concentrated.

In many disciplines, postdoctoral positions are often an expected step between doctoral education and an initial tenure-track position and are generally supported indirectly, by grants led by more senior researchers. Postdoctoral awards are often open to international competition or include budgets for long stays abroad, in order to support international mobility linked to career progress. As an extended traineeship, they provide access to research opportunities, resources, and recognition. Yet, such postdoctoral funding streams are temporary (typically one to four years), focus on the research agenda of the PI and may reduce opportunities to develop research leadership capacities, posing similar challenges and potential career disruptions at completion as at the pre-doctoral stage. The very nature of these 'soft money' project-based appointments has created a postdoctoral 'generation at risk' (Daniels, 2015), presented with well-recognized challenges associated with the inability to advance to faculty appointments in an increasingly competitive global academic market (Cantwell, 2011; Huisman et al., 2002). In the US, increased criticism and attention to these serial postdoctoral appointments has identified significant and negative impacts on equality and advancement to the professoriate and to research independence (Gaughan and Bozeman, 2019). A critical challenge for postdoctoral fellows is that US research funders often require a permanent faculty position as a requirement for PI grants. The effectiveness of training and advancement of postdoctoral scholars has been a major policy issue in the sciences for more than two decades (Åkerlind, 2005; Heggeness et al., 2018; Nerad and Cerny, 1999; Scaffidi and Berman, 2011), and will probably continue given recent trends.

A significant population of postdocs in the US are supported by direct competitive funding awards, which typically require postdoc mentoring plans, demonstrating recognition of the role of this support in career transitions. NSF postdoctoral fellowships (Table 18.1), for example, are intended to support not just the performance of research but also the move to leadership roles. In Europe, the European Research Council career awards are open to researchers of any nationality in the early-career stage (two to seven years after completion of the PhD). EU-funded Marie Skłodowska-Curie fellowships are also available at the postdoctoral stage, with many such grants requiring researchers to move to a different country for two years, followed by a third year supporting their reintegration in their home country. In European countries, direct postdoctoral research awards are provided by national research councils and delegated agencies, on a competitive basis. Such postdoctoral awards are typically part of a sequence of career awards targeted at early, mid, and later career stages, forming a sequence of grants that support academic career scripts.

The *Veni*, *Vidi* and *Vici* awards provided by the Dutch Research Council (NWO) under their Talent Programme are a good example of this type of direct national level support for researchers to 'make a permanent career of academic research' (Dutch Research Council Science, 2021a). The *Veni* award is open to researchers who obtained their doctorate in the previous three years with the aim of supporting excellent and innovative research led by the awardee, in order to establish the *bona fides* of their independent cognitive career. Funded international research stays of one to two years through their Rubicon programme are designed to support postdoctoral researchers in the gap between obtaining their PhD and being ready to apply for a *Veni* grant. Similar career stage sequences of competitive individual awards can be found in many European science systems. For example, the Spanish *Juan de la Cierva* postdoctoral awards that lead towards *Ramon y Cajal* tenure-track fellowships. In some cases, such as The Swiss National Science Foundation Starting Grant programme for researchers with three to eight years post-PhD experience, may provide funding for both the researcher and for essential members of their research team (Swiss National Science Foundation, 2021), a characteristic more common among mid-career support grants (see below).

Charitable foundations are also active supporters of early-career researchers. Wellcome Trust (UK) Early-Career Awards are for up to three years post-PhD and provide five years of salary and research budget 'to develop their research identity' and be ready to 'lead their own research programme' by the end of the grant (Wellcome, 2021a). Similarly, the Danish Villum Foundation Young Investigator awards are for two to eight years post-PhD and run for five years, with the aim of allowing researchers to establish their independent research identity. An innovative initiative is a competitive three-year extension that is available to a select number of grantees in each annual cohort, in order to further support the stability of their career (Velux Foundation, 2021).

Each of these initiatives recognizes that the period between finishing the doctorate, obtaining a postdoctoral position and transitioning towards a pre-tenure faculty position is an uncertain phase of academic research careers in which funding support is essential. The aims of relevant funders are also consistent: that early-career researchers develop a plan for independent research; learn any additional required technical skills; and experience leadership roles. From the scientific community perspective such direct funding for pre-tenure faculty is crucial to support career transitions to research independence, the responsibility for the design and conduct of projects, whilst satisfying external accountability and governance regimes. While grant-seeking and acquisition behaviour at any career stage is dependent on both the career goals of the researcher and the institutional context in which they work (Cañibano et al., 2019), acquiring direct support at an early stage may have advantages over receiving indirect support via senior colleagues. Although much remains unknown about the causal factors that relate to the emergence of independent researchers (Laudel and Bielick, 2018), it is known that the main inhibiting factor in achieving research independence is a lack of time to devote to research (Laudel and Gläser, 2008). Thus, early-career direct-funding mechanisms are particularly important for the development of independent researchers because they create protected time to conduct research based on early-career researchers' questions and designs. In some disciplines, career scripts are known to promote mobility at this stage of the career, particularly to separate from the influence and oversight of doctoral advisers and gain vital international experience (Laudel and Bielick, 2019).

Not surprisingly, the early career stage is the focus of a major proportion of career-stage-specific funding mechanisms, for both institutions and national funders. Seed funding opportunities may exist for early-career faculty at well-resourced institutions that provide research initiation funds critical for development of competitive proposals. However, because of the transitional nature of this career stage, where demonstration of research independence is necessary for advancement, pursuit and acquisition of external competitive research funding is the predominant goal and feature of careers scripts in most disciplines. External funding mechanisms that target tenure-track, early-career researchers do so with the implicit medium-term goal of supporting the researcher in developing a successful tenure case, by providing resources to allow them to devote sufficient time to research and develop independent research programmes (Millsap et al., 2001). These funding mechanisms are typically designed to support the development of a diverse pool of independent researchers – the next generation of scientists (Nikaj and Lund, 2019). Institutional programmes are also some of the most-studied early-career mechanisms in the academic literature, although these studies feature limited interface with formal theories of research careers (Good et al., 2018; Nikaj and Lund, 2019; Pickett, 2019; Sorkness et al., 2020). Procurement of these awards is highly competitive and prestigious, and success is an important maker of progress also in the community career – with most of these early-career grants adjudicated by disciplinary leaders. Although some would suggest that such funding mechanisms primarily benefit top-performers who would be successful regardless of funding (i.e. the Matthew effect), recent scholarship has suggested a 'crowding-in' effect. That is, early-career funding frees up resources from increasingly common private and other institutional funds to support additional doctoral students and early-career researchers (Graddy-Reed et al., 2021; Lanahan et al., 2016).

Many of the early studies and particularly programme evaluations of early career stage-specific funding mechanisms (Haak and Schnell, 2011; Michie et al., 2007; Millsap et al., 2001) reflect a production function approach to scientific careers (Levin and Stephan, 1991; Merton, 1968). Assistant professors who receive early-career research awards have been shown to be more likely to show an increase in publication and grant-getting (Conte and Omary, 2018; Millsap et al., 2001; Nikaj and Lund, 2019). Conversely, an evaluation of NSF (early) CAREER awards, showed that recipients are no more likely than their peers to earn tenure (Millsap et al., 2001). This could be interpreted as a sign both award recipients and control group members enjoy a high likelihood of overall success. Yet explanations for some of these findings are mixed. There is a need for more long-term study of the outcomes of early-career funding mechanisms. This is consistent with studies of privately funded early-career awards, which have been shown to increase funding levels later in the recipient's career (Dorismond et al., 2021).

Research Funding for Mid-career Researchers (Colleague to Master Stages)

Moving along the career timeframe, individuals and their roles as faculty and researchers evolve (Laudel and Gläser, 2008), as do the opportunities and functions of supporting research funding. A key factor in consolidating an academic career at this stage is searching for and gaining access to a permanent or tenured position in a suitable organization, norms and timing of which vary from one national system to another. While a researcher may enjoy success in terms of their knowledge production activities and have these validated and recognized by their scientific community, timely availability of a secure organizational position is not guaranteed, potentially generating tension between the 'three career' processes. Researchers who have achieved the status of colleague through their independent research project will not be able to contribute fully to their community's research and broader institutional activities where they remain dependent upon their capacity to source competitive funding to maintain their salary, or dependent on more senior colleagues to do so on their behalf.

Funding mechanisms that can support progress in the organizational career of an academic researcher are therefore extremely important in the transition from being recognized colleague to being a research leader with a secure institutional base. Laudel and Gläser (2008) depict this career stage as 'master', where faculty take on a leadership and mentor role for others in their scientific community. Successful grant-getting by tenured faculty puts them in a unique position to mentor early-career researchers, inviting junior colleagues to participate in large research teams that may provide important collaborative opportunities (Boardman and Bozeman, 2007; Nikaj and Lund, 2019), and building the confidence and skills of early-career colleagues (O'Meara and Stromquist, 2015).

Direct public funding support at this stage can therefore play a vital role in supporting transition to a stable academic position. Some funding mechanisms do this directly, by making the award of a researcher's salary and other resources contingent upon the delivery of a permanent position by a hosting organization. For example, the NWO *Vidi* grant, for researchers with up to eight years' research experience post-PhD, requires the host institution to guarantee either a tenure-track position or a permanent contract for the award winner (Dutch Research Council Science, 2021b). Similarly, a five-year *Ramon y Cajal* fellowship in Spain comes with the guarantee of a permanent civil servant position. Other mid-career grants, such as Australian Research Council Future Fellowships, provide salary and research budget over multiple years and aim to reduce the loss of talented researchers to overseas opportunities, owing to the scarcity of available positions (Australian Research Council, 2021). Success in gaining competitive mid-career research awards can also be an important sign of credibility within the scientific community that can be beneficial in tenure-track job contests. Some mid-career fellowships, such as the ERC Consolidator Grant, are fully portable and can be used to negotiate a position in a preferred centre, department, or faculty.

While much of the focus of this volume is on public research funding, it is important to recognize that charitable funders are increasingly a part of the organizational context for career-relevant research funding, and provide some innovative direct awards for mid-career researchers. For example, the Wellcome Career Development Award provides support for salary, a research group of up to four researchers, and training and development of research leadership, technical and soft skills, for a period of eight years (Wellcome, 2021a). The aims of the grant are focused on excellence, achieving international standing in the scientific community, and having all the requisites to obtain a permanent position. Funds are also made available for training in responsible research and promotion of a healthy research culture, while host institutions are expected to observe the guidelines of the Concordat to Support the Career Development of Researchers (UK Research and Innovation, 2019). The Villum Foundation Investigator mid-career grant targets researchers with 10 or more years' research experience, with a 33% budget extension available for leading international researchers enticed to come or return to Denmark. Both these Foundations' mid-career awards offer substantial support for equipment (particularly in the case of Wellcome) and for a research team that is funded through the success of the researcher as PI, extending this support for relatively long periods that enhance the likelihood the grantee will be in position to obtain a permanent position and that such a position will become available in a timely manner.

Research Funding for Late Career Researchers (Master to Elite Stages)

Funding mechanisms to support early and mid-stage academic careers are the main focus of policy concern. Mechanisms designed specifically for senior researchers (elites) are somewhat less common, given that they are generally the most competitive applicants in main grant pools. While the barriers to advancement to tenure are more commonly studied, there has been increasing attention towards barriers to advancement from associate to full professor in the US, particularly for underrepresented racial/ethnic minority and female academics (Fox and Colatrella, 2006; Teelken et al., 2021; Van Miegroet et al., 2019). Notably, some funding agencies are beginning to differentiate between mid-career and advanced or elite researchers with specific funding mechanisms (Michie et al., 2007; National Institutes of Health, 2021; Pomeroy-Carter et al., 2018). Such initiatives are an acknowledgement of the challenge of earning a full professorship, the difficulty of sustaining an independent research programme, and the ongoing need for protected time for scholarship and research leadership.

To illustrate, a differential time frame (often termed a 'glass ceiling') exists for female and underrepresented minority associate professors that can only be overcome through significant scholarly achievement, above what is necessary for majority peers to advance to full professor (Fox and Colatrella, 2006; Teelken et al., 2021; Van Miegroet et al., 2019). For example, the NSF only recently (2020) initiated a new programme for mid-career researchers, named 'Mid-Career Advancement'. The programme seeks to allow associate professors to substantively enhance and advance their research programme, with the long-term goal of supporting their advancement from associate to full professor as a 'critical career-stage' that ensures a researcher's long-term productivity and creativity. While the Mid-Career Advancement funding mechanism is new, it is reflective of recent scholarship that sees critical points in every career phase (Cañibano et al., 2019). In another example, the US NIH has had dedicated funding mechanisms for both mid-career and senior researchers for over two decades, which include both funding for independent investigators and mentored research experiences for cross-training and skill development (Michie et al., 2007; Pomeroy-Carter et al., 2018).

In the EU, prestigious individual competitive awards for field leading researchers such as the ERC Advanced Grant or the NWO *Vici* grant prioritize ground-breaking scientific contributions, supporting recipients with substantial research budgets for research staff and other needs. Proposals for such awards are increasingly also evaluated on the basis of their expected societal, economic, or other impacts. For example, *Vici* grants (and other NWO talent awards) require a statement on 'knowledge utilization', describing how the proposed research can be used and the researcher's plan to facilitate this use (Dutch Research Council Science, 2021c). Wellcome Discovery grants provide budgets for research expenses for researcher leaders with international standing and a track record of leading and developing research teams (Wellcome, 2021a). Up to eight co-applicants can also be included, plus salaries for technicians, fieldworkers, and research managers and other non-academic staff supporting the grant and the research team. Assessment criteria include contributions to an inclusive research culture and career development plans for team members. We might interpret evaluation criteria related to knowledge utilization and research culture as reflecting RFO expectations regarding the societal contribution of research and the 'public value' of research careers (Bozeman and Sarewitz, 2011).

Recurrent funding for advanced careers can be substantial in chair-based university systems. Following an exacting selection process, academics who accede to a full professorship negotiate a substantial budget with their university to fund their research and research group. In other European systems, such as Italy, academics who obtain tenured civil service positions advance to top-level organizational positions through internal promotion but rely largely on earning external competitive grants to fund their research. In department models, such as the UK, professors obtain grants from multiple national research councils and private foundation to buy out time from teaching and administration duties and support research staff. Despite the diversity of these funding measures for late-stage researchers, they have in common their importance in providing salaries that can maintain the positions of early-career colleagues.

In the US, recognition and reward-based forms of research funding become more important in the late career stage as signals of research leadership and reputation. Recognition of the accomplishments and visibility of faculty at this career stage can be awarded through high reputation chaired or endowed professorships (with accompanying research funds from the university), flexible research foundation funds and other reward mechanisms. These high-reputation and sparingly available awards are a pinnacle of recognition, to which there is uneven access (Treviño et al., 2018). For those who achieve these high recognition awards, access to flexible funding aligns with the changing role of the elite faculty member. The ability to fund projects, travel and support more junior colleagues puts the senior faculty member on an elite level of career advancement.

As careers develop, particularly at the more senior levels where opportunities to lead centres and large grants are more prevalent, senior academic researchers are challenged by different interests and opportunities, and the positive effects of grant-getting do not necessarily continue on an upward trajectory for all researchers. Expanded roles and the resulting stress of managing large grants and other faculty responsibilities can be a demotivator (Hendel and Horn, 2008). For the most senior faculty who have more opportunity to assume research leadership roles, issues of role stress, conflict and administrative burden associated with managing large awards can demotivate even successful senior researchers (Boardman and Bozeman, 2007). For example, evidence suggests that more senior productive faculty may be less inclined to contribute to communal knowledge sharing (Defazio et al., 2009), which may have some other trickle-down effects.

OVERVIEW

In sum, in this chapter we have provided an overview of the relationships between research funding mechanisms and support for academic careers. The availability and accessibility of research funding matters in the pathways and opportunities that shape researchers' careers. Research funding provides resources that enable the construction of teams, and the production and advancement of scientific knowledge and discovery. In turn, these outcomes and the success and reputation signalled by the acquisition of funding have both direct and indirect effects on individual careers, and at all career stages. We summarize some of these roles and impacts in Figure 18.1. While we have primarily focused on how research funding supports researchers' careers, other chapters in this volume, particularly those by Laudel and Horta, speak to the complex interrelationships of the institutional environment and impacts of funding availability, acquisition and personal career strategies.

While we acknowledge the multiple and varied sources of research funding, our focus has been on the highly competitive nature of the public funding environment which has the clearest implications for research careers. Contextually, research funding to support academic careers relies on a policy mix that continuously evolves. The extent to which competitive funds have become dominant depends very much on the characteristics and functioning of state bureaucracies and the set of authority relations that shape the structure and autonomy of public agencies and universities (Whitley et al., 2010, 2018). As we have seen, competitive funding that supports academic careers indirectly reflects a general capacity building approach

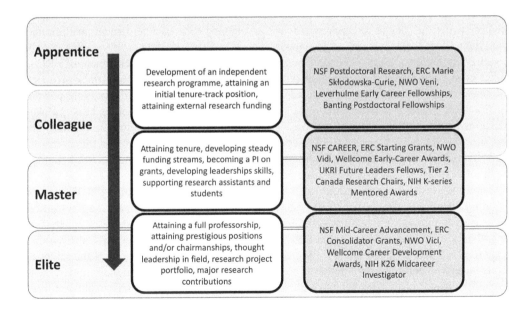

Figure 18.1   Research funding roles, by career stage (with sample funding tools)

to human and social capital (Bozeman et al., 2001), in which contract positions attached to research projects provide pathways for early-career researchers and sustain the careers of those unable to accede to more stable positions. Yet, there are costs. As scientific research teams have become more bureaucratized and the roles of individual researchers within teams more specialized (Walsh and Lee, 2015), scholars have noted the disruptive effect of placing early-career researchers as PIs in career-stage-specific funding mechanisms (Graddy-Reed et al., 2018, 2021; Nikaj and Lund, 2019). The effects of this shifting of roles and power within research teams and for developing research remains unknown, although recent scholarship suggests a positive impact on the advisor/mentee relationship (Graddy-Reed et al., 2021).

Alternatively, competitive awards to individual researchers can support the grantee to transition through critical stages of the career, particularly in establishing their independence to design and lead research, and in bridging towards the availability of tenured positions. These grants reflect institutional investment in the academic careers of the research 'talents' they identify. Both types of funding to support careers can be considered important to the quality and functioning of an academic science system. This interdependent relationship, and the form that it takes in different national systems, is an important dimension that must be considered in studies of funding and careers.

OPPORTUNITIES FOR FUTURE RESEARCH

The prevalence and prominence of sequenced individual career-stage funding schemes also raises interesting questions for future research. Many such schemes include a mechanism for incorporation into tenured or tenure-track positions. Others, including ERC Starter, Consolidator, and Advanced grants, do not, and in addition are portable between organizations and countries. Such schemes are highly selective and to some extent remove grantees from the typical career pathways of university academics. On the one hand, researchers who reach the end of such sequences of research awards without having secured a permanent position may find themselves lacking career achievements in areas such as teaching or service that may be required for tenure. On the other hand, some universities prioritize the recruitment of ERC or other prestigious research award holders, potentially impacting on the tenure-track prospects of researchers following more prosaic career trajectories that may include multiple postdoc positions or changes between employer organizations. There can therefore be significant tensions between these different pathways to building the peer community recognition and organizational requisites necessary for accessing stable positions. Research on these tensions and their effects would therefore be timely and of potential interest to multiple stakeholders with interests in the funding of scientific careers.

The future research agenda should also be one that can more meaningfully link the context of funding norms, requirements and accessibility to career advancement and transition. Scientific communities, institutions, funders and individual researchers share an understanding of a successful career path or script. Requirements for research achievements, international experience, leadership, and service, for example, will reflect the expectations of the scientific colleagues who control discipline-based peer review processes – including those reviews conducted on behalf of funding agencies. How disciplinary specific career scripts emerge from, and are maintained and institutionalized within different scientific communities is a question warranting further in-depth scholarship.

However, funders are increasingly also being tasked with designing priorities and instruments that not only distribute funding to talented researchers, but also with providing guidelines on what outcomes the researcher's work is expected to produce. Many large European research councils and private foundations and US funding agencies have also taken public positions on normative questions such as transforming the gender and ethnic composition of the research workforce and the involvement of stakeholders and citizens to improve the design and outcomes of research (Science Europe, 2021; Wellcome, 2021b). These engagements and expectations can be interpreted as also reflecting the kinds of values attaching to research and to investments in research careers. To what extent, therefore, might we see such expectations reflected in funding criteria that could contribute to a subtle shifting of career scripts? What effects the exertion of such funding pressure might have on the scientific vocation and on research career scripts over time remains uncertain, but constitutes a potentially interesting research question for the future.

There are several additional considerations and existing gaps relevant to an ongoing research agenda for the study of research funding and academic careers. The study of research funding is overly siloed, both theoretically and empirically. The inextricable relationship between research funding policies and requirements, institutional opportunities and expectations, scientific and human capital, and the scripts of research careers is not well developed in the existing literature. As we have discussed, the opportunities, relevance, and policy structures for research funding at different career stages differ considerably. Simple attributions to the Matthew effect – of success breeding success – vastly oversimplify how funding is sought, and how it matters for career transitions and advancement.

Related, this examination would also reveal the differences that exist between disciplines, both in the availability, function, and expectations for funding at different career stages. For example, researchers in laboratory-intensive disciplines with high equipment and facilities costs have wholly different needs and research team structures (and pressures) than those who are more data or field intensive. Developing an improved organizational conceptualization of these differences would help to advance our understanding of disciplinary funding structures and impacts. For example, the extent to which the productivity and career trajectory of early-career researchers who are co-PIs on standard grants compare with those with early-career research awards is also largely unknown. Evidence suggests that these early successes in prestigious early-career awards may not be universally reflected in later career impacts (van den Besselaar and Sandström, 2015). Likewise, research on setting and institutional climate are mostly disconnected from the study of the impacts of specific funding programmes on researcher experiences and work.

It is also critical to remove the social and behavioural siloing of studies of research funding and advancement. Social capital and relational resources are relevant to funding pursuit, success and (importantly) on-going management of funded research teams. Psychological barriers and confidence in pursuing funding, particularly in a highly competitive environment replete with rejection, are not well understood. The science policy research community could better incorporate psychological constructs, including efficacy and motivation, into the study of research funding and careers. Similarly, studies of mentoring could expand to examine the psychosocial and peer-related mentoring relevant to grant writing, team and research management, and career transitions (Freel et al., 2017). For example, recent work has pointed to the negative cumulative effects of rejection, where repeated unsuccessful applications reduce individual researcher confidence and motivation to pursue future proposals (Carson et al., 2013). This is consistent with self-determination theory (Deci and Ryan, 2000), which argues that individual needs and goals shape behaviour; in this case, grant-seeking. Work on 'imposter syndrome' (Bothello and Roulet, 2019), where an individual's negative reflections on their own abilities curtails their work and other engagements, highlights the cognitive aspects of seeking and managing research funding in academic careers. If an early (or later) career researcher feels a lack of confidence, this can have a detrimental and long-standing effect on their research career. The ability to move along the career pathway from apprentice to independent researcher described by Laudel and Gläser (2008) is likely to be impacted by these mutually related factors of confidence, support, and motivation.

Finally, and highly relevant to the research evaluation community, there remain significant gaps in our understanding of the relationship between funding and academic careers, and particularly career-stage-specific funding mechanisms. Despite anecdotal evidence and policy-maker narratives, surprisingly little is known about the impacts and outcomes of career-stage specific programmes over career lifetimes, and across disciplines and institutional settings. The ability to understand the career effects of the pursuit and acquisition of research funding across the range of career stages is dependent on the availability of data, the identification of appropriate metrics that address the diverse and often individual/interpersonal factors relevant to research funding, and an expanded effort by the research community concerned with STEM workforce/career effects of research funding. For example, more study is needed on the ideal order and mix of doctoral funding schemes to maximize the development of scientific and human capital and probability of degree completion (Grote et al., 2021). This is consistent with the points raised in Laudel's chapter that a more robust adaptation of organizational theory to research contexts and disciplinary norms could aid future research in important ways. Given the above, policy researchers should examine the political and agency rationales, support (as well as resistance) and expectations for the development of career-specific funding mechanisms. It is unclear whether these mechanisms' popularity, particularly at the early career stage, is a type of naive mimetic isomorphism among funders or is instead based on a foundation of theoretical arguments from the scholarly community.

CONCLUSIONS

Research careers receive important support through direct and indirect funding mechanisms. This support is primarily targeted at providing protected time and resources for the conduct of research and the development of the cognitive career. Whilst such funding typically provides temporary access (for the length of the grant) to an organizational position, it can also be made contingent upon provision of a future tenure-track position. Indirect funding of research positions remains a vital aspect of the career support system. The grant-getting success of researchers in mid and late career stages determines where project-based positions will be available. With the funding and governance of research increasingly conducted at the project level (Walsh and Lee, 2015), indirect funding for postdoctoral positions will remain a key form of labour market access that allows the initiation or continuation of many academic careers. However, the phenomenon of multiple sequential 'soft money' postdoc positions has raised questions about whether those employed in this manner are able to establish their own individual research project and become socialized into key career-relevant skillsets, such as project management and team leadership (Stephan, 2013; Stephan and Levin, 1997).

The importance of developing both research (cognitive career) and research leadership (community, organizational careers) capacities is reinforced by the prominence of these dual dimensions in prestigious career fellowships and awards. The research community must also take responsibility in their work by considering the complex and changing interplay between the availability and role of research funding across various career stages, in terms of both individual consequences and system effects. Research productivity when measured by grant acquisition risks vast oversimplification. Research careers are an irreducible mixture of intellectual and technical capabilities and the 'soft skills' necessary for productive and cohesive research teams, networks, and communities. It is essential that the design of career funding mechanisms continues to support and reinforce this holistic understanding of academic careers. Nonetheless, it is also important to recognize that transformation towards more open, inclusive, and responsible research cultures that better reflect wider society remains a desired future to which we should also expect career funding mechanisms to make a fundamental and valuable contribution.

REFERENCES

Ackers, L. (2008). Internationalisation, mobility and metrics: A new form of indirect discrimination? *Minerva, 46*(4), 411–435.

Åkerlind, G. S. (2005). Postdoctoral researchers: Roles, functions and career prospects. *Higher Education Research and Development, 24*(1), 21–40. https://doi.org/10.1080/0729436052000318550.

Australian Research Council (2021). Future Fellowships. ARC, Canberra. Retrieved from https://www.arc.gov.au/grants/discovery-program/future-fellowships December 6, 2021.

Barley, S. R. (1989). Careers, identities, and institutions: The legacy of the Chicago School of Sociology. *Handbook of Career Theory, 41*, 65.

Bazeley, P. (2003). Defining 'early career' in research. *Higher Education, 45*(3), 257–279. https://doi.org/10.1023/A:1022698529612.

Boardman, C., and Bozeman, B. (2007). Role strain in university research centers. *The Journal of Higher Education, 78*(4), 430–463.

Bosanquet, A., Mailey, A., Matthews, K. E., and Lodge, J. M. (2017). Redefining 'early career' in academia: A collective narrative approach. *Higher Education Research and Development, 36*(5), 890–902. https://doi.org/10.1080/07294360.2016.1263934.

Bothello, J., and Roulet, T. J. (2019, June 1). The imposter syndrome, or the mis-representation of self in academic life. *Journal of Management Studies, 56*(4), 854–861. https://doi.org/10.1111/joms.12344.

Bourdieu, P. (1975). The specificity of the scientific field and the social conditions of the progress of reason. *Social Science Information, 14*(6), 19–47.

Bourdieu, P. (2004). *Science of Science and Reflexivity*. Cambridge: Polity Press.

Bozeman, B., Dietz, J. S., and Gaughan, M. (2001). Scientific and technical human capital: An alternative model for research evaluation. *International Journal of Technology Management, 22*(7–8), 716–740.

Bozeman, B., and Sarewitz, D. (2011). Public value mapping and science policy evaluation. *Minerva, 49*, 1–23.

Braun, D. (1998). The role of funding agencies in the cognitive development of science. *Research Policy, 27*(8), 807–821.

Cañibano, C., Woolley, R., Iversen, E. J., Hinze, S., Hornbostel, S., and Tesch, J. (2019). A conceptual framework for studying science research careers. *Journal of Technology Transfer, 44*(6), 1964–1992. https://doi.org/10.1007/s10961-018-9659-3.

Cantwell, B. (2011). Academic in-sourcing: International postdoctoral employment and new modes of academic production. *Journal of Higher Education Policy and Management, 33*(2), 101–114.

Carson, L., Bartneck, C., and Voges, K. (2013). Over-competitiveness in academia: A literature review. https://doi.org/10.1089/dst.2013.0013.

Chapman, G. B., and McCauley, C. (1993). Early career achievements of National Science Foundation (NSF) graduate applicants: Looking for Pygmalion and Galatea effects on NSF winners. *Journal of Applied Psychology, 78*(5), 815–820. https://doi.org/10.1037/0021-9010.78.5.815.

Conte, M. L., and Omary, M. B. (2018). NIH Career Development Awards: Conversion to research grants and regional distribution. *The Journal of Clinical Investigation, 128*(12), 5187–5190. https://doi.org/10.1172/JCI123875.

Daniels, R. J. (2015). A generation at risk: Young investigators and the future of the biomedical workforce. *Proceedings of the National Academy of Sciences, 112*(2), 313–318.

Deci, E. L., and Ryan, R. M. (2000). The 'what' and 'why' of goal pursuits: Human needs and the self-determination of behavior. *Psychological Inquiry, 11*(4), 227–268. https://doi.org/10.1207/S15327965PLI1104_01.

Defazio, D., Lockett, A., and Wright, M. (2009). Funding incentives, collaborative dynamics and scientific productivity: Evidence from the EU framework program. *Research Policy, 38*(2), 293–305. https://doi.org/10.1016/j.respol.2008.11.008.

Denton, M., Choe, N. H., Borrego, M. J., and Knight, D. B. (2020). Optimal sequencing of graduate funding in a chemical engineering department: Maximizing completion and persistence rates. *2020 ASEE Virtual Annual Conference Content Access.*

Dorismond, C., Prince, A. C., Farzal, Z., and Zanation, A. M. (2021). Long-term academic outcomes of triological society research career development award recipients. *The Laryngoscope, 131*(2), 288–293. https://doi.org/https://doi.org/10.1002/lary.28714.

Dutch Research Council Science (NWO) (2021a) NWO Talent Programme: Veni 2021 Call for proposals. NWO, The Hague, Netherlands.

Dutch Research Council Science (NWO) (2021b) NWO Talent Programme: Vidi 2021 Call for proposals. NWO, The Hague, Netherlands.

Dutch Research Council Science (NWO) (2021c) NWO Talent Programme: Vici 2021 Call for proposals. NWO, The Hague, Netherlands.

Estermann, T., Nokkala, T., and Steinel, M. (2011). University autonomy in Europe II. The Scorecard. Brussels: European University Association.

Freel, S. A., Smith, P. C., Burns, E. N., Downer, J. B., Brown, A. J., and Dewhirst, M. W. (2017). Multidisciplinary mentoring programs to enhance junior faculty research grant success. *Academic Medicine: Journal of the Association of American Medical Colleges, 92*(10), 1410.

Fox, M. F., and Colatrella, C. (2006). Participation, performance, and advancement of women in academic science and engineering: What is at issue and why. *The Journal of Technology Transfer, 31*(3), 377–386.

Gaughan, M., and Bozeman, B. (2019). Institutionalized inequity in the USA: The case of postdoctoral researchers. *Science and Public Policy, 46*(3), 358–368.

Gläser, J., and Laudel, G. (2015). The three careers of an academic. Zentrum Technic und Geselshaft Discussion Paper 35/2015.

Good, M., McElroy, S. J., Berger, J. N., Moore, D. J., and Wynn, J. L. (2018). Limited achievement of NIH research independence by pediatric K award recipients. *Pediatric Research, 84*(4), 479–480.

Graddy-Reed, A., Lanahan, L., and Ross, N. M. V. (2018). The Effect of R&D investment on graduate student productivity: Evidence from the life sciences. *Journal of Policy Analysis and Management, 37*(4), 809–834. https://doi.org/https://doi.org/10.1002/pam.22083.

Graddy-Reed, A., Lanahan, L., and D'Agostino, J. (2021). Training across the academy: The impact of R&D funding on graduate students. *Research Policy, 50*(5), 104224.

Grote, D., Patrick, A., Lyles, C., Knight, D., Borrego, M., and Alsharif, A. (2021). STEM doctoral students' skill development: does funding mechanism matter? *International Journal of STEM Education, 8*(1), 50. https://doi.org/10.1186/s40594-021-00308-w.

Haak, L., and Schnell, J. (2011). *National Institutes of Health Individual Mentored Career Development Awards Program.* Alexandria, VA. Retrieved from https://researchtraining.nih.gov/sites/default/files/pdf/K_Awards_Evaluation_FinalReport_20110901.pdf#.

Heggeness, M., Ginther, D., Larenas, M., and Carter-Johnson, F. (2018). *The Impact of Postdoctoral Fellowships on a Future Independent Career in Federally Funded Biomedical Research.* Cambridge, MA. https://doi.org/10.3386/w24508.

Hendel, D. D., and Horn, A. S. (2008). The relationship between academic life conditions and perceived sources of faculty stress over time. *Journal of Human Behavior in the Social Environment, 17*(1–2), 61–88. https://doi.org/10.1080/10911350802165536.

Hicks, D., and Katz, J. S. (2011). Equity and excellence in research funding. *Minerva, 49*(2), 137–151. https://doi.org/10.1007/s11024-011-9170-6.

Horta, H., and Santos, J. M. (2016). The impact of publishing during PhD studies on career research publication, visibility, and collaborations. *Research in Higher Education, 57*(1), 28–50.

Horta, H., Cattaneo, M., and Meoli, M. (2018). PhD funding as a determinant of PhD and career research performance. *Studies in Higher Education, 43*(3), 542–570. https://doi.org/10.1080/03075079.2016 .1185406.

Huisman, J., De Weert, E., and Bartelse, J. (2002). Academic careers from a European perspective: The declining desirability of the faculty position. *The Journal of Higher Education, 73*(1), 141–160.

Knight, D., Kinoshita, T., Choe, N., and Borrego, M. (2018). Doctoral student funding portfolios across and within engineering, life sciences and physical sciences. *Studies in Graduate and Postdoctoral Education, 9*(1), 75–90.

Lam, A. (2011). What motivates academic scientists to engage in research commercialization: 'Gold', 'ribbon' or 'puzzle'? *Research Policy, 40*(10), 1354–1368, https://doi.org/10.1016/j.respol.2011.09 .002.

Lanahan, L., Graddy-Reed, A., and Feldman, M. P. (2016). The domino effects of federal research funding. *PLoS One, 11*(6), e0157325. Retrieved from https://doi.org/10.1371/journal.pone.0157325.

Laudel, G., and Bielick, J. (2018). The emergence of individual research programs in the early career phase of academics. *Science, Technology, and Human Values, 43*(6), 972–1010. https://doi.org/10 .1177/0162243918763100.

Laudel, G., and Bielick, J. (2019). How do field-specific research practices affect mobility decisions of early career researchers? *Research Policy, 48*(9), 103800.

Laudel, G., and Gläser, J. (2008). From apprentice to colleague: The metamorphosis of early career researchers. *Higher Education, 55*(3), 387–406.

Laudel, G., Bielick, J., and Gläser, J. (2019). Ultimately the question always is: 'What do I have to do to do it right?' Scripts as explanatory factors of career decisions. *Human Relations, 72*(5), 932–961.

Levin, S. G., and Stephan, P. E. (1991). Research productivity over the life cycle: Evidence for academic scientists. *The American Economic Review, 81*(1), 114–132. Retrieved from http://www.jstor.org/ stable/2006790.

Merton, R. K. (1968). The Matthew effect in science. *Science, 159*(3810), 56–62. https://doi.org/10 .1126/science.159.3810.56.

Michie, J., Zhang, X., Wells, J., Ristow, L., Pion, G., Miyaoka, A., and Frechtling, J. (2007). *Feasibility, Design and Planning Study for Evaluating the NIH Career Development Awards*. Retrieved from https://researchtraining.nih.gov/programs/career-development/K02.

Millsap, M. A., Hill, E., Brigham, N., Garcia, G., Levin, M., Martinez, A., … Silva, A. (2001). *Faculty Early Career Development (CAREER) Program: External Evaluation Summary Report*. Retrieved from https://nsf.gov/pubs/2001/nsf01134/nsf01134.pdf.

Muller-Parker, G., Brennan, S. E., and Jones, E. C. (2020). Why fellowships? A funding model worth defending. *GradEdge, 9*(01). https://cgsnet.org/why-fellowships-funding-model-worth-defending?nl =6049.

National Center for Science and Engineering Statistics. (2019). Survey of earned doctorates. https://ncses .nsf.gov/pubs/nsf21308/data-tables.

National Institutes of Health. (2021). Research Career Development ('K') Awards. In *NIH Grants Policy Statement* (pp. IIB-81 to IIB-101). Bethesda, MD: Department of Health and Human Services. Retrieved from https://grants.nih.gov/grants/policy/nihgps/nihgps.pdf.

National Science Foundation. (2019). *FY 2020 NSF Budget Request to Congress*. https://www.nsf.gov/ about/budget/fy2020/pdf/05_fy2020.pdf.

Neave, G., and Rhoades, G. (1987). The academic estate in Western Europe. In B. R. Clark (Ed.), *The Academic Profession: National, Disciplinary and Institutional Settings* (pp. 211–270). Berkeley, CA: University of California Press.

Nerad, M., and Cerny, J. (1999, September 3). Postdoctoral patterns, career advancement, and problems. *Science*. https://doi.org/10.1126/science.285.5433.1533.

Nicholas, D., Watkinson, A., Boukacem-Zeghmouri, C., Rodríguez-Bravo, B., Xu, J., Abrizah, A., Świgo, M., and Herman, E. (2017). Early career researchers: Scholarly behaviour and the prospect of change. *Wiley Online Library*, *30*(2), 157–166. https://doi.org/10.1002/leap.1098.

Nikaj, S., and Lund, P. K. (2019). The impact of individual mentored career development (K) awards on the research trajectories of early-career scientists. *Academic Medicine*, *94*(5). Retrieved from https://journals.lww.com/academicmedicine/Fulltext/2019/05000/The_Impact_of_Individual_Mentored_Career.43.aspx.

O'Meara, K. A., and Stromquist, N. P. (2015). Faculty peer networks: Role and relevance in advancing agency and gender equity. *Gender and Education*, *27*(3), 338–358. https://doi.org/10.1080/09540253.2015.1027668.

Pickett, C. L. (2019). The increasing importance of fellowships and career development awards in the careers of early-stage biomedical academic researchers. *PLoS One*, *14*(10), e0223876. https://doi.org/10.1371/journal.pone.0223876.

Pinheiro, D., Melkers, J., and Youtie, J. (2014). Learning to play the game: Student publishing as an indicator of future scholarly success. *Technological Forecasting and Social Change*, *81*, 56–66.

Pomeroy-Carter, C. A., Williams, S. R., Han, X., Elwood, W. N., and Zuckerman, B. L. (2018). Evaluation of a mid-career investigator career development award: Assessing the ability of OppNet K18 awardees to obtain NIH follow-on research funding. *PLoS One*, *13*(2), e0192543. https://doi.org/10.1371/journal.pone.0192543.

Scaffidi, A. K., and Berman, J. E. (2011). A positive postdoctoral experience is related to quality supervision and career mentoring, collaborations, networking and a nurturing research environment. *Higher Education*, *62*(6), 685. https://doi.org/10.1007/s10734-011-9407-1.

Science Europe (2021). Science Europe Strategy Plan 2021–2026. https://doi.org/10.5281/zenodo.4911426.

Serrano Velarde, K. (2018). The way we ask for money ... The emergence and institutionalization of grant writing practices in academia. *Minerva*, *56*, 85–107. https://doi.org/10.1007/s11024-018-9346-4.

Sorkness, C. A., Scholl, L., Fair, A. M., and Umans, J. G. (2020). KL2 mentored career development programs at clinical and translational science award hubs: Practices and outcomes. *Journal of Clinical and Translational Science*, *4*(1), 43–52. https://doi.org/DOI: 10.1017/cts.2019.424.

Stephan, P. (2013). How to exploit postdocs. *BioScience*, *63*(4), 245–246.

Stephan, P. E., and Levin, S. G. (1997). The critical importance of careers in collaborative scientific research. *Revue d'économie industrielle*, *79*(1), 45–61.

Swiss National Science Foundation (2021). SNSF Starting Grants 2022: Call document. SNSF, Bern. Retrieved from https://www.snf.ch/en/bUfwIrA1RmvvDcgn/news/new-funding-scheme-snsf-starting-grants-2022 December 5, 2021.

Teelken, C., Taminiau, Y., and Rosenmöller, C. (2021). Career mobility from associate to full professor in academia: micro-political practices and implicit gender stereotypes. *Studies in Higher Education*, *46*(4), 836–850. https://doi.org/10.1080/03075079.2019.1655725.

Treviño, L. J., Gomez-Mejia, L. R., Balkin, D. B., and Mixon Jr, F. G. (2018). Meritocracies or masculinities? The differential allocation of named professorships by gender in the academy. *Journal of Management*, *44*(3), 972–1000.

UK Research and Innovation (2019). *The Concordat to Support the Career Development of Researchers*. Retrieved from https://www.vitae.ac.uk/policy/concordat/full.

van den Besselaar, P., and Sandström, U. (2015). Early career grants, performance, and careers: A study on predictive validity of grant decisions. *Journal of Informetrics*, *9*(4), 826–838. https://doi.org/https://doi.org/10.1016/j.joi.2015.07.011.

Van Miegroet, H., Glass, C., Callister, R. R., and Sullivan, K. (2019). Unclogging the pipeline: Advancement to full professor in academic STEM. *Equality, Diversity and Inclusion: An International Journal*, *38*(2), 246–264. https://doi.org/10.1108/EDI-09-2017-0180.

Velux Foundation (2021). Villum Young Investigator. Retrieved from https://veluxfoundations.dk/en/teknisk-og-naturvidenskabelig-forskning/young-investigators. Accessed May 10, 2022.

Walsh, J. P., and Lee, Y.-N. (2015). The bureaucratization of science. *Research Policy*, *44*(8), 1584–1600. https://doi.org/https://doi.org/10.1016/j.respol.2015.04.010.

Wellcome (2021a) Grant funding. Retrieved from https://wellcome.org/grant-funding. Accessed December 10, 2021.

Wellcome (2021b) Diversity, equity and inclusion strategy. Retrieved from https://wellcome.org/what -we-do/our-work/diversity-and-inclusion/strategy. Accessed December 30, 2021.

Whitley, R., Gläser, J., and Engwall, L. (Eds.). (2010). *Reconfiguring Knowledge Production: Changing Authority Relationships in the Sciences and their Consequences for Intellectual Innovation.* Oxford: Oxford University Press.

Whitley, R., Gläser, J., and Laudel, G. (2018). The impact of changing funding and authority relationships on scientific innovation. *Minerva, 56,* 109–134. https://doi.org/10.1007/s11024-018-9343-7.

19. Research funding and academics' scholarly performance

Hugo Horta and Huan Li

INTRODUCTION

The past 50 years have witnessed drastic changes in the funding of research, with funding being increasingly scarce in relative terms and funding allocation being progressively conditional on performance. In the past, the state would provide funding to universities (often in lump sums), and universities could do with it as they pleased (Shapin, 2012). The state then gained greater control as public investment increased and universities were required to be more responsive to societal demands. Finally, owing to diminishing returns from this investment, constrained public budgets, and state reforms, the state settled into a role of evaluation and impact (Gunn and Mintrom, 2016). The latter role of the state was encouraged by a political turn towards neoliberal policies that urged state organisations to introduce structures and incentives inspired by practices in the private sector. Such policies returned some conditional autonomy[1] to universities based on performance-based indicators (Graffikin and Perry, 2009).

The changing landscape of research funding and the broader relationship between the state and universities have impacted both academics and their research for two reasons: funding is increasingly a prerequisite for conducting scientific research and acquiring funding helps academics to secure employment in academia. As an indispensable resource that plays a decisive role in organisational development, according to resource dependence theory, funding issues have received much attention at the organisational level. Subsequently, studies on how funding has impacted individual academics and their work have become increasingly relevant.

This chapter reviews known information regarding the effect of changing funding schemes on academics' performance in research, teaching, and service. We begin with a description of major developments that have provided a macro-historical perspective and influenced not only the evolution of funding mechanisms but also the role and focus of funding agencies. We then review the literature on the effects of the changing funding arrangements on academics and their scholarly performance, which is the focus of this chapter. The conclusion provides a critical summary of the main findings in this literature and proposes future research directions. It should be acknowledged that while we attempt to present a global overview on this salient issue, the literature we review is largely from countries in Asia, Europe, North America, and Oceania because these systems have been better documented and tend to lead or be representative of global trends.

MAJOR EVENTS IN THE HIGHER EDUCATION SECTOR WORLDWIDE

The relationship between funding and academic performance involves an evolving dynamic between the state and higher education, as the state is the primary funder of the knowledge-creation activities of academic institutions (Pavitt, 2000). Thus, when examining the effect of funding on research practices, one must consider 'the social mechanisms underlying research funding' (Gläser and Velarde, 2018, p. 7). We therefore provide a brief overview of major events in academic research and higher education and the attendant effects on funding schemes before focusing on the individual level.

We argue that the current relationship between funding and academics' performance is better understood through the contextualisation of four historical events initiated in North America and Europe before gradually spreading across the entire world. These events to some extent overlap, each reinforcing or triggering the others. The first was the adoption by policymakers and international organisations (e.g. the Organisation for Economic Co-operation and Development, OECD) of endogenous growth and human capital theories that emerged in the second half of the 20th century (Peters, 2003). The second event involved the diminishing returns of public investment in higher education observed in the late 1970s (OECD, 2018; Carnoy et al., 2012). Emerging in the 1990s, the third event was the centrality of knowledge for economic development, which influenced the development of national systems of innovation (Godin, 2009) and the continued association between triple- and quadruple-helix relations (Carayannis and Campbell, 2009; Leydesdorff and Etzkowitz, 1996) and endogenous growth theories. The fourth major event was the emergent need for policymakers to foster a more utilitarian knowledge perspective through evidence of impact, which was solidified in the early 2000s (Gunn and Mintrom, 2016).

In the first half of the 20th century, higher education was designed in most developed countries to train national elites and the obstacles to entry were high. Investment in higher education was residual, and the sector was not overly burdensome to the state owing to its small size. However, with a shift in the economic development paradigm based on the emergence of endogenous growth and human capital theories (Peters, 2003; Ulnicane, Chapter 4 in this *Handbook*), governments realised the need to invest in formal learning activities, which included both fostering the qualifications of the broader population and promoting research and development (R&D). These endeavours were part of a competitive, technology-driven race stimulated by three key events: World War II, the Cold War, and the emergence of globalisation (Castells, 2010). This shift by governments was based not only on technical functionalism but also on social and cultural emulation strongly rooted in the institutional and culturally construed globalisation of common ideals and purposes (Ramirez and Christensen, 2013). In this process, governments and populations were enticed by the potential private, social, and economic returns of education (Schofer and Meyer, 2005). The growing participation in education brought new competencies to the labour market and facilitated differentiation between individuals in terms of job skills and the associated rewards (Weeden, 2002). Consequently, higher education systems rapidly expanded, first in developed countries and then in developing countries. In the US, for instance, as this expansion occurred, the state showed commitment to investment and accumulation by increasingly contributing to R&D, which drove private companies to follow suit as they came to understand the importance of investing in knowledge to develop more sophisticated products and services (Conceição et al., 2004).

With increasing public expenditures flowing into higher education sectors, states increasingly expected universities to participate in and engage with society in general. Initially, in developed countries, universities were expected to innovate and demonstrate that the knowledge they produced had practical value to public- and private-sector organisations as well as citizens. This was part of a policy framework wherein states were striving for a more strategic perspective on the production and use of knowledge, given rising awareness of the global knowledge competition. Following World War II, in 1945–1950, the Cold War began to necessitate rearmament of the US national innovation system. The federal government provided an unprecedented level of financial support to R&D activity. The focus of federal R&D funding shifted from federal government laboratories to industry and universities, and the latter became the main producers of basic research. Aiming to catch up with the technological and economic performance of leading countries, European countries also proactively promoted national science policies and integrated universities into national innovation systems in the 1960s. With the concept of the 'national innovation system' promoted by the OECD and several renowned academics in the 1980s, universities around the world have been gradually integrated into such systems and have become one of their pillars (Godin, 2009).

As the scale of higher education expanded, expenditures and public budgets for research increased. However, the growing scale of public budgets to support higher education systems, their accessibility or universality, and a largely qualified workforce led to diminishing returns on public investment in the sector (Ionescu and Polgreen, 2009), which some scholars considered unavoidable (e.g. Jacobs and van der Ploeg, 2006). In line with the apparent diminishing returns from R&D expenditures, many economies began to consider public budgets excessive and thus implemented neoliberal reforms to achieve greater levels of accountability and effectiveness.

In the 1980s, the business sector of the most advanced economies, such as the US, France, and Germany, began to play an increasingly relevant role in funding R&D, while governmental investment in research stagnated or even declined (Etzkowitz et al., 2000; Mowery, 1998). In the late 1990s, the triple helix model of innovation began to impact the organisation of research in a larger area of the globe, including Continental Europe, Latin America, and Asia (Etzkowitz et al., 2000). This model further called for universities to contribute to the economy with the knowledge they produce, and highlighted the interaction of government, industry, and universities in building regional and national innovation systems while eroding the organisational and normative boundaries among the three sectors (Leydesdorff and Etzkowitz, 1996). This concept has somewhat challenged the collegial tradition in research by integrating other interests into the design and evaluation of academic output. Within this model, academics have been encouraged to engage in greater entrepreneurship to link academia to the market and therefore serve the knowledge economy (Etzkowitz, 2002). Public incentives have enhanced this trend by stimulating research commercialisation and university–industry collaboration. Consequently, an increasing number of universities in developed countries have begun to internalise the determinant role of technology and markets in economic development (Benner and Sandström, 2000).

Since the 1990s, governments have increasingly desired to show the public the value of public expenditures and have thus pressured funding agencies to demonstrate that the research they fund can impact daily lives (Martin, 2011). This emphasis on research impact also aligned with theoretical development from the triple- to quadruple-helix innovation framework, which highlighted the role of the media-based and culture-based public in driving innovation in democratic societies (Carayannis and Campbell, 2009). Nonetheless, assessing research impact is a difficult problem because the definition of 'impact' as well as the manner of its rigorous and reliable assessment remain ambiguous. Accordingly, the effects of research (particularly concerning research impact) developed into an emerging research topic to facilitate the design of evaluation tools with a focus on how quality can be measured and encouraged. For example, Buxton and Hanney (1996) developed a 'payback framework' for funding allocation in health sciences, which categorises research payback into five types and has been adopted in many countries.

THE ROLE OF FUNDING AGENCIES AND THEIR CHANGING FOCUS

Funding agencies serve as an important broker between academics and the state. They design and implement rules regarding research funding allocation, which are conditioned by the state but also directly influence academics. Given the importance of funding agencies, this section summarises how the role and focus of funding agencies evolved under the influence of the four major events in higher education mentioned above.

Research funding agencies played a minor role during the decades of higher education massification. With the growth of research activity and the perceived importance of qualifications, the status of academia rose globally, while its norms transformed to further highlight disciplinary knowledge production and peer recognition (Clark, 1983). Universities and academics were necessarily affected, even if this change was subtle. In many countries, scholars managed to regulate funding agencies in the decade after World War II, largely following collegially based norms and thus maintaining academic autonomy (Benner and Sandström, 2000). To increase disciplinary knowledge, both funding allocation and research evaluation emphasised academic quality and scholarly contributions (Benner and Sandström, 2000).

With the establishment of national innovation systems, funding agencies increasingly played the role of the principal in their relationships with universities and academics, who served as agents (Ferlie et al., 2008). In this context, the purpose of research funding was shifted towards fulfilling specific R&D tasks, whether policy-oriented or economically driven. To stimulate research to implement political and technological priorities, in the 1980s funding agencies in many countries introduced research projects with defined themes that coexisted with the pre-existing funding schemes (Potì and Reale, 2007).

In the era of neoliberalism, competition was widely introduced to the research funding system, such that performance-based block funding was allocated to universities and competitive grants to research projects based on either performance or 'promises of performance'. These competition-based funding reforms developed separately and in various forms globally from the mid-1980s, such as in Europe (Jongbloed and Lepori, 2015), Australasia (Hicks, 2012), and Asia (Shin et al., 2020; Shin and Lee, 2015). Although non-competitive funding methods, such as on a historical basis or via negotiation, remain in use (Auranen and Nieminen, 2010), the proportion of competitive funding has risen worldwide. For example, performance-based block funding comprised 13% of Finland's funding to universities in 2019, up from only 0.3% a decade before (Mathies et al., 2020). Through such performance-based funding reforms, funding agencies intended to increase both productivity and excellence in research per unit of investment (Hicks, 2012), which has proven fruitful in some contexts (e.g. Italy; Cattaneo et al., 2016).

The UK became the first country to implement an impact assessment and apply it to all scientific fields at the national level. The UK government uses 'impact' as an assessment dimension in the evaluation of its universities' research, namely the Research Excellence Framework of 2014, and emphasises the dual criteria of research excellence: academic contribution and societal/economic impact. The adoption of this funding rule meant that the academic quality of research was no longer the sole basis of research assessment and funding allocation. The funding aim of the Research Excellence Framework also changed to 'secur[ing] the continuation of a world-class, dynamic and responsive research base across the full academic spectrum within UK higher education' (Research Excellence Framework, n.d.). This aligns with an agenda to transform universities and ensure that university-based research is assessable in terms of the benefits of public investment. Similar impact assessment practices have also been implemented by funding agencies in other countries, such as Australia (Excellence in Research for Australia) and the Netherlands (Standard Evaluation Protocol).

To enhance research impact, some funding agencies have also included inter-sector collaborations as a requirement for funding applications, such as the Linkage funding scheme promoted by the Australian Research Council (2021), 'Knowledge-building Project for Industry' initiated by the Research Council of Norway (2021), and various programmes funded by the European Commission. Such schemes aimed to prompt universities to establish durable strategic research partnerships with other organisations.

Relatedly, given that many complex problems facing societies cannot be addressed from a single theoretical perspective or analytical method, establishing programmes that encourage interdisciplinary research has become a trend in research councils globally (Lyall et al., 2013). Interdisciplinary research proposals had long been discouraged under previous competition-based funding schemes not only because of their typical expense (Lyall et al., 2013) but also because research proposals were previously only assessed within disciplinary councils in most countries. The pressing need to address complicated global challenges and the underfunded states of certain research areas jointly prompted the establishment of special funding schemes for interdisciplinary research. Despite no direct examination of their effects owing to recent implementation, these funding schemes are expected to facilitate the advancement of science as well as address the targeted issues by fostering long-term interdisciplinary collaborations.

EFFECT OF CHANGING FUNDING ARRANGEMENTS ON ACADEMICS' SCHOLARLY PERFORMANCE

The changing funding arrangements have had pervasive effects on academics' scholarly performance. We sub-divide the relevant literature into effects on research agendas, research productivity, research collaboration, innovation and research, teaching and supervision, and the academic labour market. While these dimensions are interrelated, this categorisation enables more depth while maintaining analytical breadth.

Effect on Research Agendas

Most of the aforementioned trends in research funding have been shown to influence academics' research agendas. That is, academics have adapted their research focuses to meet funding priorities rather than following the natural next steps of their previous research. Arguably, the integration of and focus on universities by national innovation systems has affected the autonomy, and therefore the research agenda-setting, of academics, who are now restricted by competitive research grant allocations. Individual academics must consider funding opportunities when forming their strategic research agendas as they are incentivised to publish more in certain areas than in others, and to increase the range of knowledge outputs (Shin and Lee, 2015). Large-scale funding for research on topics of individual interest and for other self-directed research has become scarce in many funding systems (Gläser and Laudel, 2007) as it has been increasingly allocated to research themes of strategic interest to governments. Academics, particularly those in science, technology, engineering, and mathematics (STEM) disciplines, came to understand that individual strategic research autonomy was limited by the availability of research funding (Woelert et al., 2020). Although academia had previously concentrated on basic research, both public and private funding agencies in national innovation systems and triple-helix settings tended to prioritise applied research owing to its potential to generate monetary or social benefits (Gulbrandsen and Smeby, 2005). In addition, as private business sector funding tends to positively affect academics' participation in technology transfer (e.g. Yang et al., 2019), there was widespread concern that academics in such funding environments would swarm into applied fields and leave key fundamental research questions untouched (e.g. Mowery, 1998). However, these concerns have been partly dispelled by studies showing that most academics work on a fusion of basic and applied research, with a very small proportion specialising exclusively in applied research (Bentley et al., 2015).

Competition-based funding schemes appear to more directly influence research agendas and the direction of research advancement within a discipline. Data from several studies have suggested that owing to the importance of funding to academic career progression, most academics generally act in line with the changes in research funding schemes (Mathies et al., 2020). Evidence has shown that an exceedingly competitive funding system can inhibit academics from proposing ground-breaking research (e.g. Horta and Santos, 2020), which arguably threatens creativity and knowledge advancement. Some studies (e.g. Dougherty and Natow, 2020; Heinze et al., 2009) have reported that in pursuit of efficiency, funding agencies tend to allocate funding to projects that have already obtained preliminary research findings or to those in areas that are already trending (meaning some research foundation has already been built). Applicants are also required to specify targets and possible findings and report their research progress regularly. All of these funding allocation practices restrict the ability of academics to propose ground-breaking research owing to concerns that subsequent funding will not be guaranteed (Horta and Santos, 2020; Young, 2015). Moreover, several lines of evidence have suggested that competition-based funding schemes discourage academics in emerging disciplines, as research excellence is often assessed by mainstream researchers who lead the major research evaluation committees that determine funding allocation (e.g. Lee, 2007). As such, certain areas and research methods within a given discipline are more likely to be funded. For example, within economics, neoclassicists have dominated the 'diamond list' journals and leading economics departments, which favour their line of thinking and research over more heterodox research (Lee, 2007). Nevertheless, the effect of competition-based funding on academics' research agendas is highly context-dependent. Whitley (2007) found that strong research evaluation systems characterised by linking research performance directly to funding allocation are more likely to influence research agendas. The author also noted that as the proportion of resources supplied by competitive funding increases, the more likely it is that academics will align their research agendas with funding purposes.

Various studies have shown that evidence-of-impact funding methods are a double-edged sword for academics in terms of their research agenda-setting (Marcella et al., 2016; Stern, 2016). More positively, the introduction of impact criteria has impressed upon academics the importance of the societal impact of research (Chubb and Reed, 2018; Reale et al., 2016; Stern, 2016). In Marcella et al. (2016), interviews with library and information science academics revealed that they now proactively plan how their research can benefit stakeholders and expand the population of research beneficiaries by more deliberately considering possible research designs and methodologies before applying for research projects. To some extent, impact assessment effectively encourages academics to closely engage their stakeholders and research beneficiaries by improving their strategic thinking when forming their research agendas (Stern, 2016). However, concerns have also been raised that some components of impact assessment designs may threaten research agenda-setting (Manville et al., 2015; Marcella et al., 2016). Such assessments tend to narrow the definition of 'impact' and cause academics to form a particular notion of the desired output, such as 'instrumental impacts' with tangible benefits to non-academic stakeholders, rather than other forms including 'conceptual impacts' or 'capacity building impacts' (Ma et al., 2020; Meagher and Martin, 2017). This leads academics to propose research that is closer to real-life applications (Stern, 2016) and to avoid long-term or risky research agendas that are less likely to be regarded as impactful by review panels (Bandola-Gill and Smith, 2021). Although some funding schemes have been designed to exclusively encourage blue-sky and innovative research during the past few years, it was recently reported that such schemes still fail to understand the dynamics of scientific progress and devaluate some forms of effort towards scientific innovation (Falkenberg, 2021).

Effect on Research Productivity and Publication Patterns

One of the most prominent merits of performance-based funding and competition for project grants is their assumed incentives to improve research productivity and/or excellence (Stern, 2016), as measured by metrics such as citation numbers and publications in high-impact journals. This merit has been demonstrated by many studies at the individual (Aagaard et al., 2015), organisational (Cattaneo et al., 2016; Smart, 2009), and national levels (Aagaard et al., 2015; Checchi et al., 2019), although with several exceptions (Auranen and Nieminen, 2010). Nonetheless, inspired by the impact agenda, new funding schemes that require engagement with non-academic stakeholders have been perceived by many academics as harmful to their research productivity. A primary reason is that some academics find it difficult to publish in peer-reviewed journals if the ideas and requests of non-academic stakeholders are included in the early stages of research projects (Chubb and Reed, 2018).

Performativity and the attendant alteration of academics' publication patterns have been regarded as notable pitfalls of competition-based funding schemes (Kivistö and Mathies, Chapter 12 in this *Handbook*). To bolster evaluation efficiency, some national systems and universities have applied formulas to funding allocation, using journal-based metrics such as impact factors and indices such as Journal Citation Reports quartiles to evaluate publication quality. Additionally, scientometric evaluative techniques have become popular in universities' human resources management, including in decisions concerning academic staff appointments, promotions, and tenure (Smith et al., 2013). This evaluation method effectively stimulates academics to publish in high-impact journals; however, it has drawbacks, particularly for the humanities and social sciences (HSS) and in non-English-speaking countries (Xu et al., 2021). The high priority given to international journals also directs academics' attention to topics with international relevance, thereby discouraging both research on local issues and publishing findings in national journals (Li and Li, 2021; Mathies et al., 2020). Furthermore, several studies suggest that as competitive funding schemes and assessments often fail to fully consider disciplinary differences and place undue weight on indexed journal publications – the major publication venue of STEM fields (Sivertsen, Chapter 6 in this *Handbook*) – some HSS department leaders are pressured to request that academics place less emphasis on the publication of books and book chapters. In some cases, such as in Hong Kong, departments even administer mock evaluation exercises and display the results, placing considerable pressure on academics and making them feel 'named and shamed' (Li and Li, 2021). Such circumstances exacerbate the article-inflation phenomenon, which runs counter to the policy objectives of research funding agency managers and policymakers (Butler, 2003).

Effect on Research Collaboration

The increasing prevalence of research collaborations is a positive development in that they permit the higher levels of complexity, interdisciplinarity, and dissemination required by many modern research challenges (Bammer, 2008). Some studies have suggested that competitive funding research schemes increase collaboration, particularly within the academic sector (Bloch et al., 2014), but this phenomenon has a multi-layered explanation. First, some academics may use academic collaboration as a tactic to increase research productivity and impact and therefore secure their academic careers (Melin, 2000). Career advancement and the continuation of employment contracts greatly depend on securing research funding and maintaining productivity and impact, which tends to motivate academics to collaborate so that they can survive in academia.

Second, and more directly, collaboration has become a requirement increasingly enforced by many funding agencies. Various funding schemes, whether intended for team-based or individual research projects, require applicants to establish a team to ensure the achievement of proposed projects (Melin, 2000). Although empirical examinations of the effect of this funding rule remain insufficient, Defazio et al. (2009) reported that funding collaborative research projects contributes to establishing long-term collaborations, which is conducive to sustained individual research productivity. In addition, the funding reform characterised by increasing emphasis on the quadruple helix setting and the social impact of research has also encouraged academics to collaborate with stakeholders outside of academia. As mentioned in the previous section, some funding programmes include university–non-university partnerships as a prerequisite for application. Overall, among the scarce studies examining their effects, most have reported that such programmes, which are designed primarily to benefit industry, also benefit academics, who can augment their research networks and enhance their collaborations with industry (Langfeldt and Scordato, 2016). However, some studies have asserted that the requirement to involve non-university partners at the time of application negatively affects academics in less market-oriented disciplines because it is more difficult for them to explain the benefits of their proposed research to societal partners (Pitman and Berman, 2009).

Third, as funding for research becomes increasingly competitive, academic collaboration is normally adopted as a resource acquisition strategy for those who fail to obtain funding (Laudel, Chapter 16 in this *Handbook*). Such academics are often compelled to work with and sometimes be paid by peers who have obtained funding, but this inequality in academic collaborations can create tensions between academics and discourages those who lose their academic autonomy (Woelert et al., 2020). Moreover, status hierarchies between universities derived from competitive research funding allocation (e.g. Horta, 2008) may also make lower-end universities unable to provide necessary resources for faculty members to attract external collaborators (Heinze and Kuhlmann, 2008).

Effect on Research Malpractice

Some studies (e.g. Davis et al., 2007; Holtfreter et al., 2020) suggest that professional strains associated with the competition-based funding environment contribute to various forms of research malpractice, ranging from questionable and inappropriate conduct to research misconduct. Questionable and inappropriate conduct may include data manipulation, salami publishing, and ghost authorship (Davis et al., 2007; Hall and Martin, 2019; Holtfreter et al., 2020), while research misconduct is defined as 'fabrication, falsification, and plagiarism' (Gross, 2016, p. 694). As funding agencies increasingly expect higher quality and more commodified publications, both universities and academics experience pressure to secure funding. In response to this external requirement, universities also place extra pressure on academics by linking tenure, promotion, and reward to publications and fund acquisition. Consequently, academics bear increasing publication pressure and therefore utilise various devices to publish more papers in indexed journals (Davis et al., 2007). Some such devices may involve questionable conduct or even misconduct, ranging from the pervasive short-term strategy of spreading research across multiple publications (i.e. salami publishing) to sensational scandals of scientific fraud (see the review by Gross, 2016; Kakuk, 2009). Holtfreter et al. (2020) showed that among surveyed academics, the work pressure associated with publishing in leading journals and receiving external funds was perceived as the dominant contributor to research misconduct.

Furthermore, as the inclusion of non-academic stakeholders in research can involve conflicts of interest that are difficult to reconcile (Pitman and Berman, 2009), prior studies have reported that contract or collaborative research may contribute to research misconduct, including data withholding and hiding negative findings (e.g. Blumenthal et al., 1997). To varying degrees, such malpractices undermine research ethics, jeopardise academic culture, and slow long-term scientific advancement. However, funding agencies have taken measures to reduce misconduct, such as the recent emphasis on quality and impact in research evaluation to curb malpractices aimed at increasing the number of publications (Stern, 2016).

Effect on Teaching and Supervision

The recent funding trends have caused teaching to be regarded as less important than research, given the institutional emphasis increasingly placed on the latter under external funding pressures (Lanford, 2020). To foster grant applications and ensure research excellence, higher education institutions tend to reassign the teaching duties of those who demonstrate more grant acquisition and higher research productivity to other faculty members, including adjunct faculty or graduate teaching assistants (Tierney, 2020; Woelert et al., 2020). Studies have indeed shown that teaching competes with research for academics' time and focus (Horta et al., 2012). Although such specialisation can be wise, the degradation of teaching relative to research given the strengthened link between institutional research performance and university funding has become pervasive. Studies show that even teaching-intensive universities have begun to emphasise research productivity to increase competitive funding, which has been argued to undermine teaching and learning (Tierney, 2020). This imbalance has discouraged both academics who are devoted to teaching and early-career researchers with a stronger interest in teaching than in research from pursuing an academic career path. In addition, teaching and learning as a research field has become endangered in the current funding environment because it is seldom included in impact assessments and is the priority of neither research-focused nor teaching-focused academics (Tierney, 2020). Teaching subsequently becomes an increasingly peripheral and neglected duty for academics.

Competition-based funding schemes also tend to direct academics' attention to their own research accomplishments and thus may lead to their neglect of postgraduate students' academic guidance and progression. To balance these two tasks, many supervisory academics tactfully regard their graduate students as research resources and co-author their funded research projects with their doctoral students, which are not necessarily relevant to students' dissertations (e.g. Jung et al., 2021). Academics experience growing pressure to include graduate students and postdoctoral fellows in their own research as qualified resources who can conduct both teaching and research tasks that academics themselves are less able to devote time to. Unsurprisingly, a substantial proportion of academic research is now contributed by graduate students and postdoctoral fellows (Larivière, 2012). These practices inevitably foster some imbalances between disciplines. Co-publishing by academics and their students is common in STEM fields (even before competition-based funding schemes), whereas academics in HSS tend to adopt a 'passive availability' approach, making trade-offs between their own research output and graduate supervision (Sampson and Comer, 2010).

Effect on the Academic Labour Market

Some have argued that the funding reforms over the last decades can undermine academics' long-term career development. Most criticism points to competition-based funding schemes and the associated changes in human resources management practices that prioritise success in winning research grants, as noted above (Eigi et al., 2014; Watermeyer, 2014; Ylijoki, 2003).

First, competition-based funding schemes can increase career precarity in academia. As a buffer against changes in government policy and funding, universities hire more term-employed academics, either project-based researchers or teaching staff with short-term contracts, who are not entitled to move to permanent contracts or given satisfactory compensation packages (Ylijoki, 2003). For instance, as the impact assessment focuses on academic performance per full-time equivalent staff within an institution, some institutions have been found to strictly control the number of tenure-track positions to improve results, thus intensifying job competition (Stern, 2016). In this context, many early-career academics with short-term contracts must seek funding opportunities for the next stage of their careers without being able to consider their longer-term research agenda or career development (Eigi et al., 2014).

To secure a stable academic position, they must make it part of their daily life to remain alert to new funding and vacancy information (Carrozza and Minucci, 2014). Such pressure even follows those with permanent contracts throughout their academic careers as grant acquisition becomes a continuous process to maintain ongoing research and reputation (Cunningham et al., 2016; Ylijoki, 2003).

Second, some have criticised competitive research funding schemes for disadvantaging early-career academics, leading to further stratification of the academic labour force. Certain funding rules, such as highlighting past accomplishments, force early-career academics to rely on prestigious scholars to successfully secure funding opportunities (Laudel, Chapter 16 in this *Handbook*), thus bestowing further power on established scholarly elites (Dougherty and Natow, 2020; Hicks, 2012). Such rules may also somewhat restrict early-career researchers' academic mobility, as they must maintain connections with colleagues and be ready to dynamically participate in others' projects. The introduction of impact assessment in both grant conditions and human resources management has exacerbated this situation because early-career researchers tend to prioritise publishing to establish their professional reputation and have insufficient time to establish societal impact (Watermeyer, 2014).

Third, several studies have observed that the neoliberalism associated with competitive funding arrangements has aggravated work pressure for academics. While helping to ensure research productivity, regular evaluation of individual research output restricts academics' abilities to participate in academic entrepreneurship or other related activities, reducing the flexibility of academic careers (Stern, 2016). In addition, the incessant accountability inherent to the ubiquitous competition in academic settings can somewhat deprive academics of their autonomy, eroding their motivation to further pursue academic careers (Dougherty and Natow, 2020; Kallio and Kallio, 2014). Bureaucratic requests and barriers – such as requiring explanations for conference participation in travel grant applications and requiring the completion of highly structured case templates to showcase impact in research evaluations – have been deemed time-consuming and demotivating to early-career researchers (Manville et al., 2015; Melin, 2000).

CONCLUSIONS

The changing funding landscape owing to the evolution of global higher education over the past five decades has greatly impacted academics' scholarly performance and the academic profession. It has most directly and greatly affected research in terms of agenda setting, collaboration, productivity, and integrity. Our synthesis of the literature suggests that with the introduction of competition-based funding schemes and impact assessment, academics have become more reluctant to propose long-term, risky research projects. At least from the perspective of academics, such projects are less likely to receive funding from agencies and be published in top peer-reviewed journals (e.g. Heinze et al., 2009; Stern, 2016), which constitute crucial performance indicators in current academic evaluation. While serving their grand purposes of providing performance incentives for both universities and academics and increasing the benefits of public investment in higher education, current funding schemes remain flawed, which can lead to unintended consequences such as short-termism, research misconduct, and impeded knowledge advancement. Equally importantly, funding schemes that increasingly emphasise research and knowledge-exchange projects seem to encourage academics to disregard teaching and graduate supervision. Unpredictable public funding and growing competition also cause concerns regarding academic career precarity and undermine academic working conditions. Nonetheless, competition-based funding schemes and impact assessment have contributed to the development of the higher education sector, with benefits outweighing weaknesses overall. Although affected by funding schemes to varying degrees, most academics can recognise the positive role of such reforms in sustaining research and the higher education sector with respect to funding (Stern, 2016).

Despite the accumulated evidence of the effect of funding on academics' scholarly conduct, future work should prioritise building theory (Gläser and Velarde, 2018). While university relations with funding agencies and funding schemes can be largely explained by principal-agent theory (Ferlie et al., 2008), effective theoretical explanations of the mechanism behind the causal links between macro funding changes and individuals' scholarly conduct still require further development. Individual-level theories, such as motivation theories and role theory, may help to conceptualise academics' reactions to changing funding schemes.

We argue, first, that a closer investigation of academics' knowledge production activities is needed. Attention should be focused on both intrapersonal (e.g. research agenda-setting) and interpersonal (e.g. research collaboration) behaviours, the latter of which could greatly improve understanding. For instance, while it is largely positive that recent funding trends encourage academics to take advantage of collaboration within and beyond academia, we still need to know how academics' motivations to collaborate intersect with the changing funding arrangement to improve understanding of the underlying mechanism.

Second, situating the effect of funding reforms in the broader higher education context is vital because research is not the sole duty of academics. The majority of the literature on the effect of funding focuses on research productivity (e.g. Defazio et al., 2009; Smart, 2009), yet research on the effect of funding mechanisms on teaching and service should also be pursued and would contribute to a holistic view of this issue.

Third, it is essential to isolate the effect of funding arrangements, which are embedded in a broader social context, on scholarly performance. As summarised in this chapter, the evolution of funding purposes and the conditions of funding acquisition are part of a historical process; the relationship between funding and academics' conduct involves not only the latter's adaptation to changing policies but also academia's adaptation to broader and more complex knowledge-seeking challenges. Therefore, methods such as international comparative approaches and mixed methods are required to distinguish the effect of funding on scholarly performance from the effect of broader academic context.

Finally, more rigorous quantitative research is needed to better inform policymakers. Some funding mechanisms, such as impact assessment, were introduced relatively recently and their long-term effects must be more thoroughly assessed. Thus far, research on the effect of these recent reforms has been mostly qualitative and has primarily shown that academics do not perceive them favourably (e.g. Watermeyer, 2014). Although such studies enable a deeper understanding of the perceived effect of recent funding schemes, they tend to fill the literature with unbalanced criticisms of neoliberalism without fully recognising the positive roles of these funding reforms. This underpins the apparently negative tone of this chapter, although we do endeavour to report the current research landscape objectively. Hence, more quantitative examinations – using quasi-experimental methods and accounting for the multi-layered character of higher education systems – are needed to evaluate the net effect of specific funding mechanisms on various aspects of scholarly performance.

NOTE

1. Conditional autonomy 'recognises the role of the state in steering the system and its outcomes through procedural controls, while respecting the autonomy of (individuals and) individual institutions in the substantive fields of their intellectual work' (Hall and Symes, 2005, p. 201).

REFERENCES

Aagaard, K., Bloch, C., and Schneider, J. W. (2015). Impacts of performance-based research funding systems: The case of the Norwegian Publication Indicator. *Research Evaluation, 24*(2), 106–117.

Auranen, O., and Nieminen, M. (2010). University research funding and publication performance – An international comparison. *Research Policy, 39*(6), 822–834.

Australian Research Council (2021). *Selection Report: Linkage Projects 2021 Round 1*. https://www.arc .gov.au/grants/grant-outcomes/selection-report-linkage-projects-2021-round-1 (accessed 20 February 2022).

Bammer, G. (2008). Enhancing research collaborations: Three key management challenges. *Research Policy, 37*(5), 875–887.

Bandola-Gill, J., and Smith, K. E. (2021). Governing by narratives: REF impact case studies and restrictive storytelling in performance measurement. *Studies in Higher Education*. https://doi.org/10.1080/ 03075079.2021.1978965.

Benner, M., and Sandström, U. (2000). Institutionalizing the triple helix: Research funding and norms in the academic system. *Research Policy, 29*(2), 291–301.

Bentley, P. J., Gulbrandsen, M., and Kyvik, S. (2015). The relationship between basic and applied research in universities. *Higher Education, 70*(4), 689–709.

Bloch, C., Graversen, E. K., and Pedersen, H. S. (2014) Competitive research grants and their impact on career performance. *Minerva, 52*, 77–96.

Blumenthal, D., Campbell, E. G., Anderson, M. S., Causino, N., and Louis, K. S. (1997). Withholding research results in academic life science. Evidence from a national survey of faculty. *Jama, 277*(15), 1224–1228.

Butler, L. (2003). Explaining Australia's increased share of ISI publications – The effects of a funding formula based on publication counts. *Research Policy, 32*(1), 143–155.

Buxton, M., and Hanney, S. (1996). How can payback from health services research be assessed? *Journal of Health Services Research and Policy, 1*(1), 35–43.

Carayannis, E. G., and Campbell, D. F. (2009). 'Mode 3' and 'Quadruple Helix': Toward a 21st century fractal innovation ecosystem. *International Journal of Technology Management, 46*(3–4), 201–234.

Carnoy, M., Loyalka, P., Androushchak, G., and Proudnikova, A. (2012). The Economic Returns to Higher Education in the BRIC Countries and their Implications for Higher Education Expansion. HSE Working papers WP BRP 02/EDU/2012, National Research University Higher School of Economics.

Carrozza, C., and Minucci, S. (2014). Keep on movin'? Research mobility's meanings for Italian early-stage researchers. *Higher Education Policy, 27*(4), 489–508.

Castells, M. (2010). *The rise of the network society*. Chichester: Wiley-Blackwell.

Cattaneo, M., Meoli, M., and Signori, A. (2016). Performance-based funding and university research productivity: the moderating effect of university legitimacy. *The Journal of Technology Transfer, 41*(1), 85–104.

Checchi, D., Malgarini, M., and Sarlo, S. (2019). Do performance-based research funding systems affect research production and impact? *Higher Education Quarterly, 73*(1), 45–69.

Chubb, J., and Reed, M. S. (2018). The politics of research impact: Academic perceptions of the implications for research funding, motivation and quality. *British Politics, 13*(3), 295–311. https://doi.org/ 10.1057/s41293-018-0077-9.

Clark, B. R. (1983). *The Higher Education System*. University of California Press.

Conceição, P., Heitor, M. V., Sirilli, G., and Wilson, R. (2004). The 'swing of the pendulum' from public to market support for science and technology: Is the US leading the way? *Technological Forecasting and Social Change, 71*(6), 553–578.

Cunningham, J. A., Mangematin, V., O Kane, C., and O'Reilly, P. (2016). At the frontiers of scientific advancement: The factors that influence scientists to become or choose to become publicly funded principal investigators. *The Journal of Technology Transfer*, 41(4), 778–797.

Davis, M. S., Riske-Morris, M., and Diaz, S. R. (2007). Causal factors implicated in research misconduct: evidence from ORI case files. *Science and Engineering Ethics*, 13(4), 395–414. https://doi.org/10.1007/s11948-007-9045-2.

Defazio, D., Lockett, A., and Wright, M. (2009). Funding incentives, collaborative dynamics and scientific productivity: Evidence from the EU framework program. *Research Policy*, 38(2), 293–305.

Dougherty, K. J., and Natow, R. S. (2020). Performance-based funding for higher education: How well does neoliberal theory capture neoliberal practice? *Higher Education*, 80(3), 457–478.

Eigi, J., Põiklik, P., Lõhkivi, E., and Velbaum, K. (2014). Supervision and early career work experiences of Estonian humanities researchers under the conditions of project-based funding. *Higher Education Policy*, 27(4), 453–468.

Etzkowitz, H. (2002). *MIT and the Rise of Entrepreneurial Science*. Routledge.

Etzkowitz, H., Webster, A., Gebhardt, C., and Terra, B. R. C. (2000). The future of the university and the university of the future: Evolution of ivory tower to entrepreneurial paradigm. *Research Policy*, 29(2), 313–330.

Falkenberg, R. I. (2021). Re-invent yourself! How demands for innovativeness reshape epistemic practices. *Minerva*, 59(4), 423–444. https://doi.org/10.1007/s11024-021-09447-4.

Ferlie, E., Musselin, C., and Andresani, G. (2008). The steering of higher education systems: A public management perspective. *Higher Education*, 56(3), 325.

Gläser, J., and Laudel, G. (2007). Evaluation without evaluators: The impact of funding formulae on Australian university research. In R. Whitley and J. Gläser (Eds.), *The Changing Governance of the Sciences: The Advent of Research Evaluation Systems* (pp. 127–151). Springer.

Gläser, J., and Velarde, K. S. (2018). Changing funding arrangements and the production of scientific knowledge: Introduction to the special issue. *Minerva*, 56(1), 1–10.

Godin, B. (2009). National innovation system: The system approach in historical perspective. *Science, Technology, and Human Values*, 34(4), 476–501.

Graffikin, F., and Perry, D. C. (2009). Discourses and strategic visions: The US research university as an institutional manifestation of neoliberalism in a global era. *American Educational Research Journal*, 46(1), 115–144.

Gross, C. (2016). Scientific misconduct. *Annual Review of Psychology*, 67(1), 693–711. https://doi.org/10.1146/annurev-psych-122414-033437.

Gulbrandsen, M., and Smeby, J.-C. (2005). Industry funding and university professors' research performance. *Research Policy*, 34(6), 932–950.

Gunn, A., and Mintrom, M. (2016). Higher education policy change in Europe: Academic research funding and the impact agenda. *European Education*, 48(4), 241–257.

Hall, J., and Martin, B. R. (2019). Towards a taxonomy of research misconduct: The case of business school research. *Research Policy*, 48(2), 414–427. https://doi.org/https://doi.org/10.1016/j.respol.2018.03.006.

Hall, M., and Symes, A. (2005) South African higher education in the first decade of democracy: from cooperative governance to conditional autonomy. *Studies in Higher Education*, 30(2), 199–212.

Heinze, T., and Kuhlmann, S. (2008). Across institutional boundaries?: Research collaboration in German public sector nanoscience. *Research Policy*, 37(5), 888–899.

Heinze, T., Shapira, P., Rogers, J. D., and Senker, J. M. (2009). Organizational and institutional influences on creativity in scientific research. *Research Policy*, 38(4), 610–623. https://doi.org/https://doi.org/10.1016/j.respol.2009.01.014.

Hicks, D. (2012). Performance-based university research funding systems. *Research Policy*, 41(2), 251–261.

Holtfreter, K., Reisig, M. D., Pratt, T. C., and Mays, R. D. (2020). The perceived causes of research misconduct among faculty members in the natural, social, and applied sciences. *Studies in Higher Education*, 45(11), 2162–2174. https://doi.org/10.1080/03075079.2019.1593352.

Horta, H. (2008). On improving the university research base: The Technical University of Lisbon case in perspective. *Higher Education Policy*, 21(1), 123–146.

Horta, H., and Santos, J. M. (2020). Organisational factors and academic research agendas: An analysis of academics in the social sciences. *Studies in Higher Education, 45*(12), 2382–2397.

Horta, H., Dautel, V., and Veloso, F. M. (2012). An output perspective on teaching-research nexus: An analysis focusing on the United States higher education system. *Studies in Higher Education, 37*(2), 171–187.

Ionescu, F., and Polgreen, L. A. (2009) A theory of brain drain and public funding for higher education in the United States. *American Economic Review, 99*(2), 517–521.

Jacobs, B., and van der Ploeg, F. (2006) Guide to reform of higher education: A European perspective. *Economic Policy, 21*(47), 535–592.

Jongbloed, B., and Lepori, B. (2015). The funding of research in higher education: Mixed models and mixed results. In J. Huisman, H. de Boer, D. D. Dill and M. Souto-Otero (Eds.), *The Palgrave International Handbook of Higher Education Policy and Governance* (pp. 439–462). Palgrave Macmillan.

Jung, J., Horta, H., Zhang, L. F., and Postiglione, G. A. (2021). Factors fostering and hindering research collaboration with doctoral students among academics in Hong Kong. *Higher Education.* https://doi.org/10.1007/s10734-020-00664-6.

Kakuk, P. (2009). The legacy of the Hwang case: Research misconduct in biosciences. *Science and Engineering Ethics, 15*(4), 545–562. https://doi.org/10.1007/s11948-009-9121-x.

Kallio, K., and Kallio, T. J. (2014). Management-by-results and performance measurement in universities – Implications for work motivation. *Studies in Higher Education, 39*(4), 574–589.

Lanford, M. (2020). Institutional competition through performance funding: A catalyst or hindrance to teaching and learning? *Educational Philosophy and Theory, 53*(11), 1148–1160.

Langfeldt, L., and Scordato, L. (2016). *Efficiency and Flexibility in Research Funding. A Comparative Study of Funding Instruments and Review Criteria.* Report published by Nordic Institute for Studies in Innovation, Research and Education.

Larivière, V. (2012) On the shoulders of students? The contribution of PhD students to the advancement of knowledge. *Scientometrics, 90*, 463–481.

Lee, F. S. (2007). The research assessment exercise, the state and the dominance of mainstream economics in British universities. *Cambridge Journal of Economics, 31*(2), 309–325.

Leydesdorff, L., and Etzkowitz, H. (1996). Emergence of a triple helix of university–industry–government relations. *Science and Public Policy, 23*(5), 279–286.

Li, D., and Li, Y. (2021). Preparing for RAE 2020 in Hong Kong: Academics' research, writing and publishing trajectories in a neoliberal governance landscape. *Studies in Higher Education.* https://doi.org/10.1080/03075079.2021.1901272.

Lyall, C., Bruce, A., Marsden, W., and Meagher, L. (2013). The role of funding agencies in creating interdisciplinary knowledge. *Science and Public Policy, 40*(1), 62–71. https://doi.org/10.1093/scipol/scs121.

Ma, L., Luo, J., Feliciani, T., and Shankar, K. (2020). How to evaluate ex ante impact of funding proposals? An analysis of reviewers' comments on impact statements. *Research Evaluation, 29*(4), 431–440. https://doi.org/10.1093/reseval/rvaa022.

Manville, C., Guthrie, S., Henham, ML., Garrod, B., Sousa, S., Kirtley, A., et al. (2015). Assessing impact submissions for REF 2014: An evaluation. Rand Europe. https://www.rand.org/content/dam/rand/pubs/research_reports/RR1000/RR1032/RAND_RR1032.pdf (accessed September 2021).

Marcella, R., Lockerbie, H., and Bloice, L. (2016). Beyond REF 2014: The impact of impact assessment on the future of information research. *Journal of Information Science, 42*(3), 369–385.

Martin, B. R. (2011). The Research Excellence Framework and the 'impact agenda': Are we creating a Frankenstein monster? *Research Evaluation, 20*(3), 247–254. https://doi.org/10.3152/0958 20211x13118583635693.

Mathies, C., Kivistö, J., and Birnbaum, M. (2020). Following the money? Performance-based funding and the changing publication patterns of Finnish academics. *Higher Education, 79*(1), 21–37.

Meagher, L. R., and Martin, U. (2017). Slightly dirty maths: The richly textured mechanisms of impact. *Research Evaluation, 26*(1), 15–27. https://doi.org/10.1093/reseval/rvw024.

Melin, G. (2000). Pragmatism and self-organization: Research collaboration on the individual level. *Research Policy, 29*(1), 31–40.

Mowery, D. C. (1998). The changing structure of the US national innovation system: Implications for international conflict and cooperation in R&D policy. *Research Policy*, *27*(6), 639–654.

OECD (2018). *New trends in public research funding.* https://doi.org/doi:https://doi.org/10.1787/sti_in_outlook-2018-13-en.

Pavitt, K. (2000). Why European Union funding of academic research should be increased: A radical proposal. *Science and Public Policy*, *27*(6), 455–460.

Peters, M. A. (2003). Classical Political Economy and the Role of Universities in the New Knowledge Economy. *Globalisation, Societies and Education*, *1*(2), 153–168.

Pitman, T., and Berman, J. E. (2009). Of what benefit and to whom? Linking Australian humanities research with its 'end users'. *Journal of Higher Education Policy and Management*, *31*(4), 315–326.

Potì, B., and Reale, E. (2007). Changing allocation models for public research funding: An empirical exploration based on project funding data. *Science and Public Policy*, *34*(6), 417–430.

Ramirez, F. O., and Christensen, T. (2013). The formalization of the university: Rules, roots, and routes. *Higher Education*, *65*(6), 695–708. https://doi.org/10.1007/s10734-012-9571-y.

Reale, E., Avramov, D., Canhial, K., Donovan, C., Flecha, R., Holm, P., Larkin, C., Lepori, B., Mosoni-Fried, J., Oliver, E., Primeri, E., Puigvert, L., Scharnhorst, A., Schubert, A., Soler, M., Soòs, S., Sordé, T., Travis, C., and Van Horik, R. (2017). A review of literature on evaluating the scientific, social and political impact of social sciences and humanities research. *Research Evaluation*, *27*(4), 298–308.

Research Council of Norway (2021). *Knowledge-building Project for Industry.* https://www.forskningsradet.no/en/call-for-proposals/2020/knowledge-building-project-for-industry/#tab (accessed 2 March 2022).

Research Excellence Framework (n.d.). What is the REF? https://www.ref.ac.uk/about/what-is-the-ref/.

Sampson, K. A., and Comer, K. (2010). When the governmental tail wags the disciplinary dog: Some consequences of national funding policy on doctoral research in New Zealand. *Higher Education Research and Development*, *29*(3), 275–289.

Schofer, E., and Meyer, J. W. (2005). The worldwide expansion of higher education in the twentieth century. *American Sociological Review*, *70*(6), 898–920.

Shapin, S. (2012). The Ivory Tower: The history of a figure of speech and its cultural uses. *The British Journal for the History of Science*, *45*(1), 1–27.

Shin, J. C., and Lee, S. J. (2015). Evolution of research universities as a national research system in Korea: Accomplishments and challenges. *Higher Education*, *70*(2), 187–202.

Shin, J. C., Watanabe, S. P., Chen, R. J.-C., Ho, S. S.-H., and Lee, J.-k. (2020). Institutionalization of competition-based funding under neoliberalism in East Asia. *Studies in Higher Education*, *45*(10), 2054–2062.

Smart, W. (2009). The impact of the performance-based research fund on the research productivity of New Zealand universities. *Social Policy Journal of New Zealand*, *34*(1), 136–151.

Smith, K. M., Crookes, E., and Crookes, P. A. (2013). Measuring research 'impact' for academic promotion: Issues from the literature. *Journal of Higher Education Policy and Management*, *35*(4), 410–420.

Stern, N. (2016). *Building on success and learning from experience: an independent review of the Research Excellence Framework.* Department for Business, Energy and Industrial Strategy, London.

Tierney, A. (2020). The scholarship of teaching and learning and pedagogic research within the disciplines: Should it be included in the research excellence framework? *Studies in Higher Education*, *45*(1), 176–186. https://doi.org/10.1080/03075079.2019.1574732.

Watermeyer, R. (2014). Issues in the articulation of 'impact': The responses of UK academics to 'impact' as a new measure of research assessment. *Studies in Higher Education*, *39*(2), 359–377.

Weeden, K. A. (2002) Why do some occupations pay more than others? Social closure and earnings inequality in the United States. *American Journal of Sociology*, *108*(1), 55–101.

Whitley, R. (2007). Changing governance of the public sciences. In R. Whitley and J. Gläser (Eds.), *The Changing Governance of the Sciences: The Advent of Research Evaluation Systems* (pp. 3–27). Springer Netherlands. https://doi.org/10.1007/978-1-4020-6746-4_1.

Woelert, P., Lewis, J. M., and Le, A. T. (2020). Formally alive yet practically complex: An exploration of academics' perceptions of their autonomy as researchers. *Higher Education Policy*. Doi: https://doi.org/10.1057/s41307-020-00190-1.

Xu, X., Oancea, A., and Rose, H. (2021). The impacts of incentives for international publications on research cultures in Chinese humanities and social sciences. *Minerva, 59*(4), 469–492. https://doi.org/10.1007/s11024-021-09441-w.

Yang, X., Li, H., and Chen, B. (2019). Research funding and its influence on academic research under China's university governance system. In C. Zhu and M. Zayim-Kurtay (Eds.), *University Governance and Academic Leadership in the EU and China* (pp. 33–51). IGI Global.

Ylijoki, O. (2003). Entangled in academic capitalism? A case-study on changing ideals and practices of university research. *Higher Education, 45*(3), 307–335.

Young, M. (2015). Competitive funding, citation regimes, and the diminishment of breakthrough research. *Higher Education, 69*(3), 421–434.

PART V

SYSTEM PERSPECTIVES AND COUNTRY VARIATIONS

20. Context matters: conceptualizing research funding policies through the lens of the varieties of academic capitalism approach

Olivier Bégin-Caouette, Silvia Mirlene Nakano Koga and Émanuelle Maltais

INTRODUCTION

The globalization of the knowledge economy and of the knowledge society has pushed welfare states to increase their contribution to scientific knowledge and most have placed higher education at the core of their advances in research and innovation. This sector performs nearly 30% of the US\$ 1.7 trillion invested globally and every year in research and development (UIS-UNESCO, 2020). In addition to the total amounts invested, which vary significantly between countries (OECD, 2021), studies on academic research production focus on research funding policy (RFP) as they stipulate to whom sums are allocated, according to which allocation modes and in the pursuit of which objectives, in the geographic and temporal contexts that prevail at the time of policy formulation (Borrás and Edquist, 2019).

To conceptually highlight these multiple interactions inherent to RFP, this chapter presents and discusses the relevance of an emerging theoretical framework – the variety of academic capitalism (VoAC) approach – in explaining how countries' political–economic structures may influence RFP. After having described two intersecting competitive dynamics through the lenses of academic capitalism and following a presentation of the theoretical foundations for the VoAC approach, this chapter, based upon an integrative literature review, will explore how policy mixes, coordination and outcomes are structured in the liberal, conservative, and social-democratic welfare regimes.

ECONOMIC AND SYMBOLIC COMPETITIVE DYNAMICS

The global academic field is confronted with multiple competitive dynamics. The first dynamic stems from the knowledge economy and puts pressure on higher education systems (HES) to be economically profitable. The increase in tuition fees, financialization of student debt, recruitment of fee-paying international students, international campuses, and the marketization of academic research are some of the consequences of a global competitive landscape revolving around the accumulation of material capital (Schulze-Cleven and Olson, 2017). Slaughter and Leslie (1999) and Slaughter and Rhoades (2004) developed the first iteration of a theory they named "academic capitalism", which conceptualizes how the economic field merged with the academic field in multiple countries, partly because of RFP fostering public-private circuits of knowledge and embedding profit-oriented activities into publicly funded research. *Economic* academic capitalism has thus strengthened the interdependence relationship between HES and business actors and is propelled by a global competition for economic profits.

Scholars noted an equally transformative phenomenon strengthening and widening the deeply rooted tradition of competition for prestige based on discoveries and publications. Building upon Bourdieu's (1988) definition of capital, Münch (2014) developed a different iteration of academic capitalism to conceptualize the global competition for the accumulation of scientific capital and the symbolic power it grants to academics, institutions, and governments. While he agrees with Slaughter and Rhoades (2004) that the economic thought has seized the academic field, his theory – that we name *symbolic* academic capitalism – considers that authority in the academic field is based upon the symbolic power generated from the accumulation of scientific capital that is recognized by other actors. In symbolic academic capitalism, higher education institutions are conceived as entrepreneurial organizations that own the means of production and act strategically to maximize the symbolic profits from research.

THE MEDIATION OF POLITICAL–ECONOMIC STRUCTURES

To nuance our understanding, we argue that global dynamics of academic capitalism will produce different outcomes in different contexts. When the diversity of contexts is virtually innumerable, comparatists might rely upon Weber's (1968) ideal types, which are abstract analytical tools with a high degree of logical integration synthesizing the core features of local contexts. Like political sociology, political economy employs ideal types to compare how the interrelationships between power structures and resource distribution condition organizations' behaviour (Caporaso and Levine, 1992). For instance, Esping-Andersen (1999) defines welfare regimes as specific configurations involving the state, the market, and households, through which welfare is produced. The liberal regimes emerged in the 19th century English political economy, are found in Anglo-Saxon countries, and characterized by a faith in markets, individual responsibility, free competition, and a residual role for the State. The conservative regimes emerged in continental Europe in the mid-19th century. In these regimes, the civil service enjoys privileged treatment and the social protections offered to citizens are based on their profession and family situation, thus preserving differences in class and status. The social-democratic regimes emerged in the 1930s when social democratic parties shifted from "class parties" to "citizens' parties" and promoted social welfare, regardless of family status or employment.

Although ideal types are "logical utopias", it is worth noting that Esping-Andersen's (1999) welfare regime types have empirical resonance in comparative higher education since they depict how countries respond to policy trade-offs (such as participation rates, taxation, and public funding). For instance, performing a correspondence analysis between welfare regimes and HES in 16 Organisation for Economic Co-operation and Development (OECD) countries, Pechar and Andres (2011) found that welfare regimes could be distinguished based on the public-private funding ratio for HES. Focusing on academic research governance models, Benner (2011) noted that Anglo-Saxon (liberal), Continental European (conservative) and Nordic (social-democratic) countries varied in terms of academic self-organizations, policy discourses and support structures. Bégin-Caouette et al. (2016) performed a correspondence analysis revealing that, although both regimes were responsive to market forces, social-democratic regimes could be distinguished from liberal regimes on a "academic centrality" dimension that included variables such as higher education R&D expenditures (HERD) and R&D in the form of general university funds (GUF).

Those studies highlight contextual features that could mediate the impact of global academic capitalism and support a closer look into the VoAC. The VoAC approach is an adaptation of Hall and Soskice's (2004) varieties of capitalism approach, which was developed to examine institutional arrangements conditioning societies' adjustment paths in the face of a globalized economic system. The approach was developed to explain firms' behaviours in different contexts. Based on a comparison of five parameters – industrial relations, training and education, corporate governance, inter-firm relations, and relations with employees – in multiple countries, the authors conceptualized two ideal types: the liberal market economy and the coordinated market economy. In this approach, a comparative advantage refers to the institutional structure allowing organizations in one country to perform an activity more efficiently than others.

If Graf (2009) applied the approach to the study of internationalization in German and British universities, Olson and Slaughter (2014) were the first to compare how academic capitalism manifests itself in coordinated and liberal market economies. Kauppinen and Kaidesoja (2014) noted, however, that this bimodal categorization did not capture the particularities of the Nordic countries. While preserving the title of the approach, Schulze-Cleven and Olson (2017) opted for a categorization based on Esping-Andersen's typology. They found that academic capitalism had encouraged the financialization of the HES in liberal regimes, channelled funding to leading institutions in conservative regimes and quality assurance and performance indicators in the social-democratic variety.

While previous studies have suggested that welfare regimes were related to public–private ratios of funding for HES (Pechar and Andres, 2011), HERD and GUF (Bégin-Caouette et al., 2016) and research governance (Benner, 2011), that the varieties of capitalism influenced R&D investments (Kim 2013) and internationalization strategies (Graf, 2009), and that the VoAC could explain variations in governments' strategies to support world-class universities (Olson and Slaughter, 2014) and HES' liberalization (Schulze-Cleven and Olson, 2017), no study has applied the VoAC approach to systematically compare countries' RFPs.

RESEARCH QUESTIONS AND METHODOLOGICAL APPROACH

The objective of this chapter is to compare RFPs in three welfare regimes. To meet the objective, we conducted an integrative literature review of 75 scholarly documents and 15 OECD reports. An integrative review analyses both empirical and theoretical bodies of literature to provide a holistic understanding of a phenomenon (Whittemore and Knafl, 2005). The integrative review supports a wide range of inquiry, including non-experimental research, and typically serves to answer four questions: what is known about the phenomenon, what is the quality of what is known, what remains unknown and what the future steps for research might be. Following the prescribed steps of Toronto and Remington (2020), we formulated the three following research questions:

1. Do the competitive dynamics of academic capitalism lead to different funding policy mixes in the three welfare regimes?
2. How is policy coordination carried out in the three welfare regimes?

3. To what extent does countries' political–economic structure influence policy outcomes in the global academic capitalism?

Variables of interest were conceptualized as follows: comparative political economists pay attention to policymaking as they construe an important manifestation of public actors' strategic interaction with other sectors (Hall and Soskice, 2004). Our definition of policy *mixes* was supplemented by Borrás and Edquist's (2019) work, building upon the reconceptualization proposed by Flanagan et al. (2011). We define RFP mixes as the combination of policy instruments designed by public organizations to address the problems identified in the research system. For Borrás and Edquist, mixes include instruments whose effects can be complementary, synergetic, or contrasting, and depend on the socio-historic and political–economic context for which they are designed. Coordination is a core concept (Thelen and Kume, 2006) defined in the VoAC approach as the strategic interactions between actors in a context of diverging interests and political settlements. Although the VoAC approach is more concerned with processes than outcomes, it acknowledges that different contexts provide different comparative advantages to organizations (Bégin-Caouette, 2019). Outcomes are considered through the lenses of the specific rationales and goals set by policymakers (Flanagan et al., 2011). This chapter will focus on the reported outcomes of RFP on scientific capital accumulation, whether the goal for it is to be converted into economic profitability or symbolic power.

In an integrative literature review, the problem formulation stage includes the sampling frame. In this case, we focused on 18 OECD countries: Austria, Australia, Belgium, Canada, Denmark, Finland, France, Germany, Italy, Portugal, the Netherlands, New Zealand, Norway, Spain, Sweden, Switzerland, the UK and the US. For the literature search, we used the variables listed above to extract from multiple databases all the books, book chapters, journal articles, and research reports: (1) on one or more of the 18 countries; (2) written in French or in English; and (3) published between 2010 and 2021. We have read the abstracts of the 134 found documents and selected 75 based on their relevance and equity between varieties. We supplemented this analysis with 15 OECD reports providing specific data on R&D and funding mechanisms. For the data analysis stage, the 90 sources were placed in a double entry table in which countries were rows and variables (policy mix, coordination, and outcomes) were columns. Each author for this chapter performed a content analysis on this matrix and produced a synthesis about the VoAC in each regime. Statements were confronted and led to the common-agreed findings presented below. Although attempted to meet standards in terms of clarity, rigour, and replication, this study does not have the ambition of a systematic meta-analysis and should rather be considered as a first attempt to apply the VoAC approach to the study of RFP.

POLICY MIXES

As shown in Table 20.1, policy mixes can be characterized by expenditures (OECD, 2021), allocation mechanisms (Reale, 2017) and policy instruments (Borrás and Edquist, 2019). Thirteen OECD indicators were reported for the 18 countries in Appendix Table 20A.1 and careful readers will note that there are important intra-category variations (represented by standard deviations), sometimes even larger than inter-category variations, especially in the conservative regime's category.

Table 20.1   Expenditures, allocation modes and policy instruments

Regimes	Expenditures	Allocation mechanisms	Policy instruments
Liberal	Market sensitivity	Competitive project funding. PBIF in Australia, New Zealand and the UK.	Grant concentration and external actors on grant committees (Canada, US). Evaluation frameworks including impact-related factors (Australia, UK).
Conservative	Academic and scientific fields integration	Institutional funding. PBIF in Austria, Belgium, Germany, Spain, Italy and the Netherlands.	Block funding and excellence instruments. Regional collaboration (clusters).
Social-democratic	Academic centrality	Balance between institutional funding (PBIF component) and project funding.	Block funding, competitive grants, and two types of excellence instruments (research vs. innovation).

R&D Expenditures

As shown in Appendix Table 20A.1, gross domestic expenditures on research and development (GERD) as a percentage of the GDP (line 1) is the highest in social-democratic regimes ($\bar{x}$ = 2.83, where $\bar{x}$ = mean), followed by the conservative ($\bar{x}$ = 2.32) and the liberal ($\bar{x}$ = 1.92) regimes. HES' centrality within R&D ecosystems also varies: the proportion of GERD performed by HES systems (line 5) being, on average, the highest in the social-democratic regimes ($\bar{x}$ =29.28), followed by the liberal ($\bar{x}$ = 26.86) and conservative ($\bar{x}$ = 24.91). We conclude that the social-democratic regimes present a context of high public investments in research, and funding concentration into universities (Michavila and Martinez, 2018; Pranevičienė et al., 2017). On the contrary, some countries of conservative regime concentrate cutting-edge scientific development in research institutes outside of universities, which is visible in the proportion of higher education researchers per thousand labour force (Appendix Table 20A.1, line 9). Reale (2017) noted that public research organizations, which are more frequent in conservative regimes, receive a substantial allocation of research funding. In Germany, universities compete with the Helmholtz Centres, institutes of the Max-Planck Society and Fraunhofer institutes, which publish a higher proportion of papers (Powell and Dusdal, 2017). In France, the CNRS is the second most important research institution in the world and is ahead of leading US universities in terms of scientific publications (Musselin, 2017). However, since academic capitalism is based on universities' scientific capital, the logic of accumulation has encouraged RFPs that (re)integrate the scientific and academic fields so that the latter could appropriate capital accumulated by the former. As a reminder, a field is a setting covering one area of social life and populated by agents and positions (Bourdieu, 1988). The scientific field includes all the agents (including public research organizations) concerned with the pursuit of science, while the academic field includes agents contributing to the social functions of academia. The two fields can be more or less integrated depending on the political–economic structure. Joint initiatives, such as the International Max Planck Research Schools or mergers between institutes and universities (Powell and Dusdal, 2017), such as merger of universities, *grandes écoles*, university institutes of technology and CNRS and CEA laboratories to create University of Paris-Saclay (France), constitute examples of RFP contributing to fields' integration.

Expenditures also serves as a proxy to discern interactions between R&D sectors. The proportion of HERD financed by the business sector (line 7) is high in both conservative ($\bar{x}$

= 7.25) and liberal regimes ($\bar{x}$ = 5.49). Correspondingly, RFPs in liberal countries tend to enhance HES' market sensitivity by including business actors on granting agencies' governing councils (Sá et al., 2013), and by developing tax incentives to encourage privately funded academic research (Lester and Warda, 2014). Most OECD countries have different forms of R&D tax credits, but Canada and the UK rank among the top third of the OECD (2020), and the US remain well above the OECD (2020) average. In the liberal regimes, support for curiosity-driven research has declined in relative terms, and RFPs include instruments supporting the commodification of research, namely through the protection of intellectual property and direct support for university-industry collaborations (Link, 2019). Conservative regimes are characterized by networked coordination with the cooperation between enterprises, universities, and research institutions (Christensen and Serrano Velarde, 2019). In those regimes, economic-focused RFPs have relied upon HES' strengths to support technology transfer, such as industrial postdoctoral fellowships in Belgium (Herstad et al., 2010) or generous tax credit in Belgium, France, and the Netherlands (Vennekens et al., 2019). In social-democratic regimes, collaborations between the economic and academic fields also take the form of academic training, including the creating of industrial PhDs. These regimes have also implemented generous tax credit to trigger R&D in companies, but unlike in the liberal regimes, Bégin-Caouette et al. (2017) suggested that networking was based upon equalitarian relationships between industrial and academic partners, the latter receiving public funding to participate in technology transfer initiatives rather than being encouraged to compensate for a lack of public funding with a private one.

Allocation Mechanisms

Although governments in the liberal regimes have, on average, larger budget allocations for R&D (GBARD) in purchasing power parity (line 11), the proportion of funding allocated through non-oriented research programmes or GUF (line 13) is the lowest ($\bar{x}$ = 27.78). As reported by Reale (2017), the UK and the US allocate more than 50% of total GBARD in the form of project funding, while institutional funding accounts for more than 70% in Austria, Denmark, France, Italy, Spain, and Switzerland. Block funding is a core feature of RFP in the conservative and social-democratic regimes (Reale, 2017). Since the early 2000s, reforms have however included a performance-based institutional funding (PIBIF) in block funding, such as in the Netherlands where the formula considers PhD defences, and in Austria, and Germany, where indicators also include external research funding (Hicks, 2012). In Norway, 60% of the funding was allocated as block funding, 25% based on education outcomes and 15% on research performance (Frølich et al., 2010). The Norwegian model inspired the 2006 Danish model (Hicks, 2012). Although block funding is smaller in the liberal regimes, Australia, New Zealand, and the UK rely on performance-based research evaluation frameworks (Auranen and Nieminen, 2010; Hicks, 2012) that include institutions' publication, citations, research income, and since the mid-2000s indicators related to the economic impacts of academic research in research evaluation frameworks (Chubb and Read, 2018). The UK 2014 Research Excellence Framework, for instance, includes a 20% weighting for the demonstration of research's impacts outside the academia (Luukkonen and Thomas, 2013).

Policy Instruments

Following the channelled competition inherent to conservative regimes (Scholten et al., 2021) where the State sets criteria that only a handful of units can meet, thus creating a "consecration effect" (Münch, 2014, p. 80), additional institutional funding has been complemented by excellence instruments. In countries where research universities are prominent (such as in Germany, the Netherlands, and Switzerland), RFP built excellence upon universities' existing strengths, while in other countries (such as Austria, Belgium, France and Portugal), excellence was built upon collaboration between leading universities and other organizations. In Switzerland, the National Centres of Competence and the National Research Programmes increased host institutions' block funding (Öquist and Benner, 2012). In France, the IDEX/LabEX aimed at promoting research excellence by funding multidisciplinary projects presented by Research and Advanced Education Centres and well-established university-institutes research groups (Musselin, 2017). Portugal created centres of excellence as publicly funded laboratories located on university campuses, but almost entirely independent from universities (OECD, 2014).

Excellence funding is not unique to conservative regimes. RFPs in social-democratic countries include two types of centres of excellence, those based on the accumulation of scientific capital and those based on the accumulation of economic capital (Langfeldt et al., 2015). In Denmark, 48 centres of excellence have been funded since 1993; in Finland 33 centres of excellence since 1995; in Norway 21 centres since 2003; and in Sweden 40 Linnaeus Environments since 2006, but one could also characterize the Swedish Strategic Research Areas, which are both strategic and excellence funding. The centres of excellence for innovation are part of RFP policy mixes intending to, not only to provide industries with innovation support, but also strengthen the evolutionary dynamics of the whole economic system (Herstad et al., 2010).

While excellence funding is rarer in liberal regimes, it should be noted that competitive grants have increased in size and that success rates have decreased, thus contributing to funding concentration (Bloch and Sørensen, 2015; Polster, 2018). In Canada, 10% of researchers in the social sciences accumulate 80% of available funds, and 10% in the health sciences accumulate 50% of the funds (Larivière et al., 2010). Like the concentration prompted by performance-based institutional funding (PBIF) in Australia or the UK, the concentration of research grants seems to favour institutional and individual actors who appear the most likely to win the global symbolic race. RFPs in liberal regimes also include indicators related to the economic impacts of academic research. In Canada and the US, funding agencies have developed research programmes for which researchers or institutions must demonstrate that there is a societal or economic demand for the project (Sá et al., 2013). In Canada, 45% of the funds granted by the Natural Sciences and Engineering Research Council are linked to federal priorities, and knowledge transfer to non-academic partners (Veletanlić and Sá, 2020). These RFPs seem to support individual and institutional actors who are the most likely to convert scientific capital into economic capital and generate wealth.

POLICY COORDINATION

As shown in Table 20.2, policy coordination includes the strategic interactions between policy actors and the coordination approaches supporting policy implementation.

Table 20.2   *Policy coordination and policy actors' coordination*

Regimes	Policy actors' coordination	Policy coordination
Liberal	Competition between autonomous institutions.	Integrated approach in New Zealand and the UK.
	Hierarchies.	Fragmented in Australia, Canada and the US.
Conservative	Relational contracts between actors.	Integrated approach in France, Germany, Spain and Switzerland.
	Hierarchies.	Fragmented approach in Austria, Belgium, Italy and Portugal.
Social-democratic	Trust-based horizontal coordination between actors.	Integrated approach in Denmark, Finland, Norway and Sweden.
	Mergers.	Consensus, experts, and arm-length organizations.

Actors' Coordination

In liberal regimes, policy actors' coordination is achieved through a quasi-market competition between highly autonomous actors (Cummings and Finkelstein, 2011). In the EU Autonomy Scorecard, the UK is the only European country achieving a perfect score in terms of organizational, financial, staffing, and academic autonomy, meaning universities can select and dismiss the executive head, keep surpluses, and borrow money, decide on recruitment and salary, select students, introduce programmes, and design content (Pruvot and Estermann, 2017). A competitive dynamic between autonomous institutions would explain research performance as universities diversify revenue sources and the most competitive of them attract grants and talents (Lacroix and Maheu, 2015). The literature, however, suggests that RFP supporting competition could have accentuated vertical differentiation between institutions. A limited number of universities seem to have strengthened their position in academia through aggressive managerial strategies aimed at recruiting top scientists, increasing endowments and ultimately, converting the capital accumulated by other actors (Adams and Gurney, 2010).

In conservative regimes, coordination requires relational contracts between actors, yet this coordination is likely to accentuate existing hierarchies (Hall and Soskice, 2004). Instead of letting all players compete for grants, public authorities have channelled competition between institutions into excellence initiatives, which have increased the vertical differentiation between institutions, consolidating the symbolic authority of a limited number of universities that are the largest, oldest, and most active in natural and health sciences (Cantwell and Marginson, 2018). Flagship universities monopolize a significant part of public funding and ensure coordination by acting as a regulator setting standards for other institutions. Their graduates become professors in other universities and that their members are more strongly represented on the evaluation committees (Klemenčič, 2016). Since the 1980s, actors' coordination has also manifested itself through the imposition of accountability instruments, although the conceptualization and operationalization of these instruments vary according to the context (Capano, Chapter 5 in this *Handbook*).

Actors' coordination in social-democratic regimes has been characterized as collaborative (Woiceshyn and Eriksson, 2014), horizontal, and conducted in a context of trust. Academics have been instrumental in building the welfare state and, in the knowledge society, have justified their authority in the public sphere by their seemingly disinterested function (Bégin-Caouette, 2019). Citizens' trust towards HES is also fuelled by the egalitarian context of these regimes. Lastly, the centrality of the academic field has been reaffirmed by mergers between academic institutions, and, in Denmark and Finland, between PRO and universities (Askling, 2012). In Denmark, in 2007, 12 universities and 13 institutes were merged into five universities and three institutes. In Sweden, most of the R&D occurs in the top research universities (Brundenius et al., 2011). In Norway, however, institutes still compete with universities on the same grants and perform 25% of the country's R&D.

Policy Coordination

When it comes to policy coordination, one can distinguish between integrated and fragmented approaches. In liberal regimes, New Zealand and the UK seem to follow an integrated approach (Dawson et al., 2009). In the US, although Congress plays a critical role in providing funding and conducting oversight activities (EPTA, 2014), multiple federal and state agencies, as well as public, semi-public, private for-profit or not-for-profit organizations fund research and impose their own set of rules (Link, 2019). The OECD (2017) noted similar policy fragmentation in Australia, where government investments in R&D are spread across 15 portfolios, multiple local and national agencies, and a diversity of research programmes. Against this backdrop, Industry Innovation and Science Australia was created in 2016 to increase coordination and guide policy development. In Canada, academic research is at the crossroads of two jurisdictions as provinces have exclusive power over education and the federal government is the main funder for research (Bégin-Caouette et al., 2020). Barriers to coordination stem from a lack of clarity in the delimitation of the responsibilities of government agencies, and the absence of a tradition of federal-provincial consultations (Jones and Weinrib, 2015). In addition, various research agencies have emerged on the fringes of the three traditional research councils (Tamtik and Sà, 2020). In this decentralized and fragmented system, coordination occurs horizontally through trans-regional policy networks (Tamtik, 2018).

In conservative regimes, integration is influenced by the level of centralization in the system, and the number of state-level actors involved: Austria, Italy, and Portugal following a fragmented approach, while France, Germany, Spain, and Switzerland follow an integrated approach. Belgium is difficult to characterize since its research ecosystem is fragmented into language communities, yet both Wallonia and Flanders follow integrated approaches (Hottenrott and Thorwarth, 2011; Powell and Dusdal, 2017). Germany is also a federal system, but the central government has greater influence on RFP coordination through the intervention of the Federal Ministry of Education and Research, and the Expertenkommission für Forschung und Innovation, which, following a network-based model, increased partnerships between federal, provincial, and societal stakeholders (Christensen and Serrano Velarde, 2019). The 16 Länder have local RFP (Onestini, 2016) and co-fund the German Science Foundation, a self-governing agency that sits at the core of the German ecosystem. Spain, Switzerland, and France have fewer state-level agencies intervening on research matters and all count one institutional stronghold for RFP implementation (Langfeldt and Borlaug, 2016; Musselin, 2017; OECD, 2019). On the contrary, in Italy, academic research falls under the purview of multiple ministries and agencies, including the Ministry of University and Research mostly funding basic research, the Ministry for Economic Development that funds innovation, but also acts as a coordinating agent, and the Agency for the Evaluation of University System and Research, that evaluates institutions (Donina et al., 2015). In Portugal, the OECD (2019) indicates that the fragmented approach is the corollary of suboptimal horizontal coordination, resource dispersion and disconnection between national goals and institutions' strategies.

Lastly, coordination in social-democratic regimes follows an integrated approach characterized by consensus (Campbell and Pederson, 2010) and reliance on experts. Information feeds through networks and potent technocrats, bargaining is achieved through formal corporatist meetings, and decisions are made through consensus. The government often makes its rulings based on feedback from the social sciences, and this relationship between science and policymaking extends to the public service sector, which has institutionalized scientific expertise and its processes. RFPs are developed in collaboration with universities and implemented by arm-length organizations, such as the Swedish National Authority for Higher Education or, in the case of Finland and Norway, the main research councils (Bégin-Caouette, 2019).

POLICY OUTCOMES

Outputs refer to the immediate results of a policy and outcomes refer to the deeper changes it is intended to yield. If most RFPs attempt to enhance research production, Table 20.3 describes how the desired outcomes depend upon each global competitive dynamic's measure of success: symbolic power (Münch, 2014) or economic profitability (Slaughter and Rhoades, 2004). In other words, RFP can encourage research that will lead to indexed publications, citations, academic prizes, and universities' position in rankings (Altbach, 2012) and/or that will lead to university patents, spin-off businesses and businesses' growth (Lissoni and Montobbio, 2015).

Symbolic Power

While policy mixes in all regimes have contributed to funding concentration, the outcomes of such RFPs are nuanced (for a thorough discussion on the impact of grant sizes, please refer to Bloch, Kladakis and Sørensen, Chapter 8 in this *Handbook*). Van den Besselaar and Sandström (2017) pointed out that the Australian framework had a positive outcome on publications' impact. In the UK, Pinar and Unlu (2019) found that the Research Excellence Framework had accentuated the vertical hierarchy between institutions, since those with higher external research income performed better. In the US and Canada, an increasing number of

Table 20.3   Symbolic power and economic profitability

Regimes	Symbolic power	Economic profitability
Liberal	Limited impacts of PBIF. Negative impact of grant concentration on publications. Cultural-linguistic advantage.	Positive impact of tax incentives, direct funding, legal provisions, and access to capital ventures. Complex interactions between RFP aimed at increasing universities' prestige and economic profitability.
Conservative	Positive outcomes of prioritizing academic research and comparing institutions. A positive outcome of excellence funding as it increases universities' autonomy and postgraduate education.	Positive outcome of universities' autonomy and regional networks. Limited response of traditional universities to economically focused RFP.
Social-democratic	Positive outcome of high expenditures, accessible postgraduate education, and balance between instruments. Negative outcome of grant concentration.	Positive outcome of collaboration between sectors, but limited knowledge development and absorptive capacity on the industry side.

actors compete for a limited number of larger grants. Bloch and Sørensen (2015) found that, in the US, smaller grants from the NIH or the NSF had a stronger impact on researchers' publications than larger grants. RFP's outcome assessment should, however, consider that academic capitalism is concomitant with the linguistic hegemony of English (Altbach, 2012). Cultural hegemony of Anglo-Saxon countries is also manifest in the massive recruitment of international graduate students and top researchers (Avveduto, 2010). This context contributes to the competitive advantage of liberal regimes, which remain the most visible in the global symbolic competition (OECD, 2017).

Larger grants and lower acceptance rates are also notable in social-democratic regimes (Wendt et al., 2015), such as in Denmark where acceptance rates fell from 65% in 2001 to 16% in 2009. Like in liberal regimes, Bloch et al. (Chapter 8 in this *Handbook*) found that, in social-democratic regimes, smaller grants produced more articles (per dollar) than larger excellence instruments. Compared to their Continental European counterparts, Nordic countries, however, avoid an excessive accumulation of resources (Langfeldt et al., 2015), and this balance could contribute to research excellence (Öquist and Benner, 2015). Comparatively large block funding also ensures stable revenue sources for institutions that, in the absence of tuition fees, have little alternative for maintaining their infrastructure (Auranen and Nieminen, 2010). The PBIF may also improve quality owing to the promotion of publication in top-tier journals (Eriksson, 2013), partly thanks to a signalling effect (Bégin-Caouette et al., 2017). Any analysis of RFP outcomes in social-democratic regimes should, however, consider the positive influence of large expenditures in R&D (Michavila and Martinez, 2018) and, in agreement with egalitarian values, an improved access to a quality postgraduate education (Bégin-Caouette, 2019).

In conservative regimes, RFP tended to prioritize academic research, compare institutions' publications and citations, and provide additional funding. Belgian researchers' publications and citations have increased significantly, largely because of the well-funded research universities (Powell and Dusdal, 2017). In Spain, the Sexenio research assessment data has also improved publications and citations (Hicks, 2012), and, in Italy, PBIF increased publications in all universities, but even more in the most prestigious institutions (Cattaneo et al., 2016). The literature, however, presents important contradictions regarding the outcomes of excellence instruments. The OECD (2014) suggested that they support high-risk research and increase universities' international visibility. The German Excellence Initiative has increased publications, inter-institutional cooperation and, because of its doctoral school component, the level of research training. The success of the Swiss centres of excellence also partly stems from the improved level of doctoral education and an enhanced level of international recruitment. However, since few units succeed in obtaining excellence grants and because larger grants require complex proposals (Falavigna and Manello, 2014), their efficiency is questioned. Jonkers and Zacharewicz (2016) note that excellence initiatives work best in countries with a greater balance between institutional and project funding, such as the Netherlands, Germany, Austria, and Switzerland. Institutional autonomy is also a crucial factor to consider since it is highly variable in conservative regimes, and it could mediate the impact of various funding instruments. In the Netherlands, Scholten et al. (2021) suggest that the positive influence of excellence funding stems from the autonomy and flexibility it grants to the research unit vis-à-vis the department and central administration. For Michavila and Martinez (2018), the combination of lower funding and lower autonomy could explain why Italy, Portugal and Spain publish fewer papers per faculty than the Netherlands and Switzerland.

Economic Profitability

Institutional autonomy might also explain RFP's success in increasing universities' economic profitably in conservative regimes. For Lissoni and Montobbio (2015), the Dutch universities outperform their French and Italian counterparts in terms of producing patents, as they can more easily network with local firms and manage more effectively intellectual property matters and patent portfolios. Hottenrott and Thorwarth (2011) found that, in Germany, an increase in funding from industry is linked to a decrease in publication and citations. Many countries of conservative regimes, however, have a separate sector for applied research and teaching, and it could be that this sector responds more easily to economically oriented RFP than traditional universities, especially since performance funding and excellence initiatives have highlighted the prioritizing of internationally recognized academic research.

In liberal regimes, the OECD (2020) suggests that tax credit increases private R&D investments into academic research, but that the effects are larger in countries with higher tax rates, and that effects are smaller than directly funding university–enterprise collaborations (Becker, 2014). In the UK, Sussex et al. (2016) found that there was a statistically significant complementary relationship between RFP for academic research in the biomedical field and private pharmaceutical R&D expenditures. Tax incentives, direct funding, legal provisions, and access to capital ventures all support universities' contribution to the global economy (Loise and Stevens, 2010). With 68% of the world university-owned patents (Veugelers, 2014), the US is a special case in terms of patents, but the UK and Canada are also countries with high shares of patents owned by universities (OECD, 2009). If Leydesdorff and Meyer (2010) suggest that RFPs dedicating more resources to traditional research metrics undermine university owned patent creation, Sterzi (2013) found a correlation between patent quality and scientific productivity, and Banal-Estañol and colleagues (2015) observed a curvilinear relationship between researchers' collaborations with businesses and publication rates. In sum, in liberal regimes, there are complex interactions between RFP aimed at increasing universities' prestige and RFP aimed at increasing their economic utility.

Social-democratic regimes are characterized by small, innovative, and open economies to which the academic field contributes significantly (Woiceshyn and Eriksson, 2014). Innovation policies support collaboration between sectors rather than R&D outside academia, thus strengthening scientific capital accumulation and inducing arms-length R&D contract (Herstad et al., 2010). Falavigna and Manello (2014) however found that, when researchers spent time in conducting non-publishable research, they had less time to spend on projects with a greater impact on the scientific community. In Sweden, Öquist and Benner (2015) found that sectorial research agencies supported research perceived as economically relevant, and that it had impeded ground-breaking discoveries. For the authors, there would also be limited interaction between research units focusing on basic research and those focusing on innovation. The centrality of the academic field appears as a pillar of social-democratic regimes' competitive advantage, though it is possible the multiplication of contradictory demands put on HES limit their capacity to respond effectively.

CONCLUDING REMARKS

Relying on an integrative review of 75 scholarly documents and 15 OECD reports, this chapter compared RFPs in 18 countries and examined if there were differences in funding policy mixes, how policy coordination was carried out and to what extent the VoAC influenced policy outcomes.

Regarding policy mixes and coordination, our findings suggest that, in liberal regimes, scientific capital accumulation is based upon the following institutional arrangement: competition, market sensitivity and commodification. Competition is the main coordination mechanism and is accompanied by policy mixes including a large share of project funding granted by arm's-length publicly funded research funding agencies after a peer-reviewed evaluation of research proposals. The conservative category presents important intra-category differences, but the literature suggests that RFP policy mixes are built upon the integration of the academic and scientific fields, a competition between institutions channelled by public authorities and relational contracts between actors. PBIF would have supported scientific capital accumulation, and excellence funding contributed to institutions' autonomy and the quality of doctoral education. In social-democratic regimes, accumulation of scientific capital is partly supported by the following institutional arrangements: policy mixes based upon high expenditures, balance between instruments and the centrality of the academic field; as well as consensus-based policy coordination.

Policy outcomes are analysed with regards to the global competitive dynamics. In the *symbolic global competition*, the academic field's success stems from its capacity to accumulate scientific capital endogenously (social-democratic regimes), or convert the capital accumulated by the strongest fields in societies, whether it is the scientific field (conservative regimes) or the economic field (liberal regimes). The review however suggests that, in the three types, funding concentration is less efficient to increase publications and citations than spreading out smaller grants. We however pose that excellence instruments produce different outcomes depending on countries' balance between institutional and project funding, institutions' autonomy, and doctoral education; all of which can be influenced by the political–economic structure.

In all three regimes, policy outcomes in the *economic global race* are based upon the level of collaboration or integration between the academic and economic fields. Some differences however appear between the liberal regime and the two others when policy mixes and coordination are considered. In liberal regimes, tax incentives, legal provisions, direct subsidies, access to capital ventures, the establishment of priority areas, and the inclusion of industry representatives on grant evaluation committees have integrated both fields and supported universities' contribution to economic growth. In the conservative and social-democratic regimes, following Europe's Impact Agenda, RFPs seem to rely on HES' innovative potential for industries, and to promote intra-national linkages in the form of clusters. If those regimes follow relational- and networked-based coordination, the proportion of HERD financed by industry is higher in the conservative regimes, which corroborates equalitarian relationships between academic and economic fields, the former receiving public funding to participate in technology transfer initiatives rather than being encouraged to compensate for a lack of public funding with a private one.

This integrative review's objective was also to identify what remains unknown. Our analysis was based on a country-based conceptualization of political–economic structures, yet future studies should include two other levels. While we acknowledged the cultural and linguistic influence of liberal regimes, future studies should analyze countries' RFP in the context of the European Higher Education Area and the European Research Area, or in the context of the Canada–US–Mexico Agreement. The internationalization of research contributes to scientific capital accumulation in the three regimes, but it remains unknown how the VoAC could mediate its effects, nor if it diminishes differences between welfare regimes. Our analysis also revealed that the integrated or fragmented character of policy coordination depended less on regimes than by the number state-level actors involved in the policy implementation process and by the nature of the political system. Future studies could explore the subnational level since the VoAC may vary between jurisdictions within the same federal country (Carnoy et al., 2018). In Canada, for instance, Fisher et al. (2009) have explained how provinces' political–economic structures (liberal in Ontario and social-democratic in Quebec) influenced research and development policymaking. Regarding policy outcomes, despite the diversity of indicators, our analysis was limited to publications and citations for symbolic competition and faced difficulties in identifying the most appropriate indicators in the economic competition, which undermined our ability to draw unambiguous conclusions. Future studies could include indicators related to the research's social impacts, or equity, diversity, and inclusion.

This chapter finally presents significant limitations – to which future research could respond – including reforms occurring during the period we covered (2010 and 2021), which would have affected policy mixes. Under common global trends (such as managerialism), countries across regimes might have moved in a similar direction (Marini and Reale, 2016) or, within each regime and variety, in different directions (Öquist and Benner, 2015). An important limitation also stems from the typology itself. There was noticeable intra-category heterogeneity, and future research could examine if a framework allowing for the combination of different types may have accounted for what is observed empirically more adequately than a static approach (see Walker and Wong, 2005). Moreover, in order to maintain categories' adequacy, we limited our analysis to the 18 North American and Western European countries initially studied by Esping-Andersen (1999) and later analysed by Pechar and Andres (2011) and Bégin-Caouette et al. (2016); doing so, we omitted 20 other OECD countries and China, which does not fit the welfare regime typology (Ringen and Ngok, 2013) but produces the largest proportion of the world's scientific publications (World Bank, 2018). Future research should broaden the conceptualization to include a greater diversity of jurisdiction.

As Hayhoe (2007) posed, "ideal types are made to be broken" (p. 196), but until future research extends, nuances, or even breaks this model, we argue that the VoAC approach remains complementary to other public policy approaches, as it proposes theoretically sound ideal types to conceptualize dynamic interactions between global competitive landscapes, RFP and the deeper political–economic fabric of societies as they influence (albeit indirectly) policy choices and actors' behaviours.

REFERENCES

Adams, J. and Gurney, K. (2010). *Funding Selectivity, Concentration and Excellence: How Good is the U's Research?* Oxford: Higher Education Policy Institute.

Altbach, P. G. (2012). The globalization of college and university rankings. *Change: The Magazine of Higher Learning, 44*(1), 26–31.

Askling, B. (2012). *Integration and/or Diversification: The Role of Structure in Meeting Expectations on Higher Education*. HEIK Working Paper Series 2012/4. University of Oslo.

Auranen, O. and Nieminen, M. (2010). University research funding and publication performance – An international comparison. *Research Policy, 39*(3), 822–834.

Avveduto, S. (2010). Mobility of PhD students and scientists. Correspondence analysis. In P. Peterson, E. Baker and B. McGaw (Eds), *International Encyclopedia of Education*, 3rd ed. (pp. 286–294). Elsevier.

Banal-Estañol, A., Jofre-Bonet, M. and Lawson, C. (2015). The double-edged sword of industry collaboration: Evidence from engineering academics in the UK. *Research Policy, 44*(6), 1160–1175.

Becker, B. (2014). Public R&D policies and private R&D investment: A survey of the empirical evidence. *Journal of Economic Surveys, 29*(5), 917–942.

Bégin-Caouette, O. (2019). Behind quality, there is equality: An analysis of scientific capital accumulation in social-democratic welfare regimes. *Comparative and International Education, 48*(1), 163–185.

Bégin-Caouette, O., Askvik, T. and Cui, B. (2016). Interplays between welfare regimes typology and academic research systems in OECD countries. *Higher Education Policy, 29*(3), 287–313.

Bégin-Caouette, O., Kalpazidou Schmidt, E. and Field, C. (2017). The perceived impact of research funding streams on the level of scientific knowledge production in the Nordic higher education systems. *Science and Public Policy, 44*(6), 789–801.

Bégin-Caouette, O., Nakano Koga, S. and Karram Stephenson, G. (2020). L'influence perçue des instruments d'action publique fédéraux et provinciaux sur la production de recherche universitaire au Canada. *Canadian Journal of Higher Education, 50*(3), 49–62.

Benner, M. (2011). In search of excellence? An international perspective on governance of university research. In *Universities in Transition* (pp. 11–24). Springer.

Bloch, C. and Sørensen, M. P. (2015). The size of research funding: Trends and implications. *Science and Public Policy, 42*(1), 30–43.

Borrás, S. and Edquist, C. (2019). *Holistic Innovation Policy: Theoretical Foundations, Policy Problems, and Instrument Choices*. Oxford University Press.

Bourdieu, P. (1988). *Homo Academicus*. Stanford University Press.

Brundenius, C., Göransson, B. and Ågren, J. (2011). The role of academic institutions in the national system of innovation and the debate in Sweden. In B. Goransson and C. Brundenius (Eds), *Universities in Transition. The Changing Role and Challenges for Academic Institutions* (pp. 307–325). Springer.

Campbell, J. L. and Pederson, O. K. (2010). Knowledge regimes and comparative political economy. In D. Béland and R. H. Cox (Eds), *Ideas and Politics in Social Science Research*. Oxford Scholarship Online.

Cantwell, B. and Marginson, S. (2018). *Vertical Stratification in High Participation Systems of Higher Education*. Oxford University Press.

Caporaso, J. A. and Levine, D. P. (1992). *Theories of Political Economy*. Cambridge University Press.

Carnoy, M., Froumin, I., Leshukov, O. and Marginson, S. (Eds) (2018). *Higher Education in Federal Countries: A Comparative study*. SAGE.

Cattaneo, M., Meoli, M. and Signori, A. (2016). Performance-based funding and university research productivity: The moderating effect of university legitimacy. *The Journal of Technology Transfer, 41*(1), 85–104.

Christensen, J. and Serrano Velarde, K. (2019). The role of advisory bodies in the emergence of cross-cutting policy issues: comparing innovation policy in Norway and Germany. *European Politics and Society, 20*(1), 49–65.

Chubb, J. and Reed, M. S. (2018). The politics of research impact: Academic perceptions of the implications for research funding, motivation and quality. *British Politics, 13*(3), 295–311.

Cummings, W. K. and Finkelstein, M. J. (2011). *Scholars in the Changing American Academy: New Contexts, New Rules and New Roles* (Vol. 4). Springer Science and Business Media.

Dawson, J., van Steen, J. and van der Meulen, B. (2009). *Science Systems Compared: A First Description of Governance Innovations in Six Science Systems*. Den Haag, Rathenau Instituut.

Donina, D., Meoli, M. and Paleari, S. (2015). Higher education reform in Italy: Tightening regulation instead of steering at a distance. *Higher Education Policy, 28*(2), 215–234.

EPTA (2014). *Productivity in Europe and the United States*. European Parliamentary Technology Assessment. http://epub.oeaw.ac.at/0xc1aa500e_0x0031e598.pdf.

Eriksson, L. M. (2013). The performance-based funding model: Creating new research databases in Sweden and Norway. *Adriane*, July, 71.

Esping-Andersen, G. (1999). *Social Foundations of Postindustrial Economies*. Oxford University Press.

Falavigna, G. and Manello, A. (2014). External funding, efficiency and productivity growth in public research: The case of the Italian National Research Council. *Research Evaluation*, *23*, 33–47.

Fisher, D., Rubenson, K., Jones, G. and Shanahan, T. (2009). The political economy of post-secondary education: A comparison of British Columbia, Ontario and Québec. *Higher Education*, *57*(5), 549–566.

Flanagan, K., Uyarra, E. and Laranja, M. (2011). Reconceptualising the "policy mix" for innovation. *Research Policy*, *40*(5), 702–713.

Frølich, N., Schmidt, E. K. and Rosa, M. J. (2010). Funding systems for higher education and their impacts on institutional strategies and academia. *International Journal of Educational Management*, *24* (1), 7–21.

Graf, L. (2009). Applying the varieties of capitalism approach to higher education: Comparing the internationalisation of German and British universities. *European Journal of Education*, *44*(4), 569–585.

Hall, P. A. and Soskice, D. (2004). *Varieties of Capitalism: The Institutional Foundations of Comparative Advantage*. Oxford University Press.

Hayhoe, R. (2007). The use of ideal types in comparative education: a personal reflection, *Comparative Education*, *43*(2), 189–205. DOI: 10.1080/03050060701362342.

Herstad, S. J., Bloch, C., Ebersberger, B. and Van De Velde, E. (2010). National innovation policy and global open innovation: Exploring balances, tradeoffs and complementarities. *Science and Public Policy*, *37*(2), 113–124.

Hicks, D. (2012). Performance-based university research funding systems. *Research Policy*, *41*(2), 251–261.

Hottenrott, H. and Thorwarth, S. (2011). Industry funding of university research and scientific productivity. *Kyklos*, *64*(4), 534–555.

Jones, G. J. and Weinrib, J. (2015). Canada: Decentralization, federalism and STEM. In B. Freeman, S. Marginson and R. Tyler (Eds.), *The Age of STEM. Educational Policy and Practice across the World in Science, Technology, Engineering and Mathematics* (pp. 134–150). Routledge.

Jonkers, K. and Zacharewicz, T. (2016). *Research Performance Based Funding Systems: A Comparative Assessment*. Publications Office of the European Union. EUR, 27837.

Kauppinen, I. and Kaidesoja, T. (2014). A shift towards academic capitalism in Finland. *Higher Education Policy*, *27*(1), 23–41.

Kim, S. Y. (2013). Government R&D funding in economic downturns: Testing the varieties of capitalism conjecture. *Science and Public Policy*, *41*(1), 107–119.

Klemenčič, M. (2016). Epilogue: Reflections on a new flagship university. In J. A. Douglass (Ed.), *The new flagship university: Changing the paradigm from global ranking to national relevancy* (pp. 191–198). Springer.

Lacroix, R. and Maheu, L. (2015). *Les grandes universités de recherche: institutions autonomes dans un environnement concurrentiel*. Les Presses de l'Université de Montréal.

Langfeldt, L. and Borlaug, S. B. (2016). *Swiss National Centres of Competence in Research (NCCR): Evaluation of the Selection Process*. Nordic Institute for Studies in Innovation, Research and Education.

Langfeldt, L., Benner, M., Sivertsen, G., Kristiansen, E. H., Aksnes, D. W., Borlaug, S. B., ... and Pelkonen, A. (2015). Excellence and growth dynamics: A comparative study of the Matthew effect. *Science and Public Policy*, *42*(5), 661–675.

Larivière, V., Macaluso, B., Archambault, É. and Gingras, Y. (2010). Which scientific elites? On the concentration of research funds, publications and citations. *Research Evaluation*, *19*(1), 45–53.

Lester, J. and Warda, J. (2014). An international comparison of tax assistance for research and development: Estimates and policy implications. *The School of Public Policy Research Papers*, *7*(36), 1–42.

Leydesdorff, L. and Meyer, M. (2010). The decline of university patenting and the end of the Bayh–Dole effect. *Scientometrics*, *83*(2), 355–362.

Link, A. N. (2019). *Collaborative Research in the United States: Policies and Institutions for Cooperation among Firms*. Routledge.

Lissoni, F. and Montobbio, F. (2015). The ownership of academic patents and their impact: Evidence from five European countries. *Revue économique*, *1*(1), 143–171.

Loise, V. and Stevens, A. J. (2010). The Bayh–Dole Act turns 30. *Science Translational Medicine*, *2*(52), 1–5.

Luukkonen, T. and Thomas, D. A. (2013). Industrial engagement of university research. *ETLA Brief*, *20*, 2013.

Marini, G. and Reale, E. (2016). How does collegiality survive managerially led universities? Evidence from a European Survey. *European Journal of Higher Education*, *6*(2), 111–127.

Michavila, F. and Martinez, J. M. (2018). Excellence of universities versus autonomy, funding and accountability. *European Review*, *26*(S1), S48-S56.

Münch, R. (2014). *Academic Capitalism: Universities in the Global Struggle for Excellence*. Routledge.

Musselin, C. (2017). *La grande course des universités*. Presses de Sciences Po.

OECD (2009). *OECD Patent Statistics Manual*. OECD Publishing.

OECD (2014). *Promoting Research Excellence New Approaches to Funding*. OECD Publishing.

OECD (2017). *OECD Science, Technology and Industry Scoreboard 2017: The Digital Transformation*. OECD Publishing.

OECD (2019). *OECD Review of Higher Education, Research and Innovation: Portugal*. OECD Publishing.

OECD (2020). *Directorate for Science, Technology and Innovation: R&D Tax Incentives*. OECD Publishing.

OECD (2021). *Science, Technology and Innovation Outlook 2021: Times of Crisis and Opportunity*. OECD Publishing.

Olson, J. and Slaughter, S. (2014). Forms of capitalism and creating world-class universities. In A. Maldonado-Maldonado and R. M. Bassett (Eds), *The Forefront of International Higher Education: A Festschrift in Honor of Philip G.Altbach* (pp. 267–280). Springer.

Onestini, C. (2016). *Federalism and Länder Autonomy: The higher education policy network in the Federal Republic of Germany*. Routledge.

Öquist, G. and Benner, M. (2012). *Fostering Breakthrough Research: A Comparative Study*. Kungl. Vetenskapsakademien.

Öquist, G. and Benner, M. (2015). Why are some nations more successful than others in research impact? A comparison between Denmark and Sweden. In I. Welpe, J. Wollersheim, S. Ringelhan and M. Osterloh (ed.) *Incentives and Performance* (pp. 241–257). Springer.

Pechar, H. and Andres, L. (2011). Higher-education policies and welfare regimes: International comparative perspectives. *Higher Education Policy*, *24*(1), 25–52.

Pinar, M. and Unlu, E. (2019). Evaluating the potential effect of the increased importance of the impact component in the Research Excellence Framework of the UK. *British Educational Research Journal*, *46*(1), 140–160.

Polster, C. (2018). How and why to change the ways we try to change the corporatization of Canada's universities. In J. Brownlee, C. Hurl and K. Walby (Eds), *Corporatizing Canada: Making Business Out of Public Service* (pp. 87–109). Between the Lines.

Powell, J. J. and Dusdal, J. (2017). The European Center of science productivity: Research universities and institutes in France, Germany, and the United Kingdom. In J. J. Powell, D. P. Baker and F. Fernandez (Eds), *The Century of Science* (pp. 55–83). Emerald.

Pranevičienė, B., Pūraitė, A., Vasiliauskienė, V. and Simanavičienė, Ž. (2017, May). Comparative Analysis of Financing Models of Higher Education. In *SOCIETY. INTEGRATION. EDUCATION. Proceedings of the International Scientific Conference* (Vol. 4, pp. 330–341).

Pruvot, E. B. and Estermann, T. (2017). *University Autonomy in Europe III*. The Scorecard.

Reale, E. (2017). *Analysis of National Public Research Funding-PREF. Final Report*. Publications Office of the European Union.

Ringen, S. and Ngok, K. (2013). What kind of welfare state is emerging in China? Working Paper 2013-2. United Nations Research Institute for Social Development. https://www.unrisd.org/unrisd/website/document.nsf/(httpPublications)/28BCE0F59BDD3738C1257BE30053EBAC?OpenDocument.

Sá, C. M., Kretz, A. and Sigurdson, K. (2013). Accountability, performance assessment, and evaluation: Policy pressures and responses from research councils. *Research Evaluation*, *22*(2), 105–117.

Scholten, W., Franssen, T. P., van Drooge, L., de Rijcke, S. and Hessels, L. K. (2021). Funding for few, anticipation among all: Effects of excellence funding on academic research groups. *Science and Public Policy*, *48*(2), 265–275.

Schulze-Cleven, T. and Olson, J. R. (2017). Worlds of higher education transformed: toward varieties of academic capitalism. *Higher Education*, *73*(6), 813–831.

Slaughter, S. and Leslie, L. (1999). *Academic Capitalism: Politics, Policies and the Entrepreneurial University*. The Johns Hopkins University Press.

Slaughter, S. and Rhoades, G. (2004). *Academic Capitalism and the New Economy: Markets, State, and Higher Education*. Johns Hopkins University Press.

Sterzi, V. (2013). Patent quality and ownership: An analysis of UK faculty patenting. *Research Policy*, *42*(2), 564–576.

Sussex, J., Feng, Y., Mestre-Ferrandiz, J., Pistollato, M., Hafner, M., Burridge, P. and Grant, J. (2016). Quantifying the economic impact of government and charity funding of medical research on private research and development funding in the United Kingdom. *BMC Medicine*, *14*(1), 1–23.

Tamtik, M. (2018). "Innovation policy is a team sport" – Insights from non-governmental intermediaries in Canadian innovation ecosystem, *Triple Helix*, *5*(1), 1–19.

Tamtik, M. and Sá, C. (2020). *The Elusive Pursuit of Internationalization in Canadian Research*. International Education as Public Policy in Canada.

Thelen, K. and Kume, I. (2006). Coordination as a political problem in coordinated market economies. *Governance*, *19*(1), 11–42.

Toronto, C. E. and Remington, R. (2020). *A Step-by-Step Guide to Conducting an Integrative Review*. Springer.

UIS-UNESCO (2020). How much your country invests in R&D? http://uis.unesco.org/apps/visualisations/research-and-development-spending.

Van den Besselaar, P. and Sandström, U. (2017). Counterintuitive effects of incentives? *Research Evaluation*, *26*(4), 349–351.

Veletanlić, E. and Sá, C. (2020). Implementing the innovation agenda: A study of change at a research funding agency. *Minerva*, *58*(2), 261–283.

Vennekens, A., Koens, L. and de Jonge J. (2019). *Total Investment in Research and Innovation*. Rathenau Instituut.

Veugelers, R. (2014). *The Contribution of Academic Research to Innovation and Growth*, *71*. WWWforEurope Working Paper.

Walker, A and Wong, C. (2005). *East Asian Welfare Regimes in Transition: From Confucianism to Globalisation*. Policy Press.

Weber, M. (1968). *Economy and Society: An Outline of Interpretive Sociology*. University of California Press.

Wendt, K., Söder, I. and Leppälahti, A. (2015). *A Guide to Understanding Higher Education R&D Statistics in the Nordic Countries*. Nordic Institute for Studies in Innovation, Research and Education.

Whittemore, R. and Knafl, K. (2005). The integrative review: Updated methodology. *Journal of advanced nursing*, *52*(5), 546–553.

Woiceshyn, J. and Eriksson, P. (2014). How innovation systems in Finland and Alberta work: Lessons for policy and practice. *Innovation*, *16*(1), 19–31.

World Bank (2018). World Bank Open Data. Scientific and technical journal articles. https://data.worldbank.org/indicator/IP.JRN.ARTC.SC?end=2018&start=2000&view=chart.

APPENDIX

Table 20A.1   Research funding in 18 OECD countries

Variety / Country	Total x̄(s)	Liberal (n = 5)						Conservative (n = 9)										Social-democratic (n = 4)				
		Aus-tralia	Can-ada	UK	New Zea-land	US	x̄(s)	Aus-tria	Bel-gium	Switzer-land	Ger-many	Spain	France	Italy	Nether-lands	Portu-gal	x̄(s)	Den-mark	Fin-land	Nor-way	Swe-den	x̄(s)
1. GERD % GDP	2.32 (0.76)	1.79[a]	1.59	1.76	1.41	3.07	1.92 (0.66)	3.19	2.89	3.18[a]	3.18	1.25	2.19	1.45	2.16	1.40	2.32 (0.82)	2.96	2.79	2.15	3.40	2.83 (0.52)
2. % GERD financed by government	30.35 (6.82)	n/a	33.04	25.94[a]	31.13	22.09	28.05 (4.98)	30.20	19.96[a]	26.48[a]	27.85[a]	37.61[b]	31.58[b]	32.74[b]	29.58[b]	40.24	30.69 (5.98)	27.2[a]	27.29	48.03[b]	25.02[a]	31.89 (10.81)
3. % GERD financed by business sec.	55.46 (7.68)	n/a	41.67	54.80[a]	49.95	63.31	52.43 (9.05)	53.58	63.49[a]	68.56[a]	66.0[a]	49.49[b]	56.71[b]	54.59[b]	56.74[b]	48.26	57.49 (7.12)	58.52[a]	54.33	42.03[b]	60.76[a]	53.91 (8.36)
4. % GERD financed by foreign sources	9.77 (3.16)	n/a	9.03	13.67[a]	9.06	7.44	9.80 (2.69)	15.90	13.04[b]	5.34[a]	5.80[a]	7.90[b]	7.72[b]	10.53[b]	11.17[b]	6.82	9.36 (3.55)	8.92[a]	15.49	8.23	10.08[a]	10.68 (3.30)
5. % GERD performed by the HES	25.98 (7.81)	33.98[b]	41.49	23.08	23.79	11.97	26.86 (11.29)	22.44	19.21	28.20[a]	17.31	26.59	20.32	23.02	26.68	40.46	24.91 (6.89)	33.80	25.38	34.28	23.67	29.28 (5.54)
6. HERD % GDP	0.59 (0.20)	0.62[a]	0.66	0.41	0.34	0.37	0.48 (0.15)	0.72	0.56	0.90[a]	0.55	0.33	0.45	0.33	0.58	0.57	0.55 (0.18)	1.00	0.71	0.74	0.81	0.82 (0.13)
7. % HERD financed by business sec.	5.80 (3.29)	4.90[a]	7.99	4.45[a]	4.53	5.59	5.49 (1.47)	5.12[a]	11.71[a]	9.72[a]	13.50[b]	5.50[b]	2.83[b]	6.02[b]	8.70[b]	2.13	7.25 (3.91)	2.66[a]	3.09	2.27[b]	3.62[a]	2.91 (0.58)

Variety / Country	Total	Liberal (n = 5)						Conservative (n = 9)										Social-democratic (n = 4)				
	x̄(s)	Aus-tralia	Can-ada	UK	New Zea-land	US	x̄(s)	Aus-tria	Bel-gium	Switzer-land	Ger-many	Spain	France	Italy	Nether-lands	Portu-gal	x̄(s)	Den-mark	Fin-land	Nor-way	Swe-den	x̄(s)
8. Higher education researchers (FTE) per thousand labour force	3.97 (1.20)	5.27[a]	3.08[a]	5.08	5.65	n/a	4.77 (1.15)	3.28	4.10	4.29[a]	2.68	2.89	2.79	2.12	2.49	5.48	3.35 (1.07)	5.34	4.84	4.88	3.31	4.59 (0.88)
9. Higher education total R&D personnel (FTE) per thousand labour force	4.97 (1.26)	6.12[a]	3.81[a]	5.65	6.37	n/a	5.49 (1.16)	4.29	5.22	5.95[a]	3.46	3.61	4.04	3.24	3.75	6.01	4.40 (1.07)	7.09	6.14	5.99	3.83	5.76 (1.38)
10. Total R&D personnel (FTE) per thousand labour force	10.43 (2.47)	n/a	8.05[a]	9.35	9.52[a]	9.51[b]	9.11 (0.71)	11.53	12.29	8.70[a]	10.29	6.25	10.57	6.19	10.60	9.55	9.55 (2.15)	13.67	14.44	12.67	14.11	13.72 (0.77)
11. GBARD at constant price and PPP$	18634.70 (34252.31)	4612.97	8564.74[a]	16410.70	969.46[a]	139764.35	34064.44 (59365.45)	3544.73	3862.33	5317.99[a]	40787.16	9353.53	15917.23	12846.11	6484.67	1194.98	17518.75 (21416.48)	2749.54	2113.07	3348.90	3835.02	3011.63 (745.61)

Variety	Total	Liberal (n = 5)						Conservative (n = 9)										Social-democratic (n = 4)				
Country	x̄(s)	Aus-tralia	Can-ada	UK	New Zea-land	US	x̄(s)	Aus-tria	Bel-gium	Switzer-land	Ger-many	Spain	France	Italy	Nether-lands	Portu-gal	x̄(s)	Den-mark	Fin-land	Nor-way	Swe-den	x̄(s)
12. Civil GBARD for non-oriented research programmes as % of civil GBARD	16.81 (7.26)	9.32	12.53[c]	14.16	10.56[c]	16.54	12.62 (2.87)	12.98	26.01	28.49[a]	15.89[a]	18.05	25.50	2.24	20.54	9.29	17.67 (8.59)	14.34	28.76	15.23	22.06	20.10 (6.73)
13. GUF as % of civil GBARD	39.07 (13.39)	30.18	31.17[b]	25.98	23.80[a]	n/a	27.78 (3.48)	58.42	17.27	62.80[a]	41.16[a]	31.32	27.60	41.21	54.16	53.76	43.08 (15.37)	46.07	32.18	34.33	51.83	41.10 (9.40)

Note: Data are from 2019; [a] 2018; [b] 2017; [c] 2016; n/a: data not available.
Source: OECD (2021).

21. System-level insights into public funding of research from emerging economies
Juan D. Rogers

21.1 INTRODUCTION

Increases in public funding for research alone do not necessarily create improved scientific results. Even though scientific research cannot be carried out without resources, appropriate disbursement of funds for research requires rather sophisticated capabilities, not only by research performers, namely, good scientists, but also in the public funding entities managing such disbursement and the institutions within which research is conducted. This rather obvious statement does not receive as much attention at the overall research system level as it does on specific problems, such as increasing "transformative research" rather than "incremental research" or increasing broader social benefits from publicly funded research, for example (Mertens 2009).

In most nations with leading research systems, their status as science leaders may explain the focus on relatively narrow issues rather than the overall system operation. However, in the case of emerging economies, the system level focus is unavoidable since major improvements and upgrading are clearly needed. In this chapter, we take advantage of a recent assessment of research and innovation systems of several developing countries to get a sense of the key dimensions of research funding systems as a whole that may not only show paths of improvement for the countries in question but may also increase awareness of system-level issues that leading nations should pay attention to as well.

The landscape of public funding of scientific research in emerging economies shows a diverse collection of approaches stemming from challenges in the local context. The vast diversity in the set of countries that would fit the labels of "emerging economy" or "developing country" is a difficult challenge to overcome when attempting to find common patterns among them. This difficulty probably explains the paucity of papers addressing public funding of research in emerging economies with some generality. Almost all existing literature on the matter consists in papers that describe the situation in a single country (Benavente et al. 2012; Creso 2005; Luruli and Mouton 2016; Ubfal and Maffioli 2011).

The most focused upon dimension when referring to the support for R&D in these countries is the level of funding as a percentage of gross domestic product (GDP). Many of them have policies, at least at the level of general statements of purpose, to increase that level to at least 1% of GDP, widely considered a threshold for minimum contribution of the science system to make a difference in the economy. This measure of intensity of the effort of a nation includes the contribution of both public and private funding. One common goal in addition to increasing the investment as a percentage of GDP is to also increase the proportion of private funding.

Much less attention is paid in the literature to the management and use of resources for funding research. The agencies, instruments and research performers must be set up and have the capabilities to use the resources efficiently and productively. The features of these components of the research system are rarely analyzed carefully enough to determine how they may facilitate or hinder the research enterprise even if financial resources are increased.

The topic of the role and approach to public funding of research in emerging economies is not new. It has been hotly debated both in scholarly and policy circles for many years (Anonymous 1971). In recent times, with the increased role of scientific knowledge in economic competitiveness and, more recently, the achievement of societal development goals, the topic has increased in urgency and many developing countries are deeply involved in deliberations of the role of research in their future and the determination of the best form of government support (Mazzucato 2013).

This chapter addresses the public funding system of academic research using a comparative case study methodology of four nations from two different regions in the world, namely, Colombia and Peru in South America and Bulgaria and Croatia, new members of the European Union in Central Europe.[1]

21.2   R&D IN EMERGING ECONOMIES

Support for scientific research in emerging economies is not only confronted with the challenge of increasing its critical mass and improving quality. One of the symptoms of their development status is the weak demand for scientific knowledge (Cimoli et al. 2009; Rodrik 2007), which in turn puts the science system in a vulnerable position structurally because, in terms of the general needs of their economy and society, making scientific knowledge available is not enough. According to one view that has gained importance, policies to increase demand should be thought of as partly social policies that incentivize the development of knowledge and innovation to close the loop (Arocena and Sutz 2010).

The literature on research policy in emerging economies pays much attention to the university–industry relations that are chronically weak in emerging economies. For example, in an exploration of the university–industry–government relations in Latin America, Sutz (2010) proposed the complementarity of "bottom-up" and "top-down" approaches to policy intended to improve those relations. The "bottom-up" approach begins with pinpointing needs in the market to develop knowledge that addresses them and "top-down" begins with institutional design to enhance the flow of knowledge towards societal needs. The author presents examples of failure of both approaches suggesting the need for combining them in comprehensive policies that take real capabilities and needs simultaneously into account within the context of inequality in these nations. This proposal raises an important point addressed in this chapter, namely, that these policies require highly sophisticated professional analytical and management capabilities by the state.

In the same vein, a recent study published by the World Bank (Cirera and Maloney 2017) observed that emerging economies have the potential for greater return to investment in innovation (Griffith et al. 2004; Goñi and Maloney 2017) but spend much less than developed nations that are vulnerable to diminishing returns. One of the key findings in this work is that the policies needed to address their weaknesses put great demand on government capabilities that they generally do not have.

The focus of most work on science, technology and innovation (STI) policy in emerging economies is concerned with economic development results. Concerns over weak productivity, lack of R&D in these countries' firms, and lack of competitiveness in international markets with consequences for quality of life are central to policy makers and their constituent citizens. Many papers and reports address such issues in specific countries. A case in point is a study of the efforts by Central American countries to reform government and enhance their STI policies to increase their chances of improvement on those matters (Perez-Padilla and Gaudin 2014). The study identifies several reasons why those efforts have been largely unsuccessful in achieving the desired development results. Some of those reasons have to do with political commitment, ability to engage in long-term planning, and coordination among public organizations that is needed for policies supporting an STI system that serves the needs of the country's society. Others have to do with the institutional cultures of knowledge-producing institutions and private firms that are not conducive to collaboration (ibid.).

There is a relationship between political commitment and innovation performance according to a study by Calvo-Gonzalez et al. (2017). It shows that the frequency and consistency of references to innovation policy objectives in political speeches are positively correlated with the country's Global Innovation Index. Furthermore, the broader the dispersion of policy topics in political statements, the lower the growth of GDP per capita, which seemed to reflect weak and fluctuating commitment to policy goals, including STI objectives (ibid.).

The state should be able to properly diagnose the problems that need a solution and set up the policies and implementation mechanisms to address them. Many governments in developing countries are aware of their weaknesses in this regard and are trying to improve by engaging in government reform. In the case of STI policy, it has been noted that there is significant imitation of the organization forms and policy instruments applied in countries deemed successful. This is often discussed from the point of view of globalization and the influence of supra-national entities such as the European Union, with special attention to its effect on research funding institutions and arrangements (Lepori et al. 2007). However, these imitation processes through government reform are notoriously problematic. The formal processes of reform often do not lead to actual change in policy action and, even worse, sometimes consist in an outward form of the models they imitate that disguises a lack of improvement (Andrews and Pritchett 2013; Andrews et al. 2013). An example of this is the formulations of STI policy in Latin American countries that adopt the language of system thinking to set up a national innovation system (NSI) by law that consists only in the government entities and agencies that have roles in STI policies, completely ignoring the role of the private and academic sectors in the system (Colciencias 2016; Concytec 2016b).

These observations introduce the foci of this study of public funding for research in a set of four emerging economies. A more detailed analysis of the operations of research funding institutions, research performing organizations and the characteristics of instruments that link the two is needed to understand the challenges to achieving a research system that produces scientific results in quantity and quality commensurate with development needs of these countries.

Several studies of the research funding frameworks and mechanisms provide a backdrop to this paper by identifying components of the research funding system and their interaction. One such study tracks the evolution of research funding policies in several Western European countries over a period of three decades from the 1970s through the 1990s, focusing not only on the evolution of funding amounts but also the types of instruments, specifics of competitive project-oriented instruments and topical area emphases (Lepori et al. 2007). Another analyzes the coordination among the components of research funding systems and identifies three main configurations, namely, project-based, mixed and vertically integrated models (Lepori 2011).

This study aims to show that specific attributes of both the government side of research funding, its entities and instruments, and the research performers who are recipients of such support play a crucial role in explaining the unrealized potential of the research systems of these countries. The lessons are valuable not only for emerging economies, but also for developed nations given the complexity of evolving research systems that require continuous improvement of their own funding systems. From an analytical point of view, it aims to go beyond the characterization of research systems by means of aggregate expenditures and research output to characterize the more detailed features of the system that explain the patterns in such data.

21.3   THEORETICAL AND METHODOLOGICAL APPROACH

Public funding and performance of scientific research take place in a system of institutions, their rules and attributes, and individuals that are positioned within them with defined roles. This perspective is rooted in the systemic approach to the analysis of the creation, use and effects of scientific knowledge and technology stemming from the notion of a national innovation system (Freeman 1987; Lundvall 1992; Nelson 1993; Patel and Pavitt 1993; Metcalfe 1995). The components and structures of the research system and their interaction result in patterns of activity, outputs, and effects in the realm of research that must be understood as a whole.

A model of the publicly funded research system used in previous studies (Lepori et al. 2007; Cocos and Lepori 2020) includes the national government's entities responsible and their instruments for disbursing public funds for research and the entities and units receiving funding to engage in research activities. The government entities are ministries, research or science councils, government science agencies or foundations, and institutionalized national funds. The recipients of funds may include higher education institutions, both public and private, public research organizations and affiliated individuals. The qualification "affiliated" for individuals is pertinent since beneficiaries of public funding for research may be individuals that must be affiliated with qualifying institutions and said "affiliation" may vary. They are mostly faculty and graduate students or researchers in public research organizations. However, there are interesting variations in how the eligibility of individual researchers is defined and in the implications for management of the award when the beneficiary is an individual. In addition to the entities in the system, the model includes the research funding instruments for basic research that connect the two sides of research system, funding and performing entities, and have a combined effect on the system (Cocos and Lepori 2020).

The notion of awarding funding suggests the idea that the instruments represent a one-directional relationship that provides resources from the source to the performer. However, there is an important reverse direction in their design and implementation that reflects the response of potential and actual performance by submitting quality proposals in adequate numbers, reacting to the application requirements and procedures, requiring support for framework and complementary conditions for performance, such as infrastructure or inter-disciplinarity, among other things.

To direct funding resources productively, entities in the research funding system must have the required capabilities. The implementation of funding instruments depends on the availability of qualified staff in government entities as well as their profiles and relevant human resource policies and rules. Procedures in the evaluation and selection of proposals for

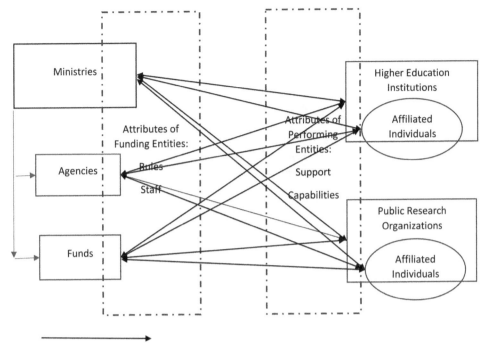

Figure 21.1   *Model of the research funding system*

making awards for competitive solicitations and engaging with and learning from evaluations to design and implement new versions of the funding instruments in the policy cycle rely on sophisticated professional competencies.

On the side of research performing entities, using funding resources effectively requires appropriate rules for integrating research project work into faculty overall labor obligations and support for preparing proposals and managing projects. Without these conditions, workloads and incentives for pursuing research will be affected negatively.

Figure 21.1 represents the resulting framework that guides the analysis of the cases.

To determine the features of components of the research system, namely, the funding entities, instruments and performers, the study applies a model of the functionality of STI policy instruments for public expenditure reviews (PER) of STI policies (Cirera and Maloney 2017).[2] The functional analysis model of policy instruments includes three areas of policy making for each instrument in the policy mix: design, implementation and governance.[3] They are illustrated in Figure 21.2.

Features of the design include several categories related to the rationale for the instrument, the intervention logic and the monitoring and evaluation scheme considered at the design stage. The dimensions of instrument implementation include types of learning during implementation, management quality and actual monitoring and evaluation of management processes and instrument performance. Finally, the governance features include four dimensions of coordination in the relation to the policy mix, namely, coordination of instruments in the same domain, coor-

Design

- Origin
- Justification
- Relationship with policy mix
- Objectives
- Choice of instrument
- Logical framework
- Inputs
- Activities
- Outputs
- Beneficiaries
- Selection criteria
- Audiences
- Results and impact
- M&E design

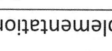

Implementation

- Learning
- Program implementation mechanisms
- Calls
- Application information
- Application process
- Information management
- Finalizing and follow-up
- Resources and management quality
- Budget adequacy
- Program management
- Autonomy
- Staff and training
- Incentives
- Process monitoring
- M&E implementation

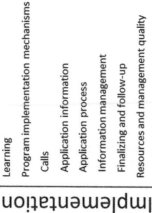

Inter-institutional integration

- Relationship between instruments
- Relationship between institutions
- Relationship with other policy frameworks – awareness and adjustment
- Relationship with other policy frameworks – severity of limitations and modifiability

Figure 21.2　Analytical framework for functional analysis

dination with other entities responsible for related instruments, and the reactive and proactive dimensions of response to background rules affecting the intervention by the instrument. In each feature, criteria derived from recommended practices are used to guide the assessment.

The information for each dimension of the model for a country of interest is gathered from two main types of sources. On the one hand, government officials provide all relevant documents for each policy instrument in the policy mix. Secondly, in person interviews with government agency staff are conducted to expand and clarify information gleaned from the documents on every category of the model. This information is compared and contrasted with the recommended practices criteria for each category in the model and a score is assigned reflecting the closeness of the observed practice to the recommended practice.[4] Analysis of the scores across all categories for all instruments leads to establishing various patterns of functionality of the instruments that are likely to affect their effectiveness.

The model aims to establish, first, whether there is a coherent rationale for the design of each policy instrument. Each instrument must aim to solve a real problem, avoid the trap of self-referential justification (e.g. "low levels of research funding justify creating instruments to increase funding") and be chosen from a set of potential alternative instruments. Interventions should follow a logical model with a clear, well-thought-through theory of change, including adequate monitoring and evaluation by design. Second, it probes the efficacy of implementation of each instrument. There is evidence that managerial practices in public service matter with better management usually leading to better outcomes (Rasul and Rogger 2016). Adequate staff profiles, capabilities and incentives can improve policy instrument management. Third, there should be policy coherence across the NSI. Stated priorities and expenditure commitments must be coherent. The notion of "enacted" versus "espoused" theory of organizational action is relevant here (Argyris and Schön 1978). Policy statements, reports and instrument documents often contain beliefs and assumptions of policy makers, managers and staff that do not match what is observable in action. Finally, policy consistency and predictability over time are important in a system where many significant outcomes occur in the long term.

21.4   FOUR-COUNTRY COMPARISON: BULGARIA, COLOMBIA, CROATIA AND PERU

The research systems of the four selected countries have been shown to need improvement (Crespi and Castillo 2020; OECD 2014; Elsevier 2019; European Commission 2015). Multilateral organizations such as the Inter-American Development Bank, for the South American countries, the European Commission, for the European countries, and the World Bank have been involved in diagnosing problems in each country's innovation system, including the research system, and supporting improvements. There are some important differences among the four countries, but also some similarities that make the comparison informative. The similarities and differences are summarized in Table 21.1.

The four countries have roughly analogous pathways and constellations of challenges over the period of the last three decades, with a period of conflict or difficult transition followed by structural changes from the early 1990s to the present. The relative measures of STI performance, such as the R&D expenditures as a percentage of GDP, seem to indicate that the European countries have a superior performance by a factor of 2 or 3. However, the research systems in these countries are roughly the same size in terms of total R&D expenditures,

Table 21.1   *Background information the four countries*

	Bulgaria	Colombia	Croatia	Peru
Population (millions)[a]	7↓	51↑	4↓	33↑
Income	Upper middle	Upper middle	Higher	Upper middle
Challenging recent history[b]	Long post-communist transition	Long internal conflict period, recent peace process	Post-communist transition	Internal conflict period
Multilateral agency influence	EU: European Regional Development Fund; European Structural Fund; World Bank	Inter-American Development Bank; World Bank	EU: European Regional Development Fund; European Structural Fund; World Bank	Inter-American Development Bank; World Bank
Total R&D expenditures (millions $US)[c]	501	780	597	283
R&D expenditures (% of GDP)[d]	0.75	0.23	0.97	0.13
Expenditures per researcher (thousands $US)[d]	30	101	76	57
Total number of researchers[e]	16 950	8 150	7 920	6 661
Annual S&E publications	4 118	9 297	4 800	2 702

Note: Arrows indicate the direction of population growth.
Sources: [a] World Bank Indicators: https://data.worldbank.org/indicator/SP.POP.TOTL, estimated for 2020; [b] for references for effects of recent history of each country on the research system see: Bulgaria (European Commission 2015; Slantcheva 2003); Colombia (Tellez 2019; OECD 2014); Croatia (Svarc 2006); and Peru (OECD 2011; Concytec 2016b); [c] World Bank World Development Indicators for 2018 and UNESCO (2021); [d] World Bank World Development Indicators for 2018; [e] World Bank World Development Indicators for 2019, and OCyT (2020).

Peru being the smallest. The expenditures per researcher suggest that the situation is more complicated and raises the question of what mediating factors in the research systems of these countries might explain the differences between them.

21.5   RESEARCH SYSTEM COMPONENTS, CAPABILITIES AND CHALLENGES

21.5.1   Research Funding Entities

The four countries have made recent efforts to adjust their institutional arrangements to improve the performance of their national research systems. They have engaged international advice and support from the European Commission, in the case of Bulgaria and Croatia, the Inter-American Development Bank in Colombia and Peru, and the World Bank in the four cases (World Bank 2019, 2020, 2021; Crespi and Castillo 2020).

In both South American cases, changes included the creation of new cabinet level ministries. The research agency of Colombia, Colciencias, created in 1968, was elevated to cabinet ministry status in 2019 with a broader mandate as the Ministry of Science, Technology and Innovation. Peru elevated its own research agency, Concytec, to the status of a cabinet ministry with the government elected in August of 2021.

In the cases of Bulgaria and Croatia, changes have to do with their recent membership in the EU and the management of funding from the European regional funding sources. Therefore, in addition to the ministries in charge of science and education, these countries have managing authorities that play a specialized planning and oversight role given by European Commission rules for the disbursement of EU funds in the country.

From the data collected in the World Bank PER projects related to the implementation categories of the model (see Figure 21.2), two key challenges for all four countries stand out. First, even though the coordination of policy across government entities is known to have an important role in facilitating or hindering the effectiveness of policies, not all coordination problems are the same. One country in each region, namely, Bulgaria and Peru, should be able to take better advantage of greater synergies between their academic research funding and the innovation policies that include university–industry collaboration. They have a strict division of labor among funding entities that hinders their ability to leverage the increased support for research in recent times (World Bank 2021; Crespi and Castillo 2020).

The division of labor required for accountability purposes by the European funding mechanisms in Croatia and Bulgaria also presents important challenges to efficient management of funding instruments. European funding generally involves a heavy auditing burden that creates delays and increases administrative costs owing to lack of clarity in the way the rules apply to specific issues raised at different times by new funding instruments (World Bank 2019, 2020, 2021).

The Latin American countries have a peculiar application of the NSI concept to their institutional arrangement that limits their coordination potential. Instead of considering the system to be a way of understanding the overall collection of institutions, research performers, private sector firms, with their interactions and knowledge flow to be analyzed and leveraged for the country's development, they are defined by law and only include a selected set of public sector entities (Colombia Competitiva 2021; Concytec 2016b). This approach also limits the ability to use the approach to design policies that properly fit the actual system rather than one defined as a political jurisdiction.

The second common challenge for the four countries is the difficulty to recruit professional-level staff. With some nuanced differences, restrictive public sector human resources policies prevail in these countries. The agencies do not provide proper professional paths for highly qualified staff. In all cases, staff tend to develop specialized skills while working in the agencies but are eventually recruited out of the agencies with significant loss of human resource investments. This leads to high turnover and the resulting costs in retraining and delays by learning on the job, loss of institutional memory and a weak organizational culture. An extreme case is Peru, which has a very rigid public administration career law that does not allow for dynamic management of human resources according to changing needs (IPEN 2019). These rules also apply to faculty in public universities, which prohibit them from receiving income from any source other than their appointed post (World Bank 2015, 2019, 2020, 2021). Therefore, there is no full-time equivalent accounting for research project-related work and virtually no consideration of indirect costs in the funding of research projects. This creates tensions in the distribution of labor between teaching and research, since there are no clear mechanisms to compensate for time taken away from teaching to do research nor for the administrative support of research activities.

21.5.2   Research Funding Instruments

The four countries devote a large proportion of their STI budgets to institutional block funding with very generic allocation criteria, mostly tied to the size of the institutions and historical trends rather than quality and performance. There has been a significant debate over the appropriateness of this sort of funding in richer countries (Hicks 2012), therefore it is no surprise that issues around block funding also arise in these cases. There is almost no mechanism in the four countries to link this funding to any measure of performance.

Peru and Colombia have dedicated a portion of the income from oil and mining natural resources to STI and HEI. The Peruvian version is a "Royalties Law"[5] that distributes funds from oil, mining and other natural resources exploitation back to the municipalities and regional governments where the natural resources are extracted. Regional universities receive these resources as block grants.

The Colombian version is the "General Royalties System".[6] Funds are also distributed back to the regions where the natural resources come from. However, the mechanism of disbursement of funds is different with a priority setting system with input from each region and a centralized proposal submission and evaluation system that reviews project portfolios from each regional government. This scheme plays a much larger role in Colombia than it does in Peru, amounting to about a third of all R&D expenditures.

The largest instruments in Bulgaria and Croatia are infrastructure programs financed largely by European funds. They fund the establishment of centers of excellence and centers of competence with programmatic foci guided by specialization strategies that have been determined at the highest strategic level for each country (European Commission 2017, 2020; World Bank 2019, 2021).

The PER carried out by the World Bank team in each one of these countries reviewed all the funding instruments and several patterns common to the four cases emerged. The design of the funding instruments is based on very generic justification arguments and objectives. It is carried out with general notions of needs that do not tie the specific arrangements of the instruments to a clear diagnosis of the situation in the research system. Justification is often stated in self-referential terms. There are no specially designed monitoring and evaluation systems that take the nature of these instruments into account, submitting instrument related information to centralized national systems that are designed for oversight of general government investments with no tailoring to the peculiarities of research and innovation (World Bank 2015, 2019, 2020, 2021).

The larger allocations from European funding in Bulgaria and Croatia and from the natural resources' royalties in Colombia and Peru have challenged the ability of the funding agencies to design appropriate solicitations and find worthy projects to disburse the funds (ibid.). There tends to be a concentration of large proportions of the budget in a few instruments and the remainder distributed across many small ones. This suggests that the smaller instruments are probably rather inefficient because the administrative costs of running them may be as large or larger than the funding they provide (ibid.; Rogers 2020).

The award processes in all four cases have difficulties related to complicated bureaucratic requirements in the application process and management of the awards. Added to this is a general difficulty in setting up application review panels that are both independent and of sufficient quality given the small size of the systems (World Bank 2015, 2019, 2020, 2019; Rogers 2020).

21.5.3 Research Performers

All four countries have some good performers in their systems as evidenced by the fact that their publications in indexed journals are growing and some areas show a share in the most highly cited journals.[7] However, some of the attributes of the performing entities seem to undermine their potential. One of the first common factors observed in these countries is that the share of faculty in universities with doctoral degrees is relatively low: only about 35% in Croatia (World Bank 2019), 18% in Peru (Renacyt 2021), less than 10% in Colombia (Mineducacion 2016) and about one-third of all R&D personnel in Bulgaria (Bulgarian National Statistical Institute 2021).

The university systems have institutional features that are not conducive to modern dynamic research activities. For example, the university governance framework in Croatia impedes collaboration even within a large university, such as the University of Zagreb that has 40% of all academic staff in the country, with 30 faculties, three academies and one autonomous department (World Bank 2019; Bilic et al. 2021). The teaching and academic professions are not highly rewarded in Bulgaria with some of the lowest salaries in the EU region at about $US13 000 per year (European Commission 2015). A very small number of universities have faculty that are active researchers in the four countries, and they all have a deficit in the number PhDs in the population and the research system. The numbers have increased somewhat in recent times but there is a long way to go to reach critical mass.

Bulgaria, Peru and Colombia have a large number of universities with a small number performing research activities. The three countries have seen an increase in private universities, which has become a challenge for quality assurance of their academic programs (Bulgarian National Statistical Institute 2021; Minciencias 2021; UniRank 2021; World Education News and Reviews 2021). In the case of Peru, a recent study of the University Superintendency (SUNEDU) revealed that only 41 percent of the PhD programs in Peru are offered by high-performing research universities (SUNEDU 2020). Many of the new universities have not met quality standards and a growing number of private universities are for-profit institutions (Asamblea Nacional de Rectores, Peru 2012). Quality assurance has been a big problem since there were no standards for the creation of new universities before 2016. A moratorium was enacted in 2012 to stop the creation of new universities until quality criteria could be established and evaluated. The moratorium was still in place in 2019 (SUNEDU 2020).

Mobility of researchers and recruitment are problematic in all four cases. Labor and public administration human resource regulations in the Latin American countries create the same problems for public universities as they do for the funding agencies. Bulgaria has not reversed the problem of the loss of qualified researchers moving abroad. The Croatian system shows a very low proportion of researchers taking advantage of research experiences abroad (World Bank 2019). The population of researchers in Peru and Bulgaria has a very high average age and the processes of recruiting and hiring faculty do not encourage applications by younger researchers (Concytec 2016a; European Commission 2015).

21.6   IMPLICATIONS FOR THE ANALYSIS OF RESEARCH FUNDING SYSTEMS

Despite some significant background differences among the countries in this analysis, there are some important similarities in the challenges facing public funding. The design and implementation of appropriate research funding policies for these countries require a much greater analytical and professional capacity in government institutions than they currently have. Furthermore, both the funding entities and research performers may also require new institutional arrangements.

The research funding systems of these countries faced coordination problems among the government entities responsible for managing and disbursing research resources. Two different types of coordination problems were observed. In the case of the South American countries, the division of labor set up by statute for the agencies does not match the interdependencies in the research and innovation system. They lack the flexibility to leverage support from different entities to create synergistic research opportunities. In the case of the Eastern European countries, the coordination problems stemmed from a tension between compliance requirements for disbursement of funds from EU sources and the functionality of the funding instruments themselves. Differences in the interpretation of EU rules by implementing agencies and managing authorities impeded timely disbursement of funding or rapid adaptation to new circumstances and opportunities.

Availability and management of skilled professional human resources impacts the research systems of these countries. The importance of this dimension is highlighted by the fact that it generates difficulties on both sides of the disbursement of research funding, namely, the government funding entities and the research performers. In all cases, there is no clear professional trajectory for staff with advanced degrees that would afford research funding agencies with the analytical and implementation capacity for modern research policy. The specifics in each country vary from fundamental public sector human resource policies to labor market incentives. However, the results are the same in terms of the reduced capacity of the funding entities.

Research performers, mainly universities, have their own human resources challenges. Across universities in these countries, a small proportion of academic faculty have doctoral level degrees and do research. The lack of clear rules for full-time equivalent accounting to enable a fruitful combination of education and research roles hinders the pursuit of research careers. There is little institutional support to manage grant awards, so research trajectories tend to develop slowly and lead to a high average age of researchers and poor recruitment of younger faculty. These countries also show a lack of insertion in the international scientific community.

The funding instruments themselves reflect the challenge of directing the resources to the right performers and activities. There has been an increase in resources for funding research in the four countries compared in this study. A significant portion is awarded in the form of block funding with no clear performance criteria to institutions that need improvement. Furthermore, instruments that disburse funding on a competitive basis have serious design and implementation problems. Among these, they lack a proper rationale for the intervention mechanism, an articulated theory of change, proper evaluation approaches, administrative cost accounting and proper definition of the target population of beneficiaries. They also face significant difficulties in setting up proposal review panels that have the expertise and independence needed for these instruments.

Performing entities, HEIs and PROs, may also have features that facilitate or hinder the realization of the objectives of research policies. Their internal organization may not align with the need for collaboration and knowledge flow that scientific research assumes. Recruitment and promotion procedures and criteria, including the requirement of having doctoral degrees, rules for the use of project funding that impede proper accounting of full-time equivalents and indirect costs, research infrastructure sharing, allowances for research mobility, and research project contract management are among the key features that affect the ability of the performing entities to deliver results upon receiving government funding.

These dimensions of the research system within which funding schemes are set up represent very general areas of concern for the support of research that apply not only to emerging economies, such as the ones included in this chapter, but also to developed nations. Attracting and retaining professional staff in government agencies is an issue of concern in leading nations as well (OECD 2002). The proper form and target of research funding instruments is also a challenge faced by the leading funding agencies in the world (Kang and Motohashi 2020; Wang et al. 2018). Similar statements can be made about the challenges for management of universities (OECD 2001; Milliken and Colohan 2004), monitoring and evaluation (Edler et al. 2012), and proposal review panels (Langfelt 2004), that even when recommended practices are codified they are difficult to apply locally without high level expertise (Manatos and Huisman 2020).

The challenges and difficulties that developing or emerging economy nations face to upgrade their research systems differ from leading nations in degree and specific symptoms but not so much in the areas or dimensions in which these challenges occur. These need continuous attention from a systems perspective to maintain quality and effectiveness of the funding schemes and the research system as a whole.

21.7 CONCLUSIONS

This chapter has highlighted challenges for the improvement in performance of the research systems of countries that are not global leaders in research nor in technological innovation. It has argued that the availability of resources without the capacity to manage and use them may not lead to the desired results. It is a visible challenge for those countries that are just behind the leaders and all the way down to those that are clearly severely disadvantaged, but also one that exists, although not as visibly, in the leading nations in science and technology.

NOTES

1. According to the World Bank classification based on gross national income per capita, Colombia, Peru and Bulgaria are upper-middle-income countries and Croatia is a high-income country. However, all four countries are recipients of external support and funding for their research systems and, as will be shown in this chapter, have research systems with similar sizes and challenges, despite other differences in population size, GDP per capita and such. In that sense we will consider them as examples or research systems in "emerging economies".
2. The full implementation of a PER requires four steps carried out sequentially: (1) determination of the policy mix, including instrument level budgets; (2) functional analysis of the instruments; (3)

374 *Handbook of public funding of research*

efficiency analysis of the instruments; and (4) effectiveness analysis of the policy mix (Cirera and Maloney 2017). Only data from steps 1 and 2 are used in this chapter.
3. The author was directly involved in the design of the method and implementation of the studies in the four cases included in this chapter.
4. To illustrate the application of the model, take the example of "Instrument Justification". The assessment criteria for this category are: (1) it is grounded on an explicit, high-quality identification and diagnosis of the problem the policy addresses; (2) it articulates the rationale for a government intervention on this problem; and (3) the problem is understood in terms that are independent of the form of intervention (i.e. not self-referential, doesn't presuppose the instrument). A full presentation of the criteria for every category is beyond the scope of this chapter.
5. "Ley del Canon" in Spanish.
6. "Sistema General de Regalías", SGR, in Spanish.
7. In the last decade, the share of published papers in top 1% journals for each country was between 0.1 and 0.3 for Bulgaria, 0.2 and 0.5 for Colombia, 0.2 and 0.4 for Croatia, and 0.2 and 0.7 for Peru (National Science Foundation Indicators 2021).

REFERENCES

Andrews, M., and L. Pritchett (2013). Escaping capability traps through problem driven iterative adaptation (PDIA). *World Development*, 51: 234–244.
Andrews, M., L. Pritchett, and M. Woolcock (2013). Looking like a state: Techniques of persistent failure in state capability for implementation. *Journal of Development Studies*, 49(1): 1–18.
Anonymous (1971). Can science be relevant in developing countries? *Nature*, 272(5306): 73.
Argyris, C., and D. A. Schön (1978). *Organizational Learning: A Theory of Action Perspective*. Reading, MA: Addison Wesley.
Arocena, R., and J. Sutz (2010). Weak knowledge demand in the South: Learning divides and innovation policies, *Science and Public Policy*, 37(8): 571–582.
Asamblea Nacional de Rectores, Peru (2012). *Datos Estadísticos Universitarios*. Dirección de Estadística, ANR.
Benavente, J.M., G. Crespi, L.F. Garone, A. Maffioli (2012). The impact of national research funds: A regression discontinuity approach to the Chilean FONDECYT. *Research Policy*, 41: 1461–1475.
Bilic, I., V. Skokic, and M. Lovrincevic (2021). Academic entrepreneurship in post-transition country – Case study of Croatia. *Journal of the Knowledge Economy*, 12(1): 41–55.
Bulgarian National Statistical Institute (2021). https://www.nsi.bg/en/content/2694/total-rd-personnel-qualification-and-sex. Last accessed November 7, 2021.
Calvo-Gonzalez, O., A. Eizmendi, and G. Reyes. 2017. Winners never quit, quitters never grow: using text mining to measure policy volatility and its link with long-term growth in Latin America. Working Paper, World Bank, Washington, DC.
Cimoli, M., C.J. Ferraz, and A. Primi 2009. Science, technology and innovation policies in global open economies: reflections from Latin America and the Caribbean. *GCG Georgetown University*, 3(1): 32–59. https://dialnet.unirioja.es/servlet/articulo?codigo=3116744. Last accessed October 31, 2021.
Cirera, X., and W. Maloney (2017). *The Innovation Paradox: Developing-country Capabilities and the Unrealized Promise of Technological Catch-up*. World Bank Group.
Cocos, M., and Lepori, B. (2020). What we know about research policy mix. *Science and Public Policy*, 47: 235–245.
Colciencias (2016). Actores del Sistema Nacional de Ciencia, Tecnología e Innovación. Adoptada mediante Resolución No. 1473 de 2016. Documento No. 1602. Departamento Administrativo de Ciencia, Tecnología e Innovación – Colciencias.
Colombia Competitiva (2021). http://www.colombiacompetitiva.gov.co/snci/el-sistema/quienes-somos.
Concytec (2016a). *National Research and Development Census to Research Centers 2016*. Lima.
Concytec (2016b). *Política Nacional para el Desarrollo de la Ciencia y la Tecnología e Innovación Tecnológica*. Gobierno del Peru.

Creso, S.A. (2005). Research policy in emerging economies: Brazil's sector funds, *Minerva*, 43(3): 245–263.

Crespi, G., and R. Castillo (2020). *Retos de la institucionalidad pública del sistema de ciencia, tecnología e innovación de Perú*. Inter American Development Bank.

Edler, J., M. Berger, M. Dinges, and A. Gök (2012). the practice of evaluation in innovation policy in Europe. *Research Evaluation*, 21(3): 167–182.

Elsevier (2019). *A Research Landscape Assessment of Croatia*. Analytical Services, Elsevier.

European Commission (2015). *Peer Review of the Bulgarian Research and Innovation system. European Commission: Horizon 2020 Policy Support Facility*. Publication Office of the European Union.

European Commission (2017). *Specific Support to Bulgaria – Background Report*, Publication Office of the European Union.

European Commission (2020). Research and Innovation Observatory – Horizon 2020 Policy Support Facility. https://rio.jrc.ec.europa.eu/country-analysis.

Freeman, C. (1987). *Technology and Economic Performance: Lessons from Japan.* London: Pinter.

Hicks, D. (2012). Performance-based university research funding, *Research Policy*, 42(2): 251–261.

Goñi, E., and W.F. Maloney (2017). Why don't poor countries do R&D? Varying rates of factor returns across the development process. *European Economic Review*, 94(C): 126–147.

Griffith, R., S. Redding, and J. Van Reenen (2004). Mapping the two faces of R&D: Productivity growth in a panel of OECD industries. *Review of Economics and Statistics*, 86(4): 883–895.

IPEN (2019). https://www.ipen.gob.pe/index.php/noticias/item/101-representantes-de-18-institutos-pub licos-del-peru-se-reunen-en-ipen-para-discutir-sobre-la-problematica-de-los-incentivos-a-los-investi gadores-del-pais. Last accessed May 12, 2022.

Kang, B., and K. Motohashi (2020). Academic contribution to industrial innovation by funding type. *Scientometrics*, 124: 169–193.

Langfeldt, L. (2004). Expert panels evaluating research: decision-making and sources of bias. *Research Evaluation*, 13(1): 51–62.

Lepori, B. (2011). Coordination modes in public funding systems. *Research Policy*, 40(3): 355–367.

Lepori, B., P. Besselaar, M. Dinges, et al. (2007). Comparing the evolution of national research policies: What patterns of change. *Science and Public Policy*, 34(6): 372–388.

Lundvall, B.-Å. (ed.) (1992). *National Innovation Systems: Towards a Theory of Innovation and Interactive Learning*. London: Pinter.

Luruli, N.M., and J. Mouton (2016). The early history of research funding in South Africa: From the research grant board to the FRD. *South African Journal of Science*, 112(5–6): 63–68.

Manatos, M.J. and J. Huisman (2020). The use of the European standards and guidelines by national accreditation agencies and local review panels. *Quality in Higher Education*, 26(1): 48–65.

Mazzucato, M. (2013). *The Entrepreneurial State: Debunking the Public vs. Private Myth in Risk and Innovation*. London: Anthem Press.

Mertens, D.M. (2009). *Transformative Research and Evaluation*. New York: Guilford Press.

Metcalfe, S. (1995). The economic foundations of technology policy: Equilibrium and evolutionary perspectives. In P. Stoneman (ed.), *Handbook of the Economics of Innovation and Technological Change*. Oxford: Blackwell.

Milliken, J., and G. Colohan (2004). Quality or control? Management in higher education. *Journal of Higher Education Policy and Management* 26(3): 381–391.

Minciencias (2021). Actores Del Sistema Nacional De Ciencia, Tecnología E Innovación Reconocidos Por El Ministerio De Ciencia, Tecnología E Innovación. https://minciencias.gov.co/sites/default/files/ actores_reconocidos_abril_2021.xlsx.

Mineducacion (2016). *Compendio Estadístico Educacion Superior Colombiana*. Ministerio de Educación de Colombia. https://www.mineducacion.gov.co/1759/articles-360739_recurso.pdf.

Nelson, R. (ed.) (1993). *National Innovation Systems. A Comparative Analysis*. Oxford: Oxford University Press.

OCyT (2020). *Indicadores de Ciencia y Tecnología – Colombia 2019*. Observatorio Colombiano de Ciencia y Tecnología, Colombia. September.

OECD (2011). OECD *Reviews of Innovation Policy: Peru*. Paris: OECD Publishing.

OECD (2001). Higher education management: Education and skills. *Journal of the Programme on Institutional Management in Higher Education*, 13(2).

OECD (2002). *Public Sector – An Employer of Choice? Report on the Competitive Public Employer Project.* OECD Publishing. https://www.oecd.org/austria/1937556.pdf.

OECD (2014). OECD *Reviews of Innovation Policy: Colombia.* Paris: OECD Publishing. http://dx.doi.org/10.17879789264204638-en.

Patel, P., and K. Pavitt (1994). The nature and economic importance of national innovation systems. STI Review 14. Paris: OECD Publishing.

Perez-Padilla, R., and Y. Gaudin (2014). Science, technology and innovation policies in small and developing economies: The case of Central America. *Research Policy*, 43(4): 749–759.

Rasul, I., and D. Rogger (2016). Management of bureaucrats and public service delivery: Evidence form the Nigerian civil service. CEPR Discussion Paper No. DP11078. SSRN: https://ssrn.com/abstract=2726558.

Renacyt (2021). Registro Nacional Científico y Tecnológico. *Datos Renacyt.* Government of Perú. https://servicio-renacyt.concytec.gob.pe/datosrenacyt/

Rodrik, D (2007). *One Economics, Many Recipes: Globalization, Institutions, and Economic Growth.* Princeton, NJ: Princeton University Press.

Rogers, J.D. (2020). Estudio de Línea Base del Gasto Público en Ciencia, Tecnología e Innovación en el Perú. Concytec–World Bank. Report to the National Government of Peru. https://repositorio.concytec.gob.pe/bitstream/20.500.12390/2208/1/Estudio_de_l%c3%adnea_base_del_gasto_p%c3%bablico_en_CTI_en_el_Per%c3%ba.

Slantcheva, S. (2003). The Bulgarian academic profession in transition. *Higher Education*, 45(3): 425–454.

SUNEDU (2020). *Informe Bienal Sobre la Realidad Universitaria de Perú.* Superintendencia Nacional de Educacion Superior Univesitaria, Gobierno Nacional de Perú.

Sutz, J. (2010). The university–industry–government relations in Latin America. *Research Policy*, 29: 279–290.

Svarc, J. (2006). Socio-political factors and the failure of innovation policy in Croatia as a country in transition. *Research Policy*, 35(1): 144–159.

Tellez, J. (2019). Peace agreement design and public support for peace: Evidence form Colombia. *Journal of Peace Research*, 56(6): 827–844.

Ubfal, D., and A. Maffioli (2011). The impact of funding on research collaboration: Evidence from a developing country. *Research Policy*, 40: 1269–1279.

UniRank (2021). https://www.4icu.org/co/. Last accessed May 12, 2022.

Wang, J., Y.N. Lee, and J.P. Walsh (2018). Funding model and creativity in science: Competitive versus block funding and status contingency effects. *Research Policy*, 47(6): 1070–1083.

World Bank (2015). Análisis Funcional y de Gobernanza del Gasto Público en Ciencia, Tecnología e Innovación en Colombia. Departemento Nacional de Planeación, Colombia. https://colaboracion.dnp.gov.co/CDT/Sinergia/Documentos/141_InformeFinal.pdf.

World Bank (2019). *Croatia Public Expenditure Review in Science, Technology, and Innovation: Analysis Of The Quality And Coherence Of The Policy Mix.* World Bank Publishing.

World Bank (2020). *Croatia Public Expenditure Review in Science, Technology, and Innovation: Functional and Governance Analysis.* World Bank Publishing.

World Bank (2021). *Bulgaria Assessment of the STI Policy Mix.* World Bank Publishing.

World Education News and Reviews (2021). https://wenr.wes.org/2020/06/education-in-colombia-2. Last accessed May 12, 2022.

Data Sites

Renacyt (National Register of Science and Technology). http://renacyt.concytec.gob.pe/. Last accessed November 5, 2021.

National Science Foundation. https://ncses.nsf.gov/pubs/nsb20213/academic-r-d-international-comparisons. Last accessed November 5, 2021.

UNESCO. http://uis.unesco.org/apps/visualisations/research-and-development-spending/. Last accessed November 5, 2021.

World Bank Indicators. https://data.worldbank.org/indicator/SP.POP.SCIE.RD.P6; https://data.world bank.org/indicator/NY.GDP.MKTP.CD?locations=CO-PE-BG-HR; https://data.worldbank.org/indic ator/GB.XPD.RSDV.GD.ZS?locations=BG-HR-PE-CO. Last accessed November 5, 2021.

22. Public research funding in Asian latecomer countries: developmental legacy and dilemmas

So Young Kim

22.1   INTRODUCTION

Investment in research and development (R&D) has soared over the last two decades in newly industrialised countries in Asia. R&D intensity measured by R&D expenditure as a share of GDP dramatically increased in these countries between 1998 and 2018, when most other countries saw a modest increase. South Korea, ranking the top on R&D intensity globally, has raised its R&D spending from 2.2 to 4.8% in the same period. Taiwan and Hong Kong have also seen a large increase – from 1.9 to 3.5% and from 0.4 to 0.8%, respectively. Most notably, the share of R&D expenditure in GDP has tripled from 0.6 to 2.2% in China. In particular, the volume of China's spending on R&D grew 10-fold in the first decade of the 2000s, surpassing that of the US in 2020 with $501 billion. South Korea and Taiwan also rank high on the absolute amount of R&D expenditure despite their country size (Figure 22.1).

While R&D intensity is one of the most representative indicators of national support for science and technology (S&T), Asian latecomer countries also score high on other indicators of national commitment to S&T such as the number of researchers and technicians per million inhabitants or per thousand labour force.

This chapter discusses the distinctive features of public research funding for S&T of Asian latecomer countries (South Korea, Singapore, Taiwan and China). Having grown rapidly over a relatively short period of time, these countries have expanded their public research funding system with strong tendencies towards strategic utilisation of public research funding to achieve national goals with S&T. Instrumental use of S&T for economic growth coupled with periodic strategic planning have left strong footprints on the modes of research funding allocation in these countries, which distinguishes Asian latecomer countries from those of other regions covered in this handbook.

S&T has been a critical element of the national economic development plans of Asian latecomer countries. Governmental promotion and mobilisation of S&T to meet national challenges have resulted in distinct features of public research funding in these countries, such as a skewed distribution of research funding towards applied research and demonstration and a designation of particular areas for strategic funding.

Relying on diverse literatures on political economy, S&T policy, and innovation studies, this chapter traces developmental legacies in public research funding regimes of Asian latecomer countries focusing on government research funding distribution and design. It then looks into the dilemmas in the design of research funding allocation, which are becoming new challenges to these countries entering a post-catch-up era. Some of these dilemmas are concerned with research funding allocations for different purposes or goals such as funding for basic vs. applied research, funding of projects to meet current vs. future needs, and funding to achieve economic vs. social goals.

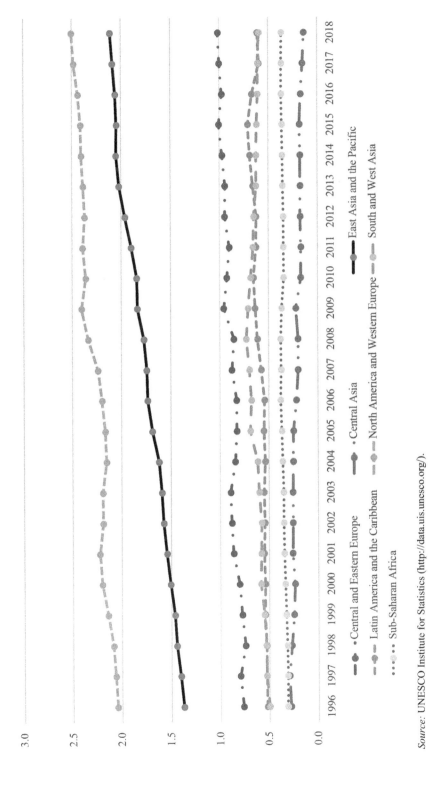

Source: UNESCO Institute for Statistics (http://data.uis.unesco.org/).

Figure 22.1   Gross expenditure on R&D (% GDP) of world regions

22.2   PREVIOUS LITERATURE

Strong commitment to S&T in Asian latecomer countries is deeply rooted in their developmental strategies as fast followers, as exquisitely elaborated in historical accounts of the origin of the Asian developmental states and their science policies (Amsden 1989, Greene 2008, Kim and Leslie 1998, Woo 1992). Such accounts emphasise the contingent nature of the historical process of building a developmental state through trial-and-error in various realms of policy in these countries.

Greene's (2008) account of the formation of Taiwanese science policy in the early years reveals that the Kuomintang state was not "developmental" all the time and only able to become developmental when state leaders previously occupied with political survival started to unite with technocrats for the vision of technology-driven growth and security.

Tracking the history of the establishment of KAIST, a higher education institution specialised in the training of skilled engineers and scientists in South Korea, Kim and Leslie (1998) elaborates early roles of the South Korean government in the late 1960s in raising indigenous technological capabilities to support the impending heavy chemical industrialisation. This part of the Korean history of S&T development is a piece of the bigger puzzle of how a country devastated by Japanese colonisation and the Korean War rose to be a middle-income country in less than a generation as documented in various accounts of South Korea's economic take-off (Amsden 1989, Woo 1992).

Remarkable success in late industrialisation of Asia's four dragons backed by technological catch-up – in marked contrast with developing countries in other regions trapped in a resource curse or rampant corruption – generated much interest from both political economists (Amsden 2001, Aoki et al. 1996, Aberbach et al. 1994, Deyo 1987, Evans 1995, Haggard 1990, Hong 1997, Johnson 1982, Lim 1983, Wade 1990, Woo-Cumings 1999) and innovation scholars (Edquist and Hommen 2009, Hobday 1995, 1997, Kim 1997, Kim and Nelson 2000, Liu and White 2001, Lundvall et al. 2006, Mathews and Cho 2002). Political economists examined closely the roles of the state in facilitating economic transformation in the newly industrialising countries in East Asia with particular attention to various institutional mechanisms and processes entailed in state-led industrialisation such as industrial policy, a pilot agency, or strategic planning. Innovation scholars were also interested in identifying strategies, policies or institutions underlying different innovation outcomes of these countries. Some of the innovation studies looked into the role of education and training as a learning-by-doing system and others policy instruments such as R&D funding as a critical enabler of catch-up innovation. In a now classic reading for Korean technological trajectory, for example, Kim (1997) analyses how South Korea made the successful transition from imitation to innovation through strategic R&D funding for indigenous technologies in South Korea's best performing sectors (e.g. automobiles, consumer electronics, and semiconductors).

With key features of the developmental strategies of Asian latecomer countries consolidated over the decades of phenomenal growth, contemporary policy designs and outcomes of these countries may well be comprehended by detecting vestiges of their developmental effort. In the realm of S&T policy, in particular, one can find strong developmental legacies in the research funding schemes and strategies in Asian countries.

First and foremost, R&D is very much often conceived as a tool of mobilising S&T for national goals in Asian latecomer countries. Indeed, frequent justifications of public research funding schemes in these countries relying on S&T serving national interests are a powerful example of the collective imagery formed from their latecomer industrialisation experience (Jasanoff and Kim 2015). Such prevailing views and practices of R&D policy in Asian countries can be subsumed under techno-nationalism that has underlain numerous governmental initiatives to develop indigenous technological capabilities as well as generally high public support for S&T in these countries.

In particular, views of science as a national endeavour (rather than an individual pursuit for curiosity) and prioritisation of technology for economic growth (rather than for social needs) dominate much of government policy discourse on public research funding in Asian latecomer countries. Not surprisingly, R&D expenditure in these countries has thus been largely devoted to applied research and experimental development rather than basic research that is of little practical or immediate utility. Dominance of applied and experimental research is evident in the composition of public research funding support in Asian latecomer countries as described later in detail. Furthermore, the governments of Asian latecomer countries have relied more on the "a few big" approach than the "many small" approach to allocate public research funding (Stephan 2015).

Another piece of developmental legacy in S&T policy can be found in the active deployment of five-year plans to draw out a vision and a roadmap for R&D investment, which is a practice very common to Asian latecomer countries. Widespread use of five-year planning in these countries provides strong vindication that S&T is largely a realm of central planning based upon long-term collective vision of these countries. As such, public research funding tends to have strategic focus grounded in the logic of concentration of limited resources, thus resulting in the government "picking winners" by periodically announcing strategic areas of research. Although the governments of Asian latecomer countries have lately attempted the "many small" approach to distribute research funding across a broader base of researchers, such initiatives are limited in impact and hold marginal importance.

The following sections provide a detailed account of these two features of developmental legacies in the public research funding of Asian latecomer countries, focusing on how such features have affected the mechanisms and tools of public research funding in these countries.

22.3   DEVELOPMENTAL LEGACIES IN PUBLIC RESEARCH FUNDING

There exist notable commonalities in the patterns and trends of research funding in Asian latecomer countries, which reflect their historical experience of S&T promotion during the developmental decades. One of the commonalities is the view of S&T as a means to achieve common goals such as economic growth or national security. As explained below, the role of the government for S&T promotion is often stipulated in the constitution, the highest level of law. Legally mandated to utilise S&T for national goals, the governments of Asian latecomer countries have generally favoured applied research over basic research, resulting in a skewed distribution of research funding towards application, development or demonstration.

Another commonality lies in the use of five-year plans to steer the direction and coordinate S&T activities. Typically, these five-year plans contain specific targets for national R&D expenditure, as the latter is considered a central instrument to raise competitiveness. Furthermore, the blueprint suggested in five-year plans provides justification for the government to select particular areas or fields of S&T for strategic promotion. This practice of "picking winners" takes on strong resemblance to selecting and concentrating government support on competitive industries and promising companies as part of industrial policy during the developmental decades of Asian countries.

22.3.1   Funding R&D to Pursue National Goals

Constitutions of Asian latecomer countries often contain a clause specifying the role of the state to support S&T – for example, requiring the state to "encourage scientific discoveries and inventions" (Republic of China Constitution Article 166), to "develop the national economy by promoting science and technology" (Republic of Korea Constitution Article 127), or to "encourage and assist creative endeavors … in education, science, technology, literature, art and other cultural work" (People's Republic of China Constitution Article 47).

As to the collective value and consequent motivation for public research funding, the clause on the role of S&T of the South Korean constitution is most pronounced for the market motivation of promoting S&T as a resource for market product or service development (see Alemán-Díaz, Chapter 3 in this *Handbook*). "Winning markets or winning Nobel prizes", the title of Kim and Leslie's study of the South Korean S&T development and late industrialisation, aptly captures the historical choice that the South Korean government made in the early years of development. Yet, S&T has long been perceived and promoted as a means to attain collective goals in other Asian latecomer countries.

The instrumental mobilisation of S&T in these countries is most prominent in the use of R&D for economic purposes such as industrial growth or transition. This is quite evident in the portion of gross R&D expenditure accounted for by the business sector in the Asian latecomer countries. As revealed in Figure 22.2, Taiwan, South Korea, and China – in addition to Japan – rank at the top on share of R&D funded or performed by industries and enterprises. The private sector of these countries accounts for more than two thirds of their total R&D expenditure, which is notably higher than other advanced countries such as the UK (53.6%), France (56.7%) and Germany (64.5%). Even the portion of the business enterprise sector of the US (65.5%), ranking the fifth in this cross-country comparison, is almost 10 percentage points smaller than that of China (76.3%), ranking fourth.

The explicit designation of the responsibility of the state for S&T promotion in the national constitutions of Asian latecomer countries has provided legal or institutional rationales to direct public funding towards specific programmes and projects of S&T that could achieve various goals of national importance. This has naturally skewed public research funding towards applied research and experimental demonstrations. Over the last two decades, as shown in Table 22.1, the governments of the three East Asian latecomer countries – China, South Korea and Taiwan – have spent comparatively more of their R&D expenditure on experimental development, between 64 and 83%, while the share of basic research funding has rarely increased.

Yet Singapore, another Asian latecomer country, shows a different pattern of R&D expenditure distribution, as it has raised the share of basic research funding from a level similar to that of the other Asian countries to a level exceeding those of Western countries. Singapore's unique path of research funding distribution may well be linked to its re-organisation of S&T governance in 2000 that brought biotechnology and biomedical research into strategic focus. Renaming the National S&T Board into A*STAR in 2000, the Singaporean government re-organised previously separate R&D activities and entities into two research bodies

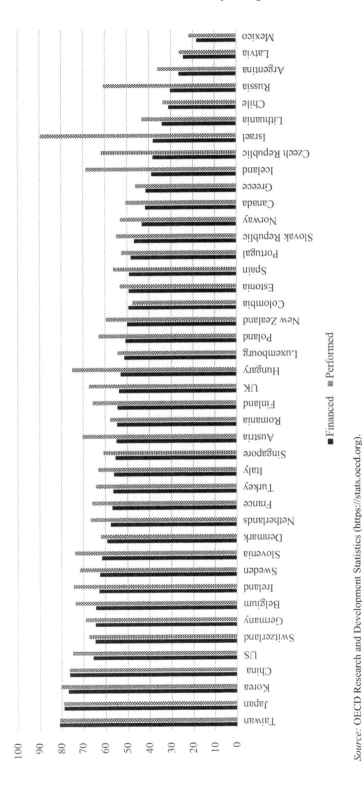

Source: OECD Research and Development Statistics (https://stats.oecd.org).

Figure 22.2 Share of gross domestic R&D financed or performed by the business enterprise sector (2019)

Table 22.1   Type of R&D activity in selected countries (percentage of gross R&D expenditure)

Type	Basic research		Applied research		Experimental development		Not specified	
Year	1996	2018	1996	2018	1996	2018	1996	2018
Asian latecomer countries								
China	5.0	5.5	24.5	11.1	70.5	83.3		
South Korea	13.2	14.2	26.9	22.0	59.9	63.8		
Singapore	11.8	23.8	39.6	31.4	48.7	44.8		
Taiwan*		7.5		22.8		69.8		
Advanced countries								
France	22.0	22.7	28.5	41.9	49.5	35.4		
Japan	12.2	12.6	22.3	19.0	59.5	64.3	6.0	4.2
UK*		18.1		44.0		37.9		
US	16.6	16.6	21.8	19.6	61.4	63.4		0.3

Notes: (1) Data source: OECD Research and Development Statistics (https://stats.oecd.org); (2) 1996 is the earliest year that the data on type of R&D distribution is available and 2018 is the latest year when the same data are available for most countries. * Data for Taiwan and the UK is unavailable for 1996.

– one focusing on biomedical research and the other on science and engineering. "Betting on biotech", the Singaporean government has raised funding for basic research to support a biotech industry that is heavily science based (Wong 2011).

In fact, a similar effort has been made in Taiwan and South Korea, as both governments began promoting biotech as the next "star" or "pillar" industry in the late 1990s (Wong 2011). Yet in these countries research funding is still dominated by the research bent on application and demonstration, which might be partially attributed to the persistence of existing strength and vested interests of the information and communication technology sector.

When it comes to R&D performed by the higher education sector, universities of Asian latecomer countries also show a distinct pattern of research funding. Compared with those of advanced countries on other continents, they are distinctively oriented to applied and experimental research, although longitudinal change in the basic-applied-experiment research portfolio is visible in some countries. According to the OECD R&D statistics, universities of major advanced countries such as the US, France and Israel have devoted more than two thirds of their research funding to basic research. In contrast, universities of Asian latecomer countries are spending less than half of their research funding for basic research. One notable change over time in the share of basic research is found in China, whose universities have more than doubled the basic research share in their funding over the last 20 years.

22.3.2   Targeting Research Funding Goals and Areas

Another distinct feature of developmental modes of S&T policymaking in Asian latecomer countries is the active use of five-year plans, which contain explicit visions and goals for S&T with specific quantitative targets to meet on way to achieve them. Rooted in planning economies such as the former Soviet Union, five-year planning as a method of economic planning for a limited period of time has been extensively utilised for the strategic planning in other policy domains. Mapping out a blueprint for policy goals to achieve in five years, the plans have functioned as a sort of a governance mechanism that coordinates various activities and stakeholders of the public and private sectors.

Table 22.2   *Type of R&D performed by the higher education sector (percentage of R&D expenditure of the higher education sector)*

Type	Basic research		Applied research		Experimental development		Capital expenditure not recorded elsewhere	
Year	1996	2018	1996	2018	1996	2018	1996	2018
Asian Latecomer countries								
China	15.6	40.5	55.8	48.8	28.6	10.7		
South Korea	44.4	35.9	26.6	32.7	29.0	31.4		
Singapore	28.3	43.5	48.5	34.1	23.2	22.4		
Taiwan*		42.5		42.3		15.2		
Advanced countries								
Australia	59.1	40.6	34.7	48.4	6.2	11.0		
France	86.9	67.0	12.3	27.3	0.9	0.6		
Israel*		68.2		24.7		0.7		
Japan	35.0	37.9	22.8	25.5	5.9	0.7	36.3	30.1
UK*		33.3		52.0		14.7		
US	67.7	62.9	24.8	27.8	7.5	0.9		0.3

Notes: (1) Data source: OECD Research and Development Statistics (https://stats.oecd.org); (2) 1996 is the earliest year that the data on type of R&D distribution is available and 2018 is the latest year when the same data are available for most countries. * Data for Taiwan, Israel and the UK is unavailable for 1996.

Notably, the governments of Asian latecomer countries have actively utilised five-year planning to advance their S&T capacity. A typical pattern found in East Asian countries including Japan is that S&T goals (mostly limited to development of technologies initially) are integrated into general five-year plans aimed at economic growth, and then separate five-year plans for S&T are developed later.

Being the first Asian country modernising the economy, Japan launched its first five-year plan for economic development in 1956, yet its first five-year plan for S&T was initiated in 1995, now entering the sixth five-year plan cycle (2021–2025). In this latest plan, the Japanese government set the goal of increasing government R&D investment to 30 trillion yen from 26 trillion yen of the previous plan period. Like the Chinese five-year plan, the Japanese five-year plan also includes strategic areas of S&T investment such as artificial intelligence, new material, space science, energy, and bio-health.

As a socialist country, China also has a long history of five-year planning dating back to the 1950s. The latest 14th Five-Year Plan for 2021–2025 places innovation as the core element of the plan, aiming to increase R&D investment by 7% every year and announcing major S&T projects (named "Innovation 2035") in frontier areas such as artificial intelligence, quantum computing, space technology, brain science, and so on.

South Korea's first five-year plan for S&T was launched in 1993, although the country had already made regular plans for technology promotion as part of the overall five-year plans in the 1960s. Similar to the five-year plans of China and Japan, South Korea's five-year S&T plans have set specific targets for R&D investment, with the latest Fourth Plan (2018–2022) announcing to double the government funding for basic research.

Singapore introduced a five-year plan for S&T in 1991, the National Technology Plan, which was renamed in 2010 as RIE (research, innovation and enterprise) to span activities beyond technology promotion. In the most recent RIE plan, RIE2025, the Singaporean government announced an R&D investment target of 1% of GDP, roughly 25 billion in S$. This

Table 22.3   Latest S&T plans and funding targets of Asian countries

Country	Name	Funding goal	Funding areas
Japan	Sixth S&T Plan (2021–2025)	30 trillion yen	Artificial intelligence, new material, space science, energy, bio-health
China	Innovation 2035	7% of GDP	Artificial intelligence, quantum computing, space technology, brain science
South Korea	Fourth S&T Plan (2018–2022)	Doubling basic research funding	30 key technologies
Singapore	RIE2025	1% of GDP	Health, sustainability, digital economy, and manufacturing

plan also contains four key areas of focus for funding support – health, sustainability, digital economy, and manufacturing.

Unveiling concrete targets for national R&D expenditure together with specific areas or projects of S&T for strategic focus, these five-year plans have served as a critical instrument for the latecomer countries in East Asia to achieve fast-track industrialisation through S&T. In particular, governmental announcement of particular areas or fields of S&T for special promotion in official plans largely meant "picking winners" for strategic funding support in anticipation of future technology trends.

With this tendency to pick winners in the provision of public research funding, the governments of Asian latecomer countries have relied more on the "a few big" approach than on the "many small" approach (Stephan 2015). While the strong propensity of public funding schemes of these countries to concentrate funding support on strategic S&T areas as well as on highly performing research institutions is frequently justified as the efficient use of public funding financed by taxpayer money, it is not clear whether the "a few big" approach is truly effective in terms of producing high-quality research output beyond simply enlarging the size of scientific publications.

For instance, Yin et al. (2018) in their study exploring the consequence of scientific research funding for knowledge output based on the Chinese research funding data, find negative effects of concentrated funding at the institutional level for research performance. This finding echoes the concerns expressed in various opinion pieces (Shi and Rao 2010, Xie 2014) on the intensification of the well-known Matthew effect in the Chinese scientific community. While negative effects of the Matthew effect are well documented, it is ironic that the performance-driven concentration of funding, the very rationale for the "a few big" approach that science policy makers of Asian latecomer countries frequently rely on, is not producing the very outcome it intends to obtain (see Bloch et al., Chapter 8 in this *Handbook*).

Related to targeted funding, increasing adoption of performance-based funding for higher education has driven universities of Asian latecomer countries to ever-fiercer competition for public research funding. Although performance-based funding swept the higher education sector in many advanced countries in the last two decades (Dougherty et al. 2016), it has had sizeable effects on the research performance of universities in Asian latecomer countries, especially in South Korea and China.

Korean universities had received general government support programmes based on the principle of uniform allocation in the earlier decades when they were relatively small in number and did not conduct much research. With the sizeable government R&D programmes introduced in the 1990s and the expansion of university research functions, such general university funding

Table 22.4   Publication output change of China/South Korea vs. other countries

Rank	Country	2008	2018	Average annual growth rate (%)
1	China	249,049	528,263	7.81
9	S. Korea	44,094	66,376	4.17
4	Germany	91,904	104,396	1.28
2	US	393,979	422,808	0.71
6	UK	91,358	97,681	0.67
10	France	66,460	66,352	−0.02
5	Japan	108,241	98,793	−0.91

Notes: (1) Data source: US National Science Board, Publication Output: US Trends and International Comparison (https://ncses.nsf.gov/pubs/nsb20206/publication-output-by-region-country-or-economy); (2) rank is the order of countries in terms of the scientific publications of 2018.

schemes began to be replaced by special-purpose programmes with targeted funding goals including the well-known World Class University project (Han et al. 2018). As the selection of universities for such targeted funding programmes is strictly based on the performance measured by mostly numeric indicators such as papers and patents, competition over performance-based research funding in Korean universities has led to the surge of scientific publications.

In a similar drive, the Chinese government tried a couple of selective university research funding programmes in the 1990s such as the 211 Project and the 985 Project targeting a small number of highly performing universities. It then made a big push for performance-based research funding in the mid-2010s with the launch of the "double first-class" plan aiming to build world class universities and disciplines (Wang 2019). As a consequence, China's scientific publications exploded, as captured in Table 22.4. Both China and South Korea had unparalleled growth of scientific publications over the 10-year period of 2008–2018, which followed the introduction of competitive funding schemes in these countries in the late 1990s and the 2000s.

22.4   POST-CATCH-UP DILEMMAS IN PUBLIC RESEARCH FUNDING

As noted earlier, Asian latecomer countries have seen phenomenal growth in their R&D investment over the last two decades, which is accompanied by a concomitant expansion of public research funding and growth in R&D output such as patents and papers. In terms of scientific publications, China's scientific articles increased at twice the rate of the rest of the world over the last decade; now China leads all other countries in the total number of scientific publications (US NSF 2018). China, Japan, and South Korea rank among the top five most active countries in patenting activity whether measured in applications or grants, with South Korea ranking at the top in relative terms (both per GDP and per million applications).

Such astonishing growth of the R&D enterprise in Asian latecomer countries over a relatively short period of time has led both policy makers and researchers to start casting doubt on the quality of research output produced with enormous research funding support. Policy documents, media reports, and scholarly articles on public research funding in Asian latecomer countries are increasingly questioning whether sizeable growth of papers and patents is indeed generating scientific discovery and technological innovation (Abrami et al. 2014, Chan 2015, Hu et al. 2021, Korea Herald 2014, Lee and Shin 2021, Schmid and Wang 2017). Such concerns are deeply tied to the so-called post-catch-up policy discourse in these countries that has proliferated in their R&D communities. The post-catch-up policy discourse represents an assemblage of a sense of urgency for change, criticisms of existing R&D policies and practices, and various calls for paradigmatic transition from a "fast follower" to a "first mover" strategy, all of which are based on the perceived need to move the R&D ecosystem beyond catching up with advanced countries to lead the global race in science and technology.

Post-catch-up has driven much of policymaking and scholarly discussions on the status of their research funding and its future, because the actual post-catch-up transition has not been easy in these countries owing to what might be called post-catch-up dilemmas in public research funding. As described below, these dilemmas directly touch upon developmental legacies, reflecting potential conflicts between the past developmental strategies and future needs or demands for structural transformation of economy and society.

22.4.1   Basic vs. Applied Research Funding

Asian latecomer countries have promoted basic research more actively over the last two decades, yet it has been a particular challenge for them to search for an optimal balance between basic and applied research (UNESCO 2015). The question of a right balance between two types of research is fundamentally a problem of redistribution, as it involves a decision to make changes in the existing research funding distribution.

On the one hand, changing a research funding structure towards basic research may be a risky choice for Asian latecomer countries, as it might weaken their existing technological strengths in ICT and related industries given an increasingly competitive global economic environment. On the other hand, it may be viewed as a natural or even an inevitable choice given an increasingly uncertain future of technological evolution as well as the contribution of basic research to the creation of knowledge and human resource pool for technological upgrading (Pavitt 1991, Salter and Martin 2001). One of the recent evaluations of China's government funding for basic research points out that basic research is now perceived as crucial in overcoming bottlenecks in leveling up its indigenous technological capabilities (Bai et al. 2021).

One of the ways to address this dilemma of preserving existing comparative advantages in the ICT sector while promoting basic research was the funding for use-inspired basic research known as the Pasteur's Quadrant (Stokes 1997; see also Alemán-Díaz, Chapter 3 in this *Handbook*). For instance, the Singaporean National Research Foundation introduced the Competitive Research Program funding scheme in 2007 to support cutting-edge research of relevance to Singapore in particular and global society in general (Chieh et al. 2015). The Korean National Research Foundation launched a similar funding scheme in 2013 called "Strategic Basic Research" within the track of the Mid-Career Researcher Program to fund basic research areas of great potential to create socioeconomic benefits in the long run (Kim 2013).

Such programmes have indeed generated discoveries of significant impact on industry and society, bringing scientific knowledge from the lab to the market. In fact, one of the rationales for infusing "strategic-ness" into basic research funding was that small countries like Singapore cannot afford to have all their academics doing blue sky research, i.e. scientific research having no immediate applications.

However, much doubt exists in the basic science communities of Asian latecomer countries on whether public research funding programmes oriented to the Pasteur's Quadrant can really foster basic research in these countries whose science policies have long been dominated by an instrumental view of science (Zastrow 2016). In the first-ever petition to the National Assembly in 2016, South Korean basic scientists called for the expansion of research funding for curiosity-driven research and greater research autonomy. This petition led to the promise to double government funding for bottom-up basic science research proposals to $2.2 billion by the incoming administration (Yeom 2018). While the promise was realised over the next five years as planned, the South Korean basic science community remains sceptical of the effect of this doubling of basic science funding, for the portion of research truly enjoying the autonomy of creativity under this funding bonanza turns out to be quite small (Kim 2022).

22.4.2   Research for Economic vs. Social Development

Another challenge for Asian latecomer countries is how to shift the balance in public research funding towards broader goals beyond industrial development and economic growth. With the developmental legacy lingering on the notion of S&T as a means for economic growth, the conception of "public" funding of research has long been confined to the roles of the government in boosting industrial and commercial applications out of scientific research by correcting market failures. It is thus a great challenge for science policy makers of Asian latecomer countries to create or re-design public funding schemes from a public values perspective (see Bozeman, Chapter 2 in this *Handbook*). Although these countries have recently introduced public funding programmes to support the research that generates few economic benefits but contributes to social problem-solving, actual projects selected for these programmes are still dominant by the research promising economic gains.

Incorporating previous R&D programmes such as "863 Program" for R&D launched in 1986 and "973 Program" for basic research launched in 1997, China revamped the National Key R&D Program (NKP) in 2015 to support R&D for social welfare and people's livelihood including environment and health. Being one of the oldest funding programmes started in 1982 and implemented through five-year plans, NKP initially aimed at technological upgrading of traditional industries. Re-organised per the Chinese government's reform plan for centrally funded S&T projects in December 2014, NKP's mission was expanded to cover R&D for social development. Now being the most active pillar of the Chinese funding programmes, NKP has funded research projects that address societal challenges such as environmental safety, infrastructure quality, public security, and control of chronic diseases.

However, the list of research projects supported through this funding mechanism still contains quite a few projects with strong economic potentials, which reveals the limitations of the funding agencies accustomed to justifying the value of science in terms of economic utility in broadening their missions to cover research funding for grand societal challenges and responsible innovation (see Bührer et al., Chapter 9 in this *Handbook*).

The Korean National Research Foundation, the largest funding agency in South Korea, revamped its Directorate for National Strategic R&D Programs in the late 2000s, introducing two funding programmes explicitly targeting societal challenges. One was the track for "Public Welfare and Safety Research" to address various social welfare and safety/security

Table 22.5   *New funding pillars of the 2014 research funding reform of China*

Funding pillars	Focus	Note
National Natural Science Fund	Basic and applied research in natural sciences (physics and mathematics; chemistry; life sciences; Earth sciences; engineering and materials; information sciences; and management sciences)	Administered by Natural Science Foundation of China, the largest research funding agency in China
National S&T Major Projects ("Megaprojects")	16 vanguard programmes focusing on major key products and technologies of strategic importance for economic competitiveness	Top-down funding divided between civil and military applications
National Key R&D Program ("NKP")	Supporting R&D in areas of social welfare and people's livelihood with some projects expected to generate well-targeted deliverables to achieve in 3–5 years	Most active pillar; integrates several pre-existing R&D programmes (e.g. "863 Program" for R&D and "973 Program" for basic research)
Technology Innovation Guidance Fund	Stimulating the transfer and commercialisation of scientific research through venture capital funds, private equity, and risk compensations	Roughly 70 new investments concluded every month
Bases and Talents Program	Promoting the establishment of scientific bases and top-notch innovative talents and teams	Relatively inactive pillar, expected to undergo structural reforms

Source: Ministry of Science and Technology of China official website (http://en.most.gov.cn/programmes1/) and European Commission (2018).

issues launched in 2010. The other was the track created in 2015 for the so-called "Social Problem-Solving R&D", which aims to raise quality of life and social safety. Numerous research projects were funded under these programmes, pursuing social values and encouraging active end-user participation in the research – especially, through living lab projects based on the co-creation of technology and demand as well as the co-designing of scientists and citizens (see Bührer et al., Chapter 9 in this *Handbook* for similar programmes in the EU).

Yet many researchers and analysts of these socially motivated research projects have observed several limitations in the design and implementation of funding, for example, under-differentiation from existing demand-driven technology projects, low participation of key stakeholders and poor coordination of multi-ministry funding (Song et al. 2018).

22.4.3   Asian R&D Paradox?

In addition to the balance in the types and purposes of public funding for research, Asian latecomer countries have faced a significant policy challenge, as their expenditure on S&T surges and public expectations for the outcomes from such investment grow in tandem. With the rapid growth of public research funding, Asian latecomer countries started to grapple with a question of how to turn huge investment in R&D into a tangible outcome, be it economic growth, national security, or quality of life. As a dramatic rise in public research funding in these countries raised public expectations of what could come out of governmental investment in S&T, public concerns and criticisms also rose about what actually has come out of S&T.

This challenge could be named the Asian R&D paradox per the well-known Swedish R&D paradox referring to the high input, low output problem of R&D. The paradox has been particularly pronounced in China and South Korea. In both countries where the central government plays a crucial role in designing and distributing public research funding, generally low levels of scientific impacts and technological commercialisation of publicly sponsored research performed by universities and government research institutes have been the target of the criticism leveled at their research funding programmes and projects.

At the centre of the paradox is the productivity of public R&D. China is now the world's largest spender on R&D in absolute terms (overtaking the US in 2020), and South Korea has consistently ranked top on in relative terms of R&D spending (i.e. R&D intensity). During the peak of fast catch-up (in the 1970s for South Korea and in the 1990s for China), public research funding in these countries could be easily justified, as general improvements in standards of living were palpable in the early phase of commercialisation. Once these countries climbed up the early growth curve and closed gaps with advanced countries in several high-tech areas, their governments have come under pressure to demonstrate tangible returns to much larger investment in S&T.

There are two manifestations of the concerns of the S&T community and the general public with the R&D paradox in these countries. One is the popular lament on the general lack of excellence and relevance of publicly funded research. For example, as to whether publicly funded research really produces impactful scientific output, the big gap between quality and quantity of China's scientific publications is a common point of reference. Despite the phenomenal growth of SCI publications by Chinese researchers pushing China over the top in both absolute numbers and relative shares of the world's SCI publications in 2019, China ranks only 15th in 2017 (Huang 2018) and 16th in 2019 (Liu 2020) on the average number of citations of SCI publications. In one of the latest moves to overcome this quality-quantity gap, the Chinese government announced a plan to move away from a simple count of international publications including the Ministry of Education guideline to prohibit universities from using SCI-related indices in faculty recruitment (Sharma 2020).

For another example as to whether publicly funded research is indeed generating relevant technological outcomes, in South Korea the often-cited reality in South Korea in reference to the R&D paradox is that 81% of 190,000 technologies developed by the government research institutes and universities with public funding support in 2014 remain "dormant", meaning that they have not been ommercialized yet (Lee and Kim 2015).

The other manifestation of the R&D paradox is the increasing call for the government to direct public research funding towards high-risk, high-return research of transformative potential, as the R&D paradox in these countries is often attributed to the tendency of researchers to fall back on safe bets in setting research goals. This is largely due to ever-fiercer competition for research funding that hardly allows a failure, resulting in the common criticism that the existing public research funding schemes have failed to encourage researchers to take up bigger challenges with out-of-the-box thinking.

Both concerns raised about the R&D paradox in China and South Korea are tied to the efficacy of the existing public research funding schemes favouring immediate results and short-term success. Even in Japan, well-known for its long-term orientation of scientific research, the government created a funding scheme to advance leading-edge R&D to counteract Japanese researchers avoiding risk in their projects (OECD 2021). It is thus a great challenge for government policy makers as well as the S&T community in these countries to provide right incentives for researchers to undertake creative and unconventional research and to ultimately align the evaluation schemes of publicly funded research with longer-term capabilities to harness S&T for national and global challenges.

22.5 CONCLUSIONS

Public funding of research in Asian latecomer countries in much of the postwar period has formed an integral part of their effort to leverage science and technology for economic modernisation and industrialisation, which resulted in distinct modalities of public research funding strategies and schemes. Some of the commonalities are easily discernible in the public research funding policy of Asian latecomer countries, such as strong commitment to S&T as a means or an instrument to achieve national goals, strategic implementation plans to monitor the timely progress of government research programmes, and explicit designation of S&T areas to target public funding in a similar fashion to the industrial policy of picking winners. These commonalities can be traced back to the developmental decades of Asian latecomer countries.

Now having successfully caught up with advanced countries in many indicators of S&T, Asian latecomer countries face a real challenge to upgrade their public research funding systems so as to compete at the frontier of scientific discovery and technological innovations and also to meet the elevated expectations of their citizens for massive public investments in S&T with tangible outcomes. Taking up this challenge would entail significant effort to move beyond those developmental legacies of public research funding policies, to handle post-catch-up dilemmas in setting the foci of funding between different types and purposes of public research funding, and ultimately to design and implement public research funding schemes that can foster transformative research with properly aligned incentives.

REFERENCES

Aberbach, J., Dollar, D., and Sokoloff, K. L. eds. (1994). *The Role of the State in Taiwan's Development*. M. E. Sharpe.

Abrami, R. M., Kirby, W. C., and McFarlan, F. W. (2014). Why China can't innovate. *Harvard Business Review*, March.

Amsden, A. H. (1989). *Asia's Next Giant: South Korea and Late Industrialisation*. Oxford University Press.

Amsden, A. H. (2001). *The Rise of "The Rest": Challenges to the West from Late-industrializing Economies*. Oxford University Press.

Aoki, M., Kim, H., and Okuno-Fujiwara, M. eds. (1996). *The Role of Government in East Asian Economic Development: Comparative Institutional Analysis*. Clarendon Press.

Bai, A., Wu, C., and Yang, K. (2021). Evolution and features of China's central government funding system for basic research. *Frontiers in Research Metrics and Analytics*. https://doi.org/10.3389/frma.2021.751497.

Chan, J. (2015). China's innovation paradox. *Perspectives: Policy and Practice in Higher Education* 19 (1): 23–27.

Chieh, H. C., Seng, L. T., and Thampuran, R. eds. (2015). *The Singapore Research Story*. World Scientific.

Deyo, F. (ed.) (1987). *The Political Economy of the New Asian Industrialism*. Cornell University Press.

Dougherty, K., Jones, S., Lahr, H., Natow, R., Pheatt, L., and Reddy, V. (2016). *Performance Funding for Higher Education*. Johns Hopkins University.

Edquist, C., and Hommen, L. eds. (2009). *Small Country Innovation Systems: Globalisation, Change and Policy in Asia and Europe*. Edward Elgar.

European Commission. (2018). Improving EU access to national and regional financial incentives for innovation in China. Project for the EU–China Joint Roadmap on Ensuring Reciprocal Access to Respective Research and Innovation Funding. http://chinainnovationfunding.eu/.

Evans, P. B. (1995). *Embedded Autonomy: States and Industrial Transformation*. Princeton University Press.

Greene, M. (2008). *The Origins of the Developmental State in Taiwan: Science Policy and the Quest for Modernisation*. Harvard University Press.

Haggard, S. (1990). *Pathways from the Periphery: The Politics of Growth in the Newly Industrializing Countries*. Cornell University Press.

Han, S.-H., Kim, S., Seo, I., and Kwon K.-S. (2018). An analysis of higher education policy: The case of government-supported university programs in South Korea. *Asian Journal of Innovation and Policy* 7 (2): 364–381.

Hobday, M. (1995). East Asian latecomer firms: Learning the technology of electronics. *World Development* 23 (7): 1171–1193.

Hobday, M. (1997). *Innovation in East Asia: The Challenge to Japan*. Edward Elgar.

Hong, S. G. (1997). *The Political Economy of Industrial Policy in East Asia: The Semiconductor Industry in Taiwan and South Korea*. Edward Elgar.

Hu, H., Devece, C., Martinez, J. M. G., and Xu, B. (2021). An analysis of the paradox in R&D. Insight from a new spatial heterogeneity model. *Technological Forecasting and Social Change* 65. https://www.sciencedirect.com/science/article/abs/pii/S004016252031297X?via%3Dihub.

Huang, F. (2018). Low quality studies belie hype about research boom in China. *Nature* 564: S70–S71.

Jasanoff, S., and Kim, S.-H. eds. (2015). *Dreamscapes of Modernity: Sociotechnical Imaginaries and the Fabrication of Power*. University of Chicago Press.

Johnson, C. (1982). *MITI and the Japanese Miracle: The Growth of Industrial Policy, 1924–1975*. Stanford University Press.

Kim, D., and Leslie, S. (1998). Winning markets or winning Nobel Prizes? KAIST and the challenges of late industrialisation. *Osiris* 13: 154–185.

Kim, L. (1997). *Imitation to Innovation: The Dynamics of Korea's Technological Learning*. Harvard Business School Press.

Kim, L., and Nelson, R. eds. (2000). *Technology, Learning and Experience: Experiences of Newly Industrializing Economies*. Cambridge University Press.

Kim, S. Y. (2013). Identification of and planning for strategic research areas in basic research. Korea National Research Foundation Report. [In Korean.]

Kim, S. Y. (2022). To boost South Korea's basic science, look to values, not just budgets. *Nature* 606 (229). https://doi.org/10.1038/d41586-022-01529-x.

Korea Herald. (2014). R&D paradox: Key is facilitating commercialisation. June 8, 2014. http://www.koreaherald.com/view.php?ud=20140608000238.

Lee, K., and Shin, H. (2021). Republic of Korea. In *Harnessing Public Research for Innovation in the 21st Century*, edited by A. Arundel, S. Athreye and S. Wunsch-Vincent. Cambridge University Press.

Lee, S.-J., and Kim, T.-Y. (2015). A study of determinants of national R&D projects. *Journal of Korea Technology Innovation Society* 18(4): 590–620. [In Korean.]

Lim, L. (1983). Singapore's success: The myth of the free market economy. *Asian Survey* 23 (6): 752–764.

Liu, W. (2020). China's SCI-indexed publications: Facts, feelings, and future directions. *ECNU Review of Education* 3 (3), https://journals.sagepub.com/doi/full/10.1177/2096531120933902.

Liu, X. L., and White S. (2001). Comparing innovation systems: A framework and application to China's transitional context. *Research Policy* 30 (7): 1091–1114.

Lundvall, B.-Å., Intarakumnerd, P., and Vang, J. (2006). *Asia's Innovation Systems in Transition*. Edward Elgar.

Mathews, J. A., and Cho, D. (2002). *Tiger Technology: The Creation of a Semiconductor Industry in East Asia*. Cambridge University Press.

OECD. (2021). Effective policies to foster high-risk/high-reward research. OECD Science, Technology and Industry Policy Papers No. 112.

Pavitt, K., (1991). What makes basic research economically useful? *Research Policy* 20: 109–119.

Salter, A. J., and Martin, B. R. (2001). The economic benefits of publicly funded research: A critical review. *Research Policy* 30: 509–532.

Schmid, J., and Wang, F-L. (2017). Beyond national innovation systems: Incentive and China's innovation performance. *Journal of Contemporary China* 26 (104): 280–296.

Sharma, Y. (2020). China shifts from reliance on international publications. *University World News.* February 25. https://www.universityworldnews.com/post.php?story=20200225181649179.

Shi, Y., and Rao, Y. (2010). China's Research Culture. *Science* 329 (5996): 1128.

Song, W., Seong J., Km, J., Kang, M., and Park, H. (2018). *Science, Technology and Innovation for Social Problem-solving.* Hanul Academy. [In Korean.]

Stephan, P. (2015). *How Economics Shapes Science.* Harvard University Press.

Stokes, D. (1997). *Pasteur's Quadrant: Basic Science and Technological Innovation.* Brooking's Institution Press.

UNESCO (2015). *UNESCO Science Report towards 2030.*

US NSF (2018). Science and Engineering Indicators. https://www.nsf.gov/statistics/2018/nsb20181/report.

Wade, R. (1990). *Governing the Market: Economic Theory and the Role of Government in East Asian Industrialisation.* Princeton University Press.

Wang, D. (2019). Performance-based resource allocation for higher education institutions in China. *Socio-Economic Planning Sciences* 65: 66–75.

Wong, J. (2011). *Betting on Biotech: Innovation and the Limits of Asia's Developmental State.* Cornell University Press.

Woo, J.-E. (1992). *Race to the Swift: State and Finance in Korean Industrialisation.* Columbia University Press.

Woo-Cumings, M. (ed.) (1999). *The Developmental State.* Cornell University Press.

Wu, Y. (2004). Rethinking the Taiwanese Developmental State. *The China Quarterly* 177: 91–114.

Xie, Y. (2014). "Undemocracy": Inequalities in science. *Science* 344 (6186): 809–810.

Yeom, H. W. (2018). Restructure science in South Korea. *Nature* 558: 511–513.

Yin, Z., Liang, Z., and Zhi, Q. (2018). Does the concentration of scientific research funding in institutions promote knowledge output? *Journal of Infometrics* 12: 1146–1159.

Zastrow, M. (2016). Why South Korea is the world's biggest investor in research. *Nature* 534: 20–23.

Index